Handbook of Psychology and Health

Volume I

Clinical Psychology and Behavioral Medicine: Overlapping Disciplines

Handbook of Psychology and Health

Volume I

Clinical Psychology and Behavioral Medicine: Overlapping Disciplines

edited by

ROBERT J. GATCHEL

The University of Texas Health Science Center, at Dallas

ANDREW BAUM
JEROME E. SINGER

Uniformed Services University of the Health Sciences

 LAWRENCE ERLBAUM ASSOCIATES, PUBLISHERS
1982   Hillsdale, New Jersey   London

Lawrence Erlbaum Associates, Inc., Publishers
365 Broadway
Hillsdale, New Jersey 07642

Library of Congress Cataloging in Publication Data
Main entry under title:

Clinical psychology and behavioral medicine.

(Handbook of psychology and health; v. 1)

Bibliography: p.
Includes index.
1. Psychology, Pathological.   2. Behavior modification.
I. Gatchel, Robert J., 1947–   . II. Baum, Andrew.
III. Singer, Jerome E.   IV. Series.   [DNLM: 1. Psychology,
Clinical.   2. Behavioral medicine. WM 100 H2337 v. 1]
RC454.H353 vol. 1   610'.1'9s   [616.89]   82-1415
ISBN 0-89859-183-X   AACR2

Printed in the United States of America
10 9 8 7 6 5 4 3 2 1

Contents

Preface

It is no coincidence that the first volume of this Handbook deals with behavioral medicine and clinical psychology. Much of what psychologists have been able to contribute to the study and treatment of health and illness has, to this point, been derived from clinical research and behavioral treatment. This volume presents some of this work, providing a fairly comprehensive view of the overlap between behavioral medicine and clinical psychology.

Although behavioral medicine is now recognized as an important area, there is still some debate among professionals in this field concerning just what behavioral medicine is. Schwartz and Weiss (1977) view the field as an amalgam of elements from behavioral science disciplines such as psychology, medical sociology, health education, and others that have relevant knowledge which can assist health care, treatment, and illness prevention. Subsequently, Pomerleau and Brady (1979) proposed a less broad definition of the field. They argue that the main "core" of this area should be viewed as the area of the *experimental analysis of behavior* since it was this area which served as the key source and inspiration of much of the current research in the field. They go on to define the discipline as: (a) consisting of methods derived from the experimental analysis of behavior—specifically behavior therapy and behavior modification—which are clinically used in the evaluation, treatment, or prevention of physical disease or physiological dysfunction (e.g., essential hypertension, addictive behaviors, obesity, etc.), and (b) emphasizing the conduct of research which will contribute to a better understanding, and the functional analysis, of behavior associated with medical disorders or health care problems.

Even more recently, Matarazzo (1980) has pointed out that the field of behavioral medicine should actually be broken down into specific areas. He suggests that the term *behavioral medicine* should be used for the broad interdisciplinary field of scientific investigation, education, and practice which concerns itself with health, illness, and related physiological dysfunctions. This is similar to the Schwartz and Weiss (1977) definition. *Behavioral health,* he proposes, is a term to describe the new interdisciplinary subspecialty within behavioral medicine which is specifically concerned with the maintenance of health and the prevention of illness and medical dysfunctions in currently healthy individuals. Finally, *health psychology* refers to a more discipline-specific term encompassing psychology's primary role as a science and profession in both of these above domains. This is more akin to the Pomerleau and Brady definition, although they are even more specific in their emphasis on the area of the experimental analysis of behavior within the field of psychology.

An interesting aspect of Matarazzo's (1980) proposal is the acknowledgment of the important role that clinical psychology has played in the field of behavioral medicine, and more specifically health psychology. In providing an enlightening historical overview of the emergence of this discipline, Matarazzo points out how Schofield (1969) emphasized that although the research and services of clinical psychologists were primarily in three health areas—psychotherapy, schizophrenia, and mental retardation—there was a growing opportunity and need for psychological research in a number of other health areas. Specifically, he indicated that the 1964 report of the President's Commission on cancer, heart disease, and stroke pointed out that these health areas were targets for well-funded research, treatment, and prevention programs. This potential research opportunity of psychology in the field of health stimulated the interest of the American Psychological Association. It ultimately eventuated in the development in 1978 of the Division of Health Psychology (Division 38 of the APA).

The purpose of this volume is to present some of the traditional areas of research and practice in clinical psychology that have directly and indirectly contributed to the development and practice of behavioral medicine. Before the "birth" of behavioral medicine, which has subsequently attracted psychologists from many different areas ranging from social psychology to operant conditioning, the chief link between psychology and medicine consisted of the relationship, albeit sometimes fragile and tumultuous, between clinical psychology and psychiatry. Many of the behavioral assessment and treatment methods now being employed in the field of behavioral medicine were originally developed in the discipline of clinical psychology. Indeed, the two treatment techniques which Pomerleau and Brady (1979) emphasize in their definition of behavioral medicine—behavior therapy and behavior modification—were originally nurtured and systematically evaluated on clinical samples by prominent clinical psychologists such as Albert Bandura, Leonard Krasner, Peter Lang, Gordon Paul, and Arnold Lazarus.

In the first chapter, James Norton reviews the area of neuropsychological assessment. Although behavioral medicine is a relatively young discipline, the collaboration between psychology and one medical specialty—neurology—has a much longer history. Beginning as a part of clinical psychology, and then taking an identity of its own, neuropsychology has a history which extends as far back as the First World War. It represents the first major category of psychological techniques addressed to a non-psychiatric medical patient population. It can be viewed as a primary forerunner of modern behavioral medicine. Norton briefly reviews the history of this specialty, and then discusses its major goal: the search for behavioral manifestations or patterns of performance aberrations that are associated with specific brain disorders.

In Chapter 2, John Hatch, Robert Gatchel, and Rick Harrington discuss clinical applications of biofeedback in medical settings. A great deal of interest was generated by the potential treatment applications of biofeedback techniques. Unfortunately, in the past, many clinicians developed an exaggerated confidence in the therapeutic efficacy of biofeedback procedures, largely on the basis of poorly controlled research studies and uncontrolled case studies. This chapter will provide the reader with a better understanding of the medical areas where biofeedback has been unequivocally shown to be clinically effective, and those areas in which it has not yet been objectively validated as clinically useful.

In Chapter 3, Terence Murphy discusses the topic of pain and pain management and treatment methods. Pain is an extremely common complaint in medical settings, with literally hundreds of thousands of individuals actively seeking relief from unbearable pain. It is a significant problem because of the frequent ineffectiveness of traditional medical approaches. In this chapter, Murphy discusses current theories of the mechanism of pain, the assessment of pain, and various pain treatment techniques (both physiological and psychological).

Neil Grunberg discusses the topic of obesity in Chapter 4. Obesity occupies a central position in the field of behavioral medicine. Historically, it was one of the first major medical concerns to be successfully subjected to systematic behavioral analysis and treatment. Grunberg discusses various treatment approaches, as well as the physiological and psychological mechanisms involved in this problem behavior.

The fifth and sixth chapters consider two major forms of addictive behavior which have significant health consequences: alcoholism and smoking, respectively. In Chapter 5, Alan Lang and Alan Marlatt present a social learning perspective of problem drinking, conceptualizing it as a maladaptive habit. They point out that the chief advantage of such an orientation is its *flexibility,* with the recognition that "problem drinking" describes an incredibly diverse population which no restrictive definition or unitary treatment approach can hope to accommodate. In discussing various treatment techniques, they point out that a major challenge to the field is to discover how to match individuals with the treatment methods that seem to suit them best. In Chapter 6, William Hunt and Joseph Matarazzo present an updated critical and evaluative overview of research directed at the control of smoking behavior. They indicate that although the results of treatments are varied, pro and con, there are encouraging signs of changes being made in smoking behavior. The prevailing "zeitgeist" is one in which there is increasing public intolerance of smoking and increased legislation against smoking. This nonsmoking *ethos* is a motivating factor important in accounting for recent statistics indicating a declining consumption rate of cigarettes. This nonsmoking *ethos* and declining consumption rate, together with the conservative estimate of 25% of subjects achieving long-term abstinence after treatment (a figure which does not include those individuals who voluntarily quit on their own), points to a reason for optimism in changing smoking behavior.

In Chapter 7, Peter Hauri discusses issues surrounding the assessment and treatment of sleep disorders. This chapter will help clinicians to effectively diagnose and treat patients who complain of sleep problems. The various specific sleep disorders are taken in turn, presenting for each one both diagnostic issues and specific treatment approaches.

Childhood hyperactivity is discussed by William Pelham in Chapter 8. Problems associated with the operational definition of this problem behavior and diagnostic heterogeneity will be discussed, as well as research on its etiology. Finally, application of behavioral assessment and treatment approaches will be reviewed.

In Chapter 9, James Geer and Madelyn Messé review the literature pertaining to sexual dysfunctions. They discuss some of the assumptions and definitions that underlie the conceptualization of sexual dysfunctions. In so doing, they show that sexual dysfunction can result from strictly physiological factors, or strictly psychological factors, but that more commonly it reflects an interaction between physiological, behavioral, and cognitive factors. The implications of this interaction for multidimensional assessment and treatment are clearly discussed in order to aid interested professionals.

In Chapter 10, Robert Gatchel, Andrew Baum, and Peter Lang discuss basic issues and future research directions in the area of psychosomatic disorders. They review the history of how psychosomatic disorders have been conceptualized over the years, some of the traditional categories of these disorders, and the major theoretical formulations proposed to account for them. They point out that any comprehensive understanding of these disorders requires an assessment of the interaction among situational variables, physiological factors, and intervening psychological processes such as personality characteristics and coping styles. Finally, they discuss a research methodology which may prove useful in the "pulling together" of the physiological and psychological factors in the integrative examination of psychosomatic disorders.

Two common psychological problems frequently seen in medical settings are the topics of the next two chapters: anxiety and affective disorders. The management and mechanism of anxiety will be discussed in Chapter 11 by Paul Skolnick and Steven Paul. They initially review issues in the measurement and clinical manifestations of anxiety, and then proceed to discuss behavioral and chemotherapeutic approaches to anxiety management. They also provide a comprehensive discussion of neurobiological mechanisms of anxiety. In Chapter 12, John Rush and Carl Fulton discuss the topic of Affective Disorders, reviewing current methods of diagnosing, subclassifying, and measuring symptom severity. They emphasize the importance of developing differential treatment procedures based on the relative contribution of biological and psychological factors involved in the affective disorder. They also offer important suggestions for how to select patients for specific treatments in this heterogeneous group of disorders.

Finally, in the last chapter, Jack Hollis, William Connor, and Joseph Matarazzo present an example of an important new trend in behavioral medicine: the application of behavioral techniques to the prevention of disease and promotion of health through lifestyle modification. They discuss their community-based nutrition intervention project known as the Family Heart Study Alternative Diet Program as one prototype for effecting health change on a relatively large scale.

This text is intended for investigators, clinicians, teachers, and both graduate and advanced undergraduate students in health-related disciplines. It will provide the reader with a comprehensive overview of many clinical and research methods, as well as important issues and controversies, relevant to the field of behavioral medicine.

Our efforts in preparing this volume were aided by a number of individuals whom we would like to gratefully acknowledge Diana Kuch and Martha Gisriel.

Robert J. Gatchel
Andrew Baum
Jerome E. Singer

REFERENCES

Matarazzo, J. D. Behavioral health and behavioral medicine: Frontiers for a new health psychology. *American Psychologist,* 1980, *35,* 897–817.

Pomerleau, O. F., & Brady, J. P. (Eds.). *Behavioral medicine: Theory and practice.* Baltimore: Williams and Wilkins, 1979.

Schwartz, G. E., & Weiss, S. What is behavioral medicine? *Psychosomatic Medicine,* 1977, *36,* 377–381.

Handbook of Psychology and Health

Volume I
Clinical Psychology and Behavioral Medicine:
Overlapping Disciplines
Robert J. Gatchel, Andrew Baum, and Jerome E. Singer

Volume II
Issues in Child Health and Adolescent Health
Andrew Baum and Jerome E. Singer

Volume III
Cardiovascular Disorders and Behavior
David S. Krantz, Andrew Baum, and Jerome E. Singer

Volume IV
Social Aspects of Health
Andrew Baum, Jerome E. Singer, and Shelley E. Taylor

Volume V
Coping and Stress
Andrew Baum and Jerome E. Singer

Handbook of Psychology and Health

Volume I

Clinical Psychology
and
Behavioral Medicine:
Overlapping Disciplines

1 Neuropsychological Assessment

James C. Norton

Veterans Administration and
University of Kentucky Medical Centers
Lexington, Kentucky

NEUROPSYCHOLOGY

Preface

In recent years there has been a rapid and evident increase in activity of psychologists in the areas of internal medicine, surgery and preventive or community medicine. This practice is termed behavioral medicine or medical psychology and the publication of books and journals with these terms in the title testifies to a spread of interest (e.g. Davidson & Davidson, 1980, Norton, 1982, Rachman, 1977). With regard to two of the medical specialties, however, collaboration with psychology has a longer history. The first of these, of course, is psychiatry with which clinical psychology has been identified virtually since the latter's inception. The other is neurology. Beginning as a part of clinical psychology, then taking on an identity of its own, neuropsychology has a history extending at least as far back as the First World War and represents the first major category of psychological practice addressed to non-psychiatric patients. It might thus be seen as the forerunner of contemporary medical psychology.

In the first section of this chapter we review briefly the history of brain-behavior relationships particularly with regard to the issue of localization. The second section summarizes some of the findings in disease of the various lobes of the cerebral hemispheres. These findings emerge from diverse sources including clinical neurology, experimental psychology, and clinical neuropsychology. Clinical diagnostic methods of neuropsychology are described in the third section which includes case examples from the writer's experience. This section also briefly discusses treatment approaches to the remediation of the behavioral con-

1

sequences of brain disease. It is hoped that the chapter will give the reader a sense of from whence neuropsychology has come and an appreciation of its current status within the general framework of relations between psychology and medicine.

HISTORICAL INTRODUCTION

Psychology and Neurology

Neurology is the medical specialty concerned with the disease of the nervous system which includes the brain. It has been known, or at least suspected, for a very long time that the brain plays a special role in relation to behavior and experience. The ancient Egyptians thought this was the case as did Hippocrates and Galen, and, in fact, the simple expedient of bashing someone on the head and observing that, if he survives, he acts funny might have convinced primitive man that the head and its contents have more to do with the way people act than do, say, the toes. The empirical observation, however, as is usual with empirical observations, raises more questions than it answers and the process of answering those questions has preoccupied physicians and philosophers for centuries. The questions have to do with mechanism, with specifying the nature of the relationship between brain and behavior. Neurologists, since they treat people with disease of the brain, have found themselves in an especially advantageous position vis a vis these questions, and neuropsychologists, by virtue of their relationship to neurologists, find themselves similarly advantaged.

The whys and wherefores of behavior and experience have been the subject matter of psychology from its beginnings and an interest in the brain as the "organ of the mind," or more contemporarily, the "organ of behavior," has always been apparent. This interest has found expression in two subdivisions of psychology: physiological and neuropsychology which differ in a number of respects. The most important difference, I think, lies in the fact that neuropsychology developed in a clinical, applied context while physiological psychology is a laboratory-based basic science. The strengths and weaknesses of these two ways of doing things have been frequently noted and will not be reiterated here. Suffice it only to note that neuropsychology quite readily became engulfed in neurology because of the shared interest in patients.

Among psychologists, probably no group has adopted the medical model as thoroughly as have neuropsychologists. Certainly many clinical psychologists working in psychiatric contexts use the medical model of inference to diagnosis from signs and symptoms, yet within clinical psychology there is a strong anti-medical trend engendered, in part at least, by the very serious problems, both conceptual and practical, with psychiatric diagnosis (Blum, 1978; Sandifer, 1972; Ullmann & Krasner, 1975). With the notable exceptions of "organic brain syndrome,'' and ''minimal brain dysfunction,'' neurologic diagnoses do not engender these problems because they are either pathologically based (e.g. tumor) or describe fairly unambiguous symptoms (e.g. seizure disorder). The distinction is not absolute, but there can be little doubt that the pathological, structural bases of neurologic diagnoses are vastly clearer than are those of psychiatric diagnoses, particularly given the inclusion in the Diagnostic and Statistical Manual (DSM III, American Psychiatric Association, 1980) of conditions for which a biological basis is not even suggested. It is not surprising, therefore, that neuropsychologists, somewhat uniquely among psychologists, are comfortable, familiar, and skilled with the application of the medical way of thinking. Certainly if psychology is to impact on the range of medical specialties, an appreciation of the medical model is of some importance and in this regard, neuropsychology might serve as a useful exemplar.

In neuropsychology, the medical model takes the form of diagnostic inference to disease of the brain on the basis of behavioral assessment. Just as the neurologist tries to discover brain disease through the techniques of history taking, physical examination, and laboratory studies, the neuropsychologist tries to discern brain disease through application of his special techniques, usually tests. What psychologists bring to this enterprise is both a technology and a paradigm. Technically, psychometric instruments are among the more sensitive methods available for assessing behavior. They are relatively objective and they yield quantitative data. As regards the paradigm, psychologists think of behavior in ways which neurologists generally do not. That is, as students of behavior, psychologists have developed a variety of taxonomies for behavior which can be brought to bear in trying to understand what is happening to behavior in neurologic disease. There is an important and constant interaction here in that, in neuropsychology, the taxonomy of behavior changes, evolves in light of what happens in neurologic disease. For the psychologist, this process inevitably raises questions about behavior in general, about what neurologic disease might tell us about the structure of behavior in normal circumstances. For example, current thinking in the field of memory has been profoundly influenced by the neuropsychological analysis of amnesic syndromes, yet these very studies rely on methods derived from experimental psychology. Thus, the neuropsychologist brings behavioral expertise to bear in neurology and in the process brings to light phenomena which may have implications for a general theory of behavior.

Brain, Behavior, and the Localization Controversy

The localization issue is an essential part of the question of mechanism, and opinion has waxed and waned over the years from localizationist to wholistic views of brain function and back again. The fundamental question can be simply stated: Are psychological functions geographically arranged in the cerebrum, or rather does the brain act as an undifferentiated whole, at least insofar as ''higher functions'' are concerned? The question is simple, but the answers have turned out to be complex in the extreme. Let us briefly survey the history of this controversy. By way of preface it is worth mentioning that opinions and speculations about localization historically far out-stripped accumulation of physiological facts, with rather dogmatic pronouncements appearing on the basis of the most meagre sort of data (Esper, 1964). Presently, this circumstance has been largely corrected with contemporary spokesmen tending toward conservatism and one might safely state as a general principle that, the more knowledgeable one is about brain and behavior, the more reluctant he is to make sweeping generalizations about how the two are related.

Bogen (1979) has usefully outlined the major historical positions, breaking them down into five categories. His interest is specifically in views of the corpus callosum, but the model applies to the localization issue more generally. The categories are: humoral theories, traffic theories, classical localization theories, wholistic critical response to classical theories, and two brain or lateralized theories.

The humoral point of view is very ancient and held sway until around the 17th century. The essence of this view which proceeds from the more general humoral theory of disease is that the critical part of the brain from a functional point of view is the ventricular system and the fluid it contains. The brain substance itself was viewed as a supporting structure analogous to the blood vessels in relation to the blood. Specific functions were associated with each of the ventricals, the structure of which had been described, albeit inaccurately, by Galen. This great interest in the ventricals and the cerebrospinal fluid fits the humoral theory of disease, but another possible reason for its preeminence may lie in the fact that dissection of the brain without fixation reveals a structure that is rather undistinguished aside from the fact that it contains huge cavities. Walsh (1978) quotes Sherrington (1951) to this effect.

Vesalius' famous anatomy text was published in the middle of the 16th century and represented a major advance in knowledge of the structure of the brain. With greater understanding of structure, the idea that the brain substance itself was of major importance grew in prominence and the corollary notion that the connections between structures played a communicative role also arose. Bogen (1979) terms those who favored this view the "traffic anatomists." Such beliefs rested almost entirely on an anatomical description, however, not physiological experimentation, a circumstance that obtained, in essence, until the 20th century. The rise of faculty psychology coincided with efforts to localize the functions so identified. Gall and Spurzheim's phrenology was part of this effort and gave rise to the localizationist point of view. Opposing phrenology were a number of writers, perhaps the most prominent among them Flourens. The later wholistic, anti-localizationist points of view claim Flourens a forebearer.

The period of the classical neurologists, beginning toward the end of the 19th century and extending into the 20th, was one of extraordinary creativity, heated debate, and discovery. During this period the issue of localization versus wholism began to be addressed on the basis of physiological knowledge and clinical pathologic correlations and the issues raised by these men remain today fundamental issues in clinical neurology and neuropsychology. The period represents one of those unusual confluences which occur episodically in science in which extraordinary men appear on the scene roughly contemporaneously and define the issues for decades to come. Among the names which punctuate this era are: Broca, Wernicke, Liepmann, Dejerine, Pierre Marie, Freud (in his prepsychoanalytic days), Head, Hughlings Jackson, and the neurohistologists Ramon y Cajal and Brodmann, the latter of whose cortical maps remain the bane of neuroanatomy students to the present day (see Fig. 1.1 and imagine trying to memorize it). The general outlines of the localization controversy can be described. In doing this, Bogen's fourth category, the critics, will be shown as a reaction to the classical neurologists and the fifth group, the two brain theorists, can be seen to arise out of the clash of these views and in response to more recently emerging data.

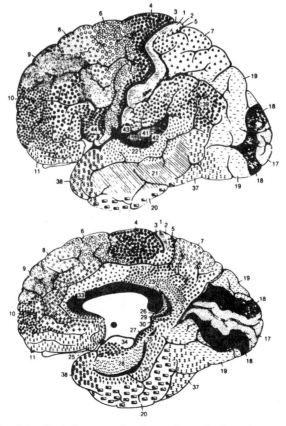

Fig. 1.1. Cortical areas numbered according to Brodmann's system.

Although the lateralization of cerebral control of motor functions had been described by the ancient physicians and demonstrated experimentally by Fritsch and Hitzig, it was Broca's studies of language impairment which brought to the fore the idea that cognitive processes might likewise rest on a local or specific cerebral region. The phrenologists had also asserted this, of course, but offered virtually no data relevant to the point. With Broca we find sustained study of the question culminating in the presentation of eight cases of loss of language in life with post mortem examination of brain tissue to show anterior left hemisphere disease in all cases. In 1885 he offered his dictum, "Nous parlons avec l'hémisphére gauche (Walsh, 1978, p. 16)." This bit of contemporary common knowledge fails now to exicte us, but at the time it represented a clarion call leading localizationists to seek regional specialization for other functions and wholists to look for examples of language loss following lesions placed elsewhere.

Roughly contemporaneous with Broca, Wernicke reported a different sort of language abnormality associated with lesions in the left hemisphere more posterior in location and including the temporal lobe. Unlike Broca's patients, who had lost the capacity to speak, Wernicke's cases seemed unable to comprehend speech. He therefore described two distinct categories of language disturbance and hypothesized a third which would result from a disconnection of the two regions. Such a patient would be able to comprehend speech and also to speak, but would be unable to transmit information from the comprehension region to the speaking region. This condition, unobserved at the time, Wernicke termed, "conduction aphasia" and predicted such a patient would be unable to repeat phrases spoken to him, though he would be able to understand the task. Such cases have since been reported. Geschwind, in a series of papers (1966, 1970), has outlined Wernicke's contribution and emphasizes the point that Wernicke was aware of the critical importance of relations among cortical areas in the generation of higher functions. This idea has a decidedly contemporary ring and might be seen as a precursor of Luria's notion of functional systems, though the latter seems not to have acknowledged the debt (Walsh, 1978).

A wholistic response to the writings of Broca, Wernicke, and others was not long in coming and found its most widespread reception in the writings of Marie (Benson, 1979). He contended that all language disturbances were derived from the receptive variety of Wernicke, the various manifestations being due to related damage to other cerebral regions. His argument seems not to have been with the lateralization of language but rather with the attempt to analyze its specific components neuroanatomically. Hughlings Jackson held a similar view and early on entertained the possibility that, if language were lateralized to the left, perhaps perception resided in the right. This idea, promulgated in 1864, proved prophetic, anticipating by many years the two brain theorists, Bogen's fifth group.

In addition to language, other functions were described during the classical period and associated with varying degrees of certitude with particular cerebral regions. Apraxia, the inability to carry out skilled movements in the absence of paralysis, weakness, or other motor abnormality, was studied around the turn of the century by Liepmann who concluded that, in addition to subserving language, the left hemisphere was the repository of motor skills (Heilman, 1979). Agnosia, the inability to identify objects in the absence of blindness or other visual disturbance, was described first by Munk in experiments with dogs. Freud coined the term, agnosia, and a variety of specific subtypes were subsequently described by various writers. Prosopagnosia, for example, the inability to recognize faces was described by Wilbrand and associated with bilateral posterior lesions (Benton, 1979a).

Argument over the localizing significance of these and many other symptoms proceeded on both conceptual and empirical grounds. Empirically it was frequently reported that a particular symptom, associated according to one authority with lesions in one region, appeared in another authority's cases with lesions placed elsewhere. Conceptually, the argument turned on whether these deficits in higher functions might not reflect subtle problems in more basic motor and sensory processes and analysis both of the component psychological processes yielding these disturbances and their neurologic basis continues to the present day.

Current Thinking

Discussion of the two brain theorists brings us essentially to the present and reflects the accumulation of data, first from the classical neurologists and their critics and subsequently from both clinical neurology and increasingly clinical neuropsychology. In simplified terms, the picture which emerged is one of lateralization of functions with language on the left and a difficult-to-describe spatial, perceptual, integrative capacity on the right. Study of the split brain preparation, first in lower animals, (e.g. Sperry, 1961) and then in humans treated for epilepsy (e.g. Gazzaniga, Bogen & Sperry, 1962) contributed tremendously to development of this point of view and revealed the critical role of commissural fibers in integration of the rather distinct contributions of the two hemispheres to higher functions. Gazzaniga's *The Bisected Brain,* (1970) is an excellent summary of this work and offers perhaps the best introduction to contemporary lateralized models of CNS function.

BEHAVIORAL ORGANIZATION OF THE CEREBRAL HEMISPHERES

Introduction

In discussing the psychological consequences of cerebral injury one can begin either from the anatomic or the behavioral side. Walsh (1978), for example, organizes his excellent text around the various lobes describing psychological changes associated with their injury. Lezak (1977) moves in the opposite direction with chapters on memory, verbal functions, and so forth. Of course, to the extent functions are localized, it should make little difference which set of chapter headings are used. A chapter on "Memory" or "The Temporal Lobes" should contain roughly the same information, assuming memory is a temporal lobe function. That chapter contents organized in these two ways are not identical results from the fact that localization, at least on the basis of the lobular geography, is far from perfect and it is worth remembering that the conventional neuroanatomic terminology for lobes of the brain based on the names of the bones of the skull overlying them is a physiologically arbitrary one (Critchley, 1953). Yet historically, it is on the basis of lobular identity that the syndromes of psychological deficit were first localized and such an organization has been chosen for the present purpose, admitting that as neurology and neuropsychology advance, an alternative anatomic conceptual model for the cerebral contents will undoubtedly emerge. It finally might be pointed out that the psychological function designations also are to a degree arbitrary, at least vis a vis their relationship to neurologic organization. While it may be psychologically useful and convenient to think of "memory" and "perception" as different processes, there is no a priori reason to assume that they are neurologically distinct.

Figure 1.2 shows the lateral aspect of the left hemisphere and can be used throughout the following sections as a point of reference. Figure 1.1 also will be mentioned when more specific loci are described. The major geographic demarcation points are the central sulcus or the fissure of Rolando separating the frontal from the parietal lobe, the lateral sulcus or the Sylvian Fissure separating the temporal lobe from the frontal and parietal, and the parieto-occipital sulcus separating the parietal and occipital lobes. Imaginary lines separating the

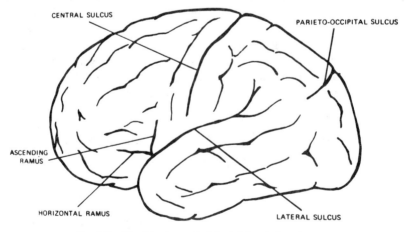

Fig. 1.2.   The lateral aspect of the left hemisphere in man.

posterior temporal lobe from both the parietal and occipital are obviously arbitrary.

Throughout this discussion, reference will be made to studies by McFie (1975) who reported the effects of lesions in various locations on Wechsler Adult Intelligence Scale (WAIS) (Wechsler, 1958) subtest scores. Given the wide familiarity with this instrument it may serve a useful purpose to mention those subtests found to be low points for each local lesion. It should be borne in mind, however, that any clinician can produce numerous individual exceptions to these group findings and that the literature contains many failures of Wechsler subtest pattern analysis to identify well-documented local disease. Occasional reference also will be made to data from the author's file of Wechsler profiles for psychiatric, neurologic and medical patients.

The Occipital Lobes

The occipital lobe contains the primary receiving areas for visual stimuli, there being a point for point representation in the contralateral hemisphere for the right and left halves of the visual field. The primary visual cortex (Brodmann's Area 17 in Figure 1.1) is surrounded by secondary or associative cortex (Brodmann's Areas 18 & 19) where it is thought the more complex formation of visual stimuli into perceptual events occurs. Area 19 has extensive interconnections with other cerebral regions and is thought, therefore, to play the critical role in integrating visual perceptual events into phenomenal wholes.

Injury of the occipital lobes results in disturbances in visual processing ranging from blindness for parts of the visual field when the damage occurs in Area 17 to perceptual disturbances such as visual agnosia with lesions in the association areas. There has been an abiding controversy in this area as to whether or not the agnosic disturbances can be accounted for by deficiencies in more basic visual processes such as elevated thresholds, reduced acuity and the like or alternatively, whether they represent not a problem in perception but rather a language disturbance. Geschwind (1965) has championed the latter point of view. Gloning, Gloning, & Hoff (1968) found only three cases of agnosic disturbance in the absence of obvious more basic visual disturbance and thus favor the idea that agnosia is a disturbance of higher functions only in the sense that disturbance of primary processes leads, in man, to disordered higher processes.

There is some evidence for hemispheric asymmetry with lesions in the left leading to object agnosia (Kleist, 1934) color naming defects (Kinsbourne & Warrington, 1964) and alexia or "word blindness (Geschwind, 1965) while lesions on the right are more frequent in prosopagnosia (DeRomanis & Benfatto, 1973) and color imperception or failure in hue discrimination tasks (Scotti & Spinnler, 1970).

With regard to the Wechsler scales, there is an abiding clinical opinion that Picture Completion is especially resistant to the effects of central nervous system disease, but that this scale will show declines with lesions of the occipital region. Impairment in Picture Completion without decline in other WAIS subtests may occur as a result of object agnosia as was reported in a case studied by Taylor and Warrington (1971). Picture Completion was not impaired in any of McFie's (1975) local lesion groups looking at mean data and the occurrence of Picture Completion as a focal low is infrequent. In the author's sample of 619 cases, Picture Completion was 3 scale scores (one standard deviation) less than the subject's subtest mean in only 6.9% of the cases, by far the lowest occurrence of focal low status among the Performance subtests. This is hardly surprising since object agnosia is also infrequent. Critchley put it nicely. "Cases of visual agnosia though a commonplace in medical textbooks represent—let us admit—an extreme rarity in clinical practice" (1964, p. 281).

The Parietal Lobes

The parietal lobes include the primary sensory receiving areas for the somatic senses (Brodmann's Areas 1,2,& 3 in Figure 1.1). There is a crossed representation here as in vision with the right body side represented in the left hemisphere and vice versa. Disorders of body sensitivity and of more complex perceptual processes are associated with lesions of the parietal lobe. These deficits represent some of the more dramatic and disabling sequelea of brain injury.

Constructional apraxia refers to the inability to assemble stick or block models, or, more generally, to put objects together. It is associated with parietal lesions, especially in the right hemisphere, (Piercy, Hacaen, & Ajuriaguerra, 1960). Kleist (1934) is credited with describing this problem and he conceived of it as a disconnection syndrome in which visual and kinesthetic processes were dissociated in the absence of visual perceptual abnormality (Walsh, 1978). The disorder is usually discovered through figure drawing tasks such as the Bender Gestalt (Bender, 1938) or through assembly tasks such as WAIS Block Design or Object Assembly.

Spatial disorientation is a more general category of deficit seen with parietal lobe disease and includes a variety of more specific defects including difficulty in route finding either on paper or in space, impaired memory for locations, difficulty in making spatial judgments, some problems in calculation and the above mentioned constructional difficulties. These defects have been studied in varying degrees of detail with constructional apraxia certainly the most extensively addressed. Likewise, the neuroanatomy of these problems is understood with degrees of specificity ranging from some to none at all. It is also obvious that spatial orientation, while expressed in motor performance, rests on sensory-perceptual processes and a failure on any specific task could result from either one or the other or both. In addition, spatial tasks may include verbal components to a greater or lesser degree, and Miller (1972) has speculated that the degree to which an apparently spatial task deteriorates with left hemisphere lesions may reflect the degree to which verbal mediation plays a role in task accomplishment.

As regards hemispheric localization of these deficits, the literature is far from wholly consistent but suggests that there is at least some degree of difference of frequency of specific defects in lesions lateralized to the left or the right. Furthermore, qualitative analysis of patient performance may reveal lateralization when examination of group mean scores shows no difference. For example, Warrington (1969) reports a qualitative difference in the figure drawings of right and left hemisphere cases. Table 1.1 adapted from Warrington by Walsh (1978), summarizes these differences and suggests the hypothesis that, for right-sided lesions, the problem may be essentially a visual-perceptual one whereas apraxic, motor difficulties characterize the left hemisphere cases (Benson & Barton, Warrington, 1969, 1970).

In addition to these visuo-spatial problems, sensory abnormalities of various kinds have been reported associated with posterior lesions. Unilateral extinction under conditions of bilateral simultaneous stimulation, for example, suggests a contralateral parietal lesion. Here the patient reports touch on the left or right body side in isolation, but fails to report stimulation to one side when both are stimulated. Finger agnosia refers to inability correctly to identify the finger touched under blindfold conditions. The term originated with Gerstmann (1940) who included finger agnosia as part of the syndrome which bears his name (finger agnosia, acalculia, right-left disorientation, and agraphia) which he localized to the left pariet-occipital region. The "syndrome" seems not to have stood the test of time (Benton, 1961; Poeck & Orgass, 1966), though there is evidence that bilateral finger agnosia is more frequent in left hemisphere disease variously located. Unilateral finger agnosia is more frequently associated with contralateral disease (Benton, 1979b).

Looking at McFie's Wechsler data, striking subtest deficits are seen in parietal lobe lesions. In lesions on the left, Arithmetic is especially impaired, followed by Digit Span and Digit Symbol. On the right, Block Design is especially impaired. The problem in arithmetic calculation has also been stressed by Luria (1974) who associates the tertiary zones of the left hemisphere with difficulty in logical and symbolic reasoning and WAIS Arithmetic seems clearly to tap such functions.

TABLE 1-1
Characteristics of Figure Drawing Impairment in Right and Left
Hemisphere Disease

Right hemisphere	Left hemisphere
Scattered and fragmented	Coherent but simplified
Loss of spatial relations	Preservation of spatial relations
Faulty orientation	Correct orientation
Energetic drawing	Slow and laborious
Addition of lines to try to make drawing correct.	Gross lack of detail

The Temporal Lobes

The temporal lobes lie laterally as elongated structures beginning at the tempor-parieto-occipital junction posteriorly and extending anteriorly beside and beneath the frontal lobe. The temporal cortex includes the transverse gyrus of Hechsel, (Brodmann's Area 41 in Figure 1.1), the primary receiving area for the auditory sense. Auditory input is incompletely crossed, though there is a preponderance of contralateral representation. Deep within the temporal lobe are a number of structures of the limbic system including the amygdala anteriorly and the hip-pocampus running within the body of the lobe to join the fornix posteriorly. The importance of the limbic system in emotional and appetitive behavior is well established as is the special role of the hippocampus in memory. The psychologi-cal manifestations of temporal lobe disease are thus multi-faceted including amnesic syndromes, auditory defects including Wernicke's aphasia, and a va-riety of poorly understood emotional disorders which may be variations of con-vulsive states.

Butters (1979) outlines the key characteristics of the amnesic disorders or disorders of memory. First, such patients show a defect in learning new material since the onset of illness. This is termed *anterograde amnesia*. Second, the patient shows a degree of difficulty in recalling events from before the beginning of illness and there is a tendency for events in the remote past to be better recalled than events just prior to the onset of illness. This phenomenon called *retrograde amnesia* is demonstrated through use of a clever test employing famous faces from decades past (Albert, Butters, & Neff, 1978). A third characteristic is termed *confabulation* and refers to a tendency amnesic patients show to "fill in the gaps" with more or less plausible stories. Confabulation was initially viewed as an essential feature of the Korsakoff's amnesic syndrome seen in alcoholics, but more recent work suggests it is an inconstant finding more frequent during acute stages of illness (Adams & Victor, 1977). Finally, the amnesic patient is characterized by generally *intact intellectual functions* independent of memory. This stands in contrast to the demented patient in whom memory loss is a prominent feature, but who shows in addition general cognitive deterioration. Clinically, amnesic patients present an extraordinary picture in seeming on initial contact so normal only to surprise the investigator by failing to recall having seen him a half an hour later.

Given its relatively high incidence, the amnesic syndrome associated with alcohol abuse (Korsakoff's disease), has been extensively studied using neuro-psychological methods. This disorder is thought to be due, in the main, to defi-ciency in B complex vitamins rather than to the direct effects of alcohol. A similar syndrome, much like alcoholic Korsakoff's, is encountered in patients deficient in these vitamins for other reasons. The classic neuropathological study of alcoholic Korsakoff's patients by Victor, Adams, & Collins (1971) reveals that lesions of the mesial thalamic nuclei are critical to the syndrome.

Walsh (1978) summarizes an interesting comparison of patients with amnesia due either to alcohol abuse or to encephalitis (Lhermitte & Signoret, 1972). Although both groups have clinically obvious memory defects, more careful neuropsychological analysis reveals important differences. In essence, while both groups have difficulty in learning new material, the Korsakoff's patients in addition show conceptual difficulties causing them to fail a task of organized spatial learning which the post-encephalitics can master. In addition, the post-encephalitics can learn a sequence of words or colored stimuli whereas the Korsakoff's patients fail. Furthermore, the function of the Korsakoff's patients is characterized by denial of the defect, by confabulation, and by a breakdown in the chronologic recall of remote material. All these attributes are lacking in the post-encephalitic group. Neuropathologically, the post-encephalitic have lesions of the hippocampi whereas, as previously noted, thalamic lesions characterize the Korsakoff's group. It would seem therefore that subtly different aspects of learning and recall are subserved by these two regions and that a careful analysis of the nature of the defect may be of help in localization.

Disorders in auditory perception follow lesions of the temporal lobes with the most profound defect being receptive aphasia with lesions of the left hemisphere. The aphasic defect ranges in severity from a total inability to comprehend spoken speech to more subtle problems with verbal memory, with naming, or with integrating verbal instructions into overt actions as when a patient is unable to draw a clock face to command while he can do it spontaneously. Auditory difficulties associated with right-sided lesions are qualitatively different. Lesions on the right impair musical abilities with problems in rhythm discrimination and tonal memory (Milner, 1962). Vignolo (1969) compared right and left temporal lesion cases on tests of auditory perception which could be failed on several different bases. The subject might mistake a sound for another similar sounding one (acoustic), for a sound of the same class (semantic), or for a completely unrelated sound. In general, left hemisphere cases tend to make the second type of error while right hemisphere cases make the first. Furthermore, the left hemisphere cases with receptive aphasia are much more likely to make semantic errors than are left hemisphere cases without aphasia or with aphasia of other types.

There is some evidence that visual perception is also affected by temporal lobe lesions. This probably reflects the fact that the posterior temporal region forms part of the so-called border zone between visual, somesthetic, and auditory association cortices and is thus likely to be involved in complex integration of perceptual events. Milner (1958), for example, found errors in interpretation of incomplete figures and in seeing pictorial anomalies in patients with right temporal lobe lesions.

With regard to Wechsler data, McFie (1975) found Picture Arrangement and Digit Symbol low in right temporal disease while Similarities, Digit Span, and Digit Symbol were impaired in left hemisphere cases. Impairment in Wechsler Memory Scale MQ relative to IQ has been frequently reported in disease of the temporal lobes (e.g. Butters, 1979) and a differentiation between the verbal and non-verbal or figural components of this test may have lateralizing significance. Russell (1975) offers suggestive data using this instrument and there is evidence of dissociation of memory defects in verbal and non-verbal material with lateralized disease using other techniques (e.g. Corkin, 1965; Milner & Teuber, 1968).

Abnormalities of emotional life associated with dysfunction of the temporal lobes cover a wide gamut. Temporal lobe seizures often include a hallucinatory component which can be confused with schizophrenic manifestations and a schizophrenic-like psychosis has been described as a consequence of temporal mass lesions (Malamud, 1967). In addition to frank hallucinations, abnormalities of temporal lobe function also give rise to a variety of unusual and bizarre experiences and behavior including *deja vu* and *jamais vu* phenomena. These refer to a sense of familiarity or strangeness respectively which precedes the seizure. There may also be experiences of vivid recollection of earlier events or of disturbing thoughts which the patient cannot force from his mind. Unusual and unpleasant visceral and oral sensations also may occur before the attack as may unpleasant smells. The seizure itself includes a clouding of consciousness, but with some degree of awareness and sometimes bizarre automatic movements like continual picking up of cigarette butts or buttoning and unbuttoning one's shirt. Oral-facial movements also are prominent. Postictally, there may be spotty recollection for the event or complete amnesia.

Small (1973) discusses the problem of misdiagnosis of temporal lobe attacks. This is especially likely if the patient does not regularly go on to have a full-blown seizure but rather experiences mainly auras and dreamy states. Once a proper diagnosis is reached, anticonvulsant medication may greatly reduce the frequency and severity of symptoms. It is worth noting, however, that the nature of temporal lobe epilepsy may give rise to reactive emotional problems independent of seizure frequency. That is, the events are frightening and unpredictable and the patient may require supportive psychotherapy as a means of coping. Thus, the psychological task in relation to temporal lobe epileptic patients may go beyond that of differential diagnosis.

A rather dramatic behavioral abnormality associated with lesions of the temporal lobe is that of episodic dyscontrol. Described by Mark and Ervin (1970), this rare syndrome includes acts of extreme violence which seem to be due to seizural events in the limbic system, particularly the amygdala. The authors list four hallmark characteristics: (1) a history of physical assault; (2) pathological intoxication or extreme drunkenness following ingestion of small quantities of alcohol; (3) a history of impulsive sexual acting out; (4) a history of many traffic violations. Their book includes a number of interesting case examples in which surgically implanted electrodes demonstrate abnormality of function in the amygdala during rage episodes and some releif of symptoms with destruction of this nucleus.

The Frontal Lobes

The frontal lobes occupy the most anterior portion of the cranial vault and include the phylogenetically newest portion of the central nervous system. It is this region that, in man, shows the most extraordinary increase in relative size and complexity as compared to lower life forms and this is especially true of those regions not directly related to motor control (Brodmann's Areas 8-13, 32, and 24 in Fig. 1.1). As this anatomic fact became known, it seemed quite reasonable to assume that the frontal lobes were the repository of the so-called higher functions, those aspects of psychological life which set humans apart from their animal cousins. The great Hughlings Jackson thought this was the case as did most of his contempories. As clinical pathological data began to accumulate, however, it soon became apparent that "thought" could not in any simple way be localized in the frontal lobes and, in fact, cases were reported in which sizable frontal lobe destruction led to virtually undetectable change in mental life. So began the "frontal lobe controversy."

Clinically a frontal lobe syndrome has been described that includes both cognitive and "personality" components. The latter are described by Benton (1968) as including a lack of future orientation, impulsiveness, a childish jocularity, and a lack of initiative and spontaneity, whereas the cognitive attributes include an inability to plan and persist in behavior over time, impaired recent memory, and a deficit in abstract thought. To these attributes may be added a tendency toward perseveration in the cognitive realm and a lack of social awareness in the personality area. These clinical descriptors appear throughout the neurologic literature and were originally based on specific cases with more or less well documented neuropathology. The questions then arose, how general a phenomenon is this, how specific to disease of the frontal lobe, and how intercorrelated are the various attributes? Resolution of these questions is an on-going process and it was in this context that the frontal lobe controversy evolved. From the neuropsychological point of view, the focus has been more on the cognitive than on the personality side of the question.

Walsh (1978) discusses with characteristic lucidity the issue of frontal lobe specificity in cognition. The controversy has to do with whether or not lesions of the frontal cortex impair higher, especially abstract functions more than do lesions placed elsewhere. A related issue concerns the distinction between abstract thinking and other types of cognitive function with some arguing that there is a qualitative difference between abstract and non-abstract thinking, while others see the functions on a continuum of complexity. Some prominent names have contributed to this at times heated discussion. Kurt Goldstein maintained that abstract thinking was quite distinct from non-abstract or concrete thinking and associated the former especially with the frontal lobe. D. O. Hebb took the contrary position seeing abstract thinking as virtually equally affected wherever the lesion was located and Reitan presented data to suggest that abstract thinking was not a qualitatively unique process affected by brain disease as Goldstein had maintained, but rather was but one of a range of abilities all of which were affected by cortical disease.

Viewing this issue in retrospect, a major source of the controversy seems to lie in the definition of "abstract ability." This is a complicated concept in any case which has been operationalized in a variety of ways and the measures employed to assess it have often been complicated procedures, inevitably requiring a variety of psychological functions. It may therefore be that failure to find impairment unique to the frontal lobes is due to the use of tests whose solution requires non-frontal as well as uniquely frontal activities. Walsh (1978) suggests that this may be true for the Halstead Category Test. What seems necessary is a component-analysis approach so that the constituent activities making up the success or failure on a given task can be delineated and localized. The work of Luria has proceeded along such lines and offers a number of empirical observations and explanatory hypotheses to account for the defects frontal patients show on testing.

Luria (1974) sees the frontal lobes as subserving the highest cognitive functions and analyzes these processes into four components. They are intentions, plans, regulating actions, and verification. Thus the frontal lobes are seen as performing a sort of executive function, overseeing the smooth execution of activities in which all brain regions participate. Damasio (1979) offers a similar conceptualization and indeed, when one looks at the accumulating experimental and clinical evidence, such a model of frontal lobe function is plausible. Let us look at a couple of examples.

Maze learning has been found to be impaired in frontal lobe disease, but also in lesions placed elsewhere (Milner, 1965). Analysis of the nature of the subject's performance, however, suggests that patients with lesions variously placed fail for different reasons. With regard to frontal patients, the problem seems often to be one of failure to learn from experience and failure to comply with instructions. The patient may be able to state the instructions so that he has not "forgotten it" in the usual sense of the term, but the instruction seems not to exert any control over his behavior. Milner (1964) makes a similar observation concerning frontal patients failure in a sorting task, remarking, "They . . . show a curious dissociation between the ability to verbalize the requirements of the test and the ability to use this verbalization . . . as a guide to action" (pg. 322–323).

Analysis of constructional tasks such as WAIS Block Design also suggests that it is the planning function that leads to failure in the frontal patient, while more basic spatial disability is at fault in the posterior lesion case. Lhermitte, Derouesne, & Signoret (1972), for example, found that provision of a plan for problem solution by the experimenter facilitated performance in the frontal cases. Such methods are not as helpful in cases of parietal lobe disease (Walsh, 1978). Contributing to the problem here also is the often noted failure of the frontal lobe patient to correct his own errors, even though he may note their presence. One would expect this defect to express itself in a great many tasks and it can be invoked as part of the explanation for the frontal lobe patient's difficulty with abstract arithmetic operations, maze-learning defects, and perhaps even some of the socially inappropriate behavior seen as part of the "frontal lobe syndrome." The patient simply fails to appreciate the effects of his actions on others and thus appears callous and insensitive. The famous case of Phineas Gage comes to mind in this regard.

What emerges, then, is a picture of the frontal lobe patient as lacking the ability to orchestrate a solution for tasks using the range of abilities which seem, in isolation, to be intact. Because these discrete abilities are not impaired, the patient may appear cognitively quite normal and may do well on those tests of intelligence which rely heavily on fund of information. When challenged with tasks requiring hypothesis formation, testing, rejection and revision, however, the frontal lobe defect comes to light.

With regard to differences in right and left hemisphere deficits, a study by Benton (1968) elegantly demonstrates that differences do exist and fit reasonably within the general conception of the left hemisphere serving language and the right hemisphere, spatial–perceptual functions. He used two verbal and two constructional type tasks and two not easily identified as purely verbal or spatial, but requiring abstract reasoning. The verbal tasks were fluency and paired associate learning; the spatial were three dimensional construction and figure drawing, while the "bilateral" tests were proverb interpretation and temporal orientation. Testing right, left, and bilateral frontal cases, Benton found the left frontals to be inferior to the right on the verbal fluency task while the reverse was true for the construction and copying tasks. The right frontal cases also were inferior to the left on the proverbs task, a result which is not easily explained.

What of the Wechsler scales? McFie (1975) found that Digit Span and Digit Symbol were impaired in left frontal disease, while Picture Arrangement and Digit Symbol were impaired in right. Walsh (1978) comments that Picture Arrangement performance in frontal patients is often characterized by expressed satisfaction with the presented order and the generation of an impoverished story compared to expectations based on educational background. McFie and Thompson (1972) also noted this tendency to leave the pictures in the presented order and suggest it reflects a specific frontal defect in self-correction. With regard to Digit Symbol, this test seems to represent the quintessential measure of efficiency and continual checking of response, attributes which seem especially lacking in the frontal lobe patient. Obviously, any tendency to preservation is going to play havoc with Digit Symbol performance.

CLINICAL METHODS

Introduction

Three general approaches to the problem of behavioral diagnosis in neurologic disease can be discerned in contemporary neuropsychology. Two of them are polar, the other, in between. At one extreme lie the purely actuarial methods advocated by Reitan and his many students (Reitan & Davison, 1974). The tools are tests and diagnostic inferences are derived from scores, literally without looking at the patient. Reitan's advocacy of this approach as a method of technique validation is incontrovertibly correct. To the extent that neuropsychological inference is confounded with other data sources, its unique diagnostic contributions cannot be known. It is necessary therefore to interpret test scores "blind" in order to show that such interpretation adds information to the diagnostic enterprise. Advocates of this approach would, however, go further than that. It can be argued that "blind" interpretation is not simply a research-validation strategy. If research indicates, as it does, that blind interpretation yields valid inferences to neuropathology, it is specifically blind in interpretation which has been validated. Subsequently to confound it with other data sources, for example the patient's chart, is to employ an unvalidated diagnostic strategy. There is thus a serious case to be made for Reitan's research approach as a viable clinical application and one is hard pressed, in fact, to find *scientific* grounds for using any other.

Another approach to neuropsychological diagnosis lies at the other extreme and is exemplified by the work of the great Russian neuropsychologist Alexander Luria (1966, 1974). The approach is clinical in the sense of being uncontrolled, non-routine, and anecdotal in terms of report. In reading Luria's books, one finds a fascinating psychological theory which mixes Pavlovian conditioning concepts with notions derived from clinical neurology, supported by case reports derived from Luria's vast exposure to focal neurological disease. Luria argues forcefully against standardized tests, stating that one must tailor the evaluation to the individual patient. One begins with interview, then notes possible areas of deficit and assesses these possible deficits with a variety of quasi-formal tasks. The direction of the evaluation follows the implicit psychological model which is Luria's theory. The result is a diagnostic inference which, judging from the writings, is almost always correct.

Recent work by Golden and his associates (Lewis, 1979; Purisch, Golden, & Hammeke, 1978) has moved the Luria approach in the direction of more quantitative methods. These writers have devised standardized tasks and scoring methods for 14 semi-discrete functions derived from Luria's theory of brain-behavior relations. The scores are similar to MMPI scale scores with 70 and above considered abnormal. Preliminary studies comparing this battery with the Halstead Reitan Battery applied to the same patients show comparable degrees of success in lesion identification and localization (Parsons, 1979). The Luria Battery has the important advantage of being much more brief in administration, taking an hour or two compared to the 5 or 6 hours required for a complete Halstead-Reitan. Equipment needs also are much more limited and less expensive, the necessary materials costing less than $100.00, while current versions of the Halstead-Reitan run into the thousands. One anticipates a prodigious amount of development and research with this newer version of the Luria approach during the 1980's, although Adams (1980) has recently criticized the existing literature on these techniques on both methodologic and conceptual grounds.

The third approach lies between the clinical and actuarial methodological extremes and probably reflects the day to day activities of the bulk of American neuropsychologists. This way of doing things is well outlined in Lezak's, *Neuropsychological Assessment* (1977). Lezak advocates an individualized examination strategy, but uses standardized tests as the medium, for example the WAIS, Purdue Pegboard, and Benton Visual Retention Test. These tests are given rather selectively and the instructions and procedures may be modified, "in a sensitive and inventive way" (page 85). This stands in contrast to Reitan who advocates rigid adherence to administration procedures, so much so that testing is done by technicians who are given limited discretion.

This issue of flexibility versus rigidity in test administration is not trivial in that it reflects a fundamental difference in the way the test scores are used. In the first place, the use of published norms, based as they are on rigorous adherence to routine administration, is legitimate only when the test is used according to standard procedures. The normative meaning of a score derived from "inventive" administration procedures is obscure. It is certainly not possible to apply to such a score assumptions about standard error or interscore comparisons which are technical niceties bound completely to methodologic constancy. To argue that one's interest is not in comparing the patient to a group norm, but rather to compare his functions with one another, does not solve the normative problem, because the inter-test comparisons are also dependent upon constancies in administration. One simply cannot know what the relative effects of inventive testing strategies are on one test as opposed to another.

It should be noted clearly that the distinction here is not one of clinical versus actuarial interpretation, but rather of differences in method of data collection. MMPI profiles may be used as a topic of psychotherapeutic discussion or as a method of patient categorization according to standardized rules. The former might be termed a clinical, the latter an actuarial utilization. If, on the other hand, the actual responses which yield the profile are obtained by interview and discussion, the resulting profile is a different sort of thing than one obtained in the conventional way and it would be absurd to "interpret it" actuarially. It would be equally absurd to interpret it clinically if one's frame of reference is his "clinical experience" with conventionally generated profiles. What we have, in essence, is a new instrument, the clinical interview—MMPI, to which the existing MMPI literature is of unknown relevance, and as with all new instruments, validation of the method is required so that we may know objectively its utility. But the only way to validate it is to standardize administration, and we have come full circle. That, it seems, is the problem with "inventive" data collection.

Granting these objections to assessment flexibility, there remains much to say on the matter, not the least important of which is that the behavioral limits of neurologic patients are, as Lezak asserts, of intrinsic interest, and standardization may obscure them. They are of special importance when one comes to issues of treatment and rehabilitation. In this situation, the patient's abilities and deficits are of interest in absolute terms. It is in the area of diagnosis where standardization is critical and when that issue is either resolved or irrelevant, adherence to the standardized method seems, except for research purposes, a methodological compulsion. One may learn much more that is of interest for retraining by helping a patient through a test, than by simply showing that he will fail, as might occur using standardized procedures.

A Model for Diagnosis

In doing neuropsychological evaluations, a number of principles can be described which seem to have relevance to the diagnostic process. They are so generally derived that I am reluctant to credit specific sources, though Dr. C. G. Matthews of the University of Wisconsin must, as my mentor, share the credit (or blame). The first three principles are implicit in what has gone before regarding the lobular syndromes, while the last two represent what might be called principles of clinical practice. In this section the principles will first be given, then two of them will be illustrated with cases.

Principle One: Psychological functions follow lateralized patterns such that motor and sensory abnormalities confined to one side of the body tend to implicate the contralateral hemisphere. In cognitive functions, verbal deficits tend to implicate the left hemisphere, nonverbal the right.

Principle Two: As we move backward on the neuraxis from frontal to temporal to parietal lobes, severity and specificity of psychological deficit increases.

Principle Three: The presence of defects in memory in the absence of equally severe deficits in other cognitive functions implicates the temporal lobes bilaterally.

Principle Four: Neuropsychological diagnosis should not rest on conventional intelligence tests alone. The evaluation must include measures specifically designed for this purpose, since in many cases of neurologic disease, standard intelligence tests are not sufficiently sensitive to reflect cognitive changes.

Principle Five: If neuropsychological testing is worth doing once, it is worth doing twice.

These last two bear comment. Principle Four means in practice that neuropsychological diagnosis, if it is to be seriously pursued, requires a considerable degree of special training beyond the usual testing courses of the graduate curriculum. In the best of cases, postgraduate training in a laboratory dedicated to this function is obtained before one presents himself as competent in the field. In the worst of cases, a one or two day "workshop" given by one neuropsychological luminary or another is offered as justification for claims of expertise in this area. This latter practice is, it seems to me, ethically questionable and in practice ludicrous. There is little worth knowing which can be learned in the morning and practiced after lunch. Since there seems generally to be a growing demand for neuropsychological services, and since postdoctoral positions are few and funding is scarce, alternative training formats seem indicated. Workshops are a short term, basically unsatisfactory sort of ad hoc solution, and it would seem that more systematic presentation of neuropsychology included in the graduate curriculum, perhaps as a minor with either a clinical or other major, would be an appropriate solution. This issue should be addressed, both by neuropsychology through its professional society, the International Neuropsychology Society (I.N.S.) and by the graduate schools. A task force addressing this issue is currently at work within the framework of the I.N.S. and the recent establishment of a division on clinical neuropsychology within the American Psychological Association augurs well for the future.

Regarding Principle Five, one of the signal contributions of Hippocratic medicine was the emphasis on history or course to differentiate and diagnose disease processes. This is true in all subspecialty fields of medicine, particularly neurology. A neurologist, or any clinician, forced to make a diagnosis on the basis either of the history of the patient's illness or the physical examination alone, would clearly prefer the former. The advantage is that one obtains far more data from a longitudinal view than from a cross-sectional view of a dynamic process. Let us look at a brief example to make this clear.

Suppose the case to be diagnosed is that of a 50-year-old man with a left hemiparesis, that is a paralysis of the left side of his body. The questions for the neurologist are "Does the patient have a central nervous system lesion? If so, where is it, and what is it?" Now if a man has a left hemiparesis, he either has a lesion in the right cerebral cortex or its efferent motor tracts, or he is "hysterical." If the patient is not hysterical, then the examination reveals little beyond the location of the lesion. The important diagnostic factors of pathophysiology, prognosis and therapy, are derived from the history. For example, if the hemiparesis in the hypothetical patient developed slowly over 2 years rather than overnight, the most likely etiology would be a tumor. The prognosis and therapy for a tumor would be quite different from that of a vascular stroke which occurred suddenly one morning. By the same token, a man with longstanding hypertension, who develops an acute headache, stiff neck, photophobia and a hemiparesis, is quite different from a man who hits his head hard on a kitchen cabinet then becomes hemiparetic within hours. The hemiparesis is evident in both cases on examination. The history gives the crucial information in terms of a more complete diagnosis beyond anatomic locus.

What is true for the neurologist is true for the neuropsychologist, only more so. When one approaches a patient the first time, that is cross-sectionally, the standard against which one compares him is the theoretical normal man, operationalized as standardized mean scores. This is true both for the neurologist and the psychologist but there is a difference. For the neurologist, the range of variability around the theoretically normal is more constricted than for the psychologist. When a patient walks into the office, our normal expectation on the Wechsler Scale is an IQ of 100 with Verbal, Performance and Full Scale IQ's equal to that value, and all subtest scores equal to 10. Now, as anyone who uses these tests will know, such a pattern almost never occurs. This normal expectation is a statistical abstraction, an expectation based on averages of large N samples. What one sees in fact is a small degree of variability in the subtests in individual cases which average out to "normal."

Still approaching the question cross-sectionally, it is further the case that deviations from 100 in a downward direction are potentially of diagnostic interest from a neurologic point of view, whereas deviations upwards are not. I am aware of no brain disease which leads to higher IQ's. It would be absurd to say that two patients, one with an IQ of 135 and one with an IQ of 65 are equally "abnormal" from the neurologic perspective, though they are equally abnormal from a statistical point of view. The problem is that the term "normal" is being used equivocally here, meaning "healthy" in the neurologic perspective and "most probable" in the statistical. Furthermore an obtained IQ of 80 is abnormal from the neurologic point of view only if we assume that it should be 100, but such an assumption is questionable since a very large number of persons in the standardization sample of presumably neurologically intact persons obtain an IQ of 80 or 85 or 90 or 75. That is, statistically "abnormal" IQ's are very frequent in healthy people, hence they cannot be used to diagnose illness cross-sectionally, hence our fifth principle.

Viewed longitudinally the IQ takes on different meaning as a sign of neurologic status. In any given case, what we are really interested in is whether the attained IQ is normal for the person being tested, not for the population at large. Thought of this way, an IQ of 120 might be abnormal if it were 135 last year, and an IQ of 75 would be viewed as normal for that patient if the patient had always functioned at this level. Neurologic disease is by its very nature locked in time, in the history of the patient, and unfolding through the course of his life. The neuropsychological evaluation offers us one unique perspective on this process, a window, if you will, or a still taken from a movie which is the patient's history. To be interpreted it must be compared to something. The ideal comparison is a previous neuropsychological evaluation, a comparable window, or a frame snipped from earlier in the film. The reason for this is quite obvious. It allows us to use the patient as his own control and thus reduces radically the variance we expect in the system from the standard deviation of the normative group to the standard error of measurement, a reduction in the case of the Wechsler Scales from plus or minus 15 to approximately 3 IQ point. Thus an IQ of 90 compared to an expected IQ of 100 based on norms is uninterpretable. An IQ of 90 compared to an expected IQ of 100 based on previous evaluation represents a very significant drop. The former pattern tells us almost nothing about neurologic status; the latter tells us the patient's brain may be diseased.

Case Examples

The principles outlined earlier represent examples of orienting ideas which neuropsychologists use in inferring brain pathology from behavioral samples. They are a sort of crude logic relating one category of event, test performance, to another, brain disease. In this respect, neuropsychology is not unlike electroencephalography or clinical neurology, disciplines which also attempt to infer brain pathology from something else—electrical waves recorded as squiggly lines on paper in the first case, reflex changes, medical history, symptoms and the like in the second. In the day to day work of neurologic diagnosis, the neurologist has the role of attempting to pull these data sources and others together to yield diagnosis. The neuropsychologist is thus a consulting specialist in the neurologic patient care system, adding more or less useful information at the diagnostic stage of the process.

It may be useful, here, to give some examples of diagnostic evaluations to give the reader a sense for how this is done. These cases have been selected from the writer's experience because they are illustrative of some of the principles listed earlier. Such cases are often presented in the clinical literature as being "representative", conveying the notion that they are "typical" of what one sees "clinically." Such a contention is, of course, absurd. If one really wished to present cases which were representative, he would choose them randomly which is almost never done in the clinical, case oriented literature. Instead what is done both in general and in the present case is to choose cases which exemplify points the author wishes to make, i.e. which support assertions which he believes are true, for example, the assertion that the right hemisphere is less involved in language production than is the left. The reader ought not to be overly convinced of the principles by the cases since the same sample of patients could be culled to offer "illustration" that the principles are false. The strength of the principles, such as it is, rests on the large N studies to which the interested reader is referred (Klove, 1974). Clinical examples are offered here because that is the level at which one works in practice and because, since a long time before anyone can remember, they have had an extraordinary ability to capture the attention of students.

Although it is beyond the present purpose to describe various neuropsychological tests in detail, it is necessary to describe the measures used in the cases to be discussed, at least in brief. It will be assumed that the reader is familiar with the standard tests, the WAIS, Wechsler Memory Scale (WMS), and Bender. If not, they are described in Anastasi (1976) or in Lezak (1977). The present section will be confined to measures to be reported in the following cases, drawn mainly from the Halstead-Reitan Battery (HRB).

The HRB was devised first by Halstead (1947) and revised by Reitan and further modified by Matthews and Klove at Wisconsin; this last revision will be described. It consists of eight tests which yield 10 scores. For each of these, an empirically derived cutoff is employed to reach a dichotomous classification of impaired or neurologic and unimpaired or normal. The impairment index (I.I.) is simply the number of scores in the impaired range and can thus range from 0.0 to 1.0. Tests making up the battery are as follows:

Category Test: This is a non-verbal concept attainment test which requires the subject to abstract a principle from a series of geometric stimuli, the application of which leads to correct choice among four alternatives in each item. For example, a series might consist of stimuli each with four squares, differing in color. The principle might be that the red is correct. Subject responds by selecting one of four numbered keys. In this example, the correct response would be the key in the position of the red square. Several series make up the whole test and the principle changes from series to series. The score is total errors, with 50 or more considered impaired.

Tactual Performance Test (TPT): This test requires the subject to perform the 10 block Sequin Form Board under blindfold conditions, first using the preferred hand, then the non-preferred, then both. The score is time to completion. After this is done, the subject is asked to draw the board placing drawings of the blocks where he remembers them to be. This yields two scores: one for memory (M), which is the number of correct shapes recalled, and one for location (L), which is the number located in the proper quadrant of the board. TPT thus yields three scores: time, memory, and location. Times over 15.7 minutes, and M and L scores under 6 and 5 respectively are considered impaired.

Trail Making Test: Figure 1.3 is a representation of a Trails like task. The subject simply connects the circles in correct numeric (A) or alpha-numeric (B) sequence. The time to completion is converted to a standard score from 1 to 10 for A and B, yielding an additive total score ranging from 2 to 20. Scores below 13 are considered impaired.

Figer Tapping: This measures rapid finger movement on a counter device. The score is the mean rate per 10 second intervals for the perferred hand. Both hands are assessed to allow right-left comparison, but only the preferred hand can contribute to the I.I. Rates below 51 are considered impaired.

Speech Perception Test: Here the subject listens to a series of tape recorded nonsense words of the type "theeks" or "theez". On an answer sheet he must select the correct word from among several alternatives. The score is total errors out of 60 items, with 8 or more considered impaired.

Rhythm Test: This test is taken from the Seashore Scale of Musical Talents (Seashore, Lewis, & Saetveit, 1960) and requires the subject to make same-different judgments of rhythmic patterns. The score is a standardized conversion based on errors, ranging from 1 to 10, with 6 or over considered impaired.

Aphasia Screening Test: This is a modification and extension of the Halstead-Wepman test which assesses fairly gross sorts of aphasic symptoms and requires the subject to draw geometric figures. It is scored as normal, impaired in language, impaired in drawing, or both and contributes to the impairment index if it is impaired in any way.

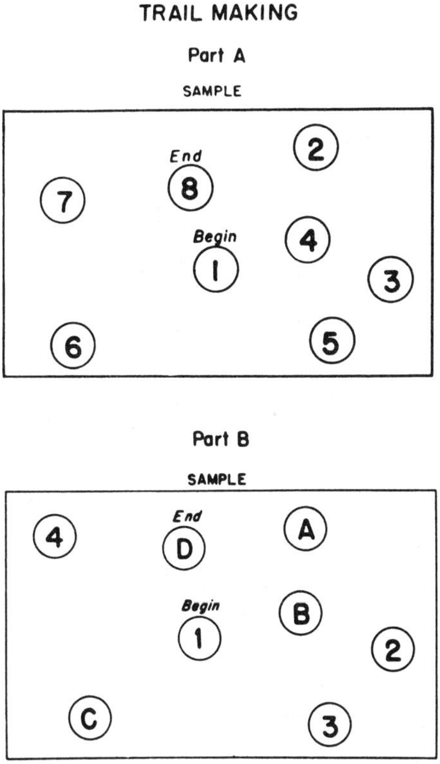

TRAIL MAKING

Part A

SAMPLE

Part B

SAMPLE

Fig. 1.3. The Trail Making Test; sample array for parts A and B.

Sensory Exam: This is a survey of touch, visual, and auditory functions derived from the classical neurologic exam. If the subject makes a sufficient number of errors on one body side, the score contributes to the I.I.

In addition to these measures, others were given in some cases. The Verbal Concept Attainment Test (VCAT) is a measure of verbal abstraction which requires the subject to choose the similar word in each of several groups. For example, an item might consist of these three series: "dog, house, cat", "phone, castle, paper", "health, record, hotel". The correct response will be left to the reader's inferential powers.

Cases Illustrating Principle One:

In examining patients with lateralized lesions, we expect in general to find contralateral impairment of motor and sensory functions. Furthermore, language functions should be impaired in diseases of the left hemisphere while non-verbal intelligence should decline in lessions of the right. Psychometrically, this implies Verbal-Performance differentiation on the WAIS with VIQ lower in the left hemisphere cases and PIQ lower in right. It has been repeatedly noted by clinical neurologists that small lesions located in the critical language regions of the left hemisphere may cause profound language impairment and thus lead to gross disability. Lesions of considerably greater size located elsewhere may lead to little apparent disability, and the right frontal region is often cited as a "silent" region for this reason.

One major issue in comparing the effects of right versus left hemisphere lesions, is to specify the comparability of the lesion size and location in the two hemispheres. Related to this is the problem of lesion type. Massive neoplastic lesions (tumor) have been shown to have distal effects so that one cannot confidently state that a left hemisphere tumor affects left hemisphere function and not right (Smith, 1966). Penetrating head injuries may similarly lead to diffuse tissue destruction even though the major traumatic injury is lateralized.

In addition to problems with lesion specification, patient variables must also be taken into account if we wish to understand the effects of lateralized disease. To the extent premorbid psychological status differs among patients, the differential effects of lesions may be obscured by pre-existing between subject differences. The reader should keep these sources of variance in mind in examining the cases to be presented.

As illustration of the differential effect of right versus left hemisphere disease two cases will be described. One, LV is a 56-year-old man who sustained a left hemisphere cerebral vascular accident (CVA) 5 months before neuropsychological evaluation, leaving him with a mild right hemiparesis. The neuropsychological and neurological picture is complicated by occasional episodes of left facial weakness, suggesting right hemisphere transient ischemic attacks (TIA's). The patient is hypertensive and has had a myocardial infarction. The second case, HI sustained a depressed skull fracture damaging the right temporal lobe 10 years before the present testing. He has had seizures since then which, following a second head injury, proved uncontrollable. He is a candidate for surgical removal of scar tissue for seizure control. Test data for these two cases appear in Table 1.2.

In comparing these protocols, one must first note that the higher subtest scores of HI suggest that his premorbid level may have been somewhat higher than LV's, though both were undoubtedly well above average. That said, the most striking finding is the Verbal-Performance differences which are large and in the expected directions. LV has difficulty in Verbal tasks such as mental arithmetic (WAIS-A) and speech sounds perception. HI shows problems in all but one Performance subtest (PC) which surely represent decline from his premorbid levels. Only on PC does his score approximate the verbal levels and this subtest is infrequently impaired in neurologic disease. Furthermore, this test has been found in factor analytic studies to load with the Verbal WAIS subtests (Berger, Burnstein, Klein, Cohen, & Lucas, 1964). HI shows a profound defect on the Rhythm Test, a measure that is reported to be particularly sensitive to right temporal lobe disease and the present case supports that belief. By contrast he has no difficulty discriminating speech sounds. Thus LV and HI show opposite and

TABLE 1.2
Test Scores for Cases Illustrating Principle One

	LV	HI
Age	56	34
Dominance	R	R
Education	12	13
WAIS V	103	124
P	118	98
F	110	113
I	11	9
C	9	19
A	7	12
S	9	15
DSp	11	11
V	12	19
DSy	10	6
PC	13	13
BD	9	11
PA	9	9
OA	10	9
Wechsler Memory Quotient	122	108
Halstead Impairment Index	.6	.6
Trails A	9	3
B	1	1
T	10*	4*
Speech	8*	1
Rhythm	1	8*
Finger Tapping R	27*	50*
L	54	34

*Contributes to Impairment Index

expected results in these two tests of qualitatively different aspects of auditory processing, one requiring verbal decoding, the other not. Trail Making is also interesting in that LV has no difficulty with A but is quite impaired on B which requires alpha-numeric sequencing. HI does poorly on both parts, reflecting a general deficit in spatial sequential processes.

In a general way then these two cases exemplify our first principle showing contralateral motor impairment on Finger Tapping and the expected cognitive findings with significant Verbal-Performance splits and a problem in particular types of auditory discrimination tasks. It is noteworthy that neither of these patients is grossly impaired with aphasic or visual constructive problems. Rather what they show are more subtle but clearly demonstrable problems which emerge when tested systematically and when viewed in terms of intrasubject rather than group differences.

Cases Illustrating Principle Three:

Two cases will be used to illustrate expected effects of dysfunction in the temporal lobes and related structures bilaterally. The first (TE) is a patient with psychomotor or temporal lobe epilepsy while the second patient (KP) has Korsakoff's syndrome following prolonged use of alcohol. TE was seen for our evaluation at the age of 23. He was a college student at that time and had a history of headache and depressed mood and some hostility. He had been observed to have occasional seizures but these were well controlled by medication. A complete medical and neurologic work-up including EEG, brain scan and lumbar puncture were within normal limits. Diagnosis of psychomotor seizures was made on basis of history as he was entirely without neurologic stigmata. Neuropsychological testing included the Wechsler Adult Intelligence Scale, the Wechsler Memory Scale and Bender as well as the Halstead-Reitan Battery. The scores are summarized in Table 1.3.

There are several striking things in TE's protocol. First is the obvious discrepancy between general intelligence (IQ 100) and memory function (MQ 84). This finding alone raises questions about the status of the temporal region. The Halstead-Reitan measures yield an impairment index of .4 which is borderline. Examination of the impaired subtests however, is consistent with the hypothesized temporal lobe problem. He has difficulty with the incidental learning or memory components (M) of the Tactual Performance Test and shows impaired scores on the two tests of sustained auditory attention, Seashore Rhythm discrimination and Speech Perception. Also possibly relevant is a relatively poor performance on the B component of the Trail Making Test, while A is well executed. The conclusions from this testing then are that the patient has temporal lobe dysfunction characterized by deficits in memory and auditory attention and discrimination. The data do not suggest a lateralizing inference. It was recommended that the patient be followed and re-evaluated on the unlikely chance that some progressive decline would be noted, suggesting active neurological disease.

KP is a 54-year-old man with a history of extreme alcohol abuse for many years. He is well educated, having completed 21 years of formal schooling and working as a professional. EEG and skull X-rays were normal, but echoencephalogram, a technique for measuring size and location of intracranial structures using reflected sound waves shows the third ventricle to be enlarged. KP's test scores appear in Table 1.3.

The differentiation of memory from other functions is clearly shown in the IQ (109) - MQ (83) difference. Some decline in abilities other than memory is suggested however by the WAIS Subtest pattern with Vocabulary, Information and Picture Completion high relative to other subtests. Also there is a significant Verbal-Performance split with PIQ lower than VIQ. Thus the Wechsler data reveal a dramatic memory defect and some other more subtle abnormalities in cognitive function.

TABLE 1.3
Test Scores for Cases Illustrating Principle Two

	TE	KP
Age	23	54
Dominance	M	R
Education	14	18
WAIS V	103	116
P	95	99
F	100	109
I	12	14
C	10	12
A	11	10
S	10	11
DSp	9	14
V	11	13
DSy	10	7
PC	10	11
BD	9	7
PA	9	7
OA	9	8
Wechsler Memory Quotient	84	83
Halstead-Reitan		
Categories	45	59*
TPT R	6.5	7
L	6.3	13.6
B	2.3	6.4
T	15.1	27*
M	4*	5*
L	1*	1*
Speech	12*	4
Rhythm	6*	3
Trails A	9	9
B	4	2
T	13	11*
Sensory	0	2*
AOH	0	0
Finger Tapping R	49	54
L	55	47
Halstead Impairment Index	4	.6

*Contributes to Impairment Index

The Halstead-Reitan Battery reinforces this impression with the subject earning an Impairment Index of .6 suggesting mild to moderate impairment of brain function. He had difficulty with the Category Test of non-verbal concept achievement. He likewise did poorly on the Verbal Concept Attainment Test. These scores reflect a loss in the highest abstract abilities, what Lezak terms "fragile functions." Memory problems are again suggested by the impaired scores in TPT posttesting for recall of shapes (M) and their location (L). A possible right hemisphere maximization of dysfunction is suggested by the Verbal-Performance split and the particular difficulty with the left hand on TPT.

Comparing TE and KP one sees a general similarity between them in that memory seems to be especially involved. In addition, KP seems to have some more general impairment of abstract ability, particularly relative to premorbid expectations based on both Vocabulary, Information and Picture Completion scores and on occupational and educational status. TE on the other hand shows evidence of a rather subtle problem in sustained auditory attention which is absent in KP whereas his abstract ability is not markedly out of line with premorbid expectations, i.e. there is no significant WAIS Subtest scatter and Categories are performed within the normal range.

The Issue of Treatment

It is sad but true that in the vast majority of cases, neurologic treatment is symptomatic and palliative, or absent altogether. Our current understanding of the diseases of the nervous system is not sufficient to allow etiologic intervention. Thus the neurologist must perform the critical function of ruling out or treating the diseases which are treatable. Once treatable illness is ruled out, however, we often face a patient with significant deficits in behavior reflecting central nervous system pathology. About the latter, often nothing can be done. If the disease is progressive like multiple sclerosis, it will progress and we can only watch. If it is static, like the residuals of a head injury, some normalization of brain function as reflected by both EEG and neuropsychological measures can be expected, but after a while, the brain reaches a steady state and no further recovery can be expected. The question is then, is there anything we can do for these patients besides watch them?

Though there can be little doubt of the theoretical relevance of psychology to rehabilitation, in practice, psychologists in this field have been notable mainly for their absence. Of the thousands upon thousands of clinical psychologists currently functioning, only a tiny fraction have interested themselves in handicaps more disabling than the depression of neurotic, affluent housewives, a preoccupation that they share, incidentally, with the bulk of psychiatrists. Neuropsychologists for their part have been engaged for decades in questions of diagnosis, lesion localization and brain-behavior relationships, with relatively little attention given to rehabilitation. This diagnostic preoccupation viewed historically is rather absurd since the actual contribution of psychological tests to neurologic diagnosis, though real, is meagre in magnitude, while the psychologist's potential contribution to the really awesome problem of remediation is huge. Thus a reordering of priorities in neuropsychology is in order and is, in fact, now beginning to take place. Papers on intervention rather than diagnosis are becoming more frequent at meetings and in the literature and one foresees an increasingly fruitful interaction between psychologists and rehabilitation specialists in the future. We will close this chapter by discussing some examples of intervention by psychologists in the rehabilitation process.

Incontinence

Nocturnal enuresis or bed wetting is a serious problem in some older patients, in certain neurological syndromes, in some chronic psychiatric disorders, and in young children. Among hospitalized patients, the control of this problem is a goal of very great importance to nursing staff, and the absence of urinary control has been shown to be a significant determinant of patient disposition. That is, patients who are enuretic are much less likely to be discharged to home care than are patients without this problem. Techniques effective in modifying this category of behavior are thus of considerable medical interest.

John Atthowe (1972) describes an aversive conditioning technique combined with a token economy which was effective in controlling nocturnal enuresis in a group of 12 chronic patients in an inpatient setting. The patients represent rather the bottom of the prognostic heap with hospital lengths of stay all over 20 years. In addition to diagnoses of chronic schizophrenia, 11 were also labeled organic brain syndrome and 6 had been lobotomized. In this population, enuresis was clearly only one of a vast number of problems, but it is an important one since its presence precluded any sort of home placement and certainly did not endear the patients to housekeeping and nursing staff.

After collection of baseline data, the treatment program began, broken into two phases. The first phase was a sort of, "We have had it with you," condition in which the patients were told that because of their bedwetting they would have to go through a "therapeutic" program. It was aversive in the following four ways: (1) they had to sleep in a crowded wing of the ward; (2) the lights came on four times per night at about 11:00 p.m., 12:30 a.m., 2:00 a.m., and 4:00 a.m.; (3) at these hours they had to go to the bathroom whether wet or not and whether they needed to urinate or not and had to stay there with the lights on for 10 minutes; (4) this treatment subjected them to social pressures from other non-enuretics on the ward who were disturbed by the routine.

These contingencies lasted 2 months and could not be avoided. After 2 months, if the patient did not wet the bed, he was rewarded with a token in the morning. The 4:00 and 2:00 a.m. trips were eliminated following dry nights and after a dry week, all bathroom trips were eliminated and the patient could buy his way out of the crowded ward with tokens. The procedure led to a dramatic reduction in enuretic episodes during the aversive phase and to their complete elimination at 8 months. Two, 22, and 43-month follow-ups show no recurrence. Two patients were able to leave the hospital for home care.

In discussing this study, Atthowe makes several points worth noting. First, the program represented a collective effort of psychologists and nursing staff which is a prerequisite to consistent application of any behavioral strategy in a ward setting. Second, the program was long in duration with successful elimination of the problem behavior in some lobotomized patients occurring as late as 8 months after starting the program. Finally, the enuresis control program operated as part of a broader behavioral intervention, the token economy, and this undoubtedly contributed to its success. We might note finally that to intervene in a population of this type and enjoy success of *any* kind is extraordinary and bears testimony of the malleability of behavior, even in patients with exceedingly protracted histories characterized by the grossest sort of deterioration.

Memory Defect

One of the more frequently occurring and disabling consequences of neurologic disease is memory loss. As we have seen, this is a sign of bitemporal lobe disease but it occurs with varying degrees of severity in brain lesions variously located. In terms of treatment for this problem, the medical armamentum is rather limited. During the acute phase, for example, of encephalitis or Korsakoff's disease, specific etiologic and symptomatic treatment will lead to some improvement in memory as function in general improves. In chronic memory loss, however, medical treatment is almost completely ineffective. Thus the stimulating drugs, caffeine or amphetamine will increase alertness or attention in demented patients as in everyone else, but they seem to have little or no effect in long term retention (Barbizet, 1970). Psychological strategies thus offer the only possibly effective modality for improving memory function in neurologic patients and a number of hopeful signs are to be found in the literature. As an example, I shall describe a project that was done in my laboratory by Michael Dolan (Dolan & Norton, 1977).

The subjects in this study were patients hospitalized because of behavior problems referable to neurologic disease and were diagnostically hetrogeneous. All of them had problems with memory as noted by staff and documented by impaired performance on the Graham-Kendall Memory For Design Test (MFD) and all were sufficiently intact to perform the Vocabulary subtest of the Verbal WAIS. Thirty such subjects were assigned to three matched groups, two experimental and one control, equated in WAIS, MFD, age, education and time in the hospital. The three groups were used to assess the efficacy of two retraining strategies as opposed to the informal activities of the ward.

Information to be learned was chosen to be relevant and useful to life in the hospital. Thus, such things as the names of staff, facts about the hospital, and general information of the sort assessed in a mental status examination were employed. At the beginning of the study all subjects were assessed as to how much of this information they already knew and this percent of correct response was the standard against which the efficacy of the procedures was judged. It should be emphasized that in the normal course of things, all patients were given frequent opportunities to learn this information. Staff frequently introduced themselves, signs announced the days of the week, the name of the hospital, etc. There was even a regularly scheduled group experience, Reality Group, devoted to teaching these bits of information. All subjects in the study were exposed to these environmental influences. General level of ward behavior was assessed using the Nurses' Observation Scale for Inpatient Evaluation, NOSIE 30 (Honigfeld, Gillis, & Klett, 1966), and this was done at both the beginning and at the end of the study.

The formal training sessions occurred twice per week for 4 weeks. During these sessions the subjects viewed slides conveying the information to be learned and gave multiple choice responses. One experimental group received praise for correct responses, the second received praise as well as a material reward, self-selected from several, e.g., cigarettes, candy, gum, money. The training involved a variety of match to sample, delayed recall and recognition procedures, the details of which need not concern us here. The training sessions lasted about one-half hour, thus involving a total time of approximately 4 hours per experimental subject over the 4 week period.

All subjects were assessed at the end of the 4 week training period and the experimental groups were reassessed one week later to assess retention. All groups began with a mean correct of approximately 20%. At post testing, the control group had shown no gain while the experimental groups had increased to about 64% and did not differ from one another. No significant loss was seen from post test scores to retention scores suggesting that the acquired information was maintained for at least a period of a week without systematic efforts to reinforce it during that period.

This study suggests that learning theory derived teaching strategems can improve the memory function of neurologic patients and that the usual pessimism about these patients is not completely warranted. It further suggests that the informal non-reinforcement based teaching strategy (Reality Group) was ineffective, the control group making no gains over the 4 week period. This lack of what might be termed incidental learning is also reflected in a near zero correlation between time on the unit and test score.

The generalized effect of this training procedure to a more global measure of behavioral effectiveness, the NOSIE 30, is notable for its absence. There were no differences as a function of training in NOSIE 30 scores, nor did they improve simply with the passage of time. NOSIE 30 scores were the same for all groups at both pre- and post-training periods. One might speculate that, had the present training procedure been part of a more general ward program, as was the case of Atthowe's study reported earlier, generalization outside the experimental setting would have been evident.

This small project illustrates that application of learning theory can improve the acquisition of information in patients who are deemed, on the basis of diagnosis, incapable of learning. This generally pessimistic expectation no doubt derives in part from the fact that these patients do not seem to benefit from the usual methods of teaching such as group discussion and informal introduction, as reflected by the present control group's total lack of progress.

Finally, it must be emphasized that the patients in this study were given truly massive amounts of support by highly skilled and sensitive staff, working in a setting with reasonably low patient staff ratios, and augmented by large numbers of enthusiastic trainees in nursing, psychology and medicine. The failure of the control group then cannot be passed of to ''back ward'' circumstances and this reinforces the fairly dramatic effectiveness of systematic as opposed to informal teaching strategies in this population.

REFERENCES

Adams, K. M. In search of Luria's battery: A false start. *Journal of Consulting and Clinical Psychology,* 1980, *48,* 511–516.

Adams, R. D., & Victor, M. *Principles of neurology.* New York: McGraw-Hill, 1977.

Albert, M., Butters, N., & Neff, J. *Retrograde amnesia of alcohol and non-alcohol related amnesias.* Paper presented at the annual meeting of the International Neuropsychological Society, Minneapolis, Minn., 1978.

American Psychiatric Association, Diagnostic and Statistical Manual (3rd ed.) Washington, D.C.: American Psychiatric Association, 1980.

Anastasi, A. *Psychological testing (4th ed.).* New York: Macmillan, 1976.

Atthowe, J. M. Controlling nocturnal enuresis in severely disabled and chronic patients. *Behavior Therapy,* 1972, *3,* 232–239.

Barbizet, J. *Human memory and its pathology.* San Francisco: W. H. Freeman, 1970.

Bender, L. A visual motor Gestalt test and its clinical use. *American Orthopsychiatric Association Research Monographs,* No. 3, 1938.

Benson, D. F. Aphasia. In K. M. Heilman & E. Valenstein (eds.), *Clinical Neuropsychology,* New York: Oxford University Press, 1979.

Benson, D. F., & Barton, M. I. Disturbances in constructional ability. *Cortex,* 1970, *6,* 19–46.

Benton, A. L. The fiction of the 'Gerstmann syndrome'. *Journal of Neurology,* Neurosurgery and Psychiatry, 1961, *24,* 176–181.

Benton, A. L. Differential behavioral effects of frontal lobe disease. *Neuropsychologia,* 1968, *6,* 53–60.

Benton, A. Visuoperceptive, visuospatial, and visuoconstructive disorder. In K. M. Heilman & E. Valenstein (eds.), *Clinical Neuropsychology,* New York: Oxford University Press, 1979a.

Benton, A., Body schema disturbances: finger agnosia and right-left disorientation, in K. M. Heilman and E. Valenstein (eds) Clinical Neuropsychology, New York, Oxford University Press, 1979b.

Berger, L., Burnstein, A., Klein, E., Cohen, J., & Lucas, G. Effects of aging and pathology on the factorial structure of intelligence. *Journal of Consulting and Clinical Psychology,* 1964, *28,* 199–207.

Blum, J. D. Changes in psychiatric diagnosis over time. *American Psychologist,* 1978, *33,* 1017–1031.

Bogen, J. E. The callosal syndrome. In K. M. Heilman & E. Valenstein (eds.), *Clinical neuropsychology,* New York: Oxford University Press, 1979.

Butters, N. Amnesic disorders. In K. M. Heilman & E. Valenstein (eds.), *Clinical neuropsychology,* New York: Oxford University Press, 1979.

Corkin, S. Tactually-guided maze learning in man: Effects of unilaterial cortical excisions and bilateral hippocampal lesions. *Neuropsychologia,* 1965, *3,* 339-351.

Critchley, M. *The parietal lobes.* London: Arnold, 1953.

Critchley, M. The problem of visual agnosia. *Journal of Neurological Science,* 1964, *1,* 274-290.

Davidson, P. O., & Davidson, S. M. (eds.). *Behavioral medicine: Changing health lifestyles.* New York: Bruner/Mazel, 1980.

Damasio, A. The frontal lobes. In K. M. Heilman & E. Valenstein (eds.), *Clinical neuropsychology,* New York: Oxford University Press, 1979.

DeRomanis, F., & Benfatto, B. Presentiazione e discussione di quattero casi di prosophanosia. *Rivista di Neurologia,* 1973, *43,* 111-132.

Dolan, M. P., & Norton, J. C. A programmed training technique that uses reinforcement to facilitate acquisition and retention in brain damaged patients. *Journal of Clinical Psychology,* 1977, *33,* 496-501.

Esper, E. A. *A history of psychology.* Philadelphia: Saunders, 1964.

Gazzaniga, M. S. *The bisected brain.* New York: Appleton-Century-Crofts, 1970.

Gazzaniga, M. S., Bogen, J. E., & Sperry, R. W. Some functional effects of sectioning the cerebral commissures in man. *Proceedings of the National Academy of Science,* 1962, *48,* 1765-1769.

Geschwind, N. Disconnexion syndromes in animals and man: *Brain,* 1965, 88, 237-294.

Geschwind, N. Karl Wernicke, the Breslau School and the history of aphasia. In E. C. Carterette (ed.), *Brain Function: Speech, Language and Communication,* Los Angeles, California: University of California Press, 1966.

Geshwind, N. The organization of language and the brain. *Science,* 1970, *170,* 940-944.

Gerstmann, J. Syndrome of finger agnosia, disorientation for right and left, agraphia and acalculia. *Archives of Neurology and Psychiatry,* 1940, *44,* 398-408.

Gloning, I., Gloning, K., & Hoff, H. *Neuropsychological symptoms and lesions of the occipital lobe and adjacent areas.* Paris: Gauthier-Villars, 1968.

Halstead, W. C. *Brain and intelligence.* Chicago: University of Chicago Press, 1947.

Heilman, K. M. Apraxia. In K. M. Hailman & E. Valenstein (eds.), *Clinical Neuropsychology,* New York: Oxford University Press, 1979.

Honigfeld, G., Gillis, R., & Klett, J. *NOSIE-30: A treatment sensitive ward behavior scale.* Report #66, Perrypoint, Maryland: Central Neuropsychiatric Research Laboratory, 1966.

Kinsbourne, N., & Warrington, E. K. Observations on colour agnosia. *Journal of Neurology, Neurosurgery and Psychiatry,* 1964, *27,* 296-299.

Kleist, K. *Gehirnpathologie.* Leipzig: Barth, 1934.

Klove, H. Validation studies in adult clinical neuropsychology. In R. M. Reitan & L. A. Davison (eds.), *Clinical neuropsychology: Current status and applications,* New York: Winston-Wiley, 1974.

Lewis, G. P., Golden, C. J., Moses, J. A., Osmon, D. C., Purisch, A. D., & Hammeke, T. A. Localization of cerebral dysfunction with a standardized version of Luria's neuropsychological battery. *Journal of Consulting and Clinical Psychology,* 1979, *47,* 1003-1019.

Lezak, M. D. *Neuropsychological assessment.* New York: Oxford University Press, 1977.

Lhermitte, F., Derouesne, J., & Signoret, J. L. Analyse neuropsychologique du syndrome frontal. *Revue Neurologique,* 1972, *127,* 415-440.

Lhermitte, F., & Signoret, J. L. Analyse neuropschologique et differenciation des syndromes amnesique. *Revue Neurologique,* 1972, *126,* 161-178.

Luria, A. R. *Higher cortical function in man.* New York: Oxford University Press, 1966.

Luria, A. R. *The working brain.* New York: Basic Books, 1974.

Malamud, N. Psychiatric Disorder with intracranial tumors of the limbic system. *Archives of Neurology,* 1967, *17,* 113-123.

Mark, B. H., & Ervin, F. R. *Violence and the brain,* New York: Harper and Row, 1970.

McFie, J. *Assessment of organic intellectual impairment.* London: Academic Press, 1975.

McFie, J., & Thompson, J. A. Picture arrangement: a measure of frontal function? *British Journal of Psychiatry*, 1972, *121*, 547-552.

Miller, E. *Clinical neuropsychology*. Harmondsworth, Middlesex: Penguin Books, 1972.

Milner, B. Psychological defects produced by temporal lobe excision. *Research Publications, Associations for Research in Nervous and Mental Disease*, 1958, *36*, 244-257.

Milner, B. Laterality effects in audition. In V. D. Mountcastle (ed.), *Interhemispheric Relations and Cerebral Dominance*, Baltimore: Johns Hopkins University Press, 1962.

Milner, B. Some effects of frontal lobectomy in man. In J. Warren & K. Akert (eds.) *The Frontal Granular Cortex in Man*. New York: McGraw-Hill, 1964.

Milner, B. Visually guided maze learning in man: effects of bilateral hippocampal, bilateral frontal, and unilateral cerebral lesions. *Neuropsychologia*, 1965, *3*, 317-338.

Milner, B., & Teuber, H. L. Alteration of perception and memory in man: reflections on methods. In L. Weiskrantz (ed.), *Analysis of behavioral change*, New York: Harper and Row, 1968.

Norton, J. C. *An introduction to medical psychology*. New York: Macmillan, 1982.

Parsons, O. A. *Recent developments in clinical neuropsychology*. Keynote Address, Advances in Clinical Neuropsychology, University of Pittsburgh, 1979.

Piercy, M., Hacaen, H., & de Ajuriaguerra, J. Constructional apraxia associated with unilateral cerebral lesions—left and right-sided cases compared. *Brain*, 1960, *83*, 225-242.

Poeck, K., & Orgass, B. Gerstmann's syndrome and aphasia, *Cortex*, 1966, *2*, 421-437.

Purisch, C. D., Golden, C. J., & Hammeke, T. A. Discrimination of schizophrenic and brain-injured patients by a standardized version of Luria's neuropsychological tests. *Journal of Consulting and Clinical Psychology*, 1978, *46*, 1266-1273.

Rachman, S. (ed.). *Contributions to medical psychology* (Vol. 1). Oxford: Pergamon, 1977.

Reitan, R. M., & Davison, L. A. *Clinical neuropsychology: Current status and applications*. New York: Winston-Wiley, 1974.

Russell, E. W. A multiple scoring method for the assessment of complex memory functions. *Journal of Consulting and Clinical Psychology*, 1975, *43*, 800-809.

Sandifer, M. G. Psychiatric diagnosis: Cross-national research findings. *Proceedings of the Royal Society of Medicine*, 1972, *65*, 497-500.

Scotti, G., & Spinnler, H. Colour imperception in unilateral hemisphere-damaged patients. *Journal of Neurology, Neurosurgery and Psychiatry*, 1970, *33*, 22-28.

Seashore, C. E., Lewis, D., & Saetveit, D. C. *Seashore measures of musical talents* (Rev. ed.). New York: Psychological Corporation, 1960.

Sherrington, C. S. *Man on his nature*. Cambridge: Cambridge University Press, 1951.

Small, L. *Neuropsychodiagnosis in psychotherapy*. New York: Bruner/Mazel, 1973.

Smith, A. Intellectual functions in patients with lateralized frontal tumors. *Journal of Neurology, Neurosurgery, and Psychiatry*, 1966, *29*, 52-59.

Sperry, R. W. Cerebral organization and behavior. *Science*, 1961, *133*, 1749-1757.

Taylor, A., & Warrington, E. K. Visual agnosia: A single case report. *Cortex*, 1971, *7*, 152-161.

Ullman, L., & Krasner, L. *A psychological approach to abnormal behavior* (2nd ed.). Englewood Cliffs, New Jersey: Prentice-Hall, 1975.

Victor, M., Adams, R. D., & Collins, G. H. *The Wernicke-Korsakoff syndrome*. Philadelphia: Davis, 1971.

Vignolo, L. Auditory Agnosia: A review and report of recent evidence. In A. Benton (ed.). *Contributions to Clinical Neuropsychology*. Chicago: Aldine, 1969.

Walsh, K. *Neuropsychology: A clinical approach*. London: Churchill Livingstone, 1978.

Warrington, E. Constructional Apraxia. In P. Vinken & G. Bruyn (eds.). *Handbook of Clinical Neurology*. Vol. 4. Amsterdam: New Holland, 1969.

Wechsler, D. *The Measurement and Appraisal of Adult Intelligence* (4th ed.). Baltimore: Williams & Wilkins, 1958.

2 Biofeedback: Clinical Applications in Medicine

John P. Hatch
The University of Texas Health Science Center at San Antonio

Robert J. Gatchel
Uniformed Services University of the Health Sciences

Rick Harrington
University of Texas at Arlington

In its broadest sense, biofeedback can be defined as any consequence of biological performance which is perceived by a behaving subject. Some of these consequences of biological behavior affect the external environment in such a way that they are directly observable to the subject through exteroceptive sensory channels. For example, we can see the position of our limbs in space, can feel our breath on the surface of our skin, and can hear the activity of our bowels. Much of our biological behavior, however, is concerned with maintaining a constant internal vegetative economy and has little or no perceptible effect on the external environment. The consequences of these behaviors do not therefore interact with exteroceptive receptors and are not readily accessible to conscious awareness. To be sure, we do consciously experience some interoceptive awareness of internal biological activity such as pain, muscle tension, or our pulse but there is normally adaptive advantage to not having to consciously attend to or control these activities. Also, interoceptors do not have the extensive afferent representation at the cortical level which is needed for a high degree of perceptual acuity or fine discriminability characteristic of vision or audition.

Primarily because their activity does not normally produce perceptible changes in the external environment, visceral and glandular behaviors were long considered not to be amenable to operant conditioning or voluntary regulation, and the autonomic nervous system was seen as being somehow "inferior" to the somatic nervous system (Miller, 1969). Beginning in the early 1960's, however, investigators pioneered research which challenged these assumptions and ultimately laid the empirical foundations for what now has come to be known as biofeedback (see Basmajian, 1963; Fowler & Kimmel, 1962; Hefferline, Keenan, & Harford, 1959; Kamiya, 1969; Lisina, 1965; Miller, 1969; Shapiro, Crider, & Tursky, 1964). Borrowing heavily from operant conditioning techniques, these investigators demonstrated some degree of operant or voluntary control in a wide variety of visceral, central nervous system, and somatomotor functions. Although many questions remain unanswered regarding the exact nature of the underlying processes and mechanisms, it is clear that some form of learning is central to the development of operant or voluntary control. Also, other psychological factors such as patient motivation, individual personality characteristics, and psychopathology are known to affect this learning process. Since these important areas represent the traditional subject matter of clinical psychology, this discipline has much to contribute to the development of biofeedback as well as much to gain through its utilization.

Today, biofeedback is broadly and loosely defined as a technique for transforming some aspect of physiological behavior into electrical signals which are made accessible to exteroception—usually vision or audition. Sometimes, the feedback signal is combined with a tangible reward such as money or the opportunity to view attractive pictures in an attempt to motivate the patient and strengthen the effect on the targeted physiological response. In other instances, the clinician provides verbal praise for success in addition to feedback. These practices also are forms of biofeedback, since they too convey information to the learner about his or her biological performance. In most instances, however, response contingent lights or tones alone can be shown to augment voluntary control.

Encouraged by the early successes which demonstrated voluntary control of normal physiological activity, medical and psychological clinicians soon began to question whether pathophysiological activity could also be controlled with the goal of restoring health or preventing illness. In this chapter, we will describe and critically evaluate the available empirical evidence bearing on this question. The biofeedback literature has grown to mammoth proportions in recent years, and discussions of the topic have appeared everywhere from the popular press to some of our most prestigeous medical journals. Unfortunately, the growth in quality has not kept pace with this growth in quantity, and there is as much variability in quality at one end of this publication continuum as there is at the other. Therefore, although almost all health professionals have by now had some introduction or exposure to the concept of biofeedback, there is tremendous variability as to what they believe its clinical capabilities to be. There are those who believe it to be a total fraud, as well as those who believe it is a panacea. Neither of these positions is of course correct, and we will review the data with cautious optimism, hoping to convert some skeptics and also to restrain some zealots.

Because of the size and qualitative variability of the biofeedback literature, it would be neither possible nor desirable to attempt an exhaustive review; but we will attempt to be as comprehensive as possible. We will limit our discussion to published studies which have used biofeedback as a treatment modality in an actual medical population. We will also focus attention on studies demonstrating a reasonable level of sophistication in design and analysis. In general, individual case studies and uncontrolled group outcome studies will receive less attention than well controlled group outcome studies or validation studies comparing biofeedback with other established therapeutic techniques.

REVIEW OF CLINICAL RESEARCH USING BIOFEEDBACK

Cardiovascular System

Essential Hypertension. Essential hypertension is an abnormal elevation of the blood pressure having no clear etiopathology. In its early stages, the disease is frequently asymptomatic, making early detection and treatment difficult. Yet, the prevalence of hypertensive disease is overwhelming, with from 10%-30% of the American population over 40 years of age afflicted to some degree. These epidemic proportions, combined with strong evidence of increased morbidity and mortality due to atherosclerosis, myocardial infarction, stroke, congestive heart disease, and renal failure, make essential hypertension one of our most insidious health problems. Fortunately, the disease can usually be treated pharmacologically once detected. However, such treatment is not without undesirable side effects and must generally be continued for the remainder of the patient's life.

The participation of psychological variables in essential hypertension is currently receiving a great deal of experimental attention, and there is an evergrowing body of literature linking blood pressure elevations with psychological variables such as personality type, life style, and reactivity to stress. Consequently, behavioral scientists have begun to advocate the desirability of developing treatment techniques which intervene at both the biological and psychological levels. Biofeedback is one such technique.

The standard auscultatory method of measuring blood pressure, involving occlusion of an artery, can itself be distressful to a subject if repeated many times, and this has posed a perennial problem in psychophysiological research. The problem has now been partially resolved through a technique described as the "constant-cuff" method (Shapiro, Tursky, Gershon, & Stern, 1969). This method involves inflating a sphygmomanometer cuff to a pressure close to median systolic pressure and holding it at that level for about 50 heart beats. The cuff is then deflated and normal circulation is allowed to occur for 30 seconds. During repeated inflation trials, a crystal microphone detects either the presence or absence of a Korotkoff sound on each heart beat. Biofeedback consists of presenting a signal, such as a light, each time a Korotkoff sound is or is not detected, indicating that momentary blood pressure is above or below median systolic pressure respectively. On successive inflation trials, cuff pressure can be adjusted as necessary to track an increasing or decreasing median pressure.

An alternative method for continuously monitoring blood pressure takes advantage of the relationship between arterial pressure and the transit time of the pulse wave between two points on the arterial tree, or the time between some electrocardiac event and the arrival of the pulse wave at some peripheral point. Although measuring pulse transit time offers potential advantages in terms of patient comfort and ability to record blood pressure continuously, its relationship to systolic and diastolic blood pressure remains to be properly demonstrated (Newlin & Levenson, 1979; Obrist, Light, McCubbin, Hutcheson, & Hoffer, 1979). Thus, there are important methodological questions which must be answered before the pulse transit time method can be unequivocably recommended. Most of the studies reviewed in the following section have used the constant-cuff method.

Studies Using Direct Systolic Blood Pressure Feedback.   Benson, Shapiro, Tursky, and Schwartz (1971) treated seven hypertensive patients, five of whom were diagnosed as suffering from essential hypertension, with biofeedback associated with the lowering of systolic blood pressure. Before therapy was begun, patients participated in up to 15 pretreatment control sessions during which basal systolic pressures were found to be stable. Biofeedback training, consisting of visual slides and monetary rewards in addition to feedback, was continued until a point was reached beyond which no further reductions in pressure were observed across five consecutive sessions. A mean reduction of 16.5 mm Hg was obtained within sessions. Although no control group was used, this problem was offset somewhat by the fact that stable performance was demonstrated both before and during treatment. No follow-up data were reported.

In another study (Kristt & Engel, 1975), five patients recorded their own blood pressures at home for a 5–7 week baseline period on a daily basis. They were then admitted to the hospital and remained in-patients for the treatment phase of the experiment. Treatment involved, in successive stages, teaching the patients first to raise, then to lower, and finally to alternately raise and lower their blood pressure. During treatment, all the patients learned to reliably raise and lower their blood pressure with biofeedback within treatment sessions. Following discharge from the hospital, patients continued to practice blood pressure regulation and once again monitored their own pressures on a daily basis. Within 3 months following treatment, systolic pressures remained approximately 18 mm Hg below pretreatment baseline levels in the four patients who provided follow-up data. Diastolic pressure also showed a significant reduction in two of the patients studied. No control group was used.

Following three baseline sessions, Kleinman, Goldman, Snow, and Korol (1977) administered systolic blood pressure feedback via the constant-cuff method to a group of eight essential hypertensive patients. Over nine training sessions subjects showed mean reductions of about 4 mm Hg in both systolic and diastolic pressure within sessions. Follow-up data collected on three patients, 4 months following therapy, showed that pressures were maintained below pre-treatment levels. This study used no control group, but in a similar experiment Goldman, Kleinman, Snow, Bidus, and Korol (1975) compared a group of seven essential hypertensive patients given nine sessions of constant-cuff type biofeedback with a group of four patients given three sessions of relaxation training. The biofeedback subjects showed a mean systolic blood pressure reduction of 7 mm Hg within sessions, whereas the control subjects reduced systolic pressure by only about 1 mm Hg. Once again, diastolic pressures also showed a reduction. Problems with this study include the short baseline period and the lack of follow-up data. Also, the control group suffered from its small sample size and the fact that it differed from the experimental group in the number of treatment sessions it received.

Studies Using Direct Diastolic Blood Pressure Feedback.   Attempts have also been made to train hypertensive patients to control diastolic blood pressure with biofeedback. In one such study, Schwartz and Shapiro (1973) provided seven essential hypertensive patients with 10 sessions of therapy consisting of biofeedback and monetary rewards contingent upon diastolic blood pressure reductions. A 5 mm Hg reduction in diastolic pressure was obtained, but the effect did not transfer from one session to the next.

In another study Elder, Ruiz, Deabler, and Dillenkoffer (1973) trained one group of hypertensives to lower diastolic blood pressure using a red light as a source of feedback and another group using the red light combined with verbal praise. A control group was instructed simply to lower blood pressure in any way they could, but were not given either biofeedback or verbal praise. By the end of seven training sessions, the group which received biofeedback alone was able to reduce diastolic pressure by an average of 9 mm Hg, and the group which received the combined treatment was able to demonstrate an average reduction of 21 mm Hg. The control group did not demonstrate any reliable blood pressure control. It was reported that these reductions in blood pressure were maintained at follow-up one week after treatment ended. In a similar procedure, Elder and Eustis (1975) used a combination of visual feedback and verbal praise with a group of 20 essential hypertensive patients. Some of the patients received spaced session (8 sessions distributed over 7 weeks) while others received massed sessions (10 sessions over 12 days). Maximum reductions in diastolic blood pressure recorded within individual sessions were approximately 9% below pretreatment levels. It was also reported that subjects receiving massed trials seemed to do somewhat better than those who received spaced trials.

Studies Using Biofeedback Other Than for the Direct Reduction of Blood Pressure.   Another approach to reducing blood pressure is to provide biofeedback contingent upon modifying some aspect of physiological function other than blood pressure which could be expected to indirectly produce the desired effect on blood pressure. For example, Patel and co-workers (e.g., Frankel, Patel, Horowitz, Friedwald, & Gaarder, 1978; Patel, 1973, 1975; Patel & North, 1975) have shown blood pressure reductions to be associated with various combinations of behavioral interventions including GSR feedback, EMG feedback, meditation, relaxation, and autogenic training. Although significant blood pressure reductions ranging from approximately 15 to 26 mm Hg have been reported, a recent study (Frankel et al., 1978) failed to show any significant reduction in blood pressure using combined blood pressure feedback, EMG feedback, and verbal relaxation beyond that produced by sham blood pressure feedback or no treatment. When such combinations of multiple treatment modalities are used it becomes impossible to evaluate the role, if any, played by the biofeedback.

Studies Comparing the Effectiveness of Biofeedback and Other Forms of Treatment. Shoemaker and Tasto (1975) compared the effectiveness of direct blood pressure biofeedback, progressive relaxation training, and no treatment in borderline hypertensive patients. In this study, an unusual form of biofeedback allowed the patients to visually monitor their own polygraph record as blood pressure was recorded every 90 seconds. Thus, the feedback was not delivered on a beat by beat basis as was done in the studies discussed earlier which used the constant-cuff technique. The results indicated that the group trained in progressive relaxation was able to reduce systolic and diastolic blood pressure by about 7 and 8 mm Hg respectively, but the other two groups showed no significant blood pressure reductions. Therefore, this study showed progressive relaxation training to be more effective than blood pressure biofeedback, but it is difficult to generalize beyond the study because the biofeedback format was atypical. The method which was used had not previously been shown to be effective in lowering blood pressure, and the changes in blood pressure which were produced (approximately 1 mm Hg) were smaller than those generally obtained with the constant-cuff method.

Surwit, Shapiro, and Good (1978) did use the constant-cuff technique in a comparative study, but they delivered the feedback contingent upon the production of an integrated physiological pattern consisting of simultaneously reducing heart rate and blood pressure, rather than blood pressure alone. A second group received biofeedback aimed at helping them reduce forearm and forehead muscle tension. A third group received relaxation training. None of the techniques produced significant reductions in blood pressure across sessions, below pretreatment, baseline levels.

In another study, Blanchard, Miller, Abel, Haynes, and Wicker (1979) compared three groups of borderline essential hypertension patients who were given either systolic blood pressure feedback, frontal EMG feedback designed to assist muscular relaxation, or self-instructed relaxation training. The blood pressure biofeedback was accomplished by reading the subject's systolic pressure from the polygraph record at one minute intervals and plotting the values on a graph which was visible to the subject on closed-circuit TV. Thus, the biofeedback was not continuous, and there was a 4 to 5 second delay between the blood pressure measurement and the time this information was available to the subject. The effect of the treatments on blood pressure was modest. In the relaxation condition, patients reduced systolic pressure by a mean of 9.5 mm Hg, and those in the biofeedback condition by 8.1 mm Hg. The EMG biofeedback group increased systolic blood pressure by 1.4 mm Hg. There were no significant reductions in diastolic pressure, and there were no significant differences among the three groups on either systolic or diastolic pressure. The authors concluded that none of the treatments could be described as successful.

One study using progressive relaxation training and pulse wave velocity biofeedback also produced equivocal results. (Walsh, Dale, & Anderson, 1977).

Assessment.   Research has shown a limited degree of success in reducing the symptoms of essential hypertension with biofeedback. The technique has not been shown, however, to reliably produce reductions in blood pressure of a clinically significant magnitude that transfer to the non-laboratory environment. Thus, it cannot be considered an alternative to pharmacologic treatment at this time. It should be noted, though, that a recent study was reported by Luborsky, Crits-Christoph, Brady, Kron, Weiss, and Engelman (1980) which compared the relative efficacy of medication, relaxation training, and biofeedback during a 6-week treatment program with mildly-moderately hypertensive individuals. It was found that although patients given medication derived the most benefit even at moderate levels of medication, some patients experienced comparable benefits from the two behavioral treatments. These investigators suggest that hypertensive individuals who are strongly motivated to adhere to a behavioral treatment program should be encouraged to undergo such treatment at first to assess whether it is beneficial, before being put on medication. This is an interesting suggestion which certainly merits additional investigation.

The usefulness of biofeedback as an adjunct to chemotherapy has not yet been evaluated, and such studies would be of much value. On the whole, research in this area has not advanced very far. Sample sizes are small, control groups are lacking and follow-up data are unavailable far too often. These are serious shortcomings, and until additional research is performed to remedy these problems, the usefulness of biofeedback in the management of essential hypertension cannot be determined.

Postural Hypotension

In some cases of high spinal cord injury, the reflex pathways which normally produce vasoconstriction upon assuming an upright posture are damaged, resulting in a lowering of the blood pressure to the point where some patients cannot stand or sit upright without fainting. There is no effective treatment for the disorder, and severely affected patients must remain in the supine position. Although controlled group outcome studies are not yet available, several good case studies have been conducted which merit mention (Brucker & Ince, 1977; Pickering, Brucker, Frankel, Mathias, Dworkin, & Miller, 1977). Using systolic blood pressure biofeedback, spinal cord injured patients have learned to raise their blood pressures by as much as 48 mm Hg. The training procedure has enabled some patients to sit upright or to stand with the crutches which prior to training produced fainting.

Cardiac Arrhythmias Treated with Heart Rate Biofeedback

Although heart rate regulation with biofeedback has probably received more experimental attention using normal volunteer subjects than any other aspect of physiological function, applications of this technique have not found many applications in clinical medicine. Engel and his coworkers pioneered the applied research in the area of treating cardiac arrhythmias with heart rate feedback, and are responsible for most of the available results. The basic paradigm employed by Engel and colleagues utilizes the presentation of visual feedback which is contingent on heart rate. The patient is typically trained over a series of sessions to speed, slow, and alternately speed and slow heart rate, first with feedback present and then with feedback gradually removed. The discussion of these experiments will be organized according to the type of arrhythmia studied.

Sinus Tachycardia. Sinus tachycardia is an abnormal acceleration of heart rate in which the dominant pacemaker remains the SA node. Heart rates usually rise to approximately 100 to 140 bpm in the condition. In most of the patients studied, there was no cardiac disease present, and the elevations in heart rate were considered secondary to a psychiatric disorder. Engel and Melmon (reported by Engel & Bleecker, 1974) treated a 53-year-old woman with biofeedback. Her resting pulse rate before treatment was 86.3 bpm, but this was reduced to 68.5 bpm during 21 treatment sessions. The ability to restrain heart rate also transferred to the natural environment as evidenced by the fact that she was able to maintain a heart rate of 75 bpm while being examined by her regular physician. Other investigators have also reported clinically meaningful reductions in the heart rates of individual sinus tachycardia patients (Blanchard & Abel, 1976; Scott, Blanchard, Edmundson, & Young, 1973).

Atrial Fibrillation. Atrial fibrillation is a common cardiac arrhythmia in which atrial rate reaches 300 bpm or more. In one study, Bleecker & Engel, (1973b) successfully trained six patients with chronic atrial fibrillation to speed and slow ventricular rate. The clinical usefulness of these results remains to be further explored.

Paroxysmal Atrial Tachycardia.   This is a condition in which heart rate increases suddenly to an abnormally high rate. One patient with this disorder did show clinical improvement following biofeedback training which included the ability to maintain a slower heart rate and a normal sinus rhythm (Engel & Bleecker, 1974).

Premature Ventricular Contractions (PVCs).   These ectopic beats occur when the heart muscle undergoes depolarization too soon following the occurrence of a normal contraction. The result is that the subsequent heartbeat is premature, that is, it occurs before the ventricles have completely filled. Several patients have now been treated with heart rate biofeedback for this condition (Engel & Bleecker, 1974; Miller, 1975; Pickering & Gorham, 1975; Pickering & Miller, 1977; Weiss & Engel, 1971). The results of these trials suggest that heart rate biofeedback can be clinically effective in reducing the frequency of premature ventricular contractions in some patients, and that these improvements can be of relatively long duration. However, as indicated by Cheatle and Weiss (1980), there may be some question about the clinical relevance of this response. Because of the spontaneous variations of PVC frequency, it is difficult to specify what constitutes a clinically meaningful change in this condition. Moreover, it is not clearly established whether a high frequency of PVCs increases a patient's risk of sudden death or is simply a concomitant of a diseased heart which adds no risk in itself.

Conduction Disorders.   Two types of cardiac conduction disorders have been investigated using heart rate biofeedback: heart block and Wolff-Parkinson-White disease. Engel & Bleecker (1974) studied three patients with third degree heart block. In this disorder, the ventricle is functionally disconnected from the atrium, and ventricular rate is usually in the range of from 30 to 40 bpm. None of the patients studied was able to significantly increase ventricular rate with biofeedback, leading to speculation that an intact conduction pathway from the SA node to the ventricle is necessary for the learning of heart rate control.

One patient suffering from Wolff-Parkinson-White disease was studied by Bleecker and Engel (1973a). This disorder is characterized by recurrent paroxysmal episodes of tachycardia caused by a defect in the arterioventricular conduction pathway. In addition to the normal conduction pathway, there is also an abnormal accessory pathway in Wolff-Parkinson-White disease. The patient studied was trained with auditory biofeedback which was presented only when a normal QRS complex was detected. Following this treatment, she was able to increase and decrease the occurrence of the abnormal heartbeats. It appeared that the patient was able to selectively exercise voluntary control over which of the two conduction pathways in her heart were used. This ability was maintained during follow-up testing 10 weeks after training.

Assessment. From the few case studies which are available, heart rate biofeedback seems to be effective in the treatment of cardiac arrhythmias. In the absence of controlled clinical trials, however, judgment must be withheld with regard to the therapeutic value of biofeedback for such disorders generally. Moreover, more information is needed about the clinical significance of PVCs before the benefits of biofeedback training can be determined.

Raynaud's Disease

Raynaud's disease is a condition characterized by recurrent attacks of paroxysmal vasospasm in the hands or feet, commonly triggered by exposure to cold or emotional stress. During the attacks, patients complain that their fingers become cold and numb, and there is sometimes considerable pain. Standard therapeutic practices include keeping the hands in a warm place, taking vasodilator drugs, and, occasionally, surgical sympathectomy.

Blanchard (1979) summarized case studies involving a total of 19 patients in which biofeedback was used to treat Raynaud's disease. Although most of these studies employed skin temperature feedback in an attempt to train the patients to warm their hands, some also used vasodilation feedback, EMG feedback, or some combination of treatment techniques. The results of these reports is encouraging, in that most of the patients reported improvements which were, in some cases, relatively long lasting.

Recently, Surwit, Pilon, and Fenton (1978) reported the first multiple group outcome study using a biofeedback approach to treating Raynaud's disease. Thirty patients suffering from idiopathic Raynaud's disease were given either autogenic training or autogenic training combined with biofeedback of skin temperature. Although both groups showed a significant reduction in the number of attacks during the treatment period, there was no reliable difference between the two treatment groups. The results thus do not show any advantage to skin temperature biofeedback beyond that which can be obtained with autogenic training alone for the treatment of Raynaud's disease.

A second study served as a partial replication of the first (Keefe, Surwit, & Pilon, 1980). It provided a more vigorous test of home biofeedback training by having patients on home practice regimens utilize more sensitive and sophisticated biofeedback equipment than used in the prior study. Twenty-one subjects were randomly assigned to one of three treatment conditions: (1) progressive muscle relaxation and home practice instructions; (2) autogenic training and home practice instructions; (3) autogenic training and skin temperature feedback with autogenic instructions and portable feedback equipment. Results indicated that all patients improved regardless of treatment. A study by Jacobson, Manschreck, and Silverberg (1979) showed relaxation training to be more effective than relaxation combined with biofeedback in establishing voluntary finger warming control, but clinical improvement was not found to be related to finger warming ability.

Finally, a follow-up study of 19 of the subjects in the initial study (Surwit et al., 1978), conducted one year after the completion of training, showed that the improvement persisted for this period of time (Keefe, Surwit, & Pilon, 1979), with again no differences between treatment conditions.

Because specific vasomotor responding has repeatedly been shown to occur with skin temperature biofeedback in normal subjects (Taub, 1977) this would seem to be an appropriate technique for reducing the vasospastic attacks of Raynaud's disease. However, several case studies and the group outcome studies reported thus far, have failed to produce conclusive evidence to this effect. Additional research is needed evaluating the specific effects of skin temperature biofeedback or direct vasomotor biofeedback in treating this disorder in order to more fully assess its clinical potential. As it stands now, biofeedback–specific effects do not appear to be the essential ingredients in producing therapeutic improvement.

Migraine Headache

Migraine is an extremely painful type of recurrent headache which affects from 3% to 12% of the population. The attacks are caused by an excessive dilation of the extracranial vasculature, and although the actual mechanism responsible for the pain is poorly understood, local edema and inflammation of the affected vessels are involved. In the classic variant of the disorder, the painful attacks are preceded by a prodromal phase during which cerebral vessels undergo vaso-constriction and the patient may experience transient neurological symptoms. The pain is intense, throbbing, and frequently unilateral in onset. Systemic symptoms such as nausea, water retention, polyuria, and constipation may also occur. The common migraine is similar, except there are no prodromal symptoms noticed by the patient. The pathophysiology underlying migraine is not well understood, but a widely accepted theory contends that it is the reaction of a hyperreactive autonomic nervous system to stress.

At present, the most common biofeedback treatment for migraine involves teaching patients to produce vasodilation in their hands. The beneficial effects of this therapy format were discovered serendipitously by Sargent, Green, and Walters (1972). While participating in an experiment involving "autogenic feedback" training, which involved a combination of autogenic training and skin temperature biofeedback, one subject reported that she had discovered that she could abort migraine headaches using the technique. Similar results using autogenic feedback were obtained in subsequent studies (Fahrion, 1977; Mitch, McGrady, & Iannone, 1976; Sargent, Green, & Walters, 1973). These early studies lacked appropriate controls for placebo effects, however, and confounded elements of autogenic training and biofeedback. Turin and Johnson (1976) were the first to employ biofeedback of finger temperature without components of autogenic training as a treatment for migraine. As a control procedure, some of the patients were taught to cool their hands prior to the finger warming therapy.

All seven patients treated with finger warming biofeedback reported headache improvements, whereas none of three patients trained to cool their fingers improved, suggesting that biofeedback alone can have a therapeutic effect on headache activity.

Studies Using Hand Temperature Biofeedback. Although numerous case studies have been reported in which hand warming biofeedback was associated with a reduction in reported migraine headache activity, upon closer examination the role played by biofeedback is less than clear. Sovak, Kunzel, Sternbach, and Dalessio (1978) treated 12 female migraineurs with a combination of relaxation training and finger temperature feedback. A 3-month follow-up using questionnaires, indicated that out of 10 patients who successfully mastered the biofeedback task, eight were "clinically improved" according to the author's criteria. No control for possible placebo effects of this treatment package were included, so it is not possible to attribute the clinical effects to the biofeedback specifically. The need for such control procedures is highlighted in a study by Mullinix, Norton, Hack, and Fishman (1978) in which one group of patients was given true auditory biofeedback of skin temperature changes while a control group received a noncontingent, placebo signal. The group which received true biofeedback was able to produce significantly greater increases in hand temperature, but both groups reported similar improvements in headaches. Mullinix et al. (1978) suggested that placebo effects do operate in the biofeedback setting, and that reported headache reductions are actually unrelated to skin temperature changes.

Another study to utilize a control for placebo effects was reported by Price and Tursky (1976). Separate groups of migraine sufferers received either (a) true feedback of hand temperature, (b) false, placebo feedback, (c) relaxation training, or (d) exposure to a neutral tape recording. Groups of normal volunteers underwent similar treatments. The results showed that, whereas normal subjects produced vasodilation, the migraine patients tended to show vasoconstriction or no change over time. Furthermore, there was no significant advantage of hand temperature biofeedback over false feedback or relaxation training in promoting vasodilation. Although clinical outcome data are lacking, these results (Price & Tursky, 1976) suggest that migraineurs may have difficulty in producing the desired response and may have little to gain from such biofeedback training.

In a recent double blind study (Kewman & Roberts, 1980), migraine patients were divided into one of three biofeedback groups: skin temperature increase, skin temperature decrease, or no training. Subjects were requested to keep headache diaries during a 9 week (10, one-hour sessions) training period and during a 6 week post-treatment period. During training, subjects were aware that they were learning to change their skin temperature but they were not informed whether the change observed on the feedback display represented an increase or a decrease. Results indicated that all three groups showed improvement in dependent variables such as number of symptoms, amount of impairment, and amount of medication taken. There was no significant difference between groups on these measures, however. Unfortunately, even when subjects were assigned to skin temperature change groups a posteriori, significant differences in skin temperature were not always evident between groups. Therefore, it is unclear what specific factors may be contributing to the results.

Studies Comparing Hand Temperature Biofeedback and Other Treatment Modalities. Andreychuk and Skriver (1974) performed an experiment to directly compare three treatment procedures: (a) autogenic training plus hand warming biofeedback; (b) autogenic training plus alpha enhancement biofeedback; and (c) self-hypnosis training. All three treatment groups showed a significant reduction in headaches, but there were no significant differences in improvement scores among the three groups. In another study, Blanchard, Theobald, Williamson, Silver, and Brown (1978) treated separate groups of migraine patients with: (a) a combination of hand temperature biofeedback, autogenic training, and regular home practice; (b) progressive relaxation training and regular home practice; or (c) a waiting-list control condition. All three groups had significantly fewer headaches following treatment, but only the active treatment groups showed significant reductions in duration and intensity of headaches and in reduced medication usage. Relaxation training was found to be the most effective treatment technique in the last week of therapy. However, the advantage of this technique over biofeedback was no longer evident at subsequent follow-up periods. A significant disadvantage to these two studies (Andreychuk & Skriver, 1974; Blanchard et al., 1978) was that the biofeedback and autogenic training were confounded. Therefore, although the goal of the Blanchard et al. (1978) study was to "isolate the biofeedback training as being responsible for the reported improvement" (p. 581), we cannot draw this conclusion from their results, nor from those of Andreychuk and Skriver (1974).

A study was reported recently which more directly does address this important question. Attfield and Peck (1979) administered six sessions of hand warming biofeedback to one group of five migraine headache patients and the same number of progressive relaxation training sessions to another group of five patients. The level of finger temperature control achieved by the biofeedback group was small ($<1°C$), but significantly greater than that produced by the relaxation group. Upon follow-up questioning 8 weeks after the last treatment session, the relaxation group showed a significant reduction in headache "pain intensity", whereas the biofeedback subjects failed to show improvement on any headache activity measure. It is difficult to draw any comparative conclusions regarding these two treatment techniques, however, because groups were very small and temperature control training was only marginally successful.

Finally, in a recent study, Lake, Rainey, and Papsdorf (1979) compared groups of migraine sufferers who were given (a) biofeedback for digit warming, (b) biofeedback for digit warming plus added rational–emotive psychotherapy,

(c) biofeedback for frontal muscle relaxation, or who were (d) placed on a waiting list and instructed to monitor their headaches. The results showed that digital temperature biofeedback, either alone or with added rational–emotive therapy, was no more effective than the control conditions in reducing migraine headache activity. Furthermore, the ability to control digital temperature did not improve with training, was not maintained over time, and was unrelated to the reported reductions in headache activity.

Studies Using Direct Cephalic Artery Biofeedback. Attempts have also been made to treat migraine headaches by training patients to directly modify the vasomotor tone of cephalic arteries. Koppman, McDonald, and Kunzel (1974) were the first to report successfully modifying temporal artery activity with biofeedback. Seven of nine patients showed signs of vasomotor control, but no effect of this ability on headache activity was reported. Using a single case design, Feurstein and Adams (1977) treated two migraine patients with cephalic vasomotor biofeedback and frontal EMG Feedback. One of the patients showed signs of headache improvement which seemed to be associated with the vasomotor feedback.

A controlled group outcome experiment comparing the effectiveness of cephalic and digital vasomotor biofeedback was conducted by Friar and Beatty (1976). One group of migraine sufferers received eight sessions of biofeedback training to vasoconstrict the temporal artery, while the other group was trained to vasoconstrict the finger. The finger was chosen as a control condition, as the authors considered vasoconstriction in the finger to be irrelevant to migraine headaches. Biofeedback training for extracranial vasoconstriction was successful, and this group reported a significant decrease in "major headache attacks." Training patients to vasoconstrict the vessels of the finger did not affect cephalic vascular activity, and the group which received this treatment did not experience headache improvement. Although the author's assumption that the control condition (digital vasoconstriction) was irrelevant to headache activity is questionable and the 30-day follow-up period was brief, this study (Friar & Beatty, 1976) does suggest that the direct control of extracranial arteries may be effective in treating migraine headaches.

Further elaboration of the relation between voluntary extracranial artery control and migraine headache activity was recently provided in a study by Bild and Adams (1980). They compared cephalic blood volume pulse biofeedback, frontal EMG biofeedback, and a waiting list control condition as treatments for migraine headaches. Both biofeedback groups did acquire the ability to control the targeted physiological response during the 10 sessions of training which were provided. The group which received cephalic artery feedback did show a statistically significant reduction in headache frequency, but at 6-week follow-up there were no significant differences among the groups. In terms of headache duration, blood volume pulse biofeedback was more effective than the control condition, but the two biofeedback groups did not differ significantly. The blood volume pulse biofeedback group also showed the largest decrease in medication usage of all the groups. Although this study (Bild & Adams, 1980) suffered from small sample size (n = 6 or 7) and a relatively brief follow-up period (6 weeks) for all subjects, the design was sound, and it adds support to the theory that direct control of the extracranial vasculature is effective in modifying migraine headaches.

Studies Using Biofeedback Other Than for the Direct Modification of Vaso-Motor Activity. Several reports have been published in which modification of some aspect of physiology other than vasomotor activity has been attempted in an effort to control migraine headaches. Many of these have embedded the biofeedback in a multifaceted treatment package approach, and these will not be discussed here since they do not advance our understanding of the specific contribution of biofeedback. A few studies which exemplify other biofeedback approaches to treating migraine headaches will, however, be briefly noted. Diamond and coworkers have reported treating several hundred patients with EMG biofeedback, hand temperature biofeedback, progressive relaxation training, and autogenic training, either alone or in various combinations (see Diamond, Diamond-Falk, & DeVeno, 1978 for a review). Many of these cases were analyzed retrospectively, and yielded generally mixed results. Biofeedback assisted EEG alpha enhancement has also been attempted as a treatment for migraine (Gannon & Sternbach, 1971).

Evaluation. Although there is an abundance of published reports in which positive claims have been made for the clinical efficacy of biofeedback in treating migraine headache, a careful and critical review of this literature suggests caution should be maintained. Many studies in the area are flawed by inadequate control groups, inappropriate statistical analysis, small sample size, brief pretreatment baseline and posttreatment follow-up periods, and the use of "treatment package" techniques which confound the effects of biofeedback with those of other components of therapy. Indeed, in a recent extensive review of the literature, Beatty (1980) concludes that there is currently no convincing evidence to indicate that biofeedback methods are any more efficacious in the treatment of migraine headache than are simple relaxation and placebo type interventions.

Another problem stems from the fact that the rationale for providing finger temperature training for the amelioration of head pain has never been properly explained. At least three possibilities exist. Finger warming biofeedback could affect patient's subjective reports of headache activity through: (a) nonspecific placebo effects; (b) induction of a relaxation-like or meditative state of lowered arousal which is incompatible with headache; or (c) a specific hemodynamic effect in which a portion of the cardiac output is somehow redirected away from congested extracranial arteries to peripheral vascular beds. Future research should attempt to provide scientific evidence which would aid in the identification of such psychological and physiological mechanisms.

RESPIRATORY SYSTEM

Asthma

Asthma is a respiratory dysfunction involving bronchospasm and edema, which increases airway resistance and impedes the normal expulsion of air from the lungs. Although asthma is generally considered an allergic reaction, it is also widely believed that psychological stress can sometimes precipitate the attacks. Standard treatment for asthma is with bronchodilators and corticosteriods.

One behavioral approach to the management of asthma is to provide forced oscillation feedback of total respiratory resistance. Feldman (1976) used this type of feedback in a study of four children with severe asthma, and reported reductions in total respiratory resistance comparable to that seen after bronchodilator inhalation therapy. One nonasthmatic child showed no significant airway resistance changes under the same training procedure. Vachon and Rich (1976) tested 46 mildly asthmatic college students with a similar biofeedback technique. The subjects given contingent biofeedback showed significant reductions in total respiratory resistance, but subjects given random biofeedback did not. The authors (Vachon & Rich, 1976) noted, however, that although the effect was approximately equivalent to the magnitude of change observed after one inhalation of Isoproterenal, "few asthmatics would be satisfied with this level of clinical relief" (p. 129).

Another approach involves using biofeedback as an adjunct to progressive muscle relaxation training in an attempt to produce an indirect effect on respiratory parameters. For example, Davis, Saunders, Creer, and Chai (1973) compared the effects of Jacobsonian relaxation training alone, relaxation training with adjunctive frontal EMG biofeedback, and a self-directed instructed relaxation control condition, using asthmatic children as subjects. The results indicated a short lived advantage for the first two treatment conditions, which did not significantly differ from each other, over the control condition in the non-severe cases treated. In severe cases, there were no significant differences among the three treatment conditions. In another study, Scherr, Crawford, Sergent, and Scherr (1975) compared a group provided EMG-assisted progressive relaxation training to a nontreated control group of asthmatic children. It was reported that the treated group showed greater improvement on a variety of dimensions than did the untreated group. The untreated group, however, must be considered a rather poor control for placebo effects.

Kotses, Glaus, Crawford, Edwards, and Sherr (1976) showed that facial muscle relaxation training with frontal EMG biofeedback was associated with increased peak expiratory flow rate in asthmatic children. Since peak expiratory flow rate was measured 3 times per day at times not coincident with training periods, the effect did not seem to be a transitory effect of the biofeedback setting. In a follow-up study (Kotses, Glaus, Bricel, Edwards, & Crawford, 1978), four groups of asthmatic children received (a) contingent frontal EMG biofeedback; (b) noncontingent frontal EMG biofeedback; (c) contingent brachioradialis EMG biofeedback; or (d) noncontingent brachioradialis EMG biofeedback. The group given contingent frontal feedback demonstrated significantly lowered frontal EMG activity and greater increases in peak expiratory flow rate immediately following the feedback sessions compared to the noncontingent frontal feedback group. Neither the contingent nor the noncontingent brachioradialis biofeedback group showed significant change in either EMG activity or peak expiratory flow rate, so it could not be determined whether the effect on respiratory behavior was specific to frontal relaxation.

Assessment.   Alexander and Smith (1979) have criticized the EMG biofeedback studies, noting that instructions to try to decrease the noncontingent biofeedback signal may lead to frustration in the control group which would be counterproductive. Alexander and Smith (1979) also commented that measurement of peak expiratory flow rate is highly dependent on patient motivation, cooperation, and physical effort, and argued that biofeedback treatment may affect that dependent outcome measures primarily through such nonspecific factors.

GASTROINTESTINAL SYSTEM

Research in the area of biofeedback directed at the modification of gastrointestinal functions has not progressed rapidly. Research that has been reported consists largely of uncontrolled case studies and small group trials. Yet, enough potentially useful information has emerged to warrant a separate analysis of this topic.

Rumination

Although not commonly identified as biofeedback, the applications of aversive stimuli contingent upon rumination was one of the first successful applications of psychological technique in the remediation of a medical problem to attract widespread attention. Lang and Melamed (1969) treated a 9-month-old child suffering from life threatening chronic ruminative vomiting by applying painful electric shock contingent on the first signs of reverse peristalsis, detected electromyographically. Since that time, a number of investigators have replicated the results. Whitehead (1978) reviewed these studies and concluded that aversive operant feedback is effective and may be the treatment of choice for very young children or mentally retarded individuals. O'Neil, White, King, and Carek (1979) recently reported successfully using a technique involving punishment of rumination with lemon juice delivered to the mouth and reinforcement of non-rumination with honey water on a differential reinforcement of other response (DRO) schedule. After training, rumination was held at a low rate using positive reinforcement alone.

Peptic Ulcer

Since the excessive secretion of hydrochloric acid is widely believed to be associated with the development and maintenance of ulcers, a few investigators have turned their attention toward developing methods for presenting biofeedback information concerning intragastric acidity. Techniques for aspirating stomach contents for extracorporeal analysis and feedback have generally not led to self control, but techniques utilizing an intragastric pH electrode would seem to hold more promise (Whitehead, Renault, & Goldiamond, 1975). Thus far, however, there have been no reports of successfully treating peptic ulcer patients with stomach acid biofeedback.

Irritable Bowel Syndrome

Furman (1973) used an electronic stethoscope to detect bowel sounds and deliver biofeedback information to five patients, all of whom reportedly were able to exercise self control. Whitehead (1978) noted, however, that others have failed to replicate these results. In another report, Bueno-Miranda, Cerulli, and Schuster (1976) reported successfully training a group of patients to inhibit spastic movements of the sigmoid colon, using a balloon inserted through the rectum as a pressure transducer.

Fecal Incontinence

Engel, Nikoomanesh, and Schuster (1974) reported successfully treating six patients suffering from fecal incontinence, due to a variety of causes, through the use of biofeedback. Balloons, which were inserted into the rectum, were used to measure pressure changes at the internal and external sphincters and provided a source of biofeedback information. As a third balloon was inflated in the rectum to elicit a sphincter response, the patients were given verbal praise for producing a response pattern consisting of internal sphincter relaxation and external sphincter constriction. The authors reported that the learning proceeded rapidly, and that all the patients either became continent or were improved following training. These results have subsequently been replicated in a much larger group of patients (Cerulli, Nikoomanesh, & Schuster, 1976).

Assessment. Although some of the research results on the biofeedback-assisted modification of gastrointestinal behaviors are encouraging, it must be remembered that controlled studies with large samples have not yet occurred. Thus, there is little information concerning the specific contribution of the biofeedback to the success of the techniques. The use of electric shock to eliminate rumination seems to work, and may be the only available technique which will work with some patients; however, nonaversive techniques using the standard, contingent feedback paradigm might find more widespread applicability among cooperative patients. Biofeedback treatments for peptic ulcer and irritable bowel syndrome require much additional testing and refinement of technique before they can be recommended for clinical use. The research suggesting the efficacy of biofeedback therapy for fecal incontinence should lead to controlled studies. Since the majority of the original patients treated showed a dysfunctional external sphincter response, which is normally under voluntary control, future studies might examine techniques for modifying this component of the response pattern without stimulating the rectum by inflating a balloon.

CENTRAL NERVOUS SYSTEM

Epileptic Seizures

Epilepsy is a family of neurological disorders, one subtype of which is characterized by paroxysmally recurring grand mal seizures. During the attacks, which may be preceded by a sensory or emotional aura, the patient experiences uncontrollable muscular convulsions and unconsciousness. Epilepsy is often idiopathic, but is also caused by injury to the brain or by inflammation. Although it has long been recognized that epileptic seizures are influenced by psychological and environmental factors, anticonvulsant medication remains the most effective treatment technique. Recently, a number of behavioral techniques attempting to modify seizure behaviors without the use of drugs have been advanced (see Mostofsky & Balaschak, 1977). One such technique is biofeedback.

Since epileptic seizures are believed to originate in a focal point of electrically abnormal brain activity which subsequently spreads through and affects larger areas of brain tissue, it is logical to presume that any technique which could modify brain electrophysiology might also affect seizure behavior. A number of single case studies and small group outcome studies have reported encouraging results employing biofeedback to regulate characteristics of the EEG (see Kuhlman & Kaplan, 1979; Sterman, 1977). Kuhlman and Allison (1977) demonstrated EEG changes and reduced seizure frequency under conditions of contingent EEG biofeedback which were not observed under conditions of pseudofeedback. It has been suggested, however, that it is difficult to reverse therapeutic effects by switching from contingent to noncontingent biofeedback (Sterman, 1977). Others have shown differential effects on seizure frequencies of administering true feedback for two different EEG frequency bandwidths (Sterman & Macdonald, 1978).

Although the aforementioned studies did control for placebo effects by using contingency reversal designs, caution should be maintained concerning placebo effects. Macdonald and Quy (1979) used a controlled group design to specifically examine the effects of the biofeedback contingency on seizure activity. Using a double–blind technique, two groups of patients received 96 sessions of either true biofeedback of EEG activity or random feedback. The patients' task was to use visual and auditory feedback to maximize EEG activity in the 8–20 Hz range and to minimize activity in the higher and lower frequency ranges. The results showed that although there was an effect of the contingent feedback on EEG which was not present with random feedback, there were no significant differences in seizure activity either between groups or between pretreatment and treatment periods.

However, in a more recent double-blind investigation, Lubar (1980) trained eight epileptics with clear evidence of brain damage to control EEG activity in an ABA cross-over design. They were trained to increase activity which would be deleterious to seizure control, as well as to increase activity found to be beneficial to seizure control. In addition, these subjects received some training with false biofeedback in order to determine the effects of placebo and other nonspecific factors. Results demonstrated that five of the eight patients showed a significant reduction in seizures from baseline when provided with appropriate training. Another interesting finding of this study was that previous notions concerning the normalizing of EEG by either increasing high frequency (11–19 HZ) or decreasing slow activity (3–8 Hz) may not be the only conditions sufficient for the reduction of seizures. Rather, the EEG changes that correlated with decreased seizures were found to be more complex. It, therefore, appears that different types of EEG conditioning may be effective for managing different types of patients.

Cott, Pavloski, and Black (1979) have noted that experiments reporting seizure reduction following biofeedback training include a signaled time out period contingent on EEG abnormalities, so that the desired EEG frequency could not be reinforced during their occurrence. They reasoned that this time out procedure might be responsible for the suppression of EEG slow wave or spiking activity rather than the biofeedback itself. They demonstrated experimentally in a small group of epileptics that a time out procedure without biofeedback was as effective as biofeedback aimed at helping patients produce a sensory motor rhythm in reducing seizures. These results suggested that sensorimotor biofeedback is not necessary for seizure reduction and, in fact, may not be related to seizure activity.

Evaluation.   At this time, the amount of controlled group research which has been done concerning possible therapeutic effects of EEG biofeedback for the treatment of epileptic seizures is extremely small, and all but the most speculative conclusions would be premature. The positive results which have been reported, however, are encouraging and would seem to justify the more time consuming and expensive research which must now occur to yield more conclusive answers. There are many important issues which remain to be resolved. One of the most basic concerns how biofeedback affects brain electrophysiology and seizures. For example, do epileptic patients undergoing biofeedback therapy (a) learn to tonically modify their EEG rhythm, (b) learn to eliminate specific electrophysiological abnormalities, (c) learn to abort an impending seizure, or (d) simply learn to relax? Much research needs to be done before EEG biofeedback can be expected to have a clinically significant effect on the psychological control of epileptic seizures.

NEUROMUSCULAR SYSTEM

Biofeedback therapy involving the presentation of EMG signals for neuromuscular reeducation and rehabilitation of neuromotor disorders has been in use for several years. Since the skeletal muscular system has traditionally been viewed as amenable to voluntary and/or operant control, it is not surprising that the presentation of performance contingent feedback facilitates motor learning in this system. However, the high degree of specific control which has been shown with biofeedback in normal subjects is impressive (Basmajian, 1963). Preliminary attempts to show therapeutic effects in the rehabilitation of a wide variety of neuromuscular dysfunctions have also produced promising results.

Upper Motor Neuron Dysfunctions

Paresis.   When parts of the brain or spinal cord involved with motor function are affected by trauma or disease, the patient usually suffers the loss of some motor function. A physical therapy exercise program is usually begun as soon as possible in an effort to restore function. EMG biofeedback has recently been utilized either as an alternative or as an adjunct to conventional physical therapy for a wide variety of neuromuscular dysfunctions. Recent reviews (Basmajian & Hatch, 1979; Fernando & Basmajian, 1978; Keefe & Surwit, 1978) suggest that many of these applications of biofeedback are associated with clinically significant improvement in patients whose conditions had been stable for years. Unfortunately, research in the area has not progressed very far beyond the case study stage, and the reports often give far too little information concerning patient characteristics, specific outcome measures used, and data reliability. Very few controlled experiments have been performed, and those which have been reported produced ambiguous results.

The first controlled experiment was that of Basmajian, Kukulka, Narayan, and Takebe (1975). In that study, two groups of hemiplegics with foot drop were randomly assigned to receive either 40 minutes of conventional therapeutic exercise or 20 minutes of exercise and 20 minutes of exercise supplemented with EMG biofeedback per day. Each patient's gait was rated on a 6-point scale, strength was measured with a dynomometer, and range of motion was evaluated clinically. Both groups showed progress in range of motion and ankle dorsiflexion strength. However, the authors reported that the biofeedback group showed approximately twice as much improvement as the group which received conventional physical therapy alone. Although the results of this study (Basmajian et al., 1975) have been frequently cited as evidence for the therapeutic value of EMG biofeedback in neuromuscular rehabilitation, they have also been sharply criticized. For example, Fish, Mayer, and Herman (1976) found the statistical analysis of the data unacceptable, and performed their own analysis of Basmajian's et al. (1975) published data. Reanalyzed this way, only the strength measure showed a significant difference. Fish et al. (1976) also noted that the two groups in the Basmajian et al. (1975) study differed in terms of the duration of their illness. When Phillips (reported by Burnside, Tobias, & Bursill, 1979) performed an analysis of covariance of the strength data, partialling out the effect of duration, even this measure failed to show a statistically significant difference between the two groups. Another problem with the study (Basmajian et al., 1975) is that the design combined biofeedback and physical therapy in to a single treatment package and precluded any evaluation of the effects of 20 minutes of EMG biofeedback alone or 20 minutes of physical therapy alone.

In another study, Lee, Hill, Johnston, and Smichoroski (1976) compared contingent EMG biofeedback, noncontingent "placebo" EMG biofeedback, and conventional physical therapy on 18 hemiplegic patients to strengthen paretic deltoid muscles. Each patient, who served as his or her own control, received one of the above three treatments in different sessions. The patients were instructed to perform 20 5-second contractions under each condition while deltoid EMG was recorded. The results showed no significant differences among the three conditions. However, when the patients were grouped according to age and the experimenters' judgments of motivation, it was found that the older and more poorly motivated patients showed greater improvements with contingent biofeedback than the younger and more highly motivated patients. In the case of the older, poorly motivated patients, the EMG biofeedback may have provided some nonspecific motivating effect, but for the younger, more highly motivated patients there was no advantage in the short term application of EMG biofeedback over conventional physical therapy for the retraining of hemiplegically paretic muscles.

A recent study by Burnside et al. (1979) provided two groups of stroke patients with either 12 15-mintue sessions of physical exercise or exercise plus supplemental EMG biofeedback from the leg. Gait, strength, and range of ankle motion were measured immediately before and after treatment as well as 6-weeks following the completion of treatment. At the end of treatment, the two groups differed significantly from one another only on the strength measure, with more people in the biofeedback group showing improvement. However, at 6-weeks follow-up, the control group had relapsed to their previous level on all three outcome measures, while the biofeedback group maintained much more of their gains.

Patient motivation can play a major role in the results obtained with biofeedback therapy, and clinicians using the technique routinely try to recruit as much patient effort and cooperation as possible. The Lee et al. (1976) study discussed earlier suggested that the ability of biofeedback to raise patient motivation may be one of its most valuable characteristics. A recent study by Santee, Keister, and Kleinman (1980) systematically examined the effects of EMG biofeedback, with and without the addition of contingent monetary incentives, on foot dorsiflexion in five stroke patients. It was found that EMG activity in the anterior tibialis muscle was significantly greater with biofeedback plus monetary incentives than with biofeedback alone. Studies such as this which systematically examine independent components of the biofeedback situation are greatly needed.

Cerebral Palsy.   Another upper motor neuron disorder which has been treated with biofeedback is cerebral palsy. Cerebral palsy is a sensorimotor dysfunction which is thought to result from brain damage occurring prenatally or near the time of birth. These people show flacid and spastic paralyses as well as stereotyped athetoid movements which affect posture and gait. Success has been reported in treating both the spastic (Finley, Ninman, Standly, & Wansley, 1977) and athetoid (Finley, Ninman, Standly, & Ender, 1976) components of cerebral palsy with EMG biofeedback designed to assist the patient in forehead relaxation. Presumably, training in forehead relaxation produced a generalized effect since improvements in fine motor control and speech production were reported.

Cataldo, Bird, and Cunningham (1978) have also reported positive results in which EMG biofeedback training was used to improve motor control in specific muscles. Biofeedback did enhance muscle control in trained muscles, and there was evidence for some generalization of the effect to untrained muscles as well.

Another biofeedback approach to treating cerebral palsy is to provide feedback contingent on gross postural adjustments. For example, Harris, Spelman, and Hymer (1974) viewed the athetoid movements in cerebral palsy as due to "inapproprioception." They viewed biofeedback as an artificial sense organ designed to compensate for a biological defect in the muscle stretch receptors. By mounting motion transducers on pendulums suspended within a helmet worn by the patient, auditory and visual feedback could be delivered contingent on head movements which deviated from vertical. Stability of limb position was trained in a similar manner. A similar technique was used by Wooldridge and Russel (1976).

Incomplete Spinal Cord Lesions.   In most cases, spinal cord lesions do not involve a complete transection of the cord and some neural pathways and residual function remain. A few cases have been reported in which EMG biofeedback has been used in an attempt to augment residual function (Brudny, Korein, Levidow, Grynbaum, Leiberman, & Fridmann, 1974; Seymour & Bassler, 1977). An additional use of biofeedback in such cases is in assisting the therapist locate muscles which have residual innervation and potential for improved function.

Assessment.   A number of studies have suggested the therapeutic effects of biofeedback in the treatment of upper motor neuron disorders. However, controlled group experiments are lacking except for the biofeedback treatment of paresis, where results are negative or ambiguous. Many of the individual and multiple case studies were well designed, showing sensitivity of behavior to changing EMG biofeedback threshold (Harris et al., 1974) and behavioral reversal with ABAB designs (Finley et al., 1977). However, the failure of therapeutic results to persist following removal of biofeedback remains problematic. Thus, although the intervention with biofeedback has been associated with therapeutic gains, it is not yet possible to distinguish between specific effects of biofeedback and nonspecific factors associated with it such as therapist attention, novelty, and placebo effects. At the present time, there is not compelling evidence for long-term clinically significant gains which are attributable to the specific effects of biofeedback for the treatment of upper motor neuron disorders.

Lower Motor Neuron Dysfunctions

Peripheral Nerve Injury.   Several instances of the successful application of EMG biofeedback therapy in the rehabilitation of patients following surgery or traumatic injury to peripheral nerves have been reported (Booker, Rubow, & Coleman, 1969; Brudny, Korein, Grynbaum, Friedmann, Weinstein, Sachs-Frankel, & Belandres, 1976; Jacobs & Felton, 1969; Kukulka, Brown, & Basmajian, 1975). However, only the study reported by Jacobs and Felton in 1969 included control procedures. In this study, 10 normal subjects and 10 who had suffered injury to the trapezius were compared for their ability to relax the trapezius muscle with and without EMG biofeedback. Both groups showed greater EMG reductions with biofeedback than they did when instructed to relax on their own. Also, both groups showed equivalent amounts of EMG activity following training, suggesting that the injured patients could relax as well as normal subjects.

Bell's Palsy.   Another peripheral disorder which has reportedly been successfully treated with biofeedback is Bell's palsy, a lesion of the facial nerve which is thought to be caused by a viral infection. Marinacci and Horande (1960) used EMG biofeedback to increase muscle activity of the paralyzed facial muscles. Jankel (1978) also reported using EMG biofeedback in the treatment of Bell's palsy.

Assessment.   The case studies reporting the successful application of EMG biofeedback in the treatment of lower motor neuron dysfunctions must be interpreted with caution due to the lack of control procedures. With the exception of the Jacobs and Felton (1969) study which showed some advantage to biofeedback over instructed relaxation, there is no basis for evaluating the effectiveness of biofeedback in comparison to either control procedures or other therapeutic procedures.

Dyskinesias

A number of different dyskinesias have been treated with various biofeedback techniques including spasmodic torticollis (Brudny, Grynbaum, & Korein, 1974; Brudny et al., 1976; Cleeland, 1973), Parkinson's disease (Netsell & Cleeland, 1973), tardive dyskinesia (Albanese & Gaarder, 1977; Sherman, 1979), Huntington's disease (MacPherson, 1967), and blepharospasm (Peck, 1977). The above individual or multiple case reports suggest a possible use for EMG biofeedback in the treatment of dyskinesias. However, the role of the biofeedback is unclear since controls were not used, treatment procedures were not adequately described for each case, and the biofeedback was sometimes combined with some other behavior modification technique such as aversive electric shock therapy.

Muscular Pain

Low Back Pain.   Low back pain caused by muscular spasm is a common disorder and one which can be extremely resistant to therapy. EMG biofeedback has been increasingly used in pain management programs, but surprisingly few formal reports of results have been published. One group of investigators (Gottlieb, Strite, Koller, Madorsky, Hockersmith, Kleeman, & Wagner, 1977) reported some success in using EMG and GSR biofeedback as one component of an eight-phase rehabilitation program for chronic low back pain patients. In another study, Hendler, Derogatis, Avella, and Long (1977) treated a group of patients suffering from back, leg, neck, shoulder, or arm pain with EMG biofeedback from the forehead muscles. Six of the 13 patients treated subjectively reported less pain following treatment, but the follow-up period was only 5 days long. Recently, Belar and Cohen (1979) reported a single case study which included a baseline, treatment, and follow-up period. The patient, suffering from chronic back pain was given EMG biofeedback from the affected back muscles designed to facilitate relaxation. Reported backache frequency declined somewhat during the treatment period, but both baseline and treatment data were highly variable. A decrease in EMG activity was also reported. However, only two sessions were statistically compared.

Myofascial Pain. In some instances, myofascial pain is thought to be caused by bruxing or clenching the teeth which strains the temporomandibular joint. Consequently, a number of attempts have been made to train patients with EMG biofeedback to relax the temporalis and masseter muscles and to stop clenching their teeth (Carlsson & Gale, 1976; 1977; Carlsson, Gale, & Ohman, 1975; Gessel, 1975; Solberg & Rugh, 1972). The procedure used by Carlsson et al. (1975) involves a two stage training process in which the patient is first made aware of tension in the jaw muscles, and is then later trained to reduce the muscle tension with EMG biofeedback. Stenn, Mothersill, and Brooke (1979) provided a group of myofascial pain sufferers a therapy consisting of relaxation training, sensory awareness training, and coping skills training. Half the patients received EMG biofeedback during relaxation training and the other half did not. The biofeedback group subjectively reported a greater reduction in pain following treatment, but the two groups did not differ in EMG activity levels. These results led the authors to question the etiological significance of muscular activity in myofascial pain dysfunction syndrome. None of the above studies used control procedures, and so the effectiveness of the treatments cannot be compared to placebo treatments or alternative active treatments. A study by Goodman, Greene, and Laskin (1976), however, suggests the positive reports should be interpreted very cautiously. These investigators treated 25 myofascial pain patients with a placebo treatment which involved a low speed grinding of nonoccluding tooth surfaces and told them that the procedure would correct occlusal dysharmonies. Sixteen of the 25 patients reported either total or nearly total remission of their symptoms. Unfortunately, Goodman et al. (1976) did not include an active treatment in their design which would have allowed a more meaningful interpretation of their results.

Although tentative results are promising with regard to the biofeedback treatment of myofascial pain, the role of placebo factors is probably a potent one, as it is in many other pain syndromes, and needs to be more carefully evaluated. It should also be recognized that the etiology of the disorder remains a mystery, and it is quite possible that similar symptom profiles can occur as a result of a host of different etiological variables. Future studies should therefore take care to obtain more homogeneous samples and to report patient characteristics more completely.

Muscle Contraction Headache

Muscle contraction or tension headache is a common disorder which, according to the Ad Hoc Committee on Classification of Headache (1962), is caused by the sustained contraction of the muscles of the head and neck. These headaches are considered psychophysiologic because they have repeatedly been reported to occur when the patient is experiencing some sort of psychological stress. The most common form of treatment is analgesic drugs, but tranquilizers and antidepressants are also occasionally used. Given the role of muscle contraction in producing the pain, however, it is not surprising that EMG biofeedback has recently become increasingly popular as a treatment technique. Budzynski, Stoyva, and Adler (1970) provided the first group outcome study showing the effectiveness of frontal EMG biofeedback in reducing tension headache activity. This study employed general relaxation procedures in addition to reduction of tension in specific head muscles, and included relaxation training as well as biofeedback.

Studies Comparing Biofeedback and Inactive Control Procedures. These positive results were later replicated in a controlled group outcome experiment (Budzynski, Stoyva, Adler, & Mullaney, 1973). Subjects were assigned to one of three groups which received either frontal EMG biofeedback, pseudo EMG biofeedback, or no treatment. The group treated with true biofeedback showed significantly lower frontal EMG levels as compared to the control groups. Also, more of the patients in the true biofeedback group reported a reduction in headache activity. The improvement was found to be maintained well at the time of a 3-month follow-up.

Subsequently, a number of additional investigations have compared EMG biofeedback, either alone or combined with relaxation instructions, to inactive control treatments including pseudo biofeedback (Kondo & Canter, 1977; Philips, 1977), and medication placebo (Cox, Freundlich & Meyer, 1975). The above studies found the treatment involving active biofeedback to be more effective than the inactive control treatment in reducing some aspect of headache activity. One study, however, (Chesney & Shelton, 1976), found no significant difference in therapeutic response to EMG biofeedback treatment alone and no treatment.

In a recent experiment by Andrasik and Holroyd (1980), three biofeedback groups and a no-treatment control group were employed. Each of the biofeedback groups was given the task of decreasing frontal muscle tension. However, only one group was given decrease feedback. The other two groups were given either increase feedback or feedback from the right forearm flexor muscles. This latter group served as a no-change control. Results indicated that all three biofeedback groups were significantly different from each other in the predicted direction in EMG level change. Relative to the no-treatment control all three groups showed significant *similar* improvement in headache symptoms. Thus, headache symptom reduction could not be attributed to any specific EMG change.

Studies Comparing Biofeedback with Other Behavioral Techniques. A number of investigations have also compared treatments including EMG biofeedback and other active treatments such as relaxation training. One study (Hutchings & Reinking, 1976) showed that frontal EMG biofeedback alone was more effective than a verbal relaxation–autogenic training procedure in reducing muscle contraction headaches. At 6 and 12-month follow-up, however, the difference was no longer apparent (Reinking & Hutchings, 1976). One study (Chesney & Shelton, 1976) has also shown relaxation instructions alone to be more effective than frontal EMG biofeedback training alone, but biofeedback training alone was no more effective than no treatment. One study (Gray, Lyle, McGuire, & Peck, 1980) has shown relaxation instructions to be superior to EMG biofeedbacks in the immediate reduction of headache frequency and intensity. In this study, EMG feedback from a site not associated with pain was as effective as feedback from a site which was associated with pain. After 1–6 months, the three treatments were equally effective. Three studies (Cox et al., 1975; Haynes, Griffin, Mooney, & Parise, 1975; Martin & Mathews, 1978) have shown EMG biofeedback and relaxation training to have similar effects on muscle contraction headache activity. Of these studies, the one by Martin and Mathews (1978) did not include a control group; however, the studies by Haynes et al. (1975) and Cox et al. (1975) showed the two experimental procedures to be superior to a self-relaxation procedure and a medication placebo respectively.

Two studies have evaluated the effects of combined EMG biofeedback and verbal relaxation training. One of these (Hutchings & Reinking, 1976) found the combination to be as effective as EMG biofeedback alone, and initially somewhat superior to a relaxation–autogenic training technique. The other study (Chesney & Shelton, 1976) showed the combination to be more effective than biofeedback alone, but equally as effective as relaxation in reducing headache frequency and duration. The combination was also the only technique shown to be significantly more effective than no treatment in reducing headache severity.

Assessment. To summarize the results of experiments using EMG biofeedback as a treatment for muscle contraction headache, a number of controlled group outcome studies have shown that treatments involving biofeedback are more effective than inactive control procedures. The exception to this is the Chesney and Shelton (1976) study which showed biofeedback alone to be no more effective than no treatment. A number of these studies have also included followup evaluations conducted several months following the end of treatment, and the results indicate that clinical gains are often maintained. When biofeedback procedures are compared to general relaxation procedures, all possible results have been reported so no comparative conclusions can be made at this time. It is also not yet possible to determine whether a combined treatment involving EMG biofeedback and verbal relaxation training is any more effective than either technique alone. A similar conclusion has been reached in a recent review of the biofeedback-tension headache literature by Cox and Hobbs (1980), who state that the only thing that can be concluded from the existing data is that EMG biofeedback is more effective than placebo in the treatment of tension headaches.

Compared to many other areas of applied biofeedback research, that aimed at reducing tension headaches has reached a relatively high degree of methodological sophistication. In general, investigators have taken care to define populations, use control groups, apply statistical analysis to their data, measure multiple dimensions of the problem, and include some sort of follow-up evaluation. Still, significant problems remain. For example, questions may be raised regarding the appropriateness of a pseudo biofeedback condition as a control for placebo effects. In order to be an appropriate control, a placebo must be credible to the patients. In the case of skeletal muscular feedback, it would be relatively simple for an observant subject to discover his or her lack of control over the stimulus and either lose interest in the task or become frustrated. The no treatment group, which has also been used, does not adequately control for such factors as therapist attention, interaction with electronic apparatus, and patient involvement. The same criticisms can be applied to the medication placebo condition. Therefore, it remains difficult to measure the specific contribution made by the biofeedback contingency to the therapeutic effect.

Another problem relates to the correlation between EMG levels and clinical improvement. Although biofeedback therapy for the purpose of reducing tension in head and neck muscles would seem a straightforward approach based on current etiological theory which attributes headache pain to sustained muscular contraction, some rather puzzling results have been reported. For example, Haynes et al. (1975) and Gray et al. (1980) reported no difference in frontal EMG levels of patients during headache attacks as compared to headache free periods. Furthermore, Martin and Mathews (1978) found frontal EMG activity was actually *lower* during headache attacks than during headache free periods. These results warn against unwarranted enthusiasm over biofeedback treatments and suggest that in future studies investigators pay very close attention to the relation between suspected pathophysiology and response to behavioral intervention.

CONCLUSIONS AND FUTURE DIRECTIONS

In spite of our lack of certainty regarding the psychological and biological mechanisms underlying the development of voluntary control over physiological functioning with biofeedback, it has been amply demonstrated that some degree of self control is possible over behaviors long assumed to be completely involuntary. It has also been shown that, with biofeedback, it is possible to extend voluntary control to pathophysiological responding in order to modify this maladaptive behavior in the direction of health. These are highly significant achievements. However, many important questions still remain as to how medically effective biofeedback will be. To date, very few well controlled clinical outcome studies have been conducted using large numbers of patients having well confirmed medical diagnoses. Moreover, the few comparative group outcome studies which have been performed compared the relative effectiveness of biofeedback to various other behavioral techniques. It would be extremely helpful to also compare biofeedback techniques with more traditional medical treatments, some of which have fairly well established success rates. Combinations of medical and behavioral techniques should also be explored and evaluated. However, these studies will be most informative if investigators design them so that the unique contribution of each individual technique, as well as the combined effect, can be isolated and reliably measured.

It is always appropriate to end a chapter by making a conclusive closing statement about the material covered. In this case, it would be extremely appropriate to answer the question, what is the current status of clinical biofeedback in medical settings? Unfortunately, it is difficult to answer this without appearing to beg the question. On the one hand, there have been a number of areas in which biofeedback has been effectively used. On the other hand, however, there have been claims for the therapeutic efficacy of biofeedback which have been grossly exaggerated and sometimes even wrong. Overall, we think it is justified to conclude that relevant and encouraging data do exist, but at the present time the value of clinical training in biofeedback is still questioned. Terms such as ''biofeedback therapist'' and ''biofeedback clinic,'' which are now regularly encountered in many medical settings, are difficult to justify. They imply that a form of treatment exists which is more or less generally applicable to a variety of ills. Worse yet, they imply, at least in the minds of some, that biofeedback is a new alternative treatment modality. Currently, in the majority of areas in which it is applied, biofeedback should be viewed merely as an adjunctive treatment.

In the future, the potential of biofeedback in diagnosis, etiology, prevention, and rehabilitation should continue to be tested. Some of its most important contributions may prove to be conceptual rather than technological or directly therapeutic. Moreover, as one of the authors emphasized earlier, in order for the field of biofeedback to effectively develop and progress:

> ... the clinician or researcher employing biofeedback needs knowledge in a number of different areas; the pathophysiology of the disorder being treated and the physiology of the response systems to be voluntarily regulated, the relation of such response systems to the etiology and symptoms of the particular disorder, the electrical functioning of the feedback device itself, the nature of the self-regulation

process involved in biofeedback "learning," and the knowledge and use of appropriate methodology. Without such expertise, it cannot be expected that useful and reliable biofeedback treatment procedures can be developed (Price & Gatchel, 1979, p. 235).

ACKNOWLEDGMENT

The authors wish to express their gratitude to Johnnie G. Fisher, M.D., for his helpful comments on a preliminary draft of this chapter.

REFERENCES

Ad Hoc Committee on Classification of Headache, Classification of Headache. *Journal of the American Medical Association,* 1962, *179,* 717–718.

Andrasik, F. & Holroyd, K. A. A test of specific and nonspecific effects in the biofeedback treatment of tension headache. *Journal of Consulting and Clinical Psychology,* 1980, *48,* 575–586.

Alexander, A. B., & Smith, D. D. Clinical applications of EMG biofeedback. In R. J. Gatchel & K. P. Price (Eds.), *Clinical applications of biofeedback: appraisal and status,* New York: Pergamon Press, 1979.

Andreychuk, T., & Skriver, C. Hypnosis and Biofeedback in the Treatment of Migraine Headache. *International Journal of Clinical and Experimental Hypnosis,* 1975, *23,* 172–183.

Attfield, M., & Peck, D. F. Temperature Self-regulation and Relaxation with Migraine Patients and Normals. *Behaviour Research and Therapy,* 1979, *17,* 591–595.

Basmajian, J. V. Control and Training of Individual Motor Units. *Science,* 1963, *141,* 440–441.

Basmajian, J. V., & Hatch, J. P. Biofeedback and the modification of skeletal muscular dysfunctions. In R. J. Gatchel & K. P. Price (Eds.), *Clinical applications of biofeedback: appraisal and status.* New York: Pergamon Press, 1979.

Basmajian, J. V., Kukulka, C. G., Narayan, M. G. & Takebe, K. Biofeedback Treatment of Foot-drop after Stroke Compared with Standard Rehabilitation Technique: Effects on Voluntary Control and Strength. *Archives of Physical Medicine and Rehabilitation,* 1975, *56,* 231–236.

Beatty, J. Biofeedback in the Treatment of Migraine: Simple Relaxation or Specific Effects. In L. White & B. Tursky (Eds.), *Clinical Biofeedback: Efficacy and Mechanisms.* New York: Guilford Press, 1980.

Belar, C. D., & Cohen, J. L. The use of EMG Feedback and Progressive Relaxation in the Treatment of a Woman with Chronic Back Pain. *Biofeedback and Self-regulation,* 1979, *4,* 345–353.

Benson H., Shapiro, D., Tursky, B., & Schwartz, G. E. Decreased Systolic Blood Pressure through Operant Conditioning Techniques in Patients with Essential Hypertension. *Science,* 1971, *173,* 740–742.

Bild, R., & Adams, H. E. Modification of Migraine Headaches by Cephalic Blood Volume Pulse and EMG Biofeedback. *Journal of Consulting and Clinical Psychology,* 1980, *48,* 51–57.

Blanchard, E. B., & Abel, G. G. An Experimental Case Study of the Biofeedback Treatment of a Rape-induced Psychophysiological Disorder. *Behavior Therapy,* 1976, *7,* 113–119.

Blanchard, E. B. Biofeedback and the modification of cardiovascular dysfunctions. In R. J. Gatchel & K. P. Price (Eds.), *Clinical applications of biofeedback: appraisal and status,* New York: Pergamon Press, 1979.

Blanchard, E. B., Miller, S. T., Abel, G. G., Haynes, M. R., & Wicker, R. Evaluation of Biofeedback in the Treatment of Borderline Essential Hypertension. *Journal of Applied Behavior Analysis,* 1979, *12,* 99–109.

Blanchard, E. B., Theobald, D. E., Williamson, D. A., Silver, B. V., & Brown, D. A. Temperature Biofeedback in the Treatment of Migraine Headaches. *Archives of General Psychiatry,*
1978, *35,* 581–588.

Bleecker, E. R. & Engel, B. T. Learned Control of Cardiac Rate and Cardiac Conduction in the
Wolff-Parkinson-White Syndrome. *New England Journal of Medicine,* 1973, *288,* 560–562. (a)

Bleecker, E. R., & Engel, B. T. Learned Control of Ventricular Rate in Patients with Atrial
Fibrillation. *Psychosomatic Medicine,* 1973, *35,* 161–175. (b)

Booker, H. E., Rubow, R. T. & Coleman, P. J. Simplified feedback in neuromuscular retraining:
An automated approach using electromyographic signals. *Archives of Physical Medicine and
Rehabilitation,* 1969, *50,* 621–625.

Brudny, J., Grynbaum, B. B. & Korein, J. Spasmodic torticollis: Treatment by feedback display
of EMG. *Archives of Physical Medicine and Rehabilitation,* 1974, *55,* 403–408.

Brudny, J., Korein, J., Levidow, L., Grynbaum, B. B., Leiberman, A., & Friedmann, L. W. Sensory Feedback Therapy as a Modality of Treatment in Central Nervous System Disorders of
Voluntary Movement. *Neurology,* 1974, *24,* 925–932.

Brudny, J., Korein, J., Grynbaum, B. B., Friedman, L. W., Weinstein, S., Sachs-Frankel, G., &
Belandres, P. V. EMG feedback therapy: Review of treatment of 114 patients. *Archives of
Physical Medicine and Rehabilitation,* 1976, *57,* 55–61.

Budzynski, T. H., Stoyva, J. M., & Adler, C. Feedback-induced Muscle Relaxation: Application to
Tension Headache. *Journal of Behaviour Therapy and Experimental Psychiatry,* 1970, *1,* 205–
211.

Budzynski, T. H., Stoyva, J. M., Adler, C. S., & Mullaney, D. J. EMG Biofeedback and Tension
Headache: A Controlled Outcome Study. *Psychosomatic Medicine,* 1973, *35,* 484–496.

Bueno-Miranda, F., Cerulli, M., & Shuster, M. M. Operant Conditioning of Colonic Motility in
Irritable Bowel Syndrome (IBS). *Gastroenterology,* 1976, *70,* 867. (Abstract)

Burnside, I. G., Tobias, H. S., & Bursill, D. Electromyographic feedback in the remobilisation of
stroke patients. In D. J. Oborne, M. M. Gruneberg, & J. R. Eiser (Eds.), *Research in Psychology
and Medicine.* London: Academic Press, 1979.

Carlsson, S. G., & Gale, E. N. Biofeedback Treatment for Muscle Pain Associated with the Temporomandibular Joint. *Journal of Behaviour Therapy and Experimental Psychiatry,* 1976, *7,*
383–385.

Carlsson, S. G., & Gale, E. N. Biofeedback in the Treatment of Longterm Temporo-Mandibular
Joint Pain: An Outcome Study. *Biofeedback and Self-regulation,* 1977, *2,* 161–172.

Carlsson, S. G., Gale, E. N., & Ohman, A. Treatment of Temporomandibular Joint Syndrome with
Biofeedback Training. *Journal of the American Dental Association,* 1975, *91,* 602–605.

Cataldo, M. F., Bird, B. L., & Cunningham, C. E. Experimental Analysis of EMG Feedback in
Treating Cerebral Palsy. *Journal of Behavioral Medicine,* 1978, *1,* 311–322.

Cerulli, M. A., Nikoomanesh, P., & Schuster, M. M. Progress in Biofeedback Conditioning for
Fecal Incontinence. *Gastroenterology,* 1976, *70,* 869. (Abstract)

Cheatle, M. D. & Weiss, T. Biofeedback in heart rate control and in the treatment of cardiac
arrhythmias. In L. White & B. Tursky (Eds.), *Clinical biofeedback: efficacy and mechanisms.*
New York: Guilford Press, 1980.

Chesney, M. A., & Shelton, J. L. A Comparison of Muscle Relaxation and Electromyogram
Biofeedback Treatments for Muscle Contraction Headache. *Journal of Behaviour Therapy and
Experimental Psychiatry,* 1976, *7,* 221–225.

Cleeland, C. S. Behavioral tactics in the modification of spasmodic torticollis. *Neurology,* 1973,
23, 1241–1247.

Cott, A., Pavloski, R. P., & Black, A. H. Reducing Epileptic Seizures through Operant Conditioning of Central Nervous System Activity: Procedural Variables. *Science,* 1979, *203,* 73–75.

Cox, D. J., Freundlich, A., & Meyer, R. G. Differential Effectiveness of Electromyograph Feedback, Verbal Relaxation Instructions, and Medication Placebo with Tension Headaches. *Journal
of Consulting and Clinical Psychology,* 1975, *43,* 892–898.

Cox, D. J., & Hobbs, W. Biofeedback as a treatment for tension headaches. In L. White & B. Tursky (Eds.), *Clinical biofeedback: efficacy and mechanisms*. New York: Guilford Press, 1980.

Daivs, M. H., Saunders, D. R., Creer, T. L., & Chai, H. Relaxation Training Facilitated by Biofeedback Apparatus as a Supplemental Treatment in Bronchial Asthma. *Journal of Psychosomatic Research*, 1973, *17*, 121–128.

Diamond, S., Diamond-Falk, J., & DeVeno, T. Biofeedback in the Treatment of Vascular Headache. *Biofeedback and Self-regulation*, 1978, *3*, 385–408.

Elder, S. T., & Eustis, N. K. Instrumental Blood Pressure Conditioning in Outpatient Hypertensives. *Behaviour Research and Therapy*, 1975, *13*, 185–188.

Elder, S. T., Ruiz, Z. R., Deabler, H. L., & Dillenkoffer, R. L. Instrumental Conditioning of the diastolic Blood Pressure in Essential Hypertensive Patients. *Journal of Applied Behavior Analysis*, 1973, *6*, 377–382.

Engel, B. T., & Bleecker, E. R. Application of operant conditioning techniques to the control of the cardiac arrhythmias. In P. A. Obrist, A. H. Black., J. Brener, & L. V. DiCara (Eds.), *Cardiovascular psychophysiology*, Chicago: Aldine, 1974.

Engel, B. T., Nikoomanesh, P., & Schuster, M. M. Operant Conditioning of Rectosphincteric Responses in the Treatment of Fecal Incontinence. *New England Journal of Medicine*, 1974, *290*, 646–649.

Fahrion, S. L. Autogenic Biofeedback Treatment for Migraine. *Mayo Clinic Proceedings*, 1977, *52*, 776–784.

Feldman, G. M. The Effect of Biofeedback Training on Respiratory Resistance of Asthmatic Children. *Psychosomatic Medicine*, 1976, *38*, 27–34.

Fernando, C. K., & Basmajian, J. V. Biofeedback in Physical Medicine and Rehabilitation. *Biofeedback and Self-regulation*, 1978, *3*, 435–455.

Feurstein, M., & Adams, H. Cephalic Vasomotor Feedback in the Modification of Migraine Headache. *Biofeedback and Self-regulation*, 1977, *2*, 241–254.

Finley, W. W., Ninman, C., Standly, J., & Ender, P. Frontal EMG Biofeedback of Athetoid Cerebral Palsy Patients: A Report of Six Cases. *Biofeedback and Self-regulation*, 1976, *1*, 169–182.

Finley, W. W., Ninman, C. A., Standly, J., & Wansley, R. A. Electrophysiologic Behavior Modification of Frontal EMG in Cerebral Palsied Children. *Biofeedback and Self-regulation*, 1977, *2*, 59–79.

Fish, D., Mayer, N., & Herman, R. Letters to the Editor: Biofeedback. *Archives of Physical Medicine and Rehabilitation*, 1976, *57*, 152.

Fowler, R. L., & Kimmel, H. D. Operant Conditioning of the GSR. *Journal of Experimental Psychology*, 1962, *63*, 563–567.

Frankel, B. L., Patel, D. J., Horowitz, D., Friedwald, W. T., Gaarder, K. R. Treatment of Hypertension with Biofeedback and Relaxation Techniques. *Psychosomatic Medicine*, 1978, *40*, 276–293.

Friar, L. R., & Beatty, J. Migraine: Management by Trained Control of Vasoconstriction. *Journal of Consulting and Clinical Psychology*, 1976, *44*, 46–53.

Furman, S. Intestinal biofeedback in functional diarrhea: A preliminary report. *Journal of Behavior Therapy and Experimental Psychiatry*, 1973, *4*, 317–321.

Gannon, L., & Sternbach, R. A. Alpha Enhancement as Treatment for Pain: A Case Study. *Jouranl of Behaviour Therapy and Experimental Psychiatry*, 1971, *2*, 209–213.

Gessel, A. H. Electromyographic Biofeedback and Tricyclic Anti-depressants in Myofascial Pain-Dysfunction Syndrome: Psychological Predictors of Outcome. *Journal of the American Dental Association*, 1975, *91*, 1048–1052.

Goldman, H., Kleinman, K., Snow, M., Bidus, D., & Korol, B. Relationship Between Essential Hypertension and Cognitive Functioning: Effects of Biofeedback. *Psychophysiology*, 1975, *12*, 569–573.

Goodman, P., Greene, C. S., & Laskin, D. M. Response of Patients with Myofascial Pain Dysfunction Syndrome to Mock Equilibration. *Journal of the American Dental Association*, 1976, *92*, 755-758.

Gottlieb, H., Strite, L. C., Koller, R., Madorsky, A., Hockersmith, V., Kleeman, M., & Wagner, J. Comprehensive Rehabilitation of Patients Having Chronic Low Back Pain. *Archives of Physical Medicine and Rehabilitation*, 1977, *58*, 101-108.

Gray, C. L., Lyle, R. C., McGuire, R. J., & Peck, D. F. Electrode Placement, EMG Feedback, and Relaxation for Tension Headaches. *Behaviour Research and Therapy*, 1980, *18*, 19-23.

Harris, F. A., Spelman, F. A., & Hymer, J. W. Electronic Sensory aids as Treatment for Cerebral-Palsied Children. Inapproprioception: Part 2. *Physical Therapy*, 1974, *54*, 354-365.

Haynes, S. N., Griffin, P., Mooney, D., & Parise, M. Electromyographic Biofeedback and Relaxation Instructions in the Treatment of Muscle Contraction Headaches. *Behavior Therapy*, 1975, *6*, 672-678.

Hefferline, R. F., Keenan, B., & Harford, R. A. Escape and Avoidance Conditioning in Human Subjects without their Observation of the Response. *Science*, 1959, *130*, 1338-1339.

Hendler, N., Derogatis, L., Avella, J., & Long, D. EMG Biofeedback in Patients with Chronic Pain. *Diseases of the Nervous System*, 1977, *38*, 505-509.

Hutchings, D. F., & Reinking, R. H. Tension Headaches: What form of Therapy is Most Effective? *Biofeedback and Self-regulation*, 1976, *1*, 183-190.

Jacobs, A. & Felton, G. S. Visual feedback of myoelectric output to train muscle relaxation in normal persons and patients with neck injuries. *Archives of Physical Medicine and Rehabilitation*, 1969, *50*, 34-39.

Jacobson, A. M., Manschreck, T. C., & Silverberg, E. Behavioral Treatment for Raynaud's Disease: A Comparative Study with Long-term Follow-up. *American Journal of Psychiatry*, 1979, *136*, 844-846.

Jankel, W. R. Bell palsy: Muscle reeducation by electromyograph feedback. *Archives of Physical Medicine and Rehabilitation*, 1978, *59*, 240-242.

Kamiya, J. Operant Control of the EEG Alpha Rhythm and Some of its Reported Effects on Consciousness. In C. Tart (Ed.), *Altered States of Consciousness*. New York: Wiley, 1969.

Keefe, F. J., & Surwit, R. S. Electromyographic Biofeedback: Behavioral Treatment of Neuromuscular Disorders. *Journal of Behavioral Medicine*, 1978, *1*, 13-24.

Keefe, F. J., Surwit, R. S., & Pilon, R. N. A 1-year Follow-up of Raynaud's Patients treated with Behavioral Therapy Techniques. *Journal of Behavioral Medicine*, 1979, *2*, 385-391.

Keefe, F. J., Surwit, R. S., & Pilon, R. N. Biofeedback, Autogenic Training, and Progressive Relaxation in the Treatment of Raynaud's Disease. *Journal of Applied Behavior Analysis*, 1980.

Kewman, D. & Roberts, A. H. Skin temperature biofeedback and migraine headaches: A double-blind study. *Biofeedback and Self-Regulation*, 1980, *5*, 327-345.

Kleinman, K. M., Goldman, H., Snow, M. Y., & Korol, B. Relationship Between Essential Hypertension and Cognitive Functioning II: Effects of Biofeedback Training Generalize to Non-laboratory Environment. *Psychophysiology*, 1977, *14*, 192-197.

Kondo, C., & Canter, A. True and False Electromyographic Feedback: Effect on Tension Headache. *Journal of Abnormal Psychology*, 1977, *86*, 93-95.

Koppman, J. W., McDonald, R. D., & Kunzel, M. G. Voluntary Regulation of Temporal Artery Diameter by Migraine Patients. *Headache*, 1974, *14*, 133-138.

Kotses, H., Glaus, K. D., Bricel, S. K., Edwards, J. E., & Crawford, P. L. Operant Muscular Relaxation and Peak Expiratory Flow Rate in Asthmatic Children. *Journal of Psychosomatic Research*, 1978, *22*, 17-23.

Kotses, H., Glaus, K. D., Crawford, P. L., Edwards, J. E., & Scherr, M. S. Operant Reduction of Frontalis EMG Activity in the Treatment of Asthma in Children. *Journal of Psychosomatic Research*, 1976, *20*, 453-459.

Kristt, D. A., & Engel, B. T. Learned Control of Blood Pressure in Patients with High Blood Pressure. *Circulation*, 1975, *51*, 370-378.

Kuhlman, W. N., & Allison, T. EEG Feedback Training in the Treatment of Epilepsy: Some Questions and Some Answers. *Paulovian Journal of Biological Science,* 1977, *12,* 112–122.

Kuhlman, W. N., & Kaplan, B. J. Clinical Applications of EEG Feedback Training. In R. J. Gatchel & K. P. Price (Eds.), *Clinical Applications of Biofeedback: Appraisal and Status.* New York: Pergamon Press, 1979.

Kukulka, C. G., Brown, D. M. & Basmajian, J. V. Biofeedback training for early finger joint mobilization. *The American Journal of Occupational Therapy,* 1975, *29,* 409–470.

Lake, A., Rainey, J., & Papsdorf, J. D. Biofeedback and Rational-Emotive Therapy in the Management of Migraine Headache. *Journal of Applied Behavior Analysis,* 1979, *12,* 127–140.

Lang, P. J. & Melamed, B. G. Case report: Avoidance conditioning therapy of an infant with chronic ruminative vomiting. *Journal of Abnormal Psychology,* 1969, *74,* 1–8.

Lee, K. H., Hill, E., Johnston, R., & Smichoroski, T. Myofeedback for Muscle Retraining in Hemiplegic Patients. *Archives of Physical Medicine and Rehabilitation,* 1976, *57,* 588–591.

Lisina, M. I. The Role of Orientation in the Transformation of Involuntary Reactions into Voluntary ones. In L. G. Voronin, A. N. Leontiev, A. R. Luria, E. N. Sokolov, & O. B. Vinogradova (Eds.), *Orienting Reflex and Exploratory Behavior.* Washington: American Institute of Biological Sciences, 1965.

Lubar, J. F. EEG Operant Conditioning in Intractable Epileptics: Controlled Multidimensional Studies. In L. White & B. Tursky (Eds.), *Clinical Biofeedback: Efficacy and Mechanisms.* New York: Guilford Press, 1980.

Luborsky, L., Cuts-Christoph, P., Brady, J. P., Kron, R. E., Weiss, T. & Englelman, K. Antihypertensive effects of behavioral treatments and medications compared. *The New England Journal of Medicine,* 1980, *303,* 386.

Macdonald, L. M., & Quy, R. J. Biofeedback of the electroencephalogram in the treatment of epilepsy. In D. J. Oborne, M. M. Gruneberg, & J. R. Eiser (Eds.), *Research in Psychology and Medicine.* London: Academic Press, 1979.

MacPherson, E. L. R. Control of involuntary movement. *Behavior Research and Therapy,* 1967, *5,* 143–145.

Marinacci, A. & Horande, M. Electromyogram in neuromuscular reeducation. *Bulletin of the Los Angeles Neurological Society,* 1960, *25,* 57–71.

Martin, P. R., & Mathews, A. M. Tension Headaches: Psychophysiological Investigation and Treatment. *Journal of Psychosomatic Research,* 1978, *22,* 389–399.

Miller, N. E. Learning of Visceral and Glandular Responses. *Science,* 1969, *163,* 434–445.

Miller, N. E. Applications of Learning and Biofeedback to Psychiatry and Medicine. In A. M. Freedman, H. I. Kaplan, & B. J. Sadock (Eds.), *Comprehensive Textbook of Psychiatry, III.* Baltimore: Williams and Wilkins Co., 1975.

Mitch, P. S., McGrady, A., & Iannone, A. Autogenic Feedback Training in Migraine: A Treatment Report. *Headache,* 1976, *15,* 267–270.

Mostofsky, D. I., & Balaschak, B. A. Psychobiological Control of Seizures. *Psychological Bulletin,* 1977, *84,* 723–750.

Mullinex, J. M., Norton, B. J., Hack, S. & Fishman, M. A. Skin temperature biofeedback and migraine. *Headache,* 1978, *17,* 242–244.

Netsell, R. & Cleeland, C. S. Modification of lip hypertonia dysarthria using EMG feedback. *Journal of Speech and Hearing Disorders,* 1973, *38,* 131–140.

Newlin, D. B., & Levenson, R. W. Pre-ejection Period: Measuring Betaadrenergic Influences upon the Heart. *Psychophysiology,* 1979, *16,* 546–553.

Obrist, P. A., Light, K. C., McCubbin, J. A., Hutcheson, J. S., & Hoffer, J. L. Pulse Transit Time: Relationship to Blood Pressure and Myocardial Performance. *Psychophysiology,* 1979, *16,* 292–301.

O'Neil, P. M., White, J. L., King, C. R., & Carek, D. J. Controlling Childhood Rumination through Differential Reinforcement of other Behavior. *Behavior Modification,* 1979, *3,* 355–372.

Peck, D. F. The use of EMG feedback in the treatment of a severe case of blepharospasm. *Biofeedback and Self-regulation*, 1977, *2*, 273–277.

Patel, C. H. Yoga and Biofeedback in the Management of Hypertension. *Lancet*, 1973, *2*, 1053–1055.

Patel, C. 12-month Follow-up of Yoga and Biofeedback in the Management of Hypertension. *Lancet*, 1975, *1*, 62–67.

Patel, C., & North, W. R. S. Randomized Controlled Trial of Yoga and Biofeedback in Management of Hypertension. *Lancet*, 1975, *2*, 93–99.

Philips, C. The Modification of Tension Headache Pain using EMG Biofeedback. *Behaviour Research and Therapy*, 1977, *15*, 119–129.

Pickering, T. G., Brucker, B. S., Frankel, H. L., Mathias, C. J., Dworkin, B. R., & Miller, N. E. Mechanisms of Learned Voluntary Control of Blood Pressure in Patients with Generalized Bodily Paralysis. In J. Beatty & H. Legewie (Eds.), *Biofeedback and Behavior*. New York: Plenum Press, 1977.

Pickering, T. G., & Gorham, G. Learned Heart-rate Control by a Patient with a Ventricular Parasystolic Rhythm. *Lancet*, 1975, *2*, 252–253.

Pickering, T. G., & Miller, N. E. Learned Voluntary Control of Heart-rate and rhythm in two Subjects with Premature Ventricular Contractions. *British Heart Journal*, 1977, *39*, 152–159.

Price, K. P., & Gatchel, R. J. A Perspective on Clinical Biofeedback. In R. J. Gatchel & K. P. Price (Eds.), *Clinical Applications of Biofeedback: Appraisal and Status*. New York: Pergamon Press, 1979.

Price, K. P., & Tursky, B. Vascular Reactivity of Migraineurs and Nonmigraineurs: A Comparison of Responses to Self-control Procedures. *Headache*, 1976, *16*, 210–217.

Reinking, R. H., & Hutchings, D. *Follow-up and Extension of "Tension Headaches—What Method is Most Effective?"* Paper presented at the meeting of the Biofeedback Research Society. Colorado Spring, Colorado, 1976.

Santee, J. L., Keister, M. E., & Kleinman, K. M. Incentives to enhance the Effects of Electromyographic Feedback Training in Stroke Patients. *Biofeedback and Self-regulation*, 1980, *5*, 51–56.

Sargent, J. D., Green, E. E., & Walters, E. D. The use of Autogenic Feedback Training in a Pilot Study of Migraine and Tension Headaches. *Headache*, 1972, *12*, 120–124.

Sargent, J. D., Green, E. E., & Walters, E. D. Preliminary Report on the Use of Autogenic Feedback Training in the Treatment of Migraine and Tension Headaches. *Psychosomatic Medicine*, 1973, *35*, 129–135.

Scherr, M. S., Crawford, P. L., Sergent, C. B., & Scherr, C. A. Effect of Biofeedback Techniques on Chronic Asthma in a Summer Camp Environment. *Annals of Allergy*, 1975, *35*, 289–295.

Schwartz, G., & Shapiro, D. Biofeedback and Essential Hypertension: Current Findings and Theoretical Concerns. *Seminars in Psychiatry*, 1973, *5*, 493–503.

Scott, R. W., Blanchard, E. B., Edmundson, E. D., & Young, L. D. A Shaping Procedure for Heart Rate Control in Chronic Tachycardia. *Perceptual and Motor Skills*, 1973, *37*, 327–338.

Seymour, R. J., & Bassler, C. R. Electromyographic Biofeedback in Treatment of Incomplete Paraplegia. *Physical Therapy*, 1977, *57*, 1148–1150.

Shapiro, D., Crider, A. B., & Tursky, B. Differentiation of an Autonomic Response through Operant Reinforcement. *Psychonomic Science*, 1964, *1*, 147–148.

Shapiro, D., Tursky, B., Gershon, E., & Stern, M. Effects of Feedback and Reinforcement on the Control of Human Systolic Blood Pressure. *Science*, 1969, *163*, 588–590.

Sherman, R. A. Successful Treatment of one Case of Tardive Dyskinesia with Electromyographic Feedback from the Masseter Muscle. *Biofeedback and Self-regulation*, 1979, *4*, 367–370.

Shoemaker, J. E., & Tasto, D. L. The Effects of Muscle Relaxation on Blood Pressure of Essential Hypertensives. *Behaviour Research and Therapy*, 1975, *13*, 29–43.

Solberg, W. K., & Rugh, J. D. The Use of Biofeedback Devices in the Treatment of Bruxism. *Journal of the Southern California Dental Association*, 1972, *40*, 852–853.

Sovak, M., Kunzel, M., Sternbach, R. A. & Dalessio, D. J. Effects of volitionally and/or thermally induced vasodilation in the upper extremities of the carotid hemodynamics of migraineurs. In J. I. Martin (Ed.), *Proceedings of the San Diego biomedical symposium* (Vol. 16) New York: Academic, 1978.

Stenn, P. G., Mothersill, K. J., & Brooke, R. I. Biofeedback and a Cognitive Behavioral Approach to the Treatment of Myofascial Pain Dysfunction Syndrome. *Behavior Therapy, 1979, 10,* 29–36.

Sterman, M. B. Effects of Sensorimotor EEG Feedback Training on Sleep and Clinical Manifestations of Epilepsy. In J. Beatty & H. Legewie (Eds), *Biofeedback and Behavior*. New York: Plenum Press, 1977.

Sterman, M. B., & Macdonald, L. R. Effects of Central Cortical EEG Feedback Training on Seizure Incidence in Poorly Controlled Epileptics. *Epilepsia, 1978, 19,* 207–222.

Surwit, R. S., Pilon, R. N., & Fenton, C. H. Behavioral Treatment of Raynaud's Disease. *Journal of Behavioral Medicine,* 1978, *1,* 323–335.

Surwit, R. S., Shapiro, D., & Good, M. I. A Comparison of Cardiovascular Biofeedback, Neuromuscular Biofeedback and Meditation in the Treatment of Boarderline Essential Hypertension. *Journal of Consulting and Clinical Psychology,* 1978, *46,* 252–263.

Taub, E. Self-Regulation of Human Tissue Temperature. In G. E. Schwartz & J. Beatty (Eds.), *Biofeedback: Theory and Research*. New York: Academic Press, 1977.

Turin, A. & Johnson, W. G. Biofeedback therapy for migraine headache. *Archives of General Psychiatry,* 1976, *33,* 517–519.

Vachon, L., & Rich, E. S. Visceral Learning in Asthma. *Psychosomatic Medicine,* 1976, *38,* 122–130.

Walsh, P., Dale, A., & Anderson, D. E. Comparison of Biofeedback Pulse Wave Velocity and Progressive Relaxation in Essential Hypertensives. *Perceptual and Motor Skills,* 1977, *44,* 839–843.

Weiss, T., & Engel, B. T. Operant Conditioning of Heart Rate in Patients with Premature Ventricular Contractions. *Psychosomatic Medicine,* 1971, *33,* 301–321.

Whitehead, W. E. Biofeedback in the Treatment of Gastrointestinal Disorders. *Biofeedback and Self-regulation,* 1978, *3,* 375–384.

Whitehead, W. E., Renault, P. F., & Goldiamond, I. Modification of Human Gastric Acid Secretion with Operant-Conditioning Procedures. *Journal of Applied Behavior Analysis,* 1975, *8,* 147–156.

Wooldridge, C. P., & Russel, G. Head Position Training with the Cerebral Palsied Child: An Application of Biofeedback Techniques. *Archives of Physical Medicine and Rehabilitation,* 1976, *57,* 407–414.

3 Pain: Its Assessment and Management

Terence M. Murphy, M.D., F.F.A.R.C.S.
Pain Clinic
University of Washington

INTRODUCTION

Pain is an enigma. Most people conceive of pain as an unpleasant signal of tissue insult. This particular concept is true for the majority of acute short duration pains as occur in response to mechanical or thermal injury. However, in many instances of chronic pain, there is no detectable evidence of a tissue damaging stimulus, and these patients frequently report considerable discomfort and distress despite appropriate treatments for pain directed at such a peripheral tissue damaging stimulus, i.e., rest, medications, surgery, etc. In fact, many of the treatments that are very effective at controlling acute tissue damaging pain often fail when applied to patients with chronic pain (Bonica, 1977).

In an attempt to explain some of the above enigmas, it has become appreciated in recent years that acute pain and chronic pain are probably caused by different mechanisms, and that if the acute pain mechanisms persist over time, they produce secondary changes in the organism which can almost become a self-perpetuating painful state. Thus, those factors which generate the pain complaint in chronic pain are often quite different from the relatively simplistic tissue damaging generators of acute pain. For this reason, many of the treatments that are effective in acute pain not only become ineffective in patients with chronic pain but can, in fact, contribute to the morbidity of such patients, such as occurs when excessive rest and inactivity or excessive medication or destructive surgical procedures are performed unsuccessfully to resolve chronic pain problems.

For the most part, there are efficient therapies for dealing with acute pain problems. The problem is primarily that of delivery of these therapies and technologies to the patients with the problem. In chronic pain however, there are

75

so many gaps in our knowledge of the mechanisms of this condition that at this time there is no consistently successful treatment of chronic pain, although present knowledge has identified sub-groups of chronic pain patients for which there are now satisfactory treatments. To better understand this, it is important to contemplate the present theories of the mechanisms of pain.

Theories of Pain

The concept of pain being a neurophysiological event whereby a tissue damaging stimulus is transmitted along nerve pathways through a specific afferent system to a "pain center" in the brain, has been conceived for many years. Anatomically, such a specific path has been demonstrated although it is now appreciated that this particular pathway is far more complex than initially conceived and involves considerable opportunities for modulating this incoming pain signal by other afferent sensations and even by descending inhibitory impulses from higher centers.

The above mechanisms whereby evidence of tissue damage is transmitted along specific nerves pathways is known as nociception. This is the phenomenon responsible for most acute pain and a significant amount of chronic pain. However, increasing knowledge has indicated that in its chronic form, pain complaints can be generated by factors other than nociception. For example, there appear to be a number of patients who have primarily a psychological or psychiatric disorder whereby they verbalize their psychological distress using the language of tissue damage as though nociception were occurring when the prime complaint appears to be that of a psychological problem such as depression or anxiety. Also, some patients with chronic pain appear to be suffering from a learned pain phenomenon whereby the initial pain complaint, due to some nociceptive stimulus, received such environmental reinforcers that the pain behavior emitted by the patient continued even after the tissue damage had healed. This form of chronic pain is generated primarily by behavioral rather than tissue damage or psychiatric problems.

Nociception

There appear to be very specific terminals in the peripheral nervous system that are sensitive to nociception. Some are specific mechanical or thermal receptors, others respond to several sensations and are called polymodal receptors. The afferent nerve pathways from these receptors tend to be along the smaller sensory nerves, the A-delta and C fibers. The A-delta fibers tend to transmit the faster pain signals which enable us to localize the site of the pain, whereas the C fibers tend to be more active in the ongoing deep, more diffuse residual pain that remains after the initial insult. These nerve fibers appear to enter the spinal cord via the posterior sensory root although there is some evidence to suggest that some may in fact enter through what was thought initially to be the exclusively motor anterior root (Coggershall, 1973). These afferent nerves impinge upon the dorsal horn and there undergo considerable modulation of a complexity that is continually undergoing elucidation. This dorsal horn of the spinal gray matter appears to be a focal area for such modulation. Initially, Melzack and Wall (1965) speculated there existed a gating mechanism whereby afferent non-pain signals could "gate out" incoming pain signals at this level or fast signals could bypass the gating mechanism to alert higher centers to produce descending suppressive signals to act on the "gate". A more recent understanding of the neurophysiology of nociception plus the ever-evolving field of neurotransmitters and the enkephalin compounds have given some support to these earlier modulation theories (Mayer, 1976). It appears now that the transmission of pain in the dorsal horn, and maybe other CNS sites, can suppress this transmission of substance P to and the liberation of enkephalin type compounds from interneurons in the dorsal horn and maybe other CNS sites, can suppress this transmission of substance P to prevent nociception and therefore produce analgesia. These enkephalin interneurons may be activated either by incoming non-pain signals or can be activated by descending signals from higher centers as may occur in such phenomena as hypnosis, biofeedback, relaxation, etc.

The traditional afferent pathway for nociception from the dorsal horn is that it crosses to the opposite anterolateral segment of the spinal cord and then ascends in the spinothalamic tract. Recent knowledge has attested to the fact that the spinothalamic tract enjoys many communications with other levels in the spinal cord and also with many of the basal ganglia and particularly the phylogenetically older paleospinal tract which freely communicates with the reticular substance in the hind brain and areas around the third ventricle which recent studies have shown to be very important sites in connection with the production of enkephalins and stimulation produced analgesia. The phylogenetically recent neospinothalamic tract runs via the thalamic nuclei to the sensory cortex and appears to be associated with the discriminative aspects of the incoming pain signal whereas the paleospinal tract and the other connections to the deeper nuclei of the brain appear to be perhaps connected with the emotional and aversive aspects of pain. This incoming signal, when it reaches higher centers, appears capable of producing a descending response which can act both at midbrain nuclei (such as the central gray matter) or the nucleus gigantocellularis. Both of these appear to be centers connected with the liberation of endogenous opiate type substances, such as the enkephalins and endorphins, which could then produce analgesia via a systemic effect. Alternately, more specific descending neural elements could liberate these substances in the dorsal horn at some of the first synapses on the afferent nociceptive pathway as described above to produce a more focal analgesia.

Nociceptive stimuli, therefore, traveling from the periphery to the cerebral cortex appear to have definite receptor endings and specific afferent paths to specific brain sites, but this path is subject to modulation probably along its afferent path in the neuraxis and certainly at such local sites as the dorsal horn of the spinal gray matter and the reticular substance in the midbrain.

This new knowledge helps explain why higher centers can influence the incoming pain signal to decrease it and maybe even augment it. Also other

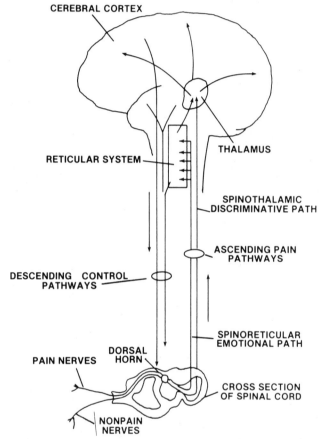

FIG. 3.1. This shows the pathways of nociceptive input whereby the signal travels along the small nerve fibers carrying such traffic and undergoes interaction with the incoming non-pain signals first at the dorsal horn levels of the spinal cord but probably at other sites in the central nervous system as well. This incoming traffic crosses to the anterolateral segment of the contralateral side of the spinal cord and ascends through a discriminative pathway to the sensory cortex via the thalamus and also by alternative pathways to the reticular system with widespread subsequent radiation to lower and higher brain centers, resulting in the emotional as opposed to the discriminative aspects of the incoming pain signal. Note also that descending control pathways appear to be able to influence this incoming nociception at probably midbrain and spinal levels.

afferent non-painful sensations, e.g., massage, physiotherapy, exercise, etc., may exert part of its salutary effect by interfering with and suppressing afferent pain signals at such peripheral sites as the dorsal horn of the spinal cord (Mayer).

Central Pain States

A specific type of pain problem encountered in Pain Clinics is known as the central pain state whereby the central nervous system receives information as though nociception were occurring when in fact it is not. This is believed to be due to a defect in the afferent nociceptive pathway previously described whereby the peripheral receptor system has been destroyed by either mechanical, thermal, or infective processes and some of the intermediate cell bodies in the afferent path undergo spontaneous nociceptive afferent activity (Taub & Collins, 1974). This is believed to be the mechanism of pain in such conditions as phantom limb phenomena, pain in post-herpetic neuralgias, tic douloureux and the pain experienced by people with spinal cord injuries. This particular form of chronic pain is very important because it does not respond to treatment directed at the peripheral nociceptor (which is often absent as in such cases as phantom limb pain) and therefore responds much better to the centrally acting agents given to suppress this abnormal activity (see the following section).

Psychological Mechanisms

Patients evaluated in Pain Clinics frequently do not appear to have significant evidence for nociception or tissue damage but when psychological evaluation is undertaken, these people often demonstrate considerable psychopathology and when treated for same, the complaint of pain can be ameliorated. A simple example of this involves those individuals where the core problem is an underlying depression whereby the patient verbalizes his suffering using a complaint of pain—headache, backache, and so forth. By treating the depression, often the complaints of pain subside suggesting that the depression is probably the cause rather than the effect of the chronic pain complaint.

With the modern theories of the neurophysiology of pain as outlined earlier, it is quite conceivable to speculate how patients with psychological problems could well have an impaired descending control mechanism, especially since 5-hydroxytryptamine has been shown to possibly be an important neurotransmitter in these descending control pathways and this chemical is known to be deficient in certain depressive states (Ward, Bloom, & Friedl, 1979).

Behavioral Generators of Chronic Pain

In its final analysis, pain complaints are a behavior. Nociception is a private sensation that is not obvious to observers, and the environment just views the behavior, limping, grimacing, pain complaints, medication taking, visiting doctors, etc. If this behavioral pattern is reinforced by the environment such as an overindulgent spouse, sympathetic employer, etc., then these behaviors can be learned and can continue even after the original pain generating nociceptive stimulus has subsided. Pain complaints can also persist as a behavioral phenomena in those circumstances where well behavior, i.e., non-pain behavior, is aversive or costly to the patient as may occur in a circumstance whereby normal behavior would lead to unpleasant demands of either a social or occupational nature on the patient and the pain behavior may provide an escape from such demands.

Chronic pain can be due to either nociception, psychological causes or even purely behavioral phenomena. More often however, chronic pain is believed to be a mix of some or all of these possible causes. For example, an individual with

BEHAVIOUR

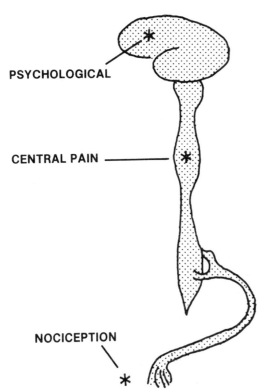

PSYCHOLOGICAL

CENTRAL PAIN

NOCICEPTION

FIG. 3.2. This shows a workable classification of the causes of chronic pain which are

(1) Nociception—i.e., tissue damage due to degenerative disease, cancer, muscle spasm, etc.

(2) Central pain—This is usually associated with some denervation process whereby the central nervous system receives input as though nociception was occurring when in fact it is not.

(3) Psychological causes—Here the patient suffering from anxieties, depression, etc., verbalizes his suffering using the language and behavior of nociception.

(4) Behavioral pain—The patient learns a repertoire of chronic pain behavior (going to doctors, taking medicine, complaining, etc.) because such behavior is sufficiently reinforced by his environment or alternatively well behavior is punished or threatening to him.

a chronic nociceptive stimulus such as arthritis or chronic degenerative joint disease may cope adequately with same, but should they develop a depression, then the combination of the nociception plus the depression can become a debilitating phenomenon and if it is persistently treated as nociception ignoring the depressive elements, the patient will not improve and both the patient and the physicians become frustrated in their attempts to resolve the continuing pain complaint. In addition, if the chronic pain complaint is also due to behavioral aspects, then to resolve the individual's dilemma may well mean active treatment both of the nociceptive source, the depressive elements, and maybe some behavioral modification techniques as well. It was with such complicated individuals in mind that Pain Clinics were developed.

PAIN CLINICS

Pain Clinics exist in many forms and at this moment in time, there is no consistent repertoire of diagnostic or treatment strategies that are offered by Pain Clinics. At extremes, the Pain Clinic can be a multidisciplinary enterprise with many diagnostic and therapeutic options in both the traditional medical and psychological behavioral therapeutic ranges, and at the other extreme, it may be some unimodal treatment facility offering just acupuncture or biofeedback to all patients without any attempts at sophisticated diagnostic evaluation.

Ideally, a Pain Clinic should possess the diagnostic facilities to evaluate a patient with chronic pain from medical, psychological, and social aspects. It should be capable of integrating this information and then offering appropriate corrective therapies which may range from the extremes of complicated medical technology through to social, occupational, or other environmental adjustments. To be able to do this requires the interaction of staff with many different talents, but all with a common purpose of helping the individual in chronic pain. This is optimally done in a multidisciplinary evaluation facility which at a minimum, should have the ability to perform a conventional and indepth medical assessment plus a comprehensive psychological evaluation of the individual who presents with the pain, and the secondary effects that the pain has produced in this individual's environment. This approach is the basic one adopted by most Pain Clinics and usually involves evaluation of such patients by a physician and a psychologist along with a social evaluation of the patient's environment which usually includes interviewing the spouse and maybe obtaining comprehensive information from the patient's employer, lawyer, etc. (Bonica, 1974).

In order to obtain an objective assessment of the pain state, most Pain Clinics usually request the patient to keep an accurate record of his pain over a set period of time such as the two weeks prior to arrival in the clinic. This is done by filling out a pain diary (see fig. 3.3). Patients in these clinics are usually seen only by a

DAY_____ Date_____

	SITTING		WALKING & STANDING		RECLINING		MEDICATIONS		PAIN LEVEL
	Major Activity	Time	Major Activity	Time	Activity	Time	Amount	Type	(0-10)
Morning A.M. 12-1 A.M.	T.V.	1 hr					2	Percodan	7
1-2 A.M.	T.V.	1hr					1	Valium	7
2-3 A.M.					Sleep	1 hr			7
3-4 A.M.					Sleep	1 hr			7
4-5 A.M.					Sleep	1 hr			7
5-6 A.M.	Bathroom	1 hr					2	Percodan	9
6-7 A.M.					Sleep	1 hr			9
7-8 A.M.					Sleep	1 hr			9
8-9 A.M.	Breakfast	1 hr							9
9-10 A.M.					Sleep	1 hr			8
10-11 A.M.			Emergency Rm. Dr. Visit	1 hr				Demerol Shot	9
11-12 A.M.	T.V.	1 hr							8
Evening P.M. 12-1 P.M.	Lunch/T.V.	1 hr							7
1-2 P.M.	T.V.	1 hr							7
2-3 P.M.			Visit to Pharmacy	1 hr					9
3-4 P.M.	Resting	1 hr					2	Percodan	8
4-5 P.M.	Resting	1 hr							8
5-6 P.M.	Meal	1 hr					2	Valium	8
6-7 P.M.	Sauna	1 hr							7
7-8 P.M.					Sleep	1 hr			7
8-9 P.M.					Sleep	1 hr			7
9-10 P.M.	T.V.	1 hr							7
10-11 P.M.	T.V.	1 hr							7
11-12 P.M.	T.V.	1 hr							7
TOTAL HOURS ➡	Sitting =	14	Walking =	2	Reclining =	8	Pain Scale; 0 = no pain		

(Hours Sitting + Hours Walking + Hours Reclining = 24 Hours)   10 = unbearable

FIG. 3.3 Diaries. This is the diary record kept by patients. Note the following characteristics: An incredibly large amount of non-activity, i.e., 22 out of the 24 hours are spent either sitting or reclining. This would suggest probably considerable behavioral reinforcers of pain complaint. Note also the only activities are health care related, i.e., Emergency Room, visit to pharmacy. Note that dependency producing medications—Percodan and Valium, are taken with little effect on the patient's pain suggesting that they are probably taken because of a pharmacological depen-

referral from their "managing physician" because most pain management strategies involve long-term care and these patients need to be returned to a managing physician to carry through on the final recommendations of the clinic. When evaluated in the Pain Clinic, after their medical and psychological evaluations with such diagnostic tests on hand as the MMPI, a decision is usually made as to the most appropriate cause of the patient's problems and what to do about it. This may be something very specific with a very specific treatment required or it may be very general whereby the patient needs a multifaceted approach. Sometimes further information is needed from other consultants and they are involved in this decision-making process.

Treatment plans fall into many categories. For example, if the patient's pain complaint is deemed to be due to a significant and overwhelming behavioral problem, he may need the elaborate behavioral modification techniques used in a prolonged inpatient pain therapeutic program. On the other hand, if his chronic pain problem is due to some more specific cause say, denervation dysesthesia due to nerve damage, he may be able to receive some appropriate medications (e.g., Tegretol) on an outpatient basis. Some patients referred to Pain Clinics arrive with a significant medication dependency problem. This often clouds the initial evaluation efforts and sometimes a formal inpatient detoxification procedure is needed prior to even starting a diagnostic or therapeutic effort.

In dealing with people with chronic pain, it is very important to acknowledge that the patient's pain is a very real problem. Attempts to explain it away as an "imagined" phenomenon or attempts to differentiate between "real" and "unreal" pain or "organic" and "psychosomatic" problems are usually fruitless and only succeed in challenging the patient to further heroic attempts to prove the validity of his suffering by seeking out more elaborate consultations and investigations and treatments. Therefore, initially, it is important to let the patient know that you believe he suffers, even if you do not have a good idea as to the diagnosis. It is very important early on for the patient and family to appreciate that there may not be some simple technological solution to his problem (such as nerve sections, etc.). It is also appropriate that the patient undergo the psychological evaluation at a very early stage. If a conventional medical approach seeking out a tissue damage diagnosis and corresponding treatment is pursued only to fail, it is then very difficult at that late stage to introduce the psychological evaluation, for the patient interprets such a move as in essence being told the pain is "all in his head" and usually becomes dissatisfied and goes elsewhere.

---

dency rather than to relieve symptoms. Note also the diurnal sleep pattern often characteristic of such patients where they catnap throughout the day. Taken altogether, such a diary suggests the patient needs switching to a detoxification regime probably via a pain cocktail with decreasing doses of long acting narcotics and sedative hypnotics and also a reactivation physical therapy program to attempt to replace the illness behavior (excess inactivity) with some well behavior patterns.

MEDICAL EVALUATION OF PATIENT WITH CHRONIC
PAIN

Basically this involves a very complete history taking and physical examination with particular stress being laid upon the patient's previous health and certainly his previous interaction with the medical and surgical professions, particularly with regard to his presenting pain complaint and to note the effects of previous therapies on same. Special attention is given to the medication history and particularly current ingestion habits, noting any overt signs of medication toxicity, i.e., slurring of speech, vague responses with regard to medication ingestion and particularly being concerned in those patients with an inappropriate sophistication with regard to pharmacological agents and their characteristics and dose forms. It is important to note the characteristics of the patient's pain complaint so that they can be compared with usual or unusual pain patterns.

Patients referred to Pain Clinics have usually undergone extensive physical examinations and it is unlikely that conventional pathological processes will have gone undetected. However, it is very important when examining people to look for unconventional generators of pain such as variations of the reflex sympathetic dystrophies, the myofascial syndromes, and areas of impaired sensation that might give rise to denervation dysesthetic pains. Also during the physical examination, specific efforts are made to determine the consistency of patient's pain complaints by testing muscle function in various positions in an attempt to determine the consistency of the patient's pain problems. It is rare that malingerers are detected in Pain Clinics but inconsistencies of claimed physical impairments is a fairly common occurrence and attests to the fact that many of the patients referred to Pain Clinics have a predominantly psychological distress which is interpreted by them as due to real, not "imagined", physical impairment (a gross example being the inappropriate responses of the true hysterical patient who is incapable of complying with straight leg raising requests when lying in the supine position and yet can accomplish comparable muscular movements when sitting). Minor variations of such inconsistencies are often detected in the examination of pain patients. A comprehensive physical examination is necessary both to confirm that no obvious pathology has been overlooked and also to reassure the patient, their relatives and referring physician that such has been completed.

PSYCHOLOGICAL EVALUATION FOR THE PATIENT
WITH CHRONIC PAIN

For the reasons mentioned earlier, it is very important to look indepth at the patient who has the pain as well as concentrating on the pain that the patient has. Many patients with chronic pain resent 'psychological' and/or 'psychiatric' evaluations of their pain inasmuch as they interpret this particular diagnostic evaluation as intimating their pain is "all in their heads". Therefore, it is very important to introduce this evaluation to the patient and their families at a very early stage in the workup. Patients will frequently accept and cooperate with such an evaluation at an early stage in the relationship but if traditional medical treatments, drugs, pills, surgeries, etc., are exhausted and then psychological measures are offered as a last resort, the patient usually complies poorly with such an approach at a late stage. Most Pain Clinics employ the services of a clinical psychologist or psychiatrist depending on availabilities. This evaluation attempts to determine if a coexisting depression, anxiety, personality or behavioral factors may be contributing to the patient's pain complaint. To help in this evaluation, such screening tests as the Minnesota Multiphasic Personality Inventory, Zung Depression Test, Illness Behavior Evaluations, etc., are often utilized by having the patient fill these in either before or at the first visit. The completion of a one or two week diary whereby the patient documents the incidence of his pain with some simple scoring scale and on the same record, identifies his activities and medication patterns can be an extremely useful screening test to ascertain the potential presence of behavioral generators of the pain complaint and if such is suspected, then the patient should undergo behavioral analysis at a very early stage in the evaluation.

Behavioral Analysis

Most patients with chronic refractory puzzling pain problems benefit from such an analysis, especially if there is little or no evidence of tissue damage factors or if they are relatively insignificant compared with the symptoms generated. If upon perusal of the diaries it appears that the pain follows inappropriate diurnal variation, (i.e., patients with behaviorally generated pain frequently do not have pain complaints at night but will complain freely of pain during daytime hours which is in contrast to most tissue damage pains which are worse at night) so that if the diaries indicate that the pain switches off at night, this would be suspicious of significant environmental factors. Also the diary can often identify those patients with a medication dependency if patients awake at regular intervals throughout the night and take medication. If they disturb the rest of the house over this time, this too would be indicative of potential environmental reinforcement of the pain problem. Behavioral analysis involves identifying those factors which increase pain behavior. If these tend to be occasions that one would regard as aversive or unpleasant, i.e., demanding occupation, chores, or threatening social situations, then it is likely that the pain behavior may be operant. It is also important to ascertain what factors decrease pain and if these are pleasant or socially reinforcing, then again one must consider operant mechanisms as a generator of the pain complaint. If the patient's pain is made worse by relaxation, inactivity, etc., it is unlikely to be a behavioral problem.

It is also important especially in the older age groups during this evaluation to ascertain cortical function and if deficits are suspected, they may well need some formal evaluation such as a Reitan test. Pain complaints can protect such patients from social or an occupational circumstance where the cortical deficit would be embarrassing.

If as a result of the behavioral analysis there appear to be significant behavioral problems, then further evaluation, and certainly treatment will almost certainly need isolating the patient in a controlled inpatient environment whereby the therapists have control over the social contingencies of pain behavior. It is also essential that the relatives are involved in this plan and process and, as will be discussed under therapy, they play an integral part in learning new non-reinforcing responses to the patient's pain complaint which will be continued after the patient leaves the inpatient setting.

TREATMENT

Often the therapies that are very effective for acute pain states such as rest, powerful medications, invasive surgical techniques, are frequently not helpful in chronic pain conditions and are usually contraindicated in same. They often contribute to the morbidity of the condition without relieving any of the symptoms.

Medication is probably the most widely prescribed form of therapy as a result of patient/physician interaction. It is very important that if chronic pain is treated by medication, that these be prescribed appropriately which will usually be quite different from their administration in acute pain states. Because many pain patients are given medications as though their problem is that of acute pain, inappropriate and excessive dependency upon narcotics and sedative hypnotics often results and a significant sub-group of patients referred to Pain Clinics present with such a problem. Detoxification from this medication dependency is a priority. As well as conventional analgesics, psychotropic agents are much used and also those drugs effective in relieving the central pain states.

Other options for treating chronic pain are to reduce any chronic nociception by means of analgesic nerve blocks and/or to increase non-pain afferent input to the central nervous system by means of stimulation produced analgesia, either with electrical stimulators, acupuncture needles, physical therapy, exercise, etc. Psychological forms of therapy have found much application in chronic pain therapy and most attempt to replace the pain behavior life style with some more appropriate non-pain behavior. In the more refractory cases, this can usually be performed in an inpatient setting. These behavioral modification techniques are usually some combination of individual and group therapeutic effort.

Neurodestructive procedures either with neurosurgical or percutaneous neurolytic agents are usually reserved for the terminally ill cancer patient and are not indicated in the chronic non-malignant pain problems.

Treatment of Acute Pain

Obviously, removal of the cause of acute pain problems is highly desirable as in the case of an inflammed appendix, a tooth abscess, the splinting of broken bones, etc. However, there are many cases of acute pain (e.g., postoperative pain), where such corrective maneuvers are not feasible and symptomatic treatment is needed.

Here the pharmacology and technology available to modern medical science if applied appropriately can usually control acute pain satisfactorily. The narcotic analgesics used in appropriate amounts at regular enough intervals can be quite effective at controlling many forms of visceral and somatic pain. Also techniques of regional anesthesia normally utilized for operative and obstetrical pain can be quite effective at controlling postoperative and other pains if the personnel and facilities are available to deliver same. The new innovative techniques of administering narcotic medications into the subarachnoid and epidural space to produce a very local analgesia on the spinal cord opiate receptors has much potential for pain control since this form of analgesia tends to last much longer than when narcotics are administered systemically.

The administration of analgesic medications at the moment and probably for sometime in the future will continue to be primarily by oral medications.

It is surprising but true that physicians tend to undertreat acute pain and overtreat chronic pain conditions with potent analgesics and sedative hypnotics. In acute pain, it is feasible by trial to determine what particular drug and dose will control an individual patient's acute pain problem. The duration of this dose should be ascertained by close observation and then administered in a time-contingent fashion at a time interval less than the duration of the analgesia so that the patient is kept pain free with regular medications, administered at a regular interval of time. With such a regime, the dosage is gradually reduced as the nociceptive stimulus wanes over time.

For those patients who are at risk for producing medication dependency, (i.e., acknowledged drug addicts or people who have over-indulged in medications in the past and chronic pain medication abusers who develop some acute problems such as an operation or trauma) then it is essential that if these people are to be prescribed powerful analagesic agents that a limit be set ahead of time for the prescribing of these medications and that the patient appreciates when this time limit is reached, no open-ended analgesic prescriptions will be forthcoming.

Other more specific technology for acute pain would involve the administration of drugs around the neuraxis to produce segmental analgesia via indwelling catheters as occurs in obstetrical anesthesia and could theoretically be extended into other acute pain situations. Unfortunately, this requires the availability of highly skilled staff in attendance plus vigilant monitoring and such facilities are only available in very limited number of locations at this time. The prescribing of rest and inactivity is entirely appropriate for most acute pain situations where this is necessary for tissue healing to occur, but for those patients who are at risk for lapsing into a chronically inactive state, then the rest and activity must be prescribed as with the dependency producing medications on a time limited base. The patient and relatives must be informed at the commencement of the rest period that after tissue healing is complete, then a gradual resumption of activity is appropriate, even though this will often frequently be accompanied by initial discomfort during the convalescent phase.

The knowledge and instruments are available for the control of the vast majority of acute pain problems at present. The problem is delivering this knowledge and technology to the large numbers of patients that require same.

Medications

Medicines are much used and abused in the treatment of chronic pain. Because as mentioned before, chronic pain is often due to several causes, both due to tissue damage and psychological and behavioral problems, so different medications may be needed depending on the cause. If nociception is the generator of the patient's pain then conventional analgesics may have a significant part to play. However, in central pain states, such drugs as carbamazipine (Tegretol) or Dilantin may be more useful. In those patients with psychological diseases, sedative tranquilizers are often used although the potent dependency producing barbiturate types are rarely if ever indicated for chronic administration. Patients whose pain problem is primarily generated by learning environmental factors may not necessarily need any specific medications.

Analgesics

Non-Narcotic Analgesics. In the majority of chronic pain problems, such drugs as aspirin and acetaminophen are most useful analgesics. What is perhaps more important than the specific drug is the fact that these agents be taken in an appropriate fashion, i.e., if a chronic nociceptive stimulus is present around the clock, then it is important to take medications by a specific time pattern rather than on a symptom oriented timetable. By taking the medication before the pain becomes a significant problem, often better relief can be obtained than by taking the medication on an ''as needed'' basis. Therefore, such drugs as acetaminophen and aspirin taken in doses of 600 to 1,000 mg every 3 to 4 hours rather than prn is often a surprisingly effective way of controlling many of the more mundane chronic pain problems. There is little, if any, evidence that suggests that any of the other non-narcotic analgesics are any more effective for pain relief than aspirin or acetaminophen. Because such patients often have secondary psychological anxieties and distress, these drugs are often combined with the non-dependency producing agents such as hydroxyzine (Vistaril) in doses of 25–50 mg.

Narcotic Analgesics.   This includes the opiate drug spectrum from codeine through to morphine. They are optimally used for the control of acute pain and are of limited application in chronic pain states. Many patients who present with a chronic pain problem already have a dependence on these drugs and it is important to address this, as discussed below. For those patients with terminal cancer pain problems that are not resolved by other maneuvers, it is justifiable to use narcotic analgesics but again these should be administered on a time-contingent rather than a symptom-contingent basis to insure adequate analgesia around the clock. The effectiveness of these drugs in acute pain states alas is not carried through into the chronic phase because all these drugs exhibit the phenomenon known as tolerance whereby the more the drug is taken, the less analgesic effect each dose has, such that an escalation of dose is frequently needed and this leads to an accumulation of side effects which usually mitigates against its satisfactory long-term use. In such situations, increased dose requirements, dependency results, and the drug seeking behavior of the dependent individual can become a major part of their problem. In brief, narcotic analgesics are usually indicated in acute pain, for short-term use in those patients who already have a narcotic dependency while they are weaned from their narcotic drugs to more appropriate therapy, and for use in terminal cancer situations where often large doses of these drugs may be needed although it must be appreciated that not all terminal cancer patients suffer from severe nociception and the fact that a patient is dying from cancer does not necessarily mean that they need narcotic analgesics although these should never be withheld in such individuals if they are necessary to control pain (Twycross, 1977).

Medication Abuse

Because many patients initially present at Pain Clinics with a pre-existing medication dependency either to the narcotics or sedative hypnotic group of drugs, a detoxification regime is often of prime importance prior to attempting meaningful diagnosis and therapy of their pain problem. This detoxification is usually quite easily carried out as follows: The patient's cooperation is necessary and usually obtained since most of these patients are iatrogenically dependent on drugs rather than primary medication abusers. They are usually willing to consider alternative medication ingestion regimes to the shorter acting narcotics and/or sedative hypnotics which usually produce a depressive state and an inadequate pain control, waxing and waning between over and under medication. An attempt therefore is made initially to stabilize these patients on long acting medications and then to gradually reduce the dose of same over time to prevent withdrawal problems and at the same time, introducing other therapeutic strategies such as physical therapy, behavioral modification, nerve blocks, etc.

Since such patients frequently erroneously report their true ingestion patterns, either under or overestimating their medication intake, an objective assessment of their medication requirements is obtained by having them undertake a "drug profile" on an inpatient basis whereby for the 48 hours following hospital admission, they are permitted to freely obtain any medications in any quantities as often as required as long as these medications are administered and documented by the nurse on the ward. This usually requires a preliminary search of patients' belongings to identify their medication and these medicines can then be dispensed by the nurse as required. With such a regime, an accurate measure of patient medication ingestion is obtained and is often quite different from the initial estimations of the patients and/or families (Ready, Sarkis, & Turner, 1981). These medications are then substituted by the longer acting narcotic (methadone) and/or sedative hypnotic (phenobarbital) according to the equivalency tables (Tables 3.1 and 3.2). Given in a masking vehicle, the active medication can be withdrawn very rapidly (10% per day) if diagnosis is the main priority. In the event that withdrawal symptoms should occur, then the withdrawal rate can be reduced and plateaued for a day or so until the symptoms resolve. With the decreasing dosages, the patient usually becomes clearer in their sensorium and often gives more meaningful pain related history and information, and a hitherto confusing pain problem may well now resolve into a more definite pattern. Also if the pain complaint had been generated by an underlying medication dependency, then the complaints of pain often become less marked with the decreasing medication and sometimes cease to be a major problem! If diagnosis is already confirmed, then the detoxification regime takes place at a much more leisurely pace while other treatment attempts to substitute a well behavior problem, i.e., behavior modification, nerve blocks, physical therapy, rehabilitation, etc.

TABLE 3.1
Analgesic Equivalents to Methadone—10 mg orally

	Dose	
Drug	Oral (mg)	IM (mg)
Alphaprodine (Nisentil)		45.0
Anilderidine (Leritine)		35.0
Codeine	200.0	130.0
Diamorphine (Heroin)		3.0
Fentanyl		0.1
Hydromorphone (Dilaudid)	7.5	1.5
Meperidine (Demerol)	400.0	100.0
Methadone (Dolophine)		8.0
Morphine	60.0	10.0
Oxycodone (Percodan)	30.0	15.0
Oxymorphone (Numorphan)		1.5
Pentazocine (Talwin)	180.0	60.0

TABLE 3.2
Sedative Hypnotic Equivalents to
Phenobarbital—30 mg orally

Drug	Oral Dose (mg)
Secobarbital (Seconal)	100
Pentobarbital (Nembutal)	100
Chlordiazepoxide (Librium)	25
Diazepam (Valium)	10
Flurazepam (Dalmane)	(?) 30
Methaqualone (Quaalude)	300
Glutethimide (Doriden)	500
Ethchlorvynol (Placidyl)	750
Chloral Hydrate (Noetec)	1000
Hydroxyzine (Vistaril)	50–100
Diphenhydramine (Benedryl)	50–100
Meprobamate (Equinil)	400
Whiskey (100 proof)	90 ml (3 oz)

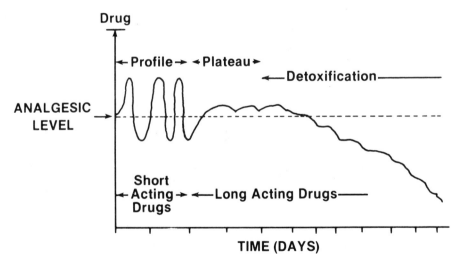

FIG. 3.4.   This shows the detoxification sequence of those patients dependent on narcotic or sedative hypnotic drugs. During the profile period of 48 hours, the patient is allowed free and liberal access to medications on demand with accurate record of the type and amount. These drugs are then switched to longacting preparations (methadone and/or phenobarbital) and during the plateau period, the patient is maintained at a drug concentration above the analgesic level. With this achieved, detoxification is commenced and proceeds rapidly (10 days) if diagnosis is the priority, or much more slowly (weeks or months) if diagnosis is known and the goal is to substitute drug seeking behavior with alternative therapies such as operant conditioning, biofeedback, physical therapy.

Non-narcotic analgesics such as acetaminophen and such non-dependency producing tranquilizers as hydroxyzine (Vistaril) or diphenhydramine (Benadryl) are usually incorporated into the masking vehicle or masking capsule so that as the narcotic and sedative hypnotic are removed, the patient still receives an appropriate analgesic and tranquilizer. Often these drugs will be continued to be given in a masking vehicle in patients who have difficulty complying with appropriate medication prescribing and sometimes this will be continued as a long time therapy although the goal is to reduce the patient's dependency on such pharmacological support. This is a very effective way of reversing medication dependencies and is incorporated by most Pain Clinics as a first line of attack in those patients with a significant drug dependency.

Antidepressants. In an attempt to control the denervation pains of post-herpetic neuralgia, the antidepressants were combined with other centrally acting drugs (Taub & Collins, 1974) and it was noted that many patients taking this combination seem to get benefits from the antidepressants themselves. Chronic pain patients frequently are mildly depressed and the use of the tricyclic antidepressants has been a significant contribution in managing these people. It helps to address their depressive elements and also if given as a once a day dose at night time, helps to reestablish sleep patterns in a group of patients that are characterized by insomnia. For this reason, Elavil or Sinequan in doses of 75 to 200 mg can be a very useful maintenance form of treatment for such patients.

Anticonvulsants. Because the mechanism of some of the denervation chronic pain problems, such as occur in tic douloureux, spinal cord injury patients, post-herpetic neuralgia, etc., appear to be due to abnormal afferent activity in the damaged nerve paths, the anticonvulsant types of drugs, Dilantin and carbamazepine (Tegretol), have been used with effect in this group (Loeser, 1978). For patients who have pain associated with nerve damage, Dilantin 100 mg qid or Tegretol in escalating doses from 200 through 1,000 mg per day are worth a trial.

It should be noted that Tegretol has significant adverse side effects—unsteadiness of gait, nausea, hemopoetic depression—and therefore it should be started in low doses, i.e., 200 mg a day and increased by 200 mg every second or third day as tolerated. If side effects occur, it should be reduced to a previously tolerated dose, plateaued and then gradually increased again. By using such a schedule, it is often feasible to obtain therapeutically effective doses in an individual who otherwise would be unable to tolerate side effects. Because of its possible anemic side effects, these patients should have a regular blood count and be warned to report any sore throats or other evidence of red or white cell depression.

Treatment of Chronic Nociception

Reduction of nociception in acute pain is classically brought about by resting the diseased part. However, rest as a therapy for chronic pain conditions has a poor success rate, for the vast majority of people presenting to chronic Pain Clinics have exploited this particular treatment to the full and are still debilitated by pain. Chronic nociception exists in many degenerative diseases, arthritis, ankylosing spondylitis, and many other chronic debilitating degenerative joint diseases. Also, cancer pain is a frequent source of chronic ongoing nociception. Chronic muscle tension disease states occur in the tension headaches and back pains often seen in Pain Clinics.

Treatment of these conditions usually involves attempts to decrease the afferent pain stimulus by nerve blocks or to introduce an alternative nonpainful stimulus that can interrupt the perception of the nociceptive painful stimulus (so called stimulation produced analgesia).

Nerve Blocks.   Attempts to remove the aversive nociceptive stimulus include injections of local anesthetic agents. These can be effective in diagnosing the origin of the patient's pain as outlined earlier and are useful therapeutically in certain kinds of chronic pain states (Arnhoff, Triplett, & Pokorney, 1977).

Trigger Point Injections.   Myofascial syndrome is a condition characterized by often exquisitely tender local areas in muscles usually around the scapulohumeral girdle but also in the low back, neck, and other body sites. The pathophysiology of this condition is imperfectly understood but clinically the patients are characterized by presenting with these painful areas and pressure upon the area or a related ''trigger zone'' can precipitate an exacerbation of the pain problem. By injecting a small quantity of weak local anesthetic (e.g., 3 cc's of 0.25% lidocaine) often dramatic relief occurs (Travell, 1976).

These trigger points classically develop in response to some preceding trauma and if vigorously treated by injections and active physical therapy in the early stages, they are reversible. However, if untreated, they can progress to chronic disability and in these circumstances, local infiltrations are often a maintenance form of therapy but not necessarily curative. In addition to actual injections of the trigger areas, topical application of vapor coolant sprays has been recommended and the addition of hydrocortisone to the local anesthetic injection is favored by some practitioners. Even needling the trigger point can be successful (Lewitt, 1979).

Trigger points are relatively safe provided large doses of anesthetic solutions are not administered sufficient to produce systemic toxic side effects, or smaller doses injected accidentally into major blood vessels which can also produce life threatening convulsions. It is therefore imperative for physicians using these techniques to appreciate the safe limits of such drugs and particularly to be facile in the emergency resuscitation that is often necessary with what are potentially life threatening toxic side effects. The other risks of this and any other needling procedures around the thorax is the risk of pneumothorax whereby pulmonary collapse can occur when a needle punctures the pleura. Again, this can be a life threatening hypoxic emergency needing urgent resuscitation.

Treatment of the Sympathetic Dystrophies

These disease entities are characterized by overactivity of the sympathetic nervous system and when good response is obtained from diagnostic sympathetic nerve blocks in either the stellate ganglion or lumbar sympathetic chain, then a course of such blocks can be most effective in rehabilitating these patients.

The technical details of these techniques are a little beyond the scope of this particular chapter, but in essence, local anesthetic agents are deposited around the sympathetic nerve supply to the effected arm or leg. This is accomplished by percutaneous needling techniques which along with other forms of nerve block, run the risk of physical needle trauma to important adjacent structures (pleura, blood vessels, nerves, spinal cord, etc.). Such sympathetic blocks are probably warranted as a diagnostic maneuver in those patients who present with puzzling pain in the extremities that is not confined to specific dermatomal patterns but instead has a more diffuse usually burning character and particularly if it is associated with signs of vascular abnormalities such as stasis, swelling, cyanosis, occurring distally in the hand or foot. Although usually associated with major nerve damage, in the more florid examples of this disease (causalgia), the minor dystrophies need have no such obvious precipitating cause and often present with very subtle signs which would not initially suggest a sympathetic dystrophy. When treated early after the onset of the disease, the sympathetic block with or without physical therapy is often curative. However, when the pain condition has been present for a matter of months or years, it becomes much more refractory, probably because it is believed this pain becomes a central phenomenon after time and peripheral sympathetic nerve blocks although helpful, are rarely curative in the chronic phase (Bonica, 1979).

Neurolytic Nerve Blocks. Permanent destruction of nerves with nerve blocks is contraindicated in non-malignant pain problems because it can result in the production of a denervation dysesthesia which can add a new pain dimension to the patient's complaints. However, in terminal cancer pain problems, neurodestructive blocks are justifiable where such agents as alcohol or phenol are used to percutaneously destroy nerves involved with the afferent nociceptive pathway. This particular procedure is optimally performed on those nerve pathways remote from the nerves controlling limb movement and sphincter control and thus it lends itself well to tumors of the breast and chest wall where a segmental neurolytic epidural or spinal block can be a very effective form of pain relief and similarily neurolytic splanchnic nerve blocks can be very useful in such cases as carcinoma of the pancreas or other upper abdominal viscera (Moore, 1979).

Because neurolytic nerve blocks have the potential for producing profound nerve destruction, meticulous accurate placement is mandatory and usually only performed by anesthesiologists with considerable experience in the technique. Many patients and their advocates enthusiastically pursue such nerve destructive blocks but because of the potential risks of spread to other vital structures, they are usually not indicated in non-malignant pain problems.

Somatic Nerve Blocks.   Local anesthetic blocks of the somatic nervous system can be utilized in a diagnostic attempt to ascertain pain pathways and can help to clarify if nociception is present or not. Such decisions can usually only be best made on the basis of repeated nerve blocks rather than a single procedure. Although somatic nerve blocks can be dramatically effective at temporarily relieving chronic pain states, they usually need to be repeated and unless prolonged periods of analgesia can be obtained between such blocks, they are not necessarily a very practical form of therapy, providing maintenance rather than cure although for some patients with limited options, they can be very helpful. Repeated epidural blocks with local anesthetics with or without added steroids (Hartman, Winnie, & Ramamorthy, 1974) have been tried extensively for low back pain with mixed results. They result in better relief in the early onset low back pain but are much less effective in the chronic refractory cases (Forrest, 1978).

Stimulation Produced Analgesia.   This form of pain relief has been used probably since time began whereby an alternative stimulus to pain is applied to the painful or related areas. Acupuncture, cupping, heat, vibration, massage, all seem to produce a pain relieving effect which in recent times has been explained by the "gate theory" whereby painful incoming sensations can be reduced or aborted by the simultaneous application of non-pain stimuli. Although there is almost certainly still a place for traditional massage and manipulation therapy, acupuncture and transcutaneous nerve stimulation have been much used in recent years as a means of producing stimulation produced analgesia in Pain Clinics.

Transcutaneous Stimulation.   Following the description of a gate theory of pain, small transcutaneous nerve stimulators were developed consisting of battery powered units which administered an electrical current via flat rubber electrodes to the painful area. These small portable units have now been so miniaturized that they can be worn in a clandestine fashion. The electrodes are usually taped in place using a conductive gel and the patient adjusts the dial setting with regard to the frequency and strength of the stimulus (usually somewhere between 5 and 200 Hz), to produce a tingling or vibration sensation which is felt rather than the pain.

This form of therapy appears to work best in myofascial syndromes, peripheral neuropathies, stump pains and phantom limb pains (Long & Hagfors, 1975). It is less effective but nevertheless much used in low back and neck pain where it can often give satisfactory supportive but non-curative therapy in this refractory group of pain patients. Along with biofeedback, transcutaneous nerve stimulation has virtually no morbidity attached to its use and is heartily endorsed by most Pain Clinics. It does not seem to help the central pain states where pain is often felt in areas of defective sensation and it appears to be dependent upon an intact sensory afferent system for its effect. Applying the electrodes to numb painful areas does not help. It has been proven to be more effective than placebo therapy (Long & Hagfors, 1975; Thorsteinson, Stonnington, Stillwell, Elveback, 1977) and although the initial units are costly ($500 to $700), they do pose an economically viable alternative to other forms of therapy at this time.

Attempts have been made to introduce the electrical stimulation at more central nervous system sites and in fact, this form of therapy was initially used by surgically placing the stimulating electrodes on dorsal columns of the spinal cord; an operative technique which has now been abandoned by most therapists in favor of the transcutaneous application of electrodes which appears to be just as effective and does not require a major invasive laminectomy. Such a dorsal column electrical stimulator can now be introduced percutaneously via an epidural needle and although still in the experimental phase, would appear to have some potential for those patients with fairly specific dermatomal pain distribution who do not have major complicating psychological or behavioral factors and cannot get adequate stimulation produced analgesia with the transcutaneous mode. Such epidural stimulating electrodes do not maintain a stable position in the more mobile parts of the spine such as the neck and are optimally placed percutaneously at a lumbar level and threaded to a thoracic placement site. Fortunately they can be undertaken as a relatively non-invasive trial for a one or two day period and if the patient gets good results from such stimulation then a catheter electrode can be subcutaneously implanted and stimulated via an external source.

Experimentally, stimulation of deep areas within the brain have produced profound analgesia in animals (Mayer & Price, 1976) and this technique is also being pioneered in human pain conditions (Richard, 1979). Here electrodes are placed in the periaqueductal central gray matter and although having some potential promise, this still remains very much an experimental procedure whose long-term value awaits confirmation.

Acupuncture. This is one of the earlier forms of stimulation produced analgesia, having been practiced in the Orient for thousands of years and which received a contemporary inpetus with the reestablishment of political and social contacts with the Peoples Republic of China during the Nixon administration. Acupuncture appears to be no better or no worse than other forms of transcutaneous stimulation and probably acts through similar mechanisms. Most informed opinion does not still ascribe to the "meridian" theories and other antique explanations for its mode of effect. In controlled studies, it has been shown to be equally effective with transcutaneous nerve stimulation (Fox & Melzack, 1976), but because of the extra time and expense and involvement of a therapist, the transcutaneous stimulators are probably more convenient and cost effective for such a therapy. Like transcutaneous stimulators, acupuncture tends to work best when the needles are applied in the area of the pain or in similar dermatome sites. It appears to be more effective for controlling pain of short onset duration and to what extent it will form a major therapeutic option for people with chronic pain remains to be seen but is unlikely (Murphy & Bonica, 1977).

Psychological Methods of Treatment. Non-specific psychological support is an integral part of maintaining patients suffering from chronic pain and is accomplished in conjunction with many of the other treatments previously mentioned. Biofeedback and some form of behavioral modification are an integral part of the repertoire of most Pain Clinics and although biofeedback is dealt with elsewhere in this book, a brief statement of its applicability in chronic pain control is given below.

Biofeedback. Here patients are taught control over bodily function not usually under voluntary control such as muscle tension and vascular reactivity. This technology helps patients to practice relaxation and is particularly effective in those painful conditions associated with muscle tension and vascular headaches. For the muscle tension pain, an EMG mode biofeedback machine is used whereby the patient practices and becomes proficient in producing relaxation in the offending muscle groups. For the vascular headache pains, the patient practices increasing skin blood flow by producing vasodilation and with this technique mastered, can often help abort or reduce the severity of vascular headaches. Both these biofeedback technologies are practiced using hardware with the eventual goal being that the patient can eventually learn to produce the effects without the technological hardware.

This technology has found its optimal place in chronic pain control using the thermal mode for migraine vascular type headaches and using the EMG mode for muscle contraction headaches, and shoulder and upper back pain. It appears to be less successful for low back muscle pain problems. Whether biofeedback is any better than conventional relaxation training is a matter for dispute (Jessup, Neufelt, & Merskey, 1979). It is however, a non-invasive, safe and benign form of treatment which is well worth a trial in head and upper dorsal pain problems since it does have a satisfactory success rate of 30 to 60%. Although it rarely is the sole cure, it is much utilized as part of the supportive therapeutic repertoire in many Pain Clinics.

Behavioral Modification Therapy.   The main goal here is primarily to reduce pain behaviors which is often readily accomplished during the early treatment phase. Of much more importance, however, is the substitution of alternate well behavior (Fordyce, 1976). Because most patients with chronic pain who are suitable for operant conditioning often have considerably reduced activity, an integral part of such programs involves increasing activity levels under the guidance of a knowledgeable psychiatrist and physical therapist whereby patient's activity tolerances are ascertained at an early stage and then working within these tolerances, a gradually increasing system of exercise quotas is planned such that the patient is then working to quota rather than to tolerance and thus gradually builds up his exercise activity. It is an interesting observation that as the exercise activity increases, the pain complaints often decrease (Fordyce, 1976).

As mentioned earlier, medication control is an integral part of such strategies and "pain cocktail" regimes are utilized with a very gradual reduction in the dependency producing drugs contained, as alternative well behavior repertoires are increased. The exercise program is increased along the quota system and this must be a pain related exercise which ideally is relatively easily measured and counted. As the medication dependency is reduced and the exercises increased, the patient is eventually introduced to a "job station" often located in the supportive hospital facilities, laundry, mail room, etc., where the patient attempts to relearn work and job related skills. This initial inpatient program can take anywhere from 3 to 6 weeks, depending on the complexity of the problem and following the inpatient phase, the patient and spouse usually continue in outpatient contact with the facility for a week or so until independence is established. Frequently upon attempts at resuming a domestic existence, there is a deterioration in the rate of improvement and the pain will worsen. The patient should be reassured that this is not unexpected and encouraged to continue in their social and physical rehabilitation program.

These behavioral modification programs seem to be quite effective at reducing medication dependencies and decreasing interaction with physicians. Although they reduce subjective complaints of pain, however, they do not eliminate same.

Neurosurgical Ablative Techniques.   With the advent of appreciation of the anatomy of the peripheral and central nervous systems, it was logical that attempts would be made to section the so-called pain pathways and virtually every part of the described pain pathway from peripheral receptor to cerebral cortex has been subject to surgical trespass in attempts to resolve pain problems. Depending on the site, these techniques can be very effective at relieving pain for finite periods of time but as with neurolytic injections, the normal pattern is that the pain returns or that a superimposed denervation pain results in a matter of months. Also, depending on which part of the nervous system is surgically incised, a price is paid for disruption of other functions: sensation, proprioception, coordination, motor power. Because of the risks and short duration of the pain relief, these invasive techniques are usually reserved for the terminal cancer patient. However, because of the invasive nature of some of the major surgical operations needed to effect spinal cord or brain ablative surgery, the patient needs to have a reasonable prognosis of 6 months or so to make it worth his while undergoing such major surgery. Probably the most common neurosurgical operation is that of cordotomy whereby the anterior spinothalamic tract is sectioned at a site proximal to the incoming painful stimulus. Dorsal rhizotomies whereby the afferent sensory root is sectioned have been much tried but do not seem to provide satisfactory long-term results (Loeser, 1972; Onofrio & Campa, 1972).

One form of trigeminal neuralgia appears to be due to an abberant artery pressing upon the rootlets of the trigeminal nerve in the posterior cranial fossa and a neurosurgical technique of intracranial operative relief of this compression has been very successful in helping this small percentage (5%) of patients with trigeminal and sometimes glossopharyngeal neuralgias (Janetta, 1967).

Because of the short-term success of cordotomy, this as mentioned is probably the most popular neurosurgical ablative technique. In an attempt to reduce the morbidity of this major operation, a percutaneous approach was developed by Mullan and has been utilized by several practitioners in specialty centers around the world whereby a coagulating probe is passed percutaneously into the high cervical cord and an electrocoagulative lesion in produced in the spinothalamic tract. There are several reports with good results from this particular procedure (Mullan et al., 1963, Lipton, 1968), such that a literature review (White & Sweet, 1979) suggests that this method is superior to open cordotomy for relieving terminal cancer pain, producing an 85% success rate in the immediate post-operative period but as with most of these neurodestructive procedures, this rate drops (down to 25%) after one year. There is a significant morbidity associated with these techniques—airways problems (8%), extremity weakness (6%), new pain, i.e., dysesthesias (8%), sleep apnea occurs in 1% with a unilateral but as high as 10% in bilateral cordotomies (White & Sweet, 1979).

Pituitary Ablation with Alcohol Injection.   Because percutaneous cordotomy is unsatisfactory for pain for the upper thorax or cervical region and also because bilateral cordotomy carries a significant mortality, alternative techniques were needed for bilaterally widespread cancer pain. This has been attempted by destruction of the pituitary gland with injections of alcohol. This is accomplished via a transnasal technique (Morrica, 1974), and 50% excellent pain relief is reported with terminal metastatic cancer pain. The needle is introduced under light general anesthesia and x-ray control into the pituitary fossa and small increments of absolute alcohol are introduced. The true mechanism of pain relief is still disputed. The injection of significant amounts of neurolytic agent in this area can obviously produce significant hormonal changes. There is significant suppression of prolactin, thyroxin, and growth hormone but to what extent these hormonal changes are responsible for the pain relief is not unknown. Although the alcohol is injected into the pituitary gland, autopsy examination has shown that neurolysis can extend to the hypothalamus via the pituitary stalk. This may explain why analgesia occurs. The original technique has recently been modified (Katz & Levin, 1979) whereby larger aliquots of alcohol (5 cc's) are injected and improved pain relief claimed.

Results of Pain Therapies

For those debilitating forms of chronic pain that lend themselves well to specific technological treatment such as sympathetic nerve blocks for analgesia, Tegretol for tic douloureux, celiac plexus block for carcinoma of the pancreas, the results of pain control in such patients are good. However, for the much larger group of patients with non-specific chronic pain problems, the results of the various pain treatment centers, Pain Clinics, etc., is still to be fully evaluated although most of these facilities which adopt a multidisciplinary approach seem to be very effective at reducing medication intake and dependency on medical treatment. They are effective at getting people mobile and functioning again, although these people frequently still have, albeit a reduced, pain complaint. In other words, pain treatment centers appear to be effective at correcting and treating the effects which pain produces in individuals especially if these effects are characterized by behavioral changes (i.e., inactivity, taking drugs, seeking health care).

REFERENCES

Arnhoff, F. N., Triplett, H. B., & Pokorney, B. 1977. Follow up status of patients treated with nerve blocks for low back pain. *Anesthesiology, 46,* 170–178.

Bonica, J. J. 1974. Organization and Function of a Pain Clinic. *Advances in Neurology, 4,* 433, Raven Press, N.Y.

Bonica, J. J. 1977. Neurophysiologic and pathologic aspects of acute and chronic pain. *Archives of Surgery, 112,* 750–761.

Bonica, J. J. 1979. Causalgia and other reflex sympathetic dystrophies. *Advances in Pain Research & Therapy, 3,* 141–166.

Coggershall, R. D., Coulter, J. D., & Willis, W. D. 1973. Unmyelinated fibers in the ventral root. *Brain Research, 57,* 229–233.

Fordyce, W. F. 1976. *Behavioral methods for chronic pain and illness.* St. Louis: C. V. Mosby.

Forrest, J. B. 1978. Management of chronic dorsal root pain with epidural steroids. *Canadian Anaesthesiology Society Journal, 25,* 218–225.

Fox, E. J., & Melzack, R. 1976. Transcutaneous nerve stimulation and acupuncture. Comparison of treatment for low back pain. *Pain, 2,* 141–148.

Jannetta, P. J. 1967. Arterial compression of the trigeminal nerve at the pons in patients with trigeminal neuralgia. *Journal of Neurosurgery, 26,* 159–162.

Jessup, B. A., Neufeld, R. W. J., & Merskey, H. 1979. Biofeedback therapy for headache and other pain. *Pain, 7,* 225–270.

Hartman, T. J., Winnie, A. P., & Ramamorthy, S., 1974. Intradural and extradural corticosteroids for sciatic pain. *Orthopedic Review, 3,* 21–24.

Katz, J., & Levin, A. B. 1979. Long term follow up study of chemical hypophysectomy and additional cases. *Anesthesiology, 51,* 167–169.

Lewitt, K. 1979. The needle effect in the relief of myofascial pain. *Pain, 6,* 83–90.

Lipton, S. 1968. Percutaneous electrical cordotomy for relief of intractable pain. *British Medical Journal, 2,* 210–212.

Loeser, J. D. 1972. Dorsal rhizotomy for the relief of chronic pain. *Journal of Neurosurgery, 36,* 745–750.

Loeser, J. D. 1978. What to do about tic douloureux. *Journal of the American Medical Association, 239,* 1153–1155.

Long, D. M., & Hagfors, N. 1975. Electrical stimulation in the nervous system: the current status of electrical stimulation in the nervous system for the relief of pain. *Pain, 1,* 109–174.

Mayer, D. J., & Price, D. D. 1976. Central nervous system mechanisms of analgesia. *Pain, 2,* 379–404.

Melzack, R., & Wall, P. D. 1965. Pain mechanisms: a new theory. *Science, 150,* 971.

Moore, D. C. 1979. Celiac Plexus Block with Alcohol for Cancer Pain of Upper Intra-abdominal Viscera. In J. J. Bonica (Ed), *Advances in Pain Research and Therapy* (Vol. 2.) 357–371, Raven Press, New York.

Morrica, G. 1974. Chemical hypophysectomy for cancer pain. *Advances in Neurology, 4,* 707–714.

Mullan, S. et al. 1963. Percutaneous interruption of spinal pain tracts by means of a strontium needle. *Journal of Neurosurgery, 20,* 931–939.

Murphy, T. M., & Bonica, J. J. 1977. Acupuncture analgesia and anesthesia. *Archives of Surgery, 112,* 896–902.

Onofrio, B. M., & Campa, H. K. 1972. Evaluation of rhizotomy review of 12 years experience. *Journal of Neurosurgery, 36,* 751–755.

Ready, L. B., Sarkis, E., & Turner, J. A. 1981. Self-reported vs. actual use of medications in clinical pain patients. *Pain* (in press).

Richard, D. E. 1979. Central grey stimulation for control of cancer pain. *Advances in Pain Research and Therapy, 2,* 487–492.

Taub, A., & Collins, W. F. 1974. Observations on the Treatment of Denervation Dysesthesia with Psychotropic Drugs: Post Herpetic Neuralgia. In J. J. Bonica (Ed.), *Advances in Neurology: International Symposium on pain. Vol. 4,* 309–315, Raven Press, New York.

Thorsteinson, G., Stonnington, H. H., Stillwell, G., & Elveback, L. R. 1977. Transcutaneous electrical stimulation: A double blind trial of its efficacy for pain. *Archives of Physical Medicine & Rehabilitation, 58,* 8–13.

Travell, J. 1976. Myofascial Trigger Points Clinical View. In Adv. in Pain Res. and Ther. 1:919–929, Raven Press, New York.

Twycross, R. G. 1977. Choice of strong analgesic in terminal cancer diamorphine or morphine. *Pain, 3,* 93–104.

Ward, N. G., Bloom, V. L., & Friedel, R. D. 1979. The effectiveness of tricyclic antidepressants in the treatment of co-existing pain and depression. *Pain, 7,* 331–341.

White, J. C., & Sweet, W. H. 1979. Anterolateral cordotomy: Open versus closed comparison of end results. *Advances in Pain Research and Therapy, 3,* 911–919.

4 Obesity: Etiology, Hazards and Treatment

Neil E. Grunberg
*Uniformed Services University
of the Health Sciences*

The opening sentence of a recent book on obesity dramatically states: ''Obesity is the most prevalent, chronic, medical condition in our society and is directly or indirectly associated with a wide variety of diseases that collectively account for 15–20% of the mortality rate'' (Powers, 1980, p. 1). In contrast, a recent review of sixteen studies dealing with the relationship between obesity and mortality argues that the data do not support the contention that increased obesity leads to increased mortality (Andres, 1980). There is no question that obesity is associated with many serious illnesses and conditions, including hypertension, diabetes, gout, arthritis, abnormal heart size and function, endometrial carcinoma, and so on (Andres, 1980; Rimm & White, 1979). However, it is presently unclear whether the relationships between obesity and these conditions are simple, linear functions (Andres, 1980).

Regardless of the controversy concerning the relationships between obesity and physical health, it is clear that: (1) many people want to lose weight, and (2) many people who are overweight (compared to their own desired weights) feel generally lousy about themselves: their mood, self-esteem, and daily behavior may be affected. Because many people will be happier and probably healthier if they lose weight, it is important to determine the most effective ways to help them lose weight.

Before discussing how to treat obesity, it is necessary to define obesity. In addition, it will be useful to have some understanding of the prevalence of obesity, biological and psychological hazards associated with obesity, and the causes of obesity. Tens of books and thousands of articles have been written on this topic, entire conferences have tackled only limited aspects of this condition, and thriving businesses (including weight loss programs and pharmaceutical houses) have devoted tremendous amounts of time and effort to develop and sell their "cures" for obesity. This chapter will not attempt to present or critically review all of this information. This chapter is designed to provide an overview of obesity, concentrating on ways to help people lose weight.

DEFINITION

Obesity results from ingesting more calories than the body uses for energy (Rodin, 1977). The word "obesity" is derived from "ob," over, and "edere," to eat (Sims, 1979). This literal meaning suggests that obesity is a single entity resulting from a single cause. This is not true. Besides overeating per se, obesity may result from genetic, endocrinological, metabolic, and a range of behavioral causes (for instance, types of foods eaten, amount of exercise). In fact, obesity probably results from a number of these factors together. It is currently estimated that a specific cause of obesity cannot be found for 95%–97% of obese patients (Powers, 1980).

"Obesity" is an excess of body fat. "Overweight" refers to an excess of body weight relative to some standards for weight which consider height, age, and sex (Bray, 1976). These terms often are used synonymously, although they are not identical. A body-builder, for example, is "overweight" but not "obese." In contrast, a "98 lb. weakling" may be "obese" and not "overweight." Most of the techniques used to determine "obesity" either estimate body fat or body weight. It is important to know which measure of "obesity" is used and what it measures in order to understand a particular patient's condition and to determine the most appropriate treatment in each case. For instance, the 98 lb. weakling, who is said to be obese because of an abnormally high percentage of body fat, will not profit from a low calorie diet program.

Some of the most common measures of obesity are described in the following section. In this chapter I sacrifice accuracy for consistency and I use the term "obesity" to refer to excesses of body fat and excesses of body weight.

HOW TO MEASURE OBESITY

Two of the simplest methods to estimate obesity are the belt test and ruler test. By the belt test, a person is said to be obese if a belt fastened tightly around the lower rib cage cannot be slipped down over the abdomen. The ruler test simply requires that a ruler be placed along the sternum of a person who is lying down. If the ruler slopes down towards the person's head, the person is obese (Sims, 1979).

Height and weight information are commonly used to estimate obesity. "Relative weight" expresses measured weight as a percentage of one's "appropriate weight" based on a standard height and weight table. A common definition is that obesity exists (in adults) when body weight exceeds by 20% the standard weight listed in height-weight charts (Rodin, 1977). Other ways to use this information include the following ratios: weight/height, weight/(height)^2 (the body mass index), and height/$^3\sqrt{\text{weight}}$ (the inverse of the ponderal index) (Bray, 1976). Of these height-weight indices, the body mass index has the lowest correlation with height and the highest correlation with measures of body fat. In contrast, the ponderal index correlates highly with height and therefore is a poor index of obesity (Powers, 1980).

All of these measures which rely on height and weight data define obesity based on a comparison to standard height-weight charts. Most of these charts were compiled by the life insurance industry and only include people who purchased life insurance. Andres (1980) argues that obesity determined from these charts is an inaccurate estimate because these tables are not representative of the total population. Nevertheless, height-weight charts provide one of the simplest techniques for comparing people to some standards, and therefore are useful. It should be noted that height-weight information estimates body weight, and not body fat.

Roughly half of total body fat is deposited in subcutaneous tissues close to the surface of the body (Powers, 1980). Therefore, skinfolds, measured with a pair of calipers, provide an estimate of body fatness. However, this technique is unreliable because different estimates are made for the same person based on different body locations (Sims, 1979). It is crucial with this technique to make skinfold measurements in specified locations and under standard conditions. Even when a particular site is defined (e.g., triceps), measurement errors may result from incorrect measurement of the mid-arm point, incorrect placement of the caliper tips, and measurement of an unrelaxed arm. If performed by an expert, this technique provides a good and simple measurement of body fat (Powers, 1980).

A variety of more sophisticated measurement techniques include: immersion of people in a tank of water and measurement of body density (densitometry); measurement of total body water by dilution of tritiated or deuterated water; injection of fat-soluble indicators (e.g., cyclopropane or radioactive krypton) and measurement of their distribution in the body (Sims, 1979). Although these techniques carefully measure body fat, they are expensive, time-consuming, and cumbersome. Therefore, they are not readily accessible to many clinicians who deal with obesity. Probably the best accessible techniques to estimate obesity are: (1) weight/height^2 (which is equivalent to log (weight) $-$ 2 log(height), and (2) "people are obese if they look fat" (Singer, 1981).

TYPES OF OBESITY

"Exogenous obesity" has been used clinically to designate obesity not due to endocrine disorder or brain damage (Sims, 1979). This term has limited value because "exogenous obesity" may result from many causes, including personal eating habits, family life-style, inactivity, occupational problems. The specific cause or causes of obesity should be determined to design the most appropriate and effective therapy.

There are other classification schemes that have been proposed and used. For instance, Hirsch distinguishes types of obesity according to number of adipocytes (fat cells). All obese individuals have enlarged adipocytes, but some of these people also have excess numbers of adipocytes (Powers, 1980). These individuals will have particular trouble losing weight because the number of adipocytes cannot be reduced; only cell size can be reduced.

Bruch divides obesity into three major types: constitutional, reactive, and developmental. Constitutional obesity is thought to result from genetic or physiological causes in psychologically normal people. Bruch suggests that reactive obesity results from overeating in response to tension or anxiety. Developmental obesity begins in childhood and involves emotional problems (Powers, 1980).

Classification schemes are useful to the clinician if they help determine the best way to treat a patient's obesity (see Powers, 1980, for a more extensive discussion of classifications). Regardless of the particular classification system used, it is generally held that it is more difficult to treat obesity that develops in childhood than adult-onset obesity.

PREVALENCE

Adults

The Health and Nutrition Examination Survey I (HANES I) conducted by the National Center for Health Statistics measured triceps skinfolds and defined obesity as greater than the sex-specific 85th percentile measurements for persons ages 20-29. That is, body fat was estimated by measuring triceps skinfolds with a caliper. People were said to be obese if their skinfold measurement exceeded the values obtained from 85% of the 20-29-year-old people of the same sex. According to this measurement, roughly 10% of 20-64-year-old men are obese, roughly 25% of women aged 20-44 are obese, and 30-50% of women aged 45-64 are obese (Bray, 1979). The HANES I also estimated the percentage of adult men and women in each five year age group who were 10-19% and 20+% overweight compared to 20-29-year-olds of the same sex. These data are presented in Table 4.1. According to HANES I, 18.1% of the 20-74-year-old men are 10%-19% overweight and 14% of them are 20+% overweight; 12.6% of the 20-74-year-old women are 10%-19% overweight and 23.8% are 20+% overweight.

Children

In a 1966 report by the U.S. Public Health Service, childhood obesity was defined as 40% or more above the median weight for a given height. According

TABLE 4.1
Prevalence of Overweight. Percent of Population Deviating by
10-19 Percent and by 20 Percent or More From Desirable Weight[a]
United States, Health and Nutrition Examination Survey, 1971-74

	Men		Women	
Age	*10-19%*	*20% or more*	*10-19%*	*20% or more*
20-74	18.1%	14.0%	12.6%	23.8%
20-24	11.1	7.4	9.8	9.6
25-34	16.7	13.6	8.1	17.1
35-44	22.1	17.0	12.3	24.3
45-54	19.9	15.8	15.1	27.8
55-64	18.9	15.1	15.5	34.7
65-74	19.1	13.4	17.5	31.5

[a] Estimated from regression equations of weight on height for men and women ages 20-29 years, obtained from HANES I.

[National Center for Health Statistics. S. Abraham and C. L. Johnson, "Overweight Adults 20-74 Years of Age: United States, 1971-74." Vital and Health Statistics. Advance Data No. 51. Hyattsville, Md.: Public Health Service, DHEW. In preparation.]

From: Bray, G. A. (Ed.). *Obesity in America*, DHEW Publication No. (NIH) 79-359. Washington, D.C.: U.S. Government Printing Office, 1979, p. 4.

to this definition and report, the incidence of childhood obesity was 2%-15% (Rodin, 1977). In other studies, estimates of the prevalence of obesity in schoolchildren range from 6%-15%. Estimates of obesity in adolescents range from 20%-30% (Powers, 1980).

HAZARDS ASSOCIATED WITH OBESITY

Biochemical and Physiological

Thirty-nine different studies indicate an association between obesity and hypertension. This relationship holds for all age groups. Obesity is commonly considered to be a cause of hypertension because blood pressure decreases when excess weight is lost (Rimm & White, 1979).

Obesity also is associated with diabetes, gout, arthritis, abnormal heart size and function, menstrual and ovarian abnormalities, endometrial carcinoma, cardiovascular diseases, and gallbladder disease (Rimm & White, 1979; Bray, 1976). There is no question that these physical ailments and conditions are associated with obesity. However, as noted at the beginning of this chapter, it is currently being questioned (cf. Andres, 1980) whether increased obesity necessarily leads to increased physical health hazards. In addition, Andres (1980) suggests that moderate obesity may provide some as yet unknown health benefits. Nevertheless, it is quite clear that many obese people suffer from a variety of health problems and that losses of weight may help alleviate some of these problems (Rimm & White, 1979; Andres, 1980).

Psychological and Social

In addition to the biological hazards associated with obesity, there are psychological and social pressures on the obese individual. These may include negative self image, feelings of alienation, anxiety, emotionality, hypochondria, negative peer attitudes, and discrimination (Rimm & White, 1979; Bray, 1976; Rodin, 1977). It is important to note that the majority of overweight people are psychologically normal. Also, when psychological or social pressures exist, they tend to be a *result,* rather than a cause of obesity (Rodin, 1977).

CAUSES OF OBESITY

Obesity results from both biological and behavioral factors. It is beyond the scope and purpose of this chapter to fully list and explain these factors. The interested reader is referred to Powers (1980) and Bray (1979) for recent summaries of the etiology and pathogenesis of obesity.

Biological Causes

To summarize briefly, the regulation of eating involves both central and peripheral biological mechanisms. Certain brain centers (e.g., the ventromedial hypothalamic and ventrolateral hypothalamic regions) and the neurochemical pathways that run through these areas (e.g., nigrostriatal dopaminergic pathway and ventral noradrenergic system) appear to be involved in hunger regulation (Powers, 1980). It is currently believed that the anterior hypothalamus and paraventricular nucleus are critical loci in the regulation of food intake. There is research indicating that norepinephrine and serotonin are involved centrally in the regulation of eating (Rodin, 1979); however, the exact role and importance of these chemicals is not at all clear. There is evidence that there are glucosensitive neurons in the hypothalamus. Also, there is evidence that free fatty acids, amino acids, and cholecystokinen affect hypothalamic neurons (Rodin, 1979). Functional or physical damage to these brain sites, neurochemical pathways, or neural receptors would affect hunger regulation and eating, and thereby affect weight gain.

The hypothalamus also receives input from peripheral receptors. This information comes from the viscera (e.g., gastric, intestinal, hepatic input) and soma (e.g., olfactory, gustatory, visual input). Additional peripheral factors that may be involved in regulating food intake are: neural regulation, humoral regulation, and hormonal regulation (Rodin, 1979; Rodin, 1977). As with the central mechanisms, functional or physical damage to these peripheral mechanisms would alter food intake and thereby alter body weight.

Another position is that obesity is determined by the number of adipocytes (fat cells) in the body. There is evidence that hypertrophy and hyperplasia of adipocytes occur with obesity and affect metabolic events (e.g., glucose transport, lipogenesis) and possibly alter food intake (Rodin, 1979). Excessive numbers of adipocytes may result from overfeeding during infancy and childhood (Powers, 1980). There appears to be a "critical period" of life (possibly through adolescence) during which the number of adipocytes is determined (Powers, 1980). However, recent data suggest that excessive growth of adipocytes at any time will eventually result in cell division (Faust, 1980). Also, research indicates that the number of fat cells is rarely or never reduced (Hirsch & Knittle, 1970). Therefore, this position suggests that excessive weight gains should be avoided, especially during any "critical periods." Even if this theory is correct, it should be noted that hypertrophy also is involved in obesity. Therefore, a reduction in adipocyte size will effectively decrease body weight (Powers, 1980).

The "set point theory" argued by Nisbett is somewhat related to the notion that number of fat cells is the key to obesity. The set point theory holds that there is a "ponderostat" (possibly in the hypothalamus) which monitors the amount of body fat (Nisbett, 1972). The ponderostat may be affected by overfeeding and adipocyte proliferation (Powers, 1980), or, the set point may be determined genetically for each of us. Nisbett maintains that pressures exist (for example, hunger) when we are below our set points (Nisbett, 1972).

Social and Psychological Causes

Besides the array of biological factors, obesity is strongly influenced by environmental, social and behavioral factors (Salans, 1979). For example, people respond to how good food looks, time of day, cultural norms, and so on. The impact of socioeconomic and cultural factors on obesity was particularly well illustrated in the Midtown Manhattan Study. This study included 110,000 adults (20–59 years old) living in an area of Manhattan selected because it included extremes in socioeconomic status. One of the striking findings of this study was the inverse relationship between obesity and socioeconomic status (Stunkard, 1975; Goldblatt, Moore, & Stunkard, 1965). The prevalence of obesity among women was 30% for the lower socioeconomic status group, 16% for the middle status group, and 5% for the upper status group. There was a similar trend among men with 32% obesity in the lower socioeconomic status group and 16% in the upper status group.

Another analysis of these data revealed an inverse relationship between generation in the United States and obesity. For instance, 24% of the first generation (i.e., foreign-born immigrants) women in this study were obese; only 5% of the fourth generation (i.e., people born in the United States to native-born parents and having all native-born grandparents) women were obese. This relationship between generation and obesity was independent of socioeconomic status (Stunkard, 1975). A thorough discussion of cultural and ethnic factors in obesity may be found in Stunkard (1975).

In the 1960's and 1970's, Schachter and his colleagues conducted a series of studies investigating the responsiveness of obese and normal weight people to external cues (Schachter, 1971; Schachter & Rodin, 1974). This research followed directly from Schachter and his colleagues' study of emotions in which they demonstrated that in the presence of physiological arousal (specifically, sympathetic nervous system activation), people label their emotions on the basis of available situational and cognitive cues. In a paragraph that bridges Schachter's (1971) work on emotions to his work on obesity, he writes:

> These simple demonstrations that the interpretation and labeling of even naturally occurring bodily states are so readily manipulable open up questions with almost metaphysical overtones. Obviously attaching a particular label to any particular internal or visceral syndrome is a learned, cognitively, and socially determined act. Though we are inclined to assume that such labels are invariant and universal, it is evident that there is no compelling reason for this to be so. As an example, consider the state of hunger. About hunger we know that food deprivation leads to various peripheral physiological changes such as modification of blood constituents, increase in gastric motility, changes in body temperature, and the like. By means of some still debated mechanism, these changes are detected by a hypothalamic feeding center. Presumably some or all facets of this activated machinery lead the organism to search out and consume food. There appears to be no doubt that peripheral changes and activation of the hypothalamic feeding center are inevitable consequences of food deprivation. On the basis of current knowledge, however, one may ask, when this biological machinery is activated, do we necessarily describe ourselves as hungry, and eat? For most of us raised on the notion that hunger is the most primitive of motives, wired into the animal and unmistakable in its cues, the question may seem farfetched, but there is increasing reason to suspect that there are major individual differences in the extent to which these physiological changes are associated with the desire to eat [p. 72].

Schachter goes on to cite a study by Stunkard (1959) in which obese and normal weight subjects swallowed gastric balloons and had their gastric motility monitored for four hours. During this period, the subjects gave regular reports indicating whether or not they were hungry. The results indicated that when the stomach was not contracting, obese and normal weight subjects gave similar reports of hunger (roughly 38% of the time). However, when the stomach was contracting, normal weight subjects usually reported hunger (71.0% of the time) but obese subjects reported hunger significantly less often (47.6% of the time). Schachter reasoned that the amount of food eaten by normal weight subjects should correspond to their physiological state of hunger. For obese, Schachter suggested that there would be little relation to physiological or internal state and that they should respond more to external cues (Schachter, 1971).

In a well-known series of studies, Schachter and his colleagues demonstrated that obese individuals: eat more food when it is placed in front of them, but eat less food when it is not salient (for example, when it is wrapped or dimly lit); eat more good-tasting food but less bad-tasting food than do normal weight people; eat when it is mealtime (e.g., noon, 6 p.m.), but have less trouble fasting on appropriate occasions (e.g., Yom Kippur for orthodox Jews); are, in general, more distracted by external stimuli than are normal weight individuals (Schachter, 1971; Schachter & Rodin, 1974). Overall, research through the mid 1970's supported the notion that obese individuals are particularly sensitive to external cues.

A number of later studies, however, have not found the obese/normal differences in responsiveness to external cues (e.g., Nisbett & Temoshok, 1976; Rodin, Slochower, & Fleming, 1977; Tom & Rucker, 1975). Explanations have been offered to reconcile the conflicting findings (e.g., Rodin, 1979; Singer, 1981). For instance, it has been pointed out that most of the research of Schachter and his colleagues examined the behavior of college students. As a result of the population sampled, the obese individuals tended to be only moderately obese. The more recent research includes a greater range of obesity, and indicates that there are people in every weight category who are responsive to external cues and people who are not responsive to external cues. In fact, some extremely obese individuals do not respond to external cues as much as do moderately obese individuals (Rodin, 1979). Therefore, the later studies do not find a clean relationship between obesity and external responsivity. Another explanation for the conflicting findings is based on the common sense notion that: Many people consciously keep their weight down by dieting, exercising, etc. If these people let themselves go, many of them might be enormous. (Supporters of the set point theory would argue that such people keep themselves below their set point and "true weight." They actually are obese individuals.) A well-designed social psychology study (which clouds the real purpose of the study with a convincing deception) would find these closet obese individuals to be externally responsive (assuming that the externality/obesity hypothesis is correct) and yet they would be classified as normal weight individuals. Possibly, the studies which failed to find clear relationships between obesity and external responsivity included more of these closet obese (Singer, 1981).

This issue is far from settled. It is likely that these conflicting findings indicate that there are individual differences among obese in their responsiveness to external cues; differences which are particularly important in designing effective weight loss programs. Current and future research will undoubtedly continue to address this phenomenon. However, even if the externality/internality hypothesis breaks down as a single, cogent explanation of obesity, it has stimulated enormous amounts of valuable research and it has encouraged the application of behavioral techniques to the treatment of obesity.

HOW TO TREAT OBESITY

This section is designed to provide a summary of the major ways to treat obesity. The reader is referred to Powers (1980) and Stuart, Mitchell, and Jensen (1981) for detailed discussions and evaluations of these and other obesity treatments.

Diets and Fasting

The simplest and oldest way to lose weight is to decrease or stop eating. The first highly publicized diet for obesity was proposed by William Harvey in 1872 (Van Itallie, Yang, & Hashim, 1974). For more than a century now, various new diets have been proposed, each outlining its own details for safe weight loss (cf. Van Itallie, 1979; Powers, 1980; Howard, 1974; Bray, 1976). According to Powers (1980), the most effective diet for weight loss is calorie-restricted but nutritionally balanced. The caloric content of the diet should be 40–45% carbohydrate, 20% protein, and 35%–40% fat. Other diets (e.g., low carbohydrate diet) may show greater weight loss in the first week or so, but these changes usually result from water loss. Long-term studies indicate that rates of weight loss are identical for equicalorie diets regardless of composition. Balanced low calorie diets are equally effective and much safer than other diets (Powers, 1980).

When diets are used, patients should be advised that the first few pounds are lost easily because of water loss. Then, 3500 calories must be expended to lose one pound of fat (Powers, 1980). Therefore, it will take time to take off pounds (for example, one pound will be lost each week by reducing the daily diet by 500 calories), but weight will be lost if the diet is maintained.

Long-term fasting may be dangerous, especially for children and adolescents (the dangers include mineral losses, metabolic acidosis, vitamin deficiencies, hyperuricemia). The fast should not exceed 2 months and the patient should be carefully monitored during the fast and for 2 to 3 years after the weight is lost (Powers, 1980).

Diets and fasting are both extremely effective ways to lose weight. However, after dieting or fasting, people tend to regain the lost weight because they stop regulating food intake (Powers, 1980; Stuart et al., 1981).

Surgery

Jejunoileal bypass surgery was introduced in the 1950's as a treatment for obesity (Bray, 1976). Since that time, it has become clear that bypass surgery (including jejunoileostomy and jejunocolostomy) effectively cause weight loss and weight loss is permanent (Sandstead, 1973; Bray, 1979; Powers, 1980; Bray, 1976). The weight loss after jejunoileal surgery probably results from malabsorption, decreased food intake, and altered taste preferences (Powers, 1980). Unfortunately, the surgery itself may be dangerous and there are side effects and complications from the surgery. The operative mortality rate has ranged from 0%–6% and other major complications include liver failure, urinary calculi, pseudo-obstructive megacolon, polyarthritis, renal failure, and malnutrition (Powers, 1980; Bray, 1979).

In 1967, gastric bypass surgery was introduced as an alternative to jejunoileal bypass. If gastric bypass is performed, the patient must be instructed to eat small amounts of solid foods and to avoid sweet beverages. Overdistension of the remaining functional gastric pouch leads to nausea and vomiting, and ingestion of sweet beverages results in diarrhea (because the pyloric mechanism is bypassed). The operative mortality rate is similar to jejunoileal bypass surgery, but there are fewer major complications (Powers, 1980).

Surgical procedures should only be considered in extreme cases. Patients who undergo bypass surgery are usually 100+% greater than their ideal weight, have been obese for more than 5 years, and have failed to lose weight by other treatments (Powers, 1980).

Drugs

Currently, there are no entirely acceptable, safe, and effective drugs to treat obesity. Amphetamines and related compounds are effective during the first few weeks of treatment; however, their long-term effectiveness has been questioned and they may produce deleterious side effects (e.g., nervousness, restlessness, irritability, insomnia, possible drug abuse) (Bray, 1979; Powers, 1980). There are four other anorexic drugs currently being used in weight reduction programs: diethylpropion (Tenuate), mazindol (sanorex), fenfluramine (pondimin), and phentermine resin (ionamin). Of these four drugs, diethylpropion appears to be the best choice considering effectiveness and side effects. However, similar to the amphetamines, these drugs seem to lose their effectiveness after a few weeks (with the possible exception of fenfluramine) and produce unwanted side effects (Powers, 1980). A variety of calorigenic drugs (e.g., thyroid hormones), drugs postulated to increase fat mobilization (e.g., human chorionic gonadotropin, indomethacin), and others have been tried (Bray, 1979). The specific effects of these drugs must be carefully evaluated and considered before they are used. For example, thyroid hormones act to decrease lean body tissue rather than body fat, and there are side effects which include increased blood pressure, tachycardia, restlessness, and sweating (Powers, 1980). Another drug treatment is methylcellulose. Once ingested, this substance acts as a sponge to absorb water, increase bulk, and presumably decrease food intake. Considering how this drug works, it is unlikely to be effective for externally responsive obese individuals (Singer, 1981).

For now, drug treatments alone do not offer much hope for effective weight management. However, some of these drugs may prove to be useful and effective adjuncts in comprehensive weight treatment programs (Powers, 1980).

Exercise

If most people were asked how to lose weight, it is a safe bet that they would say: Diet and exercise. This advice is commonly found on the back of cereal boxes and on television and radio commercials for exercise gimmicks, health spas, etc. In preparing this chapter, I even noticed this advice covering the back of a box of facial tissues. The message begins: "Overweight, a health problem for many, usually can be corrected by diet and exercise." In contrast to this commonly held belief, Feinstein wrote in 1960 (Bray, 1976):

> There has been ample demonstration that exercise is an ineffective method of increasing energy output, since it takes far too much activity to burn up calories for a significant weight loss . . . no clinical results have been cited to indicate its therapeutic effectiveness in weight reduction [pp. 336–337].

This pessimistic picture is supported by calculations of the amount of exercise required to lose weight. For instance, to lose one pound of fat requires running for three hours or walking for eleven hours at 3.5 miles per hour (Powers, 1980). However, exercise may act to reduce obesity in a number of ways not considered by this type of energy expenditure calculation. Specifically, exercise acts to decrease appetite and food intake (Bray, 1976; Powers, 1980); exercise leads to selective loss of fat and conservation of lean body mass (Stuart et al., 1981); and exercise results in a prolonged increase in basal metabolism (Powers, 1980). To date, exercise as a treatment of obesity has received little research attention (Powers, 1980). In light of the effects of exercise noted above, and the fact that mild or moderate exercise has no adverse side effects for most people, it certainly follows that regular programs of exercise should be included in comprehensive weight loss programs.

Psychotherapy

Traditional psychotherapy is considered to be ineffective in weight control for most people (Powers, 1980). However, people who receive this type of treatment for obesity may have failed on other treatments or attempts. For this and other reasons, it is difficult to assess the relative ineffectiveness of psychotherapy in weight loss. It is worth noting that success has been reported in people who have disturbances in body image, people who display the binge eating syndrome, and developmentally obese adolescents (Powers, 1980; Rodin, 1977).

Behavioral Treatment

In a recent chapter on behavioral medicine, Stunkard (1979) wrote:

> Currently, more people are receiving behavioral treatment for obesity than are receiving behavioral treatment for all other conditions combined. The behavioral treatment of obesity, furthermore, has become the most common paradigm for research in behavioral treatment [p. 279].

Two papers are considered to be classics for the application of behavioral analyses and treatment to obesity. A 1962 paper by Ferster, Nurnberger, and Levitt provided an operant analysis of eating. A 1967 paper by Stuart presented Ferster et al.'s approach in somewhat modified form and reported impressive clinical results for eight patients (Stuart, 1967). This report stimulated an enormous amount of research concerning this type of treatment for obesity (see Stunkard & Mahoney, 1976; Stunkard, 1975 for reviews of this topic).

Behavioral programs for obesity include four stages: (1) the behavior to be controlled is carefully described and documented; (2) the stimuli that precede eating are identified and controlled; (3) techniques are developed to control the act of eating; and (4) the consequences of eating are modified (Powers, 1980; Stunkard, 1979). The first stage typically involves careful record-keeping by the patient. These diaries include what is eaten, when it is eaten, where it is eaten, etc. The second stage, control of stimuli that precede eating, includes techniques such as limiting accessibility to high caloric foods, keeping low caloric foods around, and confining eating to one particular place. The third stage may include counting mouthfuls or number of chews, increasing awareness and enjoyment of food, and ending the meal when some food still remains on the plate. Finally, the consequences of eating are modified. For example, changes in eating behavior (such as those previously described) may be rewarded in ways that are best suited to the individual patient (e.g., monetary rewards, going to the movies). Frequent and prompt positive reinforcement is important (Powers, 1980; Stunkard, 1979). (The alert reader has undoubtedly realized that these techniques, drawn from the operant conditioning approach, also follow from the work of Schachter and his colleagues. That is, if obesity usually results from responsivity to external cues, then it is crucial to limit external food cues. In addition, it would be helpful to emphasize external factors which could help control eating, such as record-keeping and counting number of chews. The results of Schachter's studies also suggest additional techniques, such as keeping bad tasting food around and making food inaccessible.)

Since Stuart's (1967) report, a number of studies have been conducted to evaluate the effectiveness of behavioral treatment of obesity and reviews of these studies have been written (e.g., Wollersheim, 1970; Penick, Filion, Fox, & Stunkard, 1971; Jeffery, Wing, & Stunkard, 1978). Overall, behavioral treatment may effectively decrease body weight. However, as with so many other treatments, the weight losses are not well maintained (Stunkard, 1977; Stunkard & Penick, 1979). Unlike some of the other effective methods of weight loss, however, behavioral treatment has few or no adverse side effects and it does not require a team of highly trained personnel. In a recent evaluation of weight management therapies, Stuart, Mitchell, and Jensen (1981) wrote:

> While some earlier reviews of the outcomes of treatments in which behavior modification was the primary active agent have indicated that the results obtained are suboptimal (e.g., Stuart, 1975a; Stunkard, 1978; Stunkard & Mahoney, 1976), other reviewers who shared essentially the same methodology have reached more optimistic conclusions. As in the present review, Wilson (1979) and Wing and Jeffery (1979) found that while behavior modification did not produce the most rapid or greatest weight loss during active treatment, participants in its programs were more likely to maintain or even to improve upon the losses they achieved during treatment. Therefore, behavior modification techniques, which are low in cost and have no adverse side effects, should be included in every weight control effort [p. 335].

A Grab Bag of Additional Therapies

There are a wide variety of additional treatments of obesity to choose from, including: acupuncture, relaxation therapy, assertive training, cognitive restructuring, transswitching (a variant of classical conditioning), and hypnosis. None of these treatments has received sufficient objective evaluation to come to any conclusion regarding their effectiveness and general applicability to obesity. Some of these approaches may prove useful, but, for now, they remain as possibilities.

Maintenance of Weight Loss

Although there are effective ways to help people lose weight, maintenance of weight loss *appears to be* a major problem (except for bypass surgery patients). I write "appears to be" rather than "is" a major problem because of a fascinating, and frequently ignored, contradiction: Most of us know people who have or have ourselves successfully lost weight (sometimes tremendous amounts) and have kept it off; yet, most weight loss treatments fail miserably at maintenance of weight loss. A possible answer to this contradiction is that obese individuals who receive these treatments are people who could not lose weight on their own; people who can lose weight and keep it off have no need for weight loss programs (Schachter, 1981). This logical and rather banal suggestion should receive more attention for two major reasons: (1) if it is true that many people can lose weight and maintain weight loss on their own, then the common pessimism about weight loss is unfounded and may act to deter many people from trying to lose weight; and (2) people who have successfully maintained weight losses may offer new insights into how best to lose pounds and keep them off.

In spite of this embarrassingly obvious explanation, it is clear that there are many people who need help losing weight. Methods must now be developed to maintain weight loss. Changes in life-style (including diet and exercise) are probably the best, safest ways to maintain weight loss, and weight loss via behavior modification helps to develop these types of changes. Stuart et al (1981) note:

> It is clear that the goal of all treatments of obesity is the long-term control of the balance between food intake and energy utilization. It is equally clear that change in the energy balance cannot be achieved or maintained without the individual's active participation. To achieve and to direct this participation constructively, some form of modification of the patient's behavior must be accomplished in every successful treatment program. [p. 335]

Social support and positive reinforcement of weight loss and changes in life-style (especially from family and friends) also will help maintain decreased body weight.

New ways to treat obesity and to maintain weight loss are suggested by a few large-scale projects that have used the media to encourage weight loss and healthful life-styles (e.g., a Diet and Exercise Program conducted by the Swedish National Board of Health and Welfare; a television presentation of weight loss techniques by the German Federal Republic and the Max Planck Institute of psychiatry in Munich; the Stanford Heart Disease Prevention Program conducted in the United States)(Stunkard, 1979). These programs highlight the effectiveness of constantly reminding people about healthful life-styles. These projects also suggest cost-effective ways to communicate this information to large numbers of people.

Finally, healthful life-styles (including diet and exercise) may be most effectively established and maintained if they are integrated into our daily lives at work as well as at home. For instance, company cafeterias could sell nutritious low-calorie foods for lower prices and raise the prices on high-calorie "junk food"; exercise rooms could be added to office buildings and time could be allotted for work-outs; and weight loss reminders could be provided by signs and posters. These types of programs require minimal expense and would, for many of us, result in more pleasant work places and probably more productive work. As I think about the office or factory environment and the daily routines of most adults, I can't help but wonder why only children in our society have recess periods, gym classes, nutrition and health classes, and financially subsidized balanced lunches.

SUMMARY

Obesity results from genetic, biological, behavioral, environmental, and social factors. Obesity is associated with many physiological health hazards and may result in psychological and social pressures. There are a variety of treatments that effectively help to reduce body weight. Behavioral treatment of obesity appears to be the best, safest method for taking off pounds. However, the lost weight tends to be regained. The importance of developing effective ways to maintain weight loss is widely recognized.

New ways of encouraging weight loss are being tried and may provide powerful additions to behavioral treatments. Comprehensive treatment programs which integrate behavioral treatment, diets, exercise, group support, media reminders, and emphasis on self-help may prove to be effective in long-term weight control.

REFERENCES

Andres, R. Effect of obesity on total mortality. *International Journal of Obesity*, 1980, *4*, 381-386.

Bray, G. A. (Ed.). *Obesity in America*, DHEW Publication No. (NIH) 79-359. Washington, DC: U.S. Government Printing Office, 1979.

Bray, G. A. (Ed.). *Obesity in perspective*, DHEW Publication No. (NIH) 75-708. Washington, DC: U.S. Government Printing Office, 1973.

Bray, G. A. *The obese patient*. In L. H. Smith (Ed.), *Major problems in internal medicine*, Vol. 9. Philadelphia: W. B. Saunders Co., 1976.

Bray, G. A. Treatment of obesity with drugs and invasive procedures. In G. A. Bray (Ed.), *Obesity in America*, DHEW Publication No. (NIH) 79-359. Washington, DC: U.S. Government Printing Office, 1979.

Faust, I. M. Nutrition and the fat cell. *International Journal of Obesity*, 1980, *4*, 314-321.

Ferster, C. B., Nurnberger, J., & Levitt, E. B. Behavioral control of eating. *Journal of Mathetics*, 1962, *1*, 87-109.

Goldblatt, P. B., Moore, M. E., & Stunkard, A. J. Social factors in obesity. *Journal of the American Medical Association*, 1965, *192*, 1039-1044.

Hirsch, J., & Knittle, J. L. Cellularity of obese and nonobese human adipose tissue. *Federation Proceedings*, 1970, *29*, 1516-1521.

Howard, A. (Ed.). *Recent advances in obesity research: I., Proceedings of the 1st international congress on obesity, 8-11 October 1974*. Westport: Technomic Publishing Co., Inc., 1974.

Jeffery, R. W., Wing, R. R., & Stunkard, A. J. Behavioral treatment of obesity: The state of the art in 1976. *Behavior Therapy*, 1978, *9*, 189-199.

Nisbett, R. E. Hunger, obesity, and the ventromedial hypothalamus. *Psychological Review*, 1972, *79*, 433-453.

Nisbett, R. E., & Temoshok, L. Is there an external cognitive style? *Journal of Personality and Social Psychology*, 1976, *33*, 36-47.

Penick, S. B., Filion, R., Fox, S., & Stunkard, A. J. Behavior modification in the treatment of obesity. *Psychosomatic Medicine*, 1971, *33*, 49-55.

Powers, P. S. *Obesity, the regulation of weight*. Baltimore: Williams and Wilkins, 1980.

Reichsman, F. (Ed.). *Hunger and satiety in health and disease*, Vol. 7 of *Advances in psychosomatic medicine*. Basel: S. Karger, 1972.

Rimm, A. A., & White, P. L. Obesity: Its risks and hazards. In G. A. Bray (Ed.), *Obesity in America*, DHEW Publication No. (NIH) 79-359. Washington, DC: U.S. Government Printing Office, 1979.

Rodin, J. Bidirectional influences of emotionality, stimulus responsivity, and metabolic events in obesity. In J. D. Maser & M. E. P. Seligman, (Eds.), *Psychopathology: Experimental models*. San Francisco: W. H. Freeman and Co., 1977.

Rodin, J. Pathogenesis of obesity: Energy intake and expenditure. In G. A. Bray (Ed.), *Obesity in America*, DHEW Publication No. (NIH) 79-359. Washington, DC: U.S. Government Printing Office, 1979.

Rodin, J. The current status of the internal-external obesity hypothesis: What went wrong? *American Psychologist*, in press.

Rodin, J., Slochower, J., & Fleming, B. The effects of degree of obesity, age of onset, and energy deficit on external responsiveness. *Journal of Comparative and Physiological Psychology*, 1977, *91*, 586-597.

Salans, L. B. Natural history of obesity. In G. A. Bray (Ed.), *Obesity in America*, DHEW Publication No. (NIH) 79-359. Washington, DC: U.S. Government Printing Office, 1979.

Sandstead, H. H. Jejunoileal shunt in morbid obesity. In G. A. Brady (Ed.), *Obesity in Perspective*, DHEW Publication No. (NIH) 75-708. U.S. Government Printing Office, 1973.

Schachter, S. *Emotion, obesity and crime*. New York: Academic Press, 1971.

Schachter, S. Personal communication. (1981)

Schachter, S., & Rodin, J. *Obese humans and rats*. Potomac: Lawrence Erlbaum Associates, 1974.

Silverstone, T. (Ed.). *Appetite and food intake*. Report of the Dahlem Workshop on Appetite and Food Intake. Berlin: Dec. 8-12, 1975.

Sims, E. A. H. Definitions, criteria and prevalence of obesity. In G. A. Bray (Ed.), *Obesity in America*, DHEW Publication No. (NIH) 79-359. Washington, DC: U.S. Government Printing Office, 1979.

Singer, J. E. The social psychology of everyday life. In Λ. Baum, J. Fisher, & J. Singer (Eds.), *Basic and Applied Social Psychology*. Hillsdale, N.J.: Lawrence Erlbaum Associates, 1981.

Singer, J. E. Personal communication. (1981)

Stuart, R. B. Behavioral control of overeating. *Behavior Research and Therapy*, 1967, *5*, 357-365.

Stuart, R. B., Mitchell, C., & Jensen, J. A. Therapeutic options in the management of obesity. In C. K. Prokop & L. A. Bradley (Eds.), *Medical psychology: Contributions to behavioral medicine*. New York: Academic Press, 1981.

Stunkard, A. J. Obesity and the denial of hunger. *Psychosomatic Medicine*, 1959, *21*, 281-289.

Stunkard, A. J. From explanation to action in psychosomatic medicine: The case of obesity. *Psychosomatic Medicine*, 1975, *37*, 195-236.

Stunkard, A. J. Behavioral treatment for obesity: Failure to maintain weight loss. In R. B. Stuart (Ed.), *Behavioral self-control*. New York: Brunner/Mazel, 1977.

Stunkard, A. J. Behavioral medicine and beyond: The example of obesity. In O. F. Pomerleau & J. P. Brady (Eds.), *Behavioral medicine: Theory and practice*. Baltimore: Williams and Wilkins, 1979.

Stunkard, A. J., & Mahoney, M. J. Behavioral treatment of the eating disorders. In H. Leitenberg (Ed.), *Handbook of behavior modification and behavior therapy*. Englewood Cliffs, N.J.: Prentice Hall, 1976.

Stunkard, A. J., & Penick, S. B. Behavior modification in the treatment of obesity: The problem of maintaining weight loss. *Archives of General Psychiatry*, 1979, *36*, 801-806.

Tom, G., & Rucker, M. Fat, full and happy. *Journal of Personality and Social Psychology*, 1975, *32*, 761-766.

Van Itallie, T. B. Conservative approaches to treatment. In G. A. Bray (Ed.), *Obesity in America*, DHEW Publication No. (NIH) 79-359. Washington, DC: U.S. Government Printing Office, 1979.

Van Itallie, T. B., Yang, M., & Hashim, S. A. Dietary approaches to obesity: Metabolic and appetitive considerations. In A. Howard (Ed.), *Recent advances in obesity research: I*. Westport: Technomic Publishing Co., Inc., 1974.

Wollersheim, J. P. Effectiveness of group therapy based upon learning principles in the treatment of overweight women. *Journal of Abnormal Psychology*, 1970, *76*, 562-574.

5

Problem Drinking: A Social Learning Perspective

Alan R. Lang
Florida State University

G. Alan Marlatt
University of Washington

INTRODUCTION AND THEORETICAL CONCEPTUALIZATIONS

The Nature and Scope of the Problem

The magnitude of alcohol-related problems in the United States, and elsewhere for that matter, is staggering. Recently published statistics (NIAAA, 1978) indicate that economic costs alone, including production losses, health care expenditures, accident, crime and fire losses, and social response costs associated with U. S. drinking problems totalled nearly $43 billion as much as 5 years ago, with no signs of a recent abatement. The same report notes that approximately 205,000 alcohol-related deaths occurred in 1975—7% of this country's total mortality that year! Add to this the incalculable physical, psychological and social suffering of the estimated 10 million problem drinkers in the U. S., as well as the difficulties of those whose lives are touched by these individuals, and it is clear that problem drinking must be regarded as a major health and social concern.

While there is no disputing the fact that alcohol consumption can be associated with a wide range of serious adverse consequences, there is considerable controversy surrounding appropriate definition of terms used in reference to drinking and its attendant problems. This is true, in part, because it is not drinking per se which is viewed negatively. The majority of American adults are consumers of alcoholic beverages and consider such activity to be socially acceptable, if not desirable. Even extreme intoxication may be encouraged under certain circumstances, for example, at a bachelor party the night before one's

121

wedding. If alcohol use is normative behavior in this, and many more mundane situations, it is evident that some parameters of drinking and its concomitants must be identified to help define when alcohol consumption is problematic.

In the recently published third edition of the *Diagnostic and Statistical Manual of Mental Disorders* (DSM-III; American Psychiatric Association, 1980) some effort has been made to delineate the nature of drinking problems more specifically. The approach of DSM-III, at least where alcohol use disorders are concerned, has been to offer definitions which are primarily descriptive. This reduces complications which typically accure when diagnosis implicity or explicity suggests either unverified theories of etiology or aspects of dynamics which are irrelevant to operationalization. Though conceptual issues are alluded to in the *Manual,* and will be dealt with at some length later in this chapter, the diagnostic criteria for drinking problems basically describe two types of disorders: *alcohol abuse* and *alcohol dependence.* Alcohol abuse is characterized by: (1) "a pattern of pathological alcohol use," which includes some more or less behavioral descriptors of abusive drinking patterns, though certain key terms like "need" for alcohol and "inability" to reduce drinking are left undefined; (2) "impairment in social or occupational functioning due to alcohol use," with several objective examples of this impairment provided; *and* (3) "duration of disturbance of at least one month," a provision included to ensure that a pattern has been established. Alcohol dependence, on the other hand, is described as encompassing: (1) "either a pattern of pathological alcohol use" or "impairment in social or occupational functioning due to alcohol use" (each analogous to the criteria outlined above), *and* (2) either tolerance—"the need for markedly increased amounts of alcohol to achieve the desired effect, or markedly diminished effect with regular use of the same amount;" or withdrawal—"development of Alcohol Withdrawal . . . " (described elsewhere in the *Manual*), ". . . after cessation or reduction in drinking."

The DSM-III description of drinking problems outlined above represents a significant improvement over more simplistic approaches which heavily emphasize quantity and frequency of alcohol consumption as critical criteria. It allows for some individual differences and recognizes the importance of patterns and consequences in determining whether or not a problem exists. Furthermore, it abandons the term "alcoholism," whose utility was lost long ago in a confusing maze of connotations and surplus meanings. The contemporary psychiatric definitions are not, however, free of difficulties.

Foremost among these difficulties is the implication that alcohol abuse and alcohol dependence can be recognized as discrete from "normal" alcohol use and as separate from each other. Unfortunately, a lack of specificity in the DSM-III diagnostic criteria as well as the paucity of supportive evidence do not permit such a differentiation. Even tolerance, widely regarded as a cardinal sign of addiction in traditional conceptualizations, has been revealed to be so complex a phenomenon that it almost defies operationalization outside the laboratory.

Mello and Mendelson (1978), for example, have suggested that pharmacological, behavioral and cross-tolerance aspects of tolerance can be examined relatively independently with potentially uncorrelated results for individual subjects. Other investigators (e.g., Hinson & Siegel, 1980) have demonstrated the powerful influence of conditioning and situational variables in determining tolerance effects in any given instance. This failure of constructs such as tolerance to maintain fixed meaning belies efforts to establish qualitative differences among drinkers. All too often, however, researchers and practitioners alike, seduced by the simplicity of reified labels, pigeonhole persons according to criteria which cannot withstand logical or scientific scrutiny. It is suggested that the glib use of categorical labels does a disservice to the individual involved, while simultaneously impeding progress toward the understanding and resolution of drinking problems.

Given the above considerations, the approach of this chapter is one which views drinking problems as existing on a continuum, including largely non-deleterious alcohol use. *"Problem drinking,"* then, is used to denote *any pattern of alcohol consumption which is associated with discomfort or disability in the drinker or those around him.* The term discomfort is self-explanatory, while disability refers to impaired functioning. Such a definition encompasses multiple drinking-problem interactions, recognizing that physical, emotional, economic, social and other problems of discomfort or disability might precipitate drinking as well as be a consequence of it. Some scholars (e.g., Davies, 1976) have criticized similar notions of problem drinking by pointing out that it is often difficult to establish that problems and drinking are in fact related in a particular case. While such relations are indeed difficult to establish, there is added virtue in an approach which promotes careful efforts at problem specification rather than reinforcing the assumption that problems are better understood by the simple act of subsuming them under a label. Moreover, the breadth of the problem drinking concept can accommodate responses characteristic of psychological and/or physiological "dependence" without requiring that they be present as characteristics of the individual. This places greater emphasis on behavior and on the situation (as opposed to the person), a focus which others (e.g., Cahalan, 1970) have argued results in less permanent assignment of persons to diagnostic categories, hence minimizing the well-known pejorative effects of labeling (cf. Roman & Trice, 1968). The idea that a person does not *have* a disorder of "alcoholism" or whatever, but instead experiences problems in connection with drinking, also serves to expand theoretical and research perspectives beyond the bounds of static entities. This approach provides a stimulus for prevention and early intervention efforts aimed at multiple forms and subtypes of drinking problems. Finally, an approach which does not view the individual as a "victim" of some disorder beyond his control should encourage individuals to participate in their own problem resolution, rather than resigning themselves to their fate and/or depending on others for their care.

Whether one subscribes to our definition of problem drinking or chooses to adhere to concepts such as alcohol abuse and dependence, it is not difficult to establish the relevance of behavioral and social learning principles to questions of etiology, assessment, and remediation. Drinking is unequivocally a behavior, observable and measurable on a variety of dimensions. Moreover, many of the consequences of both acute intoxication and long-term excessive alcohol use are best identified in terms of behavioral referents—staggered gait, slurred speech, impaired intellectual performance, etc. There also can be little doubt that social learning factors, including modeling and sociocultural context, influence the way in which the behavior of drinking and its concomitants are acquired, practiced, and viewed. Thus, since drinking is the sine qua non of alcohol problems, the significance of behavioral and social learning concepts in dealing with these problems seems obvious. Yet, the importance of such factors often is neglected, if not ignored. How can this be?

Some students of problem drinking and alcoholism (e.g., Nathan & Goldman, 1979) have suggested that biological biases concerning the nature of drinking problems are a product of the often dramatic physiological effects of chronic excessive ethanol ingestion. These include, among others, physical dependence, eventual organic dysfunction and deterioration, and the apparent inability of certain individuals to exert volitional control over their drink-related behaviors. Presumably, such effects lead many to the conclusion that drinking problems represent a ''disease,'' and hence behavioral and social learning factors are irrelevant. This sequence of reasoning, however, is a decidedly weak one. Contemporary conceptualizations of the medical model (e.g., Engel, 1977) stress the need for a biopsychosocial perspective for all diseases. In addition, earlier writers (Mendelson & Mello, 1969) have advocated a similar position with respect to the disease concept of alcoholism by proposing that it be examined as an interactive function of agent (alcohol), host (individual) and environmental (including social-behavioral) factors. Thus, it appears that views of drinking problems that neglect their behavioral and social learning aspects do so without recourse to prevailing medical theories of disease processes. One can only infer that the reasons for an exclusively intrapersonal/physiological approach must lie elsewhere.

Writers like MacAndrew (1969) who are attuned to the historical, social and political dimensions of traditional conceptualizations of problem drinking offer a plausible explanation for the present state of affairs. MacAndrew argues that people *need* to believe that a certain class of problem drinkers, termed ''alcoholics,'' invariably must possess an ''alcoholic body'' or ''alcoholic personality'' or both. This is because the fundamental assumption wherever there is an organized society or social order is that ''. . . every social event must be construed as an event within that order'' (p. 498). Inasmuch as problem drinkers frequently engage in irrational conduct related to their drinking and are apparently oblivious to environmental contingencies and consequences associated with their behavior, they must be presumed to be either possessed or ill. Since the decades of the 1950s and 1960s saw a great deal of effort to reduce the moral stigma attached to problem drinking and the 1970s were marked by the decriminalization of intoxication, the only way the deviance of problem drinkers could be understood within the social order appeared to be to conclude that there is a disease "alcoholism," inherent in the individual.

The remainder of this chapter begins with a brief examination of the traditional or restricted disease model of drinking problems in light of available evidence. We then outline the alternative conceptual framework of the behavioral/social learning approach. Finally, we review some pertinent research, selected to illustrate this model in action and its potential for expanding both our understanding of problem drinking and for providing more efficacious remedies for it.

The Restricted Disease Model and Traditional Conceptualizations of Problem Drinking

Introduction.   None of the controversy over disease conceptualizations of drinking problems has arisen because anyone doubts that excessive drinking, especially over extended periods of time, can produce serious health problems which often require medical attention. Likewise, few have debated the existence of a physiological component in the development of alcohol tolerance or the occurrence of alcohol withdrawal. These biological aspects of alcohol's effects do not dictate a particular understanding of the nature, etiology, course and prognosis of drinking problems, or a specific treatment for them. They simply outline important physiological parameters of problem drinking, a disorder which legitimately might be conceived of as "disease," given the broad biopsychosocial perspective on diseases alluded to earlier. The real source of controversy is not disease notions per se, but rather what might be more appropriately referred to as a *restricted* disease model of alcoholism. This concept, pioneered by Jellinek (1960), reinforced by Keller (1976) and others, and popularized by the pervasive dogma of Alcoholics Anonymous (AA), places *primary* emphasis on the biologic aspects of disease to the serious neglect of psychologic and social factors. Let us turn now to an examination of the traditional and restricted disease model in terms of some of its major assumptions, empirical data bases, and important implications. The interested reader may wish to consult Pattison, Sobell, and Sobell (1977) for a more detailed accounting of these issues.

Assumptions and Evidence.   The principal assumption of the restricted disease model of problem drinking is that certain individuals have a genetically determined or developmentally acquired physiological defect which gives rise to and controls the course of a disease called "alcoholism." This assumption has spawned a number of etiologic theories of the specific deficit responsible for alcohol dependence, but not even a moderately convincing literature has accrued in support of any of them. For example, research has failed to substantiate claims of differences between normals and "alcoholics" in their metabolism of alcohol, as long as controls were provided for average consumption rates (Korsten & Leiber, 1976) or the "alcoholic" group tested had experienced a brief period of sobriety prior to the study (Mendelson, 1968). Another theory is that certain individuals may have "allergic" reactions to alcohol resulting in a different vulnerability to drinking problems. This idea has received some support from the finding that Orientals have more intense physiological reactions to alcohol than others (Ewing, Rouse, & Pellizzari, 1974). Ironically, however, this sensitivity has been associated with *lower,* not higher rates of problem drinking among Orientals. Overall, it seems safe to conclude that no specific physiologic dysfunction accounting for drinking problems has as yet been identified (NIAAA, 1978).

Still another tack of disease-oriented researchers, observing that drinking problems tend to run in families, has been to study the possible genetic transmission of alcohol problems under the assumption that the particular defect being transmitted would be discovered later (Goodwin, 1979). Unfortunately, these studies generally have been fraught with serious methodological complications, such as arbitrary distinctions between "alcoholics," problem drinkers and normals, making the results difficult to interpret. In any event, even if the claim of a genetic component were to be substantiated, the task of demonstrating its necessary and/or sufficient link to problem drinking would still remain.

Despite the tenuous nature of scientific evidence for a physiological cause of problem drinking, proponents of the restricted disease model have proceeded as if physical etiology were an established fact. In particular, the theory has been expanded to include assumptions about biologically-based symptomatology, course, and prognosis of the disorder. Foremost, and perhaps most problematic, among these additional assumptions is the notion that "loss of control drinking" and its attendant "craving" are physically determined. Loss of control drinking refers to the experience of a problem drinker who takes a first drink after a period of sobriety and then is so overwhelmed by an uncontrollable craving for more alcohol that he or she is unable to stop drinking until stuporous or too ill to continue. Anecdotal reports suggest that problem drinkers do sometimes exhibit such a behavior pattern—that is not the crucial issue. The question is, what underlies this phenomenon and how reliable is it? Is it, as restricted disease model theorists have assumed, a physiological reaction with one inevitable outcome, or are there alternative explanations? The answer to this question is vitally important because of its implications for the treatment of problem drinking. An examination of some of the pertinent evidence is in order.

Laboratory analogue studies represent one approach to investigating factors underlying craving and loss of control drinking. The findings of Marlatt, Demming and Reid (1973) and others (e.g., Merry, 1966; Engle, & Williams, 1972) have shed considerable light on these phenomena. Marlatt and his colleagues, for example, conducted an experiment designed to separate the physiological from the psychological processes in craving/loss of control. Under the guise of a "taste-rating task," nonabstinent (but sober) "alcoholic" subjects were offered an ad-lib supply of either alcoholic (vodka and tonic) or nonalcoholic (tonic only) beverages after first receiving a "primer" dose of the same beverage. The primer dose was designed to trigger a physiologic alcohol craving in those receiving the vodka drinks. Subjects *beliefs* about the nature of the drinks they consumed also were varied independently from actual beverage content so that four orthogonal belief/beverage conditions resulted: expect alcohol/receive alcohol, expect alcohol/receive no alcohol, expect no alcohol/receive alcohol, and expect no alcohol/receive no alcohol. According to the restricted disease model, those "alcoholics" actually receiving vodka should have experienced craving and loss of control drinking regardless of the manipulated expectations since these symptoms are presumed to be under physiologic control. However, the results showed that it was the belief that one was receiving vodka that led to the greatest beverage consumption, *regardless of the actual contents* of the drinks. These findings of course, strongly suggest that psychological and especially cognitive processes could play a major role in craving and loss of control drinking when they occur.

It might be argued that brief, single exposure analogue studies such as those just cited do not offer an adequate test of craving and loss of control phenomenon. Perhaps a more extended study of problem drinking patterns is needed. Mello and Mendelson pioneered such efforts with their "experimental drinking" research program in the late 1960s. Their projects and those of other investigators working concurrently studied the behavior of inpatient problem drinkers given access to alcohol over periods of 2 to 3 weeks or more. Such research consistently failed to demonstrate the validity of craving or loss of control drinking notions even as behavioral phenomena, let alone as symptoms under the control of involuntary, internal physiological processes (see Mello, 1972, for a review). Subjects did not "drink to oblivion" or even drink all the alcohol available. At times they spontaneously terminated drinking episodes altogether or maintained only mild intoxication for extended periods. Some individuals "tapered off" their consumption toward the end of the drinking period to avoid intense alcohol withdrawal. Moreover, several studies showed that drinking behavior could be dramatically modified and certainly "controlled" by the manipulation of external contingencies. Problem drinkers drank less if they had to work harder to obtain alcohol or if they received financial incentives for maintaining low consumption rates. Subjects' drinking was also amenable to control by access to "enriched" environments as opposed to "impoverished" ones where privileges

and pleasantries were limited. Clearly, these findings represent a serious challenge to the idea of a physiological craving and loss of control born of some
unitary biologic defect.

Finally, at the most naturalistic level are longitudinal studies of alcohol consumption in persons identified as problem drinkers. While little evidence is
available on untreated individuals (Roizen, Cahalan, & Shanks, 1978), there is a
considerable literature which follows up on the drinking behavior of those who
have been in alcohol treatment. This research ranges from small scale clinical
reports (Davies, 1962) to larger national cohort studies (Polich, Armor, &
Braiker, 1980), with some projects utilizing highly sophisticated methodologies
(e.g., Sobell & Sobell, 1978a). For the present discussion, the most important
conclusion of these studies and many others (see Lloyd & Salzberg, 1975, for a
review) is that a significant portion of severe problem drinkers, i.e., consensus
"alcoholics," are capable of returning to nonproblem levels of drinking following treatment and run no greater risk of relapse as a consequence than those
maintaining long-term abstinence. Of special import in the *4 year* follow-up
study of Polich et al. (1980) was the fact that there were more drinkers than
consistent abstainers who could be counted as treatment successes in terms of
their nonproblem drinking status, despite the fact that the treatment centers
studied in this research did not even entertain, let alone implement, nonabstinent
treatment goals. These results contrast sharply with restricted disease model
views that loss of control will inexorably follow a first drink. In fact, they also
contradict the weaker view that loss of control need not always follow all drinking, but will inevitably result from any prolonged drinking (Keller, 1972).

Longitudinal studies of drinking and drinkers such as those of Polich et al.
(1980) and Clark and Cahalan (1976) have also challenged several of the
additional restricted disease model assumptions, viz., that "alcoholism" is a
unitary disorder which is progressive and irreversible in its course. While, by
definition, there is a commonality among problem drinkers in that they have
difficulties associated with alcohol, available evidence suggests that may be as
far as the uniformity goes (cf. W. Miller, 1976). As already discussed, scant
support can be found for a single biologic etiology, and much the same can be
said about the existence of a specific "alcoholic personality" (cf. Freed, 1979).
"Alcoholism" has many faces, often shaped by sociological and contextual
factors. Cahalan and Cisin (1976), e.g., have highlighted the importance ethnic
and religious influences in the epidemiology of problem drinking. These same
investigators have raised serious questions about the hypothesized progressive
course of "alcoholism" by showing that while many problem drinkers typically
suffer from certain problems, the order of their occurrence is highly variable and
in all likelihood situationally determined. Furthermore, the general course of
drinking problems need not be a downward one since external environmental
changes apparently can lead to positive changes in status as well as to "spontaneous remissions," even in those experiencing severe problem drinking (see

Roizen et al., 1978). Finally, individual characteristics have been correlated with differences in treatment outcomes despite a general commonality in "alcoholic" symptomatology (Sobell & Sobell, 1978a). Perhaps the uniformity myth of problem drinking is a product of biased sampling (e.g., exclusive study of the most severe problem drinkers in treatment) or selective attention (e.g., the systematic exclusion or ignorance of contradictory evidence once an ideology has been established). In any event, it seems evident that the scientific tenability of the restricted disease model of problem drinking is at best questionable. In light of this conclusion one wonders about its persistence, and more importantly, about its implications for treatment.

Treatment Implications.   As any good student of science knows, a theory need not be true to be useful. Perhaps the virtues of the restricted disease model of problem drinking lie in the effective treatment methods it generates rather than its veracity. Due to the absence of any systematic medical therapy for "alcoholism," one is by default forced to examine the principal stepchild of the restricted disease model—Alcoholics Anonymous (AA). The philosophy of AA, as explicated in this self-help organization's "Big Book" (AA World Services, 1955), embraces all the basic assumptions of the restricted disease model. In fact, agreement with the notion that as "alcoholics" they are qualitatively different from others in their constitutionally-determined inability to handle alcohol is the first requisite for membership. What are the merits of this point of view?

Sociologists have shown that such a disease conception can lead the public to cease viewing deviant drinkers as morally responsible for their state (Orcutt & Cairl, 1979). And in a similar vein, Beckman (1980) has suggested that admission of illness enables the problem drinker to absolve himself of responsibility (and hence guilt) for drinking and related actions, thereby paving the way for an improved self-image and ameliorative change. Unfortunately, Orcutt and Cairl (1979) also noted that the medical worldview, even with its dissolution of responsibility, did not eliminate the stigmatization and social rejection suffered by the "alcoholic." Instead, it was shown that persons identified as "alcoholics" were perceived as threatening and were not widely tolerated. Several other investigators (Farina, Fisher, Getter, & Fischer, 1978; Fisher & Farina, 1979) also have reported relevant data showing that, compared to those provided with a social learning theory account, persons exposed to the disease concept messages about personal problems felt less able to alter their state, engaged in less direct problem-solving behavior, and were *more* inclined to use alcohol and/or other drugs to relieve distress subsequent to the manipulation. Moreover, contrary to Beckman (1980), it can be argued that absolving the "alcoholic" of responsibility for his drinking and concommitant behaviors may serve to reinforce drinking as a way of escaping blame, rather than to prepare an individual for successful treatment. Cahalan (1970), e.g., suggested that disease concepts provide an alibi for lack of change. Sterne and Pittman (1965) have further noted that assigning the problem drinker to the "sick role," with its implications of no blame or responsibility, can adversely affect client motivation both directly and by promoting indulgent and paternalistic attitudes in treatment staff. Finally, Sobell and Sobell (1978a) have pointed out that intensifying the sick role of problem drinkers by considering them to be victims of biologic defects may irrationally restrict their care to members of the medical profession. Thus, it appears that emphasis on an unproven physiologic disease etiology of alcohol problems has several liabilities from a treatment standpoint.

One also may look beyond etiologic hypotheses to the treatment implications of other assumptions of the restricted disease model. The idea that a physiologically determined loss of control over drinking is the pathognomonic symptom of "alcoholism," which itself is considered a permanent and irreversible disease subject to arrest but not cure, has significant repercussions. It means that a lifetime commitment to abstinence from alcohol is required of all who partake of treatment. The problem drinker must be constantly vigilant and exert all his will power to resist drinking since—despite the contrary evidence already reviewed—he must "know" that he is incapable of handling alcohol. Obviously, an approach which paradoxically demands both acknowledged helplessness *and* self-control necessarily entails a substantial amount of persuasion and social pressure, but with what effect and at what cost?

The efficacy of AA for its members is difficult to assess (see Bebbington, 1976, for a review), largely because of the nature of the organization itself: it is a social group with a quasi-religious character so attendance at meetings has an undetermined relation to drinking or other outcome status; it is an anonymous group so the progress of any individual member is impossible to trace; and it is a self-supporting and service-oriented group so there is little concern for data beyond that necessary to assure that its selected membership is reasonably satisfied. Nevertheless, given the frequency and intensity of AA testimonials, one cannot help but conclude that some individuals attribute the cessation of their drinking to AA. Since abstinence is the main outcome criterion of interest to AA, they usually are counted as successes. Unfortunately, several studies of the connection between drinking and more general treatment success in other important life areas such as employment, social and emotional functioning, suggest a low correlation among these variables (Finney, Moos, & Mewborn, 1980; Gerard, Saenger, & Wile, 1962; Pattison, Headley, Gleser, & Gottschalk, 1968). But, even ignoring these data, the report of Polich et al. (1980) indicating that only 7% of individuals treated in abstinence-oriented programs succeeded in maintaining abstinence over 4 years, suggests that the AA treatment approach does not have great success in promoting total abstinence among its members. Still, it may be the treatment of choice for some people. The question then becomes how many, and what of those for whom it may not work?

Leach (1973), as well as the membership figures of AA itself, suggest that less than 10% of the estimated number of problem drinkers in the U.S. belong to

AA at any given time. Thus, it appears that a substantial number of people are simply unwilling to subscribe to the ideas that they are helpless, that they can *never* drink, and that a satisfactory resolution to their problems includes associating themselves with a social support system heavily invested in the moralistic philosophy of AA. This group of resisters includes the vast majority of those responsible for the costs of problem drinking outlined in the opening paragraph of this chapter: the young, the drunken driver, and the chronic treatment failure, etc. These people are in a sense disfranchised because their inclinations and problems do not fit the unverified ideology of the restricted disease paradigm, as exemplified by AA. Must they wait until their lives are a total disaster and a ''disease'' identity has driven a wedge between them and society, hence making the fellowship of AA more palatable? Must they succumb to propaganda perhaps leading loss of control drinking to become a self-fulfilling prophesy? Must they let others determine their treatment goals, regardless of their own potentials? These appear to be some of the possibly unintended trappings of the restricted disease approach. Fortunately, there is another game in town.

Social Learning Conceptualizations of Problem Drinking

Introduction. In recent years, an alternative to the restricted disease model of problem drinking has emerged. A product of theory and research in the behavioral sciences, the social learning model conceives of *problem drinking as a maladaptive habit.* While acknowledging the potentially adverse physical consequences of excessive drinking, this approach eschews traditional disease notions, focusing instead on a complex interaction of biological, psychological, and social factors as responsible for the etiology and maintenance of problem drinking. There also is a tendency among advocates of social learning conceptualizations to view drinking problems as just one member of a larger class of appetitive or ''addictive'' behavior disorders often marked by a kind of temporary self-indulgence with short-term benefits but serious long-term liabilities. Included among such disorders are drug abuse, smoking, overeating, compulsive gambling, and perhaps some sexual deviations. Because any or all of these behaviors may be present and maladaptive to varying degrees across many individuals, they are seen as existing on a continuum rather than defining discrete categories of people, such as ''alcoholics'' and ''nonalcoholics.''

A key concept of social learning theory, as explicated by Bandura (1977a), is that behaviors are best viewed in terms of *functional relations.* Hence, a thorough analysis of the function of drinking, through examination of its determinants, behavioral topography, and consequences is an essential prerequisite to any problem management or treatment interventions. For problem drinking, determinants might include the individual's history and experience with alcohol, the physical, situational and social contexts of drinking, the emotional states an individual associates with alcohol consumption, one's cognitive set or expectations about drinking, and certain physiological reactions associated with ethanol. Drinking itself can be analyzed in terms of its frequency, quantity, rate, variability, duration, and beverage preference, among other dimensions. Finally, the consequences of drinking must be studied to ascertain how they relate to its antecedents and to what extent they influence the actual drinking behavior. Of special interest to behavioral analysts is the extent to which the probability of drinking is increased (by reinforcing consequences) or decreased (by aversive consequences). Serial and temporal relations among all these variables also are considered important to understanding the function of drinking in any particular individual or instance.

To briefly summarize, a general social learning approach assumes that drinking, like all learned behavior, is acquired and maintained through three often overlapping processes: (1) differential reinforcement; (2) modeling experiences; and (3) cognitive mediation. An examination of some specific assumptions and the empirical findings relevant to them follows.

Assumptions and Evidence.   At the outset, experimental psychologists sought an explanation for the popularity of alcohol consumption in the study of its direct pharmacological action. Operating on the assumption that the physiological consequences of drinking must be reinforcing for the behavior to continue, they explored a variety of stimulus conditions which might be affected by ethanol. Early animal research showed that "experimental neurosis" (Masserman & Yum, 1946) and approach-avoidance conflict resolution (Conger, 1951) were meliorated by alcohol. This led Conger (1956) to formulate the "tension reduction hypothesis" (TRH) which holds that alcohol reduces tension or stress. As a corollary, it also has been hypothesized that organisms will be more likely to imbibe alcohol when experiencing tension or stress. Thus, the physical effects of drinking were viewed as negative reinforcers, directly reducing averse aspects of tense, stressful or anxious states. This idea clearly fit reinforcement and drive-reduction theories of behavior central to experimental psychology at the time, while also having common sense appeal since people often seemed to drink to calm down, and ocasionally even "relaxed" to the point of passing out. Unfortunately, subsequent research on the TRH (see Brown & Crowell, 1974; Cappell & Herman, 1972, for reviews) has yielded many equivocal, negative, and contradictory results. Most of these studies, however, were conducted on infrahuman species that rarely show a preference for ethanol anyway. Perhaps the tension reducing effect of drinking was specific to man.

The first tack taken by researchers investigating the TRH in humans was to try to determine if alcohol reduces tension or anxiety. Several reviews of studies proceeding along this line (Higgins, 1976; Marlatt, 1976a) have turned up some confirmatory evidence, but mainly have served to point out important variables and methodological issues often neglected in the generally equivocal literature.

For example, the findings of Williams (1966) suggested the possibility of a nonlinear relation between alcohol dosage and affective consequences. He showed that at low doses social drinker subjects reported a lessening of anxiety and depression, while higher doses were associated with increases on the same self-report measures. Others (e.g., McNamee, Mello, & Mendelson, 1968) have noted similar results among "alcoholics," adding that the longer the drinking episode, the more negative the emotional state of the drinker, with problem drinkers perhaps experiencing only a brief initial period of minimal relief or elation. These findings gave impetus to the notion of a *biphasic action of alcohol* whereby it serves as a stimulant at low doses, but a depressant as the amount consumed increases (cf. Mello, 1968). Also indicated was the potential mediating effect of *drinking experience* as a population variable probably reflecting alcohol tolerance differences. Moreover, one was cautioned that a specific absolute level of "intoxication" might produce unique consequences depending upon its position on the ascending versus the descending limb of the blood-alcohol curve (cf. Jones & Vega, 1972).

In addition to these and other factors relating exclusively to the alcohol variable itself, there is evidence to suggest that the *social and environmental context* of drinking might influence accompanying tension, anxiety, or other affective states. Pliner and Cappell (1974) showed positive emotional states were associated with social more than with solitary drinking situations, whereas, Kalin (1972) highlighted other more physical factors in the stimulus setting that might play a role in determining alcohol's effects. Finally, inattention to the *complexity of constructs* such as tension and anxiety could contribute heavily to the lack of consistency in experimental work on the TRH. Witness, e.g., Steffen, Nathan and Taylor's (1974) finding that "alcoholics'" self-reports of subjective distress while drinking failed to correlate with electromyographic measures of their muscle tension. Obviously, validation of the hypothesis that alcohol reduces tension is not so simple as at first supposed.

Another way of exploring the relation between drinking and tension is through the corollary of the TRH, i.e., by examining the effect of stress on drinking. Several researchers have pursued this course which emphasizes antecedents and other social learning components of the functional analysis of drinking behavior. In one of the earliest studies of stress factors affecting drinking, Higgins and Marlatt (1973) created high or low levels of state anxiety in "alcoholic" and "normal" men by threatening them with either painful or painless electric shocks. Subsequent drinking then was measured unobtrusively by means of a bogus taste-rating of alcoholic beverages. This experiment yielded no differences in beverage consumption as a function of induced anxiety level. However, in a follow-up study using the same dependent measures (Higgins & Marlatt, 1975), "heavy" social drinker males, led to believe they would later be personally evaluated by a group of women, drank significantly more alcohol than those not anticipating social evaluation. Such results, of course, suggested that it may be *interpersonal* stress rather than general tension which is most closely related to problem drinking.

Along this same line, Miller, Hersen, Eisler, and Hilsman (1974) showed that "alcoholics" exposed to socially stressful situations and criticized for their social inadequacies subsequently drank more than unstressed controls. Normal drinker subjects in the same study, however, did not show such a difference, introducing the idea that the effect may be limited to those with considerable drinking experience. The importance of such individual differences in drinking history also might help to explain Holroyd's (1978) counterintuitive finding that nonabstainers receiving a negative social evaluation later drank *less* than those given a positive evaluation. Perhaps very light drinkers regard alcohol consumption as an especially inappropriate response to stress. Russell and Bond (1979) elaborated on subject variable effects by showing that among moderate social drinkers there is a tendency to use alcohol mainly to amplify positive moods rather than to try to compensate for negative ones. The latter strategy seems to be reserved for heavy or problem drinkers with a different set of expectations about alcohol's effects and different reasons for drinking (cf. Farber, Khavari, & Douglass, 1980). In any event, several very recent studies lend further credibility to the TRH corollary of stress-induced drinking while simultaneously pointing to a need for greater specificity. Noel and Lisman (1980), for example, demonstrated that female subjects increased their drinking following the evaluation-type stress of repeated failures on a series of unsolvable cognitive problems. In separate research, Gabel, Noel, Keane, and Lisman (1980) found that comparable levels of physiological arousal induced by viewing either mutilation or erotic slides led to greater drinking only in the latter case.

In an effort to reconcile the apparently disparate findings of research on the TRH, some social learning theorists have shifted their emphasis from simple tension reduction to viewing *drinking as a coping response* (cf. Marlatt, 1976a), i.e., as a way of dealing with stressful situations. Generally, this response should permit escape, avoidance, or at least temporary management of the stress. The literature reviewed earlier further suggests that the nature of the stress and/or the individual's interpretation of it are quite important. Threats to social and personal competence or control seem especially likely to prompt increased drinking if no alternative coping mechanism is readily available. A study by Marlatt, Kosturn, and Lang (1975) is illustrative of this approach. The heavy social drinker subjects in this experiment encountered an experimental confederate who either frustrated and criticized them (provocation stress conditions) or treated them in a neutral manner (control condition) in connection with their attempts to solve some very difficult anagrams. Then, half the provoked subjects were given an opportunity to retaliate (give "feedback" by means of electric shocks) against the confederate, while the others were offered no means of coping with their frustration and anger. Finally, all participants engaged in an alcoholic beverage taste-rating task.

Results showed that provoked subjects who had retaliated drank significantly less than the frustrated, angry subjects given no such coping alternative, while controls consumed an intermediate amount of alcohol. These findings were interpreted as indicating that the desire to drink might be increased by the experience of certain kinds of stress, but that that desire can be diminished if alternative coping methods are available.

Experiments like that of Marlatt et al. (1975) help explain why the stress-drinking relation is not consistent across individuals or even within the same individual at different times. If one has an adequate repertoire of coping responses for a particular stress situation or is not predisposed to interpret it as stressful, he is unlikely to engage in maladaptive drinking when it occurs. At the same time, it should be noted that among persons whose ethnic, cultural, or other social learning backgrounds promote heavy and chronic alcohol consumption there may be a greater tendency to utilize drinking as a coping response. In general, if the personal as well as socially-mediated experience of drinking to deal with stress is a reinforcing one, there will be greater expectations for its efficacy. The result should be a greater vulnerability to maladaptive "drinking to cope" patterns of alcohol consumption.

Investigations of the *effects of modeling on drinking behavior* also can be interpreted in terms of drinking as a coping response. In addition to the general drinking model influences associated with age, sex, ethno-religious background, and social class variables (cf. Cahalan & Cisin, 1976), the subtle social pressure of a particular model in a specific drinking setting can represent a stress for some individuals. Caudill and Marlatt (1975), e.g., showed that heavy drinking males exposed to a model who drank heavily in an experimental situation consumed considerably more wine than those interacting with either a "light drinker" model or no model. Moreover, subsequent research (Cooper, Waterhouse, & Sobell, 1979; Lied & Marlatt, 1979) showed the modeling effect was most profound in increasing the alcohol consumption of heavy drinking males with same sex models. Females were not as responsive to the models, perhaps because heavy drinking by women does not conform to culturally-defined role expectations. Light drinking males, on the other hand, may have had limited exposure to heavy drinking peers and may have possessed alternative means of dealing with social pressure, including a failure to construe drinking as a competitive activity or sign of masculinity.

Despite evidence supporting the idea of drinking as a coping response with different functions depending on one's experience, some important issues remain unresolved. Perhaps most significant is the question of how beliefs about the reinforcing aspects of drinking developed in the first place. Marlatt (1976a) has speculated that the biphasic physiologic action of alcohol might offer a clue. Maybe the initial arousing effect of alcohol contributes to what McClelland et al. (1972) described as increased feelings of "personal power" observed in moderately intoxicated men. He reasoned that the energy burst of released epinephrine, the warmth of dilated blood vessels, the arousal of increased heart rate, and the other initial pharmacological effects of alcohol could—if interpreted in a particular way—provide an enhanced sense of power, control or even competence to the stressed individual. These effects could be so desirable for someone feeling a lack of control or self-efficacy (cf. Bandura, 1977b) that, in a moment of great vulnerability, he or she might disregard the depressant phase of intoxication and the potential long-term consequences of drinking. At the very least one might consider them a small price to pay for some immediate relief from distress. This would account for some of the shortsightedness of the problem drinker.

An extension of the drinking to gain control idea is the suggestion that perhaps, in actuality, what is most important about alcohol from a physiological point of view is simply that it promotes a *change* in one's state of consciousness (cf. Galanter, 1976). The direction of the change, up or down, and the accompanying "objective" reactions (e.g., nausea, anxiety, etc.) may be relatively unimportant compared to the subjective experience involved. This subjective experience could function to provide a temporary escape from a dismal, constricted world of sobriety or as a means to absolve oneself of responsibility for his actions, thereby increasing the perception of freedom. It is precisely these kinds of *cognitive experiences associated with drinking* which often have been neglected in most conceptualizations of drinking put forth until just recently.

A whole set of potential reinforcers for drinking exists in the expectations of the drinker (and of those around him) about the effects of alcohol on behavior. These might include, but certainly should not be limited to cognitively-mediated tension reduction. In the past 5 years, numerous studies (see Marlatt & Rohsenow, 1980, for a review) have employed a "balanced placebo" paradigm to explore the impact of cognitive factors on the relation between drinking and various behaviors many people expect alcohol to influence. The design, patterned after that popularized by Marlatt et al. (1973), orthogonally varies both subjects' expectations about the contents of their drinks (alcoholic vs. nonalcoholic) and the actual beverage content (alcoholic vs. nonalcoholic). This procedure permits a complete separation of the physiological from the psychological effects of drinking on the behavior in question. Research results to date have repeatedly demonstrated that, especially where male subjects are concerned, the *belief* that one has consumed alcohol leads to greater aggression (Lang, Goeckner, Adesso, & Marlatt, 1975), more sexual interest and arousal (e.g., Wilson & Lawson, 1976), and less social anxiety (e.g., Wilson & Abrams, 1977) than the belief that one has consumed only tonic—*regardless of actual beverage content,* which itself has no effect at the low to moderate dosages used.

Balanced placebo research findings clearly conform to people's *expectations* about alcohol's effects (cf. Brown, Goldman, Inn, & Anderson, 1980), though *no* pharmacologic effect of alcohol on the behaviors in question has been demonstrated. Probably the most parsimonious explanation of such results is to regard drinking as a discriminative stimulus signalling that a new set of contingencies is operating to control (or fail to control) behavior. At least in much of U.S. culture, drinking apparently means that one can behave in a less "inhibited" manner with relative impunity. It is as if the boundaries of propriety, as judged by the drinker himself and reflected by the increased tolerance of those around him, have been expanded. This means that one can exercise freedom without responsibility—a state of affairs which has obvious reinforcement potential. What is further suggested is that persons who have difficulty dealing with anger, who have problems interacting sexually or socially, and who generally lack a sense of their ability to control personal or social outcomes might be most prone to depend upon drinking as a maladaptive coping device. This does not mean, however, that all drinkers are alike. On the contrary, while one person's drinking problems might be perpetuated by an inability to resist peer pressure at the club, another person who is totally competent at refusing drinks from others may seek alcohol when he is depressed. The point is that the function of drinking is unique in each case, though certain commonalities of both a psychosocial and a biological (e.g., drinking to avoid withdrawal symptoms) nature might be observed.

While most of the empirical impetus for the hypothesized function of drinking as a coping response has come from laboratory experimentation with social drinkers, some recent studies of persons having severe alcohol problems lend considerable credibility to this approach. Marlatt and Gordon (1980) followed-up a large group of patients who had been treated for "alcoholism" to determine what factors might contribute to their resumption of drinking after a period of abstinence. Data were gathered on cognitive and affective states, settings and situations, significant life events, etc. that surrounded relapses. The assumption was that an analysis of such circumstances would help illuminate the factors contributing to a general lack of control over problem drinking. Individuals were contacted as soon as possible following a relapse episode and their responses to queries on numerous treatment-relevant items were carefully classified. The results were congruent with the conceptualization of drinking as a coping response in stressful situations. Three classes of stressors were primary factors in almost 75% of respondents' relapses. These were: negative emotional states arising from nonpersonal environmental events (e.g., depression after a job layoff), interpersonal conflict (e.g., anger in marital relations), or social pressure to drink (e.g., old friends encouraging a drink "to celebrate").

In independent research, Litman, Eiser, Rawson, and Oppenheim (1979) also found that a similar set of stress-related variables (unpleasant affect, external drinking cues, social anxiety, and reduced vigilance to the need to avoid alcohol) precipitated most relapses in the sample of "alcoholics" they surveyed. In addition, it was shown that use of cognitive control coping mechanisms and greater general flexibility in the application of coping mechanisms differentiated the "survivors" (nonrelapsers) from the relapsers in the study. Investigations by the same team (Litman, Eiser, & Taylor, 1979) reported further that, contrary to restricted disease model rhetoric, individual patterns of relapse were quite variable. Erratic month-to-month variations in heavy drinking, rather than a downward spiral following the first drinking relapse, were most common. Moreover, the least favorable outcomes were associated with heavy drinking punctuated by short periods of abstinence—a pattern that traditional treatment approaches seem to foster. These findings underscore the importance of cognitive factors in problem drinking and point to the central role of providing adequate coping alternatives for "high risk" situations if problem drinking is to be controlled.

Treatment Implications.   One especially clear implication of the social learning approach is that problem drinking must be viewed as a complex problem, involving a varied set of antecedents, mediators, and consequences across individuals. As such, it is not likely to be responsive to any unitary treatment method. This, indeed, has been borne out in the failures of many traditional therapy programs as well as in the disappointing early efforts of behaviorists to treat problem drinking by a direct suppression or control of the drinking response. A sampling of such attempts will be reviewed later, however, since they might be useful components of broader treatment strategies.

Another theme implicit in the social learning model is that the goal of treatment need not be total abstinence, but simply the reduction of drinking to a nonproblem level. It is, after all, the effects of drinking not any drinking per se which define the problem. Moreover, the social learning view of the drinking aspect of problem drinking as a behavioral excess rather than a symptom of a permanent physiological disease makes a variety of drinking outcomes not only possible but also satisfactory. This does not mean that social learning approaches are synonymous with controlled drinking goals, but simply illustrates their compatibility. In all candor, however, it should be noted that many complex questions and issues surround the abstinence versus controlled drinking controversy. Some of these will be discussed in a later section on treatment goal selection.

A point of some agreement between the social learning and restricted disease model approaches is that neither necessarily holds the problem drinker responsible for his current state. Consequently, no sense of guilt, self-blame, or remorse need accompany the individual into treatment. The difference is that for social learning theorists the client is seen as being capable of changing his state, instead of having to resign himself to a life as a perpetually helpless and unfortunate individual stricken with "alcoholism." It is understood that certain experiences (modeling, differential reinforcement, associative learning, etc.) combined with more gross sociocultural and situational factors may provide conditions particularly ripe for the fostering of maladaptive drinking patterns. Persons cannot be held responsible for conditioning that takes place when such circumstances exist. However, the social learning approach views learning as a reversible process and encourages the problem drinkers to assume responsibility for and to take control of *changing* his or her behavior. Logically, these changes would include suppressing or controlling the drinking response, but also must involve developing: (1) better recognition of "high risk" problem drinking situations so that management is possible [control of antecedents]; (2) adaptive alternatives to drinking both to cope with specific stresses and to gain access to desired outcomes [control of consequences]; and (3) clearer understanding of the ways in which beliefs, expectations and other cognitive factors often act to exacerbate drinking problems, so that appropriate remedial action can be taken [cognitive control].

The remainder of this chapter will outline treatment strategies derived from social learning theory, with an emphasis on skills training and cognitive restructuring. These methods greatly enrich the classical and operant conditioning procedures which have dominated behavior therapies for problem drinking until very recently (cf. Nathan & Briddell, 1977). This broader cognitive social learning perspective seems especially important when dealing with the problem of maintaining behavior change or preventing relapse. Wilson (1978a), e.g., has pointed out that, in the absence of biological evidence, the "craving" for a first drink after a period of abstinence can be most parsimoniously understood in terms of mislabeled physiological/emotional states coupled with anticipation of positive effects from alcohol. Demonstrations that such cognitions and expectancies need not be veridical to influence behavior are available in the "balanced placebo" literature reviewed earlier. Then, once the initial drink is taken, it is probable that other cognitive processes figure prominently in "loss of control" drinking should it occur. In particular, the first drink or "slip" might easily be construed as a personal failure and could give rise to considerable guilt and internal conflict—an Abstinence Violation Effect (AVE; see Marlatt, 1978a). These stresses, in turn, can precipitate further drinking if no alternatives are readily available for coping with the discomfort. Add this to the popular, though scientifically untenable, belief that loss of control drinking is an inevitable biologic consequence of alcohol consumption in problem drinkers ("one drink, then drink"), and it is easy to see why improperly managed cognitions might lead to far more relapses than there need to be.

In sum, the contrast between social learning and restricted disease approaches is clear. The former seeks to develop skills and cognitions that foster a sense of self-efficacy, including a positive expectancy about one's ability to control outcomes in "high risk" drinking situations. The latter, on the other hand, seeks to instill a profound belief in one's helpless inability to deal with alcohol under any circumstances. This programmed insecurity and defeatist dogma of the restricted disease model would make some sense were it not for the fact that the vast majority of problem drinkers cannot always avoid contact with drinking situations and simply do not continuously abstain from alcohol following treatment. Given these facts, however, it would seem to be both more realistic and more advantageous to address ways in which high probability drinking-related events might best be dealt with, rather than pretending that such things do not happen and leaving the outcome to chance.

SOCIAL LEARNING INTERVENTION STRATEGIES

The goal of this section is to outline an approach to dealing with problem drinking which makes good clinical and theoretical sense, while simultaneously reflecting a sound empirical base. This is a formidable task since the picture of problem drinkers presented here has been one of a highly divergent population requiring complex individualized treatment; but, the research data are mostly in the form of group or program outcome studies examining very limited therapeutic strategies. The inadequacy of many of these studies is magnified by numerous design and methodological problems, making their results impossible to interpret. Though a review of important issues in psychotherapy and behavior change outcome evaluation is well beyond the scope of this chapter (see Garfield & Bergin, 1978), several problems especially critical to alcohol research deserve mention (see Nathan & Lansky, 1978a, for more comprehensive coverage).

The focus of social learning treatments on *individual* problems makes problem assessment techniques and related experimental subject selection criteria all the more important if any legitimate generalizations are to be drawn. The potential significance of these individual difference factors must also be considered in selection of treatments and treatment outcome measures. This is particularly true when social learning-based strategies offer more than one alternate treatment goal (e.g., *either* total abstinence *or* any nonproblem level of drinking). Such options add to the difficulty of matching across treatment and control groups and dictate the need for multidimensional tracking of the full range of patient behavior, rather than relying on dichotomous outcomes such as the presence or absence of any drinking. Indeed, some research (e.g., Vogler, Weissbach, Compton, & Martin, 1977) has suggested that as much as 70% of the outcome variance in programs designed to achieved moderation in problem drinkers was attributable to pre-treatment individual differences in alcohol intake and other subject variables. Hence, the selection of assessment methods, specific treatment techniques, and outcome evaluation criteria must necessarily consider individual client characteristics such as age and sex, and personal history of physical/ emotional health, education, employment, social relations, marital adjustment, etc., in addition to drinking and prior alcohol treatments.

In a similar vein, it perhaps goes without saying that the presence of an identified drinking problem should not lead the therapist, whether assessing many persons for an alcohol treatment project or dealing with an individual in clinical practice, to ignore his/her first task—to determine the client's *immediate* needs and goals. This means that critical life areas must be surveyed for current or impending crises requiring prompt attention. Arrangement for a physical examination should be mandatory so that medical status can be clarified and informed treatment choices can be made. Establishing the priorities of the client also helps organize interventions, establish clinical leverages, and facilitate relations. The point is that a relentless and exclusive focus on drinking, aside from being clinically irresponsible, often may compromise chances for treatment success.

Before proceeding, a reiteration of the social learning view of problem drinking might be helpful. Problem drinking patterns are seen as socially acquired, learned behaviors maintained by numerous antecedent cues, mediational processes, and reinforcing consequences which may be physiological, psychological and/or sociocultural in nature. The desire to cope with withdrawal symptoms, aversive cognitive/emotional states, peer pressure etc. may trigger drinking episodes. These, then, might be maintained by the immediate physiological stimulation, the sense of freedom associated with the "time out" of an altered state of consciousness, the reinforcement of group acceptance, etc. sometimes associated with drinking. Thus, effective treatment must not only control drinking directly, but must also generalize and maintain that change through the development of new ways of acting and thinking which are both adaptive and naturally reinforcing. Our general approach is one which seeks to *detach* the person from the drinking problem and to *educate* him/her in the management of it and a general lifestyle which might exacerbate it. Clients are seen as active co-investigators in a behavior change project, not as individuals to be confronted, diagnosed, converted and cared for.

Assessment of Problem Drinking

Overview.   Assessment in the social learning approach is *problem focused* rather than person focused. Its objective is to describe problems in such a way that client awareness, specific treatment planning, and change evaluation are aided. This implies a dynamic, ongoing process reflecting individual differences and the continuum on which drinking and its attendant problems might fall. In contrast, traditional scales and questionnaires typically seek to identify persons who can be given the diagnosis of "alcoholism" and consequently assigned to a unidimensional treatment. Besides being a rather stagnant approach, the various tests and diagnostic criteria designed to screen for "alcoholics" in general or patient populations have not been impressive in their reliability and validity (see Jacobson, 1975, for a review). Moreover, the goal of such instruments, to arrive at dichotomous ("alcoholic" or "nonalcoholic") classifications, ignores the problems of discontinuous definitions of problem drinking noted earlier (also see Marlatt, 1981). As W. Miller (1976) has argued in his comprehensive discussion of the differential assessment of problem drinking, a multidimensional approach focusing on the extent and pattern of alcohol use, the extent and nature of problems related to drinking, and the feasibility of various treatment approaches, is optimal. Such a prescription is consistent with the social learning emphasis on assessment of antecedent, concurrent, and consequent events associated with the presenting problem. The methods we recommend consider not only objective events (e.g., behaviors and situations), but also important cognitive or subjective variables (e.g., beliefs and expectations) which have been shown to affect outcomes in a meaningful way.

While the ideal comprehensive assessment includes direct observations of drinking and drinking-related behavior and their physiological concomitants, practitioners outside research settings often must depend on self- and/or collateral-reporting and monitoring of problem drinkers' behaviors and cognitions. Such methods have been much maligned for their alleged lack of validity and reliability (cf. Summers, 1970). However, three recent studies (Maisto, Sobell, & Sobell, 1979; Sobell & Sobell, 1975; 1978b) strongly challenged this assumption by checking the responses of "alcoholics" against official records and documents or collateral informant reports. Results showed that generally valid and reliable information was provided by clients and that when discrepancies were noted they were as likely to be overreports and underreports. Such findings argue for the utility of self-reports, especially if the social learning approach has been successful in its attempts to foster a detached, objective attitude toward problem behaviors rather than viewing them as indicative of one's personal identity as an "alcoholic."

Analyzing the Drinking Response. It is generally important to know the quantity, frequency, and variability of drinking behavior per se, but this information is of limited utility unless one also knows the antecedents, cognitive processes, and consequences surrounding the drinking response. Thus, a single instrument like the Drinking Practices Questionnaire (Cahalan, Cisin, & Crossley, 1969) could be used for preliminary screening, but more comprehensive measures should follow. As a useful starting point, an initial interview or early "homework" assignment might elicit a developmental history of the individual's drinking. This can include an appraisal of the origins and evolution of positive and negative experiences with alcohol throughout critical stages in the person's life. Such information helps to clarify attitudes and expectations about drinking as well as the possible function(s) it has served or may be serving now. Moreover, these data give the clinician a sense of the client's self-image and the extent to which he/she feels capable of managing drinking, and/or a life without drinking. Insights of this sort can be invaluable in general treatment planning.

As an aid to more specific treatment implementation, the Drinking Profile (Marlatt, 1976b) has been developed. This instrument is a structured interview questionnaire consisting of both open- and closed-ended items pertaining to drinking preferences, rates, patterns, settings, reasons, and problems. Also included are objectively scorable questions about past and present motivation for treatment as well as current outcome expectations. The Drinking Profile provides a wealth of information found to be useful in setting goals, selecting treatments, and predicting outcomes.

Though retrospective self-reports about the gross aspects of drinking have been shown to be reasonably accurate, it is helpful to complement these measures with more precise ongoing records of drinking-related behavior. This approach has the added advantage of providing a continuous indication of changes in treatment, so that program modifications can be based on data rather than speculation. Self-monitoring procedures (McFall, 1977) represent one simple way to track behavior. Clients can be asked to keep a daily record of their drinking in terms of such aspects as its time, amount, social/situational context, antecedent and consequent events/activities/experiences, intervening moods/thoughts, etc. The object is to arrive at a broadly-based topographical sketch of the drinking response so that the functional analysis of it can be fleshed out. This permits identification of important components in "high risk" drinking situations which suggest appropriate foci for treatment.

Clearly, self-monitoring procedures are not foolproof because clients must, first, comply and, second, report accurately. Where compliance is a problem, incentives might be built in. For example, Pomerleau, Pertschuk, Adkins, and d'Aquili (1978) had clients make an initial cash deposit which was refunded in installments contingent on completeness (not content) of their records. Concerns about accuracy could be diminished by having collaterals keep an independent record for comparison purposes or by making "spot check" BAL tests or direct observations for verification (all with client consent, of course). In any event, considerable research has substantiated the utility of a variety of standard self-monitoring procedures (e.g., Sobell & Sobell, 1978a; W. Miller, 1978).

Options for expanding self-monitoring might include use of drinking × situation bar graphs constructed by clients to help them become more active in pinpointing potential problem situations, to encourage their objectivity and detachment from their behavior, and to provide a clear and potentially reinforcing indication of progress being made. Even if a client were to be abstinent for a period of time before, during, or after treatment, the self-monitoring of drinking "urges" and the surrounding circumstances could still be a useful aid in developing preventive strategies. Along similar lines, clients might be asked to engage in "relapse fantasies" so that the therapist could provide treatments appropriate to the situations described. Overall, the lesson to be learned is that one of the best sources of assessment data is often the client's own reports.

In addition to the methods already described, several more direct, observational techniques have been developed for analyzing the drinking response itself. For the most part, these procedures are best suited to laboratory applications or other research settings where resources beyond those typically available to the average clinician might be found (see Marlatt, 1978b; Nathan & Briddell, 1977, for reviews). "Operant" strategies are one example. These assessment techniques rely on the reinforcing value of alcohol dispensed to subjects who are required to "work" for the drinking reward by performing simple motor tasks (lever or bar pressing) or sometimes more complex social or personal behaviors. Usually, the device which dispenses the alcohol permits automated recording of the rates and patterns of subjects' responses and their subsequent drinking. Measures obtained can be used as indicators of general motivation for alcohol and of the relative reinforcement value of alcohol for subjects, especially when reinforcement schedules and environmental circumstances are varied systematically.

"Ad libitum" drinking methods also provide direct measures of alcohol consumption and differ from the operant procedures mainly by eliminating the "work" requirement prior to gaining access to the beverages. Subjects are, in effect, permitted to drink whatever they wish in the amounts and manner of their choosing. The analogy to real life situations is sometimes enhanced by constructing simulated bars with appropriate ambience. The object is to observe and study the drinking behavior of subjects with a minimum of interference. Research along this line has reliably identified several dimensions of drinking styles which differentiate some problem drinkers from nonproblem drinkers. For example, Schaefer, Sobell, and Mills (1971) found that "alcoholics" ordered more "straight shots" and "gulped" drinks faster than "normal social drinkers." Such information helps identify potential targets for behavior change in problem drinkers, particularly if they wish only to moderate their consumption.

A variation of the ad libitum method is the "taste rating" task in which subjects are led to believe that they are involved in a test of their taste acuity using various alcoholic beverages as the stimuli. In actuality, the critical information gained from the taste test is an unobtrusive measure of the rate and total amount of beverage consumption. This approach helps reduce some of the evaluation apprehension ordinarily felt by experimental subjects, so that more accurate indicators of their relative desire for alcohol and manner of drinking can be obtained. Both taste rating and operant drinking task scores have been shown to predict treatment outcomes in problem drinking clients, with unsuccessful individuals consuming more than successful ones (Miller, Hersen, Eisler, & Elkin, 1974).

A final means of directly studying the drinking response is through naturalistic observation. This approach calls for the therapist or other observer to be physically present in some of the real life situations where the client normally drinks. Reid (1978) described a detailed system for barroom observation studies of general clientele which could be easily adapted for clinical use. By employing such procedures, the therapist can gain a clearer picture of the client's drinking pattern and how social/situational factors affect it, while simultaneously having an opportunity to become acquainted first-hand with the groups and settings in which the client operates and his/her effectiveness in them.

Assessment of Behaviors Related to Problem Drinking.   In connection with identifying the pattern of drinking excesses and a set of "high risk" drinking situations for a particular individual, one must provide for assessment of the adequacy of the client's coping responses in those stress situations which seem especially problematic. Experience has shown that these situations will often correspond to the relapse precipitants described earlier (e.g., negative affective states, interpersonal conflict, social pressure to drink), but the specifics should be gleaned from the self-reports, self-monitoring records, and other individualized data sources for each client. Then, problem situations can be role played or, where possible, directly observed (e.g., in the case of marital conflict) so that client performance can be analyzed and treatment prescriptions can be made. The technology for such individualized assessment of diverse behavioral problems has been detailed elsewhere (e.g., Hersen & Bellack, 1976). A formal approach to the general assessment of problem drinkers' coping responses in common "high risk" situations has also been developed (the Situational Competency Test; Chaney, O'Leary, & Marlatt, 1978). These methods typically provide the subject with a free response opportunity to demonstrate coping strategies in the face of stimulus situations presented via role plays or prerecorded tapes. The resultant behavioral data can be analyzed for both content and process strengths and weaknesses in client responding. Such information is directly applicable in treatment planning.

In addition to discovering the immediate stressors and corresponding inadequate or maladaptive coping responses which act to sustain problem drinking, recent treatment efforts have sought to broaden assessment to identify general problems (e.g., Miller & Mastria, 1977) and lifestyle factors (Marlatt & Gordon, 1980) that might be important considerations when attempting to prevent relapses. The rationale for these approaches is that the higher the individual's level of social-emotional functioning and the more "balanced" his or her lifestyle, the less likely that specific stresses will be encountered and/or the more likely a satisfactory outcome will follow any stress encountered. Hence, Miller and Mastria advocate overall assessment (and treatment) of social and marital, emotional, and vocational functioning. The methods applied could screen clients with traditional psychological tests and questionnaires (e.g., the MMPI), but should also include detailed self-reports, self-monitoring, and behavioral assessment interviews and observations conceptually parallelling those used in functional analysis of the drinking response and behaviors surrounding it.

One especially important aspect of the general approach to problem assessment is consideration of the client's spouse or alternative significant others who play key roles in his or her environment outside treatment. Clearly, these persons may have at their disposal reinforcements and punishments for client behavior far more potent than any therapist can hope to muster. Moreover, they are intimately involved in a "system" which has developed around an often chronic problem with drinking. The dynamics of "alcoholic" marriages, e.g., have been amply documented in recent publications (see Paolino & McCrady, 1977). Consequently, almost any change in the client will necessitate an adjustment in the "system" so that individual investments in the status quo along with costs and benefits associated with projected therapeutic outcomes need assessment. The therapist must learn to what extent a spouse or significant other can be counted on as an ally or saboteur in the treatment process. Usually, a separate interview best accomplishes these objectives.

As a preface to a spouse interview it might be helpful to explain that its purpose is not to check honesty, but rather to get another perspective on the complex set of factors which may influence the drinking problem. The spouse or others can be asked to comment on perceived determinants, behavioral variations, and consequences of drinking. Their estimate of the probability of change and the feasibility and desirability of associated posttreatment adjustments in anything from conversation topics to socioeconomic status might be assayed. Finally, the therapist should explain the rationale and procedures of the social learning approach and deal with skepticism (often born of popular restricted disease model notions), while exploring the potential and the willingness of the spouse or others to facilitate change by becoming actively involved in interventions.

Finally, at the broadest level, an effort should be made to assess the client's general lifestyle. "Lifestyle imbalance" is the term Marlatt (1979) has used to describe the experience of persons who perceive their lives as guided largely by external demands ("shoulds"), to the neglect of internal forces consonant with self-expression, fulfillment, or simple pleasure ("wants"). This state of affairs can often help set the stage for relapses because the individual soon tires of his or her virtuous overrestraint and feels a major bout of drinking or other self-indulgence has been "earned." Thus, instead of applying the principle of moderation to both "shoulds" and "wants", the problem drinker with an unbalanced lifestyle tends to make rapid, erratic and "uncontrolled" efforts at correcting disequilibrium. A proneness or vulnerability to excessive or otherwise maladaptive alcohol consumption often results. The assessment of lifestyle balance can be carried out in a variety of ways, but perhaps the simplest is to ask clients to keep a log of all discrete tasks or activities engaged in during each day over at least one typical week. These then can be rated by the client using a subjective 100 point scale on which scores from 1 to 50 suggest "wants," while those from −1 to −50 indicate "shoulds." Going to the laundromat, e.g., would typically be rated rather negatively, while leaving work early to go sunbathe at the beach could approach +50. Thus, total daily scores averaging near zero suggest a balanced lifestyle, while widely varying or consistent negative scores should signal the possible need for some remediation if the risk of vulnerability to over-indulgence is to be reduced.

In conclusion, it should be reiterated that assessment in the social learning approach should not be regarded as a terminal process. Instead, it is continuous throughout treatment, offering a means for evaluating change and redirecting treatment when necessary. Assessment techniques are best structured to enhance client involvement in decision-making and to encourage their objective detachment from the problems at hand so that they can develop and maintain a generalizable investigative frame of mind in their behavior change projects. As we turn now to a review of specific treatments for problem drinking, the ongoing nature of assessment should be borne in mind.

Treatment of Problem Drinking

Overview. As with assessment, the focus of comprehensive, social learning-based treatments is on problems. This emphasis does not ignore the strengths and assets of an individual client, but rather tries to integrate these potentials into a broad program for facilitating change. Treatment of targeted behavioral excesses or deficits and beliefs or expectations may range from direct suppression of the drinking response to a restructuring of cognitions coincident with relapse vulnerability. In the ideal case, specific intervention planning and implementation are tailored to individual clients in consideration of the great diversity of the problem drinker population. However, for the most part the general strategies discussed here, such as the development of cognitive-behavioral skills for coping with stress and for acquiring the expected or real benefits of drinking through more adaptive alternatives, appear to have wide applicability in principle.

The goal of this section is to review and evaluate the major treatment approaches to problem drinking derived from social learning theory. For the sake of brevity, a detailed coverage of marital therapy, vocational counseling and similar interventions addressing common problems encountered in general clinical practice will be sacrificed. Miller and Mastria (1977), among others, offer highly readable prescriptions for dealing with these areas as they pertain to the remediation of problem drinking. The interested reader is encouraged to consult such resources for a more complete picture of treatment planning. Overall, treatment planning should be a logical process of matching interventions to identified problems, using empirical evidence to bolster decision-making whenever possible. For at least one aspect of this process, however, often the procedure has not been quite so simple. Probably no area of therapy for alcohol-related problems has generated more emotional controversy than the choice of treatment goals pertaining to the drinking response itself—abstinence versus moderation.

Treatment Goals for Drinking: Cessation or Control?   Some of the dimensions of the paradigm clash between the restricted disease model and the social learning model have already been reviewed in an earlier section on theoretical conceptualizations. Actually, they represent only a sampling of the arguments and evidence which can be brought to bear on the feasibility of controlled drinking goals for problem drinkers (see Miller & Caddy, 1977; Nathan & Goldmen, 1979; Nathan & Lansky, 1978b; Pattison, et al., 1977; etc. for a more comprehensive coverage of the controversy). For our purposes, however, only a few points need to be made. First, research findings do not support biologically-based notions of craving, loss of control, or the permanence of drinking problems so central to abstinence orientations. Moreover, there is no firm evidence demonstrating that abstinence goals lead to better outcomes in terms of subjective (psychological) discomfort, psychosocial adjustment, or overall functioning. It is, in fact, only when there are serious medical problems liable to be directly exacerbated by further alcohol consumption that a cessation of all drinking is the unequivocal choice that should direct treatment. Otherwise, the arguments on both sides boil down to speculation, ideological preference, or simple misinformation. Given the less than overwhelming success of traditional treatments for "alcoholism" (Baekeland, 1977) and the continually mounting evidence for the efficacy of experimental programs designed to establish nonproblem levels of drinking in similar populations (Sobell, 1978), we feel compelled to entertain controlled drinking as a viable treatment option for problem drinkers.

If either abstinence or controlled drinking can be a reasonable choice for many problem drinkers, the issues then become how clients might be appropriately assigned to each goal and how the corresponding treatment is to be implemented. Both questions are subject to empirical test, but can also be approached logically. To date, little research has been done on a priori predictor variables for differential assignment to abstinence or controlled drinking treatment goals. Where data are available (e.g., Miller & Joyce, 1979), it has been found that clients with less severe drinking problems, fewer general symptoms and less family history of alcohol problems have been more successful in attaining moderate drinking patterns. Unfortunately, such potentially important variables as degree of cognitive impairment (though expected to correlate with chronicity of drinking problems) have not been included in these studies.

In general, controlled drinking programs are contraindicated for persons suffering from severe alcohol-related medical problems. Also excluded are those whose long standing excessive alcohol use, serious life complications from drinking, or personal characteristics are likely to result in cognitive dysfunction or other problems which would significantly interfere with their ability to benefit from the psycho-educational, skills acquisition procedures crucial to most controlled drinking approaches. On the other hand, certain socially or morally inclined individuals might be especially responsive to the abstinence orientation of traditional AA treatment because of the fellowship provided and the quasi-religious flavor of the organization.

By contrast, controlled drinking is perhaps best suited for clients just beginning to suffer problems in connection with their drinking. Young people and those with relatively intact support systems they wish to maintain rather than replace are often good candidates. They typically reject the "alcoholic" label and all it entails, but are willing and able to experiment with their behaviors, change their attitudes, and learn new skills. Other persons with more problematic patterns and a history of repeated failures in traditional programs also deserve an alternate approach. Whatever the client characteristics, we feel that anyone wishing to try controlled drinking should be given the best opportunity to do so. Thus, while we may point out the disadvantages associated with this goal in a particular case, no one is denied treatment on that basis. This is important because, contrary to the claims of restricted disease model proponents, the social-learning approach does not encourage "alcoholics" to try moderate drinking using only will power as a control device. Odds are that a failure perhaps even leading to death would result. What we recommend is the *systematic* application of scientifically sound social learning principles to change behaviors and alter cognitions in such a way that control of drinking becomes possible. This approach demands appropriately trained professionals with a thorough knowledge of cognitive-behavioral methods and a commitment to empirical outcome evaluation. A counselor who deals in esoteric experience with faith and advice, however dedicated, is as liable to court disaster as the uninformed problem drinker trying self-control on his own. Thus, we advocate efforts at controlled drinking only when the best techniques available are properly applied. Then, if the carefully monitored client continues to fail at moderation, it is clear that abstinence should be sought. Often this alternative goal is easier to implement when clients have had a well-conceived, but unsuccessful trial at controlled drinking.

General Alcohol Education.   Many traditional treatments of drinking problems include an "alcohol education" component. Typically, this involves a sampling of the immediate effects of ethanol on psychophysiology and an overview of the alleged causes, course and problems (medical, psychological and social) of "alcoholism." The object seems to be to frighten clients into compliance with treatment regimens which follow from restricted disease model dogma. While such "scare tactics" have not been shown to produce enduring behavior change, it would seem reasonable to provide clients with a dispassionate accounting of how drinking might affect them and with a research-based appraisal of the myths surrounding alcohol use and abuse. Particularly when controlled drinking is a treatment goal, the individuals involved should be fully apprised of factors affecting BAL (dose, weight, time, eating, etc.) and the probable physical and psychological experiences likely to be associated with particular BALs. Information about the biphasic action of alcohol discussed earlier might be especially useful to clients in choosing and maintaining BAL limits which optimize certain effects they find positive, while helping them avoid some of the depressant effects which almost inevitably accompany high doses.

A less formal aspect of alcohol education sometimes used in behavioral treatments of problem drinking is "self-confrontation" (e.g., Vogler, Compton, & Weissbach, 1975). In this method subjects' behavior while drinking is videotaped and later played back for them while sober. Originally, the procedure was designed to increase motivation for treatment by heightening the awareness of problem drinkers, many of whom have "blackouts" or only selectively recall drinking episodes and related behaviors, to the untoward or embarrassing nature of their actions while intoxicated and/or the physical consequences (vomiting, passing out, injuring themselves, etc.) of drinking. This experience could, however, be more broadly construed as alcohol education. As such, it may not be necessary that the procedure have any demonstrable direct or interactive impact on motivation or treatment outcome, but rather its value may lie in simply providing the client with a complete picture of the problem. The purpose of this and other alcohol education efforts would be to place clients in a position to make fully informed choices about drinking and about treatment. We believe this to be a desirable objective and one which is essential to ethical clinical practice.

Direct Suppression or Control of the Drinking Response. Regardless of specific treatment goals, the earliest behaviorally oriented therapies for problem drinking focused on the consumatory response itself in a very direct manner. Initial attempts employed aversive counterconditioning procedures designed to replace positive alcohol associations with negative ones by pairing inappropriate drinking with a noxious stimulus. Despite historical reports suggesting the effectiveness of electrical stimulation used as an unconditioned stimulus in Pavlovian conditioning to suppress drinking, later research has not supported such claims. In a typical study along these lines (Miller, Hersen, Eisler, & Hemphill, 1973) painful shocks were delivered to "alcoholics" on repeated experimental trials of drinking. Subjects could escape the shocks by expectorating the alcohol they had taken into their mouths. Pre- and post-treatment comparisons showed no sustained differences in the alcohol consumption rates. Wilson, Leaf and Nathan (1975) noted similar findings in their study of "alcoholics" given free access to alcohol before and after exposure to a large number of trials on which electric shocks were received in connection with drinking. The result was that drinking continued, unaffected by the efforts at aversive counterconditioning. These and other reports led Wilson (1978b) to conclude his comprehensive review of the electrical aversion literature with the suggestion that such treatment should be abandoned in view of ethical problems, high subject attrition rates, and overwhelmingly negative findings.

Chemical aversion programs based on the same principles have fared somewhat better, though they have not been tested independent of other treatments (AA, family therapy, special counseling, and inpatient milieu). And, they typically have been applied only to highly motivated clients (willing to endure a very unpleasant treatment), mostly from the upper socioeconomic strata (cf. Lemere & Voegtlin, 1950, report on Shadel Hospital; Wiens, Montague, Manaugh, & English, 1976, report on Raliegh Hills Hospital). Such clients, of course, have the highest probability of success in any treatment. Nevertheless, this simple procedure of inducing nausea and vomiting with intravenous administration of emetine, so that drinking can be paired with the aversive consequences, appears to have some merit. A few as five conditioning sessions (plus later "boosters") were required over a period of 10 days hospitalization to produce one year follow-up abstinence rates in the neighborhood of 60%. It should be reiterated, however, that a highly selected patient population was employed and that the efficacy of the aversion element of therapy was not tested alone. Furthermore, appropriate control groups were lacking in most research reported.

A variation of chemical aversion treatment is the daily administration of Antabuse (disulfiram), a drug which produces violent physical reactions if alcohol is subsequently consumed. There are, however, some problems with this method, not the least of which is getting clients to take the substance regularly. In addition, Antabuse does not decrease desire to drink, is not applicable to clients with serious medical problems, and may involve safety risks if used continuously for extended periods (see Kitson, 1977 for a review). At best one might conclude that aversion treatments, perhaps also including covert sensitization to produce aversive associations via self-elicited imagery (Cautela, 1970), could serve as useful adjuncts to more comprehensive treatments.

Another method of directly addressing the drinking response is blood-alcohol level (BAL) discrimination training, introduced by Lovibond and Caddy (1970). This procedure was designed to train "alcoholics" to recognize a range of BALs in themselves and then to use this awareness to maintain a pattern of moderation in drinking over an extended period of time. Subjects were initially taught to monitor their internal sensations as they varied in connection with different BALs (up to 0.08%). Concurrently, they were asked to give BAL estimates and were provided accurate feedback on them. Following this initial phase, patients repeated the procedure, but received electric shocks whenever their BALs exceeded 0.065%, a level considered to correspond to moderate intoxication. Follow-ups at 4 or more months after treatment found experimental subjects reporting that their drinking was "controlled," only rarely exceeding 0.07% BAL. Unfortunately, the short duration of follow-up and unverified self-reports of BAL estimates must temper this encouraging result. This is especially true since subsequent research has shown that "alcoholics" cannot maintain accurate BAL estimates once external feedback is removed (e.g., Silverstein, Nathan, & Taylor, 1974). Moreover, subjects with a high tolerance for alcohol have been shown to be poorer at BAL discrimination training than low tolerance subjects (Lipscomb & Nathan, 1980), and this basic deficit in high tolerance individuals ("alcoholics") is maintained even when the BAL range in which discrimination is tested is raised substantially (Shapiro, Nathan, Hay, & Lipscomb, 1980). Thus, the promise BAL discrimination training once held now seems unwarranted.

A similar conclusion can be drawn about efforts to teach "alcoholics" to exhibit drinking behavior more closely resembling that of "normals." For example, Mills, Sobell and Schaefer (1971) gave varied intensity finger shocks to subjects whenever they ordered "straight" drinks, "gulped" their drinks and/or accepted a fourth or fifth drink offered them. Shocks were not given in the 14 training sessions if three or fewer beer, wine or mixed drinks were ordered and sipped appropriately (social drinking). Six weeks follow-ups suggested that, while social drinking skills could be taught in the lab, their generalization and maintenance were short-lived. Miller, Becker, Foy and Wooten (1976) obtained the same disappointing results using simple instructions (no punishments) to decrease drink potency and sip size, but increase sip intervals in problem drinkers. They found the behaviors could be taught, but were not practiced.

None of the methods described above offers much in the way of incentives for reduced drinking except the avoidance of punishment or negative associations. The minimal efficacy of such approaches should not be too surprising since most problem drinkers get involved in treatment because naturally occurring environmental punishments, despite their apparent intensity, have not been enough to arrest the problem. Of course, it can be argued that the existing "punishments" or "response costs" associated with drinking technically are not punishments since they fail to reduce the probability of the behaviors that precede them (cf. Morse & Kelleher, 1977). In any event, some students of human behavior have noted that a systematic manipulation of reinforcement contingencies should be capable of altering any behavior, including alcohol consumption. Numerous laboratory studies, especially in the "experimental drinking programs" mentioned earlier, have demonstrated that this is indeed the case. Griffiths, Bigelow and Liebson (1978), e.g., reviewed studies showing that providing social and other environmental reinforcers only when abstinence or moderate drinking occurred resulted in substantial reductions in the ethanol intake of "alcoholics."

Programs to control drinking in "alcoholics" by rewarding moderation and attaching response costs to over-indulgence have also been implemented *outside* the laboratory. These procedures, sometimes referred to as "contingency contracts," spell out the consequences of abstinence or moderation versus drunkenness in advance so that it is clear to clients how their drinking behavior will affect the presence or absence of available reinforcers in the environment. Miller (1975) pioneered efforts to apply contingency contracting as an independent treatment modality by selecting 20 chronic "public drunkenness" offenders from a local city jail and implementing either contingent or noncontingent access to environmental reinforcers. Experimental subjects were provided with a wide range of opportunities, services, and goods in the community (employment, health care, counseling, shelter, food, clothing, etc.) contingent on their demonstrated maintenance of sobriety. Unannounced observations of behavior and "spot checks" of BALs enabled the investigators to monitor subjects' drinking, and whenever signs of intoxication of BALs in excess of 0.10% were observed, reinforcers were suspended for 5 days. The control subjects received all the same reinforcers, but on a noncontingent basis during the 2 month treatment period. Results showed experimental subjects were arrested less, intoxicated less, and employed more than the controls whose behavior was unaffected by the program. Despite the brevity of the follow-up period in this study, the findings are an impressive illustration of how behaviors can be changed if one has sufficient control over their consequences. Unfortunately, for most problem drinkers such external control of reinforcers would be highly intrusive, and the withholding of public services from individuals whose comportment simply deviates from arbitrary societal standards raises serious ethical issues. Nevertheless, the findings of contingency contracting research highlight a potentially critical role of behavioral consequences in treatments designed to modify problem drinking.

An appraisal of the unidimensional group treatments of drinking problems reviewed briefly above should suggest something in addition to the attractiveness of more individualized and more comprehensive programs. In particular, the futility of unitary efforts to simply eliminate drinking should be underscored. It has been some years ago that behavior modifiers taught us that it is easy to change behavior—if one is willing to pay the price. The real difficulty is in maintaining and generalizing that change. This often cannot be done by just manipulating external reinforcers and punishments because the means for continuing such contingency arrangements typically are not available or are too impractical to implement indefinitely. Moreover, inattention to the behavioral vacuum left behind when drinking diminishes or ceases would seem ill-advised since there is no guarantee that drinking will not be replaced by an even less desirable behavior. The solution would seem to lie in developing adaptive alternatives to drinking which can facilitate coping with perceived stressors and/or can provide access to the same or comparably valued reinforcers without the adverse side effects. The approach, of course, is dependent on the kind of comprehensive assessment outlined earlier. In any case, the suggestion is that a broader perspective considering the precipitators and maintainers of drinking as well as the general problems of living and lifestyle of the problem drinker should result in the most stable positive outcomes.

Skills Training and "Broad Spectrum" Approaches.   A central feature of any social learning-based treatment which conceptualizes drinking as a coping response must be the training of alternative coping skills which are more adaptive. As early as 1965, Lazarus recognized the role of stress in problem drinking and suggested that comprehensive or "broad spectrum" treatments make provisions for direct anxiety reduction, assertive and interpersonal skills training, and marital counseling. These stress management procedures were designed to augment standard medical care and direct suppression of the drinking response. His general strategy was the precursor of most of the major behaviorally-oriented treatment projects which have been evaluated to date, and it continues to be influential.

The skills training approach begins with a multidimensional assessment of client problems along the lines described above. Then, depending on the case, a variety of options may be entertained. Where practical, clients may be able to control some of their exposure to stimuli which have been antecedent cues for drinking (e.g., walking into bars), and thereby reduce drinking and its attendant problems. In other instances, it may be found that clients have the requisite coping skills in their behavioral repertoires, but that their performance is blocked by anxiety. If so, the application of systematic desensitization may be all that is necessary to disinhibit the skill and permit it to be implemented for the melioration of drinking problems. Most often, however, clients need to be taught new and different skills for coping with problems.

For clients deficient in important coping skills, a systematic training program should be applied. The approach we favor combines specific skills training with instruction and practice at general problem solving. This helps facilitate generalization and transfer of training to new problems or contexts perhaps not anticipated in the specific skills package. An array of methods including direct instruction, modeling, behavior rehearsal, coaching and therapist feedback can be usefully employed. Attention to cognitions as well as observed performance also is encouraged. For example, the modeling of self-instructional statements (Meichenbaum, 1977) may be particularly helpful in teaching clients adaptive self-statements which can be used to complement execution of the behavioral skills. The details of the skills acquisition approach can be found in numerous publications (e.g., McFall, 1975; Rimm & Masters, 1979). Miller and Mastria (1977) have reviewed a number of skills training procedures that have particular relevance for the treatment of problem drinkers.

In a recent research study (Chaney, O'Leary, & Marlatt, 1978), the additive effect of short-term skills training on outcomes experienced by chronic male "alcoholics" receiving standard 30-day inpatient hospital treatment (individual and group counseling) for problem drinking was evaluated. All subjects were administered multiple assessment measures, including the Situation Competency Test for social skills (described earlier), before being randomly assigned to one of three treatment groups: skill training, discussion, or a no additional treatment control. During hospitalization those in the skill training condition met twice weekly for 90-minute small group sessions revolving around the development of coping skills for 16 problem situations. The situations selected for training were developed to reflect circumstances other data had linked to relapses in abstinent "alcoholics." Categories included: anger/frustration (e.g., your employer criticizes you unfairly after you return to work), interpersonal temptation (e.g., social pressure from old buddies to resume drinking), negative emotional states (e.g., boredom or depression), and intrapersonal temptation (e.g., attempts to test treatment effectiveness by trying an occasional drink). In sessions, group members were taught a general problem-solving orientation to deal with the specific "high risk" situation under discussion. Participants entered into detailed discussion of the situation, trying to generate coping options and to trace their probable outcomes. Therapists then modeled a constructive coping skill appropriate to the situation, using interpersonal role plays whenever possible. For the intrapersonal situations the modeling was of internal thoughts and self-statements designed to illustrate the step-wise process of problem solving: define problem, generate alternatives, evaluate short- and long-term costs/benefits of each alternative, outline the way to implement the best solution. After every modeling demonstration, each subject chose a particular response, rehearsed it and got feedback (instruction and coaching) from the therapist and group. All subjects repeatedly revised and reenacted their responses until group approval was obtained. Finally, the group was asked to summarize the method used to generate and evaluate adequate responses to the situation.

Subjects in the discussion comparison group spent equal time in group meetings talking about the same ''high risk'' situations as the skills training clients. However, their emphasis was on the feelings and emotions elicited by the situations. The rationale was that such efforts would promote insight and self-understanding. Finally, the no treatment control participated only in the regular ward treatment with no extra meetings.

The results of the experimental treatments in this study included a predischarge demonstration of the efficacy of the skills training approach in improving coping ability as measured by the Situational Competency Test. A one year follow-up further showed that the skills training group had fewer and less severe drinking relapses than either of the other two groups (which were approximately equal). These differences were not just statistically significant, but were practically meaningful in their magnitude: one-sixth the number of intoxicated days, one-fourth the amount of alcohol consumed, and one-eighth the average duration of a drinking episode were experienced by skills trained subjects as compared to the other two groups. Moreover, it is remarkable that the results were obtained with very severe problem drinkers (''alcoholics'' by almost any definition), suggesting that the potential of skills training for younger, less chronic or problem-ridden drinkers could be even better considering the greater responsiveness to this approach expected of them.

All of the remaining major treatment outcome studies to be reviewed employ variations of the ''broad-spectrum'' approach (Lazarus, 1965). In addition, all with the exception of those by Azrin and his colleagues (Hunt & Azrin, 1973; Azrin, 1976), explicitly include controlled drinking as a treatment goal. While there are some design weaknesses in these projects, they are perhaps most noteworthy for their methodological rigor, especially as it applies to post-treatment follow-up. However, since many of the procedures in this research are extremely complex, only brief sketches will be presented here. The interested reader should consult original sources for details.

Hunt and Azrin's (1973) ''community reinforcement'' approach is actually a variation of the contingency contracting operant method discussed earlier (Miller, 1975). The difference is that here experimental subjects were first provided with an intensive skills training and cognitive-behavior therapy program designed to improve their social and vocational functioning. This treatment sought to give the ''alcoholics'' greater access to intrinsically reinforcing employment situations, and pleasant family and social contacts. Then, upon discharge, the availability of these reinforcers was made contingent upon sobriety. Control subjects were exposed to neither the psycho-educational program nor the contingency arrangements. Results showed that experimental subjects functioned far better than controls on multiple outcome dimensions, but since training and contingency were confounded it is impossible to tell to what extent each was responsible for the difference. If the skills training was most critical, there would be reason for optimism about treatment. If, on the other hand, the total environmental control necessary for the contingency program was most instrumental, its impracticality and inherent moral dilemmas would seem to mitigate its potential for widespread application. Azrin's (1976) later refinement of this approach added Antabuse to reduce impulsive drinking, a system of community informants to report early warning signs of drinking problems, a nonprofessional "buddy system" for social support and advice, and group as opposed to individual counseling. These methods improved the cost effectiveness of the program, but did not resolve the issues raised about the first study. Nevertheless, this approach shows promise especially for severe cases not amenable to less intrusive procedures.

Sobell and Sobell (1973) began the study of controlled drinking in earnest with their Individualized Behavior Therapy for Alcoholics (IBTA). Their experimental program included skills training (problem identification, generation of alternative responses, evaluation of alternatives, practice with best alternative), along with aversive avoidance conditioning for inappropriate drinking behavior, videotaped "self-confrontation" of drunken behavior and contrast with sober behavior, and exposure to impossible tests to permit analysis of failure responses. For controlled drinking subjects training in social drinking behaviors (order other than "straight" drinks, take small sips, space drinks, drink three or fewer drinks) was also included. At two year follow-up (Sobell & Sobell, 1976), 69 of the 70 male "alcoholic" subjects were reached and results showed that among subjects in the controlled drinking goal conditions, general life functioning as well as drinking status was much better in the experimental (IBTA) than in the control (traditional) treatment group. For those with abstinence goals, experimental subjects were more improved, but not significantly so.

These findings not only support the viability of controlled drinking goals, but also suggest the superiority of social learning-based treatments over some traditional approaches. Sobell and Sobell, however, are not without their detractors. Critics point to the nonrandom assignment of subjects to abstinent and nonabstinent treatment goals (despite random assignment to IBTA or traditional treatments once goals were selected), the fact that IBTA was administered in addition to conventional treatment with no attention placebo control, the use of a single follow-up worker (one of the co-investigators), etc. as flaws in the experiment. Nevertheless, this study clearly led the way in systematic alcohol treatment outcome research. As a result, social learning approaches to problem drinking have been difficult to ignore.

Vogler and his colleagues (Vogler, Compton, & Weissbach, 1975; Vogler, Weissbach, & Compton, 1977; Vogler et al., 1977) have developed and evaluated a treatment package called "integrated behavior change techniques" which was similar to that of the Sobells. The major distinction was that these investigators used BAL discrimination training to augment aversive and avoidance conditioning procedures in teaching controlled drinking to some subjects. In addition, the Vogler group applied their treatments to separate samples of both inpatient "alcoholics" and outpatient "problem drinkers." They also sought to evaluate the unique contribution of various components of their behavioral treatment package by systematically including or excluding particular procedures used in treatments of randomly selected subgroups of clients. Finally, the idea of intermittent post-discharge "booster sessions" of treatment was incorporated. A fair summary of these studies is that they reinforced the Sobells' demonstration of the overall efficacy of behaviorally-oriented treatments in reducing drinking and improving the functioning of subjects. Nearly two-thirds of the clients were still significantly improved at 12 and 18 month follow-ups. However, the data offered no clear picture of the active ingredients in the behavioral treatment package since group differences were minimal. Actually, pretreatment individual differences were the strongest predictors of subsequent drinking behavior. Younger, less chronic and less excessive drinkers with stable vocational records appeared to be the best candidates for moderation of drinking.

Other studies evaluating the relative effectiveness of behaviorally-oriented treatments to reduce alcohol consumption in self-referred and court-referred outpatient problem drinkers have been carried out by Miller and his coworkers (Miller, 1978; Miller, Taylor, & West, 1980). In the first experiment each of three randomly assigned groups received one of the following treatments: aversive counterconditioning with self-administered shocks, behavioral self-control training with self-monitoring and instruction in functional analysis, or a controlled drinking composite including BAL discrimination training and rate-control training, as well as the self-monitoring and counter-conditioning procedures. The later study employed four separate skills training treatments all based on a book entitled *How to Control Your Drinking* (Miller & Munoz, 1976) which is a self-help manual for moderating drinking through limit setting, pacing, developing assertive and other coping mechanisms through functional analysis, and cognitive behavioral change strategies. A given subject might receive: (1) simple bibliotherapy; (2) bibliotherapy plus behavioral self-control training; (3) both of the above plus relaxation, communication and assertion training; or (4) all of the above plus individually tailored "broad spectrum" modules. Both the studies showed significant decreases in drinking and improvement on multiple measures of general functioning. Again, however, no enduring differences were observed *across* treatments.

Several conclusions can be drawn from these skills-oriented and other behavioral studies. One is that such treatments can be quite successful in helping problem drinkers, with some suggestion that their efficacy far outstrips more traditional approaches. Second, the treatment goal of controlled drinking seems viable across a variety of subjects, though it appears better suited for younger clients with less severe problems. Finally, it does not seem to be too important which specific behavioral techniques are applied. This final conclusion suggests that it may be the social learning conceptualization of the problem and rationale for this general approach that account for its success. Hence, cost effectiveness and individual client characteristics might best dictate treatment selection so long as an appropriate cognitive set is maintained. That an approach which makes good sense and "feels right" is likely to meet with less resistance and realize more success should come as no surprise (cf. Frank, 1975). The observation of Miller et al. (1980) that degree of therapist empathy predicted client outcome tends to substantiate the importance of such cognitive/affective factors. Likewise, the differentially high dropout rate of middle class subjects exposed to traditional treatment (total abstinence goal, group confrontation of denial, channeling of emotions, etc.) as opposed to self-control, skills oriented behavioral treatment aimed at controlled drinking, suggests that the palatability of procedures to the individuals involved must be considered (cf. Pomerleau, et al., 1978).

Relapse Prevention: Cognitive-Behavioral Strategies.   Recent research on the determinants of posttreatment drinking status and general functioning in "alcoholics" clearly points to the importance of both general and specific stressors and to the utility of applying appropriate coping responses (Cronkite & Moos, 1980; Litman et al., 1979; Marlatt & Gordon, 1980). To date, however, the almost exclusive emphasis of empirical treatment outcome studies considering the stress-coping relation has been on the behavioral training of alternatives to drinking in relatively circumscribed "high risk" situations. As previously illustrated, this approach has proved to be highly valuable in reducing problem drinking. It also would seem to foster the increased sense of self-efficacy which Bandura (1977b) has argued is so crucial to therapeutic change. Nevertheless, there has been a relative neglect of two aspects of relapse prevention in which cognitive-behavioral strategies might be quite useful. These are: (1) modification of *general* life problems or lifestyle to improve overall functioning and reduce stress, and (2) application of interventions designed to deal with actual instances of posttreatment drinking in such a way that adverse consequences are minimized. While research on these emerging approaches is only preliminary at this time, the need for an infusion of innovative ideas in the alcohol treatment field is so acute that they will be briefly outlined. A far more extensive discussion of these issues is available elsewhere (Marlatt & Gordon, 1980; Marlatt, 1980).

As noted earlier, advocates of "broad spectrum" social learning approaches to problem drinking (cf. Hamburg, 1975) have routinely recommended that programming a higher density of various self-maintaining, nondrinking-related reinforcers into clients' natural environments should have potential for preventing future difficulties with alcohol. Some (e.g., Miller & Mastria, 1977) have even suggested specific methods of achieving such a goal through training in relaxation, vocational and recreational functioning, social/marital/sexual relations, etc. Our somewhat more global strategy, consistent with these approaches, is based on an expanded explanation of why such supplementary procedures can be so important to long-term treatment success.

It is our contention that a lifestyle imbalance (a problematic relation between the "shoulds" and "wants" in one's daily activities—see prior Assessment section) may serve to predispose individuals to "out of control" episodes of self-indulgence. In other words, problem drinkers feeling a sense of psychological constriction associated with continual restraint of pleasurable activities experience an increased desire for a major, immediate gratification such as that they expect from a drink or a binge. Similar feelings, of course, may accompany any threat to or reduction in one's perceived control over his or her world. A job layoff or many of the specific stressors described earlier would be examples of this latter kind of loss of control sensation. The point is that in either case the person experiences a desire ("craving?") for the anticipated positive effects of drinking. Moreover, since the individual is liable to be feeling deprived (due to lifestyle imbalance) or needy (due to a perceived loss of power), the stage is set for the use of cognitive distortions. These might include both *rationalization* ("I *owe* myself a drink") and *denial* ("I had nothing to do with getting into this situation" or "I need a drink now, so I'll just forget about where it might lead.") The result is that the person often begins making a series of mini-decisions which bring him or her ever closer to a bonafide "high risk" situation from which an unscathed escape will be very difficult. One such mini-decision might be to stop in the local tavern to buy cigarettes rather than getting them at the grocery as usual. In and of itself this choice seems irrelevant, but as part of a chain of similar decisions it may be charting the course to relapse. The self-monitoring procedures and relapse fantasies already discussed in connection with assessment offer one way of sensitizing clients to the early warning signs of relapse so appropriate remedial steps (e.g., implementation of trained coping skills) can be taken. A further preventive measure, however, is to correct life-style imbalances so "high risk" situations simply occur less frequently.

One approach to lifestyle intervention is to replace drinking with some form of "positive addiction" (Glasser, 1976). A positive addiction is a non-competitive daily activity or behavior requiring no more than an hour, little mental effort, and no one else to perform. One should believe that it has some value and that practice will lead to [subjective] improvement. Finally, one must be capable of engaging in the activity without self-criticism. Jogging is a particularly good example of a potential positive addiction. Unlike drinking it does not ordinarily feel good at first and prove costly later. Instead, one usually needs a bit of determination to get over initial discomfort before rewards come in the form of better health, greater relaxation, and a general sense of accomplishment. The addicting aspect is that after practicing a while, one comes to appreciate the feelings associated with jogging so that there is a kind of deprivation experienced when a session is missed.

Progressive muscle relaxation (Bernstein & Borkovec, 1973) and meditation (Carrington, 1978) are two other activities clients have found to function as positively addicting alternatives to drinking. They are simple to learn and are often accompanied by a pleasant, relaxed "high." The utility of these and other positive options as global methods of reducing predispositions to drink has been suggested by some research (Marlatt & Marques, 1977). Three groups of heavy social drinkers agreed to monitor their drinking behavior while engaging in one of the following daily activities: meditation, progressive muscle relaxation, or "bibliotherapy" (a relaxed period of pleasure reading). A no treatment control group (self-monitoring only) was also included. Subjects were trained for 6 weeks and then followed-up again after another 7. Results indicated a 50% drop from pretreatment drinking rates for all experimental groups, with no comparable change in controls after 6 weeks. Treatment subjects also showed an increased perception of internal control, apparently because of either the direct effect of training or its concomitant influence in reducing alcohol intake. While a cessation of the practice of relaxation techniques (and an increase in drinking) was found across groups in the posttraining phase, the potential utility of such methods still seems considerable for problem drinkers actually motivated to change their behavior.

Exercise programs and direct focus on relaxation represent only a few of the possible vehicles for lifestyle intervention. One need not develop a positive addiction, but could instead simply make a commitment to structuring more "wants" into his or her life. Developing hobbies or creative interests which are indulged on a regular basis is one option. Another is to simply schedule some free time each day when one can pursue whatever seems desirable—shopping, sunbathing, visiting with a friend, etc. What is important is to maintain a reasonable lifestyle economy in which "shoulds" and "wants" are in balance to the extent that one is not predisposed to overindulge.

To this point, we have discussed efforts to prevent problem drinking episodes using everything from the very direct and specific to the most global methods. However, despite the best efforts of clients and therapists alike, it is not uncommon for problem drinkers to lapse or "slip" into alcohol consumption which violates their abstinence (or even controlled drinking) goal. Many of the possible determinants of such behavior have already been discussed in this chapter, and detailed theoretical accounts of the relapse process are available elsewhere (e.g., Marlatt, 1980). Thus, the purpose of this last section is to summarize our understanding of relapse and to suggest some steps that might be taken to prevent disaster if an initial indulgence should occur.

In our view, drinking following a period of control reflects a positive expectation about the effects of alcohol coupled with a failure to enact an adequate coping response in the face of a "high risk" situation. Under these circumstances, the first drink is likely to produce a powerful cognitive-affective experience which can be called an "Abstinence Violation Effect" or AVE. The AVE has two components: (1) guilt, conflict, or other aversive psychological states similar to the cognitive dissonance phenomenon accompanying any behavior (e.g., drinking) which is inconsistent with one's prior definition of self (e.g., abstainer); and (2) impotency or self-blame associated with a personal attribution of responsibility for failure to control the urge to drink (i.e., a weakness, such as lack of "will power"). These thoughts and feelings tend to intensify already stressful aspects of the "high risk" situation the individual was apparently unprepared to cope with in the first place. Hence, the person feels more helpless and less in control so that continued drinking is likely to occur, especially if the perceived effect of the alcohol is to reduce stress, to help one forget, etc. The tendency is then to redefine oneself as "off the wagon" and "out of control," and behavior quickly follows suit. Naturally, this series of events may be all the more likely if one has been indoctrinated with the self-fulfilling prophesy of "one drink, then drunk."

An implicit assumption of the above description is that a dichotomous view of problem drinking contributes to the occurrence of relapse. However, proponents of the restricted disease model which perpetrates this view often refuse to discuss even the possibility of any drinking following treatment for fear that they will plant the seeds of destruction. This, of course, makes planning for the all too frequent eventuality of a lapse very difficult. Our approach, on the other hand, emphasizes preparation for all possible outcomes. Thus, if a drinking episode occurs, we want to be sure that its destructive aspects are minimized. Several techniques derived from the cognitive-behavioral or social learning paradigm have some promise for short-circuiting the relapse process.

While prevention of all relapses may be impossible, a first step in controlling them is to anticipate their occurrence and attempt to *limit the extent of drinking by establishing a therapeutic contact* which disrupts spontaneous patterns of abuse. Structuring an otherwise impulsive behavior can be helpful in demonstrating to clients that their drinking is often situationally controlled and that their urges will pass if given a chance. Naturally, clients are always asked to exercise restraint before "giving in" to seemingly irresistible desires for a first drink. An agreed on waiting period to reflect, reanalyze costs and benefits, change environments, let the momentary pressure die down, etc. sometimes can be profitably employed. Beyond this, the ideal contract would include agreement that the first drink be a single "dose," i.e., the client must procure his liquor by the drink (versus fifth, six pack, or whatever) to eliminate temptation to "finish off what's left." Finally, clients should be asked to delay at least an hour between the first and second drink. This not only breaks down well learned response chains, but also allows for the AVE to subside somewhat and permits a reappraisal of the decision to drink and the means of coping with the "high risk" situation. A few successful experiences with this procedure should raise expectations for self-efficacy and help prevent later relapses.

Since "forewarned is forearmed," clients should be apprised of what their reactions are likely to be after a first drink. A simple familiarization with and normalization of the AVE could go a long way in reducing its intensity. This also offers a chance for advanced practice in *cognitive restructuring* of the drinking "slip" so that it does not become a self-defeating opportunity to punish oneself or an excuse for further drinking. Instead of these catastrophizing and rationalizing thoughts, the objective and detached attitude toward behavior fostered by the social learning approach encourages conceptualization of *a drinking lapse as a learning experience*. Thus, it is viewed as a single, discrete and independent event which offers an opportunity to review antecedent decisions, cues, and other aspects of the "high risk" situation so that future encounters can be met with more adequate coping responses. Clients can also be asked to recall past experiences of successful resistance of drinking urges to prevent the generalization of this one slip into proof that a hopeless problem exists. Providing clients with a "reminder card" which outlines some of the above principles could be quite helpful in promoting self-statements which clarify thinking when distress is high.

A final relapse prevention strategy, consistent with the skills acquisition approach presented here, is the *programmed relapse*. This technique provides the client with a supervised experience of actual alcohol consumption. The rationale is that self-efficacy is best developed through performance-based treatments. Thus, if the client can learn for himself or herself that one drink need not mean a relapse, some of the cue value of alcohol for the response of "loss of control" drinking or relapse should be diminshed (cf. Hodgson & Rankin, 1976). We feel this method is probably most appropriate for clients who announce an intention to resume drinking anyway. The programmed relapse then at least permits the initial drinking to be done under optimal "low risk" conditions, rather than in an uncontrolled and potentially very stressful natural environment situation which might increase the probability of a full-blown relapse. An additional advantage of the programmed relapse is that it makes possible an explicit disconfirmation of expectations about the effects of alcohol. Before drinking, the client can be queried about what feelings are anticipated and then immediately afterward the validity of these beliefs can be tested. Often the actual experience does not live up to that which was expected so motivation for a return to drinking can be reduced. In any event, the programmed relapse seems an attractive alternative when compared to the potential for relapse when the client's indulgence is precipitated by a "high risk" situation.

In conclusion, the reader should be reminded that simply because the social learning approach plans for the possibility of posttreatment drinking does not mean it is synonymous with controlled drinking goals. On the contrary, many of the treatment methods described in this chapter are equally applicable to clients with abstinence goals. Given the high probability of some form of drinking lapse or relapse following treatment, however, it does not seem unproductive to expose problem drinkers to methods of controlling their drinking should they ever take the first swallow.

Concluding Comments. In our view, the social learning perspective presented here has as its principal virtue *flexibility*. It recognizes that "problem drinking" describes an incredibly diverse population no restrictive definition or unitary treatment can hope to accommodate. Our philosphy is that in the final analysis one must deal with individuals and honor their goals. Thus, we subcribe to a self-control approach entertaining treatment options which can be pursued independent of a static disease diagnosis. A detached and educative stance incorporating both cognitive and behavioral factors follows from our conceptualization of problem drinking as a maladaptive habit. This does not mean, however, that we reject disease models and their treatment methods out of hand. This cannot be done simply because the available data are so meager. We can only look forward to a new era of multidisciplinary empiricism which hopefully will integrate the biological, psychological, and social aspects of problem drinking in a way which is most beneficial to all. We would not be surprised to find that techniques based on diametrically opposed treatment assumptions might work equally well for different subpopulations of individuals. The challenge is to discover how to match individuals with the methods that suit them best. No such goal is likely to be accomplished unless we are willing to keep all avenues of exploration open.

REFERENCES

Alcoholics Anonymous World Services, *Alcoholics Anonymous*. New York: AA World Services, Inc., 1955.

American Psychiatric Association, *Diagnostic and statistical manual of mental disorders* (Third Edition), 1980.

Azrin, N. Improvements in the community reinforcement approach to alcoholism. *Behavior Research and Therapy*, 1976, *14*, 339–348.

Baekeland, F. Evaluation of treatment methods in chronic alcoholism. In B. Kissin & H. Begleiter (Eds.), *The biology of alcoholism* (Vol. 5). New York: Plenum, 1977.

Bandura, A. *Social learning theory*. Englewood Cliffs, N.J.: Prentice-Hall, 1977. (a)

Bandura, A. Self-efficacy: Toward a unifying theory of behavior change. *Psychological Review*, 1977, *84*, 191–215. (b)

Bebbington, P. The efficacy of Alcoholics Anonymous: The elusiveness of hard data. *British Journal of Psychiatry*, 1976, *128*, 572–580.

Beckman, L. An attributional analysis of Alcoholics Anonymous. *Journal of Studies on Alcohol*, 1980, *41*, 714–726.

Bernstein, D., & Borkovec, T. *Progressive relaxation training: A manual for helping professionals.* Champaign, IL: Research Press, 1973.

Brown, J., & Crowell, C. Alcohol and conflict resolution: A theoretical analysis. *Quarterly Journal of Studies on Alcohol,* 1974, *35,* 66–85.

Brown, S., Goldman, M., Inn, A., & Anderson, L. Expectations of reinforcement from alcohol: Their domain and relation to drinking patterns. *Journal of Consulting and Clinical Psychology,* 1980, *48,* 419–426.

Cahalan, D. *Problem drinkers.* San Francisco: Jossey-Bass, 1970.

Cahalan, D., & Cisin, I. Epidemiological and social problems associated with drinking problems. In R. Tarter & A. Sugerman (Eds.), *Alcoholism: Interdisciplinary approaches to an enduring problem.* Reading, MA: Addison-Wesley, 1976.

Cahalan, D., Cisin, I., & Crossley, H. *American drinking practices: A national study of drinking behavior and attitudes* (Monograph No. 6). New Brunswick: Rutgers Center of Alcohol Studies, 1969.

Cappell, H., & Herman, C. Alcohol and tension reduction: A review. *Quarterly Journal of Studies on Alcohol,* 1972, *33,* 33–64.

Carrington, P. *Freedom in meditation.* Garden City, N.Y.: Anchor/Doubleday, 1978.

Caudill, B., & Marlatt, G. Modeling influences in social drinking: An experimental analogue. *Journal of Consulting and Clinical Psychology,* 1975, *43,* 405–415.

Cautela, J. The treatment of alcoholism by covert sensitization. *Psychotherapy: Theory, research and practice,* 1970, *7,* 86–90.

Chaney, E., O'Leary, M., & Marlatt, G. Skill training with alcoholics. *Journal of Consulting and Clinical Psychology,* 1978, *46,* 1092–1104.

Clark, W., & Cahalan, D. Changes in problem drinking over a four year span. *Addictive Behaviors,* 1976, *1,* 251–259.

Conger, J. The effects of alcohol on conflict in the albino rat. *Quarterly Journal of Studies on Alcohol,* 1951, *12,* 1–29.

Conger, J. Reinforcement theory and the dynamics of alcoholism. *Quarterly Journal of Studies on Alcohol,* 1956, *17,* 296–305.

Cooper, A., Waterhouse, G., & Sobell, M. Influence of gender on drinking in a modeling situation. *Journal of Studies on Alcohol,* 1979, *40,* 562–570.

Cronkite, R., & Moos, E. Determinants of the post-treatment functioning of alcoholic patients. *Journal of Consulting and Clinical Psychology,* 1980, *48,* 305–316.

Davies, D. Normal drinking in recovered alcohol addicts. *Quarterly Journal of Studies on Alcohol,* 1962, *23,* 94–104.

Davies, D. Definitional issues in alcoholism. In R. Tarter & A. Sugerman (Eds.), *Alcoholism: Interdisciplinary approaches to an enduring problem.* Reading, MA: Addison-Wesley, 1976.

Engel, G. The need for a new medical model: A challenge for biomedicine. *Science,* 1977, *196,* 129–136.

Engle, K., & Williams, T. Effect of an ounce of vodka on alcoholics' desire for alcohol. *Quarterly Journal of Studies on Alcohol,* 1972, *33,* 1109–1105.

Ewing, J., Rouse, B., & Pellizzari, E. Alcohol sensitivity and ethnic background. *American Journal of Psychiatry,* 1974, *131,* 206–210.

Farber, P., Khavari, K., & Douglass, F. A factor analytic study of reasons for drinking: Empirical validation of positive and negative reinforcement dimensions. *Journal of Consulting and Clinical Psychology,* 1980, *48,* 780–781.

Farina, A., Fisher, J., Getter, H., & Fischer, E. Some consequences of changing peoples' views regarding the nature of mental illness. *Journal of Abnormal Psychology,* 1978, *87,* 272–279.

Finney, J., Moos, R., & Mewborn, C. Posttreatment experiences and treatment outcome of alcoholic patients six months and two years after hospitalization. *Journal of Consulting and Clinical Psychology,* 1980, *48,* 17–29.

Fisher, J., & Farina, A. Consequences of beliefs about the nature of mental disorders. *Journal of Abnormal Psychology,* 1979, *88,* 320-327.

Frank, J. *Persuasion and healing* (2nd Ed.). Baltimore: Johns Hopkins University Press, 1975.

Freed, E. *An alcoholic personality?* Thorofare, N.J.: Charles B. Slack, 1979.

Gabel, P., Noel, N., Keane, T., & Lisman, S. Effects of sexual versus fear arousal on alcohol consumption in college males. *Behaviour Research and Therapy,* 1980, *18,* 519-526.

Galanter, M. The "intoxication state of consciousness": A model for alcohol and drug abuse. *American Journal of Psychiatry,* 1976, *133,* 635-640.

Garfield, S., & Bergin, A. (Eds.). *Handbook of psychotherapy and behavior change: An empirical analysis* (2nd Edition). New York: Wiley, 1978.

Gerard, D., Saenger, G., & Wile, R. The abstinent alcoholic. *Archives of General Psychiatry,* 1962, *6,* 83-95.

Glasser, W. *Positive addiction.* New York: Harper & Row, 1976.

Goodwin, D. Alcoholism and heredity: A review and hypothesis. *Archives of General Psychiatry,* 1979, *36,* 57-61.

Griffiths, R., Bigelow, G., & Liebson, I. The relationship of social factors to ethanol self-administration in alcoholics. In P. Nathan, G. Marlatt, & T. Lorberg (Eds.), *Alcoholism: New directions in behavioral research and treatment.* New York: Plenum, 1978.

Hamburg, S. Behavior therapy in alcoholism: A critical review of broad spectrum approaches. *Journal of Studies on Alcohol,* 1975, *36,* 69-87.

Hersen, M., & Bellack, A. (Eds.). *Behavioral assessment: A practical handbook.* New York: Pergamon Press, 1976.

Higgins, R. Experimental investigations of tension reduction models of alcoholism. In G. Goldstein & C. Neuringer (Eds.), *Empirical studies of alcoholism.* Cambridge: Ballinger, 1976.

Higgins, R., & Marlatt, G. Effects of anxiety arousal on the consumption of alcohol by alcoholics and social drinkers. *Journal of Consulting and Clinical Psychology,* 1973, *41,* 426-433.

Higgins, R., & Marlatt, G. Fear of interpersonal evaluation as a determinant of alcohol consumption in male social drinkers. *Journal of Abnormal Psychology,* 1975, *84,* 644-651.

Hinson, R., & Siegel, S. The contribution of Pavlovian conditioning to ethanol tolerance and dependence. In H. Rigter & J. Crabbe (Eds.), *Alcohol tolerance, dependence and addiction.* Amsterdam: Elsevier/North Holland Biomedical Press, 1980.

Hodgson, R., & Rankin, H. Modification of excessive drinking by cue exposure. *Behavior Research and Therapy,* 1976, *14,* 305-307.

Holroyd, K. Effects of social anxiety and social evaluation on beer consumption and social interaction. *Journal of Studies on Alcohol,* 1978, *39,* 737-744.

Hunt, G., & Azrin, N. A community reinforcement approach to alcoholism. *Behavior Research and Therapy,* 1973, *11,* 91-104.

Jacobson, G. *Diagnosis and assessment of alcohol abuse and alcoholism.* Rockville, MD: NIAAA/DHEW Publication No. (ADM) 75-228, 1975.

Jellinek, E. *The disease concept of alcoholism.* New Haven, CT: College and University Press, 1960.

Jones, B., & Vega, A. Cognitive performance measured on the ascending and descending limbs of the blood-alcohol curve. *Psychopharmacologia,* 1972, *23,* 99-114.

Kalin, R. Social drinking in different settings. In D. McClelland, W. Davis, R. Kalin, & E. Wanner (Eds.), *The drinking man.* N.Y.: Free Press, 1972.

Keller, M. On the loss-of-control phenomenon in alcoholism. *British Journal of Addiction,* 1972, *67,* 153-166.

Keller, M. The disease concept of alcoholism revisited. *Journal of Studies on Alcohol,* 1976, *37,* 1694-1717.

Kitson, T. The disulfiram-ethanol reaction: A review. *Journal of Studies on Alcohol,* 1977, *38,* 96-113.

Korsten, M. & Lieber, C. Medical complications of alcoholism: Hepatic system. In R. Tartar & A. Sugerman (Eds.), *Alcoholism: Interdisciplinary approaches to an enduring problem*. Reading, Massachusetts: Addison-Wesley, 1976.

Lang, A., Goeckner, D., Adesso, V., & Marlatt, A. Effects of alcohol on aggression in male social drinkers. *Journal of Abnormal Psychology*, 1975, *84*, 508-518.

Lazarus, A. Towards the understanding and effective treatment of alcoholism. *South African Medical Journal*, 1965, *39*, 736-741.

Leach, B. Does Alcoholics Anonymous really work? In P. Bourne & R. Fox (Eds.), *Alcoholism: Progress in research and treatment*. New York: Academic Press, 1973.

Lemere, F., & Voegtlin, W. An evaluation of the aversion treatment of alcoholism. *Quarterly Journal of Studies on Alcohol*, 1950, *11*, 199-204.

Lied, E., & Marlatt, G. Modeling as a determinant of alcohol consumption: Effects of sex of subject and prior drinking history. *Addictive Behaviors*, 1979, *4*, 37-54.

Lipscomb, T., & Nathan, P. Blood alcohol level discrimination: The effects of family history, drinking pattern and tolerance. *Archives of General Psychiatry*, 1980, *37*, 571-576.

Litman, G., Eiser, J., Rawson, N., & Oppenheim, A. Difference in relapse precipitants and coping behavior between alcohol relapsers and survivors. *Behavior Research and Therapy*, 1979, *17*, 89-94.

Litman, G., Eiser, J., & Taylor, C. Dependence, relapse and extinction: A theoretical critique and a behavioral examination. *Journal of Clinical Psychology*, 1979, *35*, 192-199.

Lloyd, R., & Salzberg, H. Controlled social drinking: An alternative to abstinence as a treatment goal for some alcohol abusers. *Psychological Bulletin*, 1975, *82*, 815-842.

Lovibond, S., & Caddy, G. Discriminated aversive control in the moderation of alcoholics' drinking behavior. *Behavior Therapy*, 1970, *1*, 437-444.

MacAndrew, C. On the notion that certain persons who are given to frequent drunkenness suffer from a disease called alcoholism. In S. Plog & R. Edgerton (Eds.), *Changing perspectives in mental illness*. New York: Holt, 1969.

Maisto, S., Sobell, L., & Sobell, M. Comparison of alcoholics' self-reports of drinking behavior with reports of collateral informants. *Journal of Consulting and Clinical Psychology*, 1979, *47*, 106-112.

Marlatt, G. Alcohol, stress and cognitive control. In C. Spielberger & I. Sarason (Eds.), *Stress and anxiety* (Vol. 3). Washington, D.C.: Hemisphere Publishing, 1976. (a)

Marlatt, G. The drinking profile: A questionnaire for the behavioral assessment of alcoholism. In E. Mash & L. Terdal (Eds.), *Behavior therapy assessment: Diagnosis, design, and evaluation*. New York: Springer, 1976. (b)

Marlatt, G. Craving for alcohol, loss of control and relapse: A cognitive-behavioral analysis. In P. Nathan, G. Marlatt, & T. Lorberg (Eds.), *Alcoholism: New directions in behavioral research and treatment*. New York: Plenum, 1978. (a)

Marlatt, G. Behavioral assessment of social drinking and alcoholism. In G. Marlatt & P. Nathan (Eds.), *Behavioral approaches to alcoholism*. New Brunswick, N.J.: *Journal of Studies on Alcohol Inc.*, 1978. (b)

Marlatt, G. Alcohol use and problem drinking: A cognitive-behavioral analysis. In P. Kendall & S. Hollon (Eds.), *Cognitive-behavioral interventions: Theory, research, and procedures*. New York: Academic Press, 1979.

Marlatt, G. Relapse prevention: A self-control program for addictive behaviors. Unpublished manuscript, University of Washington, 1980.

Marlatt, G. The drinking history: Problems of validity and reliability. In NIAAA (Ed.), *Evaluation of the alcoholic*. Rockville, Maryland: Research Monograph Series, 1981.

Marlatt, G., Demming, B., & Reid, J. Loss of control drinking in alcoholics: An experimental analogue. *Journal of Abnormal Psychology*, 1973, *81*, 233-241.

Marlatt, G., & Gordon, L. Determinants of relapse: Implications for the maintenance of behavior change. In P. Davidson & S. Davidson (Eds.), *Behavioral medicine: Changing health lifestyles.* New York: Brunner/Mazel, 1980.

Marlatt, G., Kosturn, C., & Lang, A. Provocation to anger and opportunity for retaliation as determinants of alcohol consumption in social drinkers. *Journal of Abnormal Psychology,* 1975, *84,* 652–659.

Marlatt, G., & Marques, J. Meditation, self-control and alcohol use. In R. Stuart (Ed.), *Behavioral self-management.* New York: Brunner/Mazel, 1977.

Marlatt, G., & Rohsenow, D. Cognitive processes in alcohol use: Expectancy and the balanced placebo design. In N. Mello (Ed.), *Advances in substance abuse: Behavioral and biological research.* Greenwich: JAI Press, 1980.

Masserman, J., & Yum, K. An analysis of the influence of alcohol on experimental neurosis in cats. *Psychosomatic Medicine,* 1946, *8,* 36–52.

McClelland, D., David, W., Kalin, R., & Wanner, E. *The drinking man.* New York: Free Press, 1972.

McFall, R. Behavior training: A skill acquisition approach to clinical problems. In J. Spence, R. Carson, & J. Thibaut (Eds.), *Behavioral approaches to therapy.* Morristown, NJ: General Learning Press, 1975.

McFall, R. Parameters of self-monitoring. In R. Stuart (Ed.), *Behavioral self management: Strategies, techniques, and outcomes.* New York: Brunner/Mazel, 1977.

McNamee, H., Mello, N., & Mendelson, J. Experimental analysis of drinking patterns of alcoholics: Concurrent psychiatric observations. *American Journal of Psychiatry,* 1968, *124,* 1063–1069.

Meichenbaum, D. *Cognitive-behavior modification.* New York: Plenum, 1977.

Mello, N. Some aspects of the behavioral pharmacology of alcohol. In D. Efron (Ed.), *Psychopharmacology: A review of progress 1957–1967.* Washington: Public Health Service Publication No 1836, 1968.

Mello, N. Behavioral studies of alcoholism. In B. Kissin & H. Begleiter (Eds.), *The biology of alcoholism* (Vol. 2), 1972.

Mello, N., & Mendelson, J. Alcohol and human behavior. In L. Iversen, S. Iversen, & S. Snyder (Eds.), *Handbook of psychopharmacology* (Vol. 12). New York: Plenum, 1978.

Mendelson, J. Ethanol metabolism in alcoholics and nonalcoholics. *Science,* 1968, *159,* 319–320.

Mendelson, J., & Mello, N. A disease as an organizer for biochemical research: Alcoholism. In A. Mandell & M. Mandell (Eds.), *Psychochemical Research in Man.* New York: Academic Press, 1969.

Merry, J. The "loss of control" myth. *Lancet,* 1966, *1,* 1257–1268.

Miller, P. A behavioral intervention program for chronic public drunkenness offenders. *Archives of General Psychiatry,* 1975, *32,* 915–918.

Miller, P., Becker, J., Foy, D., & Wooten, L. Instructional control of the components of alcoholic drinking behavior. *Behavior Therapy,* 1976, *7,* 472–480.

Miller, P., Hersen, M., Eisler, R., & Elkin, T. A retrospective analysis of alcohol consumption on laboratory tasks as related to therapeutic outcome. *Behavior Research and Therapy,* 1974, *12,* 73–76.

Miller, P., Hersen, M., Eisler, R., & Hemphill, D. Electrical aversion therapy with alcoholics: An analogue study. *Behavior Research and Therapy,* 1973, *11,* 491–497.

Miller, P., Hersen, M., Eisler, R., & Hilsman, M. Effects of social stress on operant drinking of alcoholics and social drinkers. *Behavior Research and Therapy,* 1974, *12,* 67–72.

Miller, P., & Mastria, M. *Alternatives to alcohol abuse: A social learning model.* Champaign, IL: Research Press, 1977.

Miller, W. Alcoholism scales and objective assessment methods: A review. *Psychological Bulletin,* 1976, *83,* 649–674.

Miller, W. Behavioral treatment of problem drinkers: A comparative outcome study of three controlled drinking therapies. *Journal of Consulting and Clinical Psychology*, 1978, *46*, 74–86.

Miller, W., & Caddy, G. Abstinence and controlled drinking in the treatment of problem drinkers. *Journal of Studies on Alcohol*, 1977, *38*, 986–1003.

Miller, W., & Joyce, M. Prediction of abstinence, controlled drinking, and heavy drinking outcomes following behavioral self-control training. *Journal of Consulting and Clinical Psychology*, 1979, *47*, 773–775.

Miller, W., & Munoz, R. *How to control your drinking*. Englewood Cliffs, N.J.: Prentice-Hall, 1976.

Miller, W., Taylor, C., & West, J. Focused versus broad-spectrum behavior therapy for problem drinkers. *Journal of Consulting & Clinical Psychology*, 1980, *48*, 590–601.

Mills, K., Sobell, M., & Schaefer, H. Training social drinking as an alternative to abstinence for alcoholics. *Behavior Therapy*, 1971, *2*, 18–27.

Morse, W., & Kelleher, R. Determinants of reinforcement and punishment. In W. K. Honig & J. Staddon (Eds.), *Operant Behavior* (Vol. 2). Englewood Cliffs, NJ: Prentice-Hall, 1977.

Nathan, P., & Briddell, D. Behavioral assessment and treatment of alcoholism. In B. Kissin & H. Begleiter (Eds.), *Biology of alcoholism* (Vol. 5). New York: Plenum, 1977.

Nathan, P., & Goldman, M. Problem drinking and alcoholism. In O. Pomerleau & J. Brady (Eds.), *Behavioral medicine: Therapy and practice*. Baltimore: Williams and Wilkins, 1979.

Nathan, P., & Lansky, D. Common methodological problems in research on the addictions. *Journal of Consulting and Clinical Psychology*, 1978, *4*, 713–726. (a)

Nathan, P., & Lansky, D. Management of the chronic alcoholics: A behavioral viewpoint. In J. Brady & H. Brodie (Eds.), *Controversy in psychiatry*. Philadelphia: Saunders, 1978. (b)

National Institute of Alcohol Abuse and Alcoholism. *Alcohol and health: Third report to Congress*. Washington, D.C.: U.S. Government Printing Office, 1978.

Noel, N., & Lisman, S. Alcohol consumption by college women following exposure to unsolvable problems: Learned helplessness or stress-induced drinking? *Behaviour Research and Therapy*, 1980, *18*, 429–440.

Orcutt, J., & Cairl, R. Social definitions of the alcoholic: Reassessing the importance of imputed responsibility. *Journal of Health and Social Behavior*, 1979, *20*, 290–295.

Paolino, T., & McCrady, B. *The alcoholic marriage*. New York: Grune & Stratton, 1977.

Pattison, E., Headley, E., Gleser, G., & Gottschalk, L. Abstinence and normal drinking: An assessment of changes in drinking patterns in alcoholics after treatment. *Quarterly Journal of Studies on Alcohol*, 1968, *29*, 610–633.

Pattison, E., Sobel, M., & Sobell, L. (Eds.). *Emerging concepts of alcohol dependence*. New York: Springer, 1977.

Pliner, P., & Cappell, H. Modification of affective consequences of alcohol: A comparison of social and solitary drinking. *Journal of Abnormal Psychology*, 1974, *83*, 418–425.

Polich, M., Armor, D., & Braiker, H. Patterns of alcoholism over four years. *Journal of Studies on Alcohol*, 1980, *41*, 397–416.

Pomerleau, O., Pertschuk, M., Adkins, D., & d'Aquili, E. Treatment of middle income problem drinkers. In P. Nathan, G. Marlatt, & T. Lorberg (Eds.), *Alcoholism: New directions in behavioral research and treatment*. New York: Plenum, 1978.

Reid, J. Study of drinking in natural settings. In G. Marlatt & P. Nathan (Eds.), *Behavioral approaches to alcoholism*. New Brunswick, NJ: Rutgers Center of Alcohol Studies, 1978.

Rimm, D., & Masters, J. *Behavior therapy: Techniques and empirical findings* (2nd edition). New York: Academic Press, 1979.

Roizen, R., Cahalan, D., & Shanks, P. "Spontaneous remission" among untreated problem drinkers. In D. Kandel (Ed.), *Longitudinal research in drug use; empirical findings and methodological issues*. New York: Wiley, 1978.

Roman, P., & Trice, H. The sick role, labeling theory and the deviant drinker. *International Journal of Social Psychiatry*, 1968, *14*, 245–251.

Russell, J., & Bond, C. Beliefs among college students on settings and emotions conducive to alcohol and marijuana use. *International Journal of the Addictions*, 1979, *14*, 997–986.

Schaefer, H., Sobell, M., & Mills, K. Baseline drinking behavior in alcoholics and social drinkers: Kinds of drinks and sip magnitude. *Behavior Research and Therapy*, 1971, *9*, 23–27.

Shapiro, A., Nathan, P., Hay, W., & Lipscomb, T. Influence of dosage level on blood alcohol level discrimination by alcoholics. *Journal of Consulting and Clinical Psychology*, 1980, *48*, 655–666.

Silverstein, S., Nathan, P., & Taylor, H. Blood alcohol level discrimination and controlled drinking by chronic alcoholics. *Behavior Therapy*, 1974, *5*, 1–15.

Sobell, L., & Sobell, M. Outpatient alcoholics give valid self-reports. *Journal of Nervous and Mental Disease*, 1975, *161*, 32–42.

Sobell, L., & Sobell, M. Validity of self-reports in three populations of alcoholics. *Journal of Consulting and Clinical Psychology*, 1978, *46*, 901–907. (b)

Sobell, M. Alternatives to abstinence: Evidence, issues, and some proposals. In P. Nathan, G. Marlatt, & T. Lorberg (Eds.), *Alcoholism: New directions in behavioral research and treatment*. New York: Plenum, 1978.

Sobell, M., & Sobell, L. Individualized behavior therapy for alcoholics. *Behavior Therapy*, 1973, *4*, 49–72.

Sobell, M., & Sobell, L. Second year treatment outcome of alcoholics treated by individualized behavior therapy: Results. *Behavior Research and Therapy*, 1976, *14*, 195–215.

Sobell, M., & Sobell, L. *Behavioral treatment of alcohol problems*. New York: Plenum, 1978. (a)

Steffen, J., Nathan, P., & Taylor, H. Tension reducing effects of alcohol: Further evidence and some methodological considerations. *Journal of Abnormal Psychology*, 1974, *83*, 542–547.

Sterne, M., & Pittman, D. The concept of motivation: A source of institutional and professional blockage in the treatment of alcoholism. *Quarterly Journal of Studies on Alcohol*, 1965, *26*, 41–57.

Summers, T. Validity of alcoholics' self-reported drinking history. *Quarterly Journal of Studies on Alcohol*, 1970, *31*, 972–974.

Vogler, R., Compton, J., & Weissbach, T. Integrated behavior change techniques for alcoholics. *Journal of Consulting and Clinical Psychology*, 1975, *43*, 233–243.

Vogler, R., Weissbach, T., & Compton, J. Learning techniques for alcohol abuse. *Behavior Research and Therapy*, 1977, *15*, 31–38.

Vogler, R., Weissbach, T., Compton, J., & Martin, G. Integrated behavior change techniques for problem drinkers in the community. *Journal of Consulting and Clinical Psychology*, 1977, *45*, 267–279.

Wiens, A., Montague, J., Manaugh, T., & English, C. Pharmacological aversive conditioning to alcohol in a private hospital: One year follow-up. *Journal of Studies on Alcohol*, 1976, *37*, 1320–1324.

Williams, A. Social drinking, anxiety and depression. *Journal of Personality and Social Psychology*, 1966, *3*, 689–693.

Wilson, G. T. Booze, beliefs and behavior: Cognitive processes in alcohol use and abuse. In P. E. Nathan, G. A. Marlatt, & T. Lorberg (Eds.), *Alcoholism: New Directions in behavioral research and treatment*. New York: Plenum, 1978. (a)

Wilson, G. Alcoholism and aversion therapy: Issues, ethics, and evidence. In G. Marlatt & P. Nathan (Eds.), *Behavioral approaches to alcoholism*. New Brunswick, NJ: Journal of Studies on Alcohol, 1978. (b)

Wilson, G., & Abrams, D. Effects of alcohol on social anxiety: Cognitive versus pharmacological processes. *Cognitive Therapy and Research*, 1977, *1*, 195–210.

Wilson, G., & Lawson, D. Expectancies, alcohol and sexual arousal in male social drinkers. *Journal of Abnormal Psychology*, 1976, *85*, 587–594.

Wilson, G., Leaf, R., & Nathan, P. The aversive control of excessive drinking by chronic alcoholics in the laboratory setting. *Journal of Applied Behavior Analysis*, 1975, *8*, 13–26.

6 Changing Smoking Behavior: A Critique

William A. Hunt
Loyola University
Chicago, Illinois

Joseph D. Matarazzo
University of Oregon School of Medicine
Portland, Oregon

INTRODUCTION

The burgeoning of concern over the health consequences of smoking tobacco has resulted in an increased interest in the part the behavioral sciences can play in the control of smoking behavior. The last 2 years alone have seen at least six reviews of the field in the various books on behavioral medicine (Bernstein & Glasgow, 1979; Glasgow & Bernstein, 1981; Pechacek, 1979; Pechacek & Danaher, 1979; Pechacek & McAlister, 1980; Pomerleau, 1979) not to mention the monumental Surgeon General's report of 1979 which deals with all aspects of the tobacco problem. Some 60 authors are listed with innumerable consultants, each chapter has an exhaustive bibliography; and the volume as a whole has a cross-referenced index of some 64 pages (Califano, 1979).

It is not the intent of the present treatment to compete with the comprehensiveness of the Surgeon General's report, but rather to present an updated critical and evaluative overview of the field drawing upon the extant experimental evidence and where this is lacking risking a measured judgment based upon experience and common sense.

Throughout its long history the smoking of tobacco has had both its proponents and opponents. Among the latter were many prominent medical men of their time, but it took modern epidemiological methods to provide the specific statistical data to drive home the lesson that tobacco is indeed injurious to human health (Van Lanaker, 1977). With the report of the Surgeon General's Advisory committee on Smoking and Health on January 11, 1964 smoking officially graduated from a dirty messy, unhealthy habit to status as a major health hazard making an impressive contribution to human morbidity. The January, 1979 report of the Surgeon General brings the evidence up to date and fully documents the health implication of the smoking habit. As Joseph Califano, then Secretary of Health, Education, and Welfare, remarked when he forwarded the 1979 Surgeon General's report to Congress, smoking is "slow motion suicide." Briefly, the overall mortality ratio for male cigarette smokers is 70% in excess of that for non-smokers.

Lung cancer occupied much of the early attention to the smoking problem no doubt due to the active program instigated by the American Cancer Society, but cardiology was not far behind and today coronary heart disease is found to be the leading contributor to the excess mortality of cigarette smokers with lung cancer and chronic obstructive lung disease following after. Van Lanaker (1977) provided a concise discussion of the disease picture and the Surgeon General's report of 1979 offers an expanded and detailed review.

It is not our purpose to go into the details but a summary of some of the more important findings in the 1979 report is in order. The mortality ratios for smokers increase with amount smoked, duration of smoking, age at beginning, practice of inhalation, and tar and nicotine content; but decrease for former smokers as a function of years of discontinuance. The increase for cigar smokers is less than for cigarette smokers, possibly because of less inhalation, and pipe smoking shows only a slight effect. Sex differences at present are unclear. Moreover the health problems related to cigarette smoking are not limited to mortality as smoking can be shown to be related to illness, disability, and other health indicators. Thus, smokers report more chronic conditions such as chronic bronchitis, emphysema, sinusitis, peptic ulcer, and arteriosclerotic heart disease than non-smokers, and this relationship is dependent upon the amount of smoking. Smokers also show a higher rate of such other indirect measures of illness as work-days lost, days in bed, and limitation of activity. Soldatis, Kales, Scharf, Bixler, and Kales (1980) related these to difficulty in sleeping.

The exact causal relationships in many chronic conditions are as yet unclear. Thus smokers show a risk of dying from peptic ulcer which is twice that of non-smokers although the specific etiological relationship is at present unknown. In this instance, however, recent data would indicate that smoking may have some effect on pancreatic secretion and pyloric reflux. The exact relation of this to ulcer development, however, is not as yet known (Califano, 1979).

The general problem here is the old statistical difficulty with the method of correlation—although the co-relationship of two phenomena is a necessary consequence of any causal relationship, the mere establishment of a co-relationship is no guarantee of a causal relationship per se. As Vogt (1977) states it in medical terms, "Epidemiologically some of the diseases associated with smoking have not been shown to be etiologically related.'' It behooves us to remember his caution that, ''It is, perhaps, unwise to assume that the entire excess risk of disease in smokers is a result of their smoking'' (p. 228). The evidence to date, however, is overwhelmingly positive that smoking is a danger to human health, sometimes as an etiological factor in disease, although sometimes as in chronic symptoms (Liard, Perdrizet, Correman, & Bidau, 1980) it is a contributing factor.

In the last few years interest has extended beyond the health risk to the smoker per se to the passive victim of someone else's smoking (i.e., Sebben, Pimm, & Shepard, 1977) and active legislative steps have been taken to restrict smoking in enclosed public areas. While the actual extent of the health risk involved is still largely unknown there is no doubt of the personal discomfort and irritation experienced by the non-smoker under such circumstances (Weber, Fischer, & Grandjean 1979). Pachman and Frederiksen (1979) have tried a ''Yes I do mind'' program of social skills training for non-smokers to help in asserting their rights and controlling smoking behavior in their friends. Such restriction of smoking areas and occasions not only rescues the non-smoker from the predicament but offers a means of behavioral control by reducing the smoker's opportunity to indulge in the habit. A review of the problem of polutants in enclosed spaces is provided by Sterling and Kobayashe (1977). Again we must remember that tobacco is not the sole contributor to such pollution, nor is it the only contributor to health risk as Frederiksen and Martin (1979) point out in discussing carbon monoxide level and its relation to an individual's smoking pattern.

The USPHS Center for Disease Control in Atlanta issues yearly bulletins on the progress of State legislative actions in this and other smoking areas. Such legislative action seems particularly promising since the public has always resisted prohibition but seems at least grudgingly amenable to restriction, and official legislative action also has the effect of placing public opinion and social approval obviously and concretely behind the move to limit smoking, thus increasing the social pressures on the smoker.

That the tobacco industry is aware of the threat the health problem poses to the industry is evidenced by the continuing development of low tar and low nicotine popular brands which are capturing an increasing share of the market. The net benefit, however, may not be as great as was hoped for as smokers may compensate and balance their nicotine intake by increasing their consumption of low content cigarettes. Women seem more sensitive to nicotine and therefore more apt to suffer unpleasant effects early in smoking. Bennett (1980) suggests that low nicotine cigarettes may ease the introduction of women into smoking and help them in the early stages of developing tolerance to nicotine. In such cases he suggests that low content cigarettes may be the pharmacologic equivalent of the teenage training bra. Few of these complex problems as yet have evoked clear evidence to aid in resolving them.

The USPHS Office on Smoking and Health has recently extended its interest to the coverage of scientific and technical information found in the patents literature. It devotes its entire April 1980 issue of the Smoking and Health Bulletin to the pertinent patents granted between 1975 and 1979 stressing agents applied or added during the growth, curing or manufacturing of tobacco; alteration by chemical, mechanical, or biologic means; the use of tobacco substitutes; and the development of aids to cessation. The issue has 23 patents listed involving tobacco constituent alteration, 61 additives, and 31 on substitute materials. The 31 concerned with aids to cessation include devices to control the availability of cigarettes to the smoker and controlling the temporal rate of delivery. In the future such coverage will be routinely included in the Bulletin.

Extensive discussion of some of these issues will be found in Gori and Bock (1980).

EXTENT OF TOBACCO USE

The data on the extent of tobacco usage are open to the difficulties inherent in the use of retrospective reportage, but clear trends are obvious. The size of the trend is shown by the fact that 1 out of every 3 *adults* is a smoker with a total consumption of some 350 billion cigarettes per year although per capita consumption was about 11% less in 1978 than in 1963. The proportion of adult *male* smokers has declined from 53% in 1955 to 36% in 1979. Adult *females* increased from 25% in 1955 to 34% in 1966, when they began to reverse their upward trend, and fell to 29% in 1979 (Harris, 1981, p. 212–213). Smoking among teenagers did not follow a similar trend, however. Rather, between 1968–1974 smoking in 12–18-year-old *girls* increased from 8.4% to 15.3%; while smoking in 12–18-year-old *boys* remained relatively stable (14.7% to 15.8%) during the same 6 year interval (Harris, 1980, p. 36). Interestingly, the just published latest figures show a decrease in smoking for both boys and girls. Specifically, the 1979 figures reveal that only 10.7% boys and 12.7% girls in the 12–18-year-old range are current smokers; (*Sunday Oregonian,* January 25, 1981, p. 5). Reviews of the data on usage may be found in Schuman (1977), Green (1979), Moss (1979) and Harris (1980; 1981). To risk a generalization, one may hazard that the battle against smoking continues to make good headway among adult males, is beginning to show signs of decreasing numbers among adult females, and shows positive signs of reversing itself among both teenage girls and teenage boys. Data collected over the next several years will reveal the degree of confidence one should place in these seemingly clear reversals in smoking levels among children and adult age groups.

The figures on cessation are interesting. Over one-half of the current smokers have made at least one serious attempt to stop. In 1978 one out of five smokers attempting to quit were successful. Current smokers have made more unsuccessful attempts than ex-smokers did in their pre-cessation period, merely reflecting the fact that some smokers quit more easily than others. Green (1979) makes the significant point moreover that there has been a great increase in those people not liking smoking in others, even one third of actual smokers participating in this attitude. This represents a rising public opinion against smoking and should increase the public pressure on the smoker to quit as well as reinforcing public measures for its restriction.

The Status of Treatment

The preceding material leaves no doubt about the importance and the enormity of the problem. How well are we meeting it? The differential evaluation of specific types of treatment will be handled later, but first a look at the overall picture. There is no standard form for reporting success or failure for a treatment program (some programs even do not bother to report), but a frequent practice is to report the number of graduates from a cessation program that remain abstemious over a stated period of time. Such data are of course open to all the criticisms mentioned by Bernstein (1969) such as small samples, selection of subjects, poor reporting, poor controls, etc. and must be used with caution.

Hunt, Barnett, and Branch (1971) gathered some 84 studies in the literature that reported the number of subjects successfully completing treatment and that recorded the number of those subjects that returned to smoking over a period of time, usually recorded in terms of 3-month periods. The data offer the "relapse" curve shown in fig. 6.1. It is interesting to note the similarity of the smoking relapse curve to those for alcohol and heroin. With much larger samples Hunt and General (1973) have confirmed this finding for alcoholism, and Hunt and Bespalec for heroin (1974). A subsequent study by Hunt and Bespalec (1974) offers further confirmation in the smoking field. Carmody, Senner, Malinow, and Matarazzo (1980) report a like phenomenon for compliance to a physical exercise rehabilitation program, and mention it as typical phenomenon in the field. In any case frequent recidivism in the first 3 months following treatment seems typical of most programs to change a person's health life style.

These negatively accelerated relapse curves led Hunt and Matarazzo (1970) to comment on their resemblance to extinction curves in learning, with a new behavior replacing an old, but with the newer extinguishing over time, leaving the older, better established behavior in command again. This suggestion was made more on the basis of its compatibility with contemporary learning theory than on the dubious basis of the curve itself.

The most interesting aspect of these curves is their shape and not the negative acceleration. They all show a steep slope indicating the greatest amount of relapse during the first 3 months after treatment, a pronounced break around 6 months as the curve begins to asymptote, and an apparent asymptote with somewhere between 20% and 30% of the subjects remaining abstemious. These peculiarities of shape suggest that the typical curve may be a composite of two underlying functions, one governing the early part with its sharp decline, the

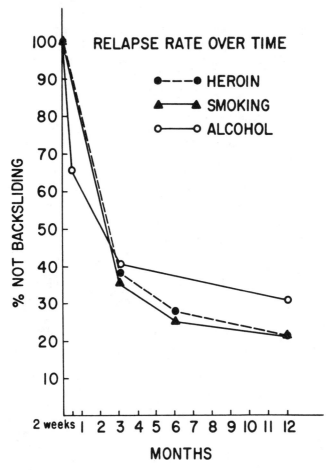

FIG. 6.1.   Relapse rate for addictive behaviors following treatment. Published with permission of *Journal of Clinical Psychology* (Hunt et al., 1971).

other the later, plateauing part as it approaches asymptote. If this is so this raises the suggestion that we may have two kinds of learning or two kinds of people involved. This of course, is only an interesting possibility but both alternatives seem compatible with present thinking.

Sutton (1979) and Litman, Eiser, and Taylor (1979) have objected to the use of such curves, pointing out that the use of cumulative relapse curves will almost always give a downward sloping negatively accelerated curve. This is obvious and Hunt and Matarazzo in suggesting a positive relation to an extinction process were going well beyond the evidence of such survival curves. Sutton further butresses his criticism by drawing a similar survival curve with data based upon survival over the first four years of life in Wales, but he does this by changing the actual coordinates on which the Hunt et al. data are plotted. The interesting aspect of the Hunt et al. survival curves is the fact that they show the same peculiarity when different sets of data from three different areas are plotted upon the *same* coordinates.

The Litman et al. objection adds the criticism that such curves are composite curves based upon group data and conceal individual differences. The use of such composite curves, however, does not reflect a deliberate disregard of such individual data but rather their relative paucity in reportage in the field where the composite survival report has been the typical method of evaluative reporting. Individual data and attention to individual differences is necessary for any complete understanding of the problem and one can only hope that as the field advances and matures its progress will be marked by more complex reportage that will shed light on the individual differences in behavior that are masked by the use of composite data. In any case the information provided by such data, however fallible it may be, supports the present trend to strengthen our treatment programs and to pay more attention to the maintenance of new health behaviors once they are acquired.

In a related vein Frederiksen (1976) has advocated the experimental use of single-case designs claiming that they are more flexible; treatment variables may be explored before they are frozen into a costly, fixed group design; subject differences are highlighted; and a fine grained analysis results in which the individual is not lost in the group mean. They may be replicated subsequently in large group designs. Frederiksen views the single-case approach as offering ''a much needed link between uncontrolled pilot work and speculation on one hand and large unwieldy group designs on the other.''

Response to the Problem

While the problem is tremendous, the response to it has been equally tremendous and has produced a spate of theoretical and experimental publication that shows little sign of abating and has resulted in what McFall (1978) wryly calls a ''secondary publishing enterprise consisting of periodic literature reviews'' (p. 703). The Bibliography on Smoking and Health for 1979 lists 113 titles in the area of cessation methods. The increasing interest in behavioral medicine, e.g. the establishment of the *Journal of Behavioral Medicine* in 1978, and the increasing participation of the social sciences and psychology in particular in the establishment of what might be called a health sciences field (Matarazzo 1980, 1981), will do nothing to decrease the flood of publication as the new field seeks to develop its identity and establish itself as a professional area.

The effort, tremendous as it has been, has by no means been concerted. It remains a fragmented melange of sometimes overlapping, sometimes isolated theoretical orientations and methodological attempts at behavior change. In part this fragmentation represents the age-old separation between the scholarsystematist whose research and experimentation furnish the basic materials from which a treatment package can be fabricated and the behavioral engineer or clinician-therapist that must develop the specific treatment program and put it in action. This in turn is fanned by scholarly systematic rivalries and professional competition.

It was an attempt to break this isolation that led the Committee on Tobacco Habituation of the American Cancer Society in 1969 and 1972 (Hunt, 1970, 1973) to sponsor two small conferences of "learning people" and "smoking people" for a free interchange of ideas rather than the development of any specific program of research or treatment. In 1972 a more ambitious, industry-sponsored conference was held by the Council for Tobacco Research U.S.A. Inc. (Dunn 1973). Subsequently the conference has become a popular means of promoting the exchange of ideas but usually with a more specific, evaluative goal, and under governmental sponsorship.

With the inclusion of smoking behavior in many of the multiple risk studies now being conducted in the health field such as the Stanford Heart Disease Prevention program (Maccoby, Farquhar, Wood, & Alexander, 1977) and the University of Oregon Medical School Family Heart Study (Matarazzo, Connor, Fey, Carmody, Pierce, Brischetto, Baker, Connor, & Sexton, 1981) some of this isolation should disappear and better and more integrated longitudinal data be available. Longitudinal data is not yet available from this latter study, but the preliminary findings indicate that the smoker is biomedically less healthy on plasma cholesterol levels, drinks more coffee, and reports more problems with alcohol than does the ex-smoker or nonsmoker. In particular the inclusion of smoking behavior in broader studies including other risk factors should give us more information concerning the interaction of the various forms of substance abuse (Miller, 1979).

The Organization of Cessation Methods

The complexity and fragmentation of the attempts to control smoking behavior become evident when one attempts to organize the cessation literature into an integrated and meaningful whole. The Hunt and Bespalec (1974) evaluative review limited itself to six categories: aversive conditioning, drug therapy, education and group support, hypnosis, behavior modification, and the inevitable "miscellaneous". This oversimplified approach, in part dictated by the requirements they set for their data, is utterly unsuitable for the complexities of the field 6 years later. Education and group support would make strange bed-fellows today even with a king-size couch.

The problem is nicely illustrated by the comprehensive evaluative review of Schwartz and Rider (1978). In discussing the complexity of the field they mention three types of approach: (1) specific studies of a research nature usually conducted in an academic setting; (2) general clinic offered by commercial as well as non-profit organizations stressing achieved results rather than methodology; and (3) professional treatment with a patient orientation toward changing smoking behavior. They then classify cessation methods into four areas according to the type of: (1) approach: medical, educational, behavior modification, etc.; (2) organization offering treatment: university, religious group, etc.; (3) investigator or leader: psychologist, psychiatrist, physician, educator, etc.; and (4) method. These categories are insightful and help in understanding the context in which treatment takes place, but for purposes of their review they offer nine categories that "represent the current work in smoking cessation."

Their nine categories are: self care, medication, non-profit programs, commercial methods, hypnosis, medically sponsored programs, research designs, mass media and community programs, and miscellaneous. There seems to be no underlying classificatory principle here. The field is covered adequately but interrelationships are not brought out clearly.

For our part we are proposing a treatment oriented classification based upon the various cessation methodologies themselves, stressing the basic psychological areas involved and recognizing the systematic and research background from which they have evolved. Our interest is in the basic principles of the methods involved and not the place (non-profit clinic, commercial setting, patient therapist relationship, etc.) nor the identity of the individual providing the service (psychologist, psychiatrist, physician, educator, etc.). These are important but we feel the ideal goal, if attainable, should be a treatment program that works wherever it is applied by whomever is responsible for executing it.

This is not to deny the importance of where the service is delivered and who delivers it. The great diversity of the reported results of treatment would suggest these as obvious factors. It also suggests that the resistance of any treatment procedure to the influence of such factors would be a positive attribute in its evaluation. This diversity led Hunt and Bespalec (1974) to report range data instead of averages for the studies they reviewed. In their category of "Education and Group Support" (including 5-day plans with health education supplemented by discussion groups and supportive patient interaction) the range of abstention at 1 year was approximately 60 percentage points. As more studies become available with adequate samples such diversity of results might be an indicator of therapist and location factors as opposed to treatment methodology per se.

Another functional sequential classification is presented by Pechacek and Danaher (1979) based upon three phases of treatment: preparation, cessation, and maintenance. This is an increasingly popular approach. While the categories are sequential, they of course overlap. Thus preparation itself may result in cessation without further treatment, aversive conditioning as a means of producing cessation may reappear as maintenance in the form of "booster shots" to reinforce abstinence, etc.

Our own treatment organizes methodology in terms of three broad categories:

1. *General Educational.* This includes such approaches as conventional classroom procedures, community programs often with media support, and clinic and industrial programs aimed perhaps more at prevention and preparation although cessation may be a goal.

2. *Behavioral learning.* Here the orientation is direct intervention to modify the target behavior. It includes behavior modification, social learning techniques, hypnosis, habit training, etc. Cessation is the goal.

3. *Component techniques.* These include such supportive procedures as group treatment, group support, and follow-up procedures. Most of them are used as ancillary to some primary treatment method. They may be used to support cessation or often as maintenance procedures. We classify psychopharmacological procedures under component processes as they are usually used to supplement other approaches.

We have stressed the interplay between systematic, experimental, and theoretical procedures and the clinical application of the treatment programs derived from them. This represents a mutual fertilization of the academic and the professional. Thus the systematic neobehaviorism of the Skinnerian school has given us the many helpful operant conditioning techniques which have formed the basics for behavior modification. As an example, Lichtenstein and Danaher (1976) point out that reduction in rate of smoking rather than abstinence remains the preferred datum of many investigators "because it is so integral to the operant research paradigm." Rate reduction data are open to more powerful parametric procedures, and likely to be a more sensitive index of group differences. In turn the applications of operant procedures in clinical practice have forced operant conditioning theory into an increased recognition of the cognitive factors previously arbitrarily ruled out by a strict behavioristic approach.

While rate reduction may offer a datum that is more discriminative and statistically amenable, its use as a treatment goal can be questioned. The goal of the health sciences is to stop smoking, to reduce the number of people who are smokers. Although rate reduction has a certain face validity because we know the health hazard correlates roughly with the amount of smoking, no valid graduated scale is available against which to evaluate the amount of reduction achieved. Nor is there any way of weighting for individual differences or history. There seems to be some ancillary benefit with either criterion since some patients achieving reduction do spontaneously at the time or later achieve abstinence, and there are reports of relapse victims under the cessation criterion who nevertheless do achieve some rate reduction. We do not have data to permit any final conclusions here.

Nor do we have data on whether rate reduction facilitates later cessation.

From the motivational standpoint it would seem that achieving rate reduction might enhance the subjects feeling of self-efficacy and contribute to self confidence in achieving cessation. On the other hand mere rate reduction might increase the subject's feelings of inability to achieve abstinence. Certainly continued smoking even at a lesser level does build up the habit strength of the undesirable behavior one is trying to eliminate, although, in Skinnerian terms the intermittent partial reinforcement provided also may enhance maintenance by inhibiting extinction rather than increasing habit strength. In any case the result is the same. Since rate reduction as compared to cessation is relatively easy to achieve it may even lull the patient into a sense of false accomplishment and unduly encourage the clinician's judgement of the efficacy of his or her procedures.

Moreover, while rate reduction per se does reduce the amount of the individual's smoking, it still leaves the subject a smoker and does not reduce the number of smokers extant. There is a chance that this may undercut the social pressure generated by non-smokers against smokers. This pressure expressed in social disapproval and restrictive measures does facilitate the social picture of smoking as an undesirable behavior.

Having stressed the continuing interplay between the theoretical and the applied, we will split our evaluative treatment into two appropriate sections. The first will deal with the theoretical backgrounds of treatment programs, the second with their applications. In dealing with recent theoretical developments affecting treatment we will select four rough areas representing common psychological interests: Personality, Motivation, Learning, and Addiction.

Before doing this we should point out certain overall developmental trends:

There is an increasing trend to stress prevention rather than cure. In part this reflects *contemporary* humanitarian trends in psychology and medicine, in part it reflects disappointment with current treatment programs.

Increasing attention is being given to the addictive aspects of smoking. Part of this may be compensation for previous neglect, but in large part it reflects the mounting importance of psychopharmacology in behavioral medicine.

Maintenance of behavior is recognized as just as important as its acquisition. While performance based measures continue to be of first importance in instituting behavior change, more attention is being placed on coping skills and health lifestyles in its maintenance.

In line with this learning increasingly is becoming a matter of cognitive concern. Social learning has taken precedence over behavior modification.

The principle of self-help and self-control with its stress on developing coping skills is substituting an internalized, single organism concept for the old two organism concept of an external advisory or guiding organism and a second, recipient organism; the single organism concept represents a sort of do-it-yourself approach with modern echoes of the old concepts of free will, and will power.

Unfortunately there seems to be an increasing pessimism regarding the potential of current treatment methods. This reflects the unduly high expectations usually accompanying any new area of therapy. One might liken it to a social manifestation of Solomon's opponent–process mechanism. The picture, however, does not seem unduly dark. If long-time abstinence can be instituted in 25%–30% of treated cases, and this is probably a concervative estimate, the comparative therapeutic picture is not a bad one, particularly since extensive effort in the field did not develop until the Surgeon General's report of 1964.

THEORETICAL DEVELOPMENTS

Personality

Coan (1967), commenting on the research on personality characteristics of smokers and nonsmokers, noted that "Common failings in personality research stem from fixation on haphazardly chosen concepts, preoccupation with particular forms of measurement, and over dependence on available instruments." This was true of much of the earlier work which was overly simplistic and at times naive. At the 1969 conference of the American Cancer Society (Hunt, 1970) Hunt and Matarazzo (1970) echoed these criticisms concluding that "the personality characteristics of smokers and nonsmokers have been well-explored and to no apparent advantage." They question whether the resulting information "is pertinent in any immediate sense to the problem of controlling smoking behavior."

Smith (1970) at the same conference took exception to these remarks. In an excellent review of the personality findings to date, he pointed out that much had been learned about smokers and nonsmokers and that it would be foolish not to accumulate information about sociological, psychological, and biological differences between them if we are trying to understand why they smoke or don't smoke.

Admittedly the Hunt and Matarazzo comments were extreme but they illustrate the difference between the theoretical, experimental approach with its acceptance of group differences, often small, as adding information to the picture, and the clinical approach which seeks specific predictive information of a higher order than can be obtained with the usual group difference paradigm.

As a result of his survey of the literature Smith stated that we can conclude safely that smokers are more extraverted than nonsmokers and that they have more antisocial tendencies. They *may* be more externally oriented, more impulsive, have more oral needs, and be in poorer mental health, but more information is needed before any conclusions can be made in these latter four areas (Matarazzo et al., 1981).

Fortunately more data have been forthcoming stimulated by the developing feeling that smoking programs must be tailored to fit the individual needs of the smoker (Best, 1975; Leventhal & Avis, 1976). This necessitates the discovery of what these needs are and what the individual differences are on which they are based.

Eysenck (1973) proposed that different people smoked for different reasons to increase or decrease cortical arousal, and in different situations depending on whether they were getting too little or too much arousal. Using the classical extraversion-introversion concept he hypothesized that if arousal is high the effects of nicotine on the cortex is depressing; if arousal is low nicotine is stimulating, with introverts having a higher level of arousal and therefore using nicotine for its tranquilizing effects and extraverts for its stimulating effects. As we learn more about the physiological effects of nicotine, interest in Eysenck's hypothesis has increased. The findings are still controversial as two recent studies by Gilbert (Gilbert, 1980; Gilbert & Hagen, 1980) illustrate. Using the Eysenck Personality Inventory and the Minnesota Multiphasic Personality Inventory as measures of introversion, and self-report measures of both reason for smoking and felt urge to smoke, Gilbert found introverts saying they smoked more for tranquilization than extroverts did, and had a greater desire to smoke in stressful situations, a finding which confirms Eysenck. Gilbert and Hagen, however, had their subjects smoke high nicotine content and low nicotine content cigarettes before viewing videotaped emotion-arousing scenes. Using a skin conductance measure of emotional arousal they confirmed Eysenck in finding lowered skin conductance responses under the high nicotine condition, but found no relation between introversion and extraversion and skin conductance response magnitude. They suggest that the emotion-reducing effects were not the result of cortical sedation, but of reduced muscular tension and reactivity.

One of the problems here would seem to be the need for further understanding of the measures involved. On the one hand we have self-report measures with their dependence on memory and faults of self-attribution and on the other more exact physiological measures of whose complex physiological interactions we still have much to learn. As Gilbert (1979) points out a wide variety of variables are involved, and until we establish a paradigm that reliably causes nicotine-induced reduction of emotion we are in trouble. We also know little of the situational factors which influence both. It seems safe at least to credit the concept of Extraversion-Introversion with generating a wealth of suggestive research.

The factors Smith mentions as promising (both anti-social tendency and mental health) are broad, loose concepts covering heterogeneous materials, potentially amenable to varying definition, and based upon data obtained from diverse instruments. They show little evidence of offering specific aid in treating smoking. Orality seems to have fallen by the wayside.

The concept of Internal-External Locus of Control (Rotter, 1966) suggests that people may view events as determined by factors intrinsic to themselves, or as determined by outside factors such as the behavior of others, fate, chance, etc. The concept is an attractive one, not because it offers information on why people smoke but because it suggests a differential approach to tailoring treatment methods to specific individuals. Best (1975) has reported some success in this way. Again, however, the I.E. scale offers little in the way of specific prediction and is subject to interaction with unique environmental and situational factors. Recently Matarazzo et al. (1981), using the Multidimensional Health Locus of Control Scale (Wallston, Wallston, & DeVellis, 1978), found no difference in health locus of control in smokers, ex-smokers and nonsmokers.

Interest shifted in time from personality factors to the *reasons why* people smoke. Drawing on his theoretical work in the field of affect, Tomkins in 1966 proposed four "general types" of smoking based on the smoker's use of smoking to control the affective experience—positive affect smoking to obtain pleasure; negative affect smoking to obtain relief from unpleasantness; habitual smoking which occurred automatically without reference to affect; and craving. This last covered the seriously addicted smoker who was subject to a craving for it whenever he or she was prevented from smoking (Tomkins, 1968). Later Horn (Horn & Waingrow, 1966; Ikard, Green, & Horn, 1969), using the Tomkin's model, constructed a questionnaire based ultimately on six factors: habitual, addictive, negative affect, pleasurable, stimulation, and sensory motor. While the validational data is meager it has remained a popular approach. Costa, McCrae, and Bosse (1980) recently have demonstrated its stability over 4 years in a repeated testing of a large sample. In another study using their own smoking attitude questionnaire on two separate samples drawn 4 years apart Dawley, Morrison and Carrol (1980) have demonstrated a like stability. However, as Schachter (1973) points out in discussing Nesbitt's Paradox (the same people who report that they smoke for sedation show the autonomic arousal typical of nicotine), such questionnaire data are subject to the failures of memory and the personal attributions of the subjects. Stated simply, self-reports are often inaccurate.

It should be kept in mind both in the construction of questionnaires and in the usually ensuing factor analysis of the data that what emerges is a function of what one puts in. Thus McKennell (1970) in England asking different questions gets different factors, but ones which in general are congruent with the American data.

As the interest in treatments tailored specifically toward meeting individual differences develops, we can expect more of this general approach. Best and Hakstian (1978) accenting intensity of urge in 63 smoking situations rather than stated reasons for smoking arrive at a different set of factors that stress *environmental* determinants rather than *internal* ones, but no basic incongruities exist that would preclude ultimate arrival of an integrated model, of necessity at a higher level of complexity.

Motivation

As we move from the older, typological orientation of *who* smokes to the current interest in *why* do they smoke, and *when* and *where* does it occur, we cross over into the problems of motivation. Bandura's (1977) exposition of social learning theory in which he proposes that psychological functioning is best understood as a reciprocal interaction of personal and environmental determinants with change mediated through cognitive processes has helped turn our attention to information processing and decision making.

Prominent here has been the development of the theory of Subjective Expected Utility (SEU) which provides an approach to the part rationality plays in human behavior (Simon, 1980). SEU states that in decision-making the person tends to maximize the expected utility of his behavior in terms of subjective extimates of the probabilities of events. In Simon's words this gives a theory of rationality that portrays "man as an organism of limited computational ability and possessing limited information and limited imagination, seeking to survive in a world rich in complexity." What better way to describe the smoker attempting to stop and the psychologist attempting to help him or her?

As Pechacek and Danaher (1979) comment "the model has resulted in only limited practical demonstrations." Mausner and Platt (1971) used an SEU and decision-making model in the studies they report with change preceded by a higher pretreatment level of SEU (benefits). Eiser and Sutton (1977) used it as a model in a choice and decision-making situation based upon acceptance of treatment. They differentiate between extrinsic and intrinsic utilities. Sutton (1979) applied SEU to questionnaire data obtained from 2,000 smokers with only mixed support for the model. Confidence and SEU combined effect intention which in turn effects subsequent behavior, but by itself the effects of SEU were small, with confidence the more important determiner of intention. Rogers, Deckner and Mewborn (1978) using an expectancy-value approach with a high fear movie manipulation in two studies report some success in achieving abstinence but the follow-up was not particularly successful; i.e., with 22% abstinent at 3 months in one study, and 18.8% at 1 year in the other, the results seem below the average for other treatments. The trend today is toward narrowing the definition of expected utility to expected self-efficacy as a more important factor in the decision to stop smoking.

Solomon's Opponent–Process Theory of Acquired Motivation (Solomon and Corbit, 1973; Solomon, 1980; Ternes, 1977; Pomerleau, 1979) may well turn out to be one of the most important theoretical advances in the motivation area in the last few decades, combining as it does elements of learning, physiology, psychopharmacology, and affectivity (hedonic tone). Solomon's 1980 paper is a very readable summary. Ternes covers the animal data and offers somewhat pessimistic suggestions for therapeutic procedure. Pomerleau discusses it at length and considers it one of the three models—social learning, nicotine addiction, and opponent-process theory—most suitable for integration into a comprehensive theoretical framework for all the phenomena of smoking.

It is important to remember that it is a general theory of acquired motivation, not limited to smoking. While in its early development it has been used widely to explain the addictive process and the consequent appearance of craving and withdrawal symptoms in smoking, alcoholism, opiate addiction, and obesity, its application is not limited to the areas conventionally defined as addiction. Solomon seems willing and ready to apply it to any strong acquired motivational system which shows an acquired craving and emotional arousal (withdrawal symptoms) when its primary affective source is removed. Speaking of any attachment (Leo, 1980) as controlled at first mainly by pleasure, with control later shifting to the threat of separation and loneliness, Solomon is quoted as saying, "The ecstasy and madness of the early love affair are going to disappear and when they do, it means that a withdrawal symptom has to emerge if you are denied the presence of your partner. We call it loneliness." In an anthropomorphic way this will touch the heart of any confirmed smoker attached to a cigarette, cigar, or pipe.

Drawing on the basic phenomena of affectivity (Beebe-Center, 1932) Solomon posits a homeostatic mechanism whereby any affective state aroused by an unconditional reflex (primary) sets off an opposite process designed to restore the hedonic balance. The original affective process is called the a state and the balancing opponent process is referred to as the b state. The hedonic tone of the moment is determined by the algebraic sum of the a and b process. Thus in the beginning the a state dominates the picture but as this fades or ceases the b state dominates. Only by reinstating the original a state can the b state be overcome. These processes are not based on conditioning or learning but are unconditional. They may, however, be conditioned to other stimuli.

Applied to smoking, the arousal provided by nicotine is pleasurable (a process), but is immediately followed by the b state which is aversive and can only be relieved by reinstating the a process through smoking another cigarette. As time passes tolerance appears and the b state becomes stronger and harder to overcome. This sets up the addictive cycle with the smoker smoking more and more in an attempt to achieve relief from the aversive b state, thus experiencing the phenomenon of "craving."

While these processes are primary and unconditional, they can subsequently be conditioned to other stimuli whose association with the b state can result in conditioned withdrawal symptoms. Stimuli conditioned to the a state will produce a brief conditioned a state and subsequently the b state with its attendant craving. The basic opponent–process model is relatively straightforward and simple, but the introduction of conditioning leads us into all the complexities of human cognitive process and suggests that any therapeutic method will ultimately be forced into a highly individualistic approach demanding the instatement, reinstatement, or removal of innumerable individual associative bonds before the smoking behavior can be effectively controlled.

No such therapeutic model has been proposed although Ternes (1977) has offered these suggestions.

1. Plan quitting to coincide with some major environmental change such as a new job in a new city, or in lesser vein moving to a new house or taking a vacation.
2. Generalize aversive responses to some situation where a mildly pleasant task is available to produce relief or where the available response is an enjoyable hobby or sport.
3. Submit the undesirable conditioning to experimental extinction.

None of these is easy and we can agree when Ternes says "The smoker trying to 'kick the habit' does not have an easy task."

At present the model is attractive both in its simplicity and its complexity, but it needs more data and more theory for its development. As Pomerleau (1979) states, "The model's major shortcoming at present is that it remains untested in the smoking area."

Leventhal and Cleary (1980) reject Schacter's pharmacological model (1978) based on nicotine regulation, and offer what they call a "multiple regulation model", an elaboration of those by Tomkins (1968) and Solomon and Corbit (1973). The model gives primacy to the regulation of emotional states with nicotine levels being regulated only because certain emotional states have been conditioned to them in a variety of settings. Thus emotional regulation is the key to smoking behavior and it is the departure from emotional or hedonic homeostasis that is responsible for smoking rather than changes in nicotine level per se.

But smoking does more than generate a positive hedonic state. It both dampens and augments arousal induced by external events and also offers direct help in coping with them. Thus it is likely that it will be associated with memories of these events, producing emotional memory schemata. The appearance of any of the elements of a schema can produce the remaining ones. Whether smokers label themselves as social, addictive, habitual, etc. will depend upon the elements of the schema and the personal experience of the smoker. While no specific treatment program is offered, Leventhal, and Cleary offer suggestions for breaking up these conditioned emotional schemata and removing the conditioned experience of craving. It is interesting to note that both the Solomon and the Leventhal and Cleary models challenge the primacy of the nicotine regulatory model of smoking and bring learning and the conditioning of emotional responses back into the picture as basic to smoking behavior.

There is an increasing interest in prevention rather than treatment springing partly from current trends in public health and partly from disillusionment with the discouraging results of contemporary treatment programs. If we have little luck in getting people to stop smoking, perhaps we may have more luck in keeping them from starting. Leventhal and Cleary (1980) separate smoking behavior into three stages: *preparation* (the experiential and educational background that sets the motivational stage for subsequent smoking behavior); *initiation* (the introduction to smoking); and *becoming* (the transition from experimentation to habitual smoking). It may be that attention to these processes would be more profitable than confining our interest to changing the behavior once it is incorporated in the individuals' behavioral repertoire. Such an approach is consistent with present trends to shift the educational stress from the horrors and evils of cigarette smoking per se to the inculcation of generalized healthy life styles that emphasize one's body as an invaluable asset and the moral responsibility one has to protect it. Thus one's coping skills are directed to health protecting behavior in general rather than a narrow caveat against the dangers of nicotine.

Prevention thus points to increased attention to the child and adolescent in the school setting and the particular and special intellectual and emotional problems involved in reaching it. Hunt (1968) has discussed the convenience and appropriateness of the school as locus for a public health program in the mental health area. Most of our attention has been directed to the adolescent. While the problem often begins earlier it is in adolescence, with the adolescent striving to cope with the emotional problems of the rites of passage involved in the transition from adolescence to adulthood, that the problem becomes obvious and demanding.

The early work of McKennel and Bynner (1969) on the difference between nonsmoking and smoking schoolboys highlighted the connection between smoking and the desire to appear tough (Marlboro Country?) and socially mature, but as Leventhal and Cleary comment these two factors are not likely to exhaust the attitudes important to their preparatory stage. The Jessors (1977) have offered an expanded model for understanding deviant adolescent behavior. Evans, Rozelle, Mittlemark, Hansen, Bane, and Havis (1978) have stressed three factors often having an overriding influence in adolescent's beginning to smoke: peers, models of smoking parents, and the media. But the problem is not a simple one.

Perhaps the most comprehensive data come from studies instigated by the National Clearing House for Smoking and Health as reported by Green (1977). A carefully developed questionnaire of 83 items was administered to some 5,200 pupils drawn from a national probability sample of school districts. Factor analysis of the data resulted in eight factors:

1. Teenagers view smoking as detrimental to health.
2. They also view it as detrimental to the environment.

3. They feel it is pleasurable.
4. They rationalize the conflict between health and pleasure by saying they don't intend to smoke enough or long enough to be hurt by it.
5. Peer pressure is the main reason for taking up smoking.
6. They feel smokers are "bad boys." They don't get good grades and tend to get in trouble.
7. There is a feeling of ambivalence toward authority. As Green puts it, they would like to be able to turn to their parents whenever they can, but they also would like to get rid of them. They feel a teenager should be able to do what he or she wants to.
8. They feel that they can do something about their lives if they want to.

These results are both encouraging and discouraging. As the recent downward trends in teenage smoking discussed earlier suggest it is obvious that the health message is getting across to teenagers, albeit still imperfectly for sure. The behavior of such youthful smokers may be influenced by teenage feelings of rebellion and resistance to authority which in turn is generated by the emotional problems attendant upon the rites of passage from childhood to adulthood. Discussion of the problem is found in Aitken (1980) and Leventhal and Cleary (1980).

Our culture seems to handle this matter of rites of passage less successfully than some primitive cultures. We need more participation for adolescents in adult rights and privileges and alternative symbols for smoking and sexual precocity as evidence of maturity. The average American parent sometimes seems to devote child rearing efforts during childhood to developing the child into conforming adult behavior but somewhere around adolescence to reverse his direction and attempt to push the adolescent back into childhood again.

We might change the old slogan, "If you can't lick 'em, join 'em to "If you can't lick 'em, let 'em join you" and offer the adolescent more participation in controlling his or her own behavior. Evans, Rozelle, Maxwell, Raines, Dill, and Guthrie (in press) seem to recognize this when they report a program that used videotapes of children of the same age as the target population. More importantly perhaps the same children served as spokespersons as well as participants in the situation depicting social pressure. At the adolescent level McAlister, Perry, and Maccoby (1979) report that in their work at Stanford and at Harvard they use "older young people (peer leaders) as the primary agents delivering the intervention" and use role playing and other methods to develop skill in resisting social pressure. Particularly important would seem to be their use of peer leaders of a type that are adventurous and unconventional but not unhealthy in their behavior, and hence judged to be attractive to the sort of person who might be attracted to smoking. We need more data on such programs particularly longitudinal studies, but so far they look promising.

Learning

For convenience we have drawn a somewhat arbitrary line between learning and motivation. The blending of the two is seen in Logan's paper on self-control as habit, drive, and incentive (1973) in which he not only recognizes the need of associating a drive for self-control with smoking behavior but also the necessity of practicing habits of not smoking so that the successful ones may achieve the incentive motivation necessary for their performance. He distinguishes between habits which are acquired through practice and incentive motivation which occurs only when the response results in an emotionally significant event. In the thinking of many practicing behavioral engineers, however, habit, drive, incentive, motivation, self-control etc. as concepts are largely reified empirical "givens." Their incorporation into learning theory demands further theoretical development as a basis for their experimental investigation and ultimate effective use in controlling smoking behavior. As Premack and Anglin (1973) point out, the development of internalized mechanisms of control are an important requisite of socialization, although Ferraro (1973) is pessimistic about the possibility of ultimate independence from some external source. He does, however, recognize the contribution of learning theory to behavioral technology, and states that smoking control seems best when the smoker controls the contingencies involved.

Of vital importance to the modification of smoking behavior has been the emergence of social learning theory under Bandura (1977). Social learning theory takes full advantage of the post-war development of cognitive psychology, a cognitive psychology largely overlooked by the operant conditioning techniques of classical behavior modification. As Bandura says, "Theoretical formulations emphasizing peripheral mechanisms began to give way to cognitive oriented theories that explained behavior in terms of central processing of direct, vicarious, and symbolic sources of information" (p. 192) Again in Bandura's view ". . . psychological functioning is explained in terms of a continuous reciprocal interaction of personal and environmental determinants. Within this approach symbolic, vicarious, and self-regulatory processes assume a prominent role" (p. 11).

Among these processes are modeling, self-control mechanisms, self-efficacy as a motivational agent, observational learning, attentional processes, vicarious expectancy learning, self-arousal functions, guided participation, and the importance of social rewards. People are seen as active agents in their own motivation, but always in reciprocal interaction with their environment. The classical mechanisms of operant conditioning are not denied, and direct intervention is considered a powerful technique particularly in changing behavior in the already confirmed smoker, but once the change is obtained, coping skills, self-control mechanisms bolstered by the experience of self-efficacy, etc. are called in to support the maintenance of the new behavior. Many traditional concepts are extended and refined to reflect a changing theoretical emphasis. Marlatt and Gordon (1980) offer an extensive treatment of the use of such cognitive concepts, stressing in particular their maintenance functions. Essentially social learning theory is eclectic in nature and brings a new (although probably temporary) unity to psychology in the behavioral control area. Actually most behavioral engineers use both approaches, with social learning procedures more popular in the educational and preventive programs and operant procedures such as aversive satiation more popular in the immediate breaking of the established smoking behavior of the confirmed smoker. Even here as we have noted social learning procedures are used in supportive fashion to help maintain the nonsmoking behavior once it is achieved.

Whether social learning theory will live up to its promise remains to be seen. It is too early for much longitudinal data to have accumulated and the complex, multi-factorial procedures render it extremely difficult to isolate and evaluate the individual factors involved. If one were to attempt to pinpoint the most important difference between classical behavior modification and social learning theory it would seem to be in the generalizability of the new behaviors introduced in social learning theory. Too often the behaviors established with operant conditioning turn out to be highly specific, stimulus specific and situation specific, and to lack the response generality and transferability of such social learning procedures as self-control, feelings of self-efficacy, life style, etc. all of which seem fairly high in any hierarchical organization of behavior.

This mixture of techniques is as well a mixture of theoretical cultures, and classical behavior modifiers as befits their behavioristic background have not always rested easily with cognitive psychologists. The basic question addresses whether cognitive factors are "mental" or not and imply a body mind dualism consistently rejected by behaviorism. Can cognitive concepts, even if disguised under the cloak of "covert" behavior, be introduced without the acceptance of such inimical terms as consciousness, sensation, etc.? Is the phrase cognitive behavior modification a confusion of concepts and should we not speak rather of cognitive therapy and behavior therapy, keeping a clear distinction between them? As Ledwidge (1979) points out these questions are largely semantic. They involve systematic and theoretical allegiances and seem of more concern to the behavioral scientist than to the behavioral engineer or practitioner who often is willing to accept the eclecticism of cognitive behavior modification if it gives him or her procedures which can be applied efficaciously in changing smoking behavior.

An interesting example of the conflicts involved is seen in the original Ledwidge paper (1978), the attack on it by Mahoney and Kazdin (1979), and Ledwidge's reply (1979). The basic situation is endemic to psychology, and is discussed historically and systematically in Howard Kendler's (1981) most recent book, *Psychology: A Science in Conflict*.

Most of the approaches to behavior change and their application to smoking behavior, neo-Hullian learning theory, classical and instrumental conditioning, and social learning theory, have in common the basic acceptance of the concept of reinforcement, although Logan's differentiation between habit and incentive motivation, and Bandura's caution that reinforcement serves principally as an informative and motivational operation rather than a mechanical strengthener of response, suggest some modification of any simplistic reinforcement process. Malone (1978) suggests the possibility of other approaches and reintroduces some of Guthrie's associative learning principles. Hunt and Matarazzo (1970, 1973) and Hunt, Matarazzo, Weiss, and Gentry (1979) in developing the concept of habit, while not denying the primacy of reinforcement, have suggested the desirability in some situations of complementing it by associative learning.

In developing their concept of habit, Hunt and Matarazzo (1970) were not interested in the "habitual" smoker of Tomkins typology but rather in the behavior itself. They defined habit as a stable behavior pattern overlearned to the point of becoming automatic and marked by decreasing awareness and increasing dependence on secondary rather than primary reinforcement. Dissatisfaction with the explanatory power of overlearning and secondary reinforcement and realization of the prominence of immediacy, automaticity, unawareness, and relative independence of reinforcement in habitual behavior then led them next to define habit as "a stable behavior pattern marked by automaticity, decreasing awareness, and a partial independence of reinforcement" (Hunt, Matarazzo, Weiss, & Gentry, 1979).

Little has been written about such habitual behavior but Kimble and Perlmuter (1970) have likened it to a transfer from voluntary to involuntary control, noting its tendency to leave the center of attention and to occur so quickly that "motivational arousal seems virtually impossible." Such automatized behavior may appear in apparent spontaneity often not only independently of the reward contingencies of the moment but sometimes in direct opposition to them. This is particularly true in the addictions. Such paradoxical behavior has puzzled psychologists since Allport's (1937) treatment of functional autonomy.

Hunt et al. (1979) have hypothesized that once a behavior has been acquired the usual reinforcement processes may be short-circuited as the behavior becomes automatized and passes to the control of associative principles of learning. Thus reinforcement becomes primary in the acquisition of new behaviors while associative learning is seen as playing an important role in their maintenance. The two processes are interactive and not independent as at any moment awareness may reinstate cognitive control and reappearance of reinforcement learning. Thus the two processes are viewed as complementary in the behavioral picture.

The treatment implications are discussed at length in Hunt et al. (1979). Thus "good" behaviors such as compliance to a treatment regimen should be automatized as habits and strengthened by repeated automatic performance in accordance with the principles of associative learning, and "bad" behaviors should be prevented and not allowed to become strengthened by practice. The reinstatement of reinforcement through awareness of the reward contingencies can act as a powerful complement in treatment. Unfortunately, the hypothesis has not as yet been subject to an experimental verification in any treatment program.

Addiction

The addictive properties of nicotine with attendant dependence and withdrawal symptoms upon deprivation have long been a part of the experience of every heavy smoker, yet for many years relatively little attention was paid them. Thanks to the work of such researchers as Jarvik (1979), Russell (1977), and particularly Schachter (1978) with his homeostatic regulatory model, they now are receiving attention. Shiffman (1979) has listed the characteristic symptoms of withdrawal as irritability, anxiety, inability to concentrate, disturbance of arousal, and intensified craving. The effects of deprivation on performance are increasingly reported, i.e. Taylor and Blezard (1979), and Tong (1980). The question has even been raised as to whether the demonstrated behavioral phenomena of withdrawal may not pose more work and health problems for the confirmed heavy smoker than the long term health benefits of not smoking can compensate for (Pertschuk, Pomerleau, Adkins & Hirsh, 1979).

Despite the acceptance of these phenomena the question remains, as we have pointed out in discussing motivation and learning, whether they are basic attributes of nicotine per se, reflection of some homeostatic regulatory mechanism (Schachter, 1978), attributable to the opponent–process mechanism of Solomon (1980), or secondary homeostatic attempts to modify emotional behaviors (Leventhal & Cleary, 1980). Like Pandora's Box the recognition of nicotine addiction has raised more questions than answers, and we need much more information on the biochemistry of nicotine, its pharmacological interactions, individual and sexual differences in human sensitivity, diurnal variation, the specific arousal mechanisms, etc. before they can be answered. The paradoxical nature of many of the problems is illustrated by the comment of Hunt, et al. (1979) on their concept of the behavior vacuum or the need of the organism for motor expression when they point out that nicotine may act as an arousal mechanism at the same time that the manipulatory activity of smoking offers an opportunity for motor expression. In a psychology increasingly attentive to cognitive process it is interesting that more time has not been given to a subjective description of the experiential nature of craving which remains an accepted, reified "given."

The expedient approach at present would seem to be the acceptance of both psychological and pharmacological addiction as indicated recently by Bossé, Garvey, and Glynn (1980). In any case little has issued as yet in the way of specific treatment models based on the pharmacological properties of nicotine.

Evaluation

Our attention here is directed to experimental evaluation rather than the theoretical approach offered in the previous section. The basic design problems cogently set forth in Bernstein's (1969) original review are still with us and probably endemic to any applied research. There has been some increase in sample size and length of follow-up attributable to the increasing attachment of nonsmoking programs to the larger clinic and at risk health programs with their better record keeping procedures. In general the additional data appearing confirm the shape of the Hunt et al. (1970) curves, with rapid relapse after treatment for the first 6 months then a gradual plateauing stabilizing around 1 year. Noticeable trends are the increasing use of physiological measures to check self-reports of smoking, and the popular use of complex, composite procedures which render difficult the evaluation of each specific factor in the package.

Educational Programs.   In general school programs follow a basic pattern of test, treatment, retest with the test and retest procedures establishing the incidence of smoking, other varying measures of knowledge of consequences of smoking, and attitudes toward health procedures. Control groups are used albeit somewhat contaminated by previous knowledge of the dangers of smoking through minimal exposure to nonsmoking materials in the general health courses standard in most school curricula. Since the goal is prevention rather than cure the criterion is subsequent incidence of smoking in the groups, measured either by the *absolute* number of smokers in the group or by the number of *new* smokers appearing.

Presently the typical program resembles that developed in Evans' (1976) pilot study in the Houston, Texas schools involving videotaped presentations with the actors congenial to the audience. These may be supplemented by group discussions, and retest monitoring which seems in itself to have some positive influence.

Evans, Rozelle, Mittlemark, Hansen, Bane, and Havis (1978) report on 750 entering seventh graders in the Houston schools. The full treatment group saw four videotapes after each of which the students answered questions and entered into group discussion. There were 3 posttest sessions at 1, 5, and 10 weeks. After each posttest, feedback was provided. The experimental groups were divided into a full treatment group, a feedback only group, and a repeated testing group. The control group had the pretest and the 10-week posttest. The reported smoking behavior for the full treatment group was 10.0%, feedback group 8.6%, and repeated testing only group 9.7%. These compare with the control groups incidence of 18.3%. The program would seem to be effective although the lack of difference in treatment groups is interesting. McAlister, Perry, and Maccoby (1979), in a pilot study involving a 7-session peer leadership program aimed at developing coping, personal and social skills, and using 550 San Jose, California seventh graders, found in a 9-month follow-up an approximately 5% difference in onset rates between the experimental groups and controls. A subsequent follow-up after another year (21 months in all) showed an increase in this difference and a concommitant difference in favor of the experimental groups in lessened drinking behavior and use of marijuana (McAlister, Perry, Killen, Slinkard, & Maccoby, 1980). Another California project (Perry, Killen, Telch, Slinkard, & Danaher, 1980) involving 498 10th grade students subjected to four consecutive 45-minute sessions showed a significant difference at the semester's end in favor of the treatment group. Pechacek and McAlister (1980 in press) report on a University of Minnesota program with which Pechacek was involved (Luepker, Hurd, Pechacek, Bast, Johnson, & Pickard, 1980) using a Houston type program involving 1530 seventh graders that found on a 1-year follow-up a 47% incidence in the control group receiving monitoring only as opposed to 10% in a school using a depersonalized film, and a *decrease* of 11% in the group using class peer leaders. This last would seem to indicate that the "preventive" program was also a "curative" one, and suggests the need for a more sensitive criterion measure than merely onset rate in future studies. Finally, Botvin, Eng, and Williams (1980), in a program involving 281 youngsters in the 8th, 9th, and 10th grades in suburban New York (using a program based upon developing coping skills through group discussion, modeling, and behavior rehearsal and onset of new smokers as a criterion over a 10-week program) report an onset rate of 16% for the control groups and only 4% for the experimental group. The results were best for 8th-graders and decreased progressively in the 9th and 10th-grade groups.

While the above results are small and perhaps not impressive they indicate the value of school programs particularly since they are aimed at one of the most important areas in controlling smoking behavior, and one in which to date little progress and interest has been manifested (Matarazzo, 1980; 1981).

Clinic Programs.   As we go from educational programs to clinic programs, from prevention to intervention, we find social learning procedures common to both. This represents an increasing realization of the potential of social learning methods for direct intervention in behavior change, the need for supportive maintenance procedures in maintaining the change once it has been obtained by the powerful tools of conventional behavior modification, and an increased interest in the cost-benefit of treatment where the cost of individual behavior modification often makes it economically less attractive than the group methods possible with social learning.

West, Graham, Swanson, and Wilkinson (1977) report a followup study after 5 years of some 800 participants in the Roswell Park Memorial Institute clinics for 1964–1965. Some 559 usuable replies were obtained. The abstinence rate 5 years after treatment was 17.8%, certainly not spectacular, but it must be remembered that many of the techniques used (i.e., lobeline as a substitute for nicotine, and amphetamine for appetite control) would be considered outmoded today. In addition the social climate for nonsmoking 15 years ago was not as favorable as it is today.

Kanzler, Jaffe, and Zeidenberg (1976) report a 4-year follow-up study of the

553 people who enrolled in Smokenders, a proprietary program, during the first 4 months of 1971. They report 70% success at the end of treatment and an abstinence rate of 39% at the end of 4 years. This would be very impressive were their definition of abstinence not so lenient, i.e., "essentially had not been smoking", and thus permitted occasional lapses if for no more than a week. Also, addresses were obtained for only 450 of the original 553 subjects, and return from a mail survey of these was only 29%. To compound this nonrepresentativeness, the final abstinence figure was obtained through the use on the non-returns of a complicated extrapolation formula based on 66 personal telephone interviews of some of those who had not answered the mailing.

Shewchuk, Dubren, Burton, Forman, Clark, and Jaffin (1977) offer a preliminary report on the American Health Foundation's midtown Manhattan programs. The 571 participants were followed for 1 year. They were given their choice of three types of treatment, group therapy, hypnosis, or individual counseling. On followup 18% were still not smoking, compared with a control group rate of 8%. There were no significant differences between type of treatment, and the authors single out group therapy as most cost effective at an estimated expense of $55 per person for the year. Harrup, Hansen, and Soghikian (1979) describe the Kaiser-Permanente Stop Smoking Clinic. The program uses an 8-week period with 13 90-minute meetings. At 3, 6, and 12 months group reunions are held. They report that of 1128 clients 57% were abstinent at 6 months and 47% at 1 year. These are excellent results but it seems to be an unusually intense program.

Evans and Lane (1980) discuss a series of clinics using the format proposed by the American Cancer Society and the American Lung Association. Each workshop met 6 times over a 3-week period. Of some 590 enrollees 372 responded to a survey conducted at one shot and covering every clinic held. This one-shot survey thus covered periods from 6 months to 5 years for the various individual clinics. An average abstinence rate of 25% is reported 1 to 2 years post workshop and remains relatively stable thereafter. Another typical program is being run by the Chicago Lung Association (1981) which is establishing a series of satellite clinics in the Chicago area run by workers trained in a 2-day workshop. The clinic program consists of six 90-minute sessions spread over 4 weeks using self-control techniques, relaxation, and group methods. A self-reinforcement procedure was added interchangeably with a covert sensitization technique. Both proved equally successful.

Standard evaluative procedures were used. While the data are still being processed, results for a 6-clinic pilot project showed that of 180 participants 41% had stopped smoking by the end of the treatment program. Of these initial abstainers 46% were still abstinent at the end of 1 year, a very good rate when compared with the average 25% to 30% rate reported in the literature. Reduction rates for those not able to stop averaged one third at the 1-year follow-up.

In a different vein Puska, Koskela, McAlister, Pallonen, Vartiainen, and

Homan (1979) and McAlister, Puska, Koskela, Pallonen, and Maccoby (1980) describe a nationwide TV program in Finland for viewers who wished to stop smoking. It combined the most successful group methods previously developed in Finland with new ideas from the United States, and its primary focus was on preventing relapse rather than achieving temporary change. Where the TV program was embellished by the participation of locally organized groups there was greater participation, but any increase in efficiency in influencing non-smoking was dubious. Owing to the size of the program evaluation had to be based on sampling procedures and inference from national health statistics. Recognizing the dangers of such extrapolation and use of inference the authors estimate 43% of those participating achieved temporary success and 27% maintained this over a period of 6 months, an estimated 1% of the smokers in Finland or some 10,000 successful cases. Based on these estimates the authors claim an unusual cost-effectiveness, about $1 spent for each 6-month success.

Some mention should be made of the development of self-help manuals designed to assist the individual who wishes to conduct a personal stop-smoking program. Notable among the non-proprietary manuals are the National Cancer Institute's (1979) "Clearing the Air", a brief pamphlet containing suggestions about quitting and subsequent maintenance, diet control, etc. and a listing of some of the popular programs available. The Institute (1979) has also prepared a Helping Smokers Quit kit, available to physicians desiring to help their patients stop smoking. Unfortunately no data are available on the success of such individual efforts. On the research side, however, the National Interagency Council on Smoking and Health (1974) has prepared what might be called a self-help manual on research procedures for those clinics that might wish to investigate follow-up procedures for evaluating the success of their efforts.

Behavioral Intervention.   Although no data are available on the independent voluntary use of manuals by individuals trying to quit smoking on their own, a manual is sometimes included in a broad spectrum program, but the only criterion for its efficacy is the success of the program as a whole. An exception is the study by Glasgow (1978) involving 69 subjects where two self-help conditions, self-help manual with minimal therapist contact and with maximal therapist contact, are compared with two aversive conditions, rapid smoking and self-paced smoking (the subject is instructed to significantly increase his or her daily consumption). No significant differences are reported but the small number in each group and the within-group variability in performance make interpretation difficult. These multicomponent programs raise problems for the evaluation of the individual components. They represent a practical philosophy expressed by Conway (1977) when he says, "Before we attempt to specify the effective components of self-management, our efforts should be directed toward demonstrating the clinical utility of complete SM packages."

Another illustration is the study by Pomerleau (1979) using 100 subjects in a broad spectrum approach based on a previous manual (Pomerleau & Pomerleau, 1977). Embedded in the procedure are two popular components, relaxation and covert conditioning. While Pomerleau quotes a respectable 32% abstinence rate at 1-year follow-up and 29% at 2 years for the complete program, no component evaluation is possible.

Aversive conditioning remains popular, with some form of rapid smoking accepted as the most powerful aversive procedure for quitting smoking. There has been some criticism of the health risks involved, but in a survey of the literature, Sachs, Hall, Pechacek, and Fitzgerald (1979) conclude that with the possible exception of cardiac and pulmonary patients the benefits justify its use, a conclusion supported by Hall, Sachs, and Hall (1979) who gathered physiologi-cal measures during a rapid smoking experiment involving 24 healthy males. Their 61% abstinence rate at 6 months is respectable. In a study using 60 subjects in four conditions—rapid smoking, covert aversive conditioning, both com-bined, and a control group—Barbarin (1978) found six of the 15 subjects (40%) in the rapid smoking group still abstinent after 1 year. The sample size is small, however, and questions are raised by the fact that only one subject in the com-bined group was successful. Tongas (1977) reporting on a Kaiser-Permanente clinic group of 72 separated into four groups—rapid smoking, covert aversive conditioning, behavioral group therapy, and a combination of all three states—that at a 2-year follow-up abstinence rates for the groups were 21%, 33%, 8%, and 62% respectively. The two aversive conditions are average but the 62% reported for the combined treatment group is phenomenal. Again the samples are small and the fact that 40 of the subjects were physician referred may have influenced motivation. Delahunt and Curran (1976) using four groups—no spe-cific treatment, negative practice, self-control, and a combination of all three, plus a control group—report at 6-months follow-up 56% abstinence for the combined group, 10% for no specific treatment, and 20% each for negative practice and for self-control. The small group samples for the short follow-up period do not inspire confidence. We have already commented on the Glasgow study. Flaxman (1978) with 64 subjects compared an aversive smoking condition with an attention control condition. The aversive condition was better at the start of the follow-up period but there was no difference at 6 months. The delay in instituting aversive conditioning in some subjects may have influenced the re-sults.

Lando (1977) reports another broad spectrum program with maintenance and aversion compared with a control group of aversion alone in a sample of 36 subjects. At 6-months follow-up 76% of the experimental group were abstinent and 35% of the "control" group. A replication with only 16 subjects was reported by Lando and McCullough (1978), but a more extensive replication by Lando (1978) involving 83 subjects failed to replicate the previous studies. Again sampling problems would seem to be involved. Lichstein and Stalgaitis (1980) used a novel form of negative practice which they call reciprocal aversion in which each member of a married couple was required to smoke a cigarette whenever the spouse did. At 6-months follow-up abstinence was 50% but only 6 couples were involved and any clinician might wonder about the dyadic dynamics involved.

Electric shock has largely been superseded in smoking control by rapid smoking but Conway (1977) used it in a study involving four types of aversive shock conditions and two self management conditions. Analysis of variance at a 20-week follow-up showed no significant differences between controls and any treatment group, although overall, self-management was more effective than aversive conditioning.

Hypnosis.   The excellent results reported by Hall and Crasilneck (1970) have not been replicated in later studies. Speigel (1970) is enthusiastic about a single-session treatment but his patients were instructed in a self-hypnosis technique for maintenance which complicates any interpretation of his results. A follow-up by mail yielded a low response rate of 44% which is unsatisfactory. A reasonable conclusion is that his method had some success but no more than other approaches. Watkins (1976) reports on a 5-session program with an abstention rate of 67% at the end of 6 months. The program eliminated the word hypnosis and used the phrase "Concentration-Relaxation Technique" with reference to a "hypnoidal" procedure. There are supportive self-control elements introduced that complicate any interpretation. Later studies, Barkley, Hastings, and Jackson (1977), Berkowitz, Ross-Townsend, and Kohberger (1979), Pederson, Scrimgeour, and Lefcoe (1975), Perry and Mullen (1975), Tori (1978) echo the general pessimism. Stanton (1978) reports a 6-month abstention rate of 45% which is not exceptional.

In general the hypnosis studies suffer from lack of long time follow-up, a failure to adequately define and control the exact procedure, and the embedding of the hypnotic technique in a wealth of other supportive procedures so that untangling the specific contribution of hypnosis is impossible. As Katz (1980) has said "To report that a client was treated with hypnosis is like reporting that one used psychotherapy or medicine to effect a cure." Pechacek (1979) succinctly refers to the data as "both chaotic and methodologically poor" (p. 101).

West (1977) is more enthusiastic. After a capsule history of hypnosis from its early days and a brief description of the technique as practiced today, he discusses the pros and cons of its use and concludes "any modern comprehensive smoking treatment program, using multiple modalities should include hypnosis as a matter of course." We would comment that where practical it might fit well into the current popular model of the three stages of treatment—preparation, cessation, and maintenance—by offering a potentially powerful and dramatic cessation technique which could then be supported in maintenance by other less costly self-help procedures.

Unfortunately, as West points out, not everyone can be hypnotized and those that can be are not all capable of achieving a deep state. West moreover has the courage to make a rough prediction of the probable success rate (defined as abstinence for 1 year) using hypnosis. He suggests that 10% of any sample of subjects would not attain any depth of hypnosis and that less than 5% *of these* would be successes, another 50% of the sample would achieve a light state with an abstinence rate of 40%, of the 30% attaining a moderate state 70% would succeed in quitting, and for the 10% achieving a deep state 90% would succeed. This would come to a success rate with a random sample of 50%, which is more than respectable. The prediction stands, but unfortunately data to check it are not available, nor is it a design that could be executed easily.

Sensory Deprivation.   Like hypnosis, sensory deprivation depends upon a subject's receiving verbal instruction in a non-distracting situation where concentration is facilitated. The subject spends 24 hours in bed in a dark room equipped with a cot and chemical toilet. Liquid food is provided. From time to time messages are transmitted concerning the danger of smoking or methods for controlling it. Perhaps because of the demands on the subject and because of the special facilities necessary it is infrequently used. Borrie and Suedfeld (1980) in a weight reducing program report a drop-out rate of 39% which certainly is high and probably testifies to its unpopularity with patients. They have renamed it Restricted Environmental Stimulation Therapy with the attractive acronym, REST, which may make it more palatable. Its infrequent use results in meager data on which to evaluate it. Follow-up procedures also complicate the picture.

Suedfeld and Ikard (1974) in a trial primarily for smoking reduction report an abstinence rate for 1 year of 27% which is about average in the field. In a more recent report Suedfeld and Best (1977) combine it with a preliminary satiation experience, a practice (satiation plus another procedure) that is becoming popular. Unfortunately they report only on 5 subjects, but do add clinical case histories of the kind advocated by Litman et al. (1979).

In any case, sensory deprivation remains a laborious technique, demanding both for the patient and the therapist and requiring a heavy investment in equipment. There seems no data available to justify the investment.

Component Processes.   We have stressed the paucity of data on individual treatment components. Kantorowitz, Walters, and Pezdek (1978) compared positive and negative monitoring (reporting resistance to urges to smoke vs. reporting actual smoking) but the paired conditions were embedded in a broad spectrum treatment and the number of subjects was small. Within these limitations no difference was found.

Lamontagne, Gagnon, Trudel, and Boisvert (1978) using 60 male volunteers in a rate reduction experiment compared three treatments—thought stopping, group discussions, and the wearing of a badge saying "I don't smoke"—all combined with self monitoring, with a self monitoring condition alone. Over 6 months, thought stopping was the most successful treatment but did not differ from self-monitoring alone. Flaxman (1974), comparing treatment successes and failures, found that successes with a reported high habit component in their smoking reported more use of thought stopping and relaxation as coping mechanisms.

The increased interest in maintenance has led Colletti and his associates to concentrate on evaluating maintenance factors. Using as subjects people who have had a 4-week non-aversive no smoking program they then compare the relative value of different procedures for improving maintenance over the post-treatment period. Colletti and Kopel (1979) with 42 subjects compared a modeling procedure in which the subjects acted as models for a new group entering treatment, a participant observer group, and a self-monitoring group. While self-monitoring seemed best, the particular strategy did not seem important but using a maintenance procedure did. They report 61% of the subjects abstinent at a 1-year follow-up. A further group of 32 replicated the findings. Colletti and Supnick (1980) using the same basic design compared a minimal contact strategy with a no maintenance procedure. At 6-months follow-up the abstinence rate was 54% for minimal contact and 19% for no maintenance strategy but at 1 year there was no between groups difference, possibly owing to an unexplained improvement by the no maintenance group during the 6 to 12-month follow-up period. Again, numbers were small and replication is needed, but the shift from treatment experimentation to maintenance is an interesting and promising development.

SUMMARY

Whether or not the past decade has seen any improvement in treatment methods per se is questionable. The reported results are varied, pro and con, which led Hunt and Bespalec (1974) to report their survey findings in terms of the *range* of reported results as well as the smoothed curve given by the use of averages, which overlooks the variation in actual reported results. The suggestion that such smoothed curves might be used for the purpose of evaluative comparison unfortunately seems to have encouraged some researchers to drop the usual control groups from their investigations. Back of the ever present demands of careful experimental investigation, there are the lurking practical demands of the systematically oriented investigator for an agreeable and consistent solution, the demands of the harried therapist for a quick justification of current therapeutic approaches, and the disregarded but quite real demands of graduate students for a time-limited satisfactory thesis proposal. The complexity of the problem might lead one to challenge the conclusion of Pechacek and McAlister (1980) that "the technology of smoking cessation is still in its infancy" and comment instead that perhaps it is a case of arrested development with no indication of special education helping the handicapped.

There is no cause for despair, however. If one accepts a conservative estimate of 25% of our subjects achieving long-term abstinence and remembers that most of these are confirmed smokers looking for relief, that the figures for those who voluntarily quit on their own individual effort are not included, that the preventive programs now getting underway are adding their bit, and that our national survey figures do show that the proportion of smokers in the population *is* decreasing, there is reason for optimism. It may well be that our immediate effort at present is best extended toward offering to as many people as possible some help at a cost efficient level as exemplified by the programs currently being sponsored by the American Cancer Society and the American Lung Association.

As Warner (1981) remarks in *Science* after a sophisticated statistical interpretation of recent trends in cigarette consumption, "declining consumption and increasing legislation probably reflect a prevalent nonsmoking ethos and the conversion of modified knowledge and attitudes into behavioral change." It could be that the increasing public intolerance of smoking is our greatest change resource (treatment). The danger is that public interest might diminish and the steam go out of the crusade.

ACKNOWLEDGMENTS

Preparation of this chapter was supported, in part, by National Heart, and Blood Institute Grants HL20910, and HL07332.

REFERENCES

Aitken, P. P. Peer group pressures, parental control, and cigarette smoking among 10–14 year olds. *British Journal of Social and Clinical Psychology*, 1980, *19*, 141–146.

Allport, G. W. *Personality*. New York: Holt, 1937.

Bandura, A. *Social learning theory*. Englewood Cliffs, N.J.: Prentice Hall, 1977.

Barbarin, O. A. Comparison of symbolic and overt aversion in the self-control of smoking. *Journal of Consulting and Clinical Psychology*, 1978, *46*, 1569–1571.

Barkley, R. A., Hastings, J. E., & Jackson, T. L. The effects of rapid smoking and hypnosis in the treatment of smoking behavior. *International Journal of Clinical and Experimental Hypnosis*. 1977, *25*, 7–17.

Beebe-Center, J. G. *The psychology of pleasantness and unpleasantness*. New York: Van Nostrand, 1932.

Bennett, W. The nicotine fix. *Harvard Magazine*, 1980, July-August, 10–14.

Berkowitz, B, Ross-Townsend, A., & Kohberger, R. Hypnotic treatment of smoking: The single-treatment method revisited. *American Journal of Psychiatry*, 1979, *136*, 83–85.

Bernstein, D. A. Modification of smoking behavior: An evaluative review. *Psychological Bulletin*, 1969, *71*, 418–440.

Bernstein, D. A., & Glasgow, R. E. Smoking. In O. F. Pomerleau & J. P. Brady (Eds.), *Behavioral medicine: Theory and practice*. Baltimore: Williams and Wilkins, 1979, pp. 233–253.

Best, J. A. Tailoring smoking withdrawal procedures to personality and motivational differences. *Journal of Consulting and Clinical Psychology*, 1975, *43*, 1–8.

Best, J. A., & Hakstian, A. R. A situation-specific model for smoking behavior. *Addictive Behaviors,* 1978, *3,* 79–92.

Borrie, R. A., & Suedfeld, P. Restricted environmental stimulation therapy in a weight reduction program. *Journal of Behavioral Medicine,* 1980, *3,* 147–161.

Bosse, R., Garvey, A. J., & Glynn, R. J. Age and addiction to smoking. *Addictive Behaviors,* 1980, *5,* 341–351.

Botvin, G. J., Eng, A., & Williams, C. L. Preventing the onset of cigarette smoking through life skills training. *Preventive Medicine,* 1980, *9,* 135–143.

Califano, J. A. Jr. *Smoking and health: A report of the Surgeon General.* Washington, D.C.: Superintendent of Documents, U.S. Government Printing Office, Stock Number 017-000-0218-0, 1979.

Carmody, T. P., Senner, J. W., Malinow, M. R., & Matarazzo, J. D. Physical exercise rehabilitation: Long-term dropout rate in cardiac patients. *Journal of Behavioral Medicine,* 1980, *3,* 163–168.

Chicago Lung Association. Personal communication from Susan Brickman, Chicago Lung Association, Chicago, January 22, 1981.

Coan, R. V. Research strategy in the investigation of personality correlates. In S. V. Zagona (Ed.), *Studies and issues in smoking behavior.* Tuscon: University of Arizona Press, 1967.

Colletti, G., & Kopel, S. A. Maintaining behavior change: An investigation of three maintenance strategies and the relationship of self-attribution to the long-term reduction of cigarette smoking. *Journal of Consulting and Clinical Psychology,* 1979, *47,* 614–617.

Colletti, G., & Supnick, J. A. Continued therapist contact as a maintenance strategy for smoking reduction. *Journal of Consulting and Clinical Psychology,* 1980, *48,* 665–667.

Conway, J. B. Behavioral self-control of smoking through aversive conditioning and self-management. *Journal of Consulting and Clinical Psychology,* 1977, *45,* 348–357.

Costa, P. T., McCrae, R., & Bosse, R. Smoking motive factors: A review and replication. *International Journal of the Addictions,* 1980, *15,* 537–549.

Dawley, H. H. Jr., Morrison, J., & Carrol, S. A comparison of hospitalized veterans' attitudes toward smoking and smoking cessation over a four year period. *Addictive Behaviors,* 1980, *5,* 241–245.

Delahunt, J., & Curran, J. P. Effectiveness of negative practice and self-control techniques in the reduction of smoking behavior. *Journal of Consulting and Clinical Psychology,* 1976, *44,* 1002–1007.

Dunn, W. L., Jr. (Ed.). *Smoking behavior: Motives and incentives.* Washington, D.C.: Winston, 1973.

Eiser, J. R., & Sutton, S. R. Smoking as a subjectively rational choice. *Addictive Behaviors,* 1977, *2,* 129–134.

Evans, D., & Lane, D. S. Long-term outcome of smoking cessation workshops. *American Journal of Public Health,* 1980, *70,* 725–727.

Evans, R. I. Smoking in children: Developing a social psychological strategy of deterrence. *Preventive Medicine,* 1976, *5,* 122–127.

Evans, R. I., Rozelle, R. M., Maxwell, S. E., Raines, B. E., Dill, C. A., & Guthrie, T. J. Social modeling films to deter smoking in adolescents: Results of a three year field investigation. *Journal of Applied Psychology,* in press.

Evans, R. I., Rozelle, R. M., Mittlemark, M. B., Hansen, W. B., Bane, A. L., & Havis, J. Deterring the onset of smoking in children: Knowledge of immediate physiological effects and coping with peer pressure, media pressure, and parent modeling. *Journal of Applied Social Psychology,* 1978, *8,* 126–135.

Eysenck, H. J. Personality and the maintenance of the smoking habit. In W. L. Dunn, Jr. (Ed.), *Smoking behavior: Motives and incentives.* Washington, D.C.: Winston, 1973, pp. 113–146.

Ferraro, D. P. Self-control of smoking: The amotivational syndrome. *Journal of Abnormal Psychology,* 1973, *81,* 152–157.

Flaxman, J. Affect-management and habit mechanisms in the modification of smoking behavior. *Addictive Behaviors*, 1979, *4*, 39–46.

Flaxman, J. Quitting smoking now or later: Gradual, abrupt, immediate, and delayed quitting. *Behavior Therapy*, 1978, *9*, 260–270.

Frederiksen, L. W. Single-case designs in the modification of smoking. *Addictive Behaviors*, 1976, *1*, 311–319.

Frederiksen, L. W., & Martin, J. E. Carbon monoxide and smoking behavior. *Addictive Behaviors*, 1979, *4*, 21–30.

Gilbert, D. G. Paradoxical tranquilizing and emotion reducing effects of nicotine. *Psychological Bulletin*, 1979, *86*, 643–661.

Gilbert, D. G. Introversion and self-reported reason for and times of urge for smoking. *Addictive Behaviors*, 1980, *5*, 97–99.

Gilbert, D. G., & Hagen, R. L. The effects of nicotine and extraversion on self-report, skin conductance, electromyography, and heart responses to emotional stimuli. *Addictive Behaviors*, 1980, *5*, 247–257.

Glasgow, R. E. Effects of a self-control manual, rapid smoking, and amount of therapist contact on smoking reduction. *Journal of Consulting and Clinical Psychology*, 1978, *46*, 1439–1447.

Glasgow, R. E., & Bernstein, D. A. Behavioral treatment of smoking behavior. In C. K. Prokop, & L. A. Bradley (Eds.), *Medical psychology: Contributions to behavioral medicine*. New York: Academic Press, 1981.

Gori, G. B. & Bock, F. G. (Eds.). *A safe cigarette?* Proceedings of a conference, Cold Spring Harbor, N.Y. Oct. 1979. Cold Spring Harbor Laboratory, Cold Spring Harbor, N.E., 1980, Banbury Report 3.

Green, D. E. Patterns of tobacco use in the United States. In N. A. Krasnegor (Ed.), *Cigarette smoking as a dependence process*. (NIDA Research Monographs No. 23), DHEW publication 79–800, Rockville, MD, 1979, pp. 44–55.

Green, D. E. Psychological factors in smoking. In M. E. Jarvik, J. W. Cullen, E. R. Gritz, T. M. Vogt & L. J. West (Eds.), *Research on smoking behavior*. (NIDA Research Monograph No 17), DHEW publication 78–581, Rockville, MD, 1977, pp. 149–155.

Hall, J. A., & Crasilneck, H. B. Development of a hypnotic technique for treating chronic cigarette smoking. *International Journal of Clinical and Experimental Hypnosis*, 1970, *18*, 283–289.

Hall, R. G., & Sachs, D. P. L., & Hall, S. M. Medical risk and therapeutic effectiveness of rapid smoking. *Behavior Therapy*, 1979, *10*, 249–259.

Harris, P. R. *The health consequences of smoking for women: A report of the Surgeon General*. Washington, D.C. Superintendent of Documents, U.S. Government Printing Office, Stock Number 1980-0326003, 1980.

Harris, P. R. *The health consequences of smoking (the changing cigarette): A report of the Surgeon General*. Washington, D.C. Superintendent of Documents, U.S. Government Printing Office, Stock Number 1980-335339:7063, 1981.

Harrup, T., Hansen, B. A., & Soghikian, K. Clinical methods in smoking cessation: Description and evaluation of a stop smoking clinic. *American Journal of Public Health*, 1979, *69*, 1226–1231.

Horn, D., & Waingrow, S. *Behavior and attitudes, questionnaire*. Bethesda, MD: National Clearing House for Smoking and Health, 1966.

Hunt, W. A. The American school system, a possible locus for a universal mental health program. *Psychology in the Schools*, 1968, *5*, 35–40.

Hunt, W. A. (Ed.). *Learning mechanisms in smoking*. Chicago: Aldine, 1970.

Hunt, W. A. (Ed.). Special Issue: New approaches to behavioral research on smoking. *Journal of Abnormal Psychology*, 1973, *81*, 107–198.

Hunt, W. A., Barnett, L. W., & Branch, L. G. Relapse rates in addiction programs. Journal of Clinical *Psychology*, 1971, *27*, 455–456.

Hunt, W. A., & Bespalec, D. A. Relapse rates after treatment for heroin addiction. *Journal of Community Psychology,* 1974, *2,* 85-87.

Hunt, W. A., & Bespalec, D. A. An evaluation of current methods of modifying smoking behavior. *Journal of Clinical Psychology,* 1974, *30,* 431-438.

Hunt, W. A., & General, W. A. Relapse rates after treatment for alcoholism. *Journal of Community Psychology,* 1973, *1,* 66-68.

Hunt, W. A., & Matarazzo, J. D. Habit mechanisms in smoking. In W. A. Hunt (Ed.), *Learning mechanisms in smoking.* Chicago: Aldine, 1970, pp. 65-106.

Hunt, W. A., & Matarazzo, J. D. Three years later: Recent developments in experimental modification of smoking behavior. *Journal of Abnormal Psychology,* 1973, *81,* 107-114.

Hunt, W. A., Matarazzo, J. D., Weiss, S. M., & Gentry, W. D. Associative learning, habit, and health behavior. *Journal of Behavioral Medicine,* 1979, *2,* 111-124.

Ikard, F. F., Green, D., & Horn, D. A scale to differentiate between types of smoking as related to the management of affect. *International Journal of Addiction,* 1969, *4,* 649-659.

Jarvik, M. E. Tolerance to the effects of tobacco. In N. A. Krasnegor (Ed.), *Cigarette smoking as a dependence process.* (NIDA Research Monograph No 23) Rockville, MD: National Institute of Drug Abuse, 1979, pp. 150-157.

Jessor, R., & Jessor, S. L. *Problem behavior and psychosocial development: A longitudinal study of youth.* New York: Academic Press, 1977.

Kantorowitz, D. A., Walters, J., & Pezdek, K. Positive versus negative self-monitoring in the self-control of smoking. *Journal of Consulting and Clinical Psychology,* 1978, *46,* 1148-1150.

Kanzler, M., Jaffe, J. H., & Zeidenberg, P. Long- and short-term effectiveness of a large-scale proprietary smoking cessation program—a 4-year follow-up of Smokenders participants. *Journal of Clinical Psychology,* 1976, *32,* 661-669.

Katz, N. W. Hypnosis and the addictions: A critical review. *Addictive Behaviors,* 1980, *5,* 41-47.

Kendler, H. *Psychology: A science in conflict.* New York: Oxford University Press, 1981.

Kimble, G. A., & Perlmuter, L. The problem of volition. *Psychological Review,* 1970, *77,* 361-384.

Lamontagne, Y., Gagnon, M. A., Trudel, G., & Boisvert, J. Thought-stopping as a treatment for reducing cigarette smoking. *International Journal of the Addictions,* 1978, *13,* 297-305.

Lando, H. A. Successful treatment of smokers with a broad-spectrum behavioral approach. *Journal of Consulting and Clinical Psychology,* 1977, *45,* 361-366.

Lando, H. A. Stimulus control, rapid smoking, and contractual management in the maintenance of nonsmoking. *Behavior Therapy,* 1978, *9,* 962-963.

Lando, H. A., & McCullough, J. A. Clinical application of a broad-spectrum behavioral approach to chronic smokers. *Journal of Consulting and Clinical Psychology,* 1978, *46,* 1583-1585.

Leo, J. A painful theory on pleasures. *Time,* November 10, 1980, 112.

Ledwidge, B. Cognitive behavior modification: A step in the wrong direction? *Psychological Bulletin,* 1978, *85,* 353-375.

Ledwidge, B. Cognitive behavior modification or new ways to change minds: Reply to Mahoney and Kazdin. *Psychological Bulletin,* 1979, *86,* 1050-1053.

Leventhal, H., & Avis, N. Pleasure, addiction and habit: Factors in verbal report or factors in smoking behavior? *Journal of Abnormal Psychology,* 1976, *85,* 478-488.

Leventhal, H., & Cleary, P. D. The smoking problem: A review of the research and theory in behavioral risk modification. *Psychological Bulletin,* 1980, *88,* 370-405.

Liard, R., Perdrizet, S., Correman, J., & Bidou, S. Smoking and chronic respiratory symptoms: Prevalence in male and female smokers. *American Journal of Public Health,* 1980, *70,* 271-273.

Lichtenstein, E., & Danaher, B. G. Modification of smoking behavior: A critical analysis of theory, research, and practice. In M. Herson, R. M. Eisler & P. Miller (Eds.), *Progress in behavior modification* (Vol. 3). New York: Academic Press, 1976.

Lichtstein, K. L., & Stalgaitis, S. J. Treatment of cigarette smoking in couples by reciprocal aversion. *Behavior Therapy*, 1980, *11*, 104–108.

Litman, G. K., Eiser, J. R., & Taylor, C. Dependence, relapse, and extinction: A theoretical critique and a behavioral examination. *Journal of Clinical Psychology*, 1979, *35*, 192–199.

Logan, F. Self-control as habit, drive, and incentive. *Journal of Abnormal Psychology*, 1973, *81*, 127–136.

Luepker, R. V., Hurd, P., Pechacek, T., Bast, P., Johnson, C. A., & Pickard, K. Prevention of cigarette smoking in 7th grade school children. *Journal of Behavioral Medicine*. 1980, *3*, 15–28.

Maccoby, N., Farquhar, J. W., Wood, P. D., & Alexander, J. Reducing the risk of cardiovascular disease: Effects of a community-based campaign on knowledge and behavior. *Journal of Community Health*, 1977, *3*, 100–114.

Mahoney, M. J., & Kazdin, A. E. Cognitive behavior modification: Misconceptions and premature evaluation. *Psychological Bulletin*, 1979, *86*, 1044–1049.

Malone, J. C. Beyond the operant analysis of behavior. *Behavior Therapy*, 1978, *9*, 584–591.

Marlatt, G. A., & Gordon, J. R. Determinants of relapse: Implications for the maintenance of behavior change. In P. D. Davidson & S. M. Davidson (Eds.), *Behavioral medicine: Changing health lifestyles*. New York: Brunner/Mazel, 1980, 410–452.

Matarazzo, J. D. Behavioral health and behavioral medicine: Frontiers for a new health psychology. *American Psychologist*, 1980, *35*, 807–817.

Matarazzo, J. D. Behavioral health's challenge to academic, scientific and professional psychology. *American Psychologist*, 1982, *37*, 1–14.

Matarazzo, J. D., Connor, W. E. Fey, S., Carmody, T. P., Pierce, D. K., Brischetto, C. S., Baker, L. H., Connor, S. L., & Sexton, G. Behavioral cardiology with emphasis on the Family Heart Study: Fertile ground for psychological and biomedical research. In T. Milton, C. J. Green & R. B. Meagher (Eds.), *Handbook of health care psychology*. New York: Plenum, 1981.

Mausner, B., & Platt, E. *Smoking: A behavioral analysis*. New York: Pergamon Press, 1971.

Miller, P. M. Interactions among addictive behaviors. *British Journal of Addictions*, 1979, *74*, 211–212.

Moss, A. J. *Changes in cigarette smoking and current smoking practices among adults: United States, 1978. Advance data*. National Center for Health Statistics, September, 1979.

McAlister, A. L., Perry, C., & Maccoby, N. Adolescent smoking: Onset and prevention. *Pediatrics*, 1979, *63*, 650–658.

McAlister, A., Perry, C., Killen, J., Slinkard, L. A., & Maccoby, N. Pilot study of smoking, alcohol and drug abuse prevention. *American Journal of Public Health*, 1980, *70*, 719–721.

McAlister, A., Puska, P., Koskela, K., Pallonen, W., & Maccoby, N. Mass communication and community organization for public health education. *American Psychologist*, 1980, *35*, 375–379.

McFall, R. M. Smoking-cessation research, *Journal of Consulting and Clinical Psychology*, 1978, *46*, 703–712.

McKennell, A. C. Smoking motivation factors. *British Journal of Social and Clinical Psychology*, 1970, *9*, 8–22.

McKennell, A. C., & Bynner, J. M. Self images and smoking behavior among school boys. *British Journal of Educational Psychology*, 1969, *39*, 27–39.

National Cancer Institute. Cause of diabetes - Helping patients stop smoking. *Journal of the American Medical Association*, 1979, *242*, 1015–1016.

National Cancer Institute. *Clearing the air: A guide to quitting smoking*. Bethesda, MD: National Cancer Institute, 1979 (DHEW Publication No [NIH] 79-1647).

National Interagency Council on Smoking and Health. Guidelines for research on the effectiveness of smoking cessation programs: A committee report. Private circulation. National Interagency Council on Smoking and Health, 419 Park Avenue South, New York, N.Y., 1974.

Pachman, J., & Frederiksen, L. "Yes I do mind": Social skills training for non-smokers. *Addictive Behaviors*, 1979, *4*, 75–81.

Pechacek, T. F. An overview of smoking behavior and its modification. In N. A. Krasnegor (Ed.), *Behavioral analysis and treatment of substance abuse*. NIDA Research Monograph 25. Washington, D.C.: DHEW, 1979.

Pechacek, T. F., & Danaher, B. G. How and why people quit smoking: A cognitive-behavioral analysis. In P. C. Kendall & S. D. Hollon (Eds.), *Cognitive-behavioral interventions: Theory, research, and procedures*. New York: Academic Press, 1979.

Pechacek, T. F., & McAlister, A. Strategies for the modification of smoking behavior: Treatment and prevention. In J. Ferguson & B. Taylor (Eds.), *A comprehensive handbook of behavior medicine*. New York: Spectrum Publications, 1980, in press.

Pederson, L. L., Scrimgeour, W. G., & Lefcoe, N. M. Comparison of hypnosis plus counseling, counseling alone, and hypnosis alone in a community service smoking withdrawal program. *Journal of Consulting and Clinical Psychology* 1975, *43*, 920.

Perry, C., Killen, B. A., Telch, M., Slinkard, M. A., & Danaher, B. K. Modifying smoking behavior of teenagers: A school-based intervention. *American Journal of Public Health,* 1980, *70*, 722-725.

Perry, C., & Mullen, G. The effects of hypnotic susceptibility on reducing smoking behavior treated by an hypnotic technique, *Journal of Clinical Psychology,* 1975, *31*, 498-505.

Pertschuk, M. J., Pomerleau, O., Adkins, D., & Hirsh, C. Smoking cessation: The psychological costs. *Addictive Behaviors,* 1979, *4*, 345-348.

Pomerleau, O. Behavioral medicine: The contribution of the experimental analysis of behavior to medical care. *American Psychologist,* 1979, *34,* 654-663.

Pomerleau O., & Pomerleau, C. *Break the smoking habit: A behavioral program for giving up cigarettes*. Champaign, Illinois: Research Press, 1980.

Premack, D., & Anglin, B. On the possibilities of self-control in man and animals. *Journal of Abnormal Psychology,* 1973, *81,* 137-151.

Puska, P., Koskela, K., McAlister, A., Pallonen, U., Vartiainen, E., & Homan, K. A Comprehensive television smoking cessation programme in Finland. *International Journal of Health Education,* 1979, *22,* 1-29.

Rogers, R. W., Deckner, C. W., & Mewborn, C. R. An expectancy-value theory approach to the long-term modification of smoking behavior. *Journal of Clinical Psychology,* 1978, *34,* 562-566.

Rotter, J. B. Generalized expectancies for internal versus external control of reinforcement. *Psychological Monographs,* 1966, *80,* (Whole No. 609).

Russell, M. A. H. Smoking problems: An overview. In M. E. Jarvik, J. W. Cullen E. R. Gritz, T. M. Vogt, & L. J. West (Eds.), *Research on smoking behavior*. (NIDA Research Monograph No 17). U.S. Department of Health, Education, and Welfare, Public Health Service, Alcohol, Drug Abuse, and Mental Health Administration, National Institute on Drug Abuse, DHEW Publication No. (ADM) 78-581, December 1977, pp. 13-33.

Sachs, D. P., Hall, R. G., Pechacek, T. F., & Fitzgerald, J. Clarification of risk-benefit issues in rapid smoking. *Journal of Consulting and Clinical Psychology,* 1979, *47,* 1053-1060.

Schachter, S. Nesbitt's paradox. In W. L. Dunn, Jr. (Ed.), *Smoking behavior: Motives and incentives*. Washington, D.C.: Winston, 1973.

Schachter, S. Pharmacological and psychological determinants of smoking. *Annals of Internal Medicine,* 1978, *88,* 104-114.

Schuman, L. M. Patterns of smoking behavior. In M. R. Jarvik, J. W. Cullen, E. R. Gritz, T. Vogt, & L. J. West (Eds.), *Research on smoking behavior*. (NIDA Monographs No 17). Rockville, MD: National Institute on Drug Abuse, 1977, pp. 36-65.

Schwartz, J. L., & Rider, G. *Review and evaluation of smoking control methods: The United States and Canada, 1969-1977*. Atlanta, GA: DHEW, Center for Disease Control, Bureau of Health Education, 1978.

Sebben, J., Pimm, P., & Shepard, R. J. Cigarette smoke in enclosed public facilities. *Archives of Environmental Health,* 1977, *32,* 53-57.

Shewchuck, L. A., Dubren, R., Burton, D., Forman, M., Clark, R. R., & Jaffin, A. R. Preliminary observations on an intervention program for heavy smokers. *International Journal of the Addictions*, 1977, *12*, 323–336.

Shiffman, S. M. The tobacco withdrawal syndrome. In N. A. Krasnegor (Ed.), *Cigarette smoking as a dependence process*. (NIDA Research Monograph #23) Rockville, MD: National Institute on Drug Abuse, 1979, 158–184.

Simon, H. A. The behavioral and social sciences. *Science*, 1980, *209*, 72–78.

Smith, G. M. Personality and smoking: A review of the empirical literature. In W. A. Hunt (Ed.), *Learning mechanisms in smoking*. Chicago: Aldine, 1970.

Soldatos, C. R., Kales, J. D., Scharf, M. B., Bixler, E. D., & Kales, A. Cigarette smoking associated with sleep difficulty. *Science*, 1980, *207*, 551–553.

Solomon, R. L. The opponent-process theory of acquired motivation: The costs of pleasure and the benefits of pain. *American Psychologist*, 1980, *35*, 691–712.

Solomon, R. L., & Corbit, J. D. An opponent-process theory of motivation: II. Cigarette addiction. *Journal of Abnormal Psychology*, 1973, *81*, 158–171.

Spiegel, H. Termination of smoking by a single treatment. *Archives of Environmental Health*, 1970, *20*, 736–742.

Stanton, H. E. A one-session hypnotic approach to modifying smoking behavior. *International Journal of Clinical and Experimental Hypnosis*, 1978, *26*, 22–29.

Sterling, T. D., & Kobayashi, D. M. Exposure to pollutants in enclosed "living spaces." *Environmental Research*, 1977, *13*, 1–35.

Suedfeld, P., & Best, J. A. Satiation and sensory deprivation combined in smoking therapy: Some case studies and unexpected side-effects. *International Journal of the Addictions*, 1977, *12*, 337–359.

Suedfeld, P., & Ikard, F. F. Use of sensory deprivation in facilitating the reduction of cigarette smoking. *Journal of Consulting and Clinical Psychology*, 1974, *42*, 888–895.

Sutton, S. R. Can subjective expected utility (SEU) theory explain smokers' decisions to try to stop smoking. In D. J. Osborne, M. M. Gruneberg & J. R. Eiser (Eds.), *Research in Psychology and Medicine (Vol. II)*. New York: Academic Press, 1979, pp. 94–101.

Sutton, S. R. Interpreting relapse curves. *Journal of Consulting and Clinical Psychology*, 1979, *47*, 96–98.

Taylor, D. H., & Blezard, P. N. The effects of smoking and urinary pH on a detection task. *Quarterly Journal of Experimental Psychology*, 1979, *31*, 635–640.

Ternes, J. An opponent process theory of habitual behavior with special reference to smoking. In M. Jarvik, J. Cullen, E. Gritz, T. Vogt & L. West (Eds.), *Research on smoking behavior*. (NIDA Monograph No 17) Rockville, MD: National Institute on Drug Abuse, 1977, pp. 157–182.

Tomkins, S. S. Psychological model for smoking behavior. *American Journal of Public Health*, 1966, *56*, 17–20.

Tomkins, S. S. A modified model of smoking behavior. In E. Borgatta, & R. Evans (Eds.), *Smoking, health and behavior*. Chicago: Aldine, 1968.

Tong, J. E. Henderson, P. R., & Chipperfield, B. G. A. Effects of ethanol and tobacco on auditory vigilance performance. *Addictive Behaviors*, 1980, *5*, 153–158.

Tongas, P. N. The long-term maintenance of non-smoking behavior. In M. E. Jarvik, J. W. Cullen, E. R. Gritz, T. M. Vogt & L. J. West (Eds.), *Research on Smoking Behavior*. (NIDA Monograph No 17) Rockville, MD: National Institute on Drug Abuse, 1977, pp. 355–363.

Tori, E. D. A smoking satiation procedure with reduced medical risk. *Journal of Clinical Psychology*, 1978, *34*, 574–577.

Van Lanaker, J. L. Smoking and disease. In M. Jarvik, J. Cullen, E. Gritz, T. Vogt & L. West (Eds.), *Research on smoking behavior*. (NIDA Monograph No 17) Rockville, MD: National Institute on Drug Abuse, 1977, pp. 230–281.

Vogt, T. M. Discussion. In M. Jarvik, J. Cullen, E. Gritz, T. Vogt & L. West (Eds.), *Research on *smoking behavior.* (NIDA Monograph No 17) Rockville, MD: National Institute on Drug Abuse, 1977, pp. 228–229.

Wallston, K. A., Wallston, B. S., & DeVellis, R. Development of the Multi-dimensional Health Locus of Control (MHLC) Scales. *Health Education Monographs,* 1978, *6,* 160–170.

Warner, K. E. Cigarette smoking in the 1970's: The impact of the antismoking campaign on consumption. *Science,* 1981, *211,* 729–731.

Watkins, H. H. Hypnosis and smoking: A five session approach. *International Journal of Clinical and Experimental Hypnosis,* 1976, *23,* 381–390.

Weber, A., Fischer, T., & Grandjean, E. Passive smoking in experimental and field conditions. *Environmental Research,* 1979, *20,* 205–216.

West, D. W., Graham, S., Swanson, M., & Wilkinson, G. Five-year follow-up of a smoking withdrawal clinic. American Journal of Public Health, 1977, *67,* 536–544.

West, L. J. Hypnosis in the treatment of the smoking habit. In M. Jarvik, J. Cullen, E. Gritz, T. Vogt & L. West (Eds.), *Research on Smoking Behavior* (NIDA Monograph No 17) Rockville, MD: National Institute on Drug Abuse, 1977.

7 Sleep Disorders

Peter J. Hauri
Dartmouth Medical School

Sleep disorders are widespread. According to a 1979 report from the Institute of Medicine (1979), about one third of all adults in the U.S. reported having had "trouble" sleeping within the last year. This is about 50 million people! About one fifth of them, about 10 million Americans, see physicians for sleep disorders within any given year, and more than half of that number receive prescriptions for sleeping pills.

Scientifically, the modern era of sleep research started when Aserinsky and Kleitmann (1953) described rapid eye movement (REM) sleep. Clinically, however, the modern era started only in the early 1970's when enough knowledge about sleep had accumulated to make it clinically useful. The 1970's then saw a phenomenal growth in clinical work, coupled with the realization that many of our previous beliefs about sleep problems may have been wrong. An Association of Sleep Disorders Centers (ASDC) was formed in 1975. This organization has now developed careful standards and certification procedures, both for sleep disorders centers and for sleep disorders specialists (called clinical polysomnographers). In addition, in 1979 the Surgeon General launched "Project Sleep," an effort to educate health professionals in the growing complexities of sleep disorders medicine.

The current chapter attempts to help clinicians to diagnose and effectively treat patients who complain of sleep problems. Relevant facts concerning sleep will first be reviewed. Some overall issues concerning diagnosis and treatment are then dealt with. Finally, the specific sleep disorders are discussed in turn, using the recently published nosology of the Association of Sleep Disorders Centers (1979) as a guide.

BASIC FACTS CONCERNING SLEEP

Research Methods

The main tool of sleep researchers is the polygraph. A one to three channel EEG is continuously recorded throughout the entire sleep period, together with other physiological variables such as eye movements, respiration, heart rate, and muscle tension. For most studies the sleepers come to the lab about 1-2 hours before their usual bedtimes. The various electrodes and sensors are then applied, and questionnaires asking about daytime activities and mood are answered. The sleeper then goes to bed in a small, sound attenuated room, and the various leads are connected to a junction box at the head of the bed. A technician monitors the polygraph throughout the night, while a two-way intercom maintains voice contact between sleeper and technician. About 1000 pages of polysomnographic record are generally obtained in this fashion per night.

Data reduction is usually done by the human eye: the technician scores each 1/2 minute epoch for its predominant features important to that study, such as the stage of sleep, the regularity of respiration, or the density of eye movements. Computer programs for data analysis and reduction are being developed, and some laboratories do use FM tapes and electronic scoring. Nevertheless, the majority of research and clinical sleep work still uses a visual analysis or the hard copy writeout. This is so because an overall ''gestalt'' of the simultaneous patterns in at least four channels is usually of interest, rather than specific frequency bands or wave forms that could be easily evaluated by electronic means.

Recording a night of sleep is expensive, costing well beyond $200.00 in most labs. This has led some researchers to use ''subjective'' evaluations as their basic data. In this approach patients usually sleep at home, and they fill out questionnaires indicating when they went to bed, when they fell asleep, how often they woke, how soundly they slept, etc.

Unfortunately, questionnaire data concerning sleep correlate very poorly with polygraphic recordings even in normal subjects, and much worse in patients with sleep problems. This has led to an unfortunate split. While the basic researcher advances new knowledge about sleep pathology using the ''objective'' polysomnographic data that he trusts, the practitioner diagnoses and treats based on the ''subjective'' interview data obtained at the office.

Actually, the problem is even more complex. When awakened from polygraphically documented, unmistakable sleep, some patients, especially insomniacs (Rechtschaffen & Monroe, 1969) report that they had been thinking and that they had felt subjectively awake. Furthermore, certain physiological measures, such as heart rate and muscle tension, seem to remain high in some of these insomniacs during sleep. Are these patients asleep, as their brain waves would suggest, or are they awake, as their continuous thinking and high autonomic arousal would suggest? The controversy has not been resolved to date.

Sleep "Architecture"

Sleep is not a uniform state, but consists of numerous and distinct stages and phases. Traditionally, these stages are distinguished by EEG (electroencephalogram), EOG (electrooculogram), and chin EMG (electromyogram). Rechtschaffen and Kales (1968) have published a manual of standardized terminology, techniques, and scoring systems for sleep stages of human subjects. This manual should be consulted whenever the outline given here proves too sketchy.

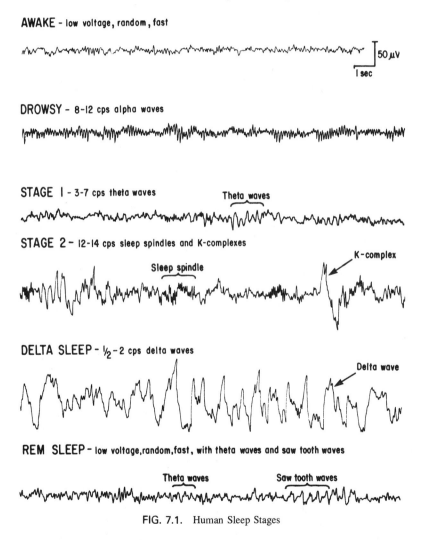

FIG. 7.1.   Human Sleep Stages

Sleep Stages.   Basically, there are two types of sleep: ordinary sleep without rapid eye movements (non-REM, NREM), also called "orthodox" sleep or "the

S-state,'' and rapid eye movement sleep (REM), also called "paradoxical" sleep, or "the D-state." NREM sleep is further subdivided into stage 2 (average, normal) sleep and delta (deep) sleep. In addition, there is a transition phase between wakefulness and sleep which is usually labelled stage 1 sleep. Figure 7.1 illustrates the typical EEG waveforms of these stages.

Stage 2, the most abundant of sleep stages, is marked by sleep spindles (bursts of 12 to 14 cps EEG activity, lasting ½ to 2 seconds) and by K-complexes (well delineated, slow, and large EEG waves starting with a negative component) on a low amplitude EEG background. Stage 2 occupies 50%–70% of adult sleep. When subjects are awakened from this stage, they usually remember short, mundane, and fragmented thoughts (Foulkes, 1962).

Delta sleep is defined by an EEG recording that contains at least 20% of the large and slow delta waves (½ to 2 cps amplitude, at least 75 uV pp when measured by standard monopolar electrodes applied over the central cortex). This is the deepest sleep of the night and, some say, the most restorative sleep. It usually occurs early at night. In the past, delta sleep had been further subdivided into stages 3 and 4 depending on the amount of delta waves produced, but this separation has proved unnecessarily detailed in most cases.

Stage 1, the transition phase between wakefulness and sleep, is characterized by a relatively low voltage, mixed-frequency EEG with a fair amount of theta waves (3–7 cps). Stage 1 occurs at sleep onset and often during sleep, especially after a body movement or after some noise. A stage 1 EEG is also found in experienced practitioners of meditation (Elson, Hauri, & Cunis, 1977). Depending on the author, stage 1 is either classified as wakefulness (Johnson, 1973) or as "light" sleep (Rechtschaffen & Kales, 1968). A frequency analysis of the EEG shows stage 1 to be more similar to wakefulness than to sleep (Johnson, 1973). Similarly, humans awakened from this sleep often feel that they had been awake. However, a decreased reactivity to external stimuli and a change in mentation from wake-type thinking to a more dreamlike experience (Foulkes & Vogel, 1965) suggest that sleep might have already begun in stage 1.

REM Sleep, the second major kind of sleep, is characterized by a low voltage, random, fast EEG. This EEG also contains many components in the theta range (3–7 cps), including some that show a characteristic saw-tooth shape. Eye movements are frequent during REM sleep, usually occurring in bursts and alternating with periods of ocular quiescence. Background muscle tonus, especially in the chin and neck muscles, is lower during REM sleep than during any other kind of sleep. However, also during REM, one often sees bursts of small twitches in many muscle groups. Heart rate and respiratory rate are higher and more variable during REM sleep than during periods of NREM sleep from the same time of the night. In general, about 80% of the awakenings from REM sleep yield reports of vivid dreaming.

Wakefulness is usually separated into alert wakefulness, with a low voltage, random, fast EEG, and drowsy wakefulness, where alpha waves (8–12 cps) predominate, at least in the occipital cortex. However, for unknown reasons there are humans who show very few, or no alpha waves even when they are subjectively drowsy.

The separation of sleeping and wakefulness into mutually exclusive, distinct stages is somewhat arbitrary. In fact, there is a gradual waxing and waning of the different stages. Delta waves, for example, start to crescendo early during stage 2, long before they are sufficiently powerful to be scored as delta sleep. Similarly, the exact beginning of REM sleep is hard to discern because the indices of REM sleep, i.e. the low voltage EEG, the lack of chin muscle tonus, and the eye movements, do not all start at the same time. In addition, these indices of REM sleep first manifest themselves tentatively, then gain in force up to the middle of the REM period, from whence they gradually fade away again.

Sleep Cycles. Figure 7.2 shows a typical night of a young adult. As illustrated there, upon going to bed, a normal sleeper usually passes through stage 1 into stage 2. After 10 to 30 minutes in stage 2 the delta waves gradually become more predominant, until the sleeper enters delta sleep. Sixty to ninety minutes later the sleeper returns to stage 2 and then enters a REM period, lasting just a few minutes. This first REM period is by far the least intense of the night, both in terms of physiological manifestations of REM sleep and in terms of the psychological intensity of the dream. Children and sleep deprived adults often skip this first REM period altogether.

The second sleep cycle begins when stage 2 reappears after the first REM period. Depending on age, the sleeper might reenter delta sleep, but there is usually less of it in the second cycle than in the first. After about 90 minutes of

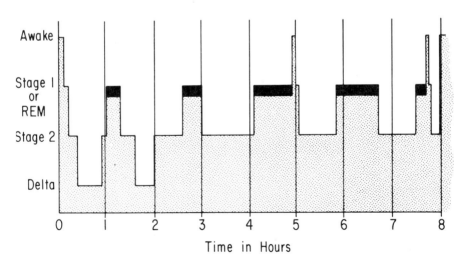

FIG. 7.2. A Typical Night's Sleep in a Young Adult (26 year old, female)

NREM sleep, the second REM period appears, usually lasting 8-10 minutes. Following it and until awakening in the morning, stage 2 sleep and REM usually alternate in approximately 90-minute cycles. REM sleep usually lasts 15-30 minutes, the rest is stage 2 sleep. Delta sleep is rarely seen in these latter sleep cycles. REM sleep becomes more intense towards morning, both physiologically and psychologically.

Sprinkled throughout REM and NREM sleep are numerous body movements, and 5-15 spontaneous awakenings. In good sleepers these awakenings last from a few seconds to a few minutes each. The sleeper is responsive to his environment during these short arousals if there is a stimulus that draws his attention, but the awakenings are habitually forgotten by morning if nothing happens during them.

Depth of Sleep is usually measured by the amount of noise it takes to awaken the sleeper. Within NREM sleep, delta sleep is clearly deeper than stage 2. However, stage 2 itself is not always of the same depth; it is lighter right after falling asleep and during the early morning hours, deeper when close in time to delta sleep (Bonnet, Johnson, & Webb, 1978).

Depth of sleep is a more complex issue for REM sleep. Rechtschaffen, Hauri, and Zeitlin (1966) found that REM sleep was as light as stage 2 sleep in humans, but Siegel and Langley (1965), and Meier and Berger (1967) report that REM sleep is the deepest of sleeps in cats and rhesus monkeys. Other indices of sleep depth are also ambiguous. The typical heart rate elevation and variability during REM sleep, the high neuronal discharge rates in some parts of the brain, and the mental activity of dreaming would all suggest that REM sleep is very active, very close to wakefulness. However, a relative lack of reactivity in skin resistance during REM, an exceedingly low muscle tonus, and the lack of reality testing in our dreams would suggest that REM might be extremely deep sleep, far removed from wakefulness.

Because REM sleep cannot be classified clearly as either light or deep sleep, most researchers now accept Snyder's (1971) view that there are three basic states of existence: Waking, NREM sleep, and REM sleep. REM sleep is conceptualized as similar to wakefulness in some aspects (e.g., cortical activation), but as similar to NREM sleep in others (e.g. diminished reactivity to the environment).

Circadian Rhythm

We call "circadian" those rhythms that take about a day to complete. Obviously, the sleep-wake cycle is one such rhythm. It is much easier to fall asleep at some points in the circadian cycle than at others.

Circadian cycles are not simple 24-hour clocks. When normal volunteers live in environments with no time clues, they usually show a sleep-wake rhythm lasting about 25 hours. Also, there appears to be more than one biological clock in our body, and these clocks do not all keep exactly the same time (Wever, 1976). Thus, unless our internal circadian cycles are regularly synchronized with the external clock of the earth's rotation, there is not only the danger that humans will drift out of phase with their social environment, but also the problem that the different biological clocks within the same human will become desynchronized. Should that happen it would mean that there never is a good time either to sleep or to be awake, because one internal rhythm may be at a low ebb when another one calls for wakefulness. People who have lost a synchronized circadian rhythm often claim that they are "always sleepy, but never sleeping well."

Experience suggests that the most powerful "Zeitgeber" (synchronizing impulse) may be a regular wake-up time. This is a signal that is clearly under voluntary control. One can force oneself into wakefulness with alarm clocks, cold showers, and similar techniques. Selecting bedtime as the "Zeitgeber" is a less powerful signal in humans because falling asleep is not under voluntary control, and cannot be easily forced by willpower.

Neurological Issues

NREM Sleep. If the brain stem is transected at the level of the mid-brain, *both* the brain stem below the lesion and the forebrain above show independent wake/NREM sleep cycling. There seems to be no single "center" for NREM sleep. There are, however, a number of regions that facilitate sleep, such as the basal forebrain, the region of the solidary tract in the medulla, and, possibly, the dorsal raphe nucleus. Similarly, there are regions that facilitate waking, primarily the ascending reticular activating system and the posterior hypothalamus.

Heuristically, it seems best to think of two far-flung, mutually inhibiting and interacting systems when considering sleep and wakefulness. Either one or the other of these two systems predominates at any one time. It follows that, neurologically, insomnia may have two basic causes: either excessive activity in the wake system (excessive arousal), or an excessive lack of activity in the sleep system. Episodic insomnia, such as the inability to sleep before an exam, is usually caused by excessive arousal. However, some patients with chronic, relentless insomnia seem able to relax quite deeply and still not to sleep well. A disturbance in the sleep system might be postulated.

Previously, it had been believed that serotonin was primarily involved in the induction and maintenance of NREM sleep. This view seems no longer tenable. Rather, it appears that a combination of serotonin, catecholamines and acetylcholine may interact in modulating the sleep-wake-REM balance.

REM Sleep. Transection of the brain stem just behind the inferior colliculus and in front of the locus coeruleus and the pontine reticular formation does not prevent REM sleep in the caudal part of the brain stem. This means that the parts rostral to this section, including the mid-brain, thalamus and cortex, are not necessary for REM sleep, although they may participate in modifying REM sleep in intact animals. On the other hand, a transection of the spinal cord does not affect REM's processes. This leads to the undisputed fact that pontine and medullary regions of the brain stem are sufficient to generate REM sleep. The major research thrust during the last 20 years has been to further localize these REM generating mechanisms within the pons and medulla.

According to a model proposed by Hobson and McCarley (e.g. Hobson, 1974), two classes of neurons (or systems) seem to be involved in the REM/NREM sleep cycle control.

1. *An aminergic system* (REM-off cells) is located in the dorsal raphe nuclei (serotonergic), the locus coeruleus (noradrenergic), and the nucleus peribrachialis lateralis (possibly noradrenergic). All cells in this system show high discharge rates during wakefulness, a progressive decline during NREM sleep, and very low discharge rates early during REM sleep. Firing in this system appears to be self inhibitory and inhibitory to post-synaptic neurons.

2. *A cholinergic reticular system* (REM-on cells) is primarily located in the medullar and pontine gigantocellular tegmental fields (FTG) and in some adjacent areas (FTC, FTL, FTP). When the animal is not moving, unit activity in these cells is opposite to that of the aminergic system previously discussed: lowest in the waking state, increasing during NREM sleep, highest during REM sleep. Cells in this system appear to be cholinoceptive, cholinergic, self- and mutually excitatory.

Hobson's model (1974) postulates that the two systems continuously interact so as to produce NREM-REM cycling. This model has now been tested by microinjections of cholinergic and anti-aminergic substances into these areas, both of which increase REM sleep in cats (Hobson, personal communication). Hobson's model is elegant in the simplicity with which it explains the REM/NREM alterations and, possibly, even WAKE/REM/NREM cycling.

The model has been questioned by Siegel (1979) who points out that Hobson's "REM-on" cells fire whenever the animal moves, be it wakefulness or REM. Siegel feels that Hobson's "REM-on" cells are simply movement cells. Hobson feels that these cells may be both: hyperpolarized cells that *can* be fired with movements during wakefulness, but whose polarization gradually decreases during sleep until they fire spontaneously as "REM-executive" cells, initiating REM sleep.

Hobson's model has also been attacked as being too simplistic by Tohyama, Sakai, Touret, Salvert, and Jouvet (1979) and by Netick, Orem, and Dement (1977). Indeed, Sastre, Sakai, and Jouvet (1979) report that a total destruction of the pontine gigantocellular tegmental field did not even produce a transient disruption of REM sleep, and they feel that the FTG cells therefore do not play *any* role in REM sleep. Hobson retorts that the "REM-on" system is much more widespread than Sakai et al.,'s lesions, and that it has never been completely lesioned.

The argument obviously has not yet been settled. The endeavor is fascinating because the most advanced single unit recordings, micro-chemical injections, and histofluorescent techniques are employed to advance our understanding of the global, overall state of the organism. Possibly, this work may soon illuminate even our understanding of the psychological act of dreaming.

Age Relationships

Age seems to be an extremely important determinant of a person's sleep pattern (Williams, Karacan, & Hursch, 1974), as Fig. 7.3 indicates. While some minor fluctuations within Fig. 7.3 (page 220) may be due to small sampling, the following seem clearly established:

1. *Total sleep time* drops from about 17 hours near birth to about 10 hours at age 4 and to about 9 hours at age 10. A precipitous drop to about 7½ hours then occurs during adolescence, and a gradual decline to about 6 hours develops from there until old age.
2. *Delta sleep* decreases steadily throughout the entire lifetime.
3. *REM sleep* comprises about 50% of total sleep at birth. It then drops to about 30% at age 4, to about 25% at age 14, and to about 20% or less in old age.
4. *Time in bed* closely parallels total time asleep up to about age 35. From then on, time in bed increases, while time asleep declines. This means that we typically become more insomniac from age 35 on, spending more and more time in bed trying to sleep, but being less and less able to do it.

The *pattern of sleep difficulties* (not graphed in Figure 7.3) also changes with age: young insomniacs typically have problems falling asleep, while middle age and older insomniacs typically have difficulties with frequent awakenings or with early morning insomnia.

Sleep Needs

Case History: Mrs. O., 75 years of age, came to the Sleep Clinic under pressure from her husband. It appears that she has rarely slept for more than 4 hours per night since early adulthood. Laboratory evaluations confirmed the finding: she slept for 3 hours on the first night, 3½ on the second, and less than 3 on the third night. However, during the day Mrs. O. felt quite well. Indeed considering her age she showed very little psychological or physiological impairment. In addition, she was still involved in town politics, and continued to hike in the summer, cross country ski in the winter. Obviously, the chronically short sleep throughout adulthood had not done any damage to Mrs. O's health.

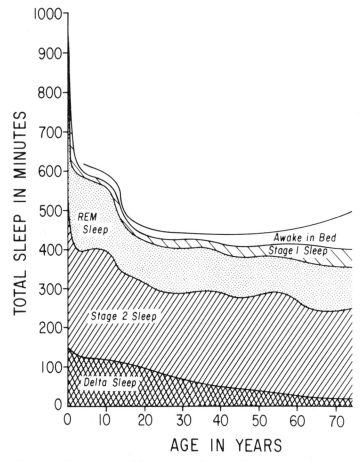

FIG. 7.3. Development of Sleep over a Human Lifetime. Data computed by permission from Williams R. L., Karacan, I., & Hursch, C. J. Electroencephalography (EEG) of Human Sleep. New York: John Wiley & Sons, 1974.

While Figure 7.3 indicated the average amount of sleep obtained during a life span, these figures should not be taken as guides for individuals. The range of customary sleep time seems surprisingly wide, even in good sleepers. Some healthy adults apparently sleep 3 hours or less per night without ill effects (Jones & Oswald, 1968; Stuss & Broughton, 1978), while others feel sleep deprived and tired when they obtain "only" 7 hours, but feel well and alert if they can sleep 10–12 hours per night. This wide range in healthy sleep makes it difficult to think of the need for sleep in the same biological way as we think of the needs for food or water. It also makes it difficult to define insomnia in an objective way. Some may sleep 7 hours or more and complain bitterly about their insomnia, while others may sleep 3 hours and feel healthy.

It is not known why humans vary so widely in their needs for sleep. Indeed, there is some argument whether, in general, we sleep too much or too little. Webb and Agnew (1975) present evidence indicating that in our Western civilization we may be chronically sleep depriving ourselves. Sleep clinicians, on the other hand, finding that insomniacs as a rule stay in bed much longer than good sleepers, advise poor sleepers to curtail their total bedtime. Indeed, Mullaney, Johnson, Naitoh, Friedmann, and Globus (1977), found that a chronic and drastic curtailment of bedtime in three couples over many months led to an appreciable decrease in their need to sleep on a one year follow-up. It appears that we can "teach" our bodies to "need" somewhat less sleep if we consistently "sleep-starve" it, but we do not yet know what the long range effects of such training may be.

Extremely large individual differences in sleep needs characterize not only adults, but children as well. Many a 2-year-old appears to need less sleep than some 10-year-olds. The best currently available yardstick of adequate sleep in children, as well as in adults, is adequate daytime functioning. As long as one remains alert and energetic during wakefulness, one apparently is getting enough sleep. If, after some weeks on a given sleep schedule, one becomes excessively tired, irritable, or frequently dozes off when not stimulated, more sleep seems indicated. However, should even drastically increased amounts of sleep not bring the expected alertness after a few nights, the possibility of pathologically excessive daytime somnolence should be investigated in children as well as in adults.

Sleep Deprivation

Case History: As a college teacher and sleep researcher, I occasionally had to teach after entire nights spent doing research at the lab. Lectures after sleepless nights often seemed awful to me. I felt worn out, without humor, and had difficulties concentrating and finding appropriate words. After some courses I then asked students to guess which lectures had been given after sleepless nights. To my great surprise, the students could not identify them! My performance, subjectively so poor after no sleep, apparently had not been as bad as I had thought when judged "objectively" from the outside.

The above anecdote illustrates a well documented and important point: The immediate effect of total sleep deprivation is a sharply increased drive to sleep, a decline in mood, and a subjective feeling of malaise. Initially, however, there is no serious impairment in objective performance. This is analogous to food: Skipping a meal usually increases our hunger quite dramatically without, initially, causing noteworthy physiological changes or medical damage. However, if sleep deprivation extends over a few nights, "mini-sleeps" start to occur during wakefulness. This means that short lapses of attention develop in which the EEG shows a few seconds of drowsiness or sleep waves. These episodes of "mini-sleep" increase in duration and number with increased sleep deprivation until, within about 10 days, it becomes almost impossible to say from the EEG or from the person's behavior whether he/she is actually awake or asleep.

Although mood after total sleep deprivation deteriorates drastically, it still follows a circadian rhythm. It is generally worse during times when one normally would be sleeping, say around 4 A.M. for most of us. Besides increased sleepiness, there is increased irritability and aggressiveness, a grim listlessness, and a feeling of depletion, not unlike the feeling insomniacs often describe (Hauri, 1979a).

After extended sleep deprivation, performance does gradually decrease. Initially, this decrease may be ascribed to the lapses of attention when taking "mini-sleeps." Later on, however, there seems to be a genuine decrease in perceptual, cognitive, and psychomotor capabilities (Pasnau, Naitoh, Stier, & Kollar, 1968). Surprisingly, in many physiological and psychological variables, the maximum disruptive effects of total sleep deprivation are found within 2-5 days. One might speculate that, after a few days, the gradually increasing mini-sleeps may be giving the body enough rest to maintain some low level of functioning.

Although experts still debate the issue, a fair amount of evidence is accumulating that artificial deprivation of *REM* sleep has different effects than artificial deprivation of *delta* sleep. While performance on work related tasks seems disturbed to about the same degree by both types of deprivation (Johnson, 1973), mood states seem to be affected differentially. REM sleep deprivation seems to heighten central neural excitability, to energize basic drives, or to weaken control over these drives (Vogel, 1975). Delta sleep deprivation, on the other hand, seems to result in more musculo-skeletal symptoms and increased sensitivity to pain (Moldofsky, Scarisbrick, England, & Smythe, 1975). This evidence does suggest, but not prove, that delta sleep may be related more to somatic recovery, while REM sleep might have more to do with the recovery of higher mental functions. Blood flow measures support such a view: during delta sleep, blood flows mainly to the muscles, while cerebral arteries are constricted. During REM sleep, cerebral blood flow increases, while blood flow to the large skeletal muscles is constricted (Townsend, Prinz, & Obrist, 1973).

The Function of Sleep

Although laymen feel they know that we sleep to restore our reserves and to recover from fatigue, science has been unable to demonstrate exactly what is being "restored" during sleep. In terms of physiological functioning, it appears that most anything that happens during sleep can also be achieved during relaxed wakefulness, albeit maybe not quite as effectively. Nevertheless, we know that a night spent asleep makes us feel much different than a night spent in relaxed wakefulness.

In the absence of firm facts about the function of sleep, it is not surprising that numerous theories have been proposed. We shall briefly review the most prominent ones.

The *restorative theory* (Hartmann, 1973; Oswald, 1974) is closest to the layman's understanding. General bodily recovery is said to occur during NREM sleep, cortical recovery may be during REM sleep. Indeed, delta sleep, the most profound of NREM sleep, is closely associated with a spurt in the secretion of growth hormone. Prolonged wakefulness, fasting, and hyperthyroidism all increase the need for recovery, and they do augment the amount of delta sleep. Nevertheless, the most powerful support for this theory rests on the common lay observation that we feel tired and worn before sleep, rested and restored after we wake up.

The *protective theory* of sleep states that we do not sleep because we are exhausted, but to *avoid* becoming exhausted (Claparede, 1905). The feeling of fatigue, and the need for sleep, appear much *before* any serious damage to tissue could occur. The neurological aspect of this theory has lost some of its credibility when it became apparent that most neurons do not rest during sleep. Indeed, some neurons become much more active during REM sleep than they ever are during wakefulness (Moruzzi, 1966).

The *energy conservation theory* rests on the observation that, ontogenetically, sleep and homeothermy developed together. Sleep is seen as an active mechanism, periodically forcing mammals and birds to conserve energy (Allison & Van Twyver, 1970). This theory is also supported by Zepelin and Rechtschaffen's (1974) observation that total sleep time and metabolic rate are correlated. The higher some species' metabolism, the more it sleeps. According to Berger (1975), "Sleep constitutes a period of dormancy, in which energy is conserved to partially off-set the increased energy demands of homeostasis."

The *instinctive theory* proposes that sleep is a species-specific, innate, organized pattern of behavior similar to nest building, migration, courtship dances, etc. While such behaviors may have survival value for the species, they are not powered by any physiological needs or drives (McGinty, 1971). This theory has problems with the fact that *all* birds and mammals (except, possibly, very primitive forms) sleep, and all show REM/NREM alternations. Why would all these animals develop the *very same* instincts?

The *behavioral-ethological theory* is impressed by the extremely wide range of sleep requirements in different species. Sleep needs seem to be finely tuned to the ecological niche any given species occupies. Animals that have few enemies, such as the large cats, or animals that are well protected, such as burrowing small rodents, sleep much of the time, while animals who are at risk during sleep, such as the large grazing animals, sleep very little.

As stated by Webb (1974), nonresponding may be beneficial for survival during certain times of the day. Sleep is used to reinforce such nonresponding. Typical sleep lengths are closely tied to the time in which it is best for the animal not to respond. To put it graphically for our own ancestors, those cavemen who slept very little probably stumbled around in the dark, broke their legs and/or were eaten by animals better adapted to hunt in the dark than man, while those who lay motionless at night were safer. On the other hand, those who slept through most of the day probably starved to death because hunting and food gathering may have used most of the daylight hours, given the primitive conditions of those times. This finally gave a survival advantage to those humans who remained unresponsive for about the length of a dark cycle, but were awake during the daylight hours.

While the behavioral-ecological theory can account for the extreme differences in the amount of time spent sleeping, it cannot, by itself, explain the fact that *all* birds and mammals sleep. It might have been even more adaptive for large grazing animals never to sleep at all. The fact that they do sleep, at great peril to themselves, suggests that the adaptive function alone is not sufficient to explain sleep.

In the forementioned, the different theories of sleep have been stated as if they were mutually exclusive. This is not true. Rather, as Webb (1979) suggests, many are compatible with each other. For example, it may well be that a certain minimal amount of sleep is required to restore some as yet unknown quantity. Once this minimal amount is satisfied, the amount of additional sleep may vary according to ecological requirements or specific needs to conserve energy. These requirements and needs may be bred into the animal by natural selection, resulting in some instinctively determined amount of sleep. Also, wakefulness serves *many* different functions such as food gathering, procreation, and the education of the young. It seems likely that sleep, too, may serve many functions, e.g. those of restoration, conservation of energy, and adaptive nonresponding.

OVERALL ISSUES IN DIAGNOSIS AND TREATMENT

A detailed classification system of sleep and arousal disorders has recently been published by the Association of Sleep Disorders Centers (ASDC). This ASDC nosology is rapidly becoming the accepted clinical standard. The current chapter therefore follows it in part, although not in the detail provided by the original publication (ASDC, 1979).

Basically, the ASDC classification recognizes four types of sleep disorders: the Insomnias (called Disorders of Initiating and Maintaining Sleep - DIMS); the Disorders of Excessive Somnolence (DOES); the Disorders of the Sleep-Wake Schedule; and the Dysfunctions Associated with Sleep, Sleep Stages, or Partial Arousals (called Parasomnias). The cumbersome title "Disorder of Initiating and Maintaining Sleep" is used by the ASDC instead of the shorter term "insomnia" because insomnia literally means *no* sleep.

Problems are classified as Disorders of the Sleep-Wake Schedule rather than DIMS if the sleep disturbance disappears whenever the patient is allowed to

TABLE 7.1
Outline of Diagnostic Classification of Sleep and Arousal Disorders
Reprinted with permission from the Association of Sleep Disorders Centers
(published in *Sleep*, Volume 2, Number 1) and from Raven Press, New York

A. *DIMS: Disorders of Initiating and Maintaining Sleep (Insomnias)*
   1. *Psychophysiological*
      a. Transient and Situational
      b. Persistent
   2. associated with
      Psychiatric Disorders
      a. Symptom and Personality Disorders
      b. Affective Disorders
      c. Other Functional Psychoses
   3. associated with
      Use of Drugs and Alcohol
      a. Tolerance to or Withdrawal from CNS Depressants
      b. Sustained Use of CNS Stimulants
      c. Sustained Use of or Withdrawal from Other Drugs
      d. Chronic Alcoholism
   4. associated with
      Sleep-induced Respiratory Impairment
      a. Sleep Apnea DIMS Syndrome
      b. Alveolar Hypoventilation DIMS Syndrome
   5. associated with
      Sleep-related (Nocturnal) Myoclonus and "Restless Legs"
      a. Sleep-related (Nocturnal) Myoclonus DIMS Syndrome
      b. "Restless Legs" DIMS Syndrome
   6. associated with
      Other Medical, Toxic, and Environmental Conditions
   7. *Childhood-Onset DIMS*
   8. associated with
      Other DIMS Conditions
      a. Repeated REM Sleep Interruptions
      b. Atypical Polysomnographic Features
      c. Not Otherwise Specified*
   9. *No DIMS Abnormality*
      a. Short Sleeper
      b. Subjective DIMS Complaint without Objective Findings
      c. Not Otherwise Specified*

B. *DOES: Disorders of Excessive Somnolence*
   1. *Psychophysiological*
      a. Transient and Situational
      b. Persistent
   2. associated with
      Psychiatric Disorders
      a. Affective Disorders
      b. Other Functional Disorders

(Continued)

TABLE 7.1 (*Continued*)

3. associated with
   Use of Drugs and Alcohol
   a. Tolerance to or Withdrawal from CNS Stimulants
   b. Sustained Use of CNS Depressants
4. associated with
   Sleep-induced Respiratory Impairment
   a. Sleep Apnea DOES Syndrome
   b. Alveolar Hypoventilation DOES Syndrome
5. associated with
   Sleep-related (Nocturnal) Myoclonus and "Restless Legs"
   a. Sleep-related (Nocturnal) Myoclonus DOES Syndrome
   b. "Restless Legs" DOES Syndrome
6. *Narcolepsy*
7. *Idiopathic CNS Hypersomnolence*
8. associated with
   Other Medical, Toxic, and Environmental Conditions
9. associated with
   Other DOES Conditions
   a. Intermittent DOES (Periodic) Syndromes
      i. Kleine-Levin Syndrome
      ii. Menstrual-associated Syndrome
   b. Insufficient Sleep
   c. Sleep Drunkenness
   d. Not Otherwise Specified*
10. *No DOES Abnormality*
   a. Long Sleeper
   b. Subjective DOES Complaint without Objective Findings
   c. Not Otherwise Specified*
C. *Disorders of the Sleep-Wake Schedule*
   1. *Transient*
      a. Rapid Time Zone Change ("Jet Lag") Syndrome
      b. "Work Shift" Change in Conventional Sleep-Wake Schedule
   2. *Persistent*
      a. Frequently Changing Sleep-Wake Schedule
      b. Delayed Sleep Phase Syndrome
      c. Advanced Sleep Phase Syndrome
      d. Non-24-Hour Sleep-Wake Syndrome
      e. Irregular Sleep-Wake Pattern
      f. Not Otherwise Specified*
D. *Dysfunctions Associated with Sleep, Sleep Stages, or Partial Arousals (Parasomnias)*
   1. *Sleepwalking* (Somnambulism)
   2. *Sleep Terror* (Pavor Nocturnus, Incubus)
   3. *Sleep-related Enuresis*
   4. *Other Dysfunctions*
      a. Dream Anxiety Attacks (Nightmares)
      b. Sleep-related Epileptic Seizures
      c. Sleep-related Bruxism
      d. Sleep-related Headbanging (Jactatio Capitis Nocturnus)

(*Continued*)

TABLE 7.1 (*Continued*)

e. Familial Sleep Paralysis
f. Impaired Sleep-related Penile Tumescence
g. Sleep-related Painful Erections
h. Sleep-related Cluster Headaches and Chronic Paroxysmal Hemicrania
i. Sleep-related Abnormal Swallowing Syndrome
j. Sleep-related Asthma
k. Sleep-related Cardiovascular Symptoms
l. Sleep-related Gastroesophageal Reflux
m. Sleep-related Hemolysis (Paroxysmal Nocturnal Hemoglobinuria)
n. Asymptomatic Polysomnographic Finding
o. Not Otherwise Specified*

*This entry is intended to leave space in the classification for both undiagnosed ("don't know") conditions and additional (as yet undocumented) conditions that may be described in the future.

follow his/her internal, biological clock. Similarly, if the main complaint is a pathological tendency towards sleeping when the patient should be awake, the problem is classified as a Disorder of Excessive Somnolence (DOES) rather than a DIMS (even though nighttime sleep may also be disturbed). Obviously, the distinction between DIMS and DOES is fluid because it relies almost entirely on the patient's primary sleep complaint.

One might be disappointed that, in this age of objective assessments and polysomnographic sophistication, the primary distinctions in the ASDC nosology depend on subjective complaints. However, as discussed under Sleep Needs, insomnia cannot be defined by a specified number of hours that the patient has to sleep, because the individually satisfying amounts of sleep are extremely varied. To date there is no easily available test of insomnia, only the patient's subjective feeling that sleep is not "adequate."

Assessment of Sleep Disturbances

Most research on sleep disorders is done in the laboratory, where all night polygraphic studies are readily available. Because of this, some clinicians have begun to feel that only certified sleep disorders centers are qualified to make diagnoses involving sleep problems. To me this appears to be a mistake. The present chapter assumes that most sleep disorders can at least be tentatively diagnosed by a sensitive interview, especially if the clinician talks not only to the patient, but also to the bed partner. Whether or not these tentative diagnoses need then to be confirmed in a laboratory is a matter of clinical judgement, depending on the clinician's trust in the diagnosis, the seriousness of the problem, and the success of the treatment that is prescribed. For example, faced with a patient complaining of serious and relentless insomnia, the clinician might want to first investigate sleep apnea, myoclonus, and other medical problems by carefully questionning the patient and bed partner. If no medical reasons are found, psychiatric problems might then be considered and, if present, vigorously treated. However, an evaluation at a sleep disorders center might become necessary later on if the sleep disturbance remains serious and if the treatment based on the interview diagnosis has yielded little relief. In sum: try everything else first, but if you have no success, do not hesitate to consult with a sleep disorders center. Only if you suspect sleep apnea or narcolepsy should a referral be made immediately, because these problems may be life threatening and, at one point or another, will need evaluation at a sleep clinic anyway.

General issues about sleep hygiene, behavioral, and pharmacological treatment have been worked out best for insomnia. They will therefore be discussed in that context, although similar statements could be made about the other kinds of sleep pathology.

Sleep Hygiene

Sleep hygiene, long the topic of folklore and folk medicine, has been the focus of some serious investigation. Table 7.2 summarizes the current scientific knowledge. While most of the points made in Table 7.2 are close to common sense, it is surprising how often these rules are overlooked by patients suffering from serious sleep disorders. For a more detailed explanation of these points, see Hauri (1977).

Behavioral Issues in Insomnia

Case History: Miss J., 32, had been a weak, but "adequate" sleeper all her life. However, since her "rather messy" divorce 2 years ago her sleep had deteriorated dramatically. At home Miss J. now took about two hours to fall asleep, then slept fitfully throughout the night. Always somewhat nervous and "high strung," Miss J. had to give up her secretarial job about 6 months before the lab evaluation because of insomnia. She felt she was desperate and there was no use to continue living unless her sleep could be cured. She had apparently complained about her poor sleep to many professionals, only to be told that poor sleep is not really a serious problem. "Nobody dies from insomnia," she was told.

On the first night in the lab, Miss J. fell asleep within 10 minutes of "light out!" Her sleep was very sound throughout the night, with an excess of delta sleep. This would indicate that she had been sleep deprived before coming to the lab. In the morning Miss J. was terribly embarrassed and stated that she had not slept as well as this for at least 6 months! Sleep on nights two and three in the laboratory was quite poor by our standards (<80% sleep efficiency), but still much better than her stated average at home. Psychiatric evaluation and psychological testing revealed a somewhat nervous and anxious person, but without psychopathology serious enough to explain the long standing insomnia.

Miss J. was first treated with relaxation therapy. This made her more relaxed during the day and more able to cope, and she slept somewhat more easily during

TABLE 7.2
Rules for Better Sleep Hygiene

1. Sleep as much as you need to feel refreshed during the next day, but not more. Most insomniacs stay in bed too long, much longer than age-matched good sleepers (Hauri, 1977).

2. A regular arousal time seems to strengthen circadian cycling and to solidify sleep (See discussion of circadian rhythm).

3. Daily exercise probably deepens sleep (Baekeland & Lasky, 1966), but occasional heavy exercise during one evening does not improve the sleep that follows (Hauri, 1968).

4. Occasional loud noises (e.g. aircraft flying over) disturb sleep even in those who feel that they have adapted to them. (Globus, Friedmann, Cohen, Pearsons, & Fidell, 1973). Insomniacs may be especially sensitive to noise.

5. A hot room causes more awakenings, more body movements during sleep, less REM, and less delta sleep than a room at 72 degrees or below. (Schmidt-Kessen & Kendel, 1973; Otto, 1973).

6. Hunger may disturb sleep. (Jacobs & McGinty, 1971). A light bedtime snack may help (Brezinova & Oswald, 1972).

7. Caffeine in the evening disturbs sleep (Karacan, Thornby, Booth, Okawa, Salis, Anch, & Williams, 1975). Some insomniacs seem to be particularly sensitive to stimulants.

8. Smoking increases arousal and makes sleeping more difficult. Sleep may be even more disturbed during withdrawal from heavy nicotine use (Myrsten, Elgerot, & Edgren, 1977).

9. Although alcohol may help tense people to relax, the ensuing sleep typically is fragmented and poor (Johnson, Burdick, & Smith, 1970).

10. According to Evans, Cook, Cohen, Orne, & Orne (1977), daytime naps may either help or hinder sleep, depending on the individual and the reasons for napping. This is controversial, Karacan, Williams, Finley, & Hursch (1970) found evidence that poor sleepers should avoid all naps.

the night. However, she still had problems falling asleep. She was then treated with Bootzin's stimulus control behavior technique (Bootzin & Nicassio, 1978). This helped dramatically after some very tough initial nights. Finally, Miss J. was given some hypnotics, to be used only if she experienced two or three poor nights in a row.

On follow-up 9 months later, Miss J. had returned to the relatively "adequate" sleep she had shown before the divorce. She still suffered through 2–5 poor nights per month, but had "learned to live with that." She had resumed her job as a secretary and was very thankful that she had been given "a new lease on life." Anxiety and agitation were no longer chronic, but only occurred when she was put under serious stress.

How can we explain the 2 year bout of severe insomnia in Miss J.? Actually, the factors that were causing it seem to be only too widespread.

Assume that a person undergoes serious and prolonged stress, such as Miss J.'s divorce. Activity in the arousal system naturally increases as a result of the stress. Sleep will become difficult in almost all of us. If the stress continues for a few weeks, the following factors usually interact to cause temporary insomnia:

1. *Trying too hard.* As one becomes more exhausted from lack of sleep, sleep itself becomes more desirable. The more one needs to sleep and the more

one tries to sleep, the more one increases arousal, and the less one actually sleeps. A maladaptive habit of "trying hard to sleep" develops. Persons with this habit can fall asleep easily when not trying to sleep, e.g., when watching T.V. or listening to lectures, but hyperalertness ensues just as soon as they make a conscious decision to try to sleep.

2. *Conditioned Wakefulness.* Lying in bed unable to sleep because of the stress may cause maladaptive conditioning. The bedroom environment, i.e. the feeling of the mattress or the darkness of the room, may become associated with frustration and arousal rather than with relaxation and sleep. Similarly, the usual bedtime rituals leading up to sleep, such as brushing teeth and turning off lights, become stimuli anticipating frustration and tension rather than relaxation. People suffering from conditioned insomnia often sleep better away from their usual sleep arrangement, e.g. in the living room, in a hammock, or in a hotel. Indeed, because the sleep laboratory is so different from their home environment, insomniacs with this problem often sleep very well during their first night in the laboratory.

3. *Disruption of the Sleep-wake Rhythm.* Sleeping poorly during most nights because of the stress, people often fall asleep towards the morning, and they then oversleep. Also, they frequently take daytime naps "to catch up." As discussed under circadian rhythms, such behavior leads to a desynchronization of the different biological clocks and to further sleep problems.

4. *Fear of insomnia.* As long as sleep is basically adequate, an occasional poor night can be taken in stride. However, in patients who have labelled themselves "insomniacs," a poor night reconfirms that label, with all the inferiority and suffering that the label implies. The fear of insomnia then often becomes a self-fulfilling prophecy. Such patients often overmedicate because their self-esteem cannot afford even a few minutes of lying in bed awake.

In basically sound sleepers, the normal extinction of unreinforced behavior gradually overcomes the maladaptive learning and poor habits that are established during the stress episode. Good sleepers recover within a few weeks after the stress has disappeared. However, if sleep had been somewhat tenuous even before the crisis, as it had been with Miss J., the naturally occurring, occasional nights of insomnia reinforce the learned maladaptive patterns. Extinction cannot occur, and the poor sleep habits may remain active over years or decades.

The learning factors discussed here seem active in almost any kind of chronic insomnia. It is unimportant whether the insomnia was originally due to psychological upheaval, to environmental stress, or to medical factors. Behavioral issues therefore often need to be considered and treated, even if the original cause of the insomnia is clearly non-behavioral. Behavioral treatments of insomnia, such as stimulus control therapy, relaxation therapy, biofeedback, environmental changes, etc. have recently been summarized by Bootzin and Nicassio (1978), by Borkovec (1979), by Hauri (1979b) and by Ware (1979).

Pharmacological Treatment

Certain drugs are clearly indicated for some specific diagnostic conditions. These cases will be discussed at the appropriate places later in this chapter. Here we are dealing with the broad symptomatic treatment of insomnia with hypnotics, an issue that is currently a matter of intensive debate.

Opponents of sleeping pills stress the following:

1. Most evidence points to a decrease in hypnotic efficacy over time. However, the speed of this loss in efficacy varies. Secobarbitol, for example, loses its hypnotic power, on the average, within a few days (Kales, Hauri, Bixler, & Silberfarb, 1976), while flurazepam hydrochloride, on the average, retains substantial hypnotic efficacy for at least a month (Dement, Carskadon, Mitler, Phillips, & Zarcone, 1978). There simply is no research evidence concerning hypnotic efficacy beyond one month of chronic use. Extrapolating the data, one might predict that sooner or later all hypnotics become ineffective.

It is also said that insomniacs who chronically use hypnotics sleep about as poorly as insomniacs who are drug-free (Kales, Bixler, Tjiauw-Ling, Scharf, & Kales, 1974). However, this evidence seems open to debate because the two groups of insomniacs evaluated in that study were not equalized for the initial severity of their problem.

2. Drug withdrawal (rebound) insomnia has been demonstrated for most currently available hypnotics. This means that for a few days or weeks after withdrawal from the chronic use of hypnotics, insomniacs usually sleep worse than they would, had they never taken the medication. Currently debated are the questions whether all hypnotics show such rebounds, and, whether or not the severity of the rebound is associated with the half-life of the drug (Kales, Scharf, & Kales, 1978; Nicholson, 1980).

3. The chronic use of hypnotics itself appears to contribute to poor sleep in some cases. In any event, most hypnotics distort natural sleep (Hauri, 1977).

4. Many hypnotics may impair waking performance on the following day (Church & Johnson, 1979; Roth, Kramer, & Lutz, 1977).

5. Prescribing sleeping pills often masks the insomniac's medical, behavioral, or psychological problem, and it may delay appropriate treatment. In addition, serious medical complications can develop both during the administration of these drugs (e.g. overdose and interaction with other medications), and during their withdrawal (e.g. seizures).

Proponents of hypnotics stress the following:

1. Modern hypnotics seem surprisingly safe. Considering the large amounts of hypnotics consumed, the incidence rates for complications and adverse reactions are exceedingly small.

2. Research evidence concerning loss of efficacy with chronic use seems not pertinent in most cases, because most insomniacs may take their hypnotics intermittently (Clift, 1975). Sleep Disorders Specialists seem to overemphasize the decrease in hypnotic efficacy over time, possibly because they deal only with those patients for whom the hypnotics have failed. Millions of current users seem well satisfied with the chronic use of their sleeping pills.

3. The detrimental side-effects of hypnotics have to be weighed against the detrimental effects of suffering from insomnia.

While a final decision about prescribing hypnotics awaits much needed research into their chronic efficacy (longer than one month), the following rules of thumb seem to have evolved for the interim:

1. Hypnotics are usually considered acceptable to help a patient get through an acute crisis, as long as the patient is also followed and supported through the inevitable drug withdrawal period.

2. A nightly prescription of hypnotics over long time spans (months and years) is rarely indicated, and it may lead to an unacceptable demand for gradually escalating dosages. However, there are some rare patients who seem satisfied with a chronic, low dose of a hypnotic. For this minority it becomes a matter of clinical judgement whether the continuous (placebo?) benefits of the medication outweigh the possible complications related to its chronic use.

3. Many hypnotics seem to maintain efficacy if used only once or twice per week. Used in this way, the occasional hypnotic helps to avoid an insomniac's panic that he may never sleep again, and it may restore his/her "reserves" after a few sleepless nights. This may prevent the development of maladaptive habits as discussed earlier.

4. Special care should be taken when prescribing hypnotics to the elderly, to patients with liver disease, and to those who are heavy snorers. Hypnotics decrease respiratory drive and may aggravate hypoventilation.

5. Customary precautions for withdrawing patients from CNS depressants need to be followed when terminating hypnotics. This means concern with nausea, nervousness, possible seizures, etc. (Shader, Caine, & Meyers, 1975).

6. Because of their relative safety and lack of interaction with other drugs, the benzodiazepines are now generally preferred over other medications. The current argument about benzodiazepines mainly concerns the question whether the long or the short acting ones are preferable. However, benzodiazepines are not totally harmless, especially when "fortified" with alcohol. Some episodes of lethal overdose have occurred. Barbiturates may be indicated in specific cases, especially where benzodiazepines have proven ineffective. There seems to be little advantage, however, in using any of the other currently available hypnotics such as glutethimide, meprobamate, methaqualone, etc. (Institute of Medicine Report, 1979).

INSOMNIAS—DISORDERS OF INITIATING AND MAINTAINING SLEEP—DIMS

Psychophysiological

Transient and Situational

Classified here are problems that have lasted for less than 3 weeks. They usually have a clearly discernible, emotional reason, such as acute stress or unfamiliar sleep environments. These transient and situational DIMS can manifest as difficulties falling asleep, difficulties remaining asleep, or early morning awakenings, mainly depending on the patient's age. We are basically dealing with a wake system that is temporarily too active, so that the sleep-inducing circuits can only overcome it in fits and spurts.

Hypnotics often seem indicated if transient and situational DIMS persist for more than 2–3 nights. The goal is not only to give the patient some rest, but also to avoid the faulty conditioning and learning that might turn the transient insomnia into a persistent one. Occasionally, relaxation exercises or hypnosis are used to calm the overly active arousal system, but these behavioral methods are usually too slow to deal with the acute crises.

Persistent Psychophysiological

"Persistent Psychophysiological DIMS" is the ASDC term for the behavioral insomnias that were described earlier. In short, a predisposition towards occasional poor sleep seems to interact in a vicious cycle with learned, maladaptive sleep habits (Hauri, 1979). Somatized tension, anxiety, and some depression are often seen in persistent psychophysiological DIMS, but not to the degree that they would warrant a purely psychiatric diagnosis. Obviously, the boundaries are fluid. They depend mainly on the diagnostician's judgment whether the tension, anxiety, and depression seen in a certain patient is primary or secondary to the insomnia. Also, persistent psychophysiological DIMS are usually more stable, while DIMS associated with psychiatric disorders are usually wax and wane in concert with the daytime symptoms of the psychiatric problems.

Persistent psychophysiological insomnias are best treated with behavioral techniques because they are based, at least in part, on faulty habits and conditioning. If somatized anxiety and tension are the main factors, various forms of relaxation training seem effective (Borkovec & Weerts, 1976). If conditioned associations between bedroom stimuli and arousal play a major role, Bootzin's (1973) stimulus control therapy seems effective. The traditional forms of psychotherapy may also be employed, depending on the amount of chronic anxiety that is present. Hypnotics seem indicated for occasional use only, no more than once or twice per week. Hypnotics are prescribed to avoid helpless panic that many psychophysiological insomniacs experience when unable to sleep for a few nights in a row. As discussed earlier, such panic, in itself, can create arousal, and it may switch a relatively minor insomnia into a chronic, relentless problem.

For the past 8 years, our own laboratory has investigated the biofeedback treatment of persistent psychophysiological insomnia. Specifically, we have tried to evaluate whether such treatment was effective, and, if so, what type of biofeedback parameter would yield the best results. In our most ambitious attempt to date (Hauri, 1981), we have carefully evaluated 48 insomniacs free of obvious medical disease and free of serious psychiatric problems. Both home sleep logs and three nights of sleep in the lab were assessed before biofeedback started. Ten insomniacs were then *randomly* assigned to one of four groups: no treatment control, treatment by frontalis EMG feedback (EMG), treatment by frontalis EMG feedback combined with EEG-theta wave feedback (Theta), or treatment by feedback of the sensory-motor rhythm (SMR). The SMR is a very low voltage 12–14 cps rhythm that can be measured over ,the sensory-motor cortex during wakefulness (Sterman, Macdonald, & Stone, 1974). It is of interest because sleep spindles have the same 12–14 cps frequency, and because cats, trained on SMR, seemed to sleep better afterwards (Sterman, Howe, & Macdonald, 1970).

After 15 to 60 feedback sessions—depending on the needs of the patient—all insomniacs were evaluated twice more: once immediately after feedback, and once for follow-up 9 months later.

Initial results were disappointing. While all three biofeedback groups improved their sleep somewhat more than the control group, *none* of the three feedback groups improved significantly more than the control group. This means that there is no difference in efficacy if one gives EMG, Theta, or SMR biofeedback to a *random* group of persistent psychophysiological insomniacs.

Baffled by these results, we looked once more at our intake data. We found that, at intake, some of our insomniacs had been quite tense at sleep onset. Others had been relatively relaxed when lights were turned out, but still could not sleep. The amount of intake tension that a patient showed correlated significantly and *positively* with improvement in the EMG and in the Theta group, but it correlated significantly and *negatively* with improvement in the SMR group! Apparently because EMG and theta feedback are basically relaxation training, they worked best in those insomniacs who initially had been tense. SMR training, with its 12–14 cps EEG rhythm, seems to be more associated with correcting a (neurological?) problem in the sleep circuits. Remember that the SMR frequency is identical to the frequency of the sleep spindles. It appears that insomniacs who could not sleep even though they were relaxed might have been suffering more from some underlying EEG problem. They might therefore benefit more from SMR training. Indeed, when we separated our feedback groups into those who, by dice, had been assigned to the appropriate feedback training according to the above speculations versus those who had not, very significant findings emerged. Those treated with feedback appropriate to their problem improved quite drastically, those treated inappropriately did not.

We have recently replicated our data in another group of 16 insomniacs (Hauri, Percy, Hartmann, & Russ, 1981). Based on results from both studies, we conclude:

1. Not all psychophysiological insomniacs are tense. Relaxation training, such as provided by EMG or theta feedback, only helps those insomniacs who are tense.
2. Insomniacs who are relaxed and still cannot fall asleep may be suffering more from the organic predisposition towards poor sleep that is also part of psychophysiological insomnia, according to our theory. Such insomniacs may be treated more effectively with SMR biofeedback.
3. The fact that both a tension component and a possible organic component emerged in our studies makes us feel more confident about the model of psychophysiological insomnia proposed in this chapter.

Associated With Psychiatric Disorders

Symptom and Personality Disorders

Classified here are insomnias associated with anxiety disorders, somatoform disorders, and personality disorders. Standard psychiatric treatment seems indicated, including psychotherapy, behavioral therapy, supportive contacts, and possibly, anxiolytics and occasional hypnotics. Kales, Kales, Bixler, and Martin (1975) advocate directive, dynamic psychotherapy. They feel that there is danger of becoming preoccupied in therapy with the symptom of insomnia, and they suggest that a discussion of that problem be confined to a specific part of the therapeutic hour, e.g. the last 5 minutes.

Affective Disorders

Case History: Mr. D. is a 50-year-old small businessman whose insomnia started while in the Navy in 1943. At that time he had been recently married, his wife was pregnant while he was on duty in the Pacific, and he was quite homesick. A Navy psychiatrist diagnosed reactive depression which cleared up after some treatment. Over the next 15 years Mr. D. had intermittent bouts with insomnia whenever serious stresses developed. This occurred on at least 8 occasions; Mr. D. expected very much from himself and occasionally became suicidal when he could not live up to these expectations. Episodes of good sleep became fewer and fewer, and for the past 15 years insomnia has been chronic and relentless. It was mainly treated with sleeping pills. About 20 years ago, Mr. D. also developed hypertension, treated with medication.

After a 4 week withdrawal period from all hypnotics, Mr. D. was studied in the lab for 3 nights. His sleep was poor, averaging about 4.5 hours per night with 5 to 15 long awakenings. On all 3 nights Mr. D. showed long REM periods only 10 to 20 minutes after sleep onset.

After psychiatric interviewing and psychological testing, it was felt that Mr. D's basic problem was insomnia secondary to depression. However, while at the beginning of his insomnia he had slept well between bouts of depression, over the decades he apparently had also developed maladaptive sleep habits (behavioral insomnia) which caused him to sleep poorly even when not depressed. He was started on the antidepressant Elavil, gradually increasing drug levels to 150 mg hs. Intensive relaxation training was also started, combined with once per week psychotherapy.

On follow-up 9 months later, Mr. D. was sleeping much better, although he still experienced occasional 1 to 2 night bouts with insomnia. He had been able to discontinue anti-hypertensive medication. Psychotherapy still continued, but anti-depressant medication was being reduced to a low maintenance level.

Insomnia secondary to affective disorders is one of the most common DIMS to be found. This type of insomnia has been studied extensively in various sleep laboratories. As summarized by Kupfer's group (e.g., Kupfer & Foster, 1978), DIMS secondary to depression is characterized by ease of falling asleep and by difficulties with sleep maintenance and early morning awakenings. One also finds early and long REM periods and some increase in REM density, as well as a decrease in delta sleep. Whether or not the total amount of REM sleep is increased in these patients remains controversial.

While the severity of insomnia often correlates with the severity of depression, the association is by no means universal (Hauri & Hawkins, 1973b). Also, the early morning awakenings that are typical for this group are more marked in older patients. Indeed, younger patients often show hypersomnia associated with their depression, rather than insomnia (Hawkins, Taub, Van de Castle, Teja, Greyson, Garland, & Talley, 1977).

In Bipolar Disorders, the manic phase is characterized by short sleep and difficulties in falling asleep. Contrary to the Major Affective Disorders, the depressive phase of a Bipolar Disorder is often associated with hypersomnia, but the typical features of short REM latency and reduced delta remain.

According to Vogel, Thurmond, Gibbons, Sloan, Boyd, and Walker (1975), REM mechanisms are intimately associated with endogenous depression. Depriving endogenously depressed patients of REM sleep by awakening them at the appropriate times appears to have potent anti-depressant effects. Indeed, all of the clinically effective anti-depressant medications show marked REM inhibition. Kupfer, Foster, Reich, Thompson, and Weiss (1976) even suggest that the reaction of the depressed patient during the first 2 nights of sleep on amitriptyline can predict whether the drug will be effective in a given patient. If REM suppression occurs secondary to the drug, the patient will respond clinically to amitriptyline after 2 to 4 weeks, but if REM suppression does not occur, a beneficial response is unlikely.

Sleep usually normalizes with the waning of depression. However, Hauri, Chernik, Hawkins, and Mendels (1974) present evidence that, at least in reactive depressives, it never actually reaches a normal level. Similarly, the dreams of patients remitted from reactive depression still show depressive content, such as more masochism and more environmental hostility (Hauri, 1976).

Hypnotics are rarely indicated in affective disorders. Karacan, Blackburn, Thornby, Okawa, Salis, and Williams (1975) present evidence that the entire daily dose of sleep inducing anti-depressant medications might be given at bedtime, making maximal use of its sedating side effects.

Other Functional Psychoses

Acute psychotic decompensation usually involves severe insomnia. Extreme anxiety, fear, racing thoughts, and preoccupation with delusional and hallucinatory material usually keep the patient awake for most of the night. Sleep then often starts in the early morning hours and the patient may sleep until midday or later. Day-night reversals are common. Treatment focuses on the relevant psychiatric problems, not on the insomnia.

Associated with Use of Drugs and Alcohol

Case History: Mrs. S., 49, was referred to the clinic because she reported sleeping less than 3 hours each night even with the nightly intake of 20 mg Valium, 200 mg Seconal, 45 mg Dalmane, and some Tylenol. However, these drugs did make her groggy, and Mrs. S. also took 25 mg of Dexedrine each morning "to wake up."

Mrs. S. apparently had been sleeping well until about 15 years ago when she was prescribed Dexedrine as a diet pill. Shortly thereafter she started Seconal because the Dexedrine kept her awake at night. Sleep then gradually deteriorated over the years, and more and more hypnotics were added.

In the lab, Mrs. S. slept about 5½ hours when on her usual medications. However, this sleep was highly fragmented with awakenings, and very atypical: the fast EEG of waking, sleep spindles, and delta waves all intermixed freely. It was extremely difficult to score Mrs. S.'s records, and in the morning she felt that she had slept less than 2 hours on each of the lab nights.

Admitted to a psychiatric inpatient service on her own initiative, Mrs. S. was gradually withdrawn from all medication. A repeat polysomnogram 2 weeks later showed marked sleep improvement. Sleep was still short (6 hours) but much freer from arousals, and the different stages of sleep and wakefulness were clearly identifiable. Mrs. S. felt that she now got "more rest out of sleep."

Psychiatrically, Mrs. S. had become much more hostile and manipulative in her interactions with the ward personnel as drug withdrawal continued. She pressed for an early discharge, claiming that she did not need a psychiatric hospital because her problem was purely biological. Although she had described her marriage as "close to ideal," a visit from her husband resulted in a drawn-out shouting match.

Attempts were made to deal with Mrs. S.'s emotional and interpersonal problems which were becoming more obvious each day. However, Mrs. S. was either unable to see, or to admit, any psychological component in her sleep disturbance. After a stormy group therapy session she signed herself out after 18 days in the hospital, against medical advice. All follow-up attempts were refused, and 3 months after admission, Mrs. S. was back on her many medications, again sleeping as poorly as before.

Although each medication has its own characteristics, the habit of avoiding emotional problems with a quick pill is common to most patients classified in this group. Treatment should not focus on the sleep disturbance, but follow the methods developed over the last few years for drug addiction.

Polysomnographic recordings under chronic and heavy use of *CNS depressants* show a disruption of the sleep architecture: decreased delta and REM sleep, increases in stages 1 and 2, frequent mixing of EEG waves, and a general loss of the REM/NREM sleep cycling. Procedures for withdrawal from CNS depressants have been described elsewhere (e.g. Renner, 1978; Shader, Caine, & Meyer, 1975). Basically, the patient is first stabilized on a steady dose of the drug and then withdrawn quite gradually in order to avoid seizures, severe insomnia, and other side effects.

The sustained use of *CNS stimulants* often relates in insomnia. This includes not only those who take amphetamines, (e.g. for weight reduction), but also excessive drinkers of caffeine beverages, depressed patients prescribed analeptics for mood elevation, and asthmatics who heavily inhale sympathomimetics. Other patients, like Mrs. S., take stimulants in the morning and hypnotics at night in ever increasing dosages "to keep going." Ultimately, such patients become susceptible to sudden episodes of sleepiness during the day, the classic "crash" of the stimulant-dependent individual begins.

Many commonly used drugs, not classified as either CNS depressants or stimulants, may also interfere with sleep. Antimetabolites, thyroid preparations, dilantin, monaminoxydase inhibitors, contraceptives and many others list insomnia as a possible side effect. It is then a matter of clinical judgment whether the beneficial effects of the drugs outweigh their detrimental side effects. In other drugs a sleep disturbing effect is highly idiosyncratic for the given individual. For still another group of drugs, such as major tranquilizers, marijuana, cocaine, it is the drug withdrawal that is associated with poor sleep (Kay, Blackburn, Buckingham, & Karacan, 1976).

Finally, heavy use of alcohol also results in a progressive disintegration of sleep. Withdrawal from alcohol is often associated with severe insomnia, a decrease in delta sleep, and a large REM rebound. Although most alcoholics show a return to almost normal sleep within 2 to 3 weeks after cessation of drinking, severe alcoholism may be followed by years of sleep that looks prematurely aged, with frequent awakenings and REM fragmentation (Gross, Goodenough, Hasten, & Lewis, 1973; Johnson, Burdick, & Smith, 1970; Pokorny, 1978).

Associated with Sleep-Induced Respiratory Impairment

For a full discussion of sleep apneas, see Disorders of Excessive Somnolence. Sleep apnea patients who complain of insomnia usually show predominantly central apneas (Guilleminault & Dement, 1978).

In many patients, breathing does not stop, but becomes excessively shallow during sleep, especially REM sleep. For some of them (e.g. "Ondine's Curse"), this seems to be a matter of seriously impaired chemoreceptor sensitivity during sleep.

Treatment is still in its infancy. Obviously, respiratory depressants (e.g. sleeping pills) should be avoided. Loss of life has been reported when giving barbiturates to patients with "Ondine's Curse." Some clinicians advocate respiratory stimulants, mechanical breathing, or phrenic pacemakers. Our own lab has reported a case treated successfully with a rocking bed (Barlow, Bartlett, Hauri, Hellekson, Nattie, Remmers, & Schmidt-Nowara, 1980).

Associated with Sleep-related (Nocturnal) Myoclonus and "Restless Legs"

Case History: Mr. C., 51, was referred for a complaint of "restless legs." Almost every night, after about 1–3 hours of sleep, Mr. C. would awaken with very uncomfortable, crawling, but not really painful sensations deep inside his calves and thighs. There usually was an overwhelming urge to move his legs vigorously. Walking or knee bends generally eliminated these sensations, but as soon as Mr. C. returned to bed, the sensations usually reappeared. This interfered seriously with sleep.

Both a psychiatric and a neurological evaluation done at a sleep disorders center were initially negative, except for a mild decrease in sensations from the legs. In the lab, Mr. C. fell asleep easily, but after about 1½–2 hours of uneventful sleep, stereotyped leg twitches started to occur at about 50 second intervals. These twitches seemed to awaken Mr. C. after a while. He then asked to get up and walk around because of his "restless legs." This occurred 2–4 times each night in the lab.

Mr. C. was first treated with clonazepan (Clonopin), ½ mg h.s. He was later switched to oxycodone (Percodan) when Clonopin proved ineffective. Increased exercise and abstinence from coffee were also prescribed. Follow-up 9 months later found a symptom free, much more relaxed patient, no longer bothered by nocturnal awakenings except maybe once or twice per month.

Nocturnal myoclonus involves episodes of repetitive, stereotyped leg muscle jerks during sleep, spaced about 40 seconds apart for periods up to an hour. These myoclonic jerks are usually, but not always, bilateral. Partial or full arousal often follows the myoclonic kick.

Sleep-related myoclonus may present either as insomnia or as a disorder of excessive somnolence. Patients usually have no knowledge of their myoclonic twitches but complain of frequent awakenings and unrefreshing sleep. Reports from bed partners are crucial to diagnose the problem, unless polysomnograms can be obtained.

Estimates of myoclonus in serious insomniacs range from 1% to 15%. The problem occurs mainly in middle-aged or older subjects. Besides the free-standing forms of myoclonus, the problem can develop in patients with chronic uremia and other metabolic disorders, in those treated with tricyclic antidepressants, and in those withdrawn from a variety of drugs, including anticonvulsants and CNS depressants.

Sleep-related myoclonus must be differentiated from sleep-related epileptic seizures, from waking myoclonus, and from the hypnic jerks that occur on occasions in many normals when falling asleep. Clonazepan, starting at ½ mg h.s., seems to be an effective treatment (Coleman, Pollak, Kokkoris, McGregor, & Weitzman, 1979; Zorick, Roth, Salis, Kramer, & Lutz, 1978).

The "restless legs" syndrome consists of extremely uncomfortable, but not really painful, deep sensations. They usually occur deep inside the calf, but occasionally also in thighs, feet, and arms. These sensations begin when the patient is relaxing, and they disappear with leg exercise.

The etiology of the "restless legs" syndrome is unknown. Some cases have been linked to motoneuron disease (Frankel, Patten, and Gillin, 1974). Inadequate circulation is suggested in other patients. The syndrome usually becomes more severe with age, is exacerbated with sleep deprivation, and often is aggravated during pregnancy. Curiously, "restless legs" often disappear with fever. A familial incidence is described in about ⅓ of the cases (Boghen & Peyronnard, 1976). Lutz (1978) has associated "restless legs" with caffeinism.

"Restless legs" need to be differentiated from painful leg cramps, "growing pains" in children, and from the agitation and restlessness of anxiety and emotional upset. Oxycodone and carbamazepine seem effective to treat "restless legs." An increase in leg exercises may also help in some cases.

While "restless legs" and myoclonus apparently are two separate entities, they often occur in the same individual, as was the case in Mr. C.

Associated with Other Medical, Toxic, and Environmental Conditions

Medical conditions in this category would include CNS disorders that result in poor sleep, endocrine and metabolic diseases, renal failure, infections, arthritis, etc. Toxic conditions would include the effects of arsenic, mercury, alcohol, etc. Environmental conditions include noise, excessive heat, humidity, etc., as long as it is the actual physical stimulus that disturbs sleep, rather than its psychiatric meaning.

Besides the obvious medical and environmental interventions, sleep in these patients is often improved by behavioral treatments, discussion of sleep hygiene, and supportive contacts. Because these conditions are often chronic, there is usually a large overlay of behavioral factors that aggravate the sleep disturbances.

Childhood Onset DIMS

Case History: Mrs. M., 52, has been sleeping poorly "ever since she can re-member." Indeed, a note from the newborn nursery, written on the second day of her life, describes her as "a very alert baby, sleeping little." As a child later on, she had been diagnosed as "hyperkinetic" and she had serious learning problems in school.

Mrs. M. was quite guarded and defensive on the initial interview, apparently worrying that we, like others, would diagnose her a neurotic. Except for this, both psychiatric and neurological evaluations were unremarkable. In an EMG biofeed-back session, however, Mrs. M. showed excessive muscle tension.

On the first night in the lab, Mrs. M. took 79 minutes to fall asleep. She awakened 35 times that night, but still rated that night as "much better than my average." On nights 2 and 3 it took her 3 hours and 3½ hours to fall asleep, and sleep throughout both nights was again riddled by many awakenings. In addition, Mrs. M.'s sleep was very difficult to score because her sleep spindles were both extremely rare and very poorly formed when present.

Mrs. M. was told that much of her insomnia seemed to be inborn, but that she had now acquired an overlay of tension and defensive denial. She was prescribed Elavil, 25 mg h.s., and occasional Dalmane, 15 mg h.s., to be used no more than once per week. EMG biofeedback was recommended, and she was encouraged to join group therapy.

This was four years ago. The yearly follow-ups since then have indicated that the Elavil, 25 mg h.s., continues to have a dramatic effect on her sleep. To assess whether she still needs that medication, she withdraws from it once a year for at least 3 weeks. On all four of these "drug holidays" she has slept as poorly as before coming to the lab. Biofeedback has also helped her to relax, but Mrs. M. has never joined the therapy group that was recommended.

In a study carried out in our own lab (Hauri & Olmstead, 1980), we compared 20 patients who had been insomniacs since childhood with 39 who had become insomniacs during adult life. The childhood onset insomniacs took significantly longer to fall asleep, slept less, and showed excessive amounts of "ambiguous" REM (REM-like EEG and EMG but no eye movements). Thus, in our study, childhood onset insomnia appeared to be relatively more serious than adult onset insomnia. Those with childhood onset insomnia also reported more evidence of possible "soft" neurological impairment, such as hyperkinesis as children, dys-lexia, a diagnosis of minimal brain dysfunction, or atypical EEG wave of un-known significance. Based on these findings, we speculated that the childhood onset group may suffer from neurological impairment in structures related to the sleep-wake balance. We also theorized that childhood onset insomnia may be similar to persistent psychophysiologic insomnia, except that the damage to the sleep/wake balance may be more severe. It therefore may manifest itself in childhood already, and does not need the episode of stress that triggers the psychophysiological insomnias.

Clinically, we have found that many childhood onset insomniacs are exquisitely sensitive to noise and to stimulants. Even one cup of tea or some chocolate many hours before bedtime often seriously interferes with their sleep. Clinically, we have also found that very low doses of Elavil (10 mg or 25 mg) often help such patients.

Associated with Other DIMS Conditions

Repeated REM Sleep Interruptions are suspected in patients who report awakening about every 1½-2 hours during the night. Greenberg (1967) has documented some cases and speculated that such insomniacs attempt to escape dreaming during REM sleep. According to the ASDC, a diagnosis of REM sleep interruptions implies that the awakenings are longer than a few minutes, and that they affect more than ¾ of all REM periods, while NREM awakenings are rare.

Atypical polysomnographic features involve a mixing of EEG waves from different stages, such as alpha-delta sleep (Hauri & Hawkins, 1973b), fast alternations between different stages, or many "mini-arousals," i.e., very short awakenings. Clinically, patients displaying these features often report feeling tired and not restored even after apparently adequate sleep length. The condition is only diagnosed if the atypical wave forms are not secondary to drugs or other toxins. No treatment for such problems has been adequately documented.

No DIMS Abnormality

> *Case History:* Mr. Q, a 25 year old graduate student, was evaluated for his chronic insomnia. Although he claimed that he had slept fitfully and for less than 5 hours in each of the 3 lab nights, the polygraph suggested that he had fallen asleep within 5 minutes each night, and had slept throughout his 8 hour bedtime. Thus, Mr. Q. was classified as suffering from "subjective DIMS complaint without objective findings." No treatment was prescribed.
>
> Shortly after the sleep lab evaluation, Mr. Q. sought the help of a therapist who taught him a combination of self-hypnosis, meditation, and relaxation training. This treatment subjectively "cured" Mr. Q.'s insomnia. He now felt that he slept soundly and throughout the night. A repeat evaluation in the lab, however, did not show any changes from before the behavioral treatment to after it, sleep being excellent on both occasions.
>
> According to subjective evaluations, there clearly was a dramatic change in Mr. Q.'s sleep after the treatment. According to the polygraph, there was none. Was there a "cure"? Sleep researchers will disagree on the answer.

Every so often, patients complaining of insomnia turn out not to have a diagnosable sleep problem when evaluated at the lab. They may be "short sleepers," seemingly needing little sleep (Jones & Oswald, 1968). Or they may be classified as having "subjective DIMS complaint without objective findings.'' This means that a convincing and honest complaint of ''insomnia'' is made by an apparently normal individual such as Mr. Q., but that this complaint cannot be substantiated with current laboratory procedures. This condition was formerly called ''pseudo'' insomnia, but it appears now that some patients presenting in this way may actually suffer from a yet undiscovered sleep problem. At the very least, personality profiles of many patients in this category do not match the narcissistic, pleading-for-help, or manipulating traits that would be expected from malingerers (Borkovec, 1979).

DISORDERS OF EXCESSIVE SOMNOLENCE - DOES

While insomnia usually has a psychological/behavioral component, pathologically excessive daytime somnolence usually has a medical origin. Indeed, in a recent survey reviewing our clinical experience, we found that over 80% of patients with *D*isorders *of E*xcessive *S*onmolence (DOES) suffered from medical diseases such as narcolepsy, sleep apnea, and drug related DOES. Psychological/behavioral components could be clearly identified in less than 20% of these patients. These figures contrasted sharply with insomnia, where over 80% showed psychological/behavioral components, whereas less than 20% showed purely medical problems.

Persons suffering from DOES report either chronic, excessive sleepiness throughout the waking hours, or an excessive tendency to nap even after relatively adequate sleep at night. This excessive somnolence should not be confused with physical tiredness, with low grade depression, or with lethargy and malaise. Rather, excessive somnolence implies the actual ability to fall asleep almost anywhere, as soon as intense stimulation ceases.

The *Multiple Sleep Latency Test* (MSLT) is currently used to objectively verify excessive daytime somnolence (Richardson, Carskadon, Flagg, Van den Hoed, Dement, & Mitler, 1978). It consists of putting patients to bed at two hour intervals throughout the usual waking hours and measuring how long it takes them to fall asleep each time. Excessive somnolence is defined as falling asleep, on the average, in less than 5 minutes whenever one is put to bed, even after adequate bedrest on the night before.

A complaint of excessive somnolence should be taken seriously. Afraid of being called lazy or worse, patients rarely complain of somnolence until it is truly serious, or after they have had some near accidents or other unpleasant occurrences. Indeed, Guilleminault and Dement (1978) found that, fearing ridicule, 35% of patients suffering from DOES delayed seeking medical advice for 5 years or more after the symptoms had originally appeared.

Based on the fact that DOES generally are purely medical diseases, they will be treated with much less detail in this chapter than the insomnias. The ASDC outline will not be followed. Rather, after some general statements, we shall discuss only narcolepsy and sleep induced respiratory impairments, because these two disorders make up the bulk of patients. For the other DOES categories mentioned on Table 7.1, consult the ASDC nosology.

Once help is sought for EDS, misdiagnosis is common. Of 100 unselected DOES patients referred to the Stanford Sleep Disorders Clinic, 92% had received glucose tolerance tests and 12% had been diagnosed as having a "hypoglycemic syndrome." Similarly, 32% of the women had been given thyroid medication to treat their somnolence. This despite the fact that *none* of the 100 patients objectively suffered either from hypoglycemia or from a thyroid problem (Guilleminault & Dement, 1978).

According to Zarcone (1977), the differential diagnosis of DOES begins with the exclusion of primary organic pathology such as brain tumors, kidney failure, liver failure, anemia or endocrine disease. Following this, the clinician should ask the following three standard questions (Guilleminault & Dement, 1977):

1. "Do you have peculiar muscular problems?" This question searches for attacks of muscular weakness, especially following strong emotions such as laughter or anger. An affirmative answer almost always indicates cataplexy, and it diagnoses the patients that are narcoleptic.

2. "Are you a heavy snorer?" If yes, the bed partner might make a tape recording of the patient's typical snoring. A large number of patients with DOES suffer from the sleep apnea syndrome, and almost all of them are heavy snorers.

3. "What about medications?" In about 5% of DOES patients the problem is secondary to pharmacological treatments or to the withdrawal from previously established pharmacological treatments.

Narcolepsy

Case History: Mrs. W. is now 32. Her sleepiness had started sometime in high school. After falling asleep on some of her movie dates, she would only accept very active engagements, e.g. dancing. Married at 20, the couple had 2 children within the next 3 years.

Mrs. W. vividly recalls her struggle to maintain an adequate home for her family, often forcing herself to take ice-cold showers 3–5 times during a morning to ward off sleepiness, or turning the stereo up full blast. Nevertheless, sleepiness gradually became worse, and, in addition, she started to experience episodes of serious muscle weakness. Because of this muscle weakness, she would nurse her babies only while lying on the floor, for fear that she might drop them. Also, she rarely ventured out of the house from that point on, fearing she might collapse in public. Her social life shriveled, much to her and her husband's chagrin.

A family physician, after a physical evaluation, first diagnosed "housewife's boredom." Later on, thyroid medication was prescribed after a test had indicated marginally low levels. It only helped for a few weeks. Still later on, Mrs. W. was diagnosed as depressive and twice hospitalized. Once she was given ECT. Her husband left her, partially because he felt she was lazy, and partially because she often fell asleep during love making.

Then, at age 29, Mrs. W. read about narcolepsy in a popular magazine. She demanded a consultation with a neurologist. Narcolepsy was diagnosed. Stimulants were described, together with imipramine. Although still more tired than most people, and still in need of 1–2 naps per day, Mrs. W. "started to live again" within a few weeks, and she has recently remarried.

A fair amount of confusion concerning narcolepsy exists in the literature. However, following an International Symposium on Narcolepsy in 1975, this term is now reserved for a syndrome of excessive daytime sleepiness combined with manifestations of abnormal REM sleep.

Excessive daytime sleepiness in the second or third decade of life is often the first sign that narcolepsy may be developing. There is a sudden and unavoidable need to nap. These naps are usually short and relatively refreshing, although most of the narcoleptics feel sleepy throughout the day. Besides these almost irresistible *sleep attacks* (naps) there usually is *cataplexy,* i.e. a sudden loss of muscle tonus, paralyzing the person for some seconds or minutes while remaining conscious. These cataplectic attacks are often triggered by emotions such as laughing, anger, or, as in Mrs. W.'s case, by the excitement of nursing her babies or making love. Also often associated with narcolepsy is *sleep paralysis,* i.e. an inability to move when falling asleep or waking up, and *hypnagogic hallucinations,* i.e. vivid dreams which occur while the person is still conscious, but close to sleep onset.

Narcolepsy seems best conceptualized as a disorder in the balance between the sleep-wake-REM systems. REM phenomena intrude into wakefulness, either as a full blown REM period (sleep attack), or as the muscle paralysis of REM sleep (cataplexy, sleep paralysis), or as the hallucination of a dream (hypnagogic hallucination). Nocturnal sleep is often poor in narcoleptics.

In the lab, narcoleptics often show *sleep onset REM periods* (Rechtschaffen, Wolpert, Dement, Mitchell, & Fisher, 1963). Indeed, the appearance of REM sleep within 10 minutes of sleep onset is considered diagnostic of narcolepsy, provided that it cannot be explained by other mechanisms such as previous REM deprivation, withdrawal from alcohol, or endogenous depression.

The rate of narcolepsy in the general population is about 4 per 10,000. However, relatives of narcoleptics are 60 times more at risk for developing narcolepsy than the general population. Genetic variables are clearly implicated. There is no evidence that narcolepsy is a psychogenic disturbance, although strict control over one's emotions may diminish the number of narcoleptic attacks.

The excessive daytime sleepiness and the inappropriate need to nap in narcolepsy are usually treated with stimulants, mainly methylphenidate, amphetamines, and pemoline (Zarcone, 1973). However, there is some evidence that the chronic use of these stimulants may aggravate the condition. Stimulant dosages are therefore kept as low as possible. "Drug-holidays" lasting a few weeks are suggested when habituation to the stimulants becomes a problem. Cataplexy, on the other hand, usually yields either to imipraminic drugs (Shapiro, 1975) or to protriptyline (Schmidt, Clark, & Hyman, 1977).

DOES Associated with Sleep-Induced Respiratory Impairment

Case History: Mr. E. is a 28 year old truck driver referred to the Sleep Disorders Center by his allergist for an evaluation of excessive somnolence. Mr. E. had been under treatment for congestion and vasomotor rhinitis since childhood, and had undergone various operations to clear the airway: trimming of turbinates, adenoidectomy and tonsillectomy, and trimming of the uvula. An ENT evaluation also noted retrognatia and "a very small airway." Nevertheless, at the time of referral, Mr. E.'s breathing seemed "adequate."

Excessive somnolence had started shortly after high school. Mr. E. started to take naps—one at first, up to five per day now. He had lost his job "because of laziness" six months before the sleep evaluation.

On the first lab night, Mr. E. slept for 373 minutes, but 85% of this sleep was stage 1. There were only 33 minutes of stage 2 sleep, 27 minutes of REM, and no delta. Subjectively, Mr. E. rated this sleep as "slightly worse than my average."

A total of 401 obstructive apneas were recorded during that night, and Mr. E. awoke for a few seconds after most of them. These apneic episodes lasted 20–150 seconds each. Oxygen saturation, measured by ear oximetry, dropped to the 60's and 70's during each apnea in NREM sleep, but it decreased to a low of 25% during REM sleep (see Figure 7.4)! Except for appropriate sinus tachycardia and a few premature ventricular contractions during the night, cardiac functioning was still normal.

Further evaluations by ENT, cardiology, and pulmonary specialists yielded the consensus that additional ENT operations would be unlikely to clear Mr. E.'s very atypical airway, and that the extremely low oxygen saturations would compromise his health seriously over a lifetime. A special type of tracheostomy was then performed, to be closed during the day, opened at night.

Mr. E.'s alertness improved dramatically just a few days after the operation. Sleep became normal, although there remained about 30 central apneas per night (indicating some damage to respiratory centers). Although the continuous care of the tracheostomy is bothersome for Mr. E., he was re-employed about 2 months after the operation and has returned to a productive life.

Sleep Apnea is a serious, potentially lethal condition. An apneic episode is usually defined as cessation of air flow lasting 10 seconds or longer. Episodes of apnea during sleep are often terminated by brief EEG arousals, usually without reaching full consciousness. Bouts of apneic sleep episodes may last from a few minutes to an entire night. In severe cases literally hundreds of apneic episodes are observed during one night.

Three types of sleep apnea are distinguished (Guilleminault & Dement, 1978):

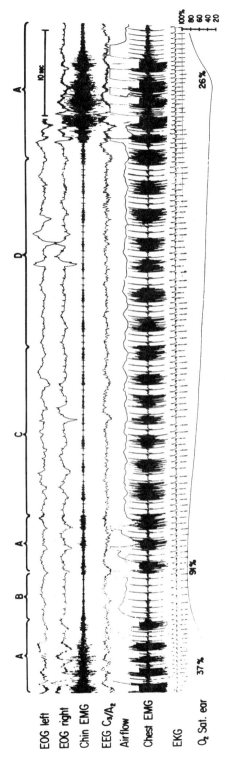

FIG. 7.4. Sleep Apnea Episode in Mr. E. A. A: Awake, breathing adequately; B: A 5 sec. episode of central apnea during wakefulness, probably due to previous overbreathing; C: Falling asleep. Obstructive apnea develops very little air flow, but continued respiratory effort; D: REM sleep. Apnea continues. Note extreme oxygen desaturation.

247

1. *Obstructive, or Upper Airway Apnea* is characterized by an obstruction in the airway, causing no air flow despite persistent respiratory efforts. This type of apnea predominates in DOES. Associated with this syndrome is a characteristic snoring pattern. Inspiratory snores gradually increase as the patient falls asleep and the obstruction develops. Then there is silence. Finally, a loud, choking, inspiratory gasp occurs 10–60 seconds later, as the patient partially arouses and his respiratory efforts succeed in overcoming the occlusion. Violent body movements often accompany this type of apnea.

2. *Central Apnea* is characterized by the cessation of airflow because respiratory drive stops. There is no obstruction. This type of apnea often results in a complaint of insomnia.

3. *Mixed Apnea* is marked by an initial central component, i.e. cessation of respiratory effort, followed by an obstructive component, i.e. no airflow despite respiratory effort.

There is considerable variation in the intensity of somnolence associated with sleep apnea. Many patients suffer from sleep attacks during the day, lasting for an hour or more. Sleep is not refreshing. Severe cases may report post-dormital disorientation, blackouts and periods of automatic behavior associated with amnesia. In children, the most prominent presenting symptom may be a reappearance of enuresis after toilet training, coupled with learning difficulties and decreases in school performance. Respiratory functioning during wakefulness is usually normal.

In a majority of cases the etiology of the sleep apnea DOES is not clear. Actual anatomic abnormalities of the upper airway exist in a small proportion of sleep apnea patients. Hypothyroidism, micrognatia and retrognatia, acromegaly, and many other problems have been linked to obstructive apneas. Many patients demonstrate a short, thick neck. Especially in children, hypertrophied tonsils and adenoids are often the source of the apnea. Although modest obesity is frequently associated with the sleep apnea DOES syndrome, many patients with this disorder are not overweight, and only about 5% fit the classical description of the obese Pickwickian patient.

Medical complications of the sleep apnea syndrome include cardiac arrhythmias, ranging from premature ventricular contractions to serious atrioventricular block and sinus arrest. Heart failure may be evident in severe cases. The condition carries an increased risk of sudden death during sleep. Hypertension is present in about 40% of the cases. Diffuse headaches and drenching nightsweats may develop. These complications are usually progressive, unless the sleep apneas are treated (Guilleminault & Dement, 1978).

Sleep apneas occur at all ages. They have been implicated in the sudden infant death syndrome and in children with mental retardation. On the other hand, they occur with increasing frequency as age increases beyond forty. For obstructive apneas, men outnumber women by a ratio of 30:1.

Variants of the sleep apnea syndrome include incomplete obstructions of the airway, heavy snoring (Lugaresi, Coccagna, & Cirignotta, 1978), decreases in diaphragmatic contractions, and alveolar hypoventilation. Air does flow with each breath in these cases, but may not be sufficient for adequate gas exchange.

A presumptive diagnosis of the sleep apnea DOES syndrome can often be made by observation of the sleeper, by interviewing the bed partner, or by listening to a recording of the patient's snoring. However, assessing the severity of the problem requires the evaluation of blood gases during the night. This is most easily performed by ear oximetry. Because the equipment involved is expensive, sleep apnea is one of the few disorders that usually require evaluation at a sleep disorders center.

Deciding on the appropriate treatment of sleep apneas involves a team of many different specialists. Besides the severity of the daytime somnolence or nocturnal insomnia, the severity of the oxygen desaturation at night needs to be considered, as well as the status of the associated medical complications such as cardiac problems, hypertension and headaches.

Sleeping in an easy chair may help in mild cases. Obviously, if there are any ENT obstructions, they need to be removed surgically. Weight loss is occasionally successful. Karacan, Derman, and Fisher (1980) suggest that gastric stapling may be a method of weight reduction that is less traumatic than the more widely known jejunoileostomy, in patients where weight reduction is crucial but cannot be achieved by dieting. Some centers advocate an "internal face lift," i.e. tightening the muscles around the pharynx. However, in many cases a special form of tracheostomy is the treatment of choice, kept closed during day, but opened at night.

Psychological/Behavioral Somnolence

DOES based on psychological/behavioral factors are rare, as discussed earlier. However, some depressions do result in excessive sleeping. This is particularly, but not exclusively, true of the depressive phase in bipolar illness, and of depression in young adults (Taub, Hawkins, & Van de Castle, 1978). In addition, it is said that confinement, boredom, some dissociative disorders, borderline states, or schizophrenia may result in DOES, but research is severly lacking.

Psychological/behavioral factors may also be involved in DOES associated with drug abuse. Some researchers even speculate that a learned form of DOES exists in individuals who have repeatedly experienced relief from their problems by sleeping. However, very little is actually known about such problems.

DISORDERS OF THE SLEEP-WAKE SCHEDULE

Disorders included here involve a mismatch between the individual's actual sleeping and waking behavior and the time when sleeping and waking "should" occur. The patient cannot sleep when he wants or needs to sleep, but sleeps well during other times.

Confronted with such problems, one searches first for psychological reasons that maintain the unusual sleep-wake schedule. A patient may like to remain awake at night, e.g. because he or she then does not have to deal with other humans. However, there are indeed people for whom the sleep/wake schedule seems to be disturbed on a purely biological basis.

In a totally time free environment (e.g. in an underground cave with artificial light and no clocks), most humans show a circadian rhythm longer than 24 hours (Aschoff, 1969). All of us, every day, have to squeeze this biologically slower rhythm into the 24-hour cycle dictated by the sun. Some patients, suffering from the *Non-24-Hour Sleep-Wake Syndrome,* may be unable to do this. They show an incremental pattern of delays in sleep onset and wake-up time, usually 1–2 hours later each day. Most patients with this problem make intermittent attempts to conform to the 24-hour rhythm, getting up at conventional morning hours. Falling asleep later and later, but still maintaining the same wake-up times then leads to episodic sleep deprivation. At other times, when their internal circadian rhythm happens to correlate with the one prescribed by society, there is no sleep difficulty.

A sleep log of at least 2 weeks duration is necessary to start diagnosing the non-24-hour syndrome. Patients rarely are aware of their problem, but complain about periodic difficulties in getting to sleep at night, coupled with extreme arousal problems.

Reasons for the non-24-hour syndrome are unclear. When put into time free environments, some patients manifesting this problem show extremely slow internal "circadian" rhythms, sleep wake cycles lasting 35–45 hours! Others, such as blind people or those with schizoid personalities, seem not to perceive the usual Zeitgebers (time markers) that synchronize the rest of us (Kokkoris, Weitzman, Pollak, Spielman, Czeisler, & Bradlow, 1978).

Another problem of the sleep wake schedule is caused by *Irregular Sleep Wake Patterns.* In the insomniac whose work is not tied to a regular clock time, in retired people, and in those without jobs, the drive to oversleep may become overwhelming after a series of poor nights. Numerous daytime naps are often taken by such people in order to catch up on sleep. Thus begins a self-reinforcing, irregular sleep wake pattern, with sleeping and waking becoming almost evenly spread over the 24 hours of a day.

The key feature in the irregular sleep wake pattern is the loss of a clear circadian rhythm. Not only is this rhythm disrupted, but as endocrine, temperature, and other circadian functions lose circadian synchronization, they may start to fluctuate erratically or may flatten altogether. The patient becomes chronically weak and groggy, always sleepy, but never sleeping well.

Treatment of the irregular sleep wake pattern consists of gradually reestablishing a regular day night cycle. Wake times during daytime hours are gradually lengthened, naps abolished, and bedtime curtailed to the usual sleeping hours. Exercise during the day may help to start circadian cycling. However, changes have to be made gradually because the patient is usually weakened and unfit from chronic bedrest. Circadian cycling, such as body temperature, are graphed daily to provide motivation. However, it is rarely possible to personally regularize a seriously disturbed sleep wake pattern. Outside "trainers" are usually necessary, or admission is made to an institution that reinforces normal sleep wake patterns and fills the waking hours with activity.

DYSFUNCTIONS ASSOCIATED WITH SLEEP, SLEEP STAGES, OR PARTIAL AROUSALS (PARASOMNIAS)

Parasomnias are problems that either occur exclusively during sleep or are exacerbated by sleep. They may be tied to certain sleep states (e.g., painful erections during REM sleep), they may occur in several stages (e.g., bruxism), or they may be related to the transition between sleeping and waking (e.g., familial sleep paralysis).

Sleepwalking (somnambulism), sleep terror (pavor nocturnus, incubus), and bed wetting (enuresis) are the three most common parasomnias and the only ones to be discussed in this chapter. Surprisingly, all three usually begin in delta sleep, typically about 1 hour after sleep onset. Broughton (1968) suggests that all three may be problems of incomplete arousal. As discussed earlier, awakening from delta sleep is difficult for all of us. Some of us, especially children with very deep delta sleep, seem to have extreme difficulties with this arousal. Rather than awakening fully when disturbed in delta sleep, such people seem to enter a confusional state which mixes sleep waves (delta) with waking waves (alpha and random fast EEG). It appears that sleep walking, night terrors, and enuresis occur in this confusional state.

Sleepwalking (Somnambulism)

Case History: Mr. E. was a 41 year old teacher working in a very difficult high school. He sought help for sleepwalking after wrecking his car on a telephone pole while driving during one of his somnambulistic episodes. It appears that over the last few years he had occasionally driven off while asleep, had twice attacked his wife during a somnambulistic state, and in the morning often found himself sleeping on the living room floor or in the bathtub. According to his wife, he sleepwalked 4–5 times almost every week, and occasionally confused the living room with the bathroom during such episodes.

Mr. E. was a slight, very nervous man. He was obviously tense about the conditions at his school, where two teachers had been brutally attacked by students during the last year. However, he refused to change jobs, feeling that this was the place where he could do the most good. Also, he had been nervous since childhood, having been diagnosed as hyperkinetic when 8-years-old. However, repeated clinical EEGs, even with nasopharyngeal leads, had never found any abnormal discharges.

Mr. E. was advised that the main concern in his condition was safety. Key locks were to be installed on all windows of his ground floor apartment. His wife was to lock them each night, as well as the hall door leading to kitchen and living room. She was told to keep these keys and those of the car during the night. Obstacles and sharp implements were to be removed from the area accessible to Mr. E. during the night. Also, Mrs. E. was advised to learn some self defense grips, and she was told, after extended interviews with both, that these nocturnal attacks were not directed against her because of some psychological anger, but because Mr. E. was biologically confused during sleepwalking.

Although medications rarely work in somnambulism, Mr. E.'s sleepwalking decreased to once per week when given very low dosages of stimulants. Furthermore, Mr. E. was advised to take plenty of rest, and to learn some relaxation procedures to help deal with daytime tension.

On follow-up 2 years later, Mr. E. was still sleepwalking, but only about twice per month. He felt much more secure with the new arrangements, but started to sleepwalk extensively whenever his wife did not sleep in the apartment.

Sleepwalking episodes usually start with EEG delta waves of extremely high amplitude. During sleepwalking, the EEG then develops into the mixture of waking and sleeping waves described earlier. Higher cortical functions are inefficient during the episodes and coordination is poor. While some visual activity occurs and sleep walkers often can avoid objects in their path, they are much clumsier when sleepwalking than they are during wakefulness. They can stumble, lose balance, fall out of windows or down fire escapes.

Occasional episodes of sleepwalking are normal in children. Indeed, most children can be induced to sleepwalk if placed on their feet during delta sleep. Stress and emotional tension may increase the frequency of sleepwalking, possibly because there are more frequent arousals from any kind of sleep during stressful times. While somnambulism in adults may be associated with significant psychological problems, sleepwalking in children does not, in itself, indicate significant psychopathology (Kales, Soldatos, Caldwell, Kales, Humphrey, Charney, & Schweitzer, 1980). There may also be a genetic component (Kales, Soldatos, Bixler, Ladas, Charney, Weber, & Schweitzer, 1980).

Sleepwalking needs to be differentiated from partial complex seizures that occur during sleep. Indeed, nasopharyngeal or sphenoidal leads in sleepwalkers may show intensive spike and wave discharges during delta sleep even when waking clinical EEGs have been read as normal. Sleepwalking also needs to be distinguished from waking fugue states that consist of longer and more purposeful behavior.

The first step in the treatment of somnambulism is to avoid injury. Adults who sleepwalk may need psychotherapy, but sleepwalking in children can usually be handled by reassurance to patients and parents. Sleep hygiene is important. The more sleep is deepened, say by previous sleep deprivation, sedatives or alcohol, the more likely are episodes of somnambulism. Although no universally helpful drug is available, some patients respond to imipramine, others to stimulants. Delta sleep suppression with benzodiazepines rarely, if ever, abolishes sleepwalking.

Sleep Terrors (Pavor Nocturnus, Incubus)

Sleep terrors almost invariably start with a terrifying scream, and they are usually accompanied by signs of intense panic. This includes a frightened expression, profuse perspiring, and quick pulse. Awakening is difficult. Full consciousness is not achieved for a few minutes, even if the patient is severely shaken by others. If aroused, the patient may remember a sense of terror or dread, a feeling of paralysis, or helplessness, but detailed dream content is rarely remembered (Fisher, Byrne, Edwards, & Kahn, 1970).

The term "sleep terror" is synonomous with "pavor nocturnus" for children, and with "incubus" for adults. Such terms should not be confused with Dream Anxiety Attacks (Kramer, 1979). This latter disturbance involves an arousal from REM sleep with terrifying dreams. Recall is usually vivid and detailed but physiological activation is slight. The patient is easy to arouse and quickly oriented to the environment. Diagnostically useful are the facts that sleep terrors usually occur early at night and show intense physiological agitation, but little dream content, while dream anxiety attacks usually occur later at night, show little physiological agitation, but fairly elaborate dream content. Sleep terrors should also not be confused with terrifying hypnagogic hallucinations that may occur in the twilight state between waking and sleeping in depressed patients, in posttraumatic stress disorders, in narcoleptics, and in schizophrenics.

Sleep terrors in children characteristically disappear in adolescence. Like somnambulism, sleep terrors may be more frequent in times of stress, but, at least in children, they are not associated with increased psychopathology.

Sleep terrors are usually non-epileptic, even in patients with known epilepsy (Gastaut & Broughton, 1964). However, partial complex seizures during sleep are occasionally mistaken for night terrors. Tricyclic anti-depressants and neuroleptics may increase the frequency of these episodes. Benzodiazepines seem to decrease attacks of sleep terror, possibly because they suppress delta sleep. Benzodiazepines also seem effective against dream anxiety attacks, possibly because they relax daytime tension.

Sleep-related Enuresis

Bed wetting after the age of 3 is called enuresis. It is a common problem, found in about 10% of girls and 15% of boys at age 5. In apparently healthy navy recruits, the incidence was 1%–3% during WWII.

Involuntary micturition typically begins in delta sleep. Generally, delta sleep changes into a body movement just prior to the urine flow, but muscular quiesence returns with the start of micturition.

In "primary" enuresis, toilet training has never been accomplished, while in "secondary" enuresis a child has been dry for at least a month before starting to wet the bed again. "Symptomatic" enuresis refers to an organic etiology, such as urogenital, renal, metabolic, endocrine or epileptic disorders, congenitally small bladders, or urethral and bladder infections. "Symptomatic" is distinguished from "idiopathic" enuresis, which seems to be a non-organic, self-limited phenomenon of delayed maturation, usually found in very deep sleepers. Idiopathic enuretics show no typical personality patterns or psychopathological features, and this phenomenon usually disappears in late childhood or adolescence.

Sleep-related enuresis must be distinguished from epileptic seizures with urinary incontinence. However, in the majority of epileptic children who are also enuretic, the bedwetting episodes are not temporally related to the epileptic discharges.

After ruling out symptomatic enuresis and significant psychopathology, excessive enuresis may be treated with behavioral techniques such as the bell and blanket technique, or bladder stretching exercises (Starfield, 1972). Imipramine is quite effective to inhibit enuresis for a while, e.g. during a visit to friends, or during summer camp. However, imipramine rarely gives a lasting cure.

Other Dysfunctions

At least a dozen other types of parasomnias have been documented, but space limitations prevent their discussion here. Suffice it to say that each has its own etiology and treatment. Also, behavior therapy, especially relaxation training, are rarely effective unless one has first demonstrated that tension, or learning factors, may be an etiological factor in the parasomnia.

CONCLUDING COMMENTS

As the reader will now appreciate, the list of disorders associated with sleep is long. It can only grow longer in the years to come. It is now a matter of debate whether existing medical and psychological specialities can absorb the new knowledge about diagnosis and treatment of these sleep disorders, or whether a new medical subspeciality, called Sleep Disorders Medicine, is gradually evolving.

Some sleep pathologies clearly have a psychological origin, while others are rooted squarely in organic pathology. Nevertheless, the main message of this chapter should be that, in most sleep problems, there are intensive interactions between psychological and medical factors. In order to become sleep disorders, psychological problems first have to disturb the balance between the arousal system and the sleep systems, and this invariably influences physiological and circadian variables. Similarly, sleep problems with purely organic etiology invariably affect mood and performance during wakefulness. Furthermore, conditioning and learning factors shape many sleep disturbances, even if the primary etiology is purely organic. Because of this, the diagnosis and treatment of sleep problems almost always involves the sensitive management of organic as well as psychological and behavioral variables. This means that much time has to be spent working with each patient.

If you have time, skill, and patience, working with sleep disorder patients is a rewarding and fascinating experience. It often feels like a detective story, as one slowly ferrets out what might cause or cure the sleep disturbance. However, anybody who does not have this time, the skills, or the patience is probably better advised to refer sleep disorders patients elsewhere. Too much damage has already been done by well meaning, but incompetent treatment, such as the psychoanalysis of narcoleptic patients or the prescription of hypnotics as soon as "insomnia" is mentioned.

REFERENCES

Allison, T., & Van Twyver, H. The evolution of sleep. *Natural History,* 1970, *79,* 56–65.

Aschoff, J. Desynchronization and Resynchronization of human circadian rhythms. *Aerospace Medicine,* 1969, 844–849.

Aserinsky, E., & Kleitman, N. Regularly occurring periods of eye motility, and concomitant phenomena during sleep. *Science,* 1953, *118,* 273–274.

Association of Sleep Disorders Centers. *Diagnostic Classification of Sleep and Arousal Disorders,* First Edition, prepared by the Sleep Disorders Classification Committee, H. P. Roffwarg, Chairman, *Sleep,* 1979, *2,* 1–137.

Baekeland, F., & Lasky, R. Exercise and sleep patients in college athletes. *Perceptual and Motor Skills,* 1966, *23,* 1203–1207.

Barlow, P. B., Bartlett, B., Jr., Hauri, P., Hellekson, C., Nattie, E. E., Remmers, J. E., & Schmidt-Nowara, W. W. Idiopathic hypoventilation syndrome: importance of preventing nocturnal hypoxemia and hypercapnia. *American Review of Respiratory Disease,* 1980, *121,* 141–145.

Berger, R. J. Bioenergetic functions of sleep and activity of rhythms and their possible relevance to aging. *Proceedings of the Federation of American Society for Experimental Biology,* 1975, *34,* 97–102.

Boghen, D., & Peyronnard, J. Myoclonus in familial restless legs syndrome. *Archives of Neurology,* 1976, *33,* 368–370.

Bonnet, M. H., Johnson, L. C., & Webb, W. W. The reliability of arousal threshold during sleep. *Psychophysiology,* 1978, *33,* 412–416.

Bootzin, R. *Stimulus control of insomnia.* Paper presented at the Symposium on the Treatment of Sleep Disorders, American Psychological Association Convention, Montreal, Canada, July 1973.

Bootzin, R. R., & Nicassio, P. N. Behavioral treatments for insomnia. In M. Hersen, R. Eisler, & P. Miller (Eds.), *Progress in Behavior Modification.* New York: Academic Press, 1978.

Borkovec, T. D. Pseudo(experiential)-insomnia and idiopathic (objective) insomnia: Theoretical and therapeutic issues. *Advanced Behavioral Research and Therapy,* 1979, *2,* 27–55.

Borkovec, T. D., & Hennings, B. L. The role of physiological attention-focusing in relaxation treatment of sleep disturbance, general tension, and specific stress reaction. *Behavioral Research and Therapy,* 1978, *16,* 7–19.

Borkovec, T. D., & Weerts, T. D. Effects of progressive relaxation on sleep disturbance: an electroencephalographic evaluation. *Psychosomatic Medicine,* 1976, *38,* 173–180.

Brezinova, V., & Oswald, I. Sleep after a bedtime beverage. *British Medical Journal,* 1972, *2,* 431–433.

Broughton, R. J. Sleep disorders—disorders of arousal. *Science,* 1968, *159,* 1070–1078.

Church, M. W., & Johnson, L. C. Mood and performance at poor sleepers during repeated use of flurazepam. *Psychopharmacology,* 1979, *61,* 309–316.

Claparede, E. Esquisse d'une theorie biologique du Sommeil. *Archives of Psychology,* 1905, *4,* 245–349.

Clift, A. D. (Ed.). *Sleep Disturbance and Hypnotic Drug Dependence.* Amsterdam: Excerpta Medica, 1975.

Coleman, R. M., Pollak, C. O., Kokkoris, C. P., McGregor, P. A., & Weitzman, E. D. Periodic nocturnal myoclonus in patients with sleep-wake disorders: A case series analysis. In Chase, M. H., Mitler, M., & Walter, P. L. (Eds.), *Sleep Research,* 1979, *8,* Brain Information Service/ Brain Research Institute, UCLA, Los Angeles, 175.

Dement, W. C., Carskadon, M. A., Mitler, M. M., Phillips, R. L., & Zarcone, V. P. Prolonged use of flurazepam: a sleep laboratory study. *Behavioral Medicine,* 1978, 25–31.

Elson, R. B., Hauri, P., & Cunis, D. Physiological changes in yoga meditation. *Psychophysiology,* 1977, *14,* 52–57.

Evans, F. J., Cook, M. R., Cohen, H. D., Orne, E. C., & Orne, M. T. Appetitive and replacement naps: EEG and behavior. *Science,* 1977, *197,* 687–689.

Fisher, C., Byrne, J., Edwards, A., & Kahn, D. A psychophysiological study of nightmares. *Journal of the American Psychoanalytic Association,* 1970, *18,* 747–782.

Foulkes, W. D. Dream reports from different stages of sleep. *Journal of Abnormal Psychology,* 1962, *65,* 14–25.

Foulkes, D., & Vogel. G. Mental activity at sleep onset. *Journal Abnormal Psychology,* 1965, *70,* 231–243.

Frankel, B. L., Patten, B. M., & Gillin, J. C. Restless legs syndrome. Sleep-electroencephalographic and neurologic findings. *Journal of the American Medical Association.* 1974, *230,* 1302–1303.

Gastaut, H., & Broughton, R. A clinical and polygraphic study of episodic phenomena during sleep. *Recent Advances in Biological Psychiatry,* 1964, *7,* 197–221.

Globus, G., Friedmann, J., Cohen, H., Pearsons, K. S., & Fidell, S. The effects of aircraft noise on sleep electrophysiology as recorded in the home. In W. D. Ward (Ed.), *Proceedings of the International Congress on Noise as a Public Health Problem.* Washington, D.C.: U.S. Environmental Protection Agency, 1973.

Greenberg, R. Dream interruption insomnia. *The Journal of Nervous and Mental Disease,* 1967, *144,* 18–21.

Gross, M. M., Goodenough, D. R., Hasten, J., & Lewis, E. Experimental study of sleep in chronic alcoholics before, during and after four days of heavy drinking, with a nondrinking comparison. *Annals New York Academy of Science,* 1973, *215,* 254–275.

Guilleminault, C., & Dement, W. C. 235 cases of excessive daytime sleepiness. Diagnosis and tentative classification. *Journal of the Neurological Sciences,* 1977, *31,* 13–27.

Guilleminault, C., & Dement, W. (Eds.). *Sleep Apnea Syndromes.* New York: Alan R. Liss, 1978.

Hartmann, E. L. *The functions of sleep.* New Haven and London: Yale University Press, 1973.

Hauri, P. Effects of evening activity on early night sleep. *Psychophysiology,* 1968, *4,* 267–277.

Hauri, P. Dreams in patients remitted from reactive depression. *Journal of Abnormal Psychology,* 1976, *85,* 1–10.

Hauri, P. The sleep disorders. *Current Concepts.* The Upjohn Company, Scope Publication, 1977.

Hauri, P. What can insomniacs teach us about the functions of sleep? In Drucker-Colin (Ed.), *The Functions of Sleep.* New York: Academic Press, 1979. (a)

Hauri, P. Behavioral treatment of insomnia. *Medical Times,* 1979, *107,* 36–47. (b)

Hauri, P. Treating psychophysiological insomnia with biofeedback. *Archives of General Psychiatry,* 1981, *38,* 752–758.

Hauri, P., Chernik, D., Hawkins, D., & Mendels, J. Sleep of depressed patients in remission. *Archives of General Psychiatry,* 1974, *31,* 386–391.

Hauri, P., & Hawkins, D. R. Individual differences in the sleep of depression. In Jovanovic, U. J. (Ed.), *The Nature of Sleep.* Stuttgart: Fisher, 1973. (a)

Hauri, P., & Hawkins, D. R. Alpha-delta sleep. *Electroencephalography and Clinical Neurophysiology,* 1973, *34,* 233–237. (b)

Hauri, P., & Olmstead, E. Childhood-onset insomnia. *Sleep,* 1980, *3,* 59–65.

Hauri, P., Percy, L., Hartmann, E., & Russ, D. Treating psychophysiological insomnia with biofeedback, a replication. *Sleep Research,* 1981 (in press) (abstract)

Hawkins, D. R., Taub, J. M., Van de Castle, R. L., Teja, J. S., Greyson, B., Garland, F., & Talley, J. E. Sleep stage patterns associated with depression in young adult patients. In W. P. Koella & P. Levin (Eds.), *Sleep.* Basel: Karger, 1977.

Hobson, J. A. The cellular basis of sleep cycle control. In D. D. Weitzman (Ed.), *Advances in Sleep Research* (Vol. 1). New York: Flushing Publications, 1974.

Hobson, J. A. The neuropharmacology of REM sleep generation. Presented in the Symposium "Advances in the Biology and Psychology of REM Sleep" at the Annual Meeting of the A.P.A. in San Francisco, California, May 3–9, 1980.

Institute of Medicine. *Sleeping Pills, Insomnia, and Medical Practice.* Washington, D.C.: National Academy of Sciences, 1979.

Jacobs, B. I., & McGinty, D. J. Effects of food deprivation on sleep and wakefulness in the rat. *Experimental Neurology,* 1971, *30,* 212–222.

Jones, H. S., & Oswald, I. Two cases of healthy insomnia. *Electroencephalography and Clinical Neurophysiology,* 1968, *24,* 378–380.

Johnson, L. C. Are stages of sleep related to waking behavior? *American Scientist,* 1973, *61,* 326–338.

Johnson, L. C., Burdick, J. A., & Smith, J. Sleep during alcohol intake and withdrawal in the chronic alcoholic. *Archives of General Psychiatry,* 1970, *22,* 406–418.

Kales, A., Bixler, E. O., Tjiauw-Ling, T., Scharf, M. B., & Kales, J. D. Chronic hypnotic-drug use. *JAMA,* 1974, *227,* 513–517.

Kales, A., Hauri, P., Bixler, E., & Silberfarb, P. Effectiveness of intermediate-term use of secobarbital. *Clinical Pharmacology and Therapeutics,* 1976, *20,* 541–545.

Kales, A., Kales, J. D., Bixler, E. O., & Martin, E. Common shortcomings in the evaluation and treatment of insomnia. In F. Kagan, T. Harwood, K. Rickels, A. Rudzik, & H. Sorer, (Eds.), *Hypnotics: Methods of Development & Evaluation,* New York: Spectrum Publications Inc, 1975.

Kales, A., Scharf, M. B., & Kales, J. D. Rebound insomnia: a new clinical syndrome. *Science,* 1978, *201,* 1039–1041.

Kales, A., Soldatos, C. R., Bixler, E. O., Ladda, R. L., Charney, D. S., Weber, G., & Schweitzer, P. K. Hereditary factors in sleepwalking and night terrors. *British Journal of Psychiatry,* 1980, *137,* 111–118.

Kales, A., Soldatos, C. R., Caldwell, A. B., Kales, J. D., Humphrey, F. J., Charney, D. S., & Schweitzer, P. K. Somnambulism. *Archives of General Psychiatry,* 1980, *37,* 1406–1410.

Karacan, I., Blackburn, A. B., Thornby, J. I., Okawa, M., Salis, P. J., & Williams, R. L. The effect of doxepin HCl (sinequan) on sleep patterns and clinical symptomatology of neurotic depressed patients with sleep disturbance. *Sinequan (doxepin HCl): A Monograph of Recent Clinical Studies,* 1975, (Monograph)

Karacan, I., Derman, S., & Fisher, P. B. Gastric stapling in the management of obstructive sleep-apnea syndrome: a case report. In M. H. Chase, D. F. Kripke, & P. L. Walter (Eds.), *Sleep Research,* 1980, *9,* Brain Information Service/ Brain Research Institute, UCLA, Los Angeles, 293.

Karacan, I., Thornby, J. I., Booth, G. H., Okawa, M., Salis, P. J., Anch, A. M., & Williams, R. L. Dose-response effects of coffee on objective (EEG) and subjective measures of sleep. In P. Levin & W. P. Koella (Eds.), *Sleep.* Basel: Karger, 1975.

Karacan, I., Williams, R. L., Finley, W. W., & Hursch, C. J. The effects of naps on nocturnal sleep. Influence on the need for stage 1 REM and stage 4 sleep. *Biological Psychiatry,* 1970, *2,* 391-399.

Karacan, I., Williams, R. L., Littell, R. C., & Salis, P. J. Insomniacs: unpredictable and idiosyncratic sleepers. In W. P. Koella & P. Lewis (Eds.), *Sleep.* Basel: Karger, 1973.

Kay, D. C., Blackburn, A. B., Buckingham, J. A., & Karacan, I. Human pharmacology of sleep. In R. L. Williams, and I. Karacan (Eds.), *Pharmacology of Sleep.* New York: Wiley, 1976.

Kokkoris, C. P., Weitzman, E. D., Pollak, C. P., Spielman, A. J., Czeisler, C. A., & Bradlow, H. Long-term ambulatory temperature monitoring in a subject with a hypernychthemeral sleep-wake cycle disturbance. *Sleep,* 1978, *1,* 177-190.

Kramer, M. Dream disturbances. *Psychiatric Annals,* 1979, *9,* 336-376.

Kupfer, D. J., & Foster, F. G. EEG sleep and depression. In R. L. Williams & I. Karacan (Eds.), *Sleep Disorders.* New York: Wiley, 1978.

Kupfer, D. J., Foster, R. G., Reich, L., Thompson, K. S., & Weiss, B. EEG sleep changes as predictors in depression. *American Journal of Psychiatry,* 1976, *133,* 622-626.

Lugaresi, E., Coccagna, G. & Cirignotta, F. Snoring and its clinical implications. In C. Guilleminault, and W. C. Dement, (Eds.), *Sleep Apnea Syndromes.* New York: Liss, 1978.

Lutz, E. G. Restless legs, anxiety and caffeinism. *Journal of Clinical Psychiatry,* 1978, *39,* 693-698.

McGinty, D. J. Encephalization and the neural control of behavior. In M. B. Sterman, D. J. McGinty, & A. M. Adinolfi (Eds.), *Brain Development and Behavior.* New York: Academic Press, 1971.

Meier, G. W., & Berger, R. J. Thresholds to arousing stimulation in the developing infant rhesus monkey. *Psychoneurologic Science,* 1967, *7,* 247-248.

Moldofsky, H., Scarisbrick, P., England, R., & Smythe, H. Musculoskeletal symptoms and non-REM sleep disturbance in patients with "fibrositis syndrome" and healthy subjects. *Psychosomatic Medicine,* 1975, *37,* 341-351.

Moruzzi, G. The functional significance of sleep with particular regard to the brain mechanisms underlying consciousness. In J. C. Eccles (Ed.), *Brain and Conscious Experience.* New York: Springer, 1966.

Mullaney, D. J., Johnson, L. C., Naitoh, P., Friedmann, J. K., & Globus, G. G. Sleep during and after gradual sleep reduction. *Psychophysiology,* 1977, *14,* 237-244.

Myrsten, A. L., Elgerot, A., & Edgren, B. Effects of abstinence from tobacco smoking on physiological and psychological arousal levels in habitual smokers. *Psychosomatic Medicine,* 1977, *39,* 25-38.

Netick, A., Orem, J., & Dement, W. Neuronal activity specific to REM sleep and its relationship to breathing. *Brain Research,* 1977, *120,* 197-207.

Nicholson, A. N. Hypnotics: rebound insomnia and residual sequelae. *British Journal of Clinical Pharmacology,* 1980, *9,* 223-225.

Oswald, I. *Sleep.* Harmondsworth, Middlesex: Penguin Books, 1974.

Otto, E. Physiological analysis of human sleep disturbances induced by noise and increased room temperature. In W. P. Koella & P. Levin (Eds.), *Sleep.* Basel: Karger, 1973.

Pasnau, R. O., Naitoh, P., Stier, S., & Kollar, E. J. The psychological effects of 205 hours of sleep deprivation. *Archives of General Psychiatry*, 1968, *18*, 496–505.

Pokorny, A. D. Sleep disturbances, alcohol, and alcoholism: A review. In R. L. Williams & I. Karacan (Eds.), *Sleep Disorders: Diagnosis and Treatment*. New York: John Wiley, 1978.

Rechtschaffen, A., Hauri, P., & Zeitlin, M. Auditory awakening thresholds in REM and NREM sleep stages. *Perceptual and Motor Skills*, 1966, *22*, 927–942.

Rechtschaffen, A., & Kales, A. (Eds.). *A Manual of Standarized Terminology, Techniques and Scoring System for Sleep Stages of Human Subjects*. Los Angeles: Brain Information Service/ Brain Research Institute, UCLA, 1968.

Rechtschaffen, A., & Monroe, J. Laboratory studies of insomnia. In A. Kales (Ed.), *Sleep Physiology & Pathology*. Philadelphia: J. B. Lippincott Co., 1969.

Rechtschaffen, A., Wolpert, E. A., Dement, W. C., Mitchell, S. A., & Fisher, C. Nocturnal sleep of narcoleptics. *Electroencephalography and Clinical Neurophysiology*, 1963, *15*, 599–609.

Renner, J. A. Drug addiction. In T. Hackett & N. Cassem (Eds.), *Massachusetts General Hospital Handbook of General Hospital Psychiatry*. St. Louis: C. V. Mosby, 1978.

Richardson, G. S., Carskadon, M. A., Flagg, W., Van den Hoed, J., Dement, W. C., & Mitler, M. M. Excessive daytime sleepiness in man: multiple sleep latency measurement in narcoleptic and control subjects. *Electroencephalography and Clinical Neurophysiology*, 1978, *45*, 621–627.

Roth, T., Kramer, M., & Lutz, T. The effects of hypnotics on sleep, performance, and subjective state. *Drugs and Experimental Clinical Research*, 1977, *1*, 279–286.

Sastre, J. P., Sakai, K., & Jouvet, M. Persistance du sommeil paradoxal chez le Chat apres destruction de l'aire gigantocellulaire du tegmentum pontique par l'acide kainique. *C. R. Acad. Sc. Paris*, 1979, *289*. 959–964.

Schmidt, H. S., Clark, R. W., & Hyman, P. R. Protriptyline: an effective agent in the treatment of the narcolepsy-cataplexy syndrome and hypersomnia. *American Journal of Psychiatry*, 1977, *2*, 183–185.

Schmidt-Kessen, W., & Kendel, K. (Influence of room temperature on night-sleep in man.) Einfluss der Raumtemperatur auf den Nachtschlaf. *Research and Experimental Medicine*, 1973, *160*, 222–233.

Shader, R. I., Caine, E. D., & Meyer , R. E. Treatment of dependence on barbiturates and sedative-hypnotics. In R. I. Shader (Ed.), *Manual of Psychiatric Therapeutics*, Boston: Little, Brown and Co., 1975.

Shapiro, W. R. Treatment of cataplexy with clomipramine. *Archives of Neurology*, 1975, *32*, 653–656.

Siegel, J. M. Reticular formation activity and REM sleep. In R. Drucker-Colin, M. Shkurovich, & M. B. Sterman (Eds.), *The Functions of Sleep*. New York: Academic Press, 1979.

Siegel, J., & Langley, T. D. Arousal threshold in the cat as a function of sleep phase and stimulus significance. *Experientia*, 1965, *21*, 740–741.

Snyder, R. Psychophysiology of human sleep. *Clinical Neurosurgery*, 1971, *18*, 503–536.

Starfield, B. Enuresis: its pathogenesis and management. *Clinical Pediatrics*, 1972, *11*, 343–348.

Sterman, M. B., Howe, R. C., & MacDonald, L. R. Facilitation of spindle-burst sleep by conditioning of electroencephalographic activity while awake. *Science*, 1970, *167*, 1146–1148.

Sterman, M. B., Macdonald, L. T., & Stone, R. K. Biofeedback training of the sensorimotor electroencephalographic rhythms in man. *Epilepsia*, 1974, *15*, 395–416.

Stuss, D., & Broughton, R. Extreme short sleep: personality profiles and a case study of sleep requirement. *Waking and Sleeping*, 1978, *2*, 101–105.

Taub, J. M., Hawkins, D. R., & Van De Castle, R. L. Electrographic analysis of the sleep cycle in young depressed patients. *Biological Psychology*, 1978, *7*, 203–214.

Tohyama, M., Sakai, K., Touret, M., Salvert, D., & Jouvet, M. Spinal projections from the lower brain stem in the cat as demonstrated by the horseradish peroxidase technique. ii. projections from the dorsolateral pontine tegmentum and raphe nuclei. *Brain Research*, 1979, *176*, 215–231.

Townsend, R. E., Prinz, P. N., & Obrist, W. D. Human cerebral blood flow during sleep and waking. *Journal of Applied Physiology*, 1973, *6*, 225–230.

Vogel, G. W. A review of REM sleep deprivation. *Archives of General Psychiatry*, 1975, *32*, 749–761.

Vogel, G. W., Thurmond, A., Gibbons, P., Sloan, K., Boyd, M., & Walker, M. REM sleep reduction effects on depression syndromes. *Archives of General Psychiatry*, 1975, *32*, 765–777.

Ware, J. C. The symptom of insomnia: causes and cures. *Psychiatric Annals*, 1979, *9*, 353–366.

Webb, W. B. Sleep as an adaptive response. *Perceptual and Motor Skills*, 1974, *38*, 1023–1027.

Webb, W. B. Theories of sleep functions and some clinical implications. In R. Drucker-Colin, M. Shkurovich, & M. B. Sterman (Eds.), *The Functions of Sleep*. New York: Academic Press, 1979.

Webb, W. B., & Agnew, H. W. Are we chronically sleep deprived? *Bulletin of the Psychonomic Society*, 1975, *6*, 47–48.

Wever, von R. (Problems of circadian periodicity and its disorders) Probleme der zirkadianen Periodik und ihrer Stoerungen. *Drug Research*, 1976, *26*, 2–6.

Williams, R. L., Karacan, I., & Hursch, C. J. Electroencephalography (EEG) of human sleep. *Clinical Applications*. New York: Wiley, 1974.

Zarcone, V. Narcolepsy. *The New England Journal of Medicine*, 1973, *288*, 1156–1166.

Zarcone, V. P. Diagnosis and treatment of excessive daytime sleepiness. In H. L. Klawans (Ed.), *Clinical Neuropharmacology*. New York: Raven Press, 1977.

Zepelin, H., & Rechtschaffen, A. Mammalian sleep, longevity, and energy metabolism. *Brain Behavior and Evolution*, 1974, *10*, 425.

Zorick, R., Roth, R., Salis, P., Kramer, M., & Lutz, T. Insomnia and excessive daytime sleepiness as presenting symptoms in nocturnal myoclonus. In M. H. Chase, M. Mitler, & P. L. Walter (Eds.), *Sleep Research*, 1978, *7*, Brain Information Service/Brain Research Institute, UCLA, Los Angeles. (Abstract)

8 Childhood Hyperactivity: Diagnosis, Etiology, Nature and Treatment

William E. Pelham
Florida State University

Hyperactivity is a psychological disorder of childhood that is presumed to affect approximately 5% of the elementary-aged population of North America (predominantly males). It is one of the most prevalent psychological disorders of childhood, accounting for a very large percentage of the child referrals to mental health and pediatric facilities. From birth or a very young age, hyperactive children exhibit symptoms of inattention, impulsivity, and overactivity that result in extreme disruptions in their academic performance, self concept, and relationships with parents, teachers, peers, and siblings. The adolescent and adult prognoses for hyperactive children are poor and there is little evidence that treatments in current use improve prognosis or even effect maximal short-term improvement.

Although the high prevalence, refractoriness, and poor prognosis of hyperactivity make it one of the most vexing treatment problems for mental health professionals, at the same time it is one of the most relevant for those interested in behavioral medicine. Most of the research in and treatment of the disorder draws from both medical and psychological disciplines. The professional who conducts research with hyperactive children needs to be familiar with neurology, electrophysiology, neurochemistry, and psychopharmacology on the medical side, and information processing, factor analysis, social learning theory and observational methodology from the psychological perspective. Similarly, the professional who treats hyperactive children should be knowledgeable in behavior therapy and behavioral assessment, as well as in applied pediatric psychopharmacology. The purpose of this chapter is to provide information regarding hyperactivity that will prove useful to clinicians and researchers from both the medical and the psychological disciplines.

DEFINITION OF THE DISORDER

There is no consensual definition of hyperactivity, but there are common facets among the definitions that have been offered. Although widely used and generally accepted as a label, the term *hyperactivity* does not provide an accurate description of the disorder to which it refers. Beginning with the early descriptions of the disorder, a variety of symptoms in addition to excessive motor activity have been noted. For example, Laufer, Denhoff, and Solomons (1957) listed symptoms of short attention span, poor concentration, unpredictable and explosive behavior, impulsivity, and low frustration tolerance. Many professionals now focus more on these symptoms of the disorder than on the excessive motor activity which gave the disorder its name. Thus one influential conceptualization is that hyperactivity is a constitutional predisposition toward deficits in three major aspects of cognition; (1) impaired ability to sustain attention and effort; (2) poor inhibitory control; and (3) poorly modulated arousal and a tendency to seek stimulation and salience (Douglas & Peters, 1979).

Similarly, Routh (1980) states that hyperactivity "refers to a child's frequent failure to comply in an age-appropriate fashion with situational demands for restrained activity, sustained attention, resistance to distracting influences, and inhibition of impulsive response," and that the term is applied to children "whose behavior problems are severe enough to have come to professional attention, and whose difficulties are manifest in several situations over a considerable period of time [p. 56]". These two conceptualizations are similar in their emphasis on deficits in attention and impulse control. Most definitions also include the qualifications that symptoms be exhibited across situations and from a young age, both delimiters with the purpose of increasing the diagnostic homogeneity of the category. Notably, an excessive activity level or "hyperactivity" is viewed as only one possible manifestation of the impulse control deficit, rather than a necessary component of these definitions.

In an attempt to operationalize the definition of hyperactivity, many researchers have employed standardized parent and teacher rating scales. A parent-teacher checklist that has been used to define hyperactivity in a number of studies is the Abbreviated Conners Rating Scale, ACRS, also known as the hyperkinesis index (Conners, 1969; Goyette, Conners, & Ulrich, 1978). This scale requires the parent or teacher to rate 10 aspects of the target child's behavior: (1) restless or overactive; (2) excitable, impulsive; (3) disturbs other children; (4) fails to finish things he starts—short attention span; (5) constantly fidgeting; (6) inattentive, easily distracted; (7) demands must be met immediately—easily frustrated; (8) cries often and easily; (9) mood changes quickly and drastically; and (10) temper outbursts, explosive and unpredictable behavior. Each item is scored as applying (a) not at all, (b) just a little, (c) pretty much, or (d) very much. Weights from zero to three are assigned to check marks in the categories (a) to (d), respectively, and a total score is summed for the rated child. For normative samples, both the mean and the standard deviation (SD) are

5 for both parent and teacher ratings, and a cutoff score of 15, two SD's above the mean, is widely used to define hyperactivity operationally (Goyette et al., 1978; Werry, Sprague, & Cohen, 1975).

In contrast to the rationally-derived ACRS, there are several checklists on which item clusters labeled "hyperactive" or "inattention" have been identified in factor analyses. The Hyperactive and Inattention factors on the full Connors Teacher Rating Scale (CTRS) are examples of these (Goyette et al., 1978). Similarly, a factor labeled "Impulsive-hyperactive" has been identified on the full Connors Parent Rating Scale (Goyette et al., 1978), and factors variously labeled "Hyperactive," "Immature," or "Immature-Hyperactive" have emerged from factor analyses of different forms of the Child Behavior Checklist, CBCL (Achenbach, 1978; Achenbach & Edelbrock, 1979). For all of these checklists, extensive normative data are available, and cutoff scores two SD's above normative means on Hyperactivity factors are usually utilized to define hyperactivity.

Finally, hyperactivity has been defined in the *Diagnostic and Statistical Manuals of Mental Disorders* (DSM II and III) of the American Psychiatric Association (1968, 1980). The DSM II category of hyperkinetic reaction of childhood was defined simply as a disorder "characterized by overactivity, restlessness, distractability, and short attention span, especially in young children [p. 50]." In DSM III the disorder has been relabeled "attention deficit disorder with hyperactivity (ADDH)" or "attention deficit disorder without hyperactivity (ADDNH)." The attention deficit disorders are described in terms of the three core symptoms shown in Table 8.1—inattention, impulsivity, and hyperactivity—and the descriptive phrases listed under each symptom. A diagnosis of ADDH[1] requires the presence of each of the core symptoms, while the diagnosis of ADDNH is made if the requirements for impulsivity and inattention are met, but the requisite number of hyperactive symptoms have never been present.

Problems in Definition

The definitions of hyperactivity described above are among the most promising recent definitions of the disorder. From the early description provided by Laufer et al. to the most recent DSM version, they illustrate several noteworthy points

---

[1]The terms *hyperactivity, attention deficit disorder with hyperactivity* (ADDH), and *hyperkinesis* are all used herein to refer to the diagnostic category which applies to the group of children of concern. The term *hyperactivity* is used most often for convenience. When specific studies identified their subject samples as ADDH or hyperkinetic, these terms are used instead. The reader should remain alert to the fact that "hyperactivity" is also used to describe the *symptom* of excessive activity level in some sections of the text. In other sections, "hyperactivity" is used to refer to the degree of symptomatology exhibited on a dimension which includes the symptoms of inattention and impulsivity as well as excessive activity level. I apologize for the confusion. It is an unfortunate product of research and practice in this area of psychopathology.

TABLE 8.1
DSM III Diagnostic Criteria for Attention Deficit Disorders

The child displays for his or her mental and chronological age, signs of developmentally inappropriate inattention, impulsivity, and hyperactivity. The signs must be reported by adults in the child's environment, such as parents and teachers. Because the symptoms are typically variable, they may not be observed directly by the clinician. When the reports of teachers and parents conflict, primary consideration should be given to the teacher reports because of greater familiarity with age-appropriate norms. Symptoms typically worsen in situations that require self-application, as in the classroom. Signs of the disorder may be absent when the child is in a new or a one-to-one situation. The number of symptoms specified is for children between the ages of eight and ten, the peak age range for referral. In younger children, more severe forms of the symptoms and a greater number of symptoms are usually present. The opposite is true of older children.

A. *Inattention.* At least three of the following:
   (1) often fails to finish things he or she starts
   (2) often doesn't seem to listen
   (3) easily distracted
   (4) has difficulty concentrating on schoolwork or other tasks requiring sustained attention
   (5) has difficulty sticking to a play activity
B. *Impulsivity.* At least three of the following:
   (1) often acts before thinking
   (2) shifts excessively from one activity to another
   (3) has difficulty organizing work (this not being due to cognitive impairment)
   (4) needs a lot of supervision
   (5) frequently calls out in class
   (6) has difficulty awaiting turn in games or group situations
C. *Hyperactivity.* At least two of the following:
   (1) runs about or climbs on things excessively
   (2) has difficulty sitting still or fidgets excessively
   (3) has difficulty staying seated
   (4) moves about excessively during sleep
   (5) is always "on the go" or acts as if "driven by a motor"
D. Onset before the age of seven.
E. Duration of at least six months.
F. Not due to Schizophrenia, Affective Disorder, or Severe or Profound Mental Retardation.

regarding the definition of hyperactivity or, as it is increasingly being called, ADDH. The diagnostic and definitional process in psychopathology is extremely complex, and none of these conceptualizations meet all of the criteria necessary to provide an adequate definition of hyperactivity as a diagnostic category.

Activity Level. Although early researchers and clinicians focused on activity level as the central diagnostic feature of hyperactivity (e.g., Douglas, 1972; Stewart, Pitts, Craig, & Dieruf, 1966), the current consensus is that excessive motoric activity is *not* the most salient characteristic of the disorder. Attempts to define activity level objectively and to compare children referred for hyperactivity with nonhyperactive children have often failed to differentiate reliably the two groups (e.g., Barkley & Ullman, 1975). For example, hyperactive children have been shown to fidget more than nonhyperactive children (normals, asthmatics, and behavior disordered) during task performance in a clinic setting (Firestone & Martin, 1979), but observational measures of fidgeting in the classroom have often failed to discriminate between hyperactive and nonhyperactive children (Douglas, 1972; O'Leary, Pelham, Rosenbaum, & Price, 1976).

Even when between-group differences in activity level have been found, the utility of these differences for individual diagnosis has been limited. In one study hyperactive children exhibited significantly higher rates of both gross motor and minor motor movement in their regular classrooms (Abikoff, Gittelman-Klein, & Klein, 1977). However, when cutpoints were used to classify group membership, the false negative and false positive rates were, respectively, 35% and 43% for minor motor movement and 42% and 20% for gross motor movement. The extensive overlap between groups in this and other studies (see Routh, 1980) casts doubt on the utility of excessive motor activity as a criterion for defining hyperactivity. Because different measures of activity in the same setting yield positive but low intercorrelations (Barkley & Ullman, 1975), and activity level covaries with a variety of situational determinants (Jacob, O'Leary & Rosenblad, 1978; Routh, 1980), an analysis of activity level that manipulated situational determinants and used converging multiple measures might yield a clearer picture of hyperactive-nonhyperactive differences in this domain.

On the other hand, even if an acceptably reliable and precise measure of activity level could be devised (see, for example, Schulman, Stevens, & Kupst, 1977) and reliable group differences were found, excessive activity level might still not be considered a *necessary* component or core symptom of the definition of hyperactivity. Excessive activity could result from a deficiency in attention or impulse control. Because he would stick with each activity he began for a shorter period of time than a comparison child, a child with a short attention span and low impulse control would be expected to move about the classroom more. Indeed, psychostimulant medication is presumed to effect a teacher-perceived decrease in activity because it lengthens a child's attention span and improves impulse control, resulting in more on-task behavior and fewer activity changes (Swanson & Kinsbourne, 1979).

Attention deficits. It has long been argued that deficits in attention are a pervasive and profound aspect of the disorder (see Douglas, 1972, for a review of these early studies). The construct of an attention deficit, however, has not been adequately operationalized, and its acceptance has surpassed the evidence for such a deficit in hyperactive children.

For example, it is commonly accepted that hyperactive children have a shorter attention span and are more easily distracted than nonhyperactive children. This belief has derived primarily from teacher ratings of classroom behavior and from analysis of hyperactive children's performance on laboratory tasks that measure sustained attention (vigilance). Teacher ratings of inattention, however, may not be valid indicators of actual attention deficits. When rating learning-disabled and normal children on the Inattention factor of the CTRS, teachers in one study discriminated accurately between the groups, but their ratings were not correlated with children's performance on four laboratory measures of selective attention, on which *no* group differences were found (Pelham, 1979; 1981). A similar lack of correspondence between laboratory and classroom measures of attention has been evident in other studies (Hallahan, 1975; Kupietz & Richardson, 1978). In addition, although "easily distracted" or "too distractible" is a symptom listed on all the major rating scales and in the DSM III definition of ADDH, there is no evidence from laboratory studies that hyperactive children are more distractible than nonhyperactive children (Douglas & Peters, 1979; Pelham, 1981).

Unless they are refined considerably, teacher ratings should not be the sole source of information regarding attention deficits in hyperactive children. Unfortunately, there are presently no viable alternatives to teacher ratings for diagnosis in an outpatient clinical setting. Although there are a variety of laboratory tasks which assess attention and yield mean differences between hyperactive and comparison children, laboratory measures are not sufficiently reliable for use in individual diagnosis (Pelham, 1981). More reliable rating scale, observational and laboratory measures of attention need to be developed, and the relationships among these measures in hyperactive children need to be delineated.

Impulsivity. Laufer et al.'s (1957) original name for hyperactivity, "hyperkinetic-impulse disorder," illustrates that impulsivity has long been presumed to be a core symptom of hyperactivity. Teachers and parents usually rate hyperactive children as more impulsive than nonhyperactive children. Standard laboratory measures of impulsivity such as the Matching Familiar Figures (MFF) test (Kagan, 1966) have often revealed that hyperactive children exhibit shorter latencies and make more errors than normal comparison children (e.g., Campbell, Douglas, & Morgenstern, 1971). When hyperactive children in one study were compared with groups of asthmatic children and behavior problem children, however, differences on the MFF were not apparent (Firestone & Martin, 1979). In addition, it has been demonstrated that performance on the MFF does not correlate with teacher ratings or observations of impulsivity in the classroom (Bentler & McClain, 1976; Sergeant, Velthoven, & Virginia, 1979). The lack of a strong relationship among these measures casts doubt on the construct validity of impulsivity as it is currently operationalized.

A separate factor describing impulsivity has often not emerged in factor analyses of teacher rating data, even though separate factors have been found for inattention and hyperactivity, the other core symptoms of hyperactivity (Goyette et al., 1978). Instead, items that describe impulsivity have loaded on factors variously labeled *Hyperactivity, Conduct Problems, Inattention,* or *Peer Problems* (Achenbach, 1978; Achenbach & Edelbrock, 1979; Lahey, Stempniak,

Robinson, & Tyroler, 1978; Pelham, Atkins, & Murphy, 1981). In general, the existence of and utility of the construct of impulsivity as a symptom of hyperactivity *independent of* inattention, excessive activity, and conduct problems have not been demonstrated. Recent efforts to improve the operationalization of impulsivity have involved the development of a teacher checklist designed specifically to measure impulsivity (Kendall & Wilcox, 1979) and adaptation of the MFF to yield a more reliable measure (Loper & Hallahan, 1980). Preliminary data appear promising, and investigation of these measures with hyperactive children appears warranted.

Attention Deficit Disorders.   Because it will have such a widespread influence on clinical practice and research over the next decade, it is worthwhile to examine briefly the DSM III definition of attention deficit disorder (ADD) shown in Table 8.1. Relative to the DSM II definition of hyperkinesis, the definition of ADD is a considerable improvement, as it focuses on attention and impulsivity as the two major symptoms of the category, and it attempts to operationalize the definition by providing descriptive statements for each category. As the discussion has shown, however, it is no simple matter to translate such descriptions of impulsive, inattentive and hyperactive behavior into objective indices of the three core symptoms. In order for the DSM III definition to be used as intended, normative data in the following domains must be generated for each symptom at different age levels throughout the developmental span: (1) laboratory measures of the core symptoms; (2) teacher and parent ratings of the descriptive criteria; and (3) objective observational measures of the descriptive criteria. Information from these different domains must be highly correlated in order to provide validity for the constructs being measured.

One step in this direction has been the development of a parent-teacher checklist for identifying ADD. The scale, the Swanson, Nolan, and Pelham (SNAP) Checklist, uses the operational criteria for ADDH and the response format of the Conners Teacher Rating Scales. Normative data have been obtained and the checklist's reliability has been shown (Pelham, Atkins, & Murphy, 1981: Swanson, 1981), but its relationship with laboratory and observational measures has not yet been demonstrated. One advantage the SNAP Checklist has over other rating scales is the use of DSM III criteria as the actual checklist items. In contrast to previous rating scales which often included but were were not limited to symptoms that defined the disorder, the SNAP Checklist information should thus be *directly* applicable to diagnosis.

In addition to parent-teacher checklists for ADD, standards for gathering direct observations of behavior in natural or standardized situations need to be established. For example, reliable normative information regarding the criterion "difficulty waiting for turn in games or group situations" needs to be developed from observations of children playing (e.g., on school playgrounds). Similar observations of a single child could then be used to determine that child's deviation from the norm on that criterion. Alternatively, a standard set of tasks could be developed in which a tester and child could interact and generate normative data as reliable as that which has been obtained with the standardized tests of intelligence. The set of tasks could then be used with individuals to determine whether the particular ADD criteria have been met. This could be accomplished relatively simply for the inattention and impulsivity symptoms, although some of the operational criteria may need to be more carefully defined in order to enable such normative data to be developed. Criteria for which there is no support in the research literature (e.g., "easily distracted") should be eliminated from the definition.

Because this ADD category has only recently been adopted, few studies have been conducted to date on children given this diagnosis. It is not clear, for example, that the use of hyperactivity as a symptom to establish a dichotomy (ADDH versus ADDNH) is justifiable (Pelham, Atkins, & Murphy, 1981). As the following discussion indicates, dichtomies based on other symptoms (i.e., aggression) have shown considerable utility (Milich & Loney, 1979), but the discriminant validity of ADDH and ADDNH has not been sufficiently investigated. In addition, the relationship between these diagnoses and previous definitions of hyperactivity have not been studied. Such research is necessary before the DSM III category of ADD is accepted as a standard part of diagnostic nomenclature.

Rating Scales

The increasing use of the rating scales described above has resulted from the desire to make the definition of hyperactivity more objective. A growing number of studies have used a cutoff score of 2 *SD*'s above the mean on the ACRS to *define* hyperactivity rather than simply to confirm other information. This trend highlights the need to examine the psychometric characteristics of the rating scales.

Regarding reliability, test-retest correlations over approximately 8 weeks were .72 for the Inattention factor and .84 for the Hyperactivity factor of the CTRS (Conners, 1969) in one study. A test-retest correlation of .89 was reported for the ACRS (Zentall & Barack, 1979). Adequate test-retest data have not been reported for related factors on the Conners Parent Rating Scales or the CBCL, and interrater reliabilities have not been reported for the teacher rating measures. On the parent rating measures, between-parent correlations on Hyperactivity factors are relatively low, ranging from .46 to .69 (Achenbach, 1978; Goyette et al., 1978). The interrater reliability is lower when correlations are examined between parent ratings and teacher ratings on the same or similar scale factors. The parent-teacher correlation on the ACRS, for example, is .49, and teacher-parent correlations between comparable factors on the CTRS and Conners Parent rating scales range from .36 to .45 (Goyette et al., 1978).

Although test-retest reliability on teacher checklists is thus acceptable where reported, the low parent-teacher correlations reported for the Conners scales show that the parent and teacher ratings share only 12% to 25% common variance. This is especially disconcerting given that the items on the parent and teacher factors are identical in most cases. Examined from the perspective of a multitrait-multimethod matrix (Campbell & Fiske, 1959), the validity of these rating scale factors is questionable. In order for the construct validity of a psychological trait to be demonstrated, it must be shown that measures made of the trait under different conditions or by different methods correlate with one another to a greater degree than they correlate with measures of *different* traits made with the same method or under the same conditions. In these data, the correlations among different factors—Hyperactivity, Inattention, and Conduct—on the CTRS, .68, .49, and .60, were considerably higher than the correlations between teacher and parent ratings on the *same* factors, .33, .36, and .45 (Goyette, et al., 1978). These findings and the low correlations between teacher ratings and laboratory measures cast serious doubt on the construct validity of these rating scale factors.

There are a variety of explanations for the low validity coefficients for the rating scales, including a possible lack of rater sensitivity for relatively specific problems (Green, Beck, Forehand, & Vosk, 1980) and psychometric difficulties in the scales themselves. One of the more obvious reasons for the low parent-teacher agreements may be that teachers and parents evaluate different behavioral samples and have different reference groups. For example, parents usually have considerably less information than teachers regarding children's behavior in task settings and peer group interactions. When discrepancies occur between teacher and parent ratings of behaviors that teachers observe, then greater weight should generally be given to the teachers' ratings. It should also be noted that rating scales are highly subject to idiosyncratic interpretations of behavior. What appears to be a short attention span to one rater may not appear that way at all to another, even if reference groups and behavioral samples are similar. Information obtained from rating scales should be evaluated with their limitations in mind.

A final point in this section concerns the heterogeneous nature of the disorder of hyperactivity as defined with rating scales. If the total score on the ACRS (or any factor on other scales) is used to define hyperactivity, then children with quite different sets of symptoms can be diagnosed as hyperactive. Given two children, for example, one could be rated negatively (i.e., "very much") by his teacher on items 3, 7, 8, 9, and 10, but not rated negatively (i.e., "not at all") on the other five items (see items previously listed), while the second child could obtain exactly the opposite pattern of ratings. Both children would be diagnosed as hyperactive using the standard ACRS cutoff of 15, but one would be exhibiting behavior characteristic of a "typical" hyperactive child while the other would be more adequately described as having a conduct disorder. The same situation could occur with the DSM III definition of ADDH (see Table 8.1), which requires presence of *any* two or three of the five or six different descriptors listed for each core symptom. Clearly the diagnostic category of hyperactivity is not a homogeneous one, and this lack of homogeneity, which is only now beginning to be resolved, has been a serious impediment to research progress (Loney & Milich, in press).

Hyperactivity as a Syndrome

For many years it was assumed that hyperactivity was a homogeneous syndrome comprised of the core symptoms described above. Children diagnosed as hyperactive were presumed to exhibit all of the core symptoms, and children with a high level of one core symptom were assumed to exhibit high levels of the other core symptoms. Although no definitional systems actually required that all symptoms be present, most professionals nonetheless believed that hyperactivity was a unitary syndrome. In contrast to the widespread belief in a syndrome, a number of studies have addressed this question, and with few exceptions have failed to provide supportive evidence. Limited evidence in support of a syndrome comes from the factor analytic studies of clinic or normal populations, which have yielded factors labeled Hyperactivity (Achenbach & Edelbrock, 1978). Although often correlated with factors reflecting conduct disorder (e.g., Werry, Sprague, & Cohen, 1975), the Hyperactivity factors have nonetheless been distinct from Conduct factors, and the failure to find Hyperactivity factors in some studies (see Quay, 1979) may have resulted from limitations in the rated sample or in the included items (Lahey et al., 1978).

The fact that a Hyperactivity factor is often found, however, is not sufficient evidence that the disorder is a unitary syndrome. Factor *labels* do not always accurately reflect the items loading on a factor. In the Lahey et al. (1978) study, for example, a number of items that described impulsivity loaded on the Conduct factor rather than the Hyperactivity factor. If hyperactivity is a syndrome, *all* of the symptoms attributed to the disorder, especially the core symptoms, should load on one factor. Very little of this type of support for the syndrome is evident. In one study, 67 variables thought to be related to hyperactivity were entered in a factor analysis with a sample of hyperactive children (Werry, 1968). Ten factors emerged from the analysis. No factor could be labeled Hyperactivity, nor were three factors present, each reflecting a core symptom. Instead, factors were related to the data sources and included neurological examination factors, psychological test factors, psychiatric evaluation factors, and so on.

Similarly, Langhorne, Loney, Paternite, and Bechtholdt (1976) performed a factor analysis of measures from four sources (raters of children's clinic charts, psychiatrist's diagnosis, teacher ratings, and parent ratings) of the following symptoms of hyperactivity: inattention and difficulty concentrating, hyperactivity and fidgetiness, lack of judgment, impulsivity and excitability, diagnosis, and problem duration. As in Werry's study, the resulting factors reflected source-related factors (a chart rating and two teacher rating factors) rather than child-related factors. Of particular interest is the observation that chart ratings and teacher ratings of the *same* symptoms loaded on *different* factors.

These and other factor analytic studies (Routh & Roberts, 1972) thus did not yield evidence for a syndrome of hyperactivity. Together with the equivocal results from the group comparisons of activity level, inattention, and impulsivity this finding shows that a homogeneous syndrome of hyperactivity, as previously described, has not been identified. Unfortunately, corresponding research on the SNAP Checklist has revealed similarly low interrater agreement and a lack of construct validity, suggesting that the new DSM III definition of attention deficit disorder has not solved the problems in diagnosis of hyperactivity (Pelham, Atkins, & Murphy, 1981; Pelham, Atkins, Murphy & White, 1981). The category of hyperactivity is a heterogeneous one which includes children with quite different symptom patterns and prognoses, and in all likelihood different etiologic and mediating variables. Much of the recent research in the field has begun to focus on the subdivision of hyperactivity with the expectation that subcategories which are homogeneous at least with respect to symptomatology can be identified.

Summary

The problems of definition outlined in the foregoing should sensitize the reader to the complexities involved in defining the disorder and in diagnosing a child as hyperactive. Given the current state of knowledge in child psychopathology, the primary purpose of definition and diagnosis is to provide groups of individuals whose etiological, mediating and prognostic similarities and differences can be studied. This discussion should alert researchers to the relative heterogeneity of the disorder, the lack of construct validity for its defining criteria, and necessary directions for future research on definition.

In contrast, the primary concern for the practitioner should not be diagnosis but assessment of the child's presenting problems. As the section on treatment details, the identification of the child's specific problem behaviors in the context of a functional analysis should be the major focus of assessment in clinical settings. The output of such an assessment provides the basis for a treatment plan. In the current state of the art in nomenclature in child psychopathology, no useful information is conveyed from a diagnosis alone (Ross & Pelham, 1981). If a diagnosis is required, for educational placement, for example, or other purposes, the diagnostic scheme for ADDH in DSM III should be used. The SNAP Checklist and the ACTRS completed by both parents and teachers appear likely to provide useful information in diagnosis. If norms for laboratory measures and classroom observational measures of attention and impulsivity are developed, then attempts should be made to tap these sources in clinical settings.

It is worth emphasizing that diagnosis of hyperactivity is independent of etiology. A common misconception is that a neurological or other medical examination is necessary before a diagnosis can be made. Although many hyperactive children present with an increased number of soft neurological signs, minor physical anomalies or abnormal EEG's, the majority of hyperactive children do not exhibit these correlates (see following discussion). Requiring their presence for diagnosis would result in a false negative rate of 40% to 50% (see discussion in section on "Etiology").

ASSOCIATED PROBLEMS

A number of behavioral correlates of hyperactivity are not included in formal diagnosis or definition of the disorder. Recent research, however, has suggested that some of these correlates play an important role in hyperactivity and should be considered in evaluation and treatment.

Aggression and Hyperactivity

Although children with predominately hyperactive symptoms have long been differentiated in clinical diagnosis from those with predominately aggressive symptoms, some researchers have recently argued that hyperactivity and conduct disorder are two subcategories of the same disorder (e.g., Quay, 1979). For example, when separate Hyperactivity and Conduct disorder factors emerge in factor analysis, on the CTRS, for example, they are highly correlated ($r = .7$; Conners, 1969; Werry et al., 1975). Such high correlations, however, do not *necessarily* mean that the two diagnostic categories cannot be differentiated. Hyperactivity and conduct disorders can be operationally defined, as in DSM III for example, in such a way that reliable differential diagnosis can be made from a structured interview with the child's parent (Stewart, Cummings, Singer, & deBlois, 1981).

Because Conduct disorder and Hyperactivity rating scale factors share common variance, the relationship between aggression, the primary symptom of conduct disorder, and hyperactivity has been a subject of considerable interest among researchers. Parents rate 59% of their hyperactive children as aggressive (Stewart, Pitts, Craig, & Dieruf, 1966), teachers reported that 24% of one sample of hyperactive children exhibited extreme rates of aggression (Prinz, Conner, & Wilson, 1981), and peers nominate 40% to 50% of ADDH children as aggressive (Pelham & Bender, 1982). Studies have thus addressed whether hyperactive children can be subdivided on a dichotomy defined by the presence of aggressive symptomatology. In the first of these studies (Loney, Langhorne, & Paternite, 1978), raters examined the clinic charts of 135 hyperactive boys and coded variables reflecting primary symptoms [judgment deficits (impulsivity), hyperactivity, inattention, uncoordination, and fidgetiness] and secondary symptoms, presumed to result from the child's flawed interactions with his environment [control deficits (e.g., delinquent acts, evasion of the rules), negative affect (e.g., irritability), and aggressive interpersonal behavior]. Factor analysis of these ratings revealed two factors: Aggression, on which the three secondary symptoms loaded; the Hyperactivity, on which the three core symptoms, hyperactivity, impulsivity, and inattention, loaded. In order to explore the meaningfulness of the two factors, factor scores were computed for each child, and the relationship between these scores (correlated with $r = .27$) and other variables were examined. Teacher ratings of a variety of acting out problems (e.g., destructive, defiant, quarrelsome, temper outbursts) correlated significantly with the Aggression factor, while teacher ratings on items more descriptive of a typical hyperactive child (e.g., restless/overactive, inattentive, disturbs other children) correlated with the Hyperactivity factor. SES was correlated with the Aggression factor, as was maternal hostility and absence of maternal control. Neurological signs were negatively correlated with the Aggression factor, and diagnosis of hyperkinesis and response to medication were correlated with the Hyperactive factor.

Thus a single-source factor analysis performed on ratings of hyperactive symptoms yielded two distinct dimensions of the disorder, Hyperactivity and Aggression, demonstrating that aggressive behavior is an important dimension in hyperactive children. These results have been replicated using the same measures with a sample of consecutive referrals to a clinic (Milich, Loney & Landau, 1981), and they have been replicated with a different sample of hyperactive children using teacher ratings rather than chart raters as the source of information (O'Leary & Steen, 1980).

Scores on these Aggression and Hyperactivity factors have been correlated with a number of variables in addition to the ones previously noted, and it is becoming widely accepted that discriminating among hyperactive children on the basis of aggressive symptomatology provides critical information regarding etiologic, treatment, and prognostic variables (Loney & Milich, in press; Milich & Loney, 1979; Paternite & Loney, 1980). The relationships among hyperactivity, aggression, and each of the domains that have been investigated are discussed in the appropriate following sections. It should be noted that the presence of aggressive symptomatology was not considered in most early studies of the disorder, and results from those studies must be evaluated with this omission in mind.

Peer Relationships

Only recently have peer relationships in hyperactive children been studied. In child psychopathology, the domain of peer relationships is thought to be important because several studies have shown that the best childhood predictor of adult maladjustment is the number of negative nominations received on classroom peer rating measures (Cowen, Pederson, Babigian, Izzo, & Trost, 1973; Roff, Sells, & Golden, 1972). Because peer relationships are considered one of the most critical facets of the socialization process (Hartup, 1970), disturbances in peer relationships may thus be both important predictors and important mediators of outcome in hyperactive children (Milich & Landau, 1982).

Data regarding peer relationships in hyperactive children have been drawn from several different sources. Teachers have rated hyperactive children as having more disturbed peer interactions than comparison children (Campbell & Paulauskas, 1979). Teacher ratings of peer problems in one study discriminated between hyperactive and comparison children *as well as* did teacher ratings on the core symptoms of the disorder (Pelham & Murphy, 1981). Peer evaluations have also been examined (e.g., Klein & Young, 1979). In one sample of 49 hyperactive children (consecutive referrals for treatment studies), 47 children received a higher number of negative nominations (named as disliked) than did their average classmate (Pelham & Bender, 1982). Twelve percent of the sample obtained negative nominations between their class mean and one *SD* above it; 22% obtained negative nominations between 1 and 2 *SD*'s above the class mean; 28% obtained negative nominations between 2 and 3 *SD*'s above class means, and 32% obtained negative nominations greater than 3 *SD*'s above class means. Seventy-four percent of these same children failed to receive as many positive nominations (named as liked) as their average classmate, including 27% who received *no* positive nominations.

These peer reports have been corroborated by data from direct observations of hyperactive children in playgroups with nonhyperactive peers (Pelham & Bender, 1982). Large significant differences were apparent in both structured and unstructured play situations. Compared to controls, hyperactive children exhibited three times as much negative nonverbal behavior (e.g., fighting), five times as much high rate behavior (e.g., yelling, running around), twice as much verbal initiation, and eight times as many negative verbalizations. After only two 90-minute play periods the peers who interacted with these hyperactive children rated them so negatively that the hyperactive children could be distinguished from controls almost perfectly on the basis of the peer ratings alone.

Similar results were obtained in an extensive sociometric study (Pelham & Bender, 1982). Using the Pupil Evaluation Inventory (PEI) (Pekarik, Prinz, Liebert, Weintraub, & Neale, 1976), a group of 52 boys and 12 girls who fit teacher rating criteria for ADDH were compared to 251 nonhyperactive boys and 272 nonhyperactive girls in two large elementary schools. The PEI consists of 35 descriptive statements on which all children in a classroom nominate classmates to whom each statement applies. Factors named Aggression, Withdrawal, and Likeability have been identified (Pekarik et al., 1976), and these results revealed that ADDH children were significantly different from comparison children on each of these three factors. The results are presented for individual PEI items in Table 8.2, which reveals that ADDH children were consistently rated as different from comparison children on items that tapped aggression, interruptions, disruption, teasing, and annoying behaviors. Their peers perceived ADDH children as having more difficulty sitting still and as doing more things which bothered the teacher, but it is noteworthy that ADDH children were rated as most different from comparison children on items that referred to peer relationships.

In addition to the ADDH-normal comparison, the relationship between the Aggressive/Hyperactive dichotomy discussed earlier and these peer ratings was examined in this study. Using teacher ratings, four groups of ADDH boys were formed by crossing high and low scores on Aggression and Hyperactivity factors (O'Leary & Steen, in press), and the PEI data were reanalyzed using these group-ings (Pelham & Murphy, 1981). Results revealed that high Aggressive children were nominated most frequently by peers on items related to aggression. In contrast, both high Aggressive and high Hyperactive boys were nominated fre-quently on items such as "those who bother other people when they are trying to work" and "those who are chosen last to join in group activities." Thus, al-though high levels of both Hyperactivity and Aggression were related to negative nominations, the factors were related to different types of negative nominations. Which, if either, of the two dimensions is predictive of or mediates outcome in adolescence and adulthood is unclear (see succeeding discussion of *Prognosis*), and additional research on this point is needed (Milich & Landau, 1982; Pelham & Bender, 1982).

It is clear that hyperactive children have very serious disturbances in peer relationships, and it is not unlikely that these disturbances play an important role in both the current severity and the long-term outcome of the disorder. Informa-tion in this domain should be routinely gathered both in research settings (espe-cially in studies that examine prognosis) and in clinical practice. In the latter case, such information should alert clinicians to the need for a treatment compo-nent which focuses on problems in peer relationships.

Learning Problems

Although it is commonly noted that 25% to 50% of hyperactive children have serious problems in learning (Safer & Allen, 1976), no studies have adequately analyzed the prevalence of learning disabilities in hyperactive samples. The difficulties of defining learning disabilities are as great as those involved in defining hyperactivity (Ross, 1976), making investigation of the relationship between the disorders especially problematic. One recent study showed that the prevalence of learning disabilities ranged from 4% to 53% in a sample of hyperactive children, depending on the criteria used to define the two disorders. More stringent criteria were associated with the lower prevalence rate (Lambert & Sandoval, 1980). The commonly cited rates of 25% to 50% should thus probably be interpreted as the upper limits of the prevalence of learning disability in a hyperactive sample.

Obtaining information on learning in hyperactive children is important for both research and clinical purposes. In research, hyperactive children with and

TABLE 8.2
Means and Standard Deviations for the Hyperactive and Nonhyperactive Samples on Items from the Pupil Evaluation Inventory and Results from the 2 (Group) × 2 (Sex) ANOVAs on Each Item[a]

Item	Boys[b] Hyperactive	Nonhyperactive	Girls[c] Hyperactive	Nonhyperactive	Group Effect[d]	Group × Sex[d] Interaction
1.[e] Those who are tall	25.6 (31.9)	21.3 (26.8)	12.9 (16.3)	20.6 (26.9)	$F < 1.0$	$F = 1.8$
2. Those who help others	9.4 (6.3)	25.0 (19.6)	18.2 (13.8)	37.2 (24.0)	$F = 24.5$*****	$F < 1.0$
3. Those who can't sit still	58.2 (18.0)	24.8 (21.4)	39.3 (28.8)	15.2 (18.5)	$F = 100.2$*****	$F = 1.6$
4. Those who try to get other people into trouble	50.7 (23.9)	17.2 (18.6)	30.1 (18.9)	10.1 (14.4)	$F = 127.0$*****	$F = 4.4$*
5.[e] Those who are too shy to make friends easily	10.8 (10.3)	8.5 (10.0)	8.5 (9.3)	13.6 (14.6)	$F < 1.0$	$F = 3.3$
6.[e] Those whose feelings are too easily hurt	13.5 (13.6)	9.8 (10.9)	18.7 (16.0)	15.4 (14.0)	$F = 4.3$*	$F < 1.0$
7. Those who act stuck-up and think they are better than everyone else	38.2 (18.3)	16.1 (14.8)	23.3 (15.2)	13.0 (12.7)	$F = 77.1$*****	$F = 5.1$*
8. Those who play the clown and get others to laugh	40.2 (18.5)	19.3 (18.9)	16.7 (15.2)	8.1 (10.6)	$F = 56.3$*****	$F = 4.6$*
9.[e] Those who start a fight over nothing	47.8 (22.5)	19.1 (19.2)	24.9 (18.2)	9.0 (12.2)	$F = 133.0$*****	$F = 5.4$*
10. Those who never seem to be having a good time	17.4 (12.4)	7.9 (8.6)	16.3 (15.2)	9.4 (10.5)	$F = 33.3$*****	$F < 1.0$
11. Those who are upset when called on to answer questions in class	25.5 (16.2)	9.5 (9.7)	15.9 (13.3)	7.6 (9.8)	$F = 76.7$*****	$F = 4.1$*
12. Those who tell other children what to do	41.2 (22.9)	15.7 (14.0)	21.7 (15.4)	14.7 (13.1)	$F = 88.2$*****	$F = 12.1$***
13. Those who are usually chosen last to join in group activities	27.0 (16.5)	13.2 (12.2)	26.7 (23.7)	13.6 (13.3)	$F = 43.1$*****	$F < 1.0$
14.[e] Those who are liked by everyone	15.9 (12.7)	23.9 (18.1)	15.7 (7.8)	24.8 (19.4)	$F = 11.0$***	$F < 1.0$
15. Those who always mess around and get into trouble	61.9 (21.0)	24.0 (23.8)	30.9 (23.5)	8.9 (13.7)	$F = 127.9$*****	$F = 4.9$*
16.[e] Those who make fun of people	47.0 (18.5)	22.1 (17.5)	25.1 (18.3)	11.8 (13.3)	$F = 110.5$*****	$F = 5.0$*

276

Item					F (group)	F (interaction)
17.[e] Those who have very few friends	31.5 (17.3)	15.9 (15.7)	22.9 (19.7)	15.4 (15.7)	$F = 41.8$*****	$F = 2.4$
18. Those who do strange things	36.0 (16.1)	19.2 (14.3)	23.3 (16.8)	10.2 (10.4)	$F = 63.0$*****	$F < 1.0$
19. Those who are your best friends	14.6 (8.5)	24.0 (12.9)	20.6 (9.2)	24.8 (13.7)	$F = 16.3$***	$F = 1.2$
20.[e] Those who bother people when they are trying to work	45.0 (18.7)	20.0 (17.1)	22.4 (16.4)	11.0 (12.5)	$F = 114.7$*****	$F = 7.1$**
21. Those who get mad when they don't get their way	51.3 (23.4)	17.6 (15.3)	30.1 (23.7)	13.2 (14.2)	$F = 147.6$*****	$F = 8.4$**
22.[e] Those who don't pay attention to the teacher	55.3 (20.3)	25.3 (23.7)	28.1 (23.2)	15.3 (19.6)	$F = 82.0$*****	$F = 5.8$*
23. Those who are rude to the teacher	50.8 (26.0)	19.0 (22.8)	25.0 (17.1)	11.1 (17.1)	$F = 74.9$*****	$F = 5.5$*
24.[e] Those who are unhappy or sad	16.0 (13.6)	8.2 (9.7)	13.1 (8.5)	9.3 (11.1)	$F = 22.9$*****	$F = 1.3$
25. Those who are especially nice	9.2 (8.0)	17.1 (14.1)	16.8 (8.6)	27.8 (18.8)	$F = 11.8$***	$F < 1.0$
26.[e] Those who act like a baby	30.2 (21.8)	10.3 (12.4)	16.6 (12.6)	9.5 (12.3)	$F = 89.6$*****	$F = 8.2$**
27. Those who are mean and cruel to other children	41.0 (24.1)	12.6 (14.0)	14.3 (11.1)	7.6 (10.2)	$F = 125.8$*****	$F = 19.4$*****
28.[e] Those who often don't want to play	13.6 (10.4)	6.7 (8.4)	7.2 (4.9)	8.8 (8.4)	$F = 19.0$****	$F = 8.9$**
29. Those who give dirty looks	38.5 (22.2)	13.1 (13.1)	17.7 (17.0)	7.9 (10.3)	$F = 117.5$*****	$F = 10.9$**
30. Those who want to show off in front of the class	44.5 (21.4)	17.7 (18.8)	16.0 (13.2)	9.0 (12.1)	$F = 78.6$*****	$F = 11.2$***
31.[e] Those who say they can beat everybody up	56.9 (21.9)	27.1 (22.1)	26.3 (22.6)	9.4 (12.1)	$F = 121.7$*****	$F = 4.6$*
32.[e] Those who aren't noticed much	15.7 (13.6)	10.1 (10.2)	14.3 (10.2)	13.8 (12.7)	$F = 8.4$**	$F = 1.8$
33.[e] Those who exaggerate and make up stories	36.3 (20.5)	15.2 (14.3)	20.3 (12.9)	8.9 (10.5)	$F = 110.8$*****	$F = 4.7$*
34.[e] Those who complain, nothing makes them happy	26.1 (16.7)	9.2 (10.3)	13.7 (12.7)	7.8 (10.0)	$F = 97.9$*****	$F = 9.3$**
35.[e] Those who always seem to understand things	12.3 (10.3)	18.8 (15.9)	13.7 (10.4)	26.7 (18.7)	$F = 12.0$***	$F = 1.3$

[a] The Pupil Evaluation Inventory is scored by calculating the percentage of a child's classmates who nominate him or her on an item. The means in the table are thus the average percentages of classmates who nominated children in the four groups. The standard deviations are reported in parentheses.

[b] Hyperactive $N = 37$; nonhyperactive $N = 217$ except on items marked with an e, where hyperactive $N = 52$; nonhyperactive $N = 251$

[c] Hyperactive $N = 10$; nonhyperactive $N = 236$ except on items marked with an e, where hyperactive $N = 12$; nonhyperactive $N = 272$

[d] These univariate ANOVAs were run after a MANOVA revealed a significant effect of group, $F(35,462) = 6.99$, $p < .00001$, and a significant group $\times$ sex interaction, $F(35,462) = 1.67$, $p < .05$. The degrees of freedom in each ANOVA were 1 and 496, except on items marked with an e, where df $= 1,583$.

[e] Items which were on both the first grade form and the upper form of the sociogram.

*$p < .05$ **$p < .01$ ***$p < .001$ ****$p < .0001$ *****$p < .00001$

without associated learning problems should be examined separately in order to insure that findings regarding cognitive and physiological correlates are a function of hyperactivity per se rather than associated learning disabilities. Unfortunately, this separation has not been made in most studies of cognitive deficit in hyperactivity, and interpretation of these studies' results is consequently seriously limited (Ross & Pelham, 1981). In clinical practice, information regarding learning difficulties should be obtained because treatment must include a focus on learning problems, if present, as well as problem social behaviors. A discussion of the diagnosis and treatment of learning disabilities is beyond the scope of this chapter, but informative discussions are available (e.g., Hallahan & Kauffman, 1976; Ross, 1976).

PROGNOSIS

Adolescent Outcome

Although the clinical lore for many years has been that hyperactive children outgrow their problems when they reach puberty, recent research fails to support this belief. Several studies that have followed hyperactive children into adolescence are in general agreement that their outcome is poor. One sample of 83 hyperactive children from 12 to 16 years of age were followed-up 2 to 5 years after initial contact with a psychiatric clinic or a private practice (Mendelson, Johnson, & Stewart, 1971). Five percent of the interviewed mothers reported that their children showed no signs of hyperactivity or other current psychological disturbances. An additional 5% said that their children were well-adjusted as long as they continued to take prescribed stimulant medication. Fifty-five percent of the children were reported to be improved relative to initial contact but still exhibiting problems, and the remaining 35% were seen by their mothers as unchanged or worse. The mothers' chief complaints at referral had been overactivity, poor school performance and poor school and home behavior. At follow-up, 74% were described as defiant and hard to discipline; 56% exhibited temper tantrums; and 40% to 50% had feelings of rejection from peers, failure in school, and low self confidence. Fifty-nine percent of the children had had some contact with the police, and according to the psychiatric interviewer, 22% were exhibiting sufficient antisocial behavior that a diagnosis of sociopathy in adulthood was seen as likely.

Other studies have reported similar findings. Two thirds of hyperactive adolescents were serious discipline problems in school, with a high rate of school suspensions and expulsions (Mendelson et al., 1971; Weiss, Minde, Werry, Douglas, & Nemeth, 1971). In addition, 50% to 70% of adolescent hyperactives have average failing grades in high school and have failed at least one grade in school, and half of these have failed two grades (Dykman & Ackerman, 1980;

Huessy & Cohen, 1976; Weiss, Hechtman, Perlman, Hopkins, & Wener, 1979; Weiss et al., 1971). Adolescent hyperactives were found to be much more likely than controls to drop out of school before high school graduation (Huessy, Metoyer, & Townsend, 1974). Finally, 50% to 70% of adolescent hyperactives have been reported to have chronically low levels of self esteem (Weiss et al., 1971).

Regarding drug use, one study found that 19-year-old hyperactives differed only slightly from controls in the estimated severity or frequency with which they reported using a variety of nonmedical drugs other than alcohol (Weiss et al., 1979). Interestingly, however, these hyperactives were more than four times as likely as controls to have *sold* a nonmedical drug during the previous five years. Two studies have reported that adolescent hyperactives consumed alcohol more frequently than comparison groups (Blouin, Bornstein, & Trites, 1978; Feldman, Denhoff, & Denhoff, 1979). This finding is noteworthy in that the fathers of hyperactive children are more likely than comparison fathers to be diagnosed as alcoholic (Cantwell, 1972; Morrison & Stewart, 1971). Although there is thus far only limited evidence that adolescent hyperactives are involved in substance abuse to a greater extent than comparison adolescents, later outcome in this area is uncertain (Kramer & Loney, 1981).

Adult Outcome

Because the diagnosis has been in extensive use only recently, few studies have followed a group of hyperactive children into adulthood. One of the first studies examined functioning in a small group of adults who had been seen in a child psychiatric clinic 25 to 30 years previously and who were retrospectively diagnosed as hyperkinetic (Menkes, Rowe, & Menkes, 1967). At follow-up, four patients were institutionalized psychotics and two were mentally retarded, living with and dependent upon their families. The remaining eight patients were self-supporting, but half of them had spent some time in an institution—two as delinquents, one as mentally retarded and one as a criminal.

In contrast to these dismal results, another study examined adult adjustment in a group of 20 men who had been seen in a child guidance clinic 25 years earlier (Borland & Heckman, 1976). Cases which conformed to present descriptions of hyperactivity were selected if the proband had a living brother with whom he could be compared. The probands and their brothers, with average ages of 28 years and 30 years, respectively, participated in an extensive interview during which information regarding symtomatology and vocational variables was gathered.

The percentages of probands and brothers, respectively, reporting each of the following psychological problems were: nervousness (60% vs. 20%), restlessness (60% vs. none), difficulty with temper (60% vs. 15%), depressed feelings (50% vs. 15%), impulsiveness (40% vs. 10%), lack of friends (40% vs. 10%), and easily upset (35% vs. 5%). Perhaps related to the nervous and restless feelings reported was the finding that 80% of the probands smoked cigarettes compared to 25% of their brothers. Only 20% of the probands were considered by the interviewers to qualify for a psychiatric diagnosis, however, and those men were diagnosed as sociopathic. An additional 25% of the probands reported that they had sought professional help in the past for their "nervous" problems, and the remainder of the probands were apparently free of psychopathology. None of the probands' brothers were given a diagnosis by the interviewers or reported ever having sought professional help for psychological problems. In the vocational sphere, probands had changed jobs much more frequently than their brothers, having an average job tenure of 3.4 years compared to 7.3 years for their brothers. The brothers' mean SES was above that of their fathers, while the probands' mean SES was below that of their fathers and significantly below that of their brothers.

The hyperactive adults studied by Borland and Heckman were for the most part free of serious psychopathology but were characterized by high rates of adjustment problems and less than expected SES levels. Nonetheless, this outcome was considerably more positive than that reported by Menkes et al. The difference in findings between the two retrospective studies highlights the need for prospective studies which might be expected to yield more reliable results. As part of a long series of studies, Weiss et al., (1979) followed prospectively a group of 75 hyperactive children from early childhood until a mean age of 19.5 years (range: 17 to 24 years). Hyperactives were compared with normal controls selected through advertisement in local high schools and matched on age, sex and SES. Generally, the results were very similar to those reported by Borland and Heckman, suggesting that young adult hyperactives had a variety of adjustment difficulties but few exhibited serious psychopathology. There were, for example, no group differences in self-rated job satisfaction, and employers did not rate the hyperactive young adults differently from the controls on rating scales measuring job competence. However, 40% of the hyperactive group were diagnosed as having characterological personality trait disorders (compared to 23% of the controls), and two of the 75 hyperactives were diagnosed as borderline psychotic (compared to none of the controls).

Although a variety of adjustment problems in both the social and vocational domains characterized young adult hyperactives in these two large follow-up studies, only a minority of them appeared to exhibit the *serious* psychopathology which their childhood and adolescent symptoms were thought to foreshadow. Several points should be considered, however, before it is firmly concluded that hyperactive children are not at great risk for serious psychopathology. It has recently been demonstrated, for example, that a high proportion, 28%, of the offspring of continuous (chronic) schizophrenics show extreme symptoms of hyperactivity, raising the possibility that hyperactivity may be an early manifestation of a "genetic diathesis that leads to schizophrenia" (Reider & Nichols, 1979). These authors noted that a number of studies have related the presence of *aggressive, antisocial behavior* in childhood to adult sociopathy, schizophrenia, and alcoholism (e.g., Robins, 1966; Watt, 1978). They speculate that *hyperactivity* has not been related to serious adult psychopathology because these studies were retrospective and a diagnosis of hyperactivity was not common at the time of initial contact, the late 1920's in Robins' (1966) study, for example. Although the children followed-up were most often diagnosed as conduct disorder or unsocialized aggressive, a substantial number of them may have exhibited behaviors which would now result in a diagnosis of hyperactivity. For example 37% of the boys referred with antisocial symptoms in Robins' (1966) study also showed signs of inattentiveness and daydreaming, and these symptoms were significantly related to a later diagnosis of alcoholism.

The prevalence of psychopathology in the Borland and Heckman and Weiss et al. studies may have been underestimated because the hyperactive adults were relatively young at the time of follow-up. For example, the period of risk for onset of schizophrenia lasts until age 55. At age 20 only 11% of the risk period for onset has been passed and at age 30 only 51% of the risk period has been survived (Slater & Cowie, 1971). The prevalence of psychoses over the life span of formerly hyperactive adults might be expected to be two to nine times higher than reported by Borland and Heckman and Weiss et al., whose samples' average ages were 28 and 19 years, respectively. Similarly, the cumulative incidences of alcoholism, sociopathy, interpersonal and vocational difficulties, and anxiety-related disorders would all be expected to increase over the adult life span of a hyperactive sample (see, for example, Kramer & Loney, 1981). The data currently available from the relatively short-term follow-ups should thus be interpreted as indicating the *maximum positive* outcome for hyperactive adults. The maximum negative outcome remains to be demonstrated, and the exact nature of the relationship between childhood hyperactivity and adult outcome will not be clear until studies have followed target individuals until they are past the risk periods for onset of major forms of psychopathology and other adjustment difficulties.

One variable that has demonstrated some utility in facilitating prediction of outcome in hyperactive children is the aggression-hyperactivity dichotomy described earlier (Loney et al., 1978; Loney & Milich, in press). Milich and Loney (1979) argued that childhood aggressive behavior is predictive of poor outcome in hyperactive adolescents. Loney and her colleagues have shown that chart rater Aggression factor scores predict parent and chart ratings of aggression, hyperactivity, and general behavior problems in adolescence. In contrast, chart rating scores on the hyperactivity factor were not differentially related to outcome measures (Paternite & Loney, 1980). Similarly, very poor adult outcome has been demonstrated for aggressive children (Robins, 1966). These data suggest that the precision of outcome predictions can be increased if information regarding the level of aggressive behavior in hyperactive children is evaluated.

ETIOLOGY

The Construct of Brain Damage

During the 1950's and 1960's the prevailing assumption was that hyperactivity resulted from brain damage. Studies on World War I veterans with confirmed brain injury often showed a behavioral syndrome which included difficulties in abstract thinking, attentional processes and emotional lability. Because children labeled hyperactive or learning-disabled exhibited similar behaviors, their disturbances were also assumed to result from brain damage (Hallahan & Kauffman, 1976). Although many brain damaged children did not exhibit these behaviors and not all hyperactive children showed evidence of brain damage, the notion of brain damage as a cause of hyperactivity and learning disabilities persisted. When it gradually became clear that no evidence of gross brain damage was apparent in the majority of these children (Ross, 1976), the term *minimal brain damage* came into prominence.

The concept of minimal brain damage implied that brain damage was so slight that its existence could not be demonstrated with traditional measures of gross brain damage. Thus "hard" signs of neurological damage were usually not found in hyperactive children, but many hyperactive children had a greater number of "soft" or equivocal signs of neurological damage (Werry, Minde, Guzman, Weiss, Dogan, & Hoy, 1972). Many hyperactive children, however, did not evidence even equivocal signs of neurological damage (Dubey, 1976), and a history of perinatal events presumed to be associated with minimal brain damage could not be demonstrated in most cases (Minde, Webb, & Sykes, 1968). Finally, neurological and behavioral variables did not relate to one another in a manner that supported a construct of minimal brain damage (Werry, 1968).

Because no minimal brain damage could be demonstrated it was assumed that hyperactivity must result from a minimal brain *dysfunction* (MBD) even more difficult to detect than minimal brain *damage* (see Rie & Rie, 1980). The notion that hyperactivity is correlated with a dysfunction in the central nervous system (CNS) is widely accepted and has been the stimulus for a large body of research, the current thrust of which is to discover both the nature of that dysfunction at cognitive and physiological levels and its etiological correlates. If the term is used only among professionals as a probable description of the current state of a child's CNS, it may be heuristically useful. Nonetheless, neither the precise nature of this dysfunction nor the etiological variables associated with it are yet known. To say that a child suffers from minimal brain dysfunction is to describe his problem rather than to explain it. The clinician needs to be particularly careful with the use of the term MBD. Any label which includes the word *brain* can have connotations for parents, teachers and uninformed professionals which go far beyond those that may be intended (Ross, 1976).

Perinatal Variables

Since the late 1950's there have been frequent suggestions that behavioral and learning problems often result from a variety of biological disturbances in pregnancy and birth. The term "continuum of reproductive casualty" has been used to imply not only that *severe* biological disturbances result in *profound* psychological problems (for example, children with extremely low birthweights, below 1500 g, are often mentally retarded), but also that less serious deviations of pregnancy can result in a variety of less profound behavior disorders (Pasamanick & Knobloch, 1960; Knobloch & Pasamanick, 1966). In retrospective interviews, mothers of hyperactives were more likely than mothers of control children to report bleeding in pregnancy, toxemia, high blood-pressure, low birthweight, and anoxia (Werry, Weiss, & Douglas, 1964). When the same information was obtained from actual medical records, however, substantially fewer differences were reported (Minde et al., 1968). Because perinatal disturbances cannot be identified for all hyperactive children (Dubey, 1976), at the least, perinatal disturbances must interact with other variables if they are to result in hyperactivity.

Several prospective studies have examined the relationships between perinatal disturbances and later behavior and learning disorders. The Kauai study (Werner, Bierman, & French, 1971) followed 1000 children from pregnancy to the age of 10. No relationship was found between (a) 60 selected complications or events which could have occurred during prenatal, labor, delivery and neonatal periods, and (b) teacher-rated presence of symptoms associated with hyperkinesis at age 10. A second study, the Educational Follow-up Study (EFS), is following 1600 of the children originally included in the Collaborative Project of the National Institute of Neurological Diseases and Stroke (Rubin & Balow, 1977). A multiple regression analysis of 8 subclasses of 76 perinatal factors and teacher identification of behavior problems at age 10 revealed that perinatal factors such as maternal reproductive and medical history, variables related to the target pregnancy and delivery, and other neonatal factors accounted for only 13% of the variance of teacher-rated problems. Similar results with another part of the NINDS sample were reported by Nichols and Chen (1981).

In summary, there are small mean differences between hyperactive and control children in the reported frequencies of a variety of perinatal disturbances, but their use to predict diagnostic group membership or degree of behavior disturbance is not possible except in extreme cases (Rubin & Balow, 1977). It is not clear that perinatal variables are exclusively related to hyperactivity. The EFS results, for example, suggest that they may be weakly related to behavior and learning disorders in general. Similarly, Nichols and Chen (1981) found that frequency of maternal smoking during pregnancy was related both to hyperactivity and to learning disabilities.

Minor Physical Anomalies

Several investigators have examined minor physical anomalies, a set of neurologically related variables that appear to be more predictive of behavioral disorders than the perinatal factors already discussed. There are 17 anomalies (e.g., epicanthus, low-set ears, curved fifth finger, elongated middle toe) that are formed in early fetal development, known to be affected by genetic, toxic, and other environmental factors and found in children with Down's syndrome and a wide variety of other behavior disorders (Rapoport, Quinn, Burg, & Bartley, 1979; Rubin & Balow, 1977). They are presumably caused by whatever agent causes the neurological dysfunction later manifested in behavioral and learning disorders. In addition, there is some evidence that there may be a genetic component to the anomalies (Quinn & Rapoport, 1974). Study of the anomalies' relationship with behavioral and neurological variables might thus implicate potential etiological factors in hyperactivity.

Several studies have revealed a relatively strong correlation between the number of anomalies (total anomaly score) and teacher or peer ratings of hyperactivity and other behavior problems (Halverson & Victor, 1976; Waldrop, Bell, McLaughlin, & Halverson, 1978; Waldrop, Pederson, & Bell, 1968). Waldrop et al. (1978) measured anomalies in 30 newborn males and 3 years later in 36 additional 3-year-olds. All the boys then attended a nursery school where observations of play behavior and peer interactions were made. Scores from factors representing short attention span and peer aggression and impulsivity were highly correlated ($r = .67$) with the newborn anomaly scores but less highly related to anomaly scores at age 3 ($r = .35$). The lower of the two correlations is closer to that reported in other studies when anomalies and behavior have been measured concurrently (e.g., Halverson & Victor, 1976). Nonetheless, the relationship between this single predictor and criterion variables is considerably larger than shown by the entire group of perinatal variables previously discussed.

Similarly, Rapoport and her colleagues (reviewed in Rapoport et al., 1979) examined minor physical anomalies in children diagnosed as hyperactive and reported the following seven findings: (1) hyperactive children had a higher average anomaly score, 3.58, than comparison children with neurotic problems, 2.53 (Quinn & Rapoport, 1974); (2) the number of anomalies was positively correlated with teacher ratings on the Conduct ($r = .35$) and the Hyperactivity ($r = .28$) factors of the CTRS (Rapoport, Quinn, & Lamprecht, 1974); (3) the high-anomaly children were more likely (57%) than low-anomaly children (19%) to have a father who remembered himself to have been hyperactive as a child (Quinn & Rapoport, 1974); (4) mothers of high-anomaly children were more likely (53%) than mothers of low-anomaly children (18%) to have had obstetrical complications during pregnancy, especially bleeding during the first trimester (Rapoport et al., 1974); (5) anomaly score was unrelated to the presence of neurological signs and EEG abnormalities (Quinn & Rapoport, 1974); (6) hyperactive children with high-anomaly scores were more likely (88%) than low-anomaly hyperactives (35%) to have been considered problems by their parents before the age of 3 years (Rapoport et al., 1979); and (7) there was a significant correlation ($r = .38$) between anomaly score and plasma level of dopamine-β-hydroxylase, the enzyme that converts dopamine to norepinephrine (Rapoport et al., 1974). A stepwise discriminant analysis using age of onset, plasma level of dopamine-β-hydroxylase, paternal history of hyperactivity, and maternal history of obstetrical complications predicted level of anomaly score (high or low) with false positive and false negative rates of only 7% and 11%, respectively (Rapoport et al., 1979).

Although these data suggest that a major biologic *subgroup* of hyperactive children has been identified, additional research is necessary. The fact that no relationship was identified between anomaly scores and signs of neurological dysfunction contradicts the basic assumption underlying the study of the anomalies—that is, whatever caused the anomaly also caused a neurological dysfunction which resulted in hyperactivity. Similarly, even though anomaly scores in one study was correlated both with plasma level of dopamine-β-hydroxylase and with teacher ratings on the CTRS, no relationship was found between teacher ratings and dopamine-β-hydroxylase levels. Similarly there was no correlation between changes in dopamine-β-hydroxylase levels and medication-related improvement in teacher ratings (Rapoport et al., 1974). Such findings cast doubt on the validity of the theoretical relationship among anomalies, dopamine-β-hydroxylase level, and behavior. In addition, the mean hyperactive anomaly score in one study, 3.58 (Quinn & Rapoport, 1974), was apparently obtained by more than 30% of the male infants examined in a normative study (Quinn, Renfield, Burg, & Rapoport, 1977), implying a very high false positive rate when a high anomaly score *alone* is used to infer deviance (Rapoport et al., 1979). Finally, in one study (Quinn & Rapoport, 1974) the mean anomaly score was higher for children labeled unsocialized aggressive (4.0) than for children labeled hyperactive (3.58), suggesting that anomalies are not limited to a role in hyperactivity (Rubin & Balow, 1977). Rapoport's studies indicated that both paternal history of hyperactivity and maternal prenatal complications were related to anomaly score but the relationships were separate. They speculated that the relationship between anomalies and hyperactivity was a genetic one "frequently mimicked (phenocopied) by an insult early in pregnancy (Quinn & Rapoport, 1974, p. 746)." These two etiologically distinct subgroups may show differential relationships with other etiologic, mediating and behavioral/cognitive variables and should be studied with this in mind. This line of research appears promising because it attempts to examine empirically defined subgroups of hyperactivity. If it is to prove fruitful, however, it will be necessary to postulate and then demonstrate comprehensive theoretical relationships linking specific anomalies, genetic or teratogenic mechanisms, resulting neurological dysfunction, and behavior patterns and diagnostic categories.

Genetic Variables

Studies with less than optimal designs have provided evidence suggestive of genetic involvement in hyperactivity, but the research necessary to confirm this involvement has not been conducted. For example, it has been shown that there is an increased prevalence of sociopathy, alcoholism, hysteria, and retrospective diagnosis of hyperactivity among the biological parents but not among the adoptive parents of hyperactive children (Morrison & Stewart, 1971; 1973). An increased prevalence of hyperactivity has been reported among full siblings (as opposed to half siblings) and among second-degree relatives of hyperactive children (Cantwell, 1975; Safer, 1973). As noted above, a recent investigation suggested that hyperactivity may be genetically linked to "continuous" schizophrenia (Rieder & Nichols, 1979), but this hypothesized connection will not be clarified until ongoing studies of children at risk are completed.

Other researchers have argued that evidence for heritability of activity level in humans and other animals suggests that hyperactivity may have a genetic etiology. For example parental ratings of activity level are higher for monozygotic than for dizygotic twins (Willerman, 1973). Given the current conceptualization of hyperactivity as a dysfunction in attention rather than activity level, such extrapolations seem unwarranted.

It is clear that either separated twin studies or genetic marker studies must be conducted before a final conclusion can be reached regarding genetic involvement in hyperactivity. Subgroup analysis in such studies is more likely to yield useful information than are global questions regarding heritability. Note, for example, that the frequency of retrospective diagnosis of parental hyperactivity was considerably higher in Rapoport's high-anomaly children than in her low-anomaly children (see previous discussion) or groups not separated on this variable (e.g., Morrison & Stewart, 1971). Finally, the nature of the putative genetic transmission in hyperactivity is unclear. Simple recessive, dominant or sex-linked explanations do not match available data, and some type of polygenetic mechanism seems likely (Cantwell, 1975).

Diet

Feingold (1975) hypothesized that hyperactivity resulted from hypersensitivity to certain dietary substances, including artificial colors, artificial flavorings, preservatives BHA and BHT, and naturally-occurring salicylates, and he suggested that elimination of these substances from the child's diet would result in remission of the hyperactivity. Though widely believed, Feingold's hypothesis has not fared well under the scrutiny of scientific inquiry. A large, well-controlled study, using a variety of objective dependent measures (including classroom and laboratory observations, neurological and psychological evaluations, and parent and teacher ratings) and a cross-over trial of the Feingold and a placebo diet, failed to reveal any consistent effects of the Feingold diet (Harley, Ray, Tomasi, Eichman, Matthews, Chun, Cleeland, and Traisman, 1978). Similar results were reported by Conners, Goyette, Southwick, Lees, and Andrulonis (1976).

As a further test of the diet, nine children in the Harley et al. (1978) study who were rated by parents as diet-improved underwent additional evaluation during which they were given multiple weekly challenges with a blend of food dyes. This analysis failed to reveal adverse effects of the dietary challenges in these parent-rated, improved children (Harley, Matthews, & Eichman, 1978). In another challenge study, 22 preschool children with behavior problems were maintained on the Feingold diet and given weekly challenges of food dye or placebo. The mother of one child was able to discriminate reliably between multiple challenges of placebo and dye (Weiss, Williams, Margen, Abrams, Caan, Citron, Cox, McKibben, Ogar, & Schultz, 1980). These challenge studies suggest that the reported improved behavior of the majority of children placed on the Feingold diet is unrelated to the elimination of artificial colors from their diets. Improvement in these children either may be illusory or may result from parental expectations of improvement or from the increased attention given the child as the diet is implemented. A very small minority of hyperactive children do appear to show an adverse response to artificial food colors.

In contrast to these equivocal results, Swanson and Kinsbourne (1980) reported dye-induced performance decrements in 17 of 20 hyperactive children performing a paired-associates learning task. These children were given a much larger dose of color (100 to 150 mg) than previous studies (for example, Weiss et al. administered 35 mg), suggesting that the effect may be pharmacological rather than immunological (allergic) (Logan & Swanson, 1979). Swanson & Kinsbourne's results, which need to be replicated could have been a function of high dosages, the sensitivity of the dependent measure, or subject selection procedures, all of which were different from previous studies.

Finally, regarding the neural basis for putative dietary influences, individual dyes or a blend of food dyes inhibit CNS neurotransmitter uptake in rat brain homogenate (Lafferman & Silbergeld, 1979; Logan & Swanson, 1979), although the specific mechanism underlying this inhibition remains uncertain (Augustine & Levitan, 1980; Mailman, Ferris, Tang, Vogel, Kilts, Lipton, Smith, Mueller, & Breeze, 1980). In addition, the relationship between these effects and behavioral effects has not been clarified (Mailman et al., 1980).

Additional research in this domain should focus on three areas: (1) investigation of the other substances which Feingold identified (e.g. artificial flavorings), as they may affect children *not* affected by the dyes, yielding a higher total percentage of children adversely affected by dietary substances; (2) dose-response and task-response studies; and (3) the study of individual differences in response to dyes (i.e., subgroup analysis).

Socio-environmental Influences

Drawing on the literatures regarding child-parent temperament interactions and social learning theory, some authors have speculated that hyperactivity results in part from the nature of the child's interactions with his environment, especially with significant others (e.g., Ross & Ross, 1976). Although several observational studies have shown that mothers exerted more control towards their hyperactive children and imposed greater structure on their task performance than mothers of comparison children (Campbell, 1975; Cunningham & Barkley, 1979), and that teachers exhibited a much higher frequency of controlling statements to hyperactive boys than to control boys (Whalen, Henker, & Dotemoto, 1981), the directionality of these relationships are unclear.

The major approach to the socio-environmental issue has employed multivariate techniques to examine the relationships among environmental variables and measures of symptomatology in hyperactive children. Loney and her colleagues (Loney, Langhorne, Paternite, Whaley-Klahn, Broeker, & Hacker, in press; Paternite & Loney, 1980) examined the relationship between their two symptom factors of Aggression and Hyperactivity and environmental variables derived primarily from chart raters' evaluations of intake and assessment information. A stepwise multiple regression with score on the Aggression factor as the criterion yielded a multiple correlation of .55 for father's love-to hostility rating, mother's autonomy-to-control rating, and parental SES, suggesting that high levels of aggression were associated with low SES, hostile fathers, and undercontrolling mothers. The only variable significantly related to score on the Hyperactivity factor was the mother's autonomy-to-control rating. In addition, chart rater evaluation of disharmony in the parent-child relationship at referral was positively associated with the Aggression factor ($r = .47$) but not with the Hyperactivity factor. Interestingly, disharmony in the mother-father relationship was positively correlated with both the Aggression and the Hyperactivity factors (both r's $= .42$). In addition, chart rating of parental disturbance (e.g., social incompetence, heavy drinking, police contacts, mental illness) was positively correlated with the Aggression factor but not with the Hyperactivity factor (Paternite & Loney, 1980).

A somewhat different picture of the relationship between these environmental factors and symptomatology was obtained when environmental measures taken at referral and measures of symptomatology at follow-up were examined (Paternite & Loney, 1980). Mother and father autonomy-to-control, family SES, and disharmony in the parent-child relationship at referral all predicted score on the Aggression factor at five-year follow-up. Degree of Hyperactivity at follow-up was predicted by mother's love-to-hostility rating, father's autonomy-to-control and love-to-hostility, SES, parental disturbance, disharmony in the parent-child relationship, and disharmony in the mother-father relationship. Behavior problems in general at follow-up were predicted by disharmony in the parent-child relationship, parental disturbance and a change (from referral) of parent figure. Change of parent figure also predicted degree of Aggression and Hyperactivity at follow-up.

Similar results were reported in the Kauai follow-up study described earlier (Werner et al., 1971). The relationships were examined between groups of children defined as hyperkinetic and overaggressive on the basis of teacher ratings and three variables of interest here: (1) SES; (2) educational stimulation (opportunities and structures provided in the home for educationally stimulating activities); and (3) emotional support (stable home, both parents present, affection, approval and reasoning used in parent-child interaction). Compared to homes with average ratings on these variables, the prevalence of ''hyperkinesis'' was increased by 77% in homes with below average ratings of educational stimulation and by 40% in homes with below average ratings of emotional support. The comparable increases in prevalence of overaggressiveness were 240% and 311%. ''Hyperkinesis'' was not related to SES, but overaggresiveness was strongly related to SES.

Although firm conclusions are prohibited because the data are correlational and are based on chart or other ratings relatively far removed from actual behavior, these studies suggest that measures of the quality of the home environment are correlated with outcome in children who show symptoms of hyperactivity and aggression. In both sets of studies the relationships were clearly stronger for aggressive than for hyperactive symptoms, showing again that level of aggressive symptomatology provides important information that is not available from examination of hyperactive symptomatology alone. Both at referral and at follow-up, there was a strong association between aggressive symptoms and disturbances in the home environment. The same association was only apparent at follow-up for hyperactive symptoms, suggesting that a considerable period of time must pass before the association between hyperactive symptoms and the home situation becomes as strong as the association between aggressive symptoms and the home situation. The causal nature of the relationship between home environment and symptomatology cannot be determined from these correlational data. The relationship is no doubt a reciprocal one with severe symptoms causing disruption in the family and disruption in the family in turn exacerbating symptoms, and research addressing this issue directly is badly needed. At the least, these data certainly highlight the need for a focus on parent-child interactions and other familial variables in the treatment of hyperactive children (see following discussion of parent training in *Treatment* section).

Summary

There is inconclusive but accumulating evidence for a variety of biological factors in the etiology of some hyperactive children. Environmental influences do not appear to cause hyperactivity, but they may exert a strong influence on the nature and severity of the problem in many children. The research just reviewed suggests, however, that no single variable accounts for all or even most cases of hyperactivity. As research designs continue to include more fine grained analyses of subgroup patterns, the relationships between different etiological factors and empirically defined subgroups of hyperactive children may be elucidated. It seems likely that such studies will reveal that most cases of hyperactivity are determined through interactions among these etiological variables. For example, it may be the case that a genetic diathesis for prenatal insult yields a biochemical dysfunction in the CNS which causes a particular hyperactive child to show a toxic response to artificial food dyes. Further, the extent to which that child will exhibit the behavioral syndrome of hyperactivity will be influenced by the home environment in which he is raised.

MEDIATING VARIABLES

Physiological Arousal

The nature of the behavioral disturbances exhibited by hyperactive children led to early speculation that they suffered from a chronic state of *overarousal* (Laufer et al., 1957), whereas more recent theorists have argued that at least a subgroup of hyperactive children are in a chronic state of *underarousal* (Satterfield, Cantwell, & Satterfield, 1974).

Autonomic arousal.   Comparisons of hyperactive and nonhyperactive children on basal skin conductance level (SCL) and nonspecific galvanic skin responses (GSRs) have not shown hyperactive children to be reliably overaroused on these measures (e.g., Cohen & Douglas, 1972). One study reported that hyperactives had lower arousal levels on these measures than comparison children (Satterfield & Dawson, 1971), but subsequent research failed to replicate this result (Ferguson, Simpson, & Trites, 1976; Spring, Greenberg, Scott, & Hopwood, 1974; Zahn, Abate, Little, & Wender, 1975). Studies which measured heart rate as an indicator of autonomic arousal also failed to document differences between hyperactives and controls (Barkley & Jackson, 1977; Ferguson et al., 1976; Zahn et al., 1975). There is general agreement that hyperactive children as a group do not differ from nonhyperactive children on measures of basal autonomic arousal (Hastings & Barkley, 1978).

Other studies examined autonomic responsivity or arousal differences during task performance with equivocal results. In some studies hyperactives showed lower frequencies and/or lower amplitudes of specific GSR responses to tones or reaction time (RT) stimuli (Cohen & Douglas, 1972; Firestone & Douglas, 1975; Zahn et al., 1975), but others failed to replicate those findings (Ferguson et al.,

1976). On another measure of autonomic responsivity, heart rate deceleration to an expected stimulus, hyperactives were not different from comparison children in at least two studies (Zahn et al., 1975; Ferguson et al., 1976), and one study that did not include controls revealed that hyperactives exhibited a reliable and significant deceleration during a RT foreperiod (Porges, Walter, Korb, & Sprague, 1975). In contrast, one study showed that hyperactives exhibited less deceleration than control children (Zahn, Little & Wender, 1978).

Although several reviews concluded that hyperactive children are autonomically less responsive than comparison children (Ferguson & Pappas, 1979; Hastings & Barkley, 1978; Rosenthal & Allen, 1977), this conclusion should be viewed as tentative. For example, a study by Sroufe, Sonies, West, and Wright (1973) which is widely cited as providing evidence that *hyperactive* children show reduced heart rate deceleration to an expected stimulus, actually employed learning-disabled children as subjects. Similarly, Rosenthal and Allen's (1978) otherwise heuristically valuable review paper is flawed by its failure to discriminate between learning-disabled, hyperactive, and other groups of subjects. In other studies, hyperactive-normal differences on multiple measures of autonomic responsivity (e.g., heart rate deceleration, pupillary dilation and skin conductance responses) fail to show convergent validity (Zahn et al., 1975; Zahn et al., 1978).

Cortical Arousal. In general, differences in tonic or background EEG have not been found when hyperactive children have been compared to appropriate controls (Dubey, 1976). Excessive slow wave activity was reported in a number of early studies in a minority of hyperactive children (Hastings & Barkley, 1978). Because those studies usually did not include a deviant control, and because there is a 10% to 12% base rate of these abnormalities in normal children (Hastings & Barkley, 1978), the significance of these findings is unclear. Recent advances in EEG methodology might yield more meaningful findings and should be investigated with a hyperactive sample (e.g., Ahn, Prichep, John, Baird, Trepetin, & Kaye, 1980).

Other studies have measured cortical arousal by comparing hyperactive and control children on their averaged evoked cortical responses (AERs or EPs) to auditory or visual stimuli. Satterfield (1973) and Buchsbaum and Wender (1973) obtained results that they interpreted as indicating cortical immaturity and a lower cortical responsivity than age-matched nonhyperactive children. In a later study that included an initial and a replication sample, however, Hall, Griffin, Moyer, Hopkins, and Rapoport (1976) completely failed to replicate those results. The relationships between the various components of the EP and other physiological and behavioral measures of arousal and attention are not clear, especially in children, a fact that makes interpretation of data in this area difficult (Donchin, Ritter, & McCallum, 1978; Hillyard, Picton, & Regan, 1978; Klorman, Thompson, & Ellingson, 1978). Consider, for example, a study by Satterfield and Braley (1977), who examined auditory EP's that occurred from 50 msec to 330 msec after auditory clicks in three age groups of hyperactive and control children (72–84 months, 96–108 months, and 120–144 months). On both early (P_1-N_1) and late (P_2-N_2) components of the EP, young hyperactive subjects had lower amplitudes than controls, the middle groups did not differ, and older hyperactives had higher amplitudes than controls. Satterfield and Braley interpreted the P_1-N_1 component as indexing selective attention and the late component as inversely related to arousal. A strict interpretation of their findings would suggest that young hyperactive children are hyperaroused and underselective, 8 and 9-year-old hyperactives are not different from normals, and older hyperactive children are overselective and underaroused. There is no evidence, however, from information processing studies of selective attention to support any of these findings.

Much more needs to be known about EPs and their relationship to external events before results from hyperactive-normal comparisons will prove useful (Klorman et al., 1978). For example, most research on hyperactive children has focused on analysis of rather early or exogenous EP peaks. The endogenous or event-related potentials that are presumed to be related to complex information processing (e.g., P300) occur later in the EP sequence (Donchin et al., 1978; Hillyard et al., 1978), and have not been extensively studied in hyperactive children. As these later components are presumed to be related to attentional variables they are likely candidates for analysis (e.g., Loiselle, Stamm, Maitinsky, & Whipple, 1980).

Attention Deficits

Despite many studies and the consequent adoption of the term *attention deficit disorder,* relatively little is known about the specific nature of the cognitive deficits in hyperactive children (Rosenthal & Allen, 1977). Early studies of attention compared the performance of hyperactive and control children on a number of different laboratory tasks with results that have been widely replicated (Douglas, 1972). Hyperactive children showed poorest performance on tasks in which attention had to be maintained over a period of time and in which impulsive responding interfered with performance. Thus hyperactives had longer and more variable simple reaction times (RTs) following preparatory intervals (Cohen & Douglas, 1972), and made more errors of omission on a continuous performance test of vigilance (Sykes, Douglas, Weiss, & Minde, 1971). In contrast, hyperactives performed as well as controls in choice RT tasks or self-paced serial RT tasks (Sykes, Douglas, & Morgenstern, (1973). In addition, hyperactives performed more poorly than controls on the MFF Test, which measures the child's ability to match a sample figure with an identical standard and in which careful visual scanning and impulse control are important performance-facilitating characteristics (Campbell, Douglas, & Morgenstern,

1971). Finally, Douglas and her colleagues found no evidence that hyperactive children were more distracted than controls when irrelevant stimuli were presented during task performance (Campbell et al., 1971; Sykes et al., 1971, 1973). Reviewing these and other studies, Douglas drew two conclusions: (1) hyperactive children have a constitutional inability to sustain attention and to inhibit responding in situations which require focused, directed and organized effort, and (2) because of these deficits hyperactive children fail to apply sufficient, organized, and strategic effort to information processing in task settings (Douglas & Peters, 1979). This failure is presumed to account for the problems that the children exhibit in a wide variety of academic and social situations.

While Douglas' is the most prominent contemporary formulation, additional research is necessary before it can be accepted with certainty as the explanation for the cognitive deficits shown by hyperactive children. Most researchers would have little quarrel with Douglas' conclusion that hyperactive children lack an organized approach to tasks. Recent studies have suggested that deficits in basic cognitive processes other than sustained attention and response inhibition may underlie these higher level difficulties, however. For example, clinical observations reveal that the great majority of children diagnosed as hyperactive are able to sustain attention for a substantial period of time in high interest situations, such as watching favorite television shows or playing video games. If hyperactive children who show deficient sustained attention in a standard vigilance task maintain attention when watching an interesting television show, it would not be valid to conclude that their problem is due to the *inability* to sustain attention. At the least there must be some interaction between subject and task variables.

Two other aspects of attention which are invoked as important basic cognitive processes more often than vigilance and which therefore might offer more insight into the nature of the cognitive deficit in hyperactivity are selective attention and attentional capacity (Posner, 1978). Conners (1976), for example, has hypothesized that hyperactive children exhibit a basic deficit in selective attention. When selective attention is defined as the degree to which performance is disrupted by the presence of irrelevant stimuli, however, no differences in such distractibility have been detected between hyperactive and control children in a large number of studies (Douglas & Peters, 1979; Pelham, 1981; Zentall & Zentall, 1976).

Attentional capacity is a construct that refers to the amount of attentional effort allocated to a task or available for allocation. Although hyperactive children's difficulties on tasks in which cognitive strategies would facilitate performance could be explained by failure to sustain attention and to inhibit impulsive responding (Douglas & Peters, 1979), they could also result from a limitation in the capacity hyperactives had available for allocation to the task. For example, a recent study compared ADDH children with controls matched for age, sex, and reading ability on performance in a series of visual and memory scanning tasks (Schnedler, Pelham, Bender, & Pass, 1982). There was no group difference in memory scanning rate when the visual display consisted of one digit, but as display size increased to four digits, ADDH children showed a steeper increase in the rate of memory scanning than did controls. Thus, hyperactive children exhibited increasing performance deficits as the limits of their attentional capacity were taxed. Hyperactive children have also been shown to exhibit performance deficits on measures of span of apprehension, reflecting group differences in basic cognitive operations involving rate of information pick-up and decay (Denton & McIntyre, 1978; McIntyre, Blackwell, & Denton, 1978).

In summary, the precise nature of the information processing deficit in hyperactive children is undetermined. Studies on the convergent validity of the laboratory measures of attention employed need to be conducted (cf. Pelham, 1979), and more research that focuses on processes other than sustained attention are needed. Although Douglas's theory is the most influential, cognitive processes other than sustained attention and impulse control may be critical. For example, recent data suggest that hyperactive children may have memory deficits (Weingartner, Rapoport, Buchsbaum, Bunney, Ebert, Mikkelson, & Caine, 1980).

Neurochemical Variables

Several hypotheses have been advanced relating the function of the CNS neurotransmitters, serotonin, norepinephrine, and dopamine, to hyperactivity. Studies usually assess the levels of transmitter metabolites in urine or cerebrospinal fluid or they measure blood levels of the transmitters, their precursors, or relevant enzymes. Such studies have failed to indicate a role for serotonin in hyperactivity (Shaywitz, Cohen, & Bowers, 1977). In addition and contrary to early speculation (Wender, 1971), there appears to be no evidence supporting a role for norepinephrine in hyperactivity (Ferguson & Pappas, 1979).

Dopamine is presumed to play an important role in the regulation of motoric and aggressive behavior (Seiden & Dykstra, 1977), and it has been postulated that hyperactive children have low brain levels of dopamine or some specific damage or dysfunction in dopaminergic pathways in the CNS (Shaywitz, Cohen, & Shaywitz, 1978; Wender, 1978). Shaywitz et al. (1977) compared cerebrospinal fluid level of homovanillic acid, a major metabolite of dopamine, in a small group of hyperactive children and controls and found tentative indications of low CNS dopamine levels in hyperactives. Shaywitz et al. (1978), however, noted the need for replication of their results with a larger sample of children.

Thus despite considerable interest in this approach and despite the challenging theoretical implications, there is no clear indication that hyperactive children differ from controls in levels of CNS neurotransmitters. The major obstacle to research in this area is that brain levels of neurotransmitters cannot be directly measured in humans and must consequently be inferred from cerbrospinal fluid levels or peripheral measures. If techniques for measuring brain levels of neurotransmitters were developed, this area of research might become especially promising.

Summary

The nature of physiological, cognitive and neurochemical mediators in hyperactivity remain undetermined. To date various methodological problems have impeded progress in this area. In addition to these noted earlier, the major difficulty is that the subject samples have usually been identified without regard to correlated pathological states. Thus most of the research has examined hyperactive children heterogeneous with respect to learning ability and aggression. There is considerable evidence that learning-disabled (LD) children have deficits in basic electrophysiological and cognitive processes that result in performance deficits on a variety of tasks (Ahn et al., 1980; Douglas & Peters, 1979; Ross, 1976; Pelham, 1979; Torgesen & Kail, 1980), and unless LD children are excluded from hyperactive samples, results cannot be unambiguously interpreted as pertaining to hyperactivity per se. Further, the physiological substrates of sociopathy and hyperactivity are presumed to differ (Porges, 1976), and the separation of high aggressive and low aggressive hyperactive children therefore appears warranted. The search for mediating variables in hyperactivity is likely to benefit from subgroup analysis involving all possible combinations of aggressive, LD, and hyperactive symptomatology. In addition, mediating factors may depend on etiology. Recall, for example, that Rapoport et al. (1979) reported that plasma levels of dopamine-β-hydroxylase were correlated with minor physical anomalies in a hyperactive sample. Examination of interactions between etiological and mediating variables are clearly necessary.

TREATMENT

Psychopharmacological Intervention

Approximately 2% to 2.5% of all elementary-aged children in North America (600,000 children) have received or are currently receiving pharmacological intervention with one of the CNS stimulants as a treatment for hyperactivity (Bosco & Robin, 1980; Krager & Safer, 1974; Sprague & Gadow, 1976). Although other classes of drugs have been used as a treatment for hyperactivity, the psychostimulants, dextroamphetamine, methylphenidate, and pemoline, have been shown to be the most effective in the short-term management of the disorder (Conners & Werry, 1979; Sroufe, 1975).

The psychostimulants, sympathomimetic amines, are presumed to enhance central and peripheral catecholaminergic effects by blocking catecholamine (both dopamine and norepinephrine) re-uptake into presynaptic nerve endings

(Cantwell & Carlson, 1978). Behavioral effects are observed within 30 min. (methylphenidate and dextroamphetamine) to 90 min. (pemoline) after ingestion of a psychostimulant. Methylphenidate and dextroamphetamine have very short half lives, and their behavioral effects peak approximately 2 hours after ingestion and disappear from 3 to 5 hours after ingestion (Cantwell & Carlson, 1978). The behavioral effects of pemoline peak four hours after ingestion and last from 6 to 10 hours (Pelham, Swanson, Bender, & Wilson, 1980). Methylphenidate and dextroamphetamine are usually administered in two daily dosages of .3 to 1.0 mg/kg for methylphenidate and .15 to .5 mg/kg for dextroamphetamine (Cantwell & Carlson, 1978). The optimal dosing regimen for pemoline is not certain, but a single daily dose of 1.0 to 2.0 mg/kg appears to produce effects comparable to those of low to moderate dosates of methylphenidate (Pelham et al., 1980). The effects of these three psychostimulants are relatively similar, and unless otherwise noted, the following discussion is applicable to all three drugs.

Effects on attention and learning. The psychostimulants have clear beneficial effects on measures of sustained attention and impulsivity. Medicated hyperactive children make fewer errors of omission on vigilance tasks and exhibit longer latencies on tasks such as the MFF (e.g., Campell et al., 1971; Cohen, Douglas, & Morgenstern, 1971; Sykes et al., 1971):. Normal comparison children also show improved performance on these tasks when receiving a psychostimulant (Rapoport, Buchsbaum, Zahn, Weingartner, Ludlow, & Mikkelsen, 1978).

There is considerable debate regarding the effects of psychostimulant medication on performance on more complex cognitive tasks (Cantwell & Carlson, 1978). Psychostimulants improve performance on measures of paired associate learning (Swanson & Kinsbourne, 1979), matching-to-sample short-term memory tasks (Sprague & Sleator, 1977), both cued and free recall (Weingartner et al., 1980), auditory comprehension (Rie & Rie, 1977), mathematical computations (Pelham, Swanson, Bender, & Wilson, 1980), and reading comprehension (Pelham, Bender, Caddell, & Booth, 1982). Whether improvement on these tasks is independent of medication-facilitated improvement in sustained attention and impulsivity is unclear (cf. Swanson & Kinsbourne, 1979; Weingartner et al., 1980).

Unfortunately, these short-term positive effects do not translate into long-term beneficial effects on academic achievement (e.g., Rie, Rie, Stewart, & Ambuel, 1976). This discrepancy between short-term and long-term effects on learning is perplexing. There are at least three possible explanations for it. First, although 20% to 40% of treated children do not respond positively to stimulants (Swanson & Kinsbourne, 1979), reported results are usually averaged over an entire sample. If hyperactives whose long-term achievement is studied were divided into groups of short-term positive responders and nonresponders on learning tasks, the responders might demonstrate stimulant-enhanced long-term achievement gains (Swanson & Kinsbourne, 1979). Swanson and Kinsbourne (1979) have argued that teacher ratings overpredict medication responsivity and have advocated a paired associates learning task for this purpose, but its predictive validity has not yet been demonstrated.

Secondly, the dosages necessary to result in maximal improvement in teacher-rated behaviors may actually impair cognitive performance (Brown & Sleator, 1979; Sprague & Sleator, 1977). Because teacher report is usually the criterion which is used to determine effective dosage, many children may be maintained on dosages of psychostimulants which impair their performance on tasks involving learning, memory and attention. Lower dosages than typically administered might yield a beneficial long-term effect on achievement. On the other hand, although performance on a short-term memory task is maximized at a methylphenicate dose of .3 mg/kg (Sprague & Sleator, 1977), equivalent doses of all three psychostimulants from two to three times this size have been shown to facilitate performance on other laboratory memory tasks and classroom measures of mathematics and reading (Pelham, Swanson, Bender, & Wilson, 1980; Pelham, Bender, Caddell, & Booth, 1981; Weingertner et al., 1980). More research in this area is needed.

A third possible explanation for the short-term/long-term learning discrepancy is state dependent learning (SDL). In one study when hyperactive children were tested for paired-associates retention in a placebo state after they had learned associations while medicated, their performance was impaired relative to children who had not changed drug states (Swanson & Kinsbourne, 1976). The retention performance of these children was actually *worse* than subjects who had both learned and been tested for retention in placebo states. This finding, which needs to be replicated (cf. Stephens & Pelham, 1982), suggests that the short-term benefits of stimulants on learning may actually *adversely* affect future performance and at the least may disappear when medication is discontinued.

Effects in the Classroom. The most widely used measure in drug research with hyperactive children has been the ACRS (Goyette et al., 1978). This 10-item checklist (see item listing in section on *Definition*) has been used to *define* medication response in many studies, and in approximately 70% of cases, hyperactive children have been rated as improved by their teachers on this scale (Conners & Werry, 1979; Sroufe, 1975). Placebo-controlled direct observations of behavior reveal that medicated children are more likely to be on-task and less likely to engage in disruptive classroom behavior (Gittelman-Klein, Klein, Abikoff, Gloisten, & Kates; 1976; O'Leary & Pelham, 1978; Whalen, Henker, Collins, Finck, & Dotemoto, 1979). Unmedicated hyperactive children initiate interactions with their teacher at a higher rate than comparison children, but this difference decreases when the hyperactives receive medication (Whalen et al., 1979; 1981), and teachers give fewer commands to medicated hyperactive children than to hyperactive children on placebo (Whalen et al., 1981). Finally, relative to placebo, medicated hyperactive children complete more math problems and more reading comprehension workbook questions with no loss in accuracy (Pelham, Swanson, Bender, & Wilson, 1980; Pelham, Bender, Caddell, & Booth, 1982).

Although psychostimulants often effect dramatic changes in classroom behavior, several limitations should be noted. First, improvement is apparent only while the medication exerts a pharmacological effect—3 to 10 hours, depending on the drug and dose. When the medication wears off or if the child does not take his pill, his behavior reverts to its unmedicated state immediately, even after months or years of medication. In addition, the average group improvement on teacher rating scales in most drug studies only approaches 1 *SD* above the normative mean. Despite improvement, most medicated children are not viewed as ''normal'' and continue to exhibit serious problems even after one or two years on medication (Quinn & Rapoport, 1975; Riddle & Rapoport, 1976). Only 10% of hyperactive children respond so positively to stimulants that their behavior falls in the normal range (Sleator & von Neumann, 1974). Additional interventions are thus usually needed when psychostimulants are utilized as treatments for hyperactivity.

Stimulant-related improvement in classroom behavior is a function of dose, with higher dosages related to more improved teacher rating scores (Pelham, Swanson, Bender, & Wilson, 1980; Werry & Sprague, 1974). Relatively higher doses increase the percentage of children both who respond to medication and also who demonstrate maximal improvement. As noted earlier, however, dosages necessary to maximize improvement on teacher ratings may actually impair cognitive abilities (Brown & Sleator, 1979; Sprague, & Sleator, 1977), and the trends in both research and clinical practice are to minimize dosages even though maximal improvement may thus not be reached with medication alone. Fortunately, however, relatively low psychostimulant dosages (.25 to .3 mg/kg methylphenidate) in combination with behavior modification programs can result in short-term improvement in classroom behavior as great as that shown with high dosages of medication (Pelham, Schnedler, Bologna & Contreras, 1980; Pelham, Schnedler, Miller, Ronnei, Paluchowski, Budrow, Marks, Nilsson, & Bender, 1979).

Effects on Social Interactions.   Relatively little is known about psychostimulant effects on social interaction. In one study mother-child interactions in a task setting were considerably more positive and cooperative when children received medication as opposed to placebo (Humphries, Kinsbourne, & Swanson, 1978). Barkley & Cunningham (1979) reported similar results in a task setting, also demonstrating that the child's rate of compliance increased on medication. In a free play setting, however, medicated children were only slightly more likely than unmedicated children to comply with maternal requests, and they were more likely to play independently and less likely to initiate interactions with their mothers (Barkley & Cunningham, 1979). These differences were noteworthy, as they indicated that medication moved hyperactive children *away* from normative means on initiation and independent play (Cunningham & Barkley, 1979), suggesting that, although interactions are improved in task situations, hyperactive children may become less sociable on medication in less structured settings.

Whalen, Henker, Collins, McAuliffe, and Vaux (1979) studied hyperactive children engaged in a highly interesting "Space Flight" game with a peer in which a child took one of two roles: Mission control, in which he provided instructions to another child regarding how to complete a block design puzzle; and Astronaut, in which he received instructions from Mission Control and completed the puzzle. Methylphenidate had no effect on the communicative efficiency or task completion measures in the study. Although medication reduced the intensity of hyperactive children's communication during the task, the change was in the direction of normal children's communicative intensity.

In a study of hyperactive children's interactions with nonhyperactive peers in playgroup settings without an adult present, methylphenidate (.3 mg/kg and .6 mg/kg) was found to exert no effect either on the nature of hyperactive children's observed interactions with peers or on peers' ratings on a sociogram, both of which were largely negative (Pelham & Bender, 1982). Although teachers have rated the peer interactions of many medicated children as improved (Gadow, 1981), both teachers and peers have been reported to view hyperactive children as dysfunctional in this domain after 4 months to 2 years on medication (Pelham et al., 1979; Riddle & Rapoport, 1976).

Finally, hyperactive children receiving different doses of pemoline were observed during school recesses, and positive and negative peer interactions were coded, as were intervals during which the children were not interacting with anyone. Although averaged group results revealed no effect of medication on these observational categories (Pelham, Swanson, Bender, & Wilson, 1980), when the data were reanalyzed with initial level of negative interaction as a grouping variable, the high negative interaction children were found to exhibit a drug-related decrease in negative interactions, an increase in positive interactions, and no consistent effect on no interaction codings (see Fig. 8.1). In contrast, the low negative interaction children showed no change in negative interaction codings, a decrease in positive interaction codings and an increase in no interaction codings. Drug effects on these measures thus depended on subject characteristics similar to Loney's Aggressive/Hyperactive dichotomy (described earlier). The aggressive hyperactive children's playground behavior apparently improved with medication, while that of the nonaggressive children became more withdrawn, an adverse reaction similar to but stronger than that noted during free play in the mother-child interaction studies. Notably, teacher ratings on the ACRS showed equivalent and large dose-related improvements for *both* groups of children, providing support for the argument that teachers may not be sensitive to certain types of adverse drug effects in medicated children.

On the whole, these studies suggest that psychostimulants have relatively

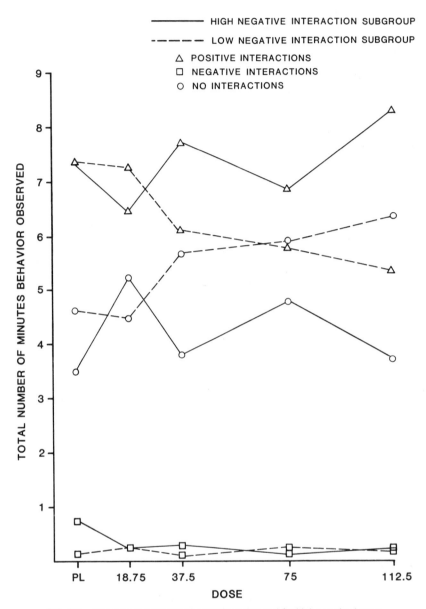

FIG. 8.1. Minutes of playground interactions observed for high negative interaction and low negative interaction subgroups of hyperactive children, plotted by dose of pemoline.

weaker effects on measures of social interaction than on measures of classroom performance and laboratory tasks. The medication-induced social withdrawal reported in several studies is alarming, and needs to be further investigated. The potentially beneficial effect on aggressive behavior is interesting in light of the widespread clinical belief that aggression is a negative sign for drug response in hyperactive children. Studies which examine the interactions between type of drug, dose, subject characteristics, and setting are needed to provide a clearer understanding of psychostimulant effects on social interactions.

Long-term Effects.   No study has reported that long-term use of psychostimulant medication improves the expected prognosis of hyperactive children in adolescence, and it is now widely accepted that long-term use of psychostimulant medication alone will not cure hyperactivity (Riddle & Rapoport, 1976; Weiss & Hechtman, 1979; Weiss, Kruger, Danielson, & Elman, 1975). There is much debate regarding the explanation for medication's failure to improve prognosis. If learning ability and peer relations are important mediators of outcome, the lack of unequivocal drug effects in these domains may explain the poor outcome. On the other hand, if the psychostimulants act simply by suppressing symptomatology, then long-term effects when medication is terminated would not be expected. Thus if medication were terminated when the child reached adolescence, then symptoms would no longer be suppressed. Although there is no data-based reason for terminating medication in adolescence, that is the most common practice.

Follow-up studies thus far have been limited to adolescence, and it is not known how adult outcome is affected by psychostimulant treatment. Some authors (e.g., Wender, 1978) argue that medication should not be terminated in adolescence, and that it may be necessary to administer it through adulthood in some cases (e.g., Wood, Reimherr, Wender, & Johnson, 1976). Whether adult prognosis would be improved with life-long use is an important question which warrants investigation.

Side Effects.   There are a number of treatment emergent symptoms (TES) of the psychostimulants. Irritability, tearfulness, withdrawal, anxiety, insomnia, loss of appetite, stomachaches, headaches, and psychotic episodes have been reported with varying frequencies (Cantwell & Carlson, 1978; Conners & Werry, 1979). In most children these symptoms are dose-related, though some respond adversely to any dose. Although some authors report that TES are not a problem with doses equivalent to 1.0 mg/kg methylphenidate and lower, they have often been reported at doses as low as .6 mg/kg methylphenidate (Pelham & Bender, 1982; Pelham, Schnedler, Bologna, & Contreras, 1980). TES often disappear after several days of treatment.

Although early studies showed that psychostimulant administration was correlated with a decrease in children's growth rate (Safer & Allen, 1973), this problem apparently can be avoided if a maximum dosage of 20 mg per day (methylphenidate) is established, and if the drug is not given on weekends or holidays (Conners & Werry, 1979). The upper dose limits to avoid growth reduction for dextroamphetamine and pemoline have not been established. Finally, increases in blood pressure and heart rate have been reported for some children on psychostimulants (Cantwell & Carlson, 1978), and regular checks of these cardiovascular functions while the child is in a medicated state should be made. Because a visit to the doctor's office is often impractical, these checks could be made by the school nurse. It should be emphasized that adverse effects such as the impairment of cognitive ability and playground withdrawal noted earlier cannot be detected as readily as more obvious TES and often go unnoticed. Especially careful monitoring is therefore required for those potential problems.

Assessment of Medication Effects. Gadow (1981) surveyed parents and teachers of a large sample of special education children receiving medication for behavior disorders and reported that only 59% of teachers had had *any* contact with parents regarding medication during the current school year. In 84% of these cases the contact was limited to a subjective verbal report of the child's response. In 9% of the cases, a teacher rating scale was used to evaluate medication effects. When parent-teacher contacts did occur, they were relatively infrequent, with the majority of cases having only one or two contacts over the entire school year. Only 19% of cases had had a drug-free period scheduled, and only 8% of the teachers had *ever* been contacted by the prescribing physician. With such inadequate monitoring procedures in the natural setting, it would be surprising if maximally beneficial medication effects were being obtained by many children. These findings suggest that a major role in the evaluation of the behavioral effects of medication can be played by the behavioral psychologist.

The behavioral psychologist working in a clinical setting can measure medication effects using the same procedures which have been used in recent studies of psychostimulant effects in hyperactive children (Pelham, 1977; Pelham, Schnedler, Bologna, & Contreras, 1980; Pelham, Swanson, Bender, & Wilson, 1980; Pelham, Bender, Caddell, & Booth, 1982). Behavioral assessment procedures can be used with individual cases to make determinations about initial drug and dose response and to monitor the child's ongoing response to medication. My colleagues and I have worked with local physicians, pharmacists and school personnel to develop a medication assessment procedure which meets three criteria: (1) it yields useful information in clinical settings; (2) it is reliable in individual cases; and (3) it is sufficiently practical that it can be implemented in a regular classroom setting (Pelham, Schnedler, & Bender, 1981). The procedure is still undergoing evaluation and modification, but it can be briefly described.

In conjunction with the referred child's physician, low dosages of several psychostimulants are selected if a medication trial is deemed appropriate. Using commercially available material, a local pharmacist prepares indistinguishable capsules of active medication and placebo. A random schedule is prepared in which the child's medication varies on a daily basis.[2] For 2 to 8 weeks the parents administer medication and along with the teacher monitor its effects. Parents, teachers and child are all blind to medication condition. Parents and teachers are taught behavioral observational and recording procedures (see section on "Behavior Therapy"), and the child's target behaviors are tracked daily. For example, in the classroom teachers often monitor the child's compliance ratio (the proportion of times the child complies with teacher requests), the number of times the target child bothers other children, and the number of times the child disrupts the classroom. Because this assessment is often being conducted after a behavioral intervention has been established, the teacher may already be monitoring these behaviors. In addition to direct observation and recording, which provide the best information, the teacher and parents complete the ACRS and a side effects checklist several times for each drug condition. Information is also gathered daily on the child's academic work output and accuracy. Either the child's regular classroom assignments are saved and compared by drug or dose, or the teacher is provided with a set of standardized materials that can replace regular seatwork and that can be easily compared across days.

This procedure provides physicians with quite useful information regarding children's short-term medication responses on ecologically valid measures. The interested professional should be aware of six considerations before attempting such an assessment.

1. Five to ten days of complete data per condition are necessary before stable responses can be identified.

2. The daily dose randomization is critical to rule out confounding order effects.

3. Teacher contact needs to be made on a daily or bidaily basis to insure accurate data collection, and behaviors the teacher is to track should be kept at a manageable number.

4. In order to detect changes in academic performance, the dependent measures need to be relatively standard from day to day. This can be insured by providing the teacher with standardized materials (e.g., reading workbooks, math worksheets). In addition, psychostimulant effects on academic performance appear to depend in part on whether the child is acquiring a new skill, mastering a

---

[2]It is not clear whether pemoline can be manipulated on a daily basis, as can methylphenidate and dextroamphetamine. The acute effects of a single dose can be detected within two hours, but there may be some residual effects of the drug on the day following ingestion of relatively high dosages (Pelham et al, Note 6). Manipulating dose on an every-other-day basis with placebo washout days on either side of the two pemoline days, or manipulating dose or drug on a weekly basis may be the way to proceed with pemoline until its span of action is more clearly established.

skill, or practicing a previously learned skill (Pelham, Swanson, Bender, & Wilson, 1980; Pelham, Bender, Caddell, & Booth, 1982), and measuring each of these levels often yields a complex but complete picture of drug effects.

5. We have not yet been able to develop a reliable sociogram that can be used on a daily basis to measure peer responses to medication. Where school aides are available, direct observations can be used to monitor the child's playground interactions, and a classroom sociogram should be administered prior to a medication trial and 3 or 4 months afterward if the child is placed on medication (see section on "Behavior Therapy").

6. Because teacher ratings *alone* are not sensitive measures of all aspects of medication response (Sprague & Sleator, 1977), each component included in the assessment appears necessary to yield a complete profile of drug response.

If the target child is placed on medication, the psychologist should play a role in following the child's response to medication. The same domains should be measured by having a double blind placebo trial of one week or longer every 3 or 4 months. Such checks are necessary because a substantial number of children who show an initial response to psychostimulants fail to show a positive response to the same dose upon follow-up (Sleator, von Neumann, & Sprague, 1974).

Although this assessment is complicated and time consuming, no alternative is available. There are no laboratory measures, for example, that reliably predict medication response in individuals (Barkley, 1976; Conners & Werry, 1979). The only way to evaluate a hyperactive child's classroom response to a drug is to measure that response directly. Although it is not certain that careful evaluation of short-term response to medication will improve long-term outcome of psychostimulant use, it seems likely that the best predictors of *future* adjustment in critical domains of functioning are *current* measures of adjustment in those domains. Because the pediatrician in private practice has neither the training nor the time necessary to conduct a comprehensive medication assessment, this area highlights the potential interaction between psychology and medicine. The common goal, the best treatment for the child, can be reached only through cooperative collaboration between physicians and psychologists.

Behavior Therapy

Behavior therapy or behavior modification has emerged as the treatment for hyperactivity with greatest promise as an alternative to medication. Although many early studies demonstrated that behavioral procedures substantially improved the classroom behavior of problem children (O'Leary & O'Leary, 1972, 1977), the approaches were not applied with children specifically diagnosed as hyperactive until relatively recently (Ayllon, Laymen, & Kandell, 1975). Since then a number of studies have shown that behavior modification can be an effective treatment for hyperactivity in classroom and home settings. Compared to the volume of research on psychostimulants, however, relatively little is known about behavioral interventions in hyperactivity. For example, there is only sparse information available regarding the effects of behavior modification on learning or achievement in hyperactive children, and no information exists regarding long-term effects. This discussion of the effects of behavior therapy is thus less extensive than that regarding medication effects. A relatively larger portion of the discussion is devoted to practical issues in the implementation of behavior therapy with hyperactive children (see also Pelham, 1978).

The rationale for using behavior modification with hyperactive children is the same as the rationale for its application to other problems in clinical and medical psychology. Behavior modification with hyperactive children thus draws on the principles of social learning theory to analyze the continuing reciprocal interaction between individuals, their behavior, and the environment, with the goal of first identifying the environmental and intrapersonal correlates of problem behaviors and then using contingency management procedures to manipulate those correlated events and change the behaviors (Bandura, 1969). It is interesting to note that early theorists argued that behavior modification would not be effective with hyperactive children because their defective CNS arousal mechanisms interfered with the influences of rewards and punishments (e.g., Wender, 1971). Subsequent empirical investigation has not supported this argument, but the belief that hyperactivity is not amenable to behavioral treatment is still common among physicians.

Assessment

Beyond diagnosis (discussed earlier), the primary purposes of assessment is to gather information necessary to conceptualize the child's problem in social learning terms, to implement treatment, and to evaluate the effects of treatment procedures. The first step in assessment is thus a functional analysis defining the child's hyperactivity as a set of specific cognitive and behavioral problems and identifying the variables that currently determine the nature of the problem and can be modified to produce behavioral and cognitive change. Assessment continues throughout intervention, allowing continual evaluation of response to treatment and modifications in treatment strategy. Assessment information is gathered through interviews, rating scales (previously discussed), and observations.

Interviews. A behavior therapist's interview differs from others in several ways. Much information is gathered through interviews with the parents and teachers, who are seen first, rather than with the child himself. Rather than a detailed history, emphasis is placed on a complete description of the current problems, which become the focus of treatment. The formats and goals of the interviews with parents and teachers are similar. After the problem has been described in general terms, the therapist guides the interviewee through a series of three steps:

(1) major problem areas are identified; (2) each major problem is then broken down into more specific problem behaviors; and (3) the relationships between the specific problem behaviors and their setting and consequent events are analyzed. The resulting set of material constitutes a comprehensive description of the problem at home and in school and provides the targets for intervention.

Consider the following main problem areas identified for one hyperactive child seen in a clinic: (1) task completion; (2) bedwetting; (3) following directions; (4) behavior away from home; (5) telling the truth; and (6) playing with other children. Each major problem area was broken down into more circumscribed problems. Regarding the first problem area, task completion, three subproblems were generated: (a) not getting dressed in the morning before school; (b) taking too long to walk to the school bus stop; and (c) taking too long to clean his room. Discussion of (a) and (b) revealed that a typical morning began with the child taking longer than necessary to eat breakfast before his mother then asked him to get dressed. Because he had a history of not getting dressed promptly, his mother frequently nagged him to hurry up, often growing impatient and dressing him herself. In addition, the child often took so long to walk to the school bus stop that he missed the bus and had to be driven to school by his mother. Thus one aspect of the "task completion" problem was identified along with associated environmental events that could be manipulated to affect it. During initial interviews, the same procedure is followed for each major problem area. Discussion moves from the general to the specific and to an analysis of the correlated setting and consequent events. In addition to information regarding the child's behavior, familial factors which may interfere with treatment (e.g., parental pschopathology, marital status, parents' work schedules) should be explored and evaluated.

Although most hyperactive children are initially referred for treatment by teachers, teachers are not obligated to cooperate with treatment programs. While the therapist's only concern is the referred child, the teacher is responsible for 20 to 30 other children under his or her care. The therapist should remain sensitive to the teacher's situation, be supportive of efforts to cooperate, and make the teacher's role in assessment and intervention interfere as little as possible with his or her other responsibilities. For example, teachers should not be expected to come to the clinic for interviews. Although the therapist's going out to the school marks a major departure from traditional approaches to therapy with children, where all client contact occurs within the therapist's office, a hyperactive child's problems simply cannot be treated without substantive teacher contact.

Because most hyperactive children come into contact with professionals at ages of 7 or 8 years, it is unlikely that valid information can be obtained from questioning them directly about their problems. Instead, the interviewing period should be used to obtain a sample of the child's behavior. The therapist should interact with the child in several different situations and should observe the child's behavioral and cognitive *style* as well as the *content* of his responses. The interview can begin with the child drawing pictures or playing with blocks while the therapist talks with him. To learn about peer relationships, the therapist might ask: Who did you play with at recess today? What did you do? Who are your best friends? What did you do after school yesterday? The general rule is to ask specific questions that will allow inferences to be made but will not threaten the child. Throughout the session, the therapist should watch for the specific problems identified in the teacher and parent interviews (e.g., noncompliance) and observe how they are manifested in the therapist-child interaction. Finally it should be emphasized that children are often anxious and inhibited in the clinic and may not show their usual symptoms. As Table 8.1 notes, failure to observe a serious problem in the clinic does not necessarily mean that one does not exist.

Observation.   Trained observers and elaborate coding schemes, common in research settings, are difficult to implement in clinical settings. Instead, parents and teachers are trained to observe and record children's behavior at home and at school. This information should corroborate that obtained in interviews, validating the functional analysis generated therein, and it should also serve as a baseline for comparing treatment changes. In the classroom, for example, the teachers should record the target behaviors which they and the therapists have identified in interviews (see O'Leary & O'Leary, 1977). Infrequent problems, such as fighting, should be monitored with a continuous frequency count maintained throughout the school day. High frequency problems such as "out of seat" behavior should be monitored for only a portion of the day (for 15 min. during morning seatwork activity, for example) to prevent the teacher from being overwhelmed by data collection. Problems such as non-compliance need to be monitored in conjunction with correlated stimuli such as teachers requests or commands. The exact nature of the monitoring system for any case depends on the identified target behaviors, and the structure of the classroom or home settings. The therapist must insure that the amount of observational data gathered is sufficient to portray an accurate picture of the child's functioning, generally 1 or 2 weeks of assessment, without overburdening parents and teachers and without giving measurement considerations priority over treatment.

In addition to training parents and teachers in observation, it is often helpful for the clinician initially to observe the parent-child interaction in a structured setting in the clinic (e.g., Barkley & Cunningham, 1979; Pelham, Schnedler, Bologna, & Contreras, 1980) and to observe the child in the classroom and on the playground at school.

Peer Relationships.   The presumed importance of peer relationships in hyperactivity emphasizes the need to evaluate that domain in assessment. An extensive discussion of this area is beyond the scope of this chapter and the interested reader should consult other sources (Foster & Ritchey, 1979; Hops & Greenwood, 1980; Milich & Landau, 1981). One type of sociogram which can be used in clinical practice is the simple positive and negative nomination technique in which each child in a classroom is asked (in a brief private interview) to name three classmates he or she likes and three he or she dislikes. Nomination sums can be used to determine the extent to which the target child is disliked. This instrument can be administered by the involved professional, the classroom teacher, or an aide. Other procedures provide more extensive information, but administration and scoring are quite complicated (e.g., Pekarik et al., 1976). In either case, confidentiality issues usually require that permission to administer a classroom sociogram be obtained at the school or district level. A relatively simple observational code can be used to gather data regarding hyperactive children's interactions on school playgrounds (Walker, Street, Garrett, Crossen, Hops, & Greenwood, 1978). The data reported in Fig. 8.1 were generated with this code, which was designed specifically for use by aides in public school settings and can provide reliable data with very little training. These measures of peer relationships are necessary because adults are often unaware of the specific nature of peer interaction problems.

Summary.   The importance of objective records of the child's behavior cannot be overemphasized. The correspondence between teacher and parent interview reports and actual behavior may often be low because teachers and parents are not aware of the functional relationships involved in their interactions with the target child. A therapist who successfully teaches a child's teacher and parents to monitor and record behavior makes them aware of these relationships and is on the way to a successful intervention. Manuals which are helpful in teaching these techniques are available (Madsen & Madsen, 1981; Patterson, 1976). This section has provided only an overview of a behavioral approach to assessment in treatment of hyperactivity, and the interested clinician should pursue additional reading (Evans & Nelson, 1977; O'Leary & Johnson, 1979).

Treatment

The behavior therapist's role in treatment is to teach parents and teachers to change their behavior and restructure the environment to facilitate improvement in the referred child. Before specific treatment strategies are discussed, six general points should be noted.

1. In the initial interviews it is important to emphasize to both parents and teachers that the focus of therapy will be on teaching them procedures they can use to help the child and that the responsibility for changing the child is primarily theirs. A therapist's first job is to convince parents and teachers that they can help the child and to motivate them to try. If commitment on the part of parent and teacher is absent, these potentially powerful change strategies will not work.

2. Changing the behavior of a hyperactive child is a long and arduous pro-

cess, and it is imperative that parents become sufficiently proficient that they can continue treatment long after clinic contact has ended.

3. It often needs to be made clear to parents and teachers that behavior therapy can be used to treat hyperactivity regardless of the etiology of the problem, that is even if hyperactivity is caused by a central processing dysfunction.

4. Before treatment begins the child should be made aware of the need for treatment, its purpose, and its nature.

5. Because behavior therapy involves highly individualized treatment programs that depend on each referred child's problems and response to specific procedures, the present discussion should not be considered a list of necessary or sufficient components of treatment.

6. The treatment procedures described have been used primarily with hyperactive children of elementary school age. Treatment for older hyperactive children has not been studied, but it could be similar to that used with rebellious adolescents, including contracting, negotiation, and parent-child communication training (see O'Leary & Wilson, 1975).

Parent and Teacher Training.   Treatment begins with the parents and teacher reading about social learning approaches to treatment of child behavior problems (e.g., Madsen & Madsen, 1981; Patterson, 1976) and discussing the readings with the therapist. After initial assessment and in series of 8 to 12 weekly sessions held separately with parents at the clinic and with the teacher at school, the therapist works with them to develop detailed programs designed to modify the target behaviors. The general procedures employed include: (1) praise and social reinforcement for appropriate behavior, and ignoring for minor inappropriate behaviors; (2) environmental restructuring (Premack contingencies); (3) token reinforcement; and (4) time out from positive reinforcement (brief isolation).

For example, for children who take too long to get dressed in the morning, a program can be instituted which makes breakfast contingent upon being dressed and having morning chores completed. For aggressive and severe noncompliant behavior at school, a multi-level time-out program can be established in which the child is punished with brief (5 to 10 min.) periods of isolation for initial transgressions and with longer periods (e.g., being sent home from school) for serious or repeated offenses. Token reinforcement programs can be established in which the child earns or loses points for engaging in appropriate behavior or avoiding the commission of a prohibited behavior. Points at school can be earned for completing academic work or getting along well with other children, for example. With hyperactive children it is usually necessary to have the points exchangeable both for consequences delivered immediately after the appropriate behavior (e.g., free time as soon as work is completed), as well as for privileges delivered at home upon parental receipt of a positive Daily Report Card (O'Leary, Pelham, Rosenbaum, & Price, 1976). Each of the goals set for a child should be carefully shaped. It is unreasonable to expect a hyperactive child who completes none of his academic assignments to complete all of them during the first week of treatment. A 25% completion rate might be acceptable initially, to be increased gradually as the child's on-task behavior improves (O'Leary & Pelham, 1978).

Implementation of behavior modification programs with hyperactive children especially in the classroom setting is quite involved. School visits may need to be twice-weekly initially, with frequent telephone contact with the teacher while the program is being developed. Once the intervention is going well, weekly contact may suffice. This description provides only a brief overview of behavioral treatment, and more extensive sources should be consulted before an intervention is attempted (e.g., O'Leary & O'Leary, 1977; Ross, 1981).

Child Training.   Rather than focusing entirely on parent and teacher training, recent approaches have employed self-control training and social skills training. Self-control training is designed to teach the children to give themselves verbal instructions to slow down, evaluate their behavior and act planfully in academic or social situations (e.g., Camp, 1980; Douglas, Parry, & Marton, 1976). Unfortunately, in spite of the hope initially raised by these cognitive behavioral procedures, they have not resulted in clinically significant behavior change in the natural environment (Friedling & O'Leary, 1979; Hobbs, Moguin, Lea, Tyroler, & Lahey, 1980). While such interventions, which place much of the responsibility for implementation on the target child, may benefit children with relatively mild disturbances, they are unlikely to prove effective with hyperactive children. Hyperactive children are often not motivated to change their behavior, and their impulsivity and inattention are incompatible with the self-generated procedures involved in self-control programs.

Similarly, social skills training programs that rely on modeling, role playing, practice, and didactic instruction (Oden & Asher, 1977), have been shown to be ineffective with hyperactive children (Pelham & Bender, 1982). There is preliminary indication that an intensive social skills training program that includes extensive group practice and reinforcement for appropriate behavior might be a useful *adjunct* to a standard parent and teacher training program (Pelham et al., 1979), but additional research is needed before this time-consuming and expensive treatment can be recommended. There is no corresponding evidence that self-control training has incremental value for a standard behavioral intervention (Friedling & O'Leary, 1979; Pelham, Schnedler, Bologna, & Contreras, 1980).

Effects of Behavioral Interventions

Although research in the area is not abundant, behavior therapy appears to be an effective treatment for hyperactive children. The form of behavior therapy that has been used in most research endeavors is very similar to that offered in clinical settings (described earlier). Such interventions have been shown to result in improvement on a number of dimensions. In the classroom it has been shown: (a) that some hyperactive children treated with behavior therapy show the same degree of improvement on standard teacher rating scales as children on low to moderate dosages of medication (Pelham, 1977; O'Leary & Pelham, 1978); (b) that they improve more on these measures than untreated controls (O'Leary et al., 1976; Pelham et al., 1979); (c) that hyperactives' observed on-task behavior increases with behavioral intervention as much as with medication (Ayllon et al., 1975; O'Leary & Pelham, 1978); (d) that a behavioral intervention results in a significant decrease in negative nominations on a classroom peer nomination inventory (Pelham et al., 1979); and (e) that a behavioral intervention increases academic output (Ayllon et al., 1975; Rapport, Murphy, & Bailey, 1980). Regarding parent training, it has been shown: (a) that parents rate their children as improved following behavioral intervention (Dubey & Kaufman, 1979; Pelham et al., 1979); (b) that observed parent-child interactions improve with behavioral intervention (Pelham, Schnedler, Bologna, & Contreras, 1980); and (c) that trained parents are more able to effect an increase in their child's academic output than before training (Pelham, Schnedler, Bologna, & Contreras, 1980).

Although a variety of positive effects of behavior therapy with hyperactives have been demonstrated both at home and at school, as is the case with medication, it has become apparent that the interventions are beneficial but not sufficient to bring hyperactive behavior into the normal range. For example, in most of the studies previously noted the average posttreatment ACRS score was 1 *SD* above normative means. In addition, in the two studies which used the measure, the average number of sociometric negative nominations were between 1 and 2 *SD*'s above the mean even after behavioral intervention (Pelham, Schnedler, Bologna, & Contreras, 1980; Pelham et al., 1979). The only studies which showed that behavioral interventions were both effective and sufficient examined only limited aspects of the child's behavior for short periods of the day (Ayllon et al., 1975; Rapport, Murphy, & Bailey, in press). For example, although a behavioral program in one study kept a child on-task for as much of his seatwork time as a "good" comparison child, the teacher nonetheless rated his behavior over the entire school day as extremely problematic—16 on the ACRS (Pelham, Schnedler, Bologna, & Contreras, 1980).

Enhancing the Effects of Behavioral Interventions

The importance of socio-environmental variables and peer relationships in prognosis clearly indicate that behavioral interventions which impact on these areas should be necessary components of treatment. The important question is what can be done to enhance the effects of behavioral interventions?

In the past decade the trend in behavioral interventions has been away from a tightly controlled, laboratory approach to the control of behavior and toward a more loosely structured, clinical approach to therapy. The major impetus for this thrust has been the desire to increase the practicality of behavioral interventions so that they could be more easily implemented in clinical settings. In the classroom setting, for example, highly structured token programs in which children were constantly monitored and behavior was immediately consequated were very effective but difficult to implement without considerable help for the teacher (see O'Leary & O'Leary, 1972, for examples). The clinical approach that evolved required less constant monitoring, consequences delivered at home for school behavior, and natural consequences that were often less motivating than those used in early studies. These programs could be implemented easily by an individual teacher with a problem child, but what they gained in ease of implementation, they lost in effectiveness (e.g., Kent & O'Leary, 1976).

This clinical approach to behavior therapy has characterized most research with hyperactive children. The programs or components of programs that have demonstrated the strongest effects have been those that maintained the tightly structured control characteristic of early behavior modification studies (e.g., Ayllon et al., 1975; Rapport, Murphy, & Bailey, 1980). Elsewhere I have offered several suggestions for the types of behavioral interventions that may prove maximally effective for hyperactivity (Pelham & Bender, 1982). In general, a return to the highly structured procedures used in early studies appears necessary to maximize the effectiveness of behavioral interventions with hyperactive children.

Regarding peer interactions, effective treatments await increased knowledge of peer relationships in normal and hyperactive children (Furman, 1980; Milich & Landau, 1982). Most current social-skills training programs have relied on a shotgun approach, focusing on cognitions and behaviors presumed but not proven to be important components of childhood social adjustment (e.g., Pelham et al., 1979). Until we know more about peer relationships, a more reasonable approach might be to focus on decreasing negative peer interactions by using the same intensive treatments that have been employed with conduct disordered children (e.g., Patterson, 1974). In addition, a fruitful area for investigation in the classroom is the use of group contingencies, in which the classmates of a target child earn or lose consequences contingent upon the target child's behavior. There is some indication that such contingencies may both reduce disruptive behavior and enhance peer relationships (Hayes, 1976; Patterson, 1965).

From an experimental design perspective, studies of behavioral interventions have not made use of the subgroup analyses that have been employed with important results in pharmacological research. Just as there may be hyperactive children who respond positively to medication and others who do not, there may be hyperactive subgroups that are more or less responsive to behavioral interventions. For example, O'Leary & Pelham (1978) reported that their behavioral intervention appeared to be more effective for those hyperactive children with social problems rather than attention deficits. Similarly, Firestone (1980) reported that certain parental characteristics were associated with successful completion of a parent training program. The investigation of such variables might result in a less prevalent but more effective application of behavioral interventions.

Finally, most investigations of behavior therapy with hyperactive children have been of relative brief duration, 8 to 16 weeks, and the target children are often back in the clinic or on medication the year following such a brief intervention. At least during the first months a behavioral intervention is no different from medication in the sense that it serves to suppress symptomatology rather than to cure the disorder. When the intervention is removed, the behavior often reverts to baseline. Behavioral interventions need to be continued with a hyperactive child for a number of years before maximal improvement is reached. It should be noted that belief in the necessity of a long-term and intensive intervention for hyperactive children is shared by therapists from a nonbehavioral perspective (Satterfield, Cantwell, & Satterfield, 1979; Satterfield, Satterfield, & Cantwell, 1981). The refractoriness and poor prognosis of hyperactivity appear to warrant such a long-term intervention.

Multimodality Treatment

Although it has long been recommended, only recently has the combination of pharmacological and behavioral interventions been studied. Two children I have studied were maintained on medication as behavior therapy was implemented, and both showed positive clinical responses to the combination treatment, though they were eventually withdrawn from medication (O'Leary & Pelham, 1978; Pelham, 1977). These cases suggested that the most effective short-term treatment for hyperactivity might be the combination of these two complementary interventions. Such a combination would in many ways be the ideal treatment. A low dose of medication might enhance the treated child's cognitive abilities, while a behavioral program could be established to modify the disruptive behavior which would be relatively unaffected by that dose (Sprague & Sleator, 1977). Alternatively, medication might make a child who might otherwise have been placed in a special class sufficiently controllable that his regular classroom teacher could implement a behavioral program.

Pelham, Schnedler, Bologna, & Contreras (1980) treated eight children and examined the incremental value of methylphenidate by giving medication probes before behavioral intervention began, after it had been in effect for three weeks and after it had been in effect for 13 weeks. Low and high doses of methylphenidate (.25 mg/kg and .75 mg/kg) and placebo were given under blind conditions during the 3-week probe periods. Results revealed that both medication before behavioral intervention and the behavioral intervention itself were effective in improving teacher ratings and on-task behavior. However, maximum improvement on all measures was reached *only* during the final medication probe when the low or high dose was given. In other words, the greatest short-term improvement in behavior was shown when the children were receiving medication after a behavioral intervention had been in effect for 13 weeks. For some of the children the combination of the low dose and behavior therapy resulted in maximum improvement, while for others the higher dose was necessary. Of particular note was an apparent interaction between dosage and behavioral treatment. Before behavioral intervention, the high dose of methylphenidate produced higher on-task behavior than the low dose, but after behavioral intervention, the two doses had equivalent effects. The behavioral intervention apparently enhanced the effectiveness of the low dose of methylphenidate.

A second study (Pelham et al., 1979) addressed the question of whether children receiving a low dose of methylphenidate (.3 mg/kg b.i.d.) for the duration of a behavioral intervention would show increased improvement. Twenty-two hyperactive children received a standard behavioral intervention focusing on parent and teacher training for 4 months. Eleven children concurrently received active medication and eleven received placebo. Dependent measures taken pre- and posttreatment (off medication) included parent and teacher ratings, classroom sociograms, and classroom observations. Results revealed that children improved significantly and substantially on all measures relative to no-treatment and contrast treatment groups, but those in the medication group failed to show any greater improvement than children in the placebo group. Blind teacher ratings on the ACRS were also obtained at midtreatment (on medication—either methylphenidate or placebo) as well as at pre- and posttreatment (off medication). As Figure 8.2 shows, the results from pre-to midtreatment revealed that .3 mg/kg medication clearly added to improvement shown with a behavioral intervention, but the posttreatment results showed that the beneficial effects of medication ended when the medication did.

These results suggest that medication's effect was not to facilitate the acquisition of information being taught in the behavioral programs, an effect which might be expected to maintain after medication was terminated. Rather, the medication exerted a main effect which disappeared when medication was discontinued. Thus one hoped-for outcome of the combination studies, that medication would improve the outcome of therapy, was not apparent. At the same time, however, this study replicated its predecessor in demonstrating that the combination of a low dose of methylphenidate and a behavioral intervention was a very effective short-term intervention.

In contrast to these results, another study showed that a combination treatment was not significantly superior to a medication alone condition, and both of these interventions were more effective than behavior therapy alone (Gittelman-Klein et al., 1976; 1980). These authors concluded that behavioral interventions offer little incremental value to pharmacological treatments. One major difference between the results of these studies and ours is a function of the medication

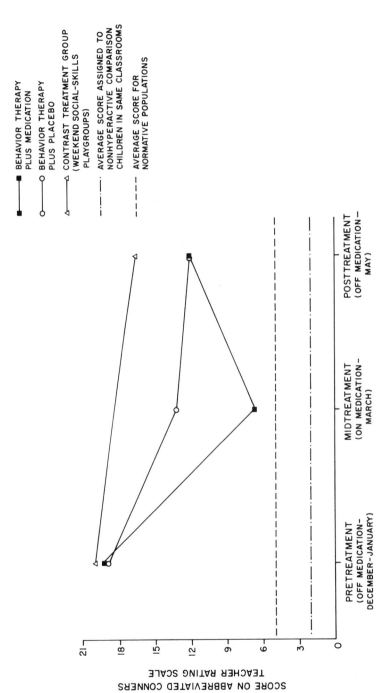

FIG. 8.2. Pretreatment, midtreatment, and posttreatment teacher ratings on the Abbreviated Conners Rating Scale for three groups of hyperactive children followed in a treatment study.

dosage employed. Pelham et al. (1979) used a mean total daily dose (.3 mg/kg ×
2) of 17 mg methylphenidate (range 12.5 mg to 20 mg), while Gittelman-Klein et
al. (1976, 1980) employed an individually titrated mean daily dose of 38.2 mg
methylphenidate (range 10 mg to 60 mg). Although behavior therapy apparently
does not enhance effects of those high doses of methylphenidate, the reasons to
avoid such dosages of and sole reliance on psychostimulants are numerous.
These results, while no doubt replicable, are thus not particularly helpful for
practitioners.

Summary

Although it has been used that way for many years, it is clear that there is no
justification for the use of psychostimulant medication as the sole treatment for
hyperactivity. There is some indication that pharmacotherapy may have potentially beneficial effects with hyperactive children if careful individual assessments are conducted and if attention is paid to dose effects, response domains, and subject characteristics, but additional research is necessary. Behavior
therapy has been shown to be a beneficial short-term treatment for hyperactive
children, but additional research is necessary to develop *maximally effective*
short-term behavioral interventions, especially which impact on the domain of
peer relationships, and to address the question of long-term effectiveness.

The most effective short-term treatment for the average hyperactive child
appears to be the combination of a low dose of a psychostimulant and a behavioral intervention. However, some children may not respond to medication,
and less severely disturbed children and those with exceptionally dedicated parents and teachers may not need it. In our clinic, medication is added to a
behavioral intervention only if maximal improvement with the behavioral program alone is not reached *and* if a medication assessment provides evidence for a
short-term incremental benefit. Each child's treatment is thus individually tailored, and unnecessary medication is avoided. Additional research on the combination approach to treatment is needed. The development of more powerful
behavioral interventions might render medication unnecessary for a large number
of children. Alternatively, psychostimulants other than methylphenidate may
yield even better combined effects (cf. Conners & Taylor, 1980). Whether this
combination approach to treatment will result in a more positive long-term prognosis for hyperactive children is a critical question that remains unanswered.

REFERENCES

Abikoff, H., Gittelman-Klein, R., & Klein, D. F. Validation of a classroom observational code for
    hyperactive children. *Journal of Consulting and Clinical Psychology*, 1977, *45*, 772–783.
Achenbach, T. M. The Child Behavior Profile: I. Boys aged 6–11. *Journal of Consulting and
    Clinical Psychology*, 1978, *46*, 478–488.

Achenbach, T. M., & Edelbrock, C. S. The classification of child psychopathology: A review and analysis of empirical efforts. *Psychological Bulletin,* 1978, *85,* 1275-1301.

Achenbach, T. M., & Edelbrock, C. S. The Child Behavior Profile: II. Boys aged 12-16 and girls aged 6-11 and 12-16. *Journal of Consulting and Clinical Psychology,* 1979, *46,* 223-233.

Ahn, H., Prichep, L., John, E., Baird, H., Trepetin, M., & Kaye, H. Developmental equations reflect brain dysfunctions. *Science,* 1980, *210,* 1259-1262.

American Psychiatric Association. *Diagnostic and statistical manual of mental disorders* (2nd Edition). Washington, D.C.: 1968.

American Psychiatric Association. *Diagnostic and statistical manual of mental disorders* (3rd Edition). Washington, D.C.: 1980.

Augustine, G. J., & Levitan, H. Neurotransmitter release from a vertebrate neuromuscular synapse affected by a food dye. *Science,* 1980, *207,* 1489-1490.

Ayllon, T., Laymen, D., & Kandell, H. A behavioral-educational alternative to drug control of hyperactive children. *Journal of Applied Behavior Analysis,* 1975, *8,* 179-188.

Bandura, A. *Principles of behavior modification.* New York: Holt, Rinehart & Winston, 1969.

Barkley, R. Predicting the response of hyperactive children to stimulant drugs. *Journal of Abnormal Child Psychology,* 1976, *4,* 327-348.

Barkley, R. A., & Cunningham, C. E. The effects of methylphenidate on the mother-child interactions of hyperactive children. *Archives of General Psychiatry,* 1979, *36,* 201-208.

Barkley, R., & Jackson, T. Hyperkinesis, autonomic nervous system activity, and stimulant drug effects. *Journal of Child Psychology and Psychiatry,* 1977, *18,* 247-257.

Barkley, R. A., & Ullman, D. G. A comparison of objective measures of activity and distractibility in hyperactive and nonhyperactive children. *Journal of Abnormal Child Psychology,* 1975, *3,* 213-244.

Bentler, P. M. & McClain, J. A multitrait-multimethod analysis of reflection-impulsivity. *Child Development,* 1976, *47,* 218-226.

Blouin, A., Bornstein, R., & Trites, R. Teenage-alcohol use among hyperactive children: A 5-year follow-up study. *Journal of Pediatric Society,* 1978, *3,* 188-194.

Borland, B., & Heckman, K. Hyperactive boys and their brothers: A follow-up study. *Archives of General Psychiatry,* 1976, *33,* 669-675.

Bosco, J., & Robin, S. Hyperkinesis: Prevalence and treatment. In C. Whalen & B. Henker (Eds.), *Hyperactive children: The social ecology of identification and treatment.* New York: Academic Press, 1980.

Brown, R., & Sleator, E. Methylphenidate in hyperactive children: Differences in dose effects on impulsive behavior. *Pediatrics,* 1979, *64,* 408-410.

Buchsbaum, M., & Wender, P. Average evoked responses in normal and minimally brain dysfunctioned children treated with amphetamine: A preliminary report. *Archives of General Psychiatry,* 1973, 764-770.

Camp, B. Two psychoeducational treatment programs for young aggressive boys. In C. Whalen & B. Henker (Eds.), *Hyperactive children: The social ecology of identification and treatment.* New York: Academic Press, 1980.

Campbell, D. T., & Fiske, D. W. Convergent and discriminant validation by the multitrait-meltimethod matrix. *Psychological Bulletin,* 1959, *56,* 81-105.

Campbell, S. Mother-child interaction: A comparison of hyperactive, learning-disabled, and normal boys. *American Journal of Orthopsychiatry,* 1975, *45,* 51-57.

Campbell, S. B., Douglas, V. I., & Morgenstern, G. Cognitive styles in hyperactive children and the effect of methylphenidate. *Journal of Child Psychology and Psychiatry,* 1971, *12,* 55-67.

Campbell, S., & Paulauskas, S. Peer relations in hyperactive children. *Journal of Child Psychology and Psychiatry,* 1979, *20,* 233-246.

Cantwell, D. Psychiatric illness in the families of hyperactive children. *Archives of General Psychiatry,* 1972, *27,* 414-417.

Cantwell, D. P. Familial-genetic research with hyperactive children. In D. P. Cantwell (Ed.), *The hyperactive child: Diagnosis, management, current research,* Hollywood, NY: Spectrum, 1975.

Cantwell, D. P., & Carlson, G. Stimulants. In J. S. Werry (Ed.) *Pediatric psychopharmacology.* New York: Brunner/Mazel, 1978.

Cohen, N. J., & Douglas, V. I. Characteristics of the orienting response in hyperactive and normal children. *Psychophysiology,* 1972, *9,* 238–245.

Cohen, N., Douglas, V., & Morgenstern, G. The effect of methylphenidate in attentive behavior and autonomic activity in hyperactive children. *Psychopharmacologia,* 1971, *22,* 282–294.

Cohen, N., Weiss, G., & Minde, K. Cognitive styles in adolescents previously diagnosed as hyperactive. *Journal of Child Psychology and Psychiatry,* 1972, *13,* 203–209.

Conners, C. A rating scale for use in drug studies with children. *American Journal of Psychiatry,* 1969, 884–888.

Conners, C. K. Learning disabilities and stimulant drugs in children: Theoretical implications. In R. Knights & D. Bakker (Eds.), *The Neuropsychology of learning disorders.* Baltimore: University Park, 1976.

Conners, C. K., Goyette, C., Southwick, D., Less, J., & Andrulonis, P. Food additives and hyperkinesis: A controlled, double-blind experiment. *Pediatrics,* 1976, *58,* 154–166.

Conners, C. K., & Taylor, E. Pemoline, methylphenidate, and placebo in children with minimal brain dysfunction. *Archives of General Psychiatry,* 1980, 922–932.

Conners, C. K., & Werry, J. S. Psychopharmacology. In H. Quay & J. Werry (Eds.) *Psychopathological disorders of childhood,* (2nd Edition). New York: Wiley, 1979.

Cowen, E., Pederson, A., Babigian, H., Izzo, L., & Trost, M. Long-term follow-up of early detected vulnerable children. *Journal of Consulting and Clinical Psychology,* 1973, *41,* 438–446.

Cunningham, C., & Barkley, R. The interactions of normal and hyperactive children with their mothers in free play and structured tasks. *Child Development,* 1979, *50,* 217–224.

Denton, C., & McIntyre, C. Span of apprehension in hyperactive boys. *Journal of Abnormal Child Psychology,* 1978, *6,* 19–24.

Donchin, E., Ritter, W., & McCallum, W. Cognitive psychophysiology: The endogenous components of the ERP. In E. Callaway, P. Tueting, & S. Koslow (Eds.), *Event-related brain potentials in man.* New York: Academic Press, 1978.

Douglas, V. I. Stop, look and listen: The problem of sustained attention and impulse control in hyperactive and normal children. *Canadian Journal of the Behavioral Sciences,* 1972, *4,* 259–282.

Douglas, V., Parry, P., & Marton, P. Assessment of a cognitive training program for hyperactive children. *Journal of Abnormal Child Psychology,* 1976, *4,* 389–410.

Douglas, V., & Peters, K. Toward a clearer definition of the attentional deficits of hyperactive children. In G. Hale & M. Lewis (Eds.), *Attention and the development of cognitive skills.* New York: Plenum, 1979.

Dubey, D. R. Organic factors in hyperkinesis: A critical evaluation. *American Journal of Orthopsychiatry,* 1976, *46,* 353–366.

Dubey, B., & Kaufman, K. Training parents of hyperactive children in behavior management. *International Journal of Mental Health,* 1979, *8,* 110–120.

Dykman, R., & Ackerman, P. Long-term follow-up studies of hyperactive children. *Advances in Behavioral Pediatrics,* 1980, *1,* 97–128.

Evans, I., & Nelson, R. Assessment of child behavior problem. In A. Ciminero, K. Calhoun, & H. Adams (Eds.), *Handbook of behavioral assessment.* New York: Wiley, 1977.

Feingold, B. F. *Why your child is hyperactive.* New York: Random, 1975.

Feldman, S., Denhoff, E., & Denhoff, J. The attention disorders and related syndromes: Outcome in adolescence and young adult life. In E. Denhoff & L. Stern (Eds.), *Minimal brain dysfunction.* New York: Masson, 1979.

Ferguson, B., & Pappas, B. Evaluation of physiological, neurochemical and animal models of hyperactivity. In R. Trites (Ed.), *Hyperactivity in children*. Baltimore: University Park Press, 1979.

Ferguson, H. G., Simpson, S., & Trites, R. L. Psychophysiological study of methylphenidate responders and nonresponders. In R. Knight's & D. Bakker (Eds.), *Neuropsychology of learning disorders*. Baltimore: University Park Press, 1976.

Firestone, P. Characteristics of adherents and nonadherents to behavioral and pharmacological interventions. In S. Campbell (Chair), *Treatment outcome studies with hyperactive children from a developmental perspective*. Symposium presented at the annual meeting of the American Psychological Association, Montreal, September 1980.

Firestone, P., & Douglas, V. The effects of reward and punishment on reaction times and autonomic activity in hyperactive and normal children. *Journal of Abnormal Child Psychology*, 1975, *3*, 201–216.

Firestone, P., & Martin, J. An analysis of the hyperactive syndrome: A comparison of hyperactive, behavior problem, asthmatic and normal children. *Journal of Abnormal Child Psychology*, 1979, *1*, 261–274.

Foster, S., & Ritchey, W. Issues in the assessment of social competence in children. *Journal of Applied Behavior Analysis*, 1979, *12*, 625–638.

Friedling, C., & O'Leary, S. Effects of self-instructional training on second- and third-grade hyperactive children: A failure to replicate. *Journal of Applied Behavior Analysis*, 1979, *12*, 211–219.

Furman, W. Promoting social development: Developmental implications for treatment. In B. Lahey & A. Kazdin (Eds.), *Advances in clinical child psychology*, (Vol. 3). New York: Plenum, 1980.

Gadow, K. Drug therapy for hyperactivity: treatment procedures in natural settings. In K. Gadow & J. Loney (Eds.) *Psychosocial aspects of drug treatment for hyperactivity*, Boulder, Colorado: Westview Press, 1981.

Gittleman-Klein, R., Klein, D. F., Abikoff, H., Katz, S., Gloisten, A. W., & Kates, W. Relative efficacy of methylphenidate and behavior modification in hyperactive children: An interim report. *Journal of Abnormal Child Psychology*, 1976, *4*, 461–472.

Gittleman-Klein, R., Abikoff, H., Pollack, E., Klein, D., Katz, S., & Mattes, J. A controlled trial of behavior modification and methylphenidate in hyperactive children. In C. Whalen & B. Henker (Eds.), *Hyperactive children: the social ecology of identification and treatment*. New York: Academic Press, 1980.

Goyette, C. H., Conners, C. K., & Ulrich, R. F. Normative data on revised Conners parent and teacher rating scales. *Journal of Abnormal Child Psychology*, 1978, *6*, 221–236.

Green, K., Beck, S., Forehand, R., & Vosk, B. Validity of teacher nominations of child behavior problems. *Journal of Abnormal Child Psychology*, 1980, *8*, 397–404.

Hall, R. A., Griffin, R. B., Moyer, D. L., Hopkins, K. H., & Rapoport, M. Evoked potential, stimulus intensity and drug treatment in hyperkinesis. *Psychophysiology*, 1976, *13*, 405–418.

Hallahan, D. P. Distractibility in the learning-disabled child. In W. M. Cruickshank & D. P. Hallahan (Eds.), *Perceptual and learning disabilities in children*, (Vol. 2). *Research and theory*. Syracuse, New York: Syracuse University Press, 1975.

Hallahan, D. P., & Kauffman, J. M. *Introduction to Learning Disabilities: A Psycho-behavioral Approach*. Englewood Cliffs, New Jersey: Prentice-Hall, 1976.

Halverson, C. F., & Victor, J. B. Minor physical anomalies and problem behavior in elementary school children. *Child Development*, 1976, *47*, 281–285.

Harley, J. P., Matthews, C. G., & Eichman, P. Synthetic food colors and hyperactivity in children: A double-blind challenge experiment. *Pediatrics*, 1978, *61*, 975–983.

Harley, J. P., Ray, R. S., Tomasi, L., Eichman, P. L., Matthews, C. G., Chun R., Cleeland, C. S., & Traisman, E. Hyperkinesis and food additives: Testing the Feingold hypothesis. *Pediatrics*, 1978, *61*, 818–828.

Hartup, W. Peer interaction and social organization. In P. Mussen (Ed.), *Carmichael's Manual of Child Psychology*, (Vol. 2). New York: Wiley, 1970.

Hastings, J. E., & Barkley, R. A. A review of psychophysiological research with hyperactive children. *Journal of Abnormal Child Psychology*, 1978, *6*, 413-448.

Hayes, L. The use of group contingencies for behavioral control. *Psychological Bulletin*, 1976, *83*, 628-648.

Hillyard, S., Picton, T., & Regan, D. Sensation, perception and attention: Analysis using ERPs. In E. Callaway, P. Tueting, & S. Koslow (Eds.), *Event-related potentials in man*. New York: Academic Press, 1978.

Hobbs, S. A., Moguin, L. E., Tyroler, M., & Lahey, B. B. Cognitive behavior therapy with children: Has clinical utility been demonstrated? *Psychological Bulletin*, 1980, *87*, 147-165.

Hops, H., & Greenwood, C. Social skills deficits. In E. Mash & L. Terdal (Eds.), *Behavioral assessment of childhood disorders*. New York: Guilford, 1980.

Huessy, H., & Cohen, A. Hyperkinetic behaviors and learning disabilities followed over seven years. *Pediatrins*, 1976, *54*, 4-10.

Huessy, M., Metoyer, M., & Townsend, M. Eight-ten year follow-up of 84 children treated for behavioral disorder in rural Vermont. *Acta Paedopsychiatrica*, 1974, *40*, 230-235.

Humphries, T., Kinsbourne, M., & Swanson, J. Stimulant effects on cooperation and social interactions between hyperactive children and their mothers. *Journal of Child Psychology and Psychiatry*, 1978, *19*, 13-22.

Jacob, R., O'Leary, K., & Rosenblad, C. Formal and informal classroom settings: Effects on hyperactivity. *Journal of Abnormal Child Psychology*, 1978, *6*, 47-59.

Kagan, J. Reflection-impulsivity: The generality and dynamics of conceptual tempo. *Journal of Abnormal Psychology*, 1966, *71*, 17-24.

Kendall, P., & Wilcox, L. Self-control in children: Development of a rating scale. *Journal of Consulting and Clinical Psychology*, 1979, *47*, 1020-1027.

Kent, R., & O'Leary, K. D. A controlled evaluation of behavior modification with conduct problem children. *Journal of Consulting and Clinical Psychology*, 1976, *44*, 586-596.

Klein, A., & Young, R. Hyperactive boys in their classroom: Assessment of teacher and peer perceptions, interactions and classroom behavior. *Journal of Abnormal Child Psychology*, 1979, *7*, 425-442.

Klorman, R., Thompson, L.,,Ellingson, R. Event-related brain potentials across the life span. In E. Callaway, P. Tueting, & S. Koslow (Eds.), *Event-related potentials in man*. New York: Academic Press, 1978.

Knobloch, H., & Pasamanick, B. Prospective studies on the epidemiology of reproductive casualty: Methods, findings and some implications. *Merrill-Palmer Quarterly*, 1966, *12*, 27-43.

Krager, J., & Safer, D. Type and prevalence of medication used in the treatment of hyperactive children. *New England Journal of Medicine*, 1974, *291*, 1118-1120.

Kramer, J., & Loney, J. Childhood hyperactivity and substance abuse: A review of the literature. In K. Gadow & I. Bialer (Eds.), *Advances in learning and behavioral disabilities* (Vol. 1). Greenwich, CT: JAI Press, 1981.

Kupietz, S., & Richardson, E. Children's vigilance performance and inattentiveness in the classroom. *Journal of Child Psychology and Psychiatry*, 1978, *19*, 145-154.

Lafferman, J., & Silbergeld, E. Erythrosin B inhibits dopamine transport in rat caudate synaptosomes. *Science*, 1979, *205*, 408-410.

Lahey, B. B., Stempniak, M., Robinson, E. J., & Tyroler, M. Hyperactivity and learning disabilities as independent dimensions of child behavior problems. *Journal of Abnormal Psychology*, 1978, *87*, 333-340.

Lambert, N., & Sandoval, J. The prevalence of learning disabilities in a sample of children considered hyperactive. *Journal of Abnormal Child Psychology*, 1980, *8*, 33-51.

Langhorne, J., Loney, J., Paternite, C., & Bechtoldt, H. Childhood hyperkinesis: A return to the source. *Journal of Abnormal Psychology, 1976, 85,* 201–210.

Laufer, M., Denhoff, E., & Solomons, G. Hyperkinetic impulse disorder in children's behavior problems. *Psychosomatic Medicine, 1957, 19,* 38–49.

Loiselle, D., Stamm, J., Maitinsky, S., & Whipple, S. Evoked potential and behavioral signs of attention dysfunctions in hyperactive boys. *Psychophysiology, 1980, 17,* 193–201.

Logan, W. J., & Swanson, J. M. Erythrosin B. inhibition of neurotransmitter accumulation by rat brain homogenate. *Science, 1979, 206,* 363–364.

Loney, J., Langhorne, J., & Paternite, C. An empirical basis for subgrouping the hyperkinetic/MBD syndrome. *Journal of Abnormal Psychology, 1978, 87,* 431–439.

Loney, J., Langhorne, J., Paternite, C., Whaley-Klahn, M., Broeker, C., & Hacker, M. The Iowa HABIT: Hyperkinetic/Aggressive Boys in Treatment. In S. Sells (Ed.), *Life History Research in Psychopathology, Vol. 6.* New York: Williams & Wilkins, 1980.

Loney, J. & Milich, R. Hyperactivity, inattention, and aggression in clinical practice. In M. Wolraich & D. Routh (Eds.), *Advances in behavioral pediatrics,* (Vol. 2). Greenwich, Connecticut: JAI Press, in press.

Loper, A., & Hallahan, D. A comparison of the reliability and validity of the standard MFF and MFF20 with learning-disabled children. *Journal of Abnormal Child Psychology, 1980, 8,* 377–384.

Madsen, C., & Madsen, C. *Teaching/Discipline: A positive approach for educational development* (3rd edition). Boston: Allyn & Bacon, 1981.

Mailman, R. B., Ferris, R. M., Tang, F. L. M., Vogel, R. A., Kilts, C. D., Lipton, M. A., Smith, D. A., Mueller, R. A., & Breese, G. R. Erythrosin (Red No. 3) and its nonspecific biochemical actions: What relation to behavioral changes? *Science, 1980, 207,* 535–537.

McIntyre, C., Blackwell, S., & Denton, C. Effect of noise distractibility on the spans of apprehension of hyperactive boys. *Journal of Abnormal Child Psychology, 1978, 6,* 483–492.

Mendelson, W., Johnson, N., & Stewart, M. A. Hyperactive children as teenagers: A follow-up study. *Journal of Nervous and Mental Disease, 1971, 153,* 273–279.

Menkes, M., Row, J., & Menkes, J. A 25 year follow-up study on the hyperkinetic child with minimal brain dysfunction. *Pediatrics, 1967, 39,* 393–399.

Milich, R., & Landau, S. Socialization and peer relations in the hyperactive child. In K. Gadow & I. Bialer (Eds.), *Advances in learning and behavioral disabilities* (Vol. 1). Greenwich, CT: JAI Press, 1981.

Milich, R., & Loney, J. The role of hyperactive and aggressive symptomatology in predicting adolescent outcome among hyperactive children. *Journal of Pediatric Psychology, 1979, 4,* 93–112.

Milich, R., Loney, J., & Landau, S. The independent dimensions of hyperactivity and aggression: A replication and further validation. Unpublished manuscript. University of Iowa, Iowa City, IA, 1982.

Minde, K., Webb, G., & Sykes, D. Studies on the hyperactive child. VI. Prenatal and paranatal factors associated with hyperactivity. *Developmental Medicine and Child Neurology, 1968, 10,* 355–363.

Morrison, J., & Stewart, M. A family study of the hyperactive child syndrome. *Biological Psychiatry, 1971, 3,* 189–195.

Morrison, J., & Stewart, M. The psychiatric status of the legal families of adopted hyperactive children. *Archives of General Psychiatry, 1973, 28,* 888–891.

Nichols, P., & Chen, T. *Minimal brain dysfunction: A prospective study.* Hillsdale, N.J.: Erlbaum, 1981.

Oden, S., & Asher, S. Coaching children in social skills for friendship making. *Child Development, 1977, 48,* 495–506.

O'Leary, K. D., & O'Leary, S. G. *Classroom management: the successful use of behavior modification* (1st edition). New York: Pergamon Press, 1972.

O'Leary, K. D., & O'Leary, S. G. *Classroom management: the successful use of behavior modification* (2nd edition). New York: Pergamon Press, 1977.

O'Leary, K. D., & Johnson, S. B. Psychological assessment. In H. Quay & J. Werry (Eds.), *Psychopathological disorders of childhood* (2nd Ed.). New York: Wiley, 1979.

O'Leary, S., & Pelham, W. Behavior therapy and withdrawal of stimulant medication with hyperactive children. *Pediatrics*, 1978, *61*, 211–217.

O'Leary, K., Pelham, W., Rosenbaum, A., & Price, G. Behavioral treatment of hyperkinetic children: An experimental evaluation of its usefulness. *Clinical Pediatrics*, 1976, *15*, 511–515.

O'Leary, S. G., & Steen, P. Independent assessment of hyperactivity and aggression in hyperactive children. In B. Lahey (Chair), *Is there an independent syndrome of hyperactivity in children?* Symposium presented at the annual meeting of the American Psychological Association, Montreal, September 1980.

O'Leary, K. D., & Wilson, T. *Behavior therapy: application and outcome*. Englewood Cliffs, New Jersey: Prentice-Hall, 1975.

Pasamanick, B., & Knobloch, H. Brain damage and reproductive casualty. *American Journal of Orthopsychiatry*, 1960, *30*, 298–305.

Paternite, C., & Loney, J. Childhood hyperkinesis: Relationships between symptomatology and home environment. In C. Whalen & B. Henker (Eds.), *Hyperactive children: the social ecology of identification and treatment*. New York: Academic Press, 1980.

Patterson, G. An application of conditioning techniques to the control of a hyperactive child. In L. Ullman & L. Krasner (Eds.), *Case studies in behavior modification*. New York: Holt, Rinehart & Winston, 1965.

Patterson, G. Intervention for boys with conduct problems: Multiple settings, treatment and criteria. *Journal of Consulting and Clinical Psychology*, 1974, *42*, 471–481.

Patterson, G. *Families: Application of social learning to family life*. Champaign: Research Press, 1976.

Pekarik, G., Prinz, R., Liebert, D., Weintraub, S., & Neale, J. The pupil evaluation inventory: a sociometric technique for assessing children's social behavior. *Journal of Abnormal Child Psychology*, 1976, *4*, 83–97.

Pelham, W. Withdrawal of a stimulant drug and concurrent behavioral intervention in the treatment of a hyperactive child. *Behavior Therapy*, 1977, *8*, 473–479.

Pelham, W. E. Hyperactive children. In R. P. Liberman (Ed.), Symposium on Behavior Therapy in Psychiatry. *Psychiatric Clinics of North America*, 1978, *1*, 227–246.

Pelham, W. E. Selective attention deficits in poor readers? Dichotic listening, speeded classification, and auditory and visual central and incidental learning tasks. *Child Development*, 1979, *50*, 1050–1061.

Pelham, W. E. Attention deficits in hyperactive and learning-disabled children: A reconceptualization. *Exceptional Education Quarterly*, 1981, *2*, 13–24.

Pelham, W. E., Atkins, M. S., & Murphy, H. A. ADD with and without hyperactivity: Parent, teacher and peer rating correlates. In W. Pelham (Chair), *DSM III Category of attention deficit disorder: Rationale, operationalization and correlates*. Symposium presented at the annual meeting of the American Psychological Association, Los Angeles, September 1981.

Pelham, W. E., Atkins, M. S., Murphy, H. A. & White, K. S. Operationalization and validity of attention deficit disorders. Paper presented in W. Pelham (Chair), *Toward the objective diagnosis of hyperactivity and attention deficit disorders*. Symposium presented at the annual meeting of the Association for the Advancement of Behavior Therapy, Toronto, November, 1981.

Pelham, W. E., & Bender, M. E. Peer relationships in hyperactive children: Description and treatment. In K. Gadow & I. Bialer (Eds.), *Advances in learning and behavioral disabilities (Vol. 1)*. Greenwich, CT: JAI Press, 1982.

Pelham, W. E., Bender, M. E., Caddell, J., & Booth, S. *Dose-response effects of methylphenidate on academic measures and classroom performance in hyperactive children.* Unpublished manuscript. Department of Psychology, Florida State University, Tallahassee, Florida, 1981.

Pelham, W. E., & Murphy, H. A. *Peer perceptions of hyperactive children: Sex differences, symptom differences, and relation to teacher perceptions.* Paper presented at the biennial meeting of the Society for Research in Child Development, Boston, April 1981.

Pelham, W. E., Schnedler, R. W., & Bender, M. E. *Behavioral and pharmacological treatment of hyperactive children in the classroom.* Paper presented at the annual meeting of the Association for Children with Learning Disabilities, Atlanta, February 1981.

Pelham, W. E., Schnedler, R. W., Bender, M. E., & Pass, J. E. *Attentional capacity in hyperactive and nonhyperactive children: Interaction between memory scanning and visual scanning.* Unpublished manuscript. Department of Psychology, Florida State University, Tallahassee, Florida, 1981.

Pelham, W. E., Schnedler, R. W., Bologna, N. C., & Contreras, J. A. Behavioral and stimulant treatment of hyperactive children: A therapy study with methylphenidate probes in a within-subject design. *Journal of Applied Behavioral Analysis,* 1980, *13,* 221–236.

Pelham, W., Schnedler, R., Miller, J., Nilsson, D., Paluchowski, C., Ronnei, M., Budrow, M., Marks, D., & Bender, M. *The combination of behavior therapy and psychostimulant medication in the treatment of hyperactive children: A therapy outcome study.* Paper presented at the annual meeting of the Association for the Advancement of Behavior Therapy, San Francisco, December 1979.

Pelham, W., Swanson, J., Bender, M., & Wilson, J. *Effects of pemoline on hyperactivity: Laboratory and classroom measures.* Paper presented at the annual meeting of the American Psychological Association, Montreal, September 1980.

Porges, S. W. Peripheral and neurochemical parallels of psychopathology: A psychophysiological model relating autonomic imbalance to hyperactivity, psychopathy and autism. In H. W. Reese (Ed.), *Advances in Child Behavior and Development* (Vol. 11). London: Academic Press, 1976.

Porges, S. W., Walter, G. F., Korb, R. J., & Sprague, R. L. The influences of methylphenidate on heart rate and behavioral measures of attention in hyperactive children. *Child Development,* 1975, *46,* 727–733.

Posner, M. I. *Chronometric Explorations of Mind.* Hillsdale, New Jersey: Lawrence Erlbaum Associates, 1978.

Prinz, R., Connor, P., & Wilson, C. The intertwined dimensions of aggression and hyperactivity in childhood. *Journal of Abnormal Child Psychology,* 1981, *9,* 191–202.

Quay, H. C. Classification. In H. Quay & J. Werry (Eds.), *Psychopathological disorders of childhood,* (2nd edition). New York: Wiley, 1979.

Quinn, P. O., & Rapoport, J. L. Minor physical anomalies and neurologic status in hyperactive boys. *Pediatrics,* 1974, *53,* 742–747.

Quinn, P., & Rapoport, J. A one year follow-up of hyperactive boys treated with imipramine of methylphenidate. *American Journal of Psychiatry,* 1975, *132,* 241–245.

Quinn, P., Renfield, M., Burg, C., & Rapoport, J. Minor physical anomalies: A newborn screening and a 1-year follow-up. *Journal of the American Academy of Child Psychiatry,* 1977, *16,* 662–669.

Rapoport, J., Buchsbaum, M., Zahn, T., Weingartner, H., Ludlow, C., & Mikkelson, E. Dextroamphetamine: Cognitive and behavioral effects in normal prepubertal boys. *Science,* 1978, *199,* 560–563.

Rapoport, J. L., Quinn, P. O., Burg, C., & Bartley, L. Can hyperactives be identified in infancy? In R. Trites (Ed.) *Hyperactivity in children.* Baltimore, MD: University Park Press, 1979.

Rapoport, J., Quinn, P., & Lamprecht, F. Minor physical anomalies and plasma dopamine B-hydroxylase activity in hyperactive boys. *American Journal of Psychiatry,* 1974, *131,* 386–390.

Rapport, M., Murphy, A., & Bailey, J. The effects of a response cost treatment tactic on hyperactive children. *Journal of School Psychology,* 1980, *18,* 98-111.

Riddle, D., & Rapoport, J. A 2-year follow-up of 72 hyperactive boys. *Journal of Nervous and Mental Disease,* 1976, *162,* 126-134.

Rie, E. D., & Rie, H. E. Recall, retention and Ritalin. *Journal of Consulting and Clinical Psychology,* 1977, *44,* 250-260.

Rie, H., & Rie, E. *Handbook of minimal brain dysfunctions.* New York: Wiley, 1980.

Rie, H., Rie, E., Stewart, S., & Ambuel, J. Effects of methylphenidate on underachieving children. *Journal of Consulting and Clinical Psychology,* 1976, *44,* 250-260.

Rieder, R., & Nichols, P. Offspring of schizophrenics III. *Archives of General Psychiatry,* 1979, *36,* 665-674.

Robins, L. *Deviant children grown up.* Baltimore, MD: Williams & Wilkins, 1966.

Roff, M., Sells, S., & Golden, M. *Social adjustment and personality development in children.* Minneapolis: University of Minnesota Press, 1972.

Rosenthal, R., & Allen, T. An examination of the attention, arousal and learning dysfunctions of hyperactive children. *Psychological Bulletin,* 1977, *85,* 689-716.

Ross, A. O. *Psychological aspects of learning disabilities and reading disorders.* New York: McGraw-Hill, 1976.

Ross, A. O. *Child behavior therapy.* New York: Wiley, 1981.

Ross, A., & Pelham, W. Child Psychopathology. In M. Rosenzweig & L. Porter (Eds.), *Annual Review of Psychology,* (Vol. 32). Palo Alto: Annual Reviews, Inc., 1981.

Ross, S., & Ross, D. *Hyperactivity: Theory, research and action.* New York: Wiley, 1976.

Routh, D. Developmental and social aspects of hyperactivity. In C. Whalen & B. Henker (Eds.), *Hyperactive children: The social ecology of identification and treatment.* New York: Academic Press, 1980.

Routh, D., & Roberts, R. Minimal brain dysfunction in children: Failure to find evidence for a behavioral syndrome. *Psychological Reports,* 1972, *31,* 307-314.

Rubin, R. A., & Balow, B. Perinatal influences on the behavior and learning problems of children. In B. Lahey & A. Kazdin (Eds.) *Advances in clinical child psychology,* (Vol. 1). New York: Plenum, 1977.

Safer, D. A familial factor in minimal brain dysfunction. *Behavior Genetics,* 1973, *3,* 175-187.

Safter, D. M., Allen, R. P. Factors influencing the suppressant effects of two stimulant drugs on the growth of hyperactive children. *Pediatrics,* 1973, *51,* 660-667.

Safer, D. J., & Allen, R. P. *Hyperactive children: Diagnosis and Management.* Baltimore, MD: University Park Press, 1976.

Satterfield, J. EEG issues in children with minimal brain dysfunction. *Seminars in Psychiatry,* 1973, *5,* 35-46.

Satterfield, J. H., & Braley, B. W. Evoked potentials and brain maturation in hyperactive and normal children. *Electroencephalography and Clinical Neurophysiology,* 1977, *43,* 43-51.

Satterfield, J. H., Cantwell, D. P., & Satterfield, B. T. Pathophysiology of the hyperactive child syndrome. *Archives of General Psychiatry,* 1974, *31,* 839-844.

Satterfield, J. H., Cantwell, D. P., & Satterfield, B. T. Multimodality treatment. *Archives of General Psychiatry,* 1979, *36,* 965-978.

Satterfield, J. H., Cantwell, D. P., Schell, A., & Blaschke, T. Growth of hyperactive children treated with methylphenidate. *Archives of General Psychiatry,* 1979, *36,* 212-219.

Satterfield, J. H., Satterfield, B. T., & Cantwell, D. P. Multimodality treatment: A two-year evaluation of 61 hyperactive boys. *Archives of General Psychiatry,* 1981, *37,* 915-919.

Satterfield, J. H., & Dawson, M. E. Electrodermal correlates of hyperactivity in children. *Psychophysiology,* 1971, *8,* 191-197.

Schulman, J., Stevens, T., & Kupst, M. The biomotometer: A new device for the measurement and remediation of hyperactivity. *Child Development,* 1977, *48,* 1152-1154.

Seiden, L., & Dykstra, L. *Psychopharmacology.* New York: Van Nostrand & Reinhold, 1977.

Sergeant, J., Velthoven, R., & Virginia, A. Hyperactivity, impulsivity and reflectivity: An examination of their relationship and implications for clinical child psychology. *Journal of Child Psychology and Psychiatry,* 1979, *20,* 47-60.

Shaywitz, B., Cohen, C., & Bowers, M. CSF monoamine metabolites in children with minimal brain dysfunction—evidence for alteration of brain dopamine. *Journal of Pediatrics,* 1977, *90,* 67-71.

Shaywitz, S. E., Cohen, D. J., & Shaywitz, B. A. The biochemical basis of minimal brain dysfunction. *Journal of Pediatrics,* 1978, *92,* 179-187.

Slater, E., & Cowie, V. *The genetics of mental disorders.* London: Oxford University Press, 1971.

Sleator, E., & von Neumann, A. Methylphenidate in the treatment of hyperkinetic children. *Clinical Pediatrics,* 1974, *13,* 19-24.

Sleator, E., von Neumann, A., & Sprague, R. Hyperactive children: A continuous long-term placebo controlled follow-up. *Journal of the American Medical Association,* 1974, *229,* 316-317.

Sprague, R., & Gadow, K. The role of the teacher in drug treatment. *School Review,* 1976, *85,* 109-140.

Sprague, R., & Sleator, E. Methylphenidate in hyperkinetic children: Differences in dose effects on learning and social behavior. *Science,* 1977, *198,* 1274-1276.

Spring, C., Greenberg, L., Scott, J., & Hopwood, J. Electrodermal activity in hyperactive boys who are methylphenidate responders. *Psychophysiology,* 1974, *11,* 436-442.

Sroufe, L. Drug treatment of children with behavior problems. In F. Horowitz (Ed.), *Review of child development research* (Vol. 4), Chicago: University of Chicago Press, 1975.

Sroufe, L. A., Sonies, B. C., West, W. D., & Wright, F. S. Anticipatory heart rate deceleration and reaction time in children with and without referral for learning disability. *Child Development,* 1973, *44,* 267-273.

Stephens, R. S., & Pelham, W. E. The state-dependent and main effects of pemoline and methylphenidate on paired-associates learning and spelling in hyperactive children. Paper presented at the annual meeting of the American Psychological Association, Washington, August, 1982.

Stewart, M., Cummings, C., Singer, C., & de Blois, C. The overlap between hyperactive and unsocialized aggressive children. *Journal of Child Psychology and Psychiatry,* 1981, *22,* 35-46.

Stewart, M., Pitts, F., Craig, A., & Dieruf, W. The hyperactive child syndrome. *American Journal of Orthopsychiatry,* 1966, *36,* 861-867.

Swanson, J. A parent-teacher checklist and norms for identifying attention deficit disorders. In W. Pelham (Chair), *DSM III Category of attention deficit disorder: Rationale, operationalization and correlates.* Symposium presented at the annual meeting of the American Psychological Association, Los Angeles, September 1981.

Swanson, J. M., & Kinsbourne, M. Stimulant-related state dependent learning in hyperactive children. *Science,* 1976, *192,* 1754-1755.

Swanson, J., & Kinsbourne, M. The cognitive effects of stimulant drugs on hyperactive (inattentive) children. In G. Hale & M. Lewis (Eds.), *Attention and the development of cognitive skills.* New York: Plenum, 1979.

Swanson, J. M., & Kinsbourne, M. Food dyes impair the performance of hyperactive children on a laboratory learning test. *Science,* 1980, *207,* 1485-1487.

Sykes, D. H., Douglas, V. I., & Morgenstern, G. Sustained attention hyperactive children. *Journal of Child Psychology and Psychiatry,* 1973, *14,* 213-220.

Sykes, D. H., Douglas, V. I., Weiss, G., & Minde, K. K. Attention in hyperactive children and the effect of methylphenidate (Ritalin). *Journal of Child Psychology and Psychiatry,* 1971, *12,* 129-139.

Torgesen, J. K., & Kail, R. V. Memory processes in exceptional children. In B. Keogh (Ed.), *Advances in Special Education,* (Vol. 1). Greenwich, CT: JAI Press, 1980.

Waldrop, M. F., Bell, R. Q., McLaughlin, B., & Halverson, C. F. Newborn minor physical anomalies predict short attention span, peer aggression, and impulsivity at age 3. *Science*, 1978, *199*, 563-565.

Waldrop, M., Pederson, F., & Bell, R. Minor physical anomalies and behavior in preschool children. *Child Development*, 1968, *39*, 391-400.

Walker, H., Street, A., Garrett, B., Crossen, J., Hops, H., & Greenwood, C. *RECESS consultant interval recording system.* Eugene: CORBEH, 1978.

Watt, N. Patterns of childhood social development in adult schizophrenics. *Archives of General Psychiatry*, 1978, *35*, 160-165.

Weingartner, H., Rapoport, J. L., Buchsbaum, M. S., Bunney, W. E., Ebert, M. H., Mikkelsen, E. J., & Caine, E. D. Cognitive processes in normal and hyperactive children and their responses to amphetamine treatment. *Journal of Abnormal Psychology*, 1980, *89*, 25-37.

Weiss, B., Williams, J. H., Margen, S., Abrams, B., Cann, B., Citron, L. T., Cox, C., McKibben, J., Ogar, D., & Schultz, S. Behavioral response to artificial food colors. *Science*, 1980, *207*, 1487-1488.

Weiss, G., & Hechtman, L. The hyperactive child syndrome. *Science*, 1979, *206*, 309-314.

Weiss, G., Hechtman, L., Perlman, T., Hopkins, J., & Wener, A. Hyperactives as young adults. *Archives of General Psychiatry*, 1979, *36*, 675-681.

Weiss, G., Minde, K., Werry, J., Douglas, V., & Nemeth, E. Studies on the hyperactive child: VIII. Five-year follow-up. *Archives of General Psychiatry*, 1971, *24*, 409-414.

Weiss, G., Kruger, E., Danielson, U., & Elman, M. Effect of long-term treatment of hyperactive children with methylphenidate. *Canadian Medical Association Journal*, 1975, *112*, 159-165.

Wender, P. *Minimal Brain Dysfunction in Children.* New York: John Wiley & Sons, 1971.

Wender, P. H. Minimal brain dysfunction: An overview. In *Psychopharmacology: A Generation of Progress*, M. A. Lipton, A. DiMascio, & K. F. Killan, Eds., New York: Raven, 1978.

Werner, E. E., Bierman, J., & French, F. *The Children of Kauai.* Honolulu: University of Hawaii Press, 1971.

Werry, J. S. Studies on the hyperactive child. IV. An empirical analysis of the minimal brain dysfunction syndrome. *Archives of General Psychiatry*, 1968, *19*, 9-16.

Werry, J., Minde, K., Guzman, A., Weiss, G., Dogan, K., & Hoy, E. Studies on the hyperactive child. VII. Neurological status compared with neurotic and normal children. *American Journal of Orthopsychiatry*, 1972, *42*, 441-451.

Werry, J. S., & Sprague, R. L. Methylphenidate in Children: effect of dosage. *Australian and New Zealand Journal of Psychiatry*, 1974, *8*, 9-19.

Werry, J., Sprague, R., & Cohen, M. Conner's Teacher Rating Scale for use in drug studies with children—an empirical study. *Journal of Abnormal Child Psychology*, 1975, *3*, 217-229.

Werry, J., Weiss, G., & Douglas, V. Studies on the hyperactive child. I. Some preliminary findings. *Canadian Psychiatric Association Journal*, 1964, *9*, 120-130.

Whalen, C. K., Henker, B., Collins, B. E., Finck, D., & Dotemoto, S. A social ecology of hyperactive boys: Medication effects in structured classroom environments. *Journal of Applied Behavior Analysis*, 1979, *12*, 65-81(b).

Whalen, C., Henker, B., Collins, B., McAuliffe, S., & Vaux, A. Peer interaction in a structured communication task: Comparisons of normal and hyperactive boys and of methylphenidate (Ritalin) and placebo effects. *Child Development*, 1979, *50*, 388-401(a).

Whalen, C., Henker, B., & Detemote, S. Teacher response to the methylphenidate (Ritalin) versus placebo status of hyperactive boys in the classroom. *Child Development*, 1981, *52*, 1004-1014.

Willerman, L. Activity level and hyperactivity in twins. *Child Development*, 1973, *44*, 228-293.

Wood, D., Reimherr, F., Wender, P., & Johnson, G. Diagnosis and treatment of minimal brain dysfunction in adults. *Archives of General Psychiatry*, 1976, *33*, 1453-1461.

Zahn, T. P., Abate, F., Little, B. C., & Wender, P. H. Minimal brain dysfunction, stimulant drugs and autonomic nervous system activity. *Archives of General Psychiatry*, 1975, *32*, 381-387.

Zahn, T. P., Little, B. C., & Wender, P. H. Pupillary and heart rate reactivity in children with minimal brain dysfunction. *Journal of Abnormal Child Psychology,* 1978, *6,* 135-148.

Zentall, S., & Barack, R. Rating scales for hyperactivity: Concurrent validity, reliability, and decisions to label for the Conners and Davids abbreviated scales. *Journal of Abnormal Child Psychology,* 1979, *2,* 179-190.

Zentall, S., & Zentall, T. Activity and task performance of hyperactive children as a function of environmental stimulation. *Journal of Consulting and Clinical Psychology,* 1976, *44,* 693-697.

9 Sexual Dysfunctions

James H. Geer
Madelyn Messé
State University of New York at Stony Brook

This chapter presents a selective survey of behavioral and medical phenomena that through their interaction impact on the field of human sexuality. As we began this survey, it immediately became apparent that the scope of material available was so extensive as to require that any single chapter be relatively superficial. Therefore, the purpose of this chapter is to point out major areas of concern to interested professionals and to highlight certain points of overlap between medicine and the behavioral sciences. The chapter will not provide an exhaustive description of all possible points of interface between these disciplines but rather will be issue-oriented. We begin with a discussion of some of the assumptions and definitions that underlie the material on sexual dysfunctions.

ASSUMPTIONS AND DEFINITIONS OF THE AREA OF STUDY

Organic versus Psychogenic

The dichotomy, organic versus psychogenic, is often proposed to separate sexual disorders into distinct categories. One of the first issues that must be addressed is the distinction between organic versus psychogenic origin. It will be the thesis of this chapter that such a dichotomy is rarely if ever adequate to explain sexual dysfunctions. Seldom will the professional meet with an instance of either "pure" organic or "pure" psychogenic etiology. Rather, what would appear to be the case is that most disorders can be approached more meaningfully by applying an interactive model in which both organic and psychogenic factors play a role. It is true, of course, that in any case under consideration there can be a relative preponderance of organic or psychogenic factors. However, to fail to search for one when one finds the other (i.e., to stop searching for psychological factors when organic problems are identified) would be a disservice to the distressed individual. Behaviorally oriented clinical psychologists are fond of pointing out that etiology of a dysfunction does not necessarily lead to treatment decisions (Goldfried & Davison, 1976). This is particularly true of sexual problems. There may well be a broad difference between the conditions that produce or contribute to dysfunctions and those that maintain them. For example, the pharmacological effects of alcohol may initially inhibit an erection, while the psychological effects of that failure may maintain the loss. The interactional model says that organic and psychogenic factors often function together. That view questions the usefulness of clinicians' tendency to "rule out" either organic or psychogenic causes. The practice of "ruling out" one or the other will often lead to inappropriate clinical decisions that may function to the disadvantage of the client or patient.

Flowing from the concern over inappropriately "ruling out" is the suggestion that treatment should focus upon a wide spectrum of issues and attack the total problem. Such an approach is almost certain to be more effective than attacking any given facet. While this push for "holistic treatment" as an ideal may be an over used platitude, it cannot be emphasized too much in this area where it so frequently goes ignored.

Definition of Sexual Dysfunction

We need to address the question, what is a sexual dysfunction? It is well recognized that definitions of sexual dysfunctions are complicated by the attitudes, values, and norms of the individual, partners, professionals, and society as a whole. This is clear, for example, in the definition of hypersexuality. The decision concerning when excessive sexual behavior (hypersexuality) becomes pathological is largely determined by the values of the society and the professional as he or she reflects society's norms. Clearly, the professional cannot escape from these concerns because he or she is and will remain a member of the society. However, awareness of the biases can help to provide an objective and more rational basis for decision making.

Dysfunction in its most general sense refers to interference with the typical, desired, or biological role of some phenomena. When this definition is applied to sexual matters we, in general, are referring to interference with "typical" sexual behavior. The nature of the interference may result from one or a combination of physiological, cognitive, affective, or behavioral factors. The multidimensional nature of sexual functioning forces the professional to broaden his or her perspective concerning both medical and behavioral events.

The definition of sexual dysfunction must include a recognition than problems can exist in one or more aspects of sexual behavior. For example, it may be that situational or stimulus components of the pattern are being affected, as when an individual is inorgasmic with one partner but not another. On the other hand, it may be that problems occur within a portion of the sexual response sequence (e.g., sex play, intromission, orgasm) or perhaps the interference may be with the social interactions that precede or follow sexual behavior. The nature of the interference can vary. It may reflect blocking or retarding of typical or desired behavior. The effects may be upon the level of sexual excitement (as in excessive as well as reduced level of arousal), and it may be that the difficulty lies with the individual's dissatisfaction with their sexual performance. Our point is that the definitions of sexual dysfunction must take into account the problems just described. We will not be able to solve all of these concerns, but we must draw attention to the issues.

Definition of Behavioral Medicine and Sexuality

Certain phenomena shall be excluded from consideration. We exclude factors that impact on reproductive functions only. We shall exclude object choice patterns such as homosexuality and the paraphilias. We exclude, other than to mention, general medical problems both transient and chronic such as fatigue, pain, and anxiety over illness. It is necessary and important to recognize the powerful impact of general pain, fatigue, and anxiety over illness has upon sexuality (Kolodny, Masters and Johnson, 1979). However, for the sake of brevity they will not be considered in depth in this chapter. Finally, behavior that leads to medical conditions will only be briefly alluded to, such as the behaviors associated with developing venereal disease and uro-genital infections. We include, however, any medical condition that has a direct impact on sexual dysfunction, and we include medical treatment decisions that impact on sexual functioning.

Interactional Model

An interactional model insists that influences upon sexuality cannot be compartmentalized into independent factors. It is necessary to look at the over-all pattern of sexual behavior in order to understand it fully. The interactional model makes explicit the fact that physiological, behavioral, affective, and cognitive factors do not exist independently but rather feed back, one upon another. The model recognizes that different perspectives will lead to emphasizing different elements in the set. These varying perspectives lead to different types of analysis; but, hopefully, the interactional model forces one to recognize that without referring to the interaction the full picture will be missed. There are a number of clear advantages associated with continuing to recognize the interaction between cognitive, physiological, affective, and behavioral events. The first is that the completeness of the model should lead to a decrease in the likelihood that important factors will be missed because they are ignored. Secondly, the recognition of different perspectives for viewing dysfunctions should yield increased awareness of the need for developing interdisciplinary skills and ties. In some sense, this makes explicit the position that medical practitioners need to evidence more sensitivity to psychological phenomena, and that psychological professionals need to be more sensitive to medical phenomena. It is directing professionals toward these goals that this chapter aspires.

ASSESSMENT STRATEGIES, METHODS, AND DEVICES

The goal of this section is to briefly outline the range of assessment techniques that are available. In addition to describing these techniques, we will comment upon some of their advantages and limitations. Assessment of sexual dysfunctions should be multi-modal. It is not enough to examine dysfunctional sexuality from a single perspective, and it is not appropriate to stop assessment when one procedure identifies a problem. It is our contention that assessment should always examine the full range of factors that may influence sexuality. We arrange assessment techniques in a sequence that is aligned from medical to behavioral. The order refers to how the data are collected rather than the nature of the data. For example, should an individual during an interview discuss information concerning their physiological reactions, we would categorize that assessment technique as behavioral. For each assessment procedure, we describe its potential utility in evaluating some aspect of sexual dysfunction.

Karyotyping

Karyotyping is an assessment procedure that allows the detection of genetic anomilies (Caspersson & Zech, 1973). A karyotype is an arrangement of chromosome photo-micrographs according to standard classification such that the full array of chromosomes in a given cell nucleus is obtained. This assessment allows the evaluation of the number, form, and size of chromosomes, as well as their groupings within the cell nucleus. Karyotyping is used to identify important information concerning the individual's genetic make-up. For our purposes karyotyping can be used to uncover genetic anomolies that impact on human sexuality. For example, it can be used in the case of ambiguous genitals to determine the genetic sex of the individual. Sex assignment can then be made on the basis of genetic characteristics when the genitals do not provide sufficient information. Also, karyotyping can be used as a research tool to evaluate the role of genetic factors in sexuality.

Hormone Assay

Hormone assays refer to a cluster of techniques that determine the concentration of hormones in fluids or tissues under study. The techniques vary considerably both in terms of the method used for assay and the aspect of the hormone actually assayed. For example, the analysis of testosterone may refer to determining the concentration of free testosterone circulating in the blood or it may refer to the amount of testosterone bound to substances in the blood (Ismail, 1976). In this instance, there is considerable controversy concerning what information is actually of most interest; is it free hormone circulating in the blood? or is it the amount of hormone bound to the receptor sites in the various cells? or is it some other aspect of hormone function?

Hormone analyses are time dependent. Hormone levels will vary according to the time of day the samples are obtained. Interpretations are heavily affected by the number of samples since assay values obtained vary dramatically across time. There are difficulties in comparing hormone assays across laboratories since the standards used in the assays (as well as other aspects of the protocol) vary from one setting to another.

Hormone assays are important as a diagnostic technique in determining the advisability of hormone replacement therapy in those individuals who have deficient hormone production. They are important in determining the presence of hyperthyroid conditions, pituitary malfunctions and other endrocrine phenomena which affect sexuality. Hormone assays may also be used to evaluate the control that hormones exert over sexual dysfunctions. They may be useful in the assessment of the success and/or the progress of physiological treatments whose goal is the modification of hormone levels.

Thermography

Thermography is a relatively new assessment procedure. In this technique the patient's or subject's body is scanned by heat sensors that determine temperature levels (Bacon, 1976). It is generally assumed that higher heat levels result from increased blood circulation in the tissues which in turn is associated with increased sexual arousal (Masters & Johnson, 1966). The output of a thermographic analysis is a color photograph of the body in which the colors obtained are determined by the amount of heat emitted. Difficulties in thermography are related to several issues. First, it is not clear at the present time precisely what measurement unit should be used, and no comparison standards for looking across individuals have been developed. Perhaps most importantly, the technology is very expensive so that considerable cost is involved in collecting thermographic information. Thermography has potential use in the evaluation of sexual arousal in a relatively unobtrusive manner since nothing actually touches the body (Seeley, Abramson, Perry, Rothblatt, & Seeley, 1980). At this point in time, however, individuals undergoing general thermographic analysis must be unclothed as specialized cameras scan their bodies. Tordjman, Thierrie, and Michel (1980) describe the use of penile thermography for identifying vascular problems in erectile disorders. Within the foreseeable future, the use of thermographic techniques may be possible while the individual remains completely clothed.

Genital Blood Flow and Supply

Genital vascular activity has been measured in both men and women. For men, the most common procedure involves taking a measurement of the circumference of the penis with a strain gauge; although volumetric measurement is possible, there are serious methodological problems with volume measure (Geer, 1980). Penile circumference is closely related to amount of erection. The evaluation of penile blood pressure (Gaskel, 1971), measures of penile blood flow for the study of anomalies of penile vascularity (Ebbehoj, G. Wagner, 1979), and the previously mentioned penile thermographic analysis are also important measures of penile function. The measures mentioned, are affected by factors that interfere with circulation to the penis and could be used to detect conditions that intefere with erections. Some investigators have taken determination of penile blood flow a step further with the injection of radio opaque materials into the penis (Cohen, 1977). This technique allows visualization of the vascular network and evaluation of its function. The various measures of penile blood flow can be used for the study and detection of physiologically based erectile dysfunctions.

The measurement of vaginal vasocongestion through the use of photoplysmography has proven useful as an assessment device in the study of sexual arousal in women (Sintchak & Geer, 1975). This procedure entails the insertion of a vaginal photoplethysmograph which detects the amount of blood in the walls of the vagina. Vasocongestion is related to the experience of sexual arousal. Other genital measures of vascularity that have been studied include measurements of blood flow directly from vaginal tissues (Shapiro, Cohen, DiBianco, & Rosen, 1968; Levin & Wagner, 1978). Thus far devices that measure genital vasocongestion have proven to be of value in the study of normal female sexuality. However, research into the potential applications of such devices to evaluation and treatment of sexual dysfunction is continuing to yield new information.

Physical Examinations of the Genitals

The physical examination of genitals is an important step in evaluation of the relative importance of organic problems in sexual functioning. For example, the physical exam can determine the presence of Peyronie's disease in males and can assess the extent of the disease so as to evaluate its impact on sexual functioning. The occurrence of vaginal infection and pelvic inflammatory diseases can be detected through appropriate examination. A thorough physical exam is an appropriate assessment procedure for the detection of structural anomalies. One of the problems commonly associated with the physical examination is the reticence displayed by the physician to conduct a complete and thorough exam of the genitals, and a reluctance of the patient to request or submit to such an exam.

General Medical Examination

A current work-up of the medical condition of individuals experiencing sexual dysfunction is called for in all cases. There are many medical conditions that impact heavily on sexuality and an assessment can be adequate only if a thorough general medical examination has been performed. Some of the conditions and system evaluations that are particularly important and that need to be touched upon include diabetes, cardiac functioning, renal functioning, systemic infections, VD, pulmonary problems, liver problems, and spinal cord reflexes. General health is important to sexual functioning. The general medical exam provides the necessary information concerning the health of individuals who experience sexual problems. Poor health is almost universally associated with reduced sexual functioning.

Medical History Taking

This assessment procedure refers to the collection of historical information concerning the individual's previous medical conditions (excluding sexual history which we include as a separate topic in the following section). Of particular importance is information concerning any history of drug or alcohol abuse which can impact heavily on sexuality. Information concerning prior and current medications are necessary. Gathering a history of prior treatment experiences may identify medical problems that interact with sexual dysfunctions and guide treatment formulations. The practitioner also needs information regarding familial patterns of genetic disturbances that might affect sexuality. Any thorough medical history should include information concerning the use of birth control procedures, previous history of abortion, the occurrence of hysterectomies, or any surgical procedure that might provide information regarding current sexual functioning.

Sexual History Taking

Sexual histories should always gather demographic information. Education level and socio-economic class are related to sexual functioning and attitudes towards sexuality. Demographic information can be useful in allowing the assessor to anticipate responses from the patient. Collecting information on both specific sexual patterns and attitudes towards sexuality make up the major portion of the sexual history taking procedure. Thorough sexual history taking will entail collecting information on early experiences that may influence sexuality, such as incest and early sexual trauma. Detailed descriptions of the specific problem that brings the patient for treatment are elicited. Clear and specific information concerning object preferences, fantasies, marital relationships, attitudes of the partner, and acceptable social practices should be gathered at this time.

Detailed information concerning the personal attributions of the patient is critical. That is, what causal inferences does the patient make about his or her difficulty? These cognitions are additional factors that may impose limitations upon treatment and are often important in determining therapeutic procedures. Information needs to be gathered concerning frequency and duration of problems. If any limitation on sexual functioning is present, information is needed to determine any past attempts to solve these difficulties. All of this information should be carefully documented in any sexual history (LoPiccolo & Heiman, 1978; Masters & Johnson, 1970; Kaplan, 1974). Sexual histories should only be gathered by those with specific professional training in this regard. Not only can important information be missed, but there also is a risk that patients can be made more uncomfortable by poor interview techniques.

General Behavioral Interview

The general behavioral interview is primarily designed to detect environmental conditions that impact on sexuality. For example, family conditions, job stresses, and emotional states (such as fears and anxiety) are all important in assessing potential interference with sexual functioning. Evidence of psychopathology and psychosis should be evaluated, and the strengths and weaknesses of an individual should be assessed to help make appropriate treatment decisions. Interpersonal skills that impact on non-sexual aspects of relationships should be carefully assessed and marital issues of a non-sexual nature need to be evaluated.

We must recall the limitations upon behavioral interviews that stem from distortion and selective recall. Subjects may deliberately withhold information and distort it to make themselves "look good". We also need to recognize that the interviewee's responses are strongly affected by the clinician who collects the information. The clinician may be strongly conditioned by theoretical models and thus may ignore some topics and spend too much time on others. The interviewer may show anxiety which is detected by the patient and which may affect the patient's responses. Behavioral interviews may run from highly structured interviews in which specific questions are asked in specific sequences to rather open-ended interviews. They might consist of behavior samples in which the client or patient is asked to demonstrate some specific skill such as "What do you say when you first ask an individual for a date?" or "How would you tell someone that they were attractive?" The more systematic the interview the less likely the interviewer is to miss important and relevant data.

Self-report Questionnaires

Self-report questionnaires are generally filled out in privacy and often at the convenience of the individual who is giving the information. Questionnaires are a cost-efficient means of data collection and, if they are appropriately structured, the assessor has knowledge of the psychometric properties of the scale. They can be used for collecting both medical and sexual information assessed in history taking. As an added advantage, they allow the clinician to collect detailed information on private and sensitive life areas with minimal embarrassment for the respondee. Some of the more widely known scales include the scales of marital discord and distress (Weiss & Margolin, 1977) and the Sexual Arousal Inventory (Hoon, Hoon, & Wincze, 1976). Questionnaire responses have the problem of being confounded by social desirability. Subjects may simply be reporting what they think they should say rather than representing the true situation.

Self-monitoring Techniques

These procedures are used by individuals to describe their own behaviors in detail. Typically, they take the form of a diary which the individual is instructed to fill out at specified times (usually at least once a day or following the incidence of a particular behavior or event). They help clarify situations by making the client's behaviors and/or cognitions accessible to the clinician. Self-monitoring forms can be used to determine whether clients are accurately following suggestions in the course of treatment, and they can help uncover difficulties in compliance. Self-monitoring procedures have the potential to be reactive. That is, individuals may respond to the process of self-monitoring. The reaction may be positive or negative, depending upon the particular situation, but change may be an indirect result of monitoring. Self-monitoring is not distortion free. Any self-monitoring instrument that patients are given needs to be explicit and, of course, aimed at gathering only information that will be useful to the clinician.

Observation

There are serious ethical issues concerning observation of sexual behavior by any professional. It is, however, possible to observe nonsexual behavior that may reflect sexual interactions. Observation of an interaction between the patient and his or her partner in a nonsexual situation can uncover dynamics of their interpersonal system. One can study the communication patterns and the affect demonstrated, and use this behavior sample to evaluate indirectly how these prevailing conditions may affect sexual expression.

A new kind of observation technique which is being used extensively in the evaluation of the organic basis for erectile dysfunction is the recording of nocturnal penile tumescence in a sleep laboratory. Although the individual is not directly observed in this situation, changes in the diameter of the penis are measured throughout sleep. The assumption is made that the nature of the interference is psychological in those cases where individuals show normal, cyclic erections during REM sleep and yet are unable to achieve erections in interpersonal sexuality. It is likely that the information gathered by this procedure is more complex than had been originally anticipated.

FACTORS ASSOCIATED WITH SEXUAL DYSFUNCTION

Rationale

We are labeling this section, Factors Associated with Sexual Dysfunction. We chose this manner of presenting the information rather than presenting the usual array of dysfunctions and their descriptions because we feel that we can more meaningfully examine factors that are related to sexual dysfunction in this way. Classification problems make it extremely difficult to group sexual dysfunctions into valid and/or orthogonal categories. In the section that follows, we examine some of the problems that have led us to the decision to examine factors that are involved in the etiology and maintenance of sexual dysfunctions rather than grouping dysfunctions by category.

The first class of problems that one runs into in attempting to group sexual dysfunctions by categories are problems common to all typologies. First, since sexual behaviors and sexual dysfunctions appear to lie on a continuum, it is very difficult to make a determination as to where one should draw the cutoff between normal function and dysfunction. The extremes are often easy to decide, but the points between them cause difficulty. When is low sex desire a problem? There is no absolute answer to that question but the categories approach would suggest that there is an answer. Secondly, categories may not discriminate in sufficient detail. We could increase the number of categories to help discrimination among individuals; however, this leads to an increase in the number of borderline problems. If we have too few categories, then we tend to lump individuals together that should be separated. Separation should be based on differing outcome predictions or treatment of choice issues. Categories are only of value if they allow us to predict either outcome or treatment effects. Therefore, we are often caught in a dilemma of either too few or too many. Thirdly, many dysfunctional individuals have problems that fall into several categories at the same time. For example, premature ejaculation and erectile problems often coexist. This raises the question of which category is primary, or should the individual be placed into two separate categories. Fourth, there is an underlying concern that typologies are too simplistic. That is, labeling an individual as dysfunctional may lead to a failure to examine other problems that may coexist with the central or presenting sexual complaint.

Typologies may also lead the clinician to spend less time in evaluating the intensity, duration, and frequency of behaviors; the application of categorical labels tends not to reflect these dimensions. Another problem concerning individual diagnoses is that the categories available to us do not satisfactorily reflect the interaction of the behavioral dysfunction with physiological and cognitive systems. It is increasingly clear that these interactions need to be evaluated. Finally, multi-axial systems are developing in the field in which a number of dimensions are assessed simultaneously. Individuals may be categorized along these multiple dimensions, making any diagnosis more closely descriptive than topological. This multi-modal type of analysis may circumvent some of the problems noted above (Friedman, Weiler, & LoPiccolo, in press).

Certain technical problems are of considerable concern in classification systems. One of the more obvious is lack of agreement. That is, it is common for clinicians to disagree upon the defining characteristics of a category. This leads to considerable confusion and problems for both researchers and practitioners. The assignment of a patient to one of the several categories is difficult when criteria are imprecise. This is especially true when those categories are not orthogonal and relevant behaviors may appear in more than one category. These problems are not resolved by simple expansion of the categories. The problem may reflect the incompatibility of the category approach with the multi-determined problem under study. Quite often categories established for research purposes differ from those with clinical utility. Researchers may set up a category system which, while useful for them in that it is quite operational, may become essentially useless to the clinician or to another researcher. Researchers' and clinicians' varying needs lead them to develop different labels for categories and/or definitions of categories that may not be equally useful in both situations.

Perhaps an example of such a definitional confusion may be useful. In the *Diagnostic and Statistical Manual III* of the American Psychiatric Association, written in 1980, the category "Inhibited Sexual Excitement" is used for failure to attain or maintain an erection. However, the precise meaning concerning erection is unclear. The DSM III does not tell us if it is possible for the patient to get an erection, or whether the problem is that he gets an erection and then loses it. Similarly, it leaves uncertainty as to whether or not the patient gets subjectively aroused but does not get an erection, and as to whether or not he desires sex. All of these questions are left unanswered when we assign a person to the category "Inhibited Sexual Excitement".

Similar confusions surround the term "premature ejaculation". Most definitions of this term have a subjective component. Premature as compared to what? Premature as compared to the partner's response? Or premature in terms of norms concerning the time to ejaculation? We really don't have solid information concerning norms for ejaculatory latency. "Normal" must refer to a range of latencies rather than a single point. How then do we make the decision about where to cut off "normality"? When is it then that we apply the term "premature ejaculation"? If we are using a partner's response, as did Masters and Johnson (1970), does this mean a man would be a premature ejaculator if his partner were inorgasmic? Many of these concerns make it very difficult to end up with a strictly defined and valid category. Kaplan (1974) avoids this definitional issue by suggesting that it is not the latency to ejaculation or the partner's responsiveness that should be evaluated, but rather it should be absence of the male's control over the ejaculatory reflex. In her definition, control is the key, not the issue of latency nor the partner's response.

The DSM III (1980) definition of premature ejaculation is "The occurrence of ejaculation before the individual wishes it because of recurrent and persistent absence of voluntary or reasonable control of ejaculation or orgasm during sexual activity." This definition is not without fault, though on the surface it avoids the problem of partner satisfaction and actual latency. A closer examination reveals the same problems. For example, in the term "before the partner wishes it", the male is unlikely to desire to extend his latency unless he contrasts his problems to his partner's satisfaction. Men are not bothered by premature ejaculation during masturbation. Therefore, the phrase "until an individual wishes it" simply hides "can I satisfy my partner?" concerns. The notion "recurrent and persistent" is the operational definition upon which this is determined. How frequently is "persistent"? How often is "recurrent"? Who makes the judgment? the therapist? the client? the patient? or the partner? And according to what criteria? And what idea does the phrase "reasonable control" camouflage? Reasonable according to whom and relative to what? The point is that the DSM III definition which on the surface may look clear and reasonable is in actuality imprecise, subjective, and unreliable when examined closely. The application of the definition may well produce different results depending upon who applies it and the purpose to which it is applied. Research definitions might be more precise, however, they may have little clinical value and utility. Hopefully, the point is now clear: definitional issues make it very difficult to design exact, clear-cut, objective, and reliable ways of identifying dysfunctional behavior. The differing needs of researchers and practitioners often lead to seemingly disparate conclusions concerning the utility of categorizing sexual dysfunctions.

A main purpose of classification is to promote communication and to facilitate undistorted impressions of a clinical picture. Classification should be based on causative factors, as well as those that maintain conditions. The prognosis is also a central function of classification. We expect that any classification system would have implications for choice of treatment and would permit reasonable judgments as to probable outcome (Mash & Terdal, 1974). It is toward making viable treatment decisions that assessment should always be directed. Assessments should ideally have a goal above and beyond just assignment of a label. Finally, assessment should always be continuous in nature. The first assessment of a given case is not an endpoint. Continuous assessment to follow progress should be the norm.

Organismic States As Contributing Factors

Based on the preceding rationale, we now describe factors that influence sexuality rather than group by dysfunction. It should always remain in view that whereas we discuss conditions and states on an individual basis, they interact complexly and that the identification of one in a patient does not rule out the presence of others. We begin by considering physical states or conditions that impact on sexuality.

Genetic Conditions.   Genetic conditions provide a clear example of the multiple determination of sexuality. We shall not attempt to discuss this issue in detail as there are many well known discussions in the literature (Money & Schwartz, 1978; Mazur & Money, 1980; Money & Wiedeking, 1980). We shall, however, describe the most common genetic anomalies with illustrative descriptions of the impacts of those anomalies upon sexuality.

Sex Chromosomal Abberations

1. Klinefelter's Syndrome. One out of every 500 males is born with an extra X chromosome (Philip, Lundsteen, Owen, & Hirshhorn, 1976). This genetic pattern is labeled 47,XXY. Ten percent of all 47,XXY individuals exhibit a mosaic or variant of the syndrome. The genitals of infants born with Klinefelter's syndrome often appear normal and, as development proceeds, they become small and atrophied. There often is an associated delay in the onset of puberty. These individuals have sterile testes and frequently complain of low sex interest or libido. This syndrome is occasionally associated with severe mental retardation. These individuals are "vulnerable to developmental psychological defects or impairments" (Kolodny et al., 1979). Klinefelter's Syndrome, readily identified by karyotyping, is often treated with long-term testosterone replacement therapy (Mazur & Money, 1980). Such treatment has been associated with increased sexual interest and potency.

2. Turner's Syndrome. Approximately one out of every 2500 live females born has Turner's Syndrome. Turner's Syndrome is labeled as 45,XO to signify that there is a missing X chromosome. While Turner's Syndrome is associated with the failure of formation of normal gonads, the individual is still considered to be female due to the absence of a Y chromosome (Money & Schwartz, 1978). Though the external genitals do not look different, the individual is sterile and requires hormal replacement therapy to undergo a feminizing puberty. Most Turner's Syndrome individuals are short in stature, experience amenorrhea and have increased frequencies of other congenital anomalies. Hormone replacement

therapy does nothing to increase height and, of course, absolute infertility may very well cause psychological problems. In general, however, the Turner's Syndrome individual is free of psychopathological problems (Money & Mittenthal, 1970). Their gender identity, acquired early in childhood, appears normal. Early hormone treatment is suggested for this problem (Watson & Money, 1975). Other sex chromosome aberrations shall not be covered as they are quite infrequent.

Hormonal Abnormality Based on Genetic Factors

1. The Adreno-Genital Syndrome. In this condition individuals of either sex are born with a genetic fault (autosomal recessive) in which the adrenal cortex, because of changed biochemical reactions, fails to synthesize cortisol. Instead, an excessive amount of androgen is formed because the enzyme system produces excessive ACTH. The ACTH, in turn, leads to increased production of androgenic adrenal hormones (Money & Schwartz, 1978). The effect is that excessive androgens are present in the normonal environment of the developing fetus. Excessive androgens affect the formation of the external genitals in the genetic female. Depending upon the timing and extent of the metabolic fault, the individual is subject to morphological defects ranging from mild increase in the size of the clitoris to the formation of external genitals of male appearance. In the less common adreno-genital syndrome which occurs in genetic males, there is an absence of fetal testosterone (Grumbach & Van Wyk, 1974). Although the external genitals of these individuals appear female or are ambiguous, there is no development of the internal female sexual organs.

Early treatment of the female condition with cortisone can result in subsequent normal growth and normal fertility (Pang, Kenny, Foley, & Drash, 1977). If treatment is begun after age six, however, the individual is usually short in stature. Surgery can be performed on these women to construct appropriate genitals if genital anomalies are apparent (Jones, Garcia, & Klingensmith, 1977). Evidence suggests that after 2½ years of age, it is impossible to successfully reassign sex for those individuals who were misassigned based on genitals discordant with genetic sex. Sex reassignment late in the course of development appears destined to have profoundly harmful effects on both the patient and his or social milieu. Females who are masculanized by this process often show an increase in the display of male interests and increased general activity levels. Though typically these fall within acceptable limits, the increases appear to be mediated by fetal hormonal influences. While cases of hormonal abnormality based on genetic factors can result in a variety of symptom constellations, most of the individuals, of both sexes, also have serious deficiencies of a metabolic nature. For example, many have deficits in salt retention.

2. Testicular Feminization Syndrome (Androgen Intensivity Syndrome). This is a rare condition in which a genetic male undergoes all the appropriate

tissue development, but is insensitive to his own androgen production. As a result, the external genitals of this individual appear typically female. There are no internal female structures such as ovary and uterus and often testes are intraabdominal. The main cue to diagnosis of this condition is failure to menstruate. A variant of this condition exists in which there are ambiguous genitals. Such individuals are typically raised as females and surgery is commonly used to construct normal appearing feminine external genitals. Estrogen therapy is recommended at puberty to allow the individual to develop secondary sex characteristics appropriate to their female sex assignment (Kolodny, et al., 1979; Money & Schwartz, 1978; Saenger, Goldman, Levine, Korthschutz, Muecke, Katsumata, Doberne, & New, 1978). Because the upper third of the vagina is not present, these individuals will require self-dilation or vaginoplasty in order to experience coitus.

3. Micro Penis. This is a condition where the individual has a very small penis with undeveloped corporeal bodies. In some instances the penis may closely resemble a clitoris and sex mis-assignment is possible. At this time the etiology of this disorder is unknown. When sex mis-assignment occurs, practitioners should recall the warning, "Development of core gender identity seems to depend on genetic, gonadal, and early environmental influences. Once the concept is formed, gender identity and self-concept remain stable throughout life, resisting modification by environmental influence" (Wolman & Money, 1980, p. 157).

Diabetes.   Diabetes is a chronic disorder of carbohydrate metabolism due to a disturbance in the normal insulin mechanism. It has many effects upon body physiology, some of which impact directly upon sexual functioning. For example, diabetes predisposes women to develop vaginal pathology with subsequent painful intercourse or dyspareunia. Neuropathy of the sensory nervous system leads to problems with the perception of sensory input. Inasmuch as this perception is a major contributor to sexual arousal, arousal problems may occur. Neuropathy of the autonomic nervous system can lead to partial or complete loss of genital responding without a loss of desire or interest. In general, these effects can be ameliorated with sound clinical management of the diabetes, and younger individuals are more likely to have positive response to treatment (Brothers, 1975).

There is a high incidence of impotence in those who suffer from diabetes (30% in males under 40) (Brothers, 1975). It also has been found that defective sphincter control in the urogenital system commonly leads to retrograde ejaculation in the diabetic male. Brothers (1975) reported that 35% of 125 women between ages 18 and 40 who were diabetic were also inorgasmic whereas only 6% of an equivalent control group were inorgasmic. Brothers (1975) suggested the duration of the illness was correlated with orgasmic dysfunction, although Ellenberg (1978) disagrees with that position. It is known, however, that a time lag of a year or more between the onset of sexual dysfunction and the detection of diabetes may occur. In general, however, clinicians report that there is no loss in sexual interest as a result of diabetes.

Very often in males nocturnal recordings of penile tumescence are used to differentiate between organic problems related to diabetes and erectile problems of a non-organic nature. As noted previously, it is assumed that if normal cyclic erections occur during sleep the impotence is not based on organic factors. Neuropathy, of course, can be detected by neurological examinations and require detailed work-ups (Ellenberg, 1978). Renshaw (1978) has presented an outline for screening individuals who have erectile dysfunction based on diabetes.

In diabetes vascular obstructions with capillary pathology may occur and these may function to produce erectile problems in males. Bypass surgery has been attempted and may help in these situations. Another common treatment for male diabetics who experience chronic erectile dysfunction is the implantation of a penile prosthesis. There are two such classes of devices currently on the market. In one, the silicone implant, a semi-firm silicone-rubber rod, is implanted in the penis (Gottesman, Kosters, Das, & Kaufman, 1977; Small, 1978). The penis then remains partially erect from that time on. The second, a hydraulic system, is implanted so that an inflatable cylinder that can be filled with liquid is placed in the penis with a reservoir and pump elsewhere (Scott, Bradley, & Timm, 1973; Furlow, 1976). The individual can pump up the cylinder so that an erection is obtained and when he wishes the fluid can be drained back into the reservoir (Lange & Smith, 1978). This system is designed to provide erections upon demand. The clinician working with impotence in a diabetic male must take care not to induce a psychogenic influence by labeling the difficulty as organic and thus interfering with the patient's attempt to "work on" the problem. The interaction between psychological and organic factors may be sufficient to maintain an interference with sexual functioning. It also should be recognized that for some patients the physical discomfort and weakness associated with diabetes may lead to loss of sexual interest and drive, independent of any direct impact on sexuality.

Coronary Heart Disease.   This category includes several kinds of medical conditions; the patient with congestive heart failure, the post-cardiac surgery patient, and the post-myocardial infarction patient. Sexual activity for the post-coronary male has been examined by Hellerstein and Friedman (1970) who set recommendations concerning the resumption of sexual activity following the heart attack. It is suggested that the exertion associated with sexual intercourse is equivalent to the using of six to eight calories per minute; roughly equivalent to vigorous walking (Hellerstein & Friedman, 1970) or climbing two flights of stairs (Stein, 1975). If an individual is able to perform either of those activities without pain or without gross changes in pulse, EKG, or blood pressure, it is safe to recommend sexual activity. This general criteria holds equally for both sexes.

Some clinicians have expressed concern that other emotional states such as guilt or fear may interact with sexual arousal. Thus, they are concerned that when the cardiac patient is involved in an extra marital affair there is an additional stress during sexual activity. Naughton (1975) recommends the resumption of sexual activity within the eighth to fourteenth week following heart attacks if symptoms have abated.

In any coronary disease the response of the partner is important. Individuals may be anxious about being part of a situation that they perceive as a life threat to their partner and thus may withdraw from sexual activity. This may be viewed as rejection by the patient. The interaction between the patient and his or her sexual partner is a major point of interface between behavioral concerns and medicine.

Following by-pass surgery, research has demonstrated that anywhere from 35% to 50% of patients report an increase in sexual activity (Frank & Kornfeld, 1975). An additional 40% to 50% report no change and the remainder report that sexual activity is worse following such surgery. The typical report following a heart attack is that there is a decrease in the frequency of sexual activity; however, the decrease is uncorrelated with the severity of the attack, the age of the individual, or the level of marital sexual activity prior to the heart attack (Tuttle, Cook, & Fitch, 1964). Koller, Kennedy, Butler, & Wagner (1972) noted that many patients needlessly reduce sexual activity for fear of untoward physical consequences.

It is accepted as a truism that the medical profession provides poor counseling concerning sexual activity for the coronary patient (Friedman, 1978). Tuttle, et al. (1964), report that two-thirds of patients say that they receive no advice in this matter, whereas Hellerstein and Friedman (1969) reported that 94% of physicians say that they counsel on these issues. Which of these figures is accurate is not the point; the point is that patients perceive inadequate counseling whereas physicians feel that they provide sufficient counsel. Adequate counseling by physicians regarding the consequences for sexuality of a cardiac condition is a factor of major importance to the adjustment of patients.

Chronic Renal Failure. Patients with chronic renal failure experience fatigue, and lack of energy as an effect of the treatment as well as a result of the disease. These conditions often diminish interest in sex. There appears to be a difference in outcome between the patient treated by dialysis versus the patient treated by kidney transplant. In general, difficulties seem to be more pronounced in the dialysis patient, although a wide variety of individual differences occur. Impotence has been associated with dialysis (Abram, Hester, Sheridan, & Epstein, 1978) and there have been reports of improved sexual functioning as a result of kidney transplants. For example, in one study with only a few subjects, it was suggested that there were less sexual dysfunctions with transplant than dialysis patients. Additionally, it was found that the younger the patient the less likely was interference with sexual activity (Abram, et al., 1978). The relationship between renal failure and sexual functioning is heavily mediated by the generally disabling effects of the illness and less so effected by the direct impact of the disease process.

Sensory Dysfunctions: The Blind and the Deaf. (a). Blindness. There is very little research on the effects of blindness on sexual functioning (Scholl, 1974). Since there is an absence of visual cues, one might infer that as a result there are reduced opportunities for erotic stimulation. Even this is not known for certain and research is sorely needed in this area. The congenitally blind reach menarche early and show irregular menstruation. There are reports of impotence in the congenitally blind male. A difficulty in evaluating these data is that in acquired blindness, depression is often found and other medical conditions such as diabetes and multiple sclerosis often co-exist. Any of those factors may be the cause of sexual problems. Therefore, it would appear that sexual dysfunctions in blindness are more likely an outgrowth of features other than blindness per se. Attention is needed to socialization issues for the blind. The effect of social isolation that the congenitally blind experience can only be presumed to be important in the absence of research.

(b). Deafness. As a research issue the relationship between deafness and sexuality has been almost completely overlooked (Fitz-Gerald & Fitz-Gerald, 1978). The deaf individual is socially isolated, often has social skill deficits, and may have distortion of the body image. These features, when they occur, almost certainly will interact with sexual phenomena to present problems. Symptoms of depression and helplessness are common in the deaf and these conditions may very well contribute to sexual dysfunction.

Peyronie's Disease. Peyronie's disease consists of the development of fibrous plaques in the penis which leads to curvature. The effect is usually visible when the penis is partially or fully erect (Poutasse, 1973). The plaques appear most commonly in the dorsal aspect of the penis and do not always interfere with sexual functioning. However, in severe cases, pain and erectile problems occur. Severe difficulties usually do not appear until the individual is over 40. Very little is known concerning the cause of Peyronie's disease and sometimes spontaneous remission occurs. Even the frequency of Peyronie's is not known. Treatment of this illness has ranged from drugs and radiation, that show no clear effect, to the implantation of a penile prosthesis. Peyronie's disease is an example of a disorder that may directly affect sexual functioning.

Arteriosclerosis. Obstruction of the hypergastric arteries resulting from arteriosclerosis can cause impotence. This condition, known as the Leriche Syndrome (Jacobsen, 1975), can be corrected by surgery (Casey, 1979). In the organic brain syndrome associated with arteriosclerosis, individuals often experience a loss of cognitive and emotional functioning which may act to reduce sexual responsiveness. High blood pressure is commonly associated with arteriosclorosis but its effect upon sexuality, if any, is unknown. Any general debilitation or weakness is likely to interfere with sexual functioning.

Cerebro-Vascular Accident (Stroke). The stroke victim may have motor handicaps and sensory loss. In a study of 105 stroke victims under 60 years of age, 60% reported no loss of sex drive (Ford & Orfirer, 1967) although there was commonly an accompanying loss of motor functioning. A partner's concern over the patient's ability to function sexually after a stroke will often lead them to reduce sexual opportunities when such a reduction is not medically indicated (Ford & Orfirer, 1967). Depression and other psychological sequelae may very well play a role in the genesis of sexual dysfunctions that are associated with cerebral vascular accidents.

Epilepsy. Historically, epilepsy was assumed to result from excessive masturbation. In reality, we don't know if there is a relationship between epilepsy and sexuality. However, some of the medication given to epileptics may sedate them and thus reduce general responsiveness. One would anticipate that these general effects would interfere with sexual functioning. Also, since dilantin is known to affect personal appearance (Money & Pruce, 1977), this drug regimine may interfere with social interactions thus in an indirect way affecting sexuality. The epileptic is often rejected by society with adverse affects. While there are no known direct impacts of epilepsy on sexual functioning, it may very well be that the effects of societal rejection, medication, and negative emotional states do have powerful indirect effects.

Chronic Arthritis. Often there are mechanical limitations upon the arthritis victim. Bilateral hip disease interferes with mobility and placement of legs so as to disrupt coital activity. The chronic arthritic may have problems with weakness, fatigue, numbness, pain, stiffness, and a variety of disabling symptoms. The fact that the symptoms of arthritis vary during the day may affect sexuality. Arthritis itself does not seem to directly affect sexual interest or genital responding. However, limitations upon movement and pain associated with movement may seriously inhibit the expression of sexuality and this issue needs to be addressed when counseling these patients.

Asthma - Emphysema. Asthmatic spasms seldom follow sexual intercourse. However, any physician counseling the asthmatic patient should recommend intelligent and appropriate approaches to sexual activity. Chronic pulmonary obstructions, however, may be more directly related to sexual functioning. Hypoxia, associated with any form of exertion, may be accompanied by fears of suffocation. This may lead to the loss of sexual interest and avoidance of sexual activity (Agle & Baum, 1977). The severity of the disorder is directly related to the amount of loss of sexual function since disabling symptoms increase in more severe cases. Many asthmatics experience psychological sequelae such as depression and anxiety. As noted over and over these conditions impact adversely on sexuality.

Hypothyroidism. The thyroid affects all aspects of the individual's physiological functioning so that reduced thyroid activity is associated with general reduction of the individual's activity levels (Kolodny et al., 1979). Four of 700 Masters and Johnson's male and nine of 800 Masters and Johnson's female patients suffered from hypothyroidism (Kolodny, Masters, & Johnson, 1979). Hormone supplement therapy often restores sexual functioning in those individuals. Since the whole system is affected by hypothyroidism, one would expect rather generalized changes in sexual functioning. Eighty percent of hypothyroid patients report a decrease in sexual interest and desire; 40% to 50% of males report erectile dysfunctions (Kupperman, 1975). It also has been found that female hypothyroid patients report deficiency in sexual arousal and the ability to achieve orgasm (Kolodny, et al. 1979). Most of these effects appear to be the manifestation of chronic disease. In the developing child, hypothyroidism may result in retarded growth and delayed sexual maturation (Barnes, Hayles, & Ryan, 1973). There appears to be a decrease in the synthesis of testosterone in the hypothyroid adult (Kolodny, et al. 1979). Fertility is lowered in both male and female juvenile hypothyroid patients.

Hyperthyroidism (Thyrotoxicosis). An overactive thyroid is associated with divergent effects upon sexual activity. Of such patients, 10% to 20% report an increase in sexual interest, while 50% report no change and the others report a decrease. Around 40% of hyperthyroid males report erectile disturbances. Among women patients, there is a high incidence of the disruption of the menstrual cycle. Of females with the condition, 70% to 80% report reduction in sexual interest and the frequency of orgasms (Kolodny, et al. 1979). Males report growth in breast size. In many instances the interferences with sexual functioning are reversible with medication and surgical treatment of the disease.

Recreational Drugs. The recreational drugs: alcohol, nicotine (cigarettes), marijuana, amphetamines, amyl nitrate, cocaine, and heroin will be considered next. It should be noted that many of these drugs are taken in the belief that they provide a stimulant to sexual behavior. Therefore, we may well find that effects of these drugs may result from a psychological rather than a physiological mechanism or result from an interaction between the two. It is possible that the use of particular drugs acts by removing inhibitions or increasing expectations rather than acting directly upon physiological processes.

Alcohol.

The ingestion of alcohol provides a perfect example of the interaction between psychological and physiological events. Excessive long term use of alcohol may be associated with peripheral neuropathy and nutritional deficits both of which may function to suppress sexual activity. From a psychological perspective, we know that alcohol may function in very complex ways. It may, for example, act to remove inhibition and thus permit sexual activity that would not occur under other circumstances. We also note that alcohol may function to provide behavioral attributions that are harmful. For example, when a male functions sexually only after having had alcohol, he may very well attribute his functioning to the physiological effect of the alcohol and "give no credit" to himself. In this situation, we would expect the positive effect of success under alcohol not to transfer to the non-alcohol condition. Farkas and Rosen (1976) have shown that alcohol directly inhibits the achievement of an erection, and Wilson and Lawson (1976) have shown that at moderate and high levels alcohol functions to reduce vaginal pressure pulse activity. Interestingly, in the Wilson and Lawson study, while vaginal pulse activity to erotic stimuli decreased, the rating of subjective sexual arousal to erotic stimuli increased. Thus they found a divergence between pharmacological and psychological effects.

In surveying individuals, 68% of females and 48% of males say that alcohol enhances their sexuality (Athanasiou, Shaver, & Tavris, 1970). Based on Farkas's and Wilson's data, one would have to assume that this resulted primarily from psychological rather than physiological effects since alcohol appears to act as an inhibitor rather than a facilitator of physiological response. Alcohol levels have been implicated in lowering testosterone and LH production in humans (Gordon, Altman, Southren, Rubin, & Lieber, 1976).

Nicotine (Cigarettes).

While it has been reported that sexual activity increases when individuals stop smoking (Ochsner, 1975), there is very little substantial data to support that position. It is known that smoking is associated with early menapause though how that might effect sexuality is not clear (Jick, Porter, & Morrison, 1977).

Marijuana.

There is no evidence that smoking marijuana increases sex drive, but it may very well be that the relaxation that some individuals experience when smoking marijuana facilitates sexual activity. It has been reported (Weil, 1972) that time sense is distorted under the influence of marijuana and that tactile senses are affected. Through changes in sensory events marijuana use may enhance positive feelings in sexual activity. Kolodny, Masters, Kolodner, and Toro (1974), report that heavy usage of marijuana is associated with lowered testosterone levels (although in those studies the level of marijuana usage was far above that of most casual marijuana users). In the drug culture, marijuana has been regularly associated with increased sexual activity. That expectation may very well influence sexuality and lead, through psychological rather than physiological mechanisms, to enhanced sexual experience.

Amphetamines.

Amphetamines may affect sexuality through decreasing inhibition and through changes in sensory sensitivity. It seems that the effects of amphetamines are dose related and that at high dosages, withdrawal and loss of sexual interest are often reported (Dahlberg, 1975).

Amyl nitrate

Some members of the drug culture are known to use amyl nitrate immediately prior to orgasm. They report that this increases the sensation of the orgasm. Since amyl nitrate is known to increase vasodilation and to drop blood pressure, the experience of these physiological events may very well be interpreted as enhanced sexual sensations.

Cocaine.

Individuals report an alteration in sense of time when on cocaine. Many who use cocaine believe that it has positive effects upon sexuality. That may well become true due to the same psychological mechanisms previously outlined for other drugs.

Heroin.

It is generally accepted that heroin addicts have disordered lives and diminished sexuality. There are contradictory data concerning the effects of heroin on sex hormone productions with some reports of lowered levels (Azizi, Vagenakis, Longscope, Ingbar, & Braverman, 1973). It has been reported that heroin addiction is associated with amenorrhea and infertility (Bai, Greenwald, Caterini, & Kaminetsky, 1974). Many heroin addicts report that mainlining heroin yields a subjective experience similar to orgasm. The experience has been labeled as a "pharmogenetic orgasm". There are many harmful sequelea of heroin addiction, such as poor nutrition which would impact negatively upon sexuality. It is well known that many female heroin addicts turn to prostitution to obtain money to support their habit. This is an indirect effect of the drug, but it does illustrate the interaction between widely differing phenomena.

Dyspareunia From Organic Conditions.   Any condition that can cause pain associated with or occurring at the same time as sexual interactions will hamper sexual responsiveness. There is a long list of medical conditions that can produce pain in sexual activity. In the following list we note some of the more obvious ones that affect women: acute vaginitis, vaginal scars, endometriosis, intrapelvic pathology, venereal diseases, and atrophy of vaginal tissues resulting from estrogen starvation. Pain will naturally lead to avoidance of sexual contact and the avoidance may, in turn, lead to problems between partners. Males are not immune to pain in sexual activity. Prostatitis, which we will cover in greater detail later, infections of uro-genital structures, and associated scars all may lead to pain in the male. In a mechanism identical to that of females, the discomfort may lead to a reduction and/or avoidance of sexual contact. Any condition that can lead to pain in sexual activity is almost bound to interfere with sexual function.

Nutrition.   Nutritional deficiencies are associated with fatigue, and fatigue is well known to be associated with reduced interest in sexuality and withdrawal from sexual contacts. Individuals who suffer from reduced caloric intake often have lowered sexual performance (Gebhard, 1965). When the physician finds nutritional problems in the United States, it is often secondary to life style problems such as excessive dependency upon alcohol or drugs.

Spinal Cord Lesions.   In a recent text on the treatment of spinal cord injuries there was only one reference to sexual functioning (Eisenberg & Falconer, 1978). The total statement on these issues in that text was limited to the following:

> Erectile and ejaculatory incompetence and sterility are also commonly experienced. The physiological impairments often produce massive social and psychological ramifications which can threaten the life goals of the cord injured and their families, endanger their defensive systems, and disrupt their role functions (p. 3–4).

Such a lack of focus on the issue of sexuality indicates that, like other disabled people, the spinal cord injured are often treated as asexual beings. Usually, they have received inadequate counseling on how to manage future sexual behavior and how they can expect their disabilities to affect/limit the sexual aspects of their lives. In the face of the archaic attitudes expressed by some medical professionals, an increasing awareness of these issues by a number of practitioners is leading to willingness to deal with them.

Education of both the professional and the spinal cord lesion patient is crucial. It is estimated that 100,000 males in the United States have spinal cord lesions and that the site and extent of injury has significant impact upon sexual functioning (Higgins, 1978). Neurological examinations of these individuals is necessary to determine the degree and site of lesions.

There are a wide range of effects of spinal cord lesions. Between 48.2% and 91.7% of such patients retain some ability to maintain an erection (Jochheim & Wahle, 1970; Fitzpatrick, 1974). In general, it would appear that the higher the lesion the more likely the individual is to maintain his erectile capacity and as the lesions are less complete, erection is more likely (Higgins, 1978). It has been found that up to 7% (Jochheim & Wahle, 1970) of individuals with complete cord lesions can still ejaculate, whereas 27% (Comarr, 1970) to 32% (Bors & Comarr, 1960) of incomplete lesion patients still maintain the ability to ejaculate. The lower the lesion, the more likely is the occurrence of ejaculation; the reverse of the erectile dysfunction. Anywhere from 2% (Jochheim & Wahle, 1970) to 56% (Hohmann, 1966) of males can obtain sufficient erection to permit successful penetration of the vagina and thus provide a degree of self and partner satisfaction. The typical spinal cord lesion patient continues to have a high interest in sex and is powerfully influenced by many psychological factors (Evans, Halar, DeFreece, & Larsen, 1976). These must not be neglected by medical personnel dealing with the patient.

Venereal Disease.   We are not going to discuss VD in detail. We note that it has been implicated in dyspareunia and in infertility. VD, by definition, is a sexually transmitted disease and thus sexual behavior and the pathology are closely interwoven. VD is often missed in the physical examination because of reticence on the part of physicians to examine the genitals. This seems to be a particular problem in the occurrence of anal VD in the homosexual population. Since symptom free gonorrhea is common in women, physicians need to be more careful and consistent in examinations for this condition.

Prostatitis.   Prostatitis is inflammation of the prostate. It is associated with burning sensations, the feeling of need for frequent urination, and often is associated with discomfort in the testes. Prostatitis is commonly caused by bacteriological infection, the most common source of which is E. coli (80% of the time; Kolodny, et al., 1979). Prostatitis is quite difficult to treat as medicines are unable to cross the prostatic epithelium. The prostate often acts as a reservoir of infection making treatment difficult since reinfection continues. The individual experiencing prostatitis often has painful erections and ejaculations and there may be referral of pain to the rectum and to the testes. Prostatitis will usually lead to a reduction in sexual activity as the result of the associated discomfort. Treatments including abstinence and prostatic massage have been recommended. Men need to be educated as to hygienic habits that serve to reduce the likelihood of prostatitis.

Stricture.   Stricture refers to a constriction of the urethral canal. Stricture in males often results in painful ejaculation and can be treated with surgery if necessary. Such surgery is threatening to the individual, and the associated fears and anxieties can have an adverse effect upon sexuality.

The Effects of Medical Treatments that Impinge on Sexuality

Prostate Surgery.   Fifteen percent of all malignancies found in males are carcinoma of the prostate. In addition, hypertrophy of the prostate is found in approximately 30% of males aged 41 to 50 and is found in 75% of males aged 80 or older (Flocks, 1969). In many instances benign disease of the prostate results in urine retention and requires surgical intervention. It is common for patients facing this treatment to be concerned about postoperative loss of sexual functioning. A number of different surgical procedures are involved in the treatment of both benign and malignant prostatic disease. They vary in the likelihood of postoperative erectile dysfunction occurring as a complication (Madorsky, Drylie, & Finlayson, 1976). The first, a transurethreal approach, involves surgery in which the prostate is approached through the urethra. There is no accompanying nerve damage or adverse effects upon blood flow in the pelvic region. Following transurethreal surgery, retrograde ejaculation to the bladder is common. Though this has no specific effects upon sexuality, it is quite common for males experiencing retrograde ejaculation to develop psychologically based impotence due to the change in sexual function.

The second surgical approach is called the suprapubic approach. Following this kind of surgery, 75% to 80% of males report retrograde ejaculation and erectile failure occurs in 10% to 20% (Zohar, Meiraz, Maoz, & Durst, 1976). The third is the retrograde pubic approach. When this approach is employed, retrograde ejaculation occurs in 70% to 80% of patients with 10% to 20% reporting problems with erections. The fourth surgical approach, the perineal approach, results in a higher rate of postoperative erectile dysfunctions. It is reported that 40% to 50% of perineal approaches for benign prostatic disease result in erectile dysfunctions. In the case of radical disection of a wide area of tissues for malignant disease, erectile problems result in 98% of those males whose surgery involved the perineal approach (Nelson, 1978).

The psychological response of both partner and patient to changes in ejaculatory volume and to retrograde ejaculation is important. Clinicians often neglect to note that the partner may be affected by a lack of ejaculatory volume; the emphasis has typically been upon the patient who also may react negatively to this experience. It has been reported that preoperative explanation is important in the recovery of sexual function in prostatic surgery. Zohar, et al. (1976), report that if preoperative reassurance and factual explanations are given, postsurgery erectile problems come close to disappearing. In a control group of eight males who were not given reassurance and information preoperatively, five developed erectile problems (Zohar, et al., 1976). It has been suggested by Madorsky et al. (1976), that nocturnal recording of penile erection should be used if erectile problems occur following prostatic surgical procedures. They report that following transurethreal surgery that nocturnal penile tumescence is still present, but that there is a loss in quality of the response. For patients with inoperative prostatic disease, radiation, and hormone therapies are often recommended. Many of the side effects of those procedures result in nausea and weakness that will disturb sexual functioning. Of course, the fear and anxiety that accompanies knowledge of a malignancy may interfere with sexual activity as well.

General Surgery.   Following any surgical procedure there are a number of factors which may operate to interfere with sexual functioning. Pain experienced during recovery from the surgical procedure may interfere, and the weakness and fatigue which is common following surgery is also likely to act as an inhibitor of sexual functioning. Following surgery and for a period preceeding surgery, when the individual is aware of oncoming surgical intervention, he or she may be focusing on that aspect of his or her existence and as a result sexual functioning may be diminished. It is quite natural for individuals undergoing surgery to fear for the loss of their life. This fear, with the powerful emotional feelings accompanying it, may lead to sexual dysfunction.

Any surgical procedure that interferes with the nerve supply or blood supply to genitals or to secondary sex organs may have powerful, longterm, negative impact upon sexual functioning. Colon resections, which would be commonly anticipated to interfere with sexual functioning, in reality seldom directly lead to erectile problems (Lyons, 1975). Rectal resections for malignancies often result in erectile failure (Lyons, 1975). However, it is not clear whether this is the result of psychological or physiological factors. Pelvic lymph gland disection associated with these resections often leads to high levels of postsurgical erectile failure (Malin, 1975). We ought to note that the colostomy with its attendant emotional impact and concerns over personal hygiene often presents a problem in sexual functioning for both the patient and his or her sexual partner. On the other hand, we should not forget to note that there may be positive effects of surgery on sexual functioning. If the surgery results in pain reduction, it may facilitate sexual interactions. Vascular surgery and bypass surgery that permits the individual to become more active postsurgery may very well lead to positive effects upon sexual behavior. Surgical procedures which are designed to enhance or positively change body image may also have a salutary effect upon sexual functioning.

Surgery to the Genitals and Secondary Sex Organs.   The clitoris is subject to development of adhesions that produce pain when the clitoris is stimulated. Relatively straightforward and simple surgical removal of these adhesions can result in a dramatic reduction in pain and have very positive effects upon sexual functioning.

As discussed previously, an increasingly common surgical procedure is the implantation of a penile prosthesis (Lange & Smith, 1978). This procedure is used for treatment of irreversible, organically-based impotence such as that associated with some prostate surgery and some instances of diabetes. As noted, there are both fixed rods and inflatable penile prostheses (Lange & Smith, 1978). Accompanying penile implants there are rejection problems and increased risk of infections, particularly in diabetic patients. When sexual functioning is important to the individual, the impairment of erection is physiologically based, and the individual does not report a loss of sexual interest or inability to ejaculate; a prothesis may become the treatment of choice. The fixed rod prosthesis results in a permanent semi-erection which may prove discomforting and be distressful to the individual. The ''pump-up'' prosthesis requires more extensive surgical intervention with increased costs and is subject to a high rate of mechanical failure. There is, however, a greater personal acceptance of this latter device since it mimics the natural state of the flacid as well as the erect penis. Complications of penile prosthesis surgery have occurred in up to one-quarter of those who have had the surgery (Kramer, Anderson, Bredael, & Paulson, 1979).

Genetically based anomalies of the genitals may be treated with plastic surgery. Males for whom testicles are undescended can often be treated successfully with surgical intervention. A new and interesting development in penile surgery is the repair of the cavernosis system for some individuals whose impotence is based upon structural anomalies in that system. Wagner's (1980) work on this phenomena suggests that it is broader in nature than had been previously considered. Reconstructive surgery of any kind may have positive effects upon the individual. Increasing positive aspects of their self image as well as increased attractiveness to potential partners, may lead to enhanced sexuality.

Each year approximately 90,000 women in the United States develop cancer of the breast (Silverberg, 1978). Many of these women undergo breast surgery. When breast surgery involves removal (mastectomy), adverse psychological consequences may follow. The individual may experience severe concerns over their changed body image, and she may be very much concerned about partner reaction or anticipated partner reactions of either repulsion or disgust. Work on reconstruction and prosthesis of the post-mastectomy is in part a response to concerns of patients and partners. Research has been conducted concerning the impact of counseling upon the mastectomy patient. Frank, Dornbush, Webster, and Kolodny (1978) reported that only 4% to 6% of premastectomy patients were counselled concerning the impact of the procedure upon sexuality. About 50% of the patients reported wishing that such counseling had occurred. It has been reported that 49% of mastectomy patients resume intercourse within one month. However, approximately one-third have not resumed intercourse six months post surgery even though there were no physical complications that required abstinence (Frank, et al., 1978). Following mastectomy, 61% to 45% of women report a decrease in the frequency of orgasm and from a frequency of 17% prior to surgery there is an increase to 40% post surgery of women who report never or rarely engaging in intercourse (Frank, et al., 1978). The frequency of intercourse generally changes. Fifty-two percent of patients reported intercourse at once per week, preoperatively. Following surgery, only 35% reported this level as continuing in the first 3 months postoperatively. Initiation of sexual activity by the female drops and there is a considerable reduction in the use of the female above position for sexual intercourse. It has been found that roughly 40% of all males have not viewed the site of mastectomy surgery 3 months postsurgery (Malin, 1975). Complications involved in mastectomies may serve to exacerbate sexual problems. Additional treatments including radiation therapy, chemotherapy, or hormone treatments are often associated with nausea, vaginal atrophy, and other conditions which may lead to reduced sexual responding.

Penile loss through trauma or surgery is a relatively infrequent event. Cosmetic replacement is possible, and the individual can both ejaculate and experience orgasm. However, at this time, these surgical techniques have not been developed enough to construct a penis that erects naturally, although penile implants can allow for artificial erection in some cases (Noe, Sato, Coleman, & Laub, 1978).

Sometimes hysterectomy results in a reduction of sexual activity particularly if the woman feels that somehow she has become less feminine. It is not uncommon for the hysterectomized woman to view herself as incomplete and that adversely affects sexual functioning. On the other hand, in some instances, sexual functioning increases following a hysterectomy particularly if the woman had been concerned over unwanted pregnancy (Kolodny, et al., 1979). In the past, the hysterectomy was commonly used as a birth control procedure although at this point in time this is rarely the case in the U.S.A..

Obstetrical Trauma.   A number of traumas to the genital structures are associated with the delivery of infants. These include scarring from tissue tears, scars resulting from poorly performed or healed episiotomies, ligament damage, and muscular damage. Any one or a combination of these problems may result in pain during subsequent intercourse. Physicians need to make themselves aware of these problems and to apply corrective procedures when possible.

Pharmacological Effects of Prescribed Drugs on Sexuality.   There are some general issues concerning the effects of drugs upon sexuality that need to be noted. First, it is quite often difficult to differentiate placebo effects from true physiological effects. Of course, in many instances there is an interaction where both kinds of factors are operative. It is known that the effects of pharmacological agents may persist in the system far beyond the time that they are detectable and this complication may mask true pharmacological effects, making them appear psychological. Any drug that directly effects the sympathetic nervous system, the parasympathetic nervous system, the central nervous system, or sex hormone production may have specific effects upon sexual activity. The birth control pill, which modifies the hormonal environment of the individual, also must be considered as having a potential pharmacological impact upon sexuality. The point is, that many widely prescribed drugs affect sexuality, and physicians need to consider these effects when deciding upon a treatment of choice.

One prescribed drug which might be expected to have effects upon sexual functioning is the birth control pill. The pill consists of both estrogens and progestins; the principal female sex hormones. As we shall see, however, the results of studies on the effect of the pill on sexual behavior are varied. As Cohen (1977) has said, "The information reported tends to show that for the time being there are no satisfactory studies from which the effects of oral contraceptives on sexual behavior could be effectively evaluated." (p. 381). Rice-Wray, Goldzieher, and Aranda-Rosell (1963) have found an increase in frequencies of sexual intercourse for women on the pill. Udry and Morris (1970), however, reported no change in frequency of sexual intercourse. Some individuals have reported increases in sexual satisfaction (Pasini, 1974), whereas Cullberg, Gelli, & Jonsson (1969), found no change in sexual satisfaction. We could go on, but the point is that there are no consistent effects of the birth control pill on sexuality. Should effects be present, we have no way of knowing the mechanism of action. Effects could result from hormones acting upon the central nervous system or could be secondary to such changes as modifications of lining of the vagina, or the production of lubrication during arousal. Finally, the changes could be the result of the psychological effect of the reduction of anxiety or fear of becoming pregnant. Until we have more accurate information concerning the effect of the pill, speculation on mechanism of effects is premature.

There are several classes of prescribed drugs that have identified effects upon sexual functioning. Diuretic agents, used in the treatment of hypertension, have been associated with changes in peripheral circulation. While the mechanism is unknown, they have been associated with a low incidence of erectile failure (Kolodny, et al., 1979). The medication spironolactone, used in the treatment of hypertension, is known as a competitive antagonist of at least one of the androgens. The drug has been reported to be associated with decreases in sexual interest and in the occurrence of impotence and gynecomastia in men (Stripp, Taylor, Bartter, Gillette, Loriaux, Easley, & Menard, 1975); menstrual irregularity and breast tenderness in women have been reported (Levitt, 1970). It is obvious that careful monitoring of that drug for its effects upon sexuality is warranted. On the other hand, other drugs used to reduce blood pressure (e.g., alpha-methyldopa, propranolol, reserpine, hydralazine, guanethidine, and clonidine) seem to have their effects on hypertension through effects upon the autonomic nervous system. To the degree that these drugs affect autonomic functioning, it is possible that men and women using these drugs will show impaired sexual responsiveness. As can be true for any drug, psychological factors may interact with the pharmacological factors to exacerbate the problem or to continue it after the medication has been removed. Since compliance with medication for hypertension is seen as such as a serious problem, it should be recognized that compliance issues are confounded by the fact that some of these medications impact on sexuality. It is difficult to get individuals to maintain a medication regimen that adversely affects otherwise adequate sexual functioning.

Tranquilizers and sedatives are complicated in their impact on sexuality. First, the degree to which they reduce anxiety may facilitate sexual functioning that was inhibited by anxiety. Secondly, the degree to which medications impact upon the autonomic nervous system or the central nervous system can result in complicated interactions. It is difficult to tell when an effect results from direct nervous system involvement, when the effect is mediated through psychological processes, or when an interactive process is involved.

The habitual use of barbituates seems to be associated with depressed sexual interest, impotence, and loss of orgasmic responsiveness (Kolodny, et al., 1979). It is also true, however, that some individuals chronically using these medications show little or no effect on psychological functioning.

Many of the drugs used to treat psychiatric disturbances have been associated with sexual dysfunction. The phenothiazines used for treatment of severe psychiatric disturbances have a strong effect on the sympathetic nervous system and the parasympathetic nervous system and are often associated with decreased sexual interest (Story, 1974). The monoamine oxidase inhibitors are frequently associated with delays in ejaculation or ability to ejaculate, and the frequency of erectile dysfunctions runs fairly high in males on these drugs (Kolodny, et al. 1979). The tricyclic anti-depressants have been known to disturb sexual functioning perhaps due to side effects such as dizziness, tachycardia, dry mouth, etc. (Blackwell, Stefopoulos, Enders, Kuzma, & Adolphe, 1978). Perhaps the best that can be said is that drug effects vary considerably from person to person and across dose levels.

Health care professionals must be familiar with harmful side effects of pharmacological agents and must be prepared to cope with them when they arise in their patients. As Katchadourian and Lunde (1980) have pointed out, ''The main thing to remember in this connection is that whenever a person is using a drug—any drug—and develops sexual problems, the drug must be evaluated as a possible cause of the problem. This is especially true for tranquilizers and all other compounds that act on the central nervous system'' (p. 400). We would add that medications cannot be viewed independently of their interaction with psychological phenomena. Expectation of pharmacological effects, effects upon inhibitions, effects upon anxiety, and so on all can powerfully influence sexual behavior.

Experiential Factors and Conditions That Influence Sexuality

In referring to experiential factors we are beginning to move along the organic/psychogenic continuum our model proposes and away from the more exclusively physiological factors. This section considers those experiences that impact upon the emotions and/or thought processes of individuals and through those pathways have their impact upon sexuality. In this section, we discuss both conditions and experiences that are non-medical in nature but that either are experiential or result from experiential factors and that may interact with medical considerations. It is impossible to produce an exhaustive description of experiential conditions which effect sexuality. Therefore, the following list should be seen as illustrative and modal in nature.

Educational Deficits. Lack of information about the physiology and anatomy of sexual functioning may impact upon sexual behavior. For example, occasionally women are seen whose knowledge of sexual physiology is so limited that they express the concern that the lubrication that occurs during sexual arousal is a leakage of urine. Males, unaware of the tactile sensitivity of the clitoris and having learned something about its importance in sexual functioning, may almost attack that structure inadvertently inflicting considerable distress and discomfort upon their sexual partners. Some individuals become frightened by their own sexual responses. They feel that the strength of their response to sexual stimuli is beyond what they had expected. Often that feeling is accompanied by fear of the loss of control over themselves with the attendant concern that perhaps they will do things that they will later regret or find embarrassing. A very common worry that can be alleviated with the offering of some factual information is the effect of aging upon sexuality. Many people expect that major sexual deficits result directly and inevitably from aging. Most people are not aware of the fact that individuals can maintain an active, comfortable, and rewarding sex life as long as they live.

Kolodny, et. al. (1979) list six examples of misinformation about the anatomy and physiology of sex that illustrate the problem of educational deficits. The following is a paraphrase of that list.

1. Uncertainty about the location of the clitoris.
2. A woman not recognizing her own orgasm.
3. Belief that the capacity for sexual functioning is lost with aging.
4. Belief that the male must ejaculate every time he has intercourse or every time he has an erection.
5. Belief that the amount of vaginal lubrication is proportionate to the woman's sexual excitation.
6. Belief that sexual activity must cease as soon as the male has ejaculated.

Each of these common misunderstandings make clear the fact that lack of information or misinformation concerning the anatomy and physiology of the sexual response may interfere with sexual behavior. Misinformation may provide the individual with expectations concerning sexual activity which are unrealistic at best and destructive or detrimental at worst.

We also note a paucity of information concerning the impact of medical conditions upon sexual behavior. Incorrect information concerning the impact of sexual behavior upon post-coronary patients is an example. Information may be necessary to assure individuals as to the normalcy of their behavior. There are individuals who fear that oral-genital contact is a perversion and simple information concerning the frequency of that behavior among the general population may go far to alleviate worry or concern. Finally, knowledge often leads people to believe that they have greater control over themselves and their environment. It is generally acknowledged that feeling in control has positive emotional consequences (Gatchel, 1980). Thus, we would expect that sexual knowledge would lower the negative emotions that might accompany the lack of knowledge.

Attitudinal Problems. There are many attitudes which impact on sexual functioning. Strict religious unbringing may very well provide a set of values and emotional responses that produce guilt and anxiety, and inhibit sexual activity (Masters & Johnson, 1970). If individuals feel that sexual activity is dirty, sinful, or demeaning, there are bound to be negative effects upon their scope of sexual interactions. The impact of an attitude is a function of its strength rather than its source. Individual's attitudes may relate to the determination of what they consider to be acceptable behavior. Thus, attitudes can limit the range of sexual activities and such limitations have implications for interventions designed to deal with sexual dysfunctions.

Most of us have inculcated sterotyped values concerning masculinity or femininity that influence our behavior. The degree to which these standards and values effect sexuality varies from individual to individual. Those with stereotyped attitudes concerning masculine or feminine behavior are very likely to find themselves limited both in terms of behaviors and in terms of flexibility regarding what is acceptable. Clinicians should be alert to the fact that attitudes differ widely as a function of educational and economic levels within society (Kinsey, Pomeroy, Martin, & Gebhard, 1953). Physicians and professionals in the mental health disciplines need to be particularly sensitive to their own attitudes and biases and how these may affect their dealings with patients.

Communication Deficits and Deficiencies.   Even when professionals "give permission" to discuss sexual concerns by initiating such discussions, patients may show a continued reluctance to seek information or counsel. It is all right to talk about most behavior but for many people discussion of sexual behavior is extremely difficult, if not taboo. This is particularly important since there is a mutuality in the responsibility for problems that occur in sexual interactions (Masters & Johnson, 1970). Even where partners are not mutually responsible for the cause of sexual dysfunction, they are for its maintenance and are likely to be for its cure. Lack of communication between individuals very often leads to difficulty. If communication is a problem in any sphere of social interaction for sexual partners, it is virtually assured be present in the sexual sphere. Physicians and psychological professionals need to be aware that verbal and non-verbal aspects of communication are important in sexuality. In fact, much of sexual behavior occurs without direct verbal responding. Often permission to initiate or continue sexual activity is sought non-verbally. That set of conditions is ready-made to develop problems. Sometimes these problems can be dealt with by giving individuals graded experience in communication skills and by observing appropriate communication patterns. Another communication problem often seen in sexual interactions is deceit between partners. Deceit may occur in many situations. For example, the partner may hide his or her concerns over homosexual interests. Commonly, there are issues over a sexual behavior which is desired by one member and not by the other. Often in this situation the partner who does not wish the act is worried about presenting such information for fear of rejection and, therefore, hides his or her feelings. Communication problems are often seen as the focus of marital discord and almost universally spill over into sexual interactions within the marriage (Paolino & McCrady, 1978).

Environmental Conditions.   Clinicians need to be aware of the fact that there are many environmental situations which impact upon sexuality. Physical conditions that allow for intrusion on a couple's privacy will inhibit sexual intercourse. Fear of a child walking in on parents during coitus is a commonly expressed concern. Novelty in the environment may play a facilitative role in sexual interactions. It is a common observation that vacation time increases sexual activity. There are life styles that do not leave time for sex, and spouses in those situations may feel unloved or unwanted. There are environmental conditions that increase the probability of the occurrence of extra-marital affairs. Professionals need to be sensitive to the many environmental conditions that impact upon sexual behavior.

Sexual Fears.   There are many fears that disturb sexual functioning. Perhaps the most obvious are performance fears. It appears that when individuals are concerned with their sexual performance (and this fear is more common in males than females) there often is a resultant interference with that performance. In addition, the individual who is concerned about ability to perform tends to avoid sexual situations. In turn, this increase in avoidance of sexual contact may be accompanied by depression and guilt which leads to further interference and avoidance. As can be seen, there is a vicious cycle established in which fear leads to further problems and exacerbates exigent ones. Often performance fears arise from misconceptions and misperceptions of the situation or the partner's reaction. However, regardless of their source, fears almost invariably interfere with sexual functioning.

There are individuals who have specific phobias and aversions concerning either viewing or having contact with genitals. While this is a relatively infrequent phobia, its occurrence is devastating to sexual activity. Many women report fears of penetration and fears of VD and these fears usually lead to a reduction of sexual activity. The occurrence of vaginismus, the spasmodic tightening of the muscles around the introitus, is often reported by individuals who fear penetration (Fuchs, Hoch, Paldi, Abramovici, Brandes, Timor-Tritsch, & Kleinhaus, 1978). Sexual aversion may result from fears concerning the sex act itself as well as fears of "letting go" in a sexual situation. Systematic desensitization for concrete fears, such as semen phobias, have been used with some effectiveness (Friedman, et al., in press). Often clinicians forget that simple fear reduction is not enough. It may also be necessary to simultaneously train those individuals with respect to specific skills that may not have been practiced as a result of fear-motivated avoidance behaviors.

Stresses.   General stress conditions are normally reflected by an array of behavior changes. Such changes are likely to include a decrease in the frequency of sexual activity. Death of loved ones, change of jobs, and occupational concerns are general stresses that may be associated with reductions in sexual activity.

Specific stresses, such as the occurrence of rape, incest, or the existence of marital discord, also impact on sexual activity. The over-all effect of such events and circumstances is to inhibit sexual activity. Any stress may result in reduced quality and/or frequency of sexual functioning.

Transsexualism.   Transsexualism is the condition in which a genetic male or female declares that their sexual identity is that of the opposite sex. They feel that they are trapped in the body of the wrong sex. There have been no consistent demonstrations of hereditary or hormonal factors which lead to this condition (Money & Wiedeking, 1980). Its relative intransigence to psychological treatment has resulted in widespread use of surgical and hormonal interventions. Surgical treatment consists of removal of the gonads and external genitals of the individual and attempted reconstruction of the genitals so as to mimic those of the desired sex. This procedure is considered major surgery, is quite expensive and, unfortunately, has a high complication rate (Jayaram, Stuteville, & Bush, 1978). Hormone supplements are given as a treatment adjunct. After reviewing a report evaluating surgical intervention for transsexualism (Meyer & Reter, 1979), Johns Hopkins University has ceased performing sex reassignment surgery. It has been reported that they feel the outcome did not justify major surgical intervention. That view is not shared by others evaluating the same study (Fleming, Steinman, & Bocknek, 1980). The incidence of transsexualism is not very high in the population, however, its dramatic nature has made it the subject of much coverage in the popular media.

Alcohol.   As described in a previous section, alcohol interferes with the occurrence of erection. In Masters and Johnson's work on erectile dysfunction, they suggested that a common route for development of erectile dysfunction involved the use of alcohol (Masters & Johnson, 1970). In their model, while drinking, the individual experiences difficulty in obtaining or maintaining an erection based upon the pharmacological effect of the alcohol. The male subsequently attributes that failure to himself rather than to the effect of alcohol. This attribution is expressed in terms of performance anxiety, perhaps guilt, and fears of sexual functioning. These fears subsequently interfere with any attempt at sexual performance. We are left with the now familiar interaction in which a physiological effect becomes attributed to psychological factors. In turn, this results in interfering psychological states, principally negative emotions, and they continue to maintain an erectile disorder.

Hypersexuality.   Except in the rare instance of the organic Klüver-Bucy syndrome (Katchadourian & Lunde, 1980), hypersexuality is not associated with organic disease. Hypersexuality is defined principally by a judgment of society concerning standards of sexual behavior. The professional reflects societal judgment by saying that sexual activity at a given level with a given number of partners reflects dysfunctional behavior. Many individuals who are "hypersexual'' do not experience their behavior as dysfunctional. However, if they receive enough negative evaluations from their culture and society then they will begin to negatively evaluate themselves and feel that they do indeed have a sexual problem. In other instances, it appears that hypersexuality reflects the wish for attention and/or affection. Many individuals who are viewed as hypersexual seem to be using their sexual behavior to obtain close interpersonal contact and to avoid being lonely. The point is that in this instance sexual behavior reflects needs that are not strictly sexual. To look for a disturbance in the sexual system in these cases would prove futile.

Low Desire. Clinical impressions support the suggestion that there is an increase in the frequency of complaints of low sexual desire (Friedman, et al., in press). This increased level of complaints over low sexual interest may result from the push in our society towards increased sexual activity. Individuals may feel that their interest in sex does not match their perception of society's norms and, thus conclude that there must be something wrong with them. A natural consequence of this scenario would be to seek professional help. Many individuals with low sexual desire show normal arousal when stimulated (Friedman, et al., in press). Thus it is necessary to separate low desire from low arousability. Often in the clinic as well as research literature these conditions are not seen as distinct. It is a common clinical impression that many of the cases of low sexual desire are complicated by marital problems. That is, individuals expressing low sexual desire may also have disturbed marriages. It is difficult to maintain sexual interest in the context of arguments and interpersonal conflict. There has been some interest in treating low sexual desire by administration of male sex hormones (Rakoff, 1975; Bancroft & Skakkebaek, 1978). The outcome of this treatment is complex. In some instances, however, it has appeared to have been of some help.

Psychopathology. Severe psychopathology impacts on sexuality in a wide range of effects. For example, individuals with severe psychopathology are seen by other members of society as being less attractive since they exhibit behaviors that are unusual and sometimes bizarre. Also, individuals suffering from severe psychopathology often have communication deficits which function to further interfere with the development of sexual relationships. A complete description of the impact of psychopathology on sexuality would be out of scope of this chapter.

IMPLICATIONS AND WARNINGS

There are several general considerations that we wish to bring to the attention of individuals interested in behavioral medicine and sexual problems. First, we have demonstrated that sexual dysfunction can result from strictly physiological factors, from strictly psychological factors, but that more commonly it reflects an interaction between physiological, behavioral, and cognitive factors. This means, of course, that assessment of sexual functioning must be multi-dimensional in nature. It is not appropriate to restrict assessment to just the identification of the operating subset of medical or psychological factors. Assessment should always look towards decisions for intervention strategies and should be continued throughout treatment to assure the most effective management of dysfunctional behaviors. The finding of an organic problem in a sexual dysfunction does not rule out the concurrent presence of psychological components. Nor, on the other hand, does the finding of a psychological component rule out the possibility of an organic complication.

It must be recognized that uncovering the occurrence of an organic or psychological problem does not necessarily indicate that the treatment of choice must match the psychological or organic cause. For example, vaginismus, the constriction of muscles around the entrance to the vagina, seems in many instances to result from psychological tension. The treatment of choice of a psychologically determined physiological symptom is the use of dialators which are gradually introduced into the vagina. Thus we have an instance of psychological cause leading to a physiological event and a physical treatment. On the other hand, one can find instances of similar processes in which the basic cause was organic in nature but the treatment is psychological (e.g., performance fear based on alcohol-induced failure). These interactional effects emphasize the central role that can be played by the concept of behavioral medicine with its reliance on cross-disciplinary contacts and concepts.

Sex therapy may be directly relevant in medical treatment. It can help patients deal with dysfunctional behavior and make appropriate adjustments in their sexual practices. Sex therapy may help patients to cope with changes that have resulted from medical problems. Individuals with medical restrictions imposed on their behavioral repertoires may need sex therapy to modify their attitudes and approaches toward the expression of sexuality. Patients can be helped so that they can engage in mutually satisfying sex. Sex therapy functions to help clients deal with the side effects of medical treatments that impact on sexuality. Sex therapy may be a means of helping individuals increase their knowledge of the physiology and behavioral components of sexuality. This knowledge can free them from some of the limitations resulting from medical conditions.

The way information is given to patients is important. The sex therapist has the experience and methodologies that are helpful in dealing with people who are experiencing sexual dysfunctions. Members of the medical profession are not generally trained in these procedures and, therefore, the interaction between sex therapists (regardless of their training background) and medical specialists is important.

Sex therapy should be applied to special populations. The assumption that handicaps normally and automatically lead to sexual dysfunction is misguided.

Dysfunctions found in the handicapped very frequently result from the same causes as those found in the non-handicapped population. There is an increased awareness that the handicapped individual has a right to adequate sexual functioning. It is imperative that the medical profession becomes aware of both the potential as well as the existent limitations on sexuality in handicapped populations. Physicians must be certain that information is made available to handicapped individuals so as to give them the opportunity to participate in sexuality. Finally, we must note that our knowledge is limited concerning the prognoses and effects of many long term medical treatments upon sexuality.

Current training of professionals that deal with sexual problems leaves much to be desired. Medical schools tend to underevaluate the importance of interpersonal and experiential variables as they affect patients. Training of professionals in the behavioral sciences tends to ignore the serious and important impact, not only of medical treatment, but also of disease. We can do no more than reflect our concerns that these major gaps be overcome in the training of professionals. Until that is done, it remains for practicing professionals to rely heavily upon inter-disciplinary referrals and contacts to make up for deficits in their own training.

There is a tendency for physicians to avoid the topic of sex when dealing with patients. The data do not support the position that this attitude is welcomed by patients. Rather, the data suggests that patients are open to discussion of these issues, particularly if the physician initiates discussions (Kolodny, et al., 1979). Unfortunately, there is very little such counseling in the clinical practice of medicine.

Rehabilitation medicine often neglects sexual issues. These serious shortcomings must be addressed by professionals and hopefully a more positive state of affairs will eventuate for the ill. The recent appearance of the *Journal of Sexuality and Disability* reflects concern with these issues and represents a positive step.

We should not forget that basic psychological truism, "When you get individuals to change their behavior very often their attitudes change to match their behavior." A desirable goal is to get professionals in both the medical and behavioral fields to change their behavior so as to be more aware of, sensitive to, and responsive to ideas and concepts from other perspectives. We would expect that such individuals would then be more open to multi-disciplinary interactions and that ultimately patients will benefit.

REFERENCES

Abram, H. S., Hester, L. R., Sheridan, W. F., & Epstein, G. M. Sexual functioning in patients with chronic renal failure. In J. LoPiccolo & L. LoPiccolo (Eds.), *Handbook of Sex Therapy*. New York: Plenum Press, 1978.

Agle, D. P., & Baum, G. L. Psychological aspects of chronic obstructive pulmonary disease. *Medical Clinics of North America,* 61: 749–458, 1977.

American Psychiatric Association. *Diagnostic and Statistical Manual III,* 1980.

Athanasiou, R., Shaver, P., & Tavris, C. Sex. *Psychology Today, 4,* 39–52, 1970.

Azizi, F., Vagenakis, A. G., Longscope, C., Ingbar, S. H., & Braverman, L. E. Decreased serum testosterone concentration in male heroin and methadone addicts. *Steroids, 22,* 467–472, 1973.

Bacon, T. Thermography - Explanation and description. *Thermographic Quarterly, 1,* 1976.

Bai, J., Greenwald, E., Caterini, H., & Kaminetsky, H. A. Drug-related menstrual aberrations. *Obstetrics and Gynecology, 44,* 713–709, 1974.

Bancroft, J., & Skakkebaek, N. E. Androgens and human sexual behavior. CIBA funded Symposium, 62nd, March 14–16, 1978, p. 209–226.

Barnes, N. D., Hayles, A. B., & Ryan, R. J. Sexual maturation in juvenile hypothyroidism. *Mayo Clinic Proceedings.* 48: 849–856, 1973.

Blackwell, B., Stefopoulos, A., Enders, P., Kuzma, R., & Adolphe, A. Anti cholinergic activity of two tricyclic anti depressants. *American Journal of Psychiatry. 135,* 722–724, 1978.

Bors, E., & Comarr, A. E. Neurological disturbances of sexual function with special reference to 529 patients with spinal cord injury. *Urological Survey, 10,* 191–222, 1960.

Brothers, M. J. In H. I. Lief (Ed.), *Medical Aspects of Human Sexuality.* Baltimore: The Williams & Wilkins Company, 1975. p. 117.

Casey, W. C. Revascularization of corpus cavernosum for erectile failure. *Urology,* Vol. *XIV,* No. 2: 135–139, 1979.

Caspersson, T., Zech, L. Identification of mammalian chromosome. *Acta Endocrinology* (Suppl.) *168:* 67–85, 1972.

Cohen, J. The effects of oral contraceptives on sexual behavior. In R. Gemme, & C. C. Wheeler (Eds.), *Progress in Sexology.* New York: Plenum, 1977.

Comarr, A. E. Sexual function among patients with spinal cord injury. *Urologia Internationalis, 25,* 135–168, 1970.

Cullberg, J., Gelli, M. G., & Jonsson, C. O. Mental and sexual adjustment before and after six months' use of an oral contraceptive. *Acta Psychiatrica Scandinavica,* 45(3): 259–276, 1969.

Dahlberg, C. C. In H. I. Lief (Ed.), *Medical Aspects of Human Sexuality.* Baltimore: The Williams and Wilkins Company, 1975. p. 313.

Ebbehoj, M. D. & Wagner, G. Insufficient Penile erection due to abnormal drainage of cavernous bodies. *Urology,* Vol. XIII No. 5, 507–510, May 1979.

Eisenberg, M. G., & Falconer, J. A. (Eds.). *Treatment of the Spinal Cord Injured. An Interdisciplinary Perspective.* Illinois: Charles C. Thomas Publisher, 1978. p. 3–4.

Ellenberg, M. Impotence in diabetes: The neurologic factor. In J. LoPiccolo, & L. LoPiccolo (Eds.), *Handbook of Sex Therapy.* New York: Plenum Press, 1978.

Evans, R. L., Halar, E. L., DeFreece, A. B., & Larsen, G. L. Multidisciplinary approach to sex education of spinal cord-injured patients. *Physical Therapy,* May 1976, Vol. *56* (5), 541–545.

Farkas, G. M., & Rosen, R. C. Effect of alcohol on elicited male sexual response. *Journal of Studies on Alcohol, 37,* 265–272, 1976.

Fitz-Gerald, D., & Fitz-Gerald, M. Sexual implications of deafness. *Sexuality and Disability. 1,* 57–69, 1978.

Fitzpatrick, W. F. Sexual functioning in the paraplegic patient. *Archives of Physical Medicine and Rehabilitation, 55,* 221–227, 1974.

Fleming, M., Steinman, C., & Bocknek, G. Methodological problems in assessing sex-reassignment surgery. A reply to Meyer, J. and Peter, D. *Archives of Sexual Behavior, 9*(5), 451–456.

Flocks, R. H. Benign prostatic hyperplasia. *Hospital Medicine, 5*(11), 72–81. 1969.

Ford, A. B., & Orfirer, A. P. Sexual behavior and the chronically ill patient. *Medical Aspects of Human Sexuality, 1*(2), 51–61, 1967.

Frank, D., Dornbush, R. L., Webster, S. K., and Kolodny, R. C. Mastectomy and sexual behavior: A pilot study. *Sexuality and Disability. 1,* 16-26, 1978.

Frank, K. A., & Kornfeld, D. S. In H. I. Lief, (Ed.), *Medical Aspects of Human Sexuality.* Baltimore: The Williams and Wilkins Company, 1975. p. 126.

Friedman, J. M., Weiler, S. J., & LoPiccolo, J. Sexual dysfunctions and their treatment: Current status. In A. Bellack, M. Hersen, & A. Kazdin (Eds.), *The International Handbook of Behavior Modification and Behavior Therapy.* New York: Plenum (In press).

Friedman, J. M. Sexual adjustment of the postcoronary male. In J. LoPiccolo & L. LoPiccolo, *Handbook of Sex Therapy.* New York: Plenum, 1978. p. 373-386.

Fuchs, K., Hoch, Z., Paldi, E., Abramovici, H., Brandes, J. M., Timor-Tritsch, I., & Kleinhaus, M. Hypnodesensitization therapy of vaginismus: In vitro and in vivo methods. In J. LoPiccolo & L. LoPiccolo (Eds.), *Handbook of Sex Therapy.* New York: Plenum, 1978.

Furlow, W. L. Surgical management of impotence using the inflatable penile prosthesis: Experience with 36 patients. *Mayo Clinic Proceedings, 51,* 325-328, 1976.

Gaskel, P. The importance of penile blood pressure in cases of impotence. *Canadian Medical Association Journal,* Vol. *105,* 1047-1051, November 1971.

Gatchel, R. J. Perceived control: A review and evaluation of therapeutic implications. In A. Baum & J. E. Singer (Eds.), *Advances in Experimental Psychology: Applications of Personal Control, Vol. 2.* Hillsdale, NJ: Lawrence Erlbaum Associates, Publisher, 1980.

Geer, J. H. Measurement of genital arousal in human males and females. In I. Martin & P. H. Venables (Eds.), *Techniques in Psychophysiology.* New York: John Wiley & Sons, 1980.

Goldfried, M. R. & Davison, G. C. *Clinical Behavior Therapy.* New York: Holt, Rinehart & Winston, 1976.

Gordon, G. G., Altman, K., Southren, A. L., Rubin, E., & Lieber, C. S. Effect of alcohol (ethanol) administration on sex-hormone metabolism in normal men. *New England Journal of Medicine, 295,* 793-797, 1976.

Gottesman, J. E., Kosters, S., Das, S., & Kaufman, J. J. The Small-carrion prosthesis for male impotency. *Journal of Urology, 117,* 289-290, 1977.

Grumbach, M. M., & VanWyk, J. J. Disorders of sex differentiation. In R. H. Williams (Ed.), *Textbook of Endocrinology, 5th Edition.* Philadelphia: W. B. Saunders Co., 1974.

Hellerstein, H. K., & Friedman, E. H. Sexual activity and the postcoronary patient. *Archives of Internal Medicine, 125,* 987, 1970.

Hellerstein, H. K., & Friedman, E. H. Sexual activity and the postcoronary patient. *Medical Aspects of Human Sexuality, 3,* 70, March 1969.

Higgins, G. E., Jr. Aspects of sexual response in adults with spinal cord injury: A review of the literature. In J. LoPiccolo & L. LoPiccolo (Eds.), *Handbook of Sex Therapy.* New York: Plenum Press, 1978.

Hohmann, G. W. Some effects of spinal cord lesions on experienced emotional feelings. *Psychophysiology, 3,* 143-156, 1966.

Hoon, E. F., Hoon, P. W., & Wincze, J. P. An inventory for the measurement of female sexual arousability: The SAI. *Archives of Sexual Behavior. 5,* 291-300, 1976.

Ismail, A. A. A. Testosterone. In J. Loraine & T. Bell (Eds.) *Hormone Assays and Their Clinical Application.* New York: Churchill Livingstone, 1976.

Jacobson, J. N. In H. I. Lief (Ed.), *Medical Aspects of Human Sexuality.* Baltimore: The Williams and Wilkins Company, 1975.

Jayaram, B. N., Stuteville, O. H., & Bush, I. M. Complications and undesirable results of sex-reassignment surgery in male-to-female transsexuals. *Archives of Sexual Behavior,* Vol. 7, No. 4, 337-345, 1978.

Jick, H., Porter, J., & Morrison, A. S. Relation between smoking and age of natural menopause. *Lancet, 1,* 1354-1355, 1977.

Jochheim, K. A., & Wahle, H. A. A study on sexual function on 56 male patients with complete irreversible lesions of the spinal cord and cauda equina. *Paraplegia, 8.* 166-172, 1970.

Jones, H. W., Jr., Garcia, S. C., & Klingensmith, G. J. Necessity for and the technique of secondary surgical treatment of the masculinized external genitals of patients with virilizing adrenal hyperplasia. In P. A. Lee, L. P. Plotnick, A. A. Kowarski, & C. J. Migeon (Eds.), *Congenital Adrenal Hyperplasia*. Baltimore: University Park Press, 1977.

Kaplan, H. S. *The New Sex Therapy*. New York: Brunner/Mazel, 1974.

Katchadourian, H. A. & Lunde, D. T. *Fundamentals of Human Sexuality, 3rd Edition*. New York: Holt, Rinehart & Winston, 1980.

Kinsey, A. C., Pomeroy, W. B., Martin, C. E., & Gebhard, P. H. *Sexual Behavior in the Human Female*. Philadelphia: W. B. Saunders Co., 1953.

Koller, R., Kennedy, J. W., Butler, J. C., & Wagner, N. N. Counseling the coronary patient on sexual activity. *Postgraduate Medicine, 51*, 133, 1972.

Kolodny, R. C. Unpublished observation 1978 as cited in R. C. Kolodny, W. H. Masters & V. E. Johnson *Textbook of Sexual Medicine*. Boston: Little, Brown, & Company, 1978.

Kolodny, R. C., Masters, W. E., & Johnson, V. E. *The Textbook of Sexual Medicine*. Boston: Little, Brown & Co., 1979.

Kolodny, R. C., Masters, W. H., Kolodner, R. M., & Toro, G. Depression of plasma testosterone levels after chronic intensive marijauna use. *New England Journal of Medicine, 290*, 872–874, 1974.

Kramer, S. A., Anderson, E. E., Bredael, J., & Paulson, D. F. Complications of Small-carrion penile prosthesis. *Urology, 13*, 49–51, 1979.

Kupperman, H. S. In H. I. Lief, (Ed.), *Medical Aspects of Human Sexuality*. Baltimore: The Williams & Wilkins Company, 1975. p. 119-120.

Lange, P. H., & Smith, A. D. A comparison of the two types of penile prostheses used in the surgical treatment of male impotence. *Sexuality and Disability, 1*, 307–311, 1978.

Levin, R. J. & Wagner, G. Hemodynamic changes of the human vagina during sexual arousal assessed by a heated oxygen electrode. *Journal of Physiology, 275*, 23-24, 1978.

Levitt, J. I. Spironolactone therapy and amenorrhea. *Journal of the American Medical Association, 211*, 2014-2115, 1970.

LoPiccolo, J. & Heiman, J. The role of cultural values in the prevention and treatment of sexual problems. In C. B. Qualls, J. P. Wincze, and D. H. Barlow (Eds.) *The Prevention of Sexual Disorders*, New York: Plenum Press, 43-71, 1978.

Lyons, A. S. In H. I. Lief (Ed.), *Medical Aspects of Human Sexuality*. Baltimore: The Williams & Wilkins Company, 1975. p. 137–138.

Madorsky, M., Drylie, D. M., & Finlayson, B. Effect of benign prostatic hypertrophy on sexual behavior. *Medical Aspects of Human Sexuality, 10*(2), 8-22, 1976.

Malin, J. M. In H. E. Lief (Ed.), *Medical Aspects of Human Sexuality*. Baltimore: The Williams & Wilkins Company, 1975. p. 137–138.

Mash, E. J., & Terdal, I. G. Behavior therapy assessment: Diagnosis, design and evaluation. *Psychological Reports, 35*, 587-601, 1974.

Masters, W. H., & Johnson, V. E. *Human Sexual Response*. Boston: Little, Brown and Co., 1966.

Masters, W. H. & Johnson, V. E. *Human Sexual Inadequacy*. Boston: Little, Brown and Co., 1970.

Mazur, T., & Money, J. Prenatal influences and subsequent sexuality. In B. B. Wolman & J. Money (Eds.), *Handbook of Human Sexuality*. New Jersey: Prentice-Hall Inc., 1980.

Meyer, J., & Reter, D. Sex reassignment. *Archives of General Psychiatry, 36*, 1010-1015, 1979.

Money, J., & Mittenthal, S. Lack of personality pathology in Turner's syndrome: Relation to cytogenics, hormones and physique. *Behavior Genetics. 1*, 43-56, 1970.

Money, J., & Pruce, G. Psychomotor epilepsy and sexual function. In J. Money & H. Musaph (Eds.), *Handbook of Sexology*. New York: Elsevier/North Holland Biomedical Press, 1977.

Money, J., & Schwartz, M. Biosocial determinants of gender identity differentiation and development. In J. B. Hutchison (Ed.), *Biological Determinants of Sexual Behavior*. New York: John Wiley & Sons, 1978.

Money, J. & Wiedeking, C. Gender identity/role: Normal differentiation and its transpositions. In B. B. Wolman & J. Money (Eds.), *Handbook of Human Sexuality,* New Jersey: Prentice-Hall Inc., 1980.

Naughton, J. In H. I. Lief (Ed.), *Medical Aspects of Human Sexuality.* Baltimore: The Williams & Wilkins Company, 1975. p. 124.

Nelson, B. J. How to prevent impotence after prostatectomy. *Sexual Medicine Today, 2*(3), 4–41, 1978.

Noe, J. M., Sato, R., Coleman, C., & Laub, D. R. Construction of male genitalia: The Stanford experience. *Archives of Sexual Behavior.* Vol. *7,* No. 4: 297–303, 1978.

Ochsner, A. In H. I. Lief (Ed.), *Medical Aspects of Human Sexuality.* Baltimore: The Williams & Wilkins Company, 1975. p. 313.

Pang, S., Kenny, F. M., Foley, T. P., & Drash, A. L. Growth and sexual maturation in treated congenital adrenal hyperplasia. In P. A. Lee, L. P. Plotnick, A. A. Kowarski, & C. J. Migeon (Eds.), *Congenital Adrenal Hyperplasia.* Baltimore: University Park Press, 1977.

Paolino, T. J., & McCrady, B. S. (Eds.) *Marriage and Marital Therapy.* New York: Brunner Mazel Publishers, 1978.

Pasini, W. Contraception et plaisir. In G. Abraham & W. Pasini (Eds.), *Introduction a la Sexologie Medicale.* Paris: Plon, 1974.

Philip, J., Lundsteen, C., Owen, D., & Hirshhorn, K. The frequency of chromosome aberrations in tall men with special reference to 47,XYY and 47,XXY. *American Journal of Human Genetics, 28,* 404–411, 1976.

Poutasse, E. F. Peyronie's Disease. In C. E. Horton (Ed.), *Plastic and Reconstructive Surgery of the Genital Area.* Boston: Little, Brown and Co., 1973.

Rakoff, A. E. In H. I. Lief (Ed.), *Medical Aspects of Human Sexuality.* Baltimore: The William & Wilkins Company, 1975. p. 123.

Renshaw, D. C. Impotence in diabetics. In LoPiccolo, J. and LoPiccolo, L., *Handbook of Sex Therapy.* New York: Plenum Press, 1978.

Rice-Wray, E., Goldzieher, J., & Aranda-Rosell, A. Oral progestatives in fertility control: A comparative study. *Fertility and Sterility, 14,* 402, 1963.

Saenger, P., Goldman, A. S., Levine, L. S., Korthschutz, S., Muecke, E. C., Katsumata, M., Doberne, Y., & New, M. I. Prepubertal diagnosis of steroid 5 $\propto$ - reductase deficiency. *Journal of Clinical Endocrinology and Metabolism, 46,* 627–634, 1978.

Scholl, G. T. The psychosocial effects of blindness: Implications for program planning in sex education. *New Outlook for the Blind 68*(5) 201–209, May 1974.

Scott, F. B., Bradley, W. E., & Timm, G. W. Management of erectile impotence: Use of implantable inflatable prosthesis. *Urology.* 2: 80–82, 1973.

Seeley, T. T., Abramson, P. R., Perry, L. B., Rothblatt, A. B., & Seeley, D. M. Thermographic measurement of sexual arousal: A methodological note. *Archives of Sexual Behavior, 9*(2), 77–85, 1980.

Shapiro, A., Cohen, H., DiBianco, P. & Rosen, G. Vaginal blood flow changes during sleep and sexual arousal. *Psychophysiology,* Vol. *4*(3), 394, 1968.

Silverberg, E. Cancer statistics, 1978·CA. *Cancer Journal for Clinicians, 28,* 17–32, 1978.

Sintchak, G. & Geer, J. H. A vaginal plethysmograph system, *Psychophysiology,* Vol. 12, No. *1,* 113–115, 1975.

Small, M. P. The Small-carrion penile prosthesis: Surgical implant for the management of impotence. *Sexuality and Disability. 1* 282–291, 1978.

Stein, R. The effects of exercise training on peak coital heart rate in postmyocardial infarction males. *Circulation, 51,* Abstract 456, Supplement 11, 1975.

Story, N. L. Sexual dysfunction resulting from drug side effects. *Journal of Sex Research, 10*(2), 132–149, 1974.

Stripp, B., Taylor, A. A., Bartter, F. C., Gilette, J. R., Loriaux, D. L., Easley, R., & Menard R.

H. Effect of spironolactone on sex hormones in man. *Journal of Clinical Endocrinology and Metabolism, 41,* 777–781, 1975.

Tordjman, G., Thierree, R., & Michel, J. R. Advances in the vascular pathology of male erectile dysfunction. *Archives of Sexual Behavior,* Vol. *9,* No. 5, 391–398, 1980.

Tuttle, W. B., Cook, W. L., & Fitch, E. Sexual behavior in postmyocardial infarction patients. *American Journal of Cardiology.* 13, 140, 1964.

Udry, R. J., & Morris, N. Effects of contraceptive pills on the distribution of sexual activity in the menstrual cycle. *Nature.* 227: 502, 1970.

Watson, M. A., & Money, J. Behavior cytogenics and Turner's syndrome: A new principle in counseling and psychotherapy. *American Journal of Psychotherapy, 29.* 166–177, 1975.

Weil, A. *The Natural Mind. A New Way of Looking at Drugs and the Higher Consciousness.* Boston: Houghton Mifflin Co., 1972.

Weiss, R. L., & Margolin, G. Assessment of marital conflict and accord. In A. Ciminero, K. S. Calhoun, & H. E. Adams (Eds.), *Handbook of Behavioral Assessment.* New York: John Wiley & Sons, 1977.

Wilson, G. T., & Lawson, D. M. Effects of alcohol on sexual arousal in women. *Journal of Abnormal Psychology. 85,* 489–497, 1976.

Wolman, B. B., & Money, J. (Eds.) *Handbook of Human Sexuality.* New Jersey: Prentice-Hall Inc., 1980.

Zohar, J., Meiraz, D., Maoz, B., & Durst, N. Factors influencing sexual activity after prostatectomy: A prospective study. *Journal of Urology, 116.* 332–334, 1976.

10 Psychosomatic Disorders: Basic Issues and Future Research Directions

Robert J. Gatchel
The University of Texas Health Science Center at Dallas

Andrew Baum
Uniformed Services University of the Health Sciences

Peter J. Lang
University of Wisconsin

Psychophysiological disorders, traditionally called psychosomatic illnesses, are characterized by physical symptoms or dysfunction in various organs of the body that are intimately linked with psychological factors. The close interplay of psychological and physiological processes involved in these disorders makes their diagnosis and treatment particularly difficult. The symptoms of psychophysiological disorders are similar, and often identical, to those present in a systemic disease. As a result, distinctions between these types of disorders are usually made on the basis of etiology. For example, in the case of hypertension, renal hypertension is a systemic disease caused by kidney malfunctioning. Essential hypertension, on the other hand, is classified as a psychophysiological disorder because there is no known medical cause. In other words, it is *idiopathic*. However, even though psychological factors appear to cause the chronic elevation of blood pressure in the disorder, the physical problem is nevertheless very real.

In many disorders, the distinction between psychosomatic and non-psychosomatic disorders is difficult to make. Indeed, Buss (1966) pointed out that psychological factors may be sufficient but not necessary causes of certain somatic disorders so that the line between purely psychophysiological and systemic disorders is frequently blurred. For example, in the case of childhood asthma, Rees (1964) isolated three causal factors: allergic, infective, and psychological. These factors, either alone or in any combination, can trigger an asthma attack. Rees suggested that multiple causation is usually the rule, with various sequences and combinations of these factors culminating in the attack.

We still do not know enough about the process by which psychological factors produce changes in somatic factors. It should also be noted that in the field of medicine as a whole, the exact causes of many disorders are not totally understood. The general rule of assessment has therefore traditionally been that a particular case of hypertension, headache, and the like should not be diagnosed as psychophysiological until a complete medical evaluation has ruled out organic factors as the primary cause, and there is good evidence for emotional factors that are antecedent or coincident to the disorder.

In this chapter, we first briefly review the history of how psychosomatic disorders have been conceptualized over the years, as well as some of the major traditional categories of these disorders. We then discuss the major theoretical formulations proposed to account for these disorders. As will be pointed out, there is still no one theoretical formulation which can be used to comprehensively understand psychosomatic disorders. Rather, over the years, there have been two relatively disjoint orientations and resultant research literatures that have developed, one of which emphasized biological factors such as inherited autonomic response patterns or weakness in a particular body organ, while the other underlines psychological factors such as personality characteristics, unconscious emotional conflicts, or specific attitudes toward stress. We will pay special attention to research on psychological factors, and point out problems associated with it both in the past and present. It will be concluded that any comprehensive understanding of psychosomatic disorders will require an assessment of the interaction among stimulus or situational variables, physiological factors, and intervening psychological processes such as personality characteristics and coping styles. Such an integrative approach has not been taken in the bulk of past research in this area.

There have been a number of reasons for this delineation between the two research literatures—one psychological and one physiological. First, most medical explanations of disease have traditionally been *functional* in nature. That is to say, medical explanations of the symptoms of a disorder have not explained their antecedents but only the functional disturbances they express. They have basically been descriptive in nature, without much predictive power. For example, they tell us about the relationship between high blood pressure and renal dysfunction, but they do not indicate why at a particular point in time the kidneys failed. The contribution of the field of psychosomatic research to medicine has been to provide a historical explanation of a disorder as well, in order to allow the prediction of who might be at risk for a particular disorder, and under what conditions the predisposed person is most likely to develop it. Unfortunately, this field initially overemphasized the sole role of psychological predisposition in the etiological process. A great deal of psychological research was conducted without simultaneously taking into account physiological and genetic factors that interact in predisposing an individual to a particular disorder.

Another reason for this sharp delineation has been the lack of an appropriate research methodology to use with intact human subjects in order to simultaneously examine physiological components and those psychological factors suggested to be important on the basis of clinical practice and experience. Later in the chapter, we discuss a research methodology developed by Lang (1979) which may significantly contribute to the "pulling together" of physiological and psychological factors in an integrative examination of psychosomatic disorders.

CONCEPTUALIZATIONS OF PSYCHOSOMATIC DISORDERS: A BRIEF HISTORY

The relationship between the mind and the body has long been a controversial topic among philosophers, physiologists, and psychologists. Are experiences purely mental, purely physical, or an interaction of both? Are people simply complex organisms whose unique abilities and self-consciousness make us think we are different, or do people have souls apart from their bodies? Traditionally, in our western culture, it has been difficult to view the mind and body as one. One major reason for this has been the lack of an English word denoting the union of mind and body. Moreover, with the advent of physical medicine during the Renaissance, the view of the mind influencing the body came to be regarded as unscientific. The understanding of the mind and soul was relegated to the areas of religion and philosophy, further perpetuating a dualistic viewpoint.

One of the earliest and most influential attempts to deal with the mind-body problem was proposed by the French philosopher Rene Descartes in the seventeenth century. He proposed a dualistic approach—mind and body were separate—but held that the two could and did interact. This proposal was important because it suggested that the two realms could not always be considered independently. He also proposed that the pineal gland located in the midbrain was the vital connection between the mind and body.

With the discovery that microorganisms caused certain diseases during the nineteenth century, there was further acceptance of this dualistic viewpoint. However, the view began to change at about the mid-nineteenth century through the work of Claude Bernard. Bernard was the first influential physician to emphasize the contributions of psychological factors to physical ailments. Subsequently, Sigmund Freud was very influential in emphasizing the interaction of psychological and physical factors in various disorders. A more comprehensive review of the early history of mind-body dualistic view can be found in McMahon and Hastrup (1980).

Starting in the twentieth century, psychosomatic medicine became an extremely important area of medical science, with the growing interest in treating patients as "whole" human beings and the realization that psychological factors are important in the course of most any disease. In a comprehensive overview of the field of psychosomatic medicine during the 1970's, Lipowski (1977) noted a great resurgence of interest in this field. Indeed, most professionals today take the position that mind and body are not separate entities. A change in emotional state will be accompanied by a change in physiological responding, and a change in physiological functioning will frequently be accompanied by alterations in emotional affect. In clinical treatment, a *holistic* approach is now advocated, with the view that to comprehensively understand health and disease, it is important to study people as "individual mind-body complexes ceaselessly interacting with the social and physical environment in which they are embedded" (Lipowski, 1977, p. 234).

There are psychological factors involved in all diseases. In fact, Graham (1972) suggests that the psychological and physical explanations of a disease or disorder are merely different ways of describing the same event. The present view of these disorders is that they are the result of many causes—physical, psychological, and sociocultural. It is the search for the unique interaction of these factors that interests investigators of psychophysiological disorders.

The DSM-III Classification of Psychophysiological Disorders

Until recently, the Diagnostic and Statistical Manual of the American Psychiatric Association (DSM-II) recognized the existence of psychogenic illness but separated such disorders and implied that only certain ailments could have psychological causes. Nine major categories of disorders were delineated, with the major factor being the affected part or system of the body (e.g., cardiovascular disorders such as hypertension or Raynaud's disease; skin disorders such as hives or neurodermatitis). The problem with this scheme is readily apparent: With the increasing recognition that psychological or emotional factors are important in the precipitation and/or exacerbation of most organic illness, a change in this classification system was needed. Research had implicated psychological factors in the etiology and development of a number of illnesses not traditionally considered to be psychosomatic, ranging from neurological disorders (e.g., multiple sclerosis) to infectious diseases and malignancies such as tuberculosis and leukemia (Wittkower & Dudek, 1973). The DSM-II could not account for this.

Lipp, Looney, and Spitzer (1977) originally pointed out that the new DSM-III would have to take into account the degree to which psychosocial factors can influence any physical condition. In their proposal, which was subsequently adopted and incorporated in the DSM-III, they recommended that the separate section on psychophysiological disorders be deleted and a section entitled "Psychological Factors in Physical Conditions" be substituted (the title was subsequently changed to "Psychological Factors Affecting Physical Condition.'') This section includes not only the traditional psychophysiological disorders listed in the old DSM-II, but also any physical condition in which psychological factors are found to be significant in precipitating, exacerbating, or prolonging the disorder. Such a system allows clinicians to avoid considering a given condition exclusively in psychological or organic terms. This is in keeping with the view of most professionals in the field of psychosomatic medicine who take a multicausal etiological approach to disease. In describing psychosomatic disorders, the current trend is not to talk about any distinct group of disorders, but about any physical condition that is precipitated, exacerbated, or prolonged by psychological factors. Thus, the DSM-III embraces the notion that psychological factors are important in many disorders. It will hopefully have a significant impact in promoting an integrated psychological-somatic approach to patient assessment/treatment and medical research.

MAJOR FORMS OF PSYCHOPHYSIOLOGICAL DISORDERS

In this section, we briefly review a few of the traditional forms of psychophysiological disorders in order to provide a flavor for the characteristics and symptoms involved. For a more in-depth review of these as well as other psychosomatic disorders, the reader is referred to Weiner's (1977) comprehensive survey.

Bronchial Asthma

Bronchial asthma is a common psychophysiological disorder, with an estimated occurrence of approximately 5% in the general population (Mears & Gatchel, 1979). It is an obstructive disease of the bronchial airways characterized by shortness of breath, coughing, wheezing, and a sensation of choking, which is caused by a decrease in the diameter of the bronchi through which air passes to the lungs. These constrictions are produced by swelling of the bronchial mucosa and/or contraction of the bronchial muscles. Asthmatic attacks usually begin suddenly, with the symptoms lasting anywhere from less than an hour to several hours or even days. Between these attacks, no abnormal symptoms are usually detected. Two distinct forms of asthma are usually referred to: *extrinsic* in which there is strong evidence of allergy involvement with patients having a strong family history of allergy; and *instrinsic* in which there is less evidence for hereditary and allergy factors. Approximately 30%–50% of all cases of asthma are extrinsic (Holman & Muschenheim, 1972).

As we noted earlier, Rees (1964) isolated three causal factors when examining the case histories of children with asthma. The allergy factor reflected situations in which some substance (e.g., an allergen such as pollen or dust) caused a biochemical reaction that constricts the bronchi. The infection factor included microbial or pathogenic etiology, with the most common type of respiratory infection being acute bronchitis. Rees noted that 35% of the asthmatic children he studied had their first asthmatic attacks during a respiratory infection. Finally, psychological factors such as anxiety, depression, and other emotional reactions were considered as potential causes of an asthmatic attack.

Other investigators have also isolated the importance of these three factors. For example, Williams, Lewis-Faning, Rees, Jacobs, and Thomas (1958), in their study of 487 asthmatic patients of all ages, found that allergy factors played a dominant precipitating role in 29%, infection factors in 40%, and psychological factors in 30%. However, even in the latter group where psychological factors played a dominant role, asthmatic attacks were also precipitated by allergic factors in 50% of these patients. Thus, no one factor appears solely responsible for the precipitation of asthmatic attacks. Multiple causations are most common, with the majority of cases involving two or more of these factors in various sequences and combinations.

Essential Hypertension

Essential hypertension is characterized by chronically elevated blood pressure for which no organic cause is known. Hambling (1952) was the first to distinguish between stages in the development of this disorder. He distinguished three major stages. The first, or prehypertension stage, is marked by the individual consistently reacting to psychological stress or pain with a diastolic blood pressure response of over 95 mm of mercury (the normal resting diastolic blood pressure level is about 80 mm of mercury). The second, or benign hypertension stage, is characterized by a labile or fluctuating blood pressure and a permanent diastolic blood pressure level of above 95. Also, in response to this chronically elevated blood pressure, the walls of the small arteries begin to thicken slightly. Finally, in the third, or malignant hypertension stage, diastolic blood pressure level is permanently above 130. This severe elevation of blood pressure can cause physical damage to the kidneys, the retinas of the eyes, and other organs.

As indicated by Weiner (1977), there is general agreement about three features of essential hypertension—it consists of an elevation of blood pressure, an increase in peripheral resistance develops at some point in time during the development of the disorder, and genetic factors play an etiological role in most cases of the disorder—but there is disagreement concerning just about every other feature of its etiology and pathogenesis. This is because methods have not been developed to reliably predict who will develop essential hypertension, and the sequence of events leading up to the disorder have not been well delineated.

It is assumed that hypertension is related to chronic stress produced by environmental and psychological factors. Most individuals demonstrate a physiological response to stress characterized by, among other reactions, secretion of epinephrine and norepinephrine, acceleration of heart rate and constriction of the arterial walls (e.g., Selye, 1956). These responses, especially arterial constriction, lead to an elevation of blood pressure. Research has linked stress to increased blood pressure among adults and children, and has also demonstrated that psychosocial stimulation is associated with such increases in animals (cf. Weiner, 1977). Chronic hypertension, as indicated earlier, can lead to serious consequences such as kidney damage or heart attack or stroke due to the persistent stress on the heart. It is a serious disorder and is currently a critical health problem with estimates by the American Heart Association that approximately one out of every nine Americans suffers from hypertension. It is an especially dangerous disorder because it is frequently present for many years without any serious symptoms or signs except the elevated blood pressure. As a result, it may not be diagnosed and treated until it reaches a critical stage of development in which organ damage has already occurred or the person has suffered a heart attack or stroke.

Headache

Headache can result from a wide variety of organic causes such as tumors, systemic infections, concussions, etc. The vast majority of headaches, however, are psychophysiological in nature and can be divided into three major categories: (1) migraine headache; (2) muscle contraction or tension headache; and (3) a mixed headache category in which symptoms of both migraine and tension headache are present. Headache is common in the general population. The incidence of migraine is about 5% of the population, while about another 30% experience tension and mixed categories.

Migraine headache is a vascular disorder caused by a loss of tone in the major extracranial vessels, leading to painful pulsatile distention. A pain threshold chemical (bradykinin or neurokinin) is thought to be released at the site of the dilated vessels, causing an inflammatory reaction. Edema develops (i.e., the walls of the blood vessels become filled with fluid), resulting in a sharp, painful, and throbbing sensation in the head. The pain is often unilateral. The headache is frequently preceded by an aura, a subjective sensation alerting the person that the headache is about to start. Symptoms such as nausea, vomiting, and dizziness may accompany this prodromal. These headaches usually do not occur during an immediate period of stress, but rather during the post-stress period. They can last anywhere from a few hours to several days.

Muscle contraction or tension headaches are quite different from migraine headaches. They are caused by sustained contraction of the head and neck muscles. They often last for days or weeks and usually begin during an immediate stress period. There are no significant prodromal symptoms, and the headache itself consists of a nonthrobbing ache, with a sensation of tightness frequently described as the feeling of a "tight band" around the head.

Clinical observation frequently reveals an association between emotionally stressful events and the emergence of symptoms in chronic headache sufferers.

Wolff conducted a number of studies using an "emotional provocation technique" to precipitate headaches in patients (Dalessio, 1972). The psychological stress produced by this technique, in which patients were criticized and rebuked for their behavior, was found to trigger headache attacks.

More recently, Bakal (1977) thoroughly reviewed the literature on migraine and muscle contraction headaches and concluded that headache appears to be a psychological reaction to stressful stimulation.

Peptic Ulcer

A peptic ulcer is a lesion or sore in the lining of the stomach or the upper part of the small intestine or duodenum which lies immediately below the stomach. A basic problem with the term "peptic ulcer" is that it is not always precisely defined because it is generally viewed to include both gastric and duodenal ulcer. Although these two forms have certain characteristics in common, there are also significant differences between them. For example, duodenal ulcer is usually associated with an increase in gastric secretion of hydrochloric acid and pepsin, while gastric ulcer is usually characterized by either normal, subnormal, or elevated gastric secretion levels. Another important difference is that emotional factors appear to play a more important role in duodenal ulcer than in gastric ulcer (Yager & Weiner, 1970). Indeed, gastric and duodenal ulcers are viewed by clinicians as separate disorders which are associated with different predisposition and preadaptation factors (Kirsner, 1968). Thus, the general term "peptic ulcer" can be misleading since it is not one disease but several diseases which differ in their anatomical location, natural history, pathophysiology, and response to treatment.

Ulcers are quite common, with a prevalence of about 2% of the general population. They are sometimes "quiet," in the sense that they cause no pain or discomfort and remain unnoticed and therefore unreported. More often than not, however, the individual feels discomfort, ranging from a "burning sensation" in the stomach, usually the first sign of an ulcer, to severe pain (caused by enlargement of the lesion) accompanied by nausea and vomiting. If the ulcer perforates (breaking blood vessels in the walls of the stomach), vomiting of blood will occur. If hemorrhaging and internal bleeding are severe, the person may die.

Peptic duodenal ulcers are assumed to be produced by excessively high levels of gastric secretion of hydrochloric acid. The stomach produces this acid to aid in the digestive process, but the walls of the duodenum as well as the stomach have a protective mucous lining which normally is able to resist its mildly corrosive action. If the acid is secreted even when food is no longer present, though, then it may begin to eat away the protective mucous lining of those individuals who cannot tolerate this excessive secretion. When the output of acid is excessive, and a particular site is no longer resistant to the acid, an ulcer will develop.

The most popular view of why there is an excessive secretion of acid in the absence of food is that psychological stress causes an increase in secretion (e.g.,

Wolf & Wolff, 1947). This viewpoint is based on both animal and human research demonstrating a relationship between stress and secretion activity. There have been numerous examples of patients exposed to emotionally stressful situations showing an increase in the volume and acidity of gastric secretion (e.g., Wolf, 1965). In research with animals, it has been demonstrated that the persistent exposure of rats to stress (unpredictable or uncontrollable electric shock) leads to a significant increase ulceration rate (e.g., Weiss, 1968).

In passing, it should be noted that a widely publicized study by Brady, Porter, Conrad, and Mason (1958), which became known as the "executive monkey" study, reported that ulcers were not produced in all monkeys exposed to uncontrollable electric shock, but only those who could actively control the occurrence of this stressor and avoid it by pressing a bar. Brady and colleagues interpreted these findings to suggest that the ulcers were due to the pressure and responsibility of actively responding and attempting to control stressful events. These data were used to support the popular, but unsubstantiated, notion that ulcers are more common in persons in highly responsible, upper-level, executive positions (in fact, it has been reported by Kahn (1969) that ulcers are more common in blue-collar workers who are chronically discontented with their lives). However, there was a major methodological flaw in the design of this study that seriously questions the interpretability of the results. The flaw concerns the manner in which the monkeys were assigned to the two experimental groups (four monkeys in each group). All monkeys were originally placed on the "executive" schedule, and the first four who started pressing the bar became the "executives;" the last four were assigned to the uncontrollable group. Subsequent to this study, it has been shown that the more emotional a monkey is, the sooner it begins pressing the bar when it is shocked (e.g., Sines, Cleeland, & Adkins, 1963). Thus, it appears that the four most emotional animals, those possibly predisposed to develop ulcers, were assigned to the "executive" group. The four least emotional became the uncontrollable group subjects. This created a major methodological problem in the experiment.

Weiss (1968, 1971) repeated this type of "executive" study with rats, but with a truly random assignment of animals to experimental groups. The results of these studies clearly demonstrated that the executive animals who could control shock developed fewer ulcers than the nonexecutive animals. Thus, it appears that *lack* of control over aversive events is an emotional stressor associated with ulceration.

THE ROLE OF PHYSIOLOGICAL AND GENETIC FACTORS IN PSYCHOSOMATIC DISORDERS

Although a great deal of additional work still needs to be done, there have been significant developments in biomedical research which can lead to an increase in our understanding of the pathogenesis of psychosomatic disorders. Unfortunately, until relatively recently, researchers in the field of psychosomatic disorders have not kept abreast of many new developments in the delineation of physiological underpinnings of the various disorders. Today, this has greatly changed, with researchers in the field developing a more comprehensive understanding of the genetic, neural, hormonal, and psychophysiological components of the disorders. One consequence of this has been that, because of the great complexity of the interaction of these variables in various disorders, there is a trend towards greater "specialization" within the field of psychosomatic medicine, with a research focus usually on only one disorder. The investigator who is conducting research on essential hypertension, for example, may therefore not be aware of much of the current progress being made in better understanding peptic ulcer.

Before this change towards specialization, a relatively broad theoretical model was used to conceptualize the physiological contribution to psychosomatic disorders. The term *specific-response pattern approach* was used to convey the assumption that individuals tend to respond physiologically to stressful situations in their own idiosyncratic ways. It has often been shown that individuals differ in physiological responding to situations (e.g., Lacey, 1967). One person may demonstrate an increase in heart rate and blood pressure level, but little increase in muscle tension; another person in the same situation may display very little increase in heart rate and blood pressure, but a great increase in muscle tension. This difference in response patterns is known as *individual response stereotypy*. As an early example of these individual differences in an actual clinical population, Malmo and Shagass (1949) demonstrated that under stress, patients with cardiovascular symptoms showed more cardiovascular response than increase in muscle tension, whereas patients with muscle tension headaches showed an opposite pattern.

It was generally assumed that the particular physiological symptom or organ that is most constantly activated, and therefore more stressed, may be susceptible to a breakdown and the resultant development of a psychophysiological disorder. That is to say, the person who persistently responds to situations with a greatly elevated blood pressure level may sufficiently stress the cardiovascular system to cause a disruption of its homeostatic mechanism and, as a result, render it more susceptible to essential hypertension. A major problem with this general model, however, is its lack of predictive validity. It cannot answer the basic question of why all individuals who respond with a significant degree of cardiovascular activation do not eventually develop a cardiovascular disorder such as essential hypertension. Psychological factors, which will be discussed in the next section of this chapter, were assumed to play an important role in determining who did or did not develop the disease.

There was also some evidence to suggest that patterns of physiological reactivity are inherited, implying a possible genetic involvement in psychosomatic disorders. Indeed, today it is generally accepted that genetic factors likely play an important role in predisposing individuals to various psychosomatic disorders (again, the reader is referred to Weiner, 1977, for a comprehensive review of such factors in many major forms of psychosomatic disorders). With reference to one specific psychophysiological disorder, Mirsky (1958) demonstrated that *pepsinogen* levels of ulcer patients are significantly higher than those of patients without ulcers. Pepsinogen, a gastric secretion, is a good measure of gastric secretion activity. In the stomach, it is converted to the enzyme *pepsin* which digests proteins and which, together with hydrochloric acid, is the primary active agent in gastric digestive juices. Many investigators view an excess of pepsinogen as a cause of ulcers. In an initial study, Mirsky assessed significant individual differences in pepsinogen levels in newborn infants. Moreover, infants with high pepsinogen levels were likely to be members of families in which there was a high pepsinogen level. In addition, twin studies have shown that pepsinogen levels for identical twins are very similar (Mirsky, Futterman & Kaplan, 1952; Pilot, Lenkoski, Spiro, & Schaefer, 1957). This provided some early evidence that pepsinogen level, which is viewed as an important contributing factor in the development of ulcers, is an inherited characteristic.

In another study, Weiner, Thaler, Reiser, and Mirsky (1957) sought to evaluate whether oversecretors of pepsinogen were more prone to develop ulcers than undersecretors. From a group of newly inducted soldiers, a group of oversecretors were selected on the basis of a gastrointestinal examination conducted before basic training. Only soldiers who did not have ulcers at the time were chosen for the study. At the end of basic training (approximately 4 months later), the men were reexamined. It was found that 14% of the oversecretors had developed ulcers, whereas none of the undersecretors had. A similar study by Mirsky (1958), conducted with a population of children and adult civilians, showed a similar tendency for ulcers to develop in those individuals with a high pepsinogen level.

Thus, the evidence indicates that individuals who develop ulcers may be genetically predisposed because of excessive secretion of gastric acid which, in turn, produces stomach lesions and ulcerations. Family studies have also suggested the importance of genetic factors. For example, Rosen and Gregory (1965) reported that brothers of ulcer patients are about twice as likely to develop ulcers as comparable members of the general population.

A great deal of additional research, using better methodology such as twin studies, is still greatly needed to more clearly delineate the importance of genetic predispositions in many psychophysiological disorders. Although numerous family studies have shown that patients with various psychophysiological disorders came from families in which there is a high incidence of the same disorder, such findings could be attributed to common factors in learning and experience rather than to a genetic factor. A number of studies, for example, have indicated that certain patterns of disturbed parent-child relationships are common in cases of childhood asthma (e.g., Purcell, Brady, Chai, Muser, Molk, Gordon, & Means,

1969). Such common family relationship experiences could partly or totally explain the high family-incidence findings. Future research will have to partial out the relative contributions of such factors to each specific psychosomatic disorder. Moreover, as Weiner (1977) indicates, we currently know more about factors that predispose an individual to the disease than factors that initiate or sustain it. Research is also needed to isolate these latter factors.

MAJOR PSYCHOLOGICAL FORMULATIONS OF PSYCHOSOMATIC DISORDERS

In this section we review a number of diverse psychological formulations proposed to account for psychosomatic disorders. As we previously mentioned, psychological factors were assumed to play an important role in determining who did or did not develop a disorder once predisposed to it. At an early point in time, Dunbar (1943) reported some apparently reliable and consistent associations (assessed in terms of attitudes, behaviors, and traits). Subsequently, there were numerous attempts to delineate personality traits that are associated with specific psychosomatic disorders. Indeed, the unsubstantiated view that a disorder such as peptic ulcer is typical of the ambitious, hard-working, high-achieving executive is engrained in popular folklore and language. For the most part, though, these early attempts have not proven to be fruitful since it was not shown that a particular personality constellation is reliably associated with a specific disorder, or that such a constellation could be used to differentiate among individuals with other forms of emotional problem behavior. Recently, there have been some more potentially heuristic approaches suggesting a relationship between a particular constellation of personality traits and psychophysiological disorders. For example, Friedman and Rosenman (1974) have proposed a relationship between the *Type A* personality and cardiovascular disorders. Moreover, research has suggested a relationship between certain personality characteristics and the incidence of breast cancer (e.g., Greer & Morris, 1975). A great deal of additional research is needed, however, in order to assess the validity of such relationships. Due to space limitations and the lack of convincing data, we will not review the many specific relationships that have been proposed. Rather, we will focus on broader theoretical frameworks that have been proposed to account for a wide range of psychophysiological disorders.

Nuclear Conflict Theory

The first widely accepted psychological formulation of psychophysiological disorders was the psychoanalytic approach of Franz Alexander (1950). Alexander suggested that each specific psychosomatic disorder was associated with specific unconscious emotional conflicts (thus the term ''nuclear conflict''). His formulation was based to a large extent on clinical observation of patients undergoing psychoanalysis. He believed that repressed psychic energy could be discharged directly to the autonomic nervous system, leading to impairment of visceral functioning. The following are some of the emotional conflicts and associated psychosomatic disorders he hypothesized:

Asthma: Excessive unresolved dependence upon the mother, a dependence that is a wish to be encompassed or protected. Asthma occurs when there is a threat of separation of the patient from the protective mother. It is assumed to represent a suppressed cry for the mother.

Duodenal Ulcer: Frustration of oral receptive longings leading to oral aggressive response. This is assumed to be followed by overcompensation by successful accomplishment in responsible activities, leading to increased unconscious oral-dependent cravings as reactions to excessive effort and concentration.

Migraine: Repressed hostile impulses, often when the repression or inhibition occurs during the planning and preparation for a hostile attack.

Essential Hypertension: Rage is viewed as the major emotion underlying this disorder. It is assumed that the individual has a great many hostile impulses that cannot be discharged.

There has not been much research to support the validity of Alexander's formulations. As Weiner (1977) has noted, a major reason for this was the lack of adequate predictor variables that would allow investigators to choose a relevant subject population to examine *prior* to the onset of the disease. Objective and reliable inferences could therefore not be drawn about the presence of such intrapsychic conflict. Indeed, a major problem with most of the psychological formulations that have been proposed is that they are difficult to test and validate because of inherent methodological limitations. Many of these formulations were proposed when American psychiatry, which has traditionally dominated the field of psychosomatic medicine, was couched almost totally in a psychodynamic orientation during the 1950's and 1960's. These formulations were therefore built upon a framework of psychoanalytic concepts such as conflict and unconscious motivation. Such constructs are difficult to experimentally validate. Because Alexander's approach was so greatly dependent on the inference of such constructs, it has not proven to be very useful.

Alexithymia

A more recent psychoanalytic formulation of psychosomatic disorders centers around the concept of alexithymia. Sifneos (1967) and Nemiah (1973, 1975) contend that the psychosomatic process is often characterized by alexithymia, which refers to a cluster of cognitive traits marked mainly by inability of patients to describe their feelings. According to Nemiah (1975), the "alexithymic" personality displays: an inability to verbally describe feelings, a significant paucity of fantasy, and an inability to make any significant internal psychological changes in the course of psychodynamically-oriented psychotherapy. Such a description is similar to psychoanalytic writings about psychosomatic patients which emphasized that in order to produce some dissipation in a physical illness, it was necessary that patients be assisted in breaking down repression and denial defenses that were keeping feelings and fantasies in a pent-up state (Deutsch, 1953).

Nemiah, Freyberger, and Sifneos (1976) have more recently noted that alexithymic patients "... are often unable to localize effects in their bodies and appear unaware of any of the common automatic somatic reactions that accompany the experience of a variety of feelings. If there is a somatic component, it is identical with the symptoms of their bodily illness" (p. 431). It is this emotionality deficit which is assumed to be the major underpinning of psychosomatic disorders.

This alexithymic construct is currently becoming more prevalent and popular. However, there are some problems as it relates to psychosomatic disorders which will have to be dealt with in the coming years. The first problem is that alexithymic characteristics have been observed in a variety of clinical disorders, and not just the psychosomatic patient group. Research is needed to determine the relative distribution of these characteristics in the general population as well as other clinical populations. A second important question concerns whether these alexithymic characteristics are the dominant traits possessed by psychosomatic patients, or whether other major personality traits are also found among this patient group.

Unfortunately, to date, there has been no systematic research of these alexithymic characteristics. Most of the work conducted has been in the form of clinical impressions by psychoanalytically-oriented workers such as Nemiah and Sifneos. A research methodology needs to be developed to allow a more systematic and objective examination of this construct. The work by Lang (1979) on emotional imagery, to be discussed in a later section, may provide a framework to more vigorously investigate the core component of this construct—an emotionality deficit.

Specific-Attitudes Theory

Graham and colleagues conducted a series of classic experiments examining the relationship between specific attitudes toward a distressing life situation and the occurrence of particular psychophysiological disorders (cf. Graham, 1972). These attitudes, which related to what individuals felt were happening to them and what they wanted to do about it, were originally obtained in clinical interviews with patients suffering from various psychophysiological disorders. The attitudes were initially assessed in a study by Grace and Graham (1952) in which 128 patients with 12 different psychosomatic disorders or symptoms were evaluated. This evaluation indicated that patients with the same disorder showed similarities in describing their attitudes toward events that occurred just before the appearance or worsening of their symptoms. Subsequent and better-controlled studies further validated the presence of these attitudes (Graham, Lundy, Benjamin, Kabler, Lewis, Kunish, & Graham, 1962), leading these investigators to conclude that different psychophysiological disorders were indeed associated with different attitudes. Some of the associations found were:

Asthma: The person feels left out in the cold and wants to shut out another individual or the situation.

Essential Hypertension: The person feels threatened by harm by an ever present danger and, as a result, needs to be on guard, watchful, and prepared.

Migraine: The person feels that something has to be achieved and then relaxes after the effort.

Peptic Ulcer: The person feels deprived of what is due him or her and wants to seek revenge and get even.

A significant advantage of the Graham formulation over previous approaches such as that of Alexander is the more precise operational definition of constructs, and the availability of an independent variable that could be experimentally manipulated (the specific attitudes) and dependent measures that could be reliably and objectively measured (physiological responding). According to this line of reasoning, we should be able to predict the type of psychosomatic illness an individual is likely to get by assessing their attitudes towards life. This notion is intriguing, both in its inherent interest level and its potential application. However, proof for it is not easily found. In one study, Graham, Stern, and Winokur (1958) hypnotized subjects and provided them with suggestions leading either to attitudes specific to hives (you feel you are taking a beating and feel helpless to do anything about) or to Raynaud's disease (you want to take hostile physical action, but do not know what the actual act should be). Hives are accompanied by an increase in real skin temperature while Raynaud's disease is characterized by decreasing skin temperature. If the specific attitudes notion is useful in predicting these conditions, suggestions related to taking a beating (hives related attitude) should result in an increase in skin temperature while suggestions about wanting to take hostile action should lead to a decrease in skin temperature. Findings confirmed the hypothesis—attitudes specific to hives raised skin temperature while attitudes specific to Raynaud's disease lowered it.

Other studies have also provided evidence for this theory. Graham, Kabler, and Graham (1962) gave hypnotized subjects suggestions about being threatened by an ever-present danger and found that subjects' blood pressure increased. However, other studies have not found support for the specific attitudes theory

(Buss, 1966; Peters & Stern, 1971). In spite of the promise of this Specific-Attitudes Theory to better understand psychosomatic disorders, few investigators attempted to pursue and extend it during the 1960's and 1970's. Lang (1979) has recently noted several reasons for this premature abandonment. One major reason was the difficulty in replicating the results in nonhypnotized patients. Subsequent research such as that by Peters and Stern (1971) suggested that the findings in the earlier Graham studies were related mainly to the hypnosis factor rather than the specific attitudes. We will return to this issue later in the chapter.

Coping Styles

Due to dissatisfaction with earlier psychodynamic formulations, many investigators interested in the role of psychological factors in psychosomatic disorders began to shift their attention to the role of more easily and reliably quantified situational variables such as bereavement and separation as precipitating variables (e.g., Engel, 1967; Green, 1958; Schmale, 1958). An important offshoot of this research has been the establishment that behavioral and physiological responses to separation and other environmental stressors may be correlated with an important intervening psychological variable—coping mechanisms (Weiner, 1977).

The notion of coping styles is a general one, referring to consistent ways of dealing with stress, both across situations and within more specific ones. Thus, people may manifest tendencies to cope with all stressors in certain ways, or may show dispositions to deal with specific problems in certain ways. These response tendencies include psychological and physiological styles of coping (e.g., Baum, Calesnick, Davis, & Gatchel, 1980; Ilfeld, 1980; Mehrabian, 1977), and research has suggested that the ways in which people cope is associated with illness (e.g., Ilfeld, 1980; Vaillant, 1979).

Mechanic (1969) defined coping as instrumental behavior that was directed at meeting demands posed by a situation. In contrast, defense was considered to be less concerned with management of the situation and more concerned with management of emotional responses. Of course, both of these behaviors are forms of coping styles. This is consistent with differences in fear and danger control distinctions drawn by Leventhal (1970) and by Lazarus and Launier (1978). Some people (or most people in certain situations) may tend to cope either by attacking the situation or by managing emotions.

Lazarus and Launier (1978) also refer to information-seeking as a style of coping. Similarly, many studies have suggested that openness or interest in obtaining information about a stressor can determine coping success in medical settings (e.g., Andrew, 1970; Janis, 1968; Lazarus & Cohen, 1973). A fourth coping option, taking no action at all, has also been discussed, and it is apparent that these four strategies—taking direct action, managing emotional response, seeking information, and inaction—constitute major coping dimensions (e.g.,

Coyne & Lazarus, in press; Folkmann & Lazarus, 1982; Lazarus & Launier, 1978).

Research has suggested that these general classifications are useful in understanding response to stress. For example, Baum, Calesnick, Davis, and Gatchel (1982), in studying differences in coping with overload associated with crowding, found that a dimension similar to Mehrabian's (1977) screening style was effective in predicting strategy and success. Mehrabian developed a scale that assesses individual differences in coping with overload. The scale is based upon the notion that screening is associated with a hierarchical approach to information processing. It distinguishes between *screeners,* who effectively reduce the stress of numerous inputs by constructing a priority-based pattern of attention to incoming information and disregard low priority inputs, and *nonscreeners* who are less likely to impose a priority-based schema on incoming information. The Baum et al. (1980) study also indicated that the direction/emotional management distinctions drawn earlier characterized screening/nonscreening differences. One group (screeners) responded to overload by attempting to organize and prioritize their surroundings—a direct action response. The other group (nonscreeners) made more reference to being upset, anxious, or unhappy and did not exhibit many situation-oriented coping mechanisms.

Ilfeld (1980) has reported evidence that differences between instrumental, passive, and denial strategies are related to health, and Vaillant (1979) found effects of different defense mechanisms on health. Moreover, in a major research program, Glass (1977) has defined characteristics of the Type A behavior pattern (e.g., Friedman & Rosenman, 1974), a coping style associated with the incidence of coronary heart disease. The Type A pattern appears to be a coping style in which vigilance for threats to control, and hyperresponsiveness when actual threats to control materialize, are important (Glass, 1977). Behavioral response to stress or loss of control is aggressive, hostile, and time urgent, and physiological response to challenge is characterized by dramatic increases in blood pressure and blood catecholamine levels (e.g., Glass, Krakoff, Contrada, Hilton, Kehoe, Mannucci, Collins, & Snow, 1980).

Another coping dimension shown to have a significant influence on cardiovascular reactivity in humans is the active-passive coping dimension proposed by Obrist, Gaebelein, Teller, Langer, Grignolo, Light, and McCubbin (1978). According to these investigators, passive coping is exemplified by a classical aversive conditioning situation in which escape or avoidance from an aversive stimulus such as electric shock is not possible. Active coping, in contrast, is characterized by shock avoidance when the subject can exert some control over the receipt of an aversive stimulus contingent on some aspect of his or her behavior such as performance on a reaction time task. Obrist and colleagues found that during passive coping, beta adrenergic influences on the heart, as assessed by cardiovascular measures such as heart rate and diastolic and systolic blood pressure, were either minimal or rapidly dissipated. Under active coping conditions, beta adrenergic effects were more pronounced. Thus, the type of coping available to subjects has a significant impact on cardiovascular responding. This is a fruitful area for future systematic research.

Research on the Type A pattern is the most systematic investigation of a coping style to date. Unfortunately, for the most part, past research on coping has focused on a single coping variable rather than attempting to systemize findings. For example, Grinker and Speigel (1945) considered defensive coping styles focusing on denial among combat air crews in World War II and found that for some, denial was an effective way of managing fear and conflict. Wolff, Friedman, and Hofer (1964) also noted the effectiveness of denial among leukemia patients, and styles of coping have been considered among patients awaiting surgery (e.g., Andrews, 1970; Cohen & Lazarus, 1973), or recovering from burns or illness (e.g., Andreasen, et al., 1972). Further, research has attempted to link sociocultural influences to physiological response patterns by considering coping processes (e.g., Henry, Ely, Watson, & Stephens, 1975).

Given the nonsystematic nature of this literature, the relationships between coping styles and psychophysiological illness are presently merely speculative. Research has shown that psychologically-based coping processes affect physiological responding, organic dysfunction and illness, so such a link is probable. Its nature is unspecified, however. One possible link is through appraisal processes. As Lazarus (1966) and others have argued, cognitive appraisal or interpretation of environmental threats or challenges is an important determinant of stress. Hence, if styles of appraisal, or tendencies to interpret situations in ways which lead to stress and certain kinds of response exist, they may determine vulnerability to a range of ills. To some extent, the Type A pattern reflects an appraisal style as well as a type of response. The Type A individual is more prone to interpret situations as threatening to control or more likely to appraise loss of control as threatening (e.g., Glass, 1977). By the same token, Graham's (1972) notion of specific attitudes may in fact reflect differences in appraisal. The ways in which situations are interpreted may be related not only to the physiological system involved in response (e.g., Lacey, 1967), but also to the degree of stress experienced and the focus of coping.

Thus, coping and appraisal processes may prove to be important variables to consider in any comprehensive model of psychophysiological disorders. However, again, not enough systematic research has been conducted to determine the predictive validity and utility of such psychological constructs.

THE DIATHESIS-STRESS MODEL OF PSYCHOSOMATIC DISORDERS

We have reviewed various theoretical orientations and research that have highlighted the importance of either genetic, physiological, or psychological factors. Even though we have discussed these factors separately, any comprehensive model of a psychosomatic disorder will have to take all these factors into account and unravel the interaction among them. As Weiner (1977) states:

> Being predisposed to a disease does not necessarily mean that one will get it. A comprehensive theory of disease should also explain why many predisposed persons remain healthy. One reason is that additional factors, such as psychological maturity and health, may play a role in maintaining physical health in some undisclosed manner. Another reason might be that single predisposing factors are never etiologically sufficient. They must be combined with one or several additional predisposing factors. (p. 581)

Sternbach (1966) proposed a diathesis-stress model which emphasized the importance of considering all these factors in any attempt to understand a particular disorder. The *diathesis* portion of this model postulates the presence of two major factors: (1) individual response stereotypy which he sees as a constitutional predisposition to respond physiologically to various situations in a particular way, with consistent activation of certain physiological systems or organs; and (2) the existence of inadequate homeostatic restraints, which may be due to stress-induced breakdown, previous accident or infection, or genetic predisposition. The *stress* portion of the model refers to the persistent exposure of the individual to stressful, activating situations. Situational determinants are very important and must be taken into account. For example, an individual exposed to an emotional stressor in a work situation may respond to it quite differently than if he or she were at home. Socially accepted methods of dealing with stressors will differ from situation to situation, and thus the physiological consequences will similarly be expected to differ.

Along with exposure to actual external activating/stressful situations, Sternbach also includes in his model the possibility that, in the absence of such objective real-life stressors, an individual may perceive ordinary situations and events as stressors and so react to them with heightened physiological responding. These misperceptions are due to the person's chronic attitudes (e.g., *specific* attitudes) or personality characteristics that significantly affect his or her perception and interpretation of stimuli and his or her ability to effectively cope with them.

There has been some recent animal research to support a diathesis-stress model of various psychosomatic disorders. For example, Ader (1963) bred rats for their susceptibility to gastric lesions under conditions of restraint (restraint and immobilization have been found to be significant stressors for rats). These individual differences in susceptibility to gastric lesions are due to individual variations in serum pepsinogen levels. Ader found that rats which were ulcer-susceptible *and* which were exposed to restraint conditions were more likely to develop ulceration than other rats (this relationship was found only when the rats were restrained at the peak of their circadian activity cycle).

Friedman and Iwai (1976) also demonstrated that when rats were genetically made to be salt-susceptible to hypertension through selective inbreeding *and* were clinically exposed to stress (an approach-avoidance conflict), they showed persistent elevation in systolic blood pressure. In contrast, rats who were genetically resistant to salt-induced hypertension and who were exposed to the same stressor did not develop similar high blood pressure. These results indicate that stress is selectively effective in producing hypertension—type effects depending on the animal's genetic predisposition. More recently, Lawler, Barker, Hubbard, and Allen (1980) have found similar effects of conflict on tonic level of blood pressure in the genetically borderline hypertensive rat.

Clearly, the investigation of psychosomatic disorders is complex. A host of variables—genetic, physiological, situational, behavioral/personality—obviously need to be taken into account in any comprehensive understanding of the various psychophysiological, disorders. As we have noted, significant progress is being made in biomedical research in the development of a better understanding of the pathogenesis of various disorders. Unfortunately, parallel progress has not been evidenced in research on psychological factors. Such research in the past has been sorely inadequate. However, more recent evaluations of specific behavioral characteristics—such as the Type A personality and coping mechanisms—may provide useful avenues for future investigation. Of course, no one would doubt the great importance of the role of emotional factors in these disorders. However, as has been pointed out throughout this chapter, the quality of research on emotional factors, in combination with the simultaneous evaluation of physiological mechanisms, has been poor and/or incomplete. In the next section, we will review an experimental methodology which may provide a useful means of filling this research void.

THE BIO-INFORMATIONAL THEORY OF EMOTIONAL IMAGERY: IMPLICATIONS FOR THE ASSESSMENT OF EMOTION IN PSYCHOSOMATIC PATIENTS

Lang (1979) has proposed a theory of emotional imagery which conceives the visual image in the brain to be a conceptual network which controls specific somatovisceral response patterns. He has drawn upon research in psychophysiology, the information processing approach of cognitive psychology, and behavior therapy in formulating this theory. The image is viewed as a finite propositional network, and not as an analogue representation suggested by phenomenology. Furthermore, the image structure is assumed to include some propositions which are elements in a somato-motor program which controls specific patterns of physiological and behavioral responding. Lang proposes that the image is a prototype in the brain for overt behavioral responding; it has the same status as a perceptual-motor set which controls contextual behavior.

Evidence for this theory is beginning to accumulate with the demonstration that the type and content of imaginal activity is associated with specific patterns of efferent outflow as assessed by visceral and somato-motor activity (an effective training procedure has been developed by Lang and colleagues for the amplification of this efferent outflow during imagery). For example, research has shown that the imaging of relevant fearful content prompts a specific increase in the amplitude of physiological arousal, and that the discrimination between different phobic subjects can be significantly made through imagery analysis. They have also noted wide individual differences in the ability of subjects to generate an emotional response to semantic or other symbolic stimuli.

One important implication of this bio-information theory is the opportunity to more systematically study somato-visceral patterns in emotion. In the earlier reviewed specific-attitudes formulation of Graham, findings suggested that psychosomatic disorders were related to habitual patterns of physiological reactions. These specific patterns, in turn, were seen as being prompted by characteristic emotional attitudes held by the patients. The experimental procedure he employed was to hypnotize subjects and instruct them to assume a critical emotional attitude during which physiological responses were monitored. He found significant physiological reactions to different imagined emotional states. Thus, for example, the attitude assumed to be fundamental to hives led to an increase in skin temperature, with no significant effect on blood pressure. Conversely, it was found that the attitude assumed to underlay hypertension prompted increases in blood pressure, and no appreciable rise in skin temperature. Graham interpreted these results as supporting his view that specific psychosomatic disorders were a consequence of the chronic instigation of these attitude-mediated physiological reaction patterns.

There were a number of other investigations which suggested the important role that physiological response patterns played in the etiology of psychosomatic disorders. For example, both Ax (1953) and Joseph Schachter (1957) presented evidence demonstrating that fear and anger situations elicited a different pattern of muscular and cardiovascular responses in their subjects. They interpreted these data in terms of catecholamine balance: A norepinephrine pattern was generated by the anger situation (characterized by a more predominant diastolic blood pressure increase), while an epinephrine dominance determined the physiological concomitant of fear.

The experimental procedure employed by investigators such as Ax to evoke emotion involved the staging of a complex, interactional situation in which a confederate of the experimenter verbally abused the subjects (anger situation) or subjects were attached to an apparently malfunctioning apparatus which seemed to place their lives in danger (fear situation). Unfortunately, such a complex staged laboratory situation is difficult to repeat reliably. Moreover, since it involves deception and a great deal of stress, important ethical concerns can be raised about conducting such a study. These factors limited subsequent research of this type. In addition, more "cognitive" models of emotion proposed by Stanley Schachter (1964) and George Mandler (1975) dismissed the concept of specific physiological patterns of emotion. Instead, these theorists assumed an undifferentiated or undimensional state of arousal. This undifferentiated state of arousal *coupled* with the individual's cognitive appraisal of a particular situation was viewed as determining the specific emotional state experienced. Such a two-factor model of emotion was widely accepted in subsequent years. This had the unfortunate effect of causing a premature abandonment of attempts to more clearly delineate whether there were unique psychophysiological patterns associated with different emotional states.

There were also questions raised concerning the validity of the experimental procedure used to test Graham's formulation, which further contributed to a loss of interest in the evaluation of psychophysiological concomitants of emotion and psychosomatic disorders. As pointed out earlier, a major issue centered around the use of hypnosis. Peters and Stern (1971) conducted a study in which the respective attitudes were suggested to subjects either with or without hypnosis. The differences they obtained were found to be related mainly to the hypnosis factor and not to the attitude suggested. The subjects employed by Graham may therefore have been a special subsample of the population who were especially responsive to hypnosis. The inability to adequately deal with this hypnosis confound presented major problems for subsequent attempts at validating Graham's formulation of unique physiologial response patterns associated with specific emotional states.

Recently, Weerts and Roberts (1976) revived the attempt to demonstrate specific physiological patterns associated with particular emotional states. They employed an experimental procedure in which subjects were instructed to imagine as vividly as possible specific scenes which were created by the experimenter and each subject individually. Two types of scenes were evaluated: anger evoking and fear evoking experiences. Results of this study demonstrated that, similar to the findings of Ax (1953), diastolic blood pressure increased significantly more for high anger scenes (norepinephrine pattern) than for high fear scenes. Such findings provide support for the view that there may be meaningful differences in psychophysiological patterns of emotion.

Lang (1979) has previously pointed out an important feature of the Weerts and Roberts (1976) results which limit their generality—the subjects employed were specifically selected on the basis of their ability to generate strong emotional reactions through imagery. It can be argued that these subjects were a special subsample of individuals, not necessarily representative of the general population.

The bio-informational approach provides an excellent alternative experimental methodology to further assess the psychophysiological concomitants of emotional responding and psychosomatic disease. As indicated, a training procedure has been developed to train subjects to increase their verbal reports of responding in an imagery experience, and also increase their physiological responses and report of imagery vividness. Emotional imagery can therefore be brought under experimental control. This methodology may circumvent those problems produced by the use of hypnosis which plagued the earlier Graham studies, and the special subsample of subjects used in the Weerts and Roberts (1974) study. It has the potential of assessing emotional imagery/attitudes and the effects on physiological reactivity in subjects, including psychosomatic patients. In a recent study suggesting the differential responsiveness of psychosomatic patients to imagery-generated affect, Taylor, Gatchel, and Korman (1980) found that imagined scenes involving a great many somato-motor elements (e.g., driving a car; walking into a room) produced more physiological arousal in rheumatoid arthritis patients than peptic ulcer patients and normal control group subjects. These differences were interpreted as reflecting the greater impact of these somato-motor scenes on the arthritic patients because of their greater emotional impact and relevance for these patients (because physical activity is a major problem in their lives).

This bio-information theory may also provide a useful method of assessing the validity of the concept of alexithymia since it allows one to objectively evaluate imagination, to analyze the image for perceptual, semantic, and affective response structure. It also allows the exploration of the impact of training procedures which modify in predictable ways the emotional cognition of subjects.

Even in research areas examining the relationship between psychological factors and one specific physical disorder, this theoretical approach may make an important contribution. For example, the recent research on psychological concomitants of the coronary-prone individual, suggests that a hostility dimension may be important (Matthews, Glass, Rosenman, & Bortner, 1977). The bio-informational approach may provide an effective methodology to more intensively examine this emotional dimension of hostility.

The bio-information theory of emotional imagery may therefore provide an extremely useful organizational framework for the objective study of emotional reactivity among psychosomatic patients. It provides a useful experimental methodology to simultaneously assess the interaction of emotional/psychological factors and somato-visceral patterns of responding. As we indicated at the outset and throughout this chapter, it is extremely important in the field of psychosomatic medicine to simultaneously examine physiological and psychological factors in an integrative manner in order to comprehensively understand disease.

SUMMARY AND CONCLUSIONS

In this chapter, we have focused our attention primarily on research which evaluated the role of psychological factors in psychosomatic disorders. We highlighted the fact that there were a number of significant problems with this past research, both methodological as well as conceptual, which seriously limits its utility in helping develop a more comprehensive understanding of psychosomatic disorders. A major problem has been the overemphasis of much of this research on the sole role of psychological predisposition in the etiological process. The great bulk of earlier psychological research was conducted without simultaneously taking into account situational, physiological, and genetic factors that interact in predisposing an individual to a particular disorder.

Using a *diathesis-stress model* conceptualization, we pointed out that any complete understanding of psychosomatic disorders will require a careful evaluation of the interaction among stimulus or situational factors, genetic/physiological variables, and intervening psychological processes such as personality characteristics and coping styles. Significant progress is being made in biomedical research in delineating the pathogenesis of various disorders. However, for the field to progress even further, research on psychological/emotional factors, in combination with the simultaneous evaluation of physiological mechanisms, is sorely needed.

Finally, we discussed the bio-informational theory of emotional imagery proposed by Lang (1979), and the implications of this approach for the assessment of emotion in psychosomatic patients. It provides a useful research methodology for the evaluation of psychophysiological concomitants of emotional responding and psychosomatic disease. A determination of the utility of this approach to the field, however, awaits future research.

REFERENCES

Ader, R. Plasma pepsinogen level as a predictor of susceptibility to gastric erosins in the rat. *Psychosomatic Medicine*, 1963, *25*, 221–230.

Alexander, F. *Psychosomatic medicine: Its principles and applications*. New York: Norton, 1950.

Andreasen, N. J. et al. Management of emotional reactions in seriously burned adults. *New England Journal of Medicine*, 1972 (Jan.), *286* (2), 65–69.

Andrews, J. M. Recovery from surgery, with and without preparatory instruction, for three coping styles. *Journal of Personality and Social Psychology*, 1970, *15*, 223–226.

Ax, A. R. The physiological differentiation between fear and anger in humans. *Psychosomatic Medicine*, 1953, *15*, 433–442.

Bakal, D. A. Headache: A biopsychological perspective. *Psychological Bulletin*, 1977, *82*, 369–382.

Baum, A., Calesnick, L. E., Davis, G. E., & Gatchel, R. J. Individual differences in coping with crowding: Stimulus screening and social overload. *Journal of Personality and Social Psychology*, in press.

Brady, J. V., Porter, R. W., Conrad, D. G., & Mason, J. W. Avoidance behavior and the development of gastroduodenal ulcers. *Journal of Experimental Analysis of Behavior*, 1958, *1*, 69–75.

Buss, A. H. *Psychopathology*. New York: Wiley, 1966.

Cohen, F., & Lazarus, R. S. Active coping processes, coping dispositions and recovery from surgery. *Psychosomatic Medicine*, 1973, *35* 375–389.

Coyne, J. C., & Lazarus, R. Cognition, stress, and coping: A transactional perspective. I. L. Kutash, & L. B. Schlesinger (Eds.), *Pressure point: Perspectives on stress and anxiety*. San Francisco: Jossey-Bass, 1982.

Dalessio, D. J. *Wolff's headache and other head pain*. New York: Oxford University Press, 1972.

Deutsch, F. *The psychosomatic concept in psychoanalyses*. New York: International Universities Press, 1953.

Dunbar, H. F. *Psychosomatic diagnosis*. New York: Hoebar, 1943.

Engel, G. L. A psychological setting of somatic disease: The "giving up-given up complex. *Proceedings of the Royal Society of Medicine*, 1967, *60*, 553–563.

Friedman, R., & Iwai, J. Genetic predisposition and stress-induced hypertension. *Science*, 1976, *193*, 161–192.

Friedman, M., & Rosenman, R. H. *Type A behavior and your heart*. New York: Alfred Knoph, 1974.

Folkmann, S., & Lazarus, R. An analysis of coping in a middle-aged community sample. *Journal of Health and Social Behavior*, 1982.

Glass, D. Stress, behavior patterns, and coronary disease. *American Scientist*, 1977, *65* (2), 177–187.

Glass, D. C., Krakoff, L. R., Contrada, R., Hilton, W. F., Kehoe, K., Mannucci, E. G., Collins, C., Snow, B., & Elting, E. Effect of harassment and competition upon cardiovascular and plasma catecholamine responses Type A and Type B individuals. *Psychophysiology*, 1980, *17* (5), 453–463.

Graham, D. T. Psychosomatic medicine. In N. S. Greenfield & R. A. Sternbach (Eds.), *Handbook of psychophysiology*, New York: Holt, Rinehart & Winston, 1972.

Graham, D. T., Kabler, J. D., & Graham, F. K. Physiological responses to the suggestion of attitudes specific for hives and hypertension. *Psychosomatic Medicine*, 1962, *24*, 159–169.

Graham, D. T., Lundy, R. M., Benjamin, L. S., Kabler, J. D., Lewis, W. C., Kunish, N. C., & Graham, F. K. Specific attitudes in initial interviews with patients having different "psychosomatic" diseases. *Psychosomatic Medicine*, 1962, *24*, 257–266.

Graham, D. T., Stern, J. A., & Winokur, G. Experimental investigation of the specificity hypothesis in psychosomatic disease. *Psychomatic Medicine*, 1958, *20*, 446–457.

Grace, W. J., & Graham, D. T. Relationship of specific attitudes and emotions to certain bodily diseases. *Psychosomatic Medicine*, 1952, *14*, 242–251.

Green, W. A., Jr. Role of a vicarious object in the adaptation to object loss. I. Use of a vicarious object as a means of adjustment to preparation from a significant person. *Psychosomatic Medicine*, 1958, *20*, 344–350.

Greer, S., & Morris, T. Psychological attributes of women who develop breast cancer: A controlled study. *Journal of Psychosomatic Research*, 1975, *19*, 147–153.

Grinker, R. R., & Speigel, J. P. *War neuroses*. Philadelphia: Blakeston, 1945.

Hambling, J. Psychosomatic aspects of arterial hypertension. *British Journal of Medical Psychology*, 1952, *25*, 39–47.

Henry, J. P., Ely, D. L., Watson, F. M. C., & Stephens, P. M. Ethological methods as applied to the measurement of emotion. In L. Levi (Ed.), *Emotions: Their parameters and measurement*. New York: Raven, 1975.

Holman, C. W., & Muschenheim, C. *Bronchopulmonary disease and related disorders*. New York: Harper & Row, 1972.

Ilfeld, F. W., Jr. Coping styles of Chicago adults: Description. *Journal of Human Stress*, 1980, *6* (2), 2–10.

Janis, I. Stages in the decision-making process. In R. Abelson & E. Aronson (Eds.), *Theories of cognitive consistency: A sourcebook*. Chicago: Rand-McNally, 1968, 577–588.

Kahn, R. L. Stress: From 9 to 5. *Psychology Today*, 1969, *3*, 34–38.

Kirsner, J. B. Peptic ulcer: A review of the current literature on various clinical aspects. *Gastroenterology*, 1968, *54*, 610–618.

Lacey, J. I. Somatic response patterning and stress: Some revisions of activation theory. In M. H. Appley & R. Trumbull (Eds.), *Psychological Stress*. New York: McGraw-Hill, 1967.

Lang, P. J. A bio-informational theory of emotional imagery. *Psychophysiology*, 1979, *16*, 495–512.

Lawler, J. E., Barker, G. F., Hubbard, J. W., & Allen, M. T. The effects of conflict on tonic levels of blood pressure in the genetically borderline hypertensive rat. *Psychophysiology*, 1980, *17*, 363-370.

Lazarus, R. S. *Psychological stress and the coping process*. New York: McGraw-Hill, 1966.

Lazarus, R. S., & Cohen, F. Active coping processes, coping dispositions, and recovery from surgery. *Psychosomatic Medicine*, 1973, *35* (5), 375-389.

Lazarus, R. S., & Launier, R. Stress-related transactions between person and environment. In L. A. Pervin & M. Lewes (Eds.), *Perspectives in interactional psychology*, New York: Plenum, 1978.

Leventhal, H. Findings and theory in the study of far communication. *Advances in experimental social psychology*, 1970, *5*, 119-186.

Lipowski, Z. J. Psychosomatic medicine in the seventies: An overview. *American Journal of Psychiatry*, 1977, *134*, 233-243.

Lipp, M. R., Looney, J. G., & Spitzer, R. L. Classifying psychophysiologic disorders: A new idea. *Psychosomatic Medicine*, 1977, *39*, 285-287.

Malmo, R. B., & Shagass, C. Physiologic study of symptom mechanisms in psychiatric patients under stress. *Psychosomatic Medicine*, 1949, *11*, 25-29.

Mandler, G. *Mind and emotion*. New York: Wiley, 1975.

Matthews, K. A., Glass, D. C. Rosenman, R. H., & Bortner, R. W. Competitive drive, pattern A., and coronary heart disease: A further analysis of some data from the Western Collaborative Group Study. *Journal of Chronic Diseases*, 1977, *30*, 489-498.

McMahon, M., & Hastrup, J. The role of imagination in the disease process: Post-cartesian history. *Journal of Behavioral Medicine*, 1980, *3*, 205-217.

Mears, F. G., & Gatchel, R. J. *Fundamentals of abnormal psychology*. Chicago: Rand McNally, 1979.

Mechanic, D. *Mental health and social policy*. Englewood Cliffs, NJ: Prentice-Hall, 1969.

Mehrabian, A. A questionnaire measure of individual differences in stimulus screening and associated differences in arousability. *Environmental Psychology and Nonverbal Behavior*, 1977, *1*, 89-103.

Mirsky, I. A. Physiologic, psychologic, and social determinants in the etiology of duodenal ulcer. *American Journal of Digestive Diseases*, 1958, *3*, 285-314.

Mirsky, I. A., Futterman, P., & Kaplan, S. Blood plasma pepsinogen, II. The activity of the plasma from "normal" subjects, patients with duodenal ulcer and patients with pernicious anemia. *Journal of Laboratory and Clinical Medicine*, 1952, *40*, 188-195.

Nemiah, J. C. Psychology and psychosomatic illness. Reflections in theory and research methodology. In J. Freyberger (Ed.), *Topics in psychosomatic research; Proceedings of the 9th European Conference Psychosomatic Research*. London: Karger, Basel, 1973.

Nemiah, J. C. Denial revisited. Reflections on psychosomatic theory. *Psychotherapy and Psychosomatics*, 1975, *26*, 140-147.

Nemiah, J. C., Freyberger, H., & Sifneos, P. Alexthymia: A view of the psychosomatic research. In O. Hill (Ed.), *Modern trends in psychosomatic medicine*. Vol. 3. London: Buttersworths, 1976.

Obrist, P. A., Gaebelein, C. J., Teller, E. S., Langer, A. W., Grignolo, A., Light, K. C., & McCublin, J. A. The relationship among heart rate, carotid dP/dt, and blood pressure in humans as a function of the type of stress. *Psychophysiology*, 1978, *15*, 102-115.

Peters, J. E., & Stern, R. M. Specificity of attitude hypothesis in psychosomatic medicine: A reexamination. *Journal of Psychosomatic Research*, 1971, *15*, 129-135.

Pilot, M. L., Lenkoski, L. D., Spiro, H. M., & Schaeffer, R. Duodenal ulcer in one of identical twins. *Psychosomatic Medicine*, 1957, *19*, 221-229.

Purcell, K., Brady, K., Chai, H., Muser, J., Molk, L., Gordon, U., & Means, J. The effect on asthma in children of experimental separation from the family. *Psychosomatic Medicine*, 1969, *31*, 144-164.

Rees, L. The importance of psychological, allergic, and infective factors in childhood asthma. *Schizophrenia Bulletin*, 1964, *8*, 7-11.

Rosen, E., & Gregory, I. *Abnormal psychology*. Philadelphia: W. B. Saunders, 1965.

Schachter, J. Pain, fear, and anger in hypertensives and normotensives. *Psychosomatic Medicine,* 1957, *19,* 17–29.

Schachter, S. The interaction of cognitive and physiological determinants of emotional states. In. L. Berkowitz (Ed.), *Advances in Experimental Social Psychology,* Vol. 1. New York: Academic Press, 1964.

Schmale, A. H. A relationship of separation and depression to disease. *Psychosomatic Medicine,* 1958, *20,* 259–265.

Selye, H. *The stress of life.* New York: McGraw-Hill, 1956.

Sifneos, P. E. Clinical observations in some patients suffering from a variety of psychosomatic diseases. *Proceedings of the 7th European Conference of Psychosomatic Research.* London: Karger, Basel, 1967.

Sines, J. O., Cleeland, C., & Adkins, J. The behavior of normal and stomach lesion susceptible rates in several learning situations. *Journal of Genetic Psychology,* 1963, *102,* 91–94.

Sternbach, R. A. *Principles of psychophysiology.* New York: Academic Press, 1966.

Taylor, J. A., Gatchel, R. J., & Korman, M. *Psychophysiological and cognitive characteristics of ulcer and rheumatoid arthritis patients. Journal of Behavioral Medicine,* 1982.

Vaillant, G. M. Northwood history of male psychologic health. *New England Journal of Medicine,* 1979, *301* (23), 1249–1254.

Weerts, T. C., & Roberts, R. The physiologic effects of imagining anger-provoking and fear-provoking scenes. *Psychophysiology,* 1976, *13,* 174. (Abstract)

Weiner, H. *Psychological and human disease.* New York: Elsevier, 1977.

Weiner, H., Thaler, M., Reiser, M. F., & Mirsky, I. A. Etiology of duodenal ulcer: Relation of specific psychological characteristics to rate of gastric secretion (serum pepsinogen). *Psychosomatic Medicine,* 1957, *19,* 1–10.

Weiss, J. M. Effects of coping response on stress. *Journal of Comparative and Physiological Psychology,* 1968, *65,* 251–260.

Weiss, J. M. Effects of coping behavior in different warning signal conditions on stress pathology in rats. *Journal of Comparative and Physiological Psychology,* 1971, *77,* 1–13.

Williams, D. A., Lewis-Faning, E., Rees, L., Jacobs, J., & Thomas, A. Assessment of the relative importance of the allergic, infective and psychological factors in asthma. *Acta Allergologista,* 1958, *12,* 376–385.

Wittkower, E. D., & Dudek, S. Z. Psychosomatic medicine: The mind-body-society interaction. In B. Wolman (Ed.), *Handbook of general psychology.* Englewood Cliffs, NJ: Prentice-Hall, 1973.

Wolf, S. *The stomach.* New York: Oxford, 1965.

Wolf, S., & Wolff, H. G̅. *Human gastric function.* New York: Oxford, 1947.

Wolff, C. T., Friedman, S. B., Hofer, M. A., & Mason, J. W. Relationship between psychological defenses and mean urinary 17-OH-CS excretion rates: A predictive study of parents of fatally ill children. *Psychosomatic Medicine,* 1964, *26,* 576.

Yager, J., & Weiner, H. Observations in man. *Advances in Psychosomatic Medicine,* 1970, *6,* 40–55.

11 Anxiety: Mechanisms and Management

Phil Skolnick, Ph.D.
Steven M. Paul, M.D.
National Institutes of Health

INTRODUCTION

Anxiety has been acknowledged throughout history as an integral component of emotional being which is experienced throughout life. In the 55 years since the publication of Freud's "Hemmung, Symptom, und Angst" (translated as: "The Problem of Anxiety"), anxiety has become a principle focus of psychological, psychoanalytic, psychiatric, and most recently psychopharmacologic investigation. Perhaps because anxiety is such a universal experience, it defies precise definition from a psychological standpoint. However, it may be thought of as an unpleasant state, associated with feelings of uneasiness and apprehension. Anxiety is usually accompanied by heightened autonomic activity which may be manifest in a variety of somatic complaints. Although anxiety is generally associated with counterproductive behavior (i.e. behavior handicapping the "normal" functioning of an individual) and is believed to be involved in almost all neurotic symptom formation, it also is a strong motivating force for many types of adaptive behaviors. Anxiety-related motivation or arousal may therefore be related to survival and, like fear, could have evolutionary significance.

Freud considered (cf. Villeneuve, 1979) anxiety to have an inherited biological (viz. genetic) basis, with individuals being endowed with differing capacities for reacting to anxiety-provoking situations and perhaps with varying psychological and physical manifestations as well. However, the strong influence of existential concepts of anxiety coupled with its highly variable, episodic nature have (until recently) impeded efforts to develop tenable biological hypotheses regarding its biological bases.

Many investigators now separate so called "state" from "trait" anxiety. State or situational anxiety refers to anxiety experienced at a particular time in response to a specific situation (e.g. prior to an examination, late for an airplane, meeting a blind date), whereas "trait" anxiety generally refers to a habitual tendency to be anxious for protracted periods. The voluminous literature concerning the psychological theories of anxiety makes a detailed discussion of this area beyond the scope of this review. This chapter will review the characteristics and development of anxiety as a clinical problem, some behavioral and chemotherapeutic approaches successfully used to control anxiety, and finally some recent studies on the mechanisms of action of anxiolytic agents. The latter area has provided new and exciting insights into the neurochemical bases of anxiety.

MEASUREMENT AND CLINICAL MANIFESTATIONS OF ANXIETY

Despite differing criteria which makes the uniform diagnosis of anxiety impossible, most investigators report that 2-5% of the general populations in Western cultures may be considered to have pathological anxiety (Marks & Lader, 1973; Noyes, Clancy, Hoenk, & Slymen, 1980). However, within the subpopulation of psychiatric outpatients, somewhere between 6-27% have been diagnosed with moderate to severe anxiety (Marks & Lader, 1973). Studies of patients with cardiovascular symptoms encountered in general medical practice have shown that between 10-14% of these patients (cf. Marks & Lader, 1973) have demonstrable and symptomatic anxiety. It has also been suggested that anxiety is these patients may be causally related to and/or at least partially responsible for problems such as hypertension and/or cardiac arrhythmias. The incidence of females diagnosed as having pathological anxiety among patients encountered in general medical practice is remarkably constant between studies, ranging from 67-74% (Hagnell, 1966; Wheeler, White, Reed, & Cohen, 1950). However among psychiatric patients, this value drops to approximately 50% in Western cultures (Miles, Barrabee, & Finesinger, 1951; Winokur & Holeman, 1963).

Because of its highly variable and episodic nature, anxiety may manifest itself in several ways, all of which have been subject to study and experimentation. Self-reports in which patients subjectively report anxiety by the use of such descriptive terms as "clutched up", "tense", "nervous", "on edge", "jittery", and other adjectives of a similar genre are most common. Many attempts have been made to quantitate this self-assessment through psychological tests (cf. Zuckerman, 1976). Such tests have been used to assess and differentiate "state" from "trait" anxiety, and may be valuable tools in preliminary evaluation of the patient. However these tests are subject to the caveats of intentional or unintentional bias, such as attributing non-relevant stimuli to formation of symptoms.

The second means of assessing anxiety is by the degree of physiological arousal experienced by the patient. Physiological arousal is most commonly manifested through an increased activity of the autonomic nervous system resulting in altered cardiovascular function (e.g. heart rate, blood volume, blood pressure), respiration, galvanic skin response, muscle tension, and pupillary response. Usually, measurement of one parameter is inadequate, since the physiological sequelae of anxiety are highly variable. Autonomic changes caused by anxiety may also be manifest in complaints such as palpitations, dizziness, respiratory distress, sweating, irritability, and chest pains. Somatomotor alterations may also be present, such as stuttering, trembling, or tics. These may result as an observable consequence of the physiological arousal or means of avoiding certain stimuli.

A major problem in the diagnosis of anxiety is the lack of correlation between these three assessment paradigms. An anxious patient may (e.g.) display a strong physiological response but have a self-assessment score showing little anxiety with no somatomotor manifestations. This highly variable response may be related to varying social, situation, and cognitive consequences (either positive or negative) that are involved in the individuals' expression of anxiety.

Because a certain level of anxiety-related arousal or activation may be important to normal functioning, the treatment of anxiety is clearly indicated only when it interferes with normal functioning: that is, when excessive activation in terms of intensity, duration, frequency, or generality of the stimulus is encountered. Intense and prolonged periods of anxiety may result in depression, physical exhaustion, and pathophysiological conditions such as hypertension and ulcers.

Anxiety states often resemble certain forms of depression, although different courses of treatment suggest that these conditions are different disease entities. Prominent anxiety will often mask a depressive illness. In one study, 19% of patients diagnosed as anxious were subsequently re-diagnosed as having depression (Davidian, 1969). The age of the patient (mean age of anxiety state patients is 35 versus 51 for unipolar depressives) can often provide a clue to diagnosis, and thus for treatment as well. Depressed patients have a uniformly better outcome when treated with electroconvulsive therapy (ECT) and/or antidepressants than patients with anxiety alone.

Before deciding on a course of treatment, the clinician must determine whether anxiety is adaptive or maladaptive. Anxiety clearly related to a threatening situation would usually not require long-term treatment. However, when responses are deemed inappropriate, some type of psychotherapeutic or chemotherapeutic treatment is usually warranted. Most anxiety-related behaviors dealt with by clinicians involve inappropriate and maladaptive attempts to escape stimuli which would usually be deemed harmless.

TARGETS OF ANXIETY MANAGEMENT

The physiologic (i.e. autonomic) arousal that may accompany anxiety can result in pathophysiological changes including gastrointestinal disorders (e.g. colitis, ulcer), cardiovascular disorders (e.g. hypertension, tachycardia or other dysrhythmias, migraine headache), and fatigue. The physical manifestation of anxiety can be treated directly (e.g. anticholinergics, antihypertensives, etc.), and psychotherapy should be aimed at identifying and preventing or reducing inappropriate arousal.

Anxiety and overarousal which accompanies anxiety may further result in the disruption of more complex behaviors involving cognitive functions. For example, the patient may not complain of anxiety per se, but more of an inability to concentrate associated with memory impairment, disruptive daydreaming, etc. Sexual functioning, which involves physiological, motor, and cognitive responses may also be disrupted. An anxiety or phobic response to conditions not obviously (i.e. objectively) threatening is often termed a conditioned anxiety reaction. The patient will usually report feelings of anxiety to such a condition (e.g. travelling through tunnels, crowds). However, this hyperaroused state may be the result of complex behavior patterns or multiple stimuli (both external and cognitive) so that a specific cause cannot be precisely determined. This is so-called "free-floating" anxiety because of its "nonspecific" nature. Escape or avoidance of anxiety-producing stimuli may result in socially acceptable (but inconvenient and/or disruptive) behaviors. Taken to extremes, inappropriate or disruptive behaviors for escape (e.g. alcohol or drug abuse), phobic behavior, and obsessions and compulsions may also be manifest.

BEHAVIORAL TECHNIQUES IN ANXIETY MANAGEMENT

Introduction

The treatment of anxiety by behavioral modification techniques has been one of the most extensively investigated areas in contemporary psychology. Extensive reviews and treatises on specific methods are readily available and are beyond the scope of this review. The most widely used techniques are based on the assumption that anxiety responses which are maladaptive are learned, and strategies are aimed at unlearning or relearning these behaviors.

Systematic Desensitization

Systematic desensitization is one of the most widely employed behavioral techniques used in the treatment of anxiety. There are three basic elements to this technique: (1) relaxation of the patient; (2) development of a hierarchy of anxiety provoking stimuli (from least to most arousing); and (3) a coupling of the items in the hierarchy (accomplished by either imagery or actual pairing) with relaxation. The principle of reciprocal inhibition assumes in this situation that the relaxation will inhibit anxiety (Wolpe, 1958). Relaxation may be achieved by hypnosis or drugs to facilitate relaxation training and inhibit anxiety during imagination of the hierarchy. It is important that the arousing stimuli are sufficiently weak so that the induced relaxation will prevent discomfort. The anxiety provoking stimuli may either be presented by imagery or in vivo. Variations of the hierarchal theme would include breaking down the situation into components in a spatial-temporal time frame as well as within a thematic hierarchy. Vicarious desensitization, where the individual may observe others (e.g. by videotape) being desensitized rather than undergoing the technique by themselves, may also prove effective.

Modeling

Modeling is a behavioral technique based on the patients' acquiring desired responses by observing others (usually of a similar age and/or sex) in similar anxiety-generating situations, rather than by direct participation. This technique borrows on some of the basic principles of systematic desensitization, and is very similar to vicarious desensitization previously discussed. Much of the current therapeutic application of modeling is derived from the work of Bandura (1969). In the simplest form, the patient observes others (usually peers) as they confront anxiety-provoking situations and deal with them without the arousal experienced by the patient. Variations of modeling such as participant modeling uses a live model to perform the response followed by the patient performing the task. The modeling may be live, imagined, or filmed. Modeling has been used to treat a variety of behaviors such as fear of animals, heights, and unassertive behavior. This technique has been used successfully with children, adolescents, and adults. Modeling is effective when anxiety responses are related to concrete stimuli (e.g. physical, social) which can be presented in a controlled and graduated manner. The theoretical mechanisms which underlie modeling are still the subject of investigation. Some investigators believe modeling to be a cognitive process (Bandura, 1969), while others (Gewirtz, 1971) have devised operant models to explain the efficacy of this technique.

Flooding and Implosion Therapy

The techniques of systematic desensitization and modelling employ graded and gradual presentation of arousing stimuli in a setting designed to minimize discomfort. Flooding is a technique used to treat avoidance responses by presenting the patient with an intense, anxiety-provoking stimulus (either directly or via imagery) to immediately and dramatically heighten arousal. These techniques are based on the hypothesis that responses which are not reinforced will ultimately disappear or be extinguished (Masserman, 1943). Masserman demonstrated that forced exposure to an anxiety-producing stimulus could eventually extinguish the anxiety. In a clinical setting, the patient may imagine anxiety-provoking stimuli for prolonged periods. This procedure is repeated until the arousal response and associated anxiety dissipates over time. Although flooding is usually conducted by imagery, direct exposure tends to be more effective. When flooding is combined with implosion, the imagination of strongly arousing therapy is combined with scenes devised by the therapist to unrealistically exaggerate and intensify the imagined consequences of the anxiety-provoking situation. Flooding and implosion have been reported to be effective in reducing anxiety related to many social and environmental situations. Some authors have questioned the efficacy and safety of this technique, but proponents of implosion therapy feel this concern is unfounded (cf. Bernstein, 1976).

CHEMOTHERAPEUTIC APPROACHES TO THE MANAGEMENT OF ANXIETY

Introduction

The ubiquitous nature of anxiety has resulted in the widespread use and abuse of drugs used in its treatment (Marks, 1978). The anxiolytics comprise the largest class of prescribed drugs in the world (cf. Tallman, Paul, Skolnick, & Gallager, 1980). In 1977 for example, nearly 70 million prescriptions were written for diazepam (Valium[R]) and chlordiazepoxide (Librium[R]) in the United States. This represents nearly 8000 tons consumed in a single year!

The earliest anxiolytic agents in clinical use were bromides and alcohols (including ethanol and chemically related compounds such as chloral hydrate and paraldehyde). These agents were largely supplanted by barbiturates such as pentobarbital, still used for this purpose. However, over the past 25 years, these agents have been largely supplanted by safer and more efficacious compounds. Meprobamate (Miltown[R], Equanil[R]), first introduced into clinical practice in 1955, is generally regarded as the first specific anxiolytic agent. Although meprobamate continues to be used, its importance has been largely overshadowed by the benzodiazepines. This group of compounds represents the most important class of anxiolytic agents with respect to both utilization and efficacy. A third "generation" of anxiolytics, which may not have some of the undesirable side effects of benzodiazepines (e.g. ataxia, sedation, potentiation of the depressant effects of ethanol) are currently being evaluated in clinical trials.

Propanediol Carbamates

The development of "second generation" anxiolytics such as meprobamate stemmed from efforts to find non-addicting anxiolytics which lacked the potentially lethal respiratory depressant properties of the barbiturates. Meprobamate was first synthesized by Berger and colleagues in an attempt to find a more potent and long-lasting derivative of mephenesin (Berger & Bradley, 1946). Meprobamate is a simple aliphatic molecule that is rapidly absorbed after oral administration. Peak plasma levels are attained within 1–2 hours after ingestion and complete elimination occurs within 24–36 hours (half-life of approximately 11 hours). Most of the drug is oxidized to hydroxymeprobamate or eliminated as the glucuronide conjugate while about 10% of the drug is excreted unchanged. Meprobamate is widely and rather uniformly distributed throughout the body as well as in various regions of the brain.

The pharmacological effects of meprobamate are, in general, similar to other central nervous system (CNS) depressants such as the barbiturates (Berger, 1978). In addition, meprobamate has potent muscle-relaxant and anticonvulsant properties. Both of these effects are observed at subsedative doses, but their relationship to the antianxiety effects of the drug are unclear. Meprobamate does not effect "classical" conditioned responses but suppresses autonomic (i.e. visceral) responses that accompany conditioned reflexes. Similar autonomic responses are often seen in anxious patients or in normals as a response to stressful situations.

The exact mechanism of action of meprobamate is unknown. The muscle relaxant, anticonvulsant and anxiolytic properties have been proposed to result from a depressant effect on nerve conduction in interneurons (Berger, 1977). For example, meprobamate depresses various multineuronal reflexes such as the flexor or crossed extensor reflex but has little effect on monosynaptic reflexes such as the knee jerk. In relatively low doses, meprobamate will counteract the neuronal hyperexcitability produced by strychnine and tetanus toxin, effects that are believed to be mediated through central interneurons. The biochemical basis for these neurophysiological actions is unknown. Speculation of specific effects on various neurotransmitters has been generally unsupported. Meprobamate has been shown not to exert significant effects on central biogenic amine release, turnover, or metabolism. Recent experiments suggest that brain concentrations of meprobamate after pharmacologically relevant doses can affect receptor sites for anxiolytics in the CNS (E. Williams, S. Paul and P. Skolnick, unpublished observations), which could account for the therapeutic and/or side effects of this compound (see Section on CNS Receptors for Anxiolytics).

It is generally accepted that tolerance develops to the clinical effects of meprobamate. As is the case with barbiturates, meprobamate will induce hepatic microsomal drug metabolizing enzymes thereby increasing its own metabolism which would contribute to the development of tolerance. Addiction to meprobamate can occur after prolonged use at doses somewhat greater than those recommended for therapeutic purposes. Serious withdrawal reactions (probably related to the relatively short to intermediate half-life of meprobamate) have been reported and should be carefully considered in patients being managed during chronic use of the drug. Physical signs of withdrawal are not unlike those seen during alcohol withdrawal and have been reported following discontinuation of doses in the therapeutic range (1200 mg to 2400 mg, daily). Serious signs of withdrawal (e.g. seizures) are not uncommon after discontinuing larger doses(>3000 mg daily).

Adverse reactions and side effects of meprobamate are, in general, minor. Meprobamate has not been reported to produce extrapyramidal symptoms nor anticholinergic side effects. Serious adverse reactions include allergic and dermatological reactions such as urticarial or maculopapular rashes. However, these idiosyncratic reactions are uncommon and are usually observed after only a few doses. Meprobamate has a lower acute toxicity than the barbiturates, but its therapeutic index (the ratio between lethal and therapeutic dose) is much less than the benzodiazepines. Therefore, the risk of fatality following serious overdose of meprobamate should be considered significant. Because meprobamate induces hepatic drug-metabolizing enzymes, the metabolism and pharmacological effects of many other drugs can be affected, a factor which should be considered when prescribing it with other agents.

Benzodiazepines

History.   The benzodiazepines are widely used not only as anxiolytics but are also prescribed as hypnotics, anticonvulsants, and muscle-relaxants (Randall & Kappel, 1973). Clinically active benzodiazepines were first synthesized by Sternbach and colleagues in the late 1950's (cf. Sternbach, 1979). Chlordiazepoxide (Librium[R]) was the first 1,4-benzodiazepine introduced into clinical use and was followed in 1963 by the chemically similar but more potent derivative, diazepam (Valium[R]), and more recently by the popular hypnotic flurazepam (Dalmane[R]). As a result of the economic incentives resulting from the development of safe antianxiety agents, literally thousands of benzodiazepine derivatives have been synthesized and tested. At the present time there are approximately a dozen benzodiazepines (including the triazolobenzodiazepines and 1,5-benzodiazepines) in therapeutic use throughout the world. Although the various benzodiazepines differ significantly in their clinical potencies, there is no evidence that at behaviorally equivalent doses there are any major differences in efficacy. Furthermore, although several benzodiazepines such as flurazepam (Dalmane[R]) and nitrazepam (Mogadon[R]) are marketed specifically as hypnotics, recent reports suggest that these agents are no more effective as hypnotics than diazepam.

Structure-activity Relationships.   The benzodiazepines were derived from a group of compounds described in the early German literature as the 4,5-benzo-hept-1,2,6-oxidiazines (cf. Gschwend, 1979). Most clinically effective benzodiazepines contain a phenyl substituent at the 5-position. Electron-withdrawing substituents at position 7 are essential for anxiolytic activity. In contrast, substitution at positions 6, 8, 9 leads to a marked reduction or complete loss of activity. Substitution of a methyl group in position 1 of the B ring results in an enhanced anxiolytic activity, while further lengthening of the alkyl group in this position results in a decrease in activity. Substitution(s) at the ortho position of the C ring (phenyl group) by electron withdrawing groups (e.g. $-Cl$, $-NO_2$) enhances anxiolytic activity while substitution at the meta and para positions decreases activity. The phenyl group (C ring) does not appear to be essential for anxiolytic activity since bromazepam, which contains a pyridine substituent, is reported to be an effective antianxiety agent with little or no sedating effects. The addition of a triazolo moiety on the B ring (the triazolobenzodiazepines) produces compounds which have been reported to be more potent than diazepam. The chemistry of benzodiazepines has been extensively studied and the interested reader is directed to other more comprehensive reviews for more detailed structure-activity relationships (Sternbach, 1979; Gschwend, 1979).

Pharmacokinetics. Since subtle structural modification of the benzodiazepine nucleus can result in marked alterations in absorption, distribution, and metabolism, diazepam (the most widely prescribed benzodiazepine) will serve as a prototype for this discussion. Diazepam is completely and rapidly absorbed after oral administration, reaching peak plasma concentrations within one hour. The benzodiazepines are extremely lipophilic compounds which explains both the accumulation of these compounds in adipose tissue and the rapid uptake by brain. For example, brain levels of diazepam at one minute after intravenous administration are higher than corresponding blood levels (Garattini, Marcucci, & Mussini, 1977). The rapid entry of benzodiazepine into the central nervous system (CNS) also accounts for their efficacy in the acute management of seizure disorders, such as status epilepticus (Browne & Penry, 1973).

The elimination of diazepam from the body is biphasic. A rapid elimination phase with a $t_{\frac{1}{2}}$ of 2–3 hours is followed by a slower phase with a corresponding $t_{\frac{1}{2}}$ of 2–8 hours. Diazepam is metabolized by both N-dimethylation and hydroxylation at the 3-position. Both the N-demethylated (nordiazepam) and hydroxylated (oxazepam, Serax[R]) metabolites of diazepam are pharmacologically active, which may account for the long-lived effects of the parent compound. Benzodiazepines and their hydroxylated and demethylated metabolites usually conjugated as glucuronides and excreted in this form.

Pharmacological Actions. The benzodiazepines exert four distinct pharmacological actions: (a) anxiolytic; (b) anticonvulsant; (c) muscle-relaxant; and (d) sedative-hypnotic effects. Benzodiazepines have been demonstrated to be superior to placebo in reducing anxiety in numerous well-controlled clinical studies (Hollister, 1973). Nonetheless, there have been studies reporting no significant drug-placebo differences, which may relate to the highly variable and episodic nature of anxiety.

In experimental animals, the "anti-anxiety" effects of the benzodiazepines are readily demonstrable using a number of experimental paradigms. Perhaps the most impressive effect of the benzodiazepines is their ability to "release" conditioned and unconditioned behaviors previously suppressed by punishment (Lippa, Nash, & Greenblatt, 1979a). These behavioral paradigms are called "conflict" situations since the behavioral responses of the animal is both rewarded and punished. In the simplest form of this test, animals (usually rats) are food and water deprived for 24 hours. The animals are then presented with a 10% solution of sucrose from a spout. The animal is allowed a short period of free consumption, followed by an interval of intermittent punishment (receiving a shock to the feet or mouth/tongue while licking the spout) such as a 5 second "on"-5 second "off" schedule for a total of (e.g.) 5 minutes. In this "conflict" paradigm, untreated animals will be normally affected by punishment and will suppress responses for the rewarding stimulus. Benzodiazepines (and other anxiolytics) characteristically increase the behavioral responses (e.g. number of "licks" per trial) for the rewarding stimulus during conditions of punishment. Since the clinical effects of benzodiazepines in man also appears to involve a decrease in the behavioral and autonomic consequences of frustration, fear, and punishment, this "conflict" paradigm may represent a useful animal model for anxiety (Lippa, Greenblatt, & Pelham, 1977). This assumption is further supported by the relatively specific "anti-conflict" effect of the benzodiazepines since other psychotropic drugs (e.g. phenothiazines, analgesics, antidepressants) are without effect. A recent report (Crawley & Goodwin, 1980) described another potentially useful behavioral paradigm which is affected by the benzodiazepines. In this test, mice are placed in a two chamber compartment connected by a runway. The number of light/dark chamber transitions is recorded. Clinically active benzodiazepines increase in a dose dependent fashion the number of dark/light transitions. This test may also present a "conflict" situation to the animal: the desire to explore and the aversive passage from a dark to a light environment. Other animal models including the anti-pentylenetetrazol (Metrazol[R]) and cat muscle-relaxant tests are excellent predictors of anxiolytic activity in man, and are often used as initial screens for anxiolytic activity (Lippa et al., 1979a).

Mechanism of Action. Numerous studies have been directed towards elucidating the neurochemical events associated with the anxiolytic actions of benzodiazepines. Knowledge of the cellular and subcellular loci of actions of these compounds would not only provide insights into the neurochemical bases of anxiety-neuroses, but would also provide information about seizure disorders, sleep and centrally mediated muscle relaxation. These phenomena are the physiologic processes affected by the benzodiazepines (as well as other anxiolytics). In addition, there is a great economic incentive to develop effective anxiolytics which are devoid of the undesirable side effects of the benzodiazepines.

Benzodiazepines have been demonstrated to effect many "classical" neurotransmitter systems (e.g. catecholamines, serotonin, glycine, γ-aminobutyric acid (GABA)). However, both the doses necessary to effect alterations in these systems and the lack of temporal correlation between pharmacologic effect and neurochemical change make it unlikely that the therapeutic effects of the benzodiazepines are directly attributable to an alteration in any one system (cf. Koe, 1979).

There is compelling neurophysiological evidence, however, to suggest that benzodiazepines selectively facilitate the transmission of the major inhibitory neurotransmitter, GABA, in both the brain and spinal cord (cf. Haefely, Kulcsor, Mohler, Pieri, Polc, & Schaffner, 1975). More recent biochemical studies (see next section) also support an important role for GABA in potentiating benzodiazepine action at the neuronal or cellular level (cf. Tallman et al., 1980). These data suggest that some of the pharmacological effects (including side effects) of the benzodiazepines may be mediated via actions on this neurotransmitter system. Although the facilitory action of benzodiazepines on GABAergic transmission may be of importance for the anticonvulsant properties of the benzodiazepines, behavioral studies have failed to demonstrate synergistic actions between GABA and the benzodiazepines (Cook & Sepinwall, 1975; 1980). In contrast to the neurophysiological studies which fail to support a role for serotonin in the mechanism(s) of action of the benzodiazepines, behavioral studies suggest a role for serotonin pathways in punishment systems which may mediate the "anti-conflict" activity of the benzodiazepines in animals (Stein, Wise, & Berger, 1973). Nonetheless, since complex behavioral states such as anxiety may involve multiple neurotransmitter systems, it is simplistic to suggest that a single neurotransmitter system is responsible or involved in all of the pharmacologic actions of the benzodiazepines.

The recent demonstration of high affinity, saturable, and stereospecific binding sites for benzodiazepines in the CNS has provided perhaps the most useful information concerning the biochemical mechanisms of action of these compounds (Braestrup & Squires, 1977; Mohler & Okada, 1977a,b; Squires & Braestrup, 1977; cf. Tallman et al., 1980 for review). The good correlations obtained between the potencies of a series of pharmacologically active benzodiazepines as anxiolytics and their abilities to displace radiolabelled benzodiazepines from these sites, suggests that they are pharmacological receptors which mediate the therapeutic effects of the benzodiazepines. The presence and pharmacological importance of benzodiazepine receptors in brain has now been confirmed by many investigators (Tallman et al., 1980) and will be presented in detail in the next section.

Tolerance, Dependence, and Abuse.   There is still considerable controversy over the development of tolerance to the behavioral effects of the benzodiazepines. While most clinical investigators agree that tolerance develops to the sedative effects of the benzodiazepines, there is little evidence documenting the development of tolerance to the anxiolytic effects. Studies in experimental animals where tolerance has been demonstrated to develop to both the sedative and ataxic properties (after acute or subacute administration of relatively high doses of benzodiazepine) failed to demonstrate tolerance to either the anti-conflict or anti-pentylenetetrazol activity, pharmacological effects that are highly indicative of anxiolytic activity in man (Lippa et al., 1977; 1979a). Clinical studies on the development of tolerance to the anxiolytic effects of benzodiazepines are technically difficult because of the episodic and vacillating nature of anxiety. Furthermore, many clinicians agree that the benzodiazepines are most useful in the short-term treatment of relatively transient forms of anxiety, fear, and tension and thus chronic use is generally not indicated for most patients.

Recently, a controversy has developed over the incidence of psychological dependence and (or) physiological "addiction" to the benzodiazepines (Marks, 1978). There now appears to be little doubt that psychological dependence can develop especially after chronic use of relatively high doses. Serious withdrawal reactions (e.g. seizures) have been reported after discontinuation of similar doses. Physiological addiction to the benzodiazepines is unlikely unless 10–20 times the recommended daily dose is chronically used. The onset of withdrawal symptoms after discontinuing such doses of the benzodiazepines is seen considerably later than that seen with either meprobamate or the shortacting barbiturates. In toto, the potential for abusing benzodiazepines is more significant than was previously believed, requiring the careful monitoring of both the frequency and quantity prescribed are essential.

Toxicity and Side Effects.   Fatal overdoses following ingestion of even large amounts of benzodiazepines are rare. Doses between 2 to 3 grams (orally) have been reported to produce little or no serious respiratory or cardiovascular distress. However, most deliberate overdoses usually involve more than one agent and combinations of benzodiazepines with other CNS depressants (such as alcohol and barbiturates) can be lethal. The most frequent side effect of the benzodiazepines is daytime sedation and drowsiness. Ataxia is also commonly observed, especially in the elderly. Extrapyramidal or autonomic side effects are not observed with the benzodiazepines. Idiosyncratic reactions including hepatic damage, blood dyscrasias, and dermatological reactions are rare. Stimulation of appetite is not an uncommon side effect seen with both the benzodiazepines and other anxiolytics.

The benzodiazepines readily cross the placenta. No major developmental anomolies are reported to be associated with benzodiazepines use during pregnancy. However, subtle behavioral effects are now being demonstrated in experimental animals (Kellogg, Tervo, Ison, Parisi, & Miller, 1980). Diazepam, as well as its major metabolites have also been identified in human breast milk at concentrations approximately 10% those of plasma. In most cases these concentrations are probably too low to effect the nursing infant.

Miscellaneous Anxiolytics

A number of miscellaneous drugs including some antihistamines and β-adrenergic blockers are also used in the treatment of anxiety. These compounds are usually prescribed for other purposes, but their continued use in anxious patients warrants a brief discussion in this section.

Diphenylmethane Antihistaminics.   The two most common drugs in this class are hydroxyzine (Atarax[R], Vistaril[R]) and diphenhydramine (Benadryl[R]). These compounds differ significantly from the classical antianxiety agents in that they may increase muscle tone, lower seizure threshold, and are not associated with physical dependence. Furthermore, the cross tolerance observed with the commonly used sedative-tranquilizers is not observed with these drugs.

Hydroxyzine is commonly given to relieve the temporary anxiety associated with medical and dental procedures. Since it also has antiemetic properties it has been considered especially useful as a preoperative medication. The exact mechanism(s) of action of these drugs as anxiolytics is unknown; although they have been shown to depress neuronal activity in certain limbic areas of the brain that are believed to be involved in emotional behavior.

The diphenylmethane antihistamics appear to be relatively safe as few serious side effects have been reported. They do potentiate the effects of meperidine and barbiturates and their use in early pregnancy is contraindicated.

β-Adrenergic Blockers and Newer Agents.   Recently there has been increased interest in the use of β-adrenergic blockers for the treatment of anxiety. These agents are somewhat related to the propanediol carbamates since both classes of compounds possess an orthosubstituted aryloxy-propanolamine moiety. The β-blockers seem to be particularly useful in somatic manifestations of anxiety such as tachycardia, trembling, and sweating. Although a number of studies indicate the β-blockers are quite useful in acute episodes of anticipatory anxiety (e.g. stage fright), their mechanism of action remains controversial. Proctolol, a β-adrenergic blocker that does not cross the blood-brain barrier, has also been reported to be an effective anxiolytic, suggesting that the antianxiety effects of the β-adrenergic blockers involve peripheral rather than central effects. It is likely, however, that these compounds will have prominent role in the treatment of the anxiety.

A number of newer potential anxiolytics including the pyrazolopyridine, SQ 20009 and the triazolopyridazine, CL 218872 (see next section) have been shown to have "antianxiety" effects in animals and are currently being studied in man. Several of these compounds, including both SQ 20009 (Weinryb, Beer, Proctor,

& Hess, 1974) and CL 218872 (Lippa, Coupet, Greenblatt, Klepner, & Beer, 1979b) are structurally related to the purines inosine and hypoxanthine, which have been proposed to be endogenous ligands or modulators (cf. Skolnick, Paul, & Marangos, 1980a) of the "benzodiazepine receptor" (see next section). The outstanding feature of these compounds is their lack of sedative effect or potentiation of the depressant effects of ethanol. Another group of compounds which are quinoline derivatives (PK 8165 and PK 9085), also appear to be devoid of these side effects (LeFur, Mizoule, Burgevin, Ferris, Heaulme, Gauthier, Gueremy, & Uzan, 1981) and lack anticonvulsant activity. At this time, several of these compounds are about to enter the initial phases of clinical testing.

CNS RECEPTORS FOR ANXIOLYTICS–TOWARDS A NEUROBIOLOGICAL UNDERSTANDING OF ANXIETY

Introduction

Since the introduction of agents specifically designed for the relief of anxiety there have been numerous attempts to delineate the biochemical mechanisms by which these compounds exert their therapeutic effects. Because clinically useful anxiolytics usually have sedative and muscle relaxant properties as well, it had been suggested that the anxiolytic actions of benzodiazepines and propanediol carbamates could result from a combination of these two pharmacologic actions. However, these properties are insufficient to elicit an anxiolytic action. Furthermore, in experimental models of anxiety such as the "conflict" test, benzodiazepines have clearly been shown to exert an "anxiolytic" action (i.e. increase in punished responding) at concentrations below those needed to elicit sedative effects (Lippa et al., 1977). Despite the experimental observations outlined in the previous section suggesting a possible role for serotonergic and GABAergic pathways in some of the pharmacologic actions of the benzodiazepines, explanations of the molecular actions of anxiolytics and the neurochemical bases of anxiety remained obscure. However, within the past 3–4 years, a series of observations detailing the discovery of recognition sites (viz. receptors) for benzodiazepines in the mammalian CNS and putative endogenous ligands or modulators of these receptors has radically altered our concept of both the bases of mechanism of action of the benzodiazepines (as well as other minor tranquilizers) *and* the neurochemical bases of anxiety (for comprehensive reviews, cf. Tallman et al., 1980; Skolnick & Paul, 1981; Paul, Marangos, & Skolnick, 1981).

Benzodiazepine Receptors in the CNS

The discovery of high affinity, saturable and stereospecific binding sites for benzodiazepines in the mammalian CNS was reported independently by two groups of investigators in 1977 (Braestrup and Squires, 1977; Mohler & Okada,

1977a,b). The excellent correlations between a series of benzodiazepines to displace [^{3}H]diazepam from these sites in vitro and the potencies of these compounds as anxiolytics, anticonvulsants and muscle relaxants in vivo (Squires & Braestrup, 1977; Mohler & Okada, 1977) strongly suggests these binding sites were pharmacologic receptors mediating the therapeutic effects of the benzodiazepines. These receptors may be thought of as primary recognition sites for the benzodiazepines: reversible binding of a drug to this receptor would be the initial step in a cascade of events resulting in a therapeutic (e.g. anxiolytic) effect. Subsequent steps may involve the integration of other neurotransmitter systems, but the precise events have not yet been defined.

Shortly after the demonstration of benzodiazepine receptors using isolated membrane preparations in vitro, the stereospecific binding of radiolabelled benzodiazepines were demonstrated in vivo (Williamson, Paul, & Skolnick, 1978a,b; Chang & Snyder, 1978; Tallman, Thomas, & Gallager, 1979). Furthermore, while many peripheral tissues including kidney, liver, and skeletal muscle "bind" [^{3}H]benzodiazepines, only the binding in brain was displaced in a stereospecific fashion. Analogous to the observations made in vitro, the affinities of a series of benzodiazepines for the benzodiazepine receptor in vivo was highly correlated with the clinical potencies of these compounds as anxiolytics, anticonvulsants, and muscle relaxants (Chang & Snyder, 1978). Benzodiazepine receptors have also been demonstrated in both baboons (Comar, Maziere, Godot, Berger, Soussaline, Menini, Arfel, & Naquet, 1979) and man (Comar, Maziere, Sargent, Naquet, Zarifian, Sechter, & Henri, 1980) using C^{11} flunitrazepam as a probe and monitoring the drug with positron emission tomography. The use of in situ labelling technique for detecting benzodiazepine receptors may be a valuable experimental tool for assessing receptor function in various psychopathological states such as anxiety. These studies support the physiologic and pharmacologic significance of these receptors since relevant binding can be demonstrated in tissue preparations at all levels of organization including intact animals.

The benzodiazepine receptor is widely but unevenly distributed throughout the CNS. Phylogenetically older areas (e.g. pons and medulla) contain fewer receptors than phylogenetically newer areas (e.g. frontal cortex) (Braestrup & Squires, 1977; Mohler, Okada, Ulrich, & Heitz, 1978). However, the regional differences in the density of benzodiazepine receptors among the various brain regions is smaller than differences reported for other neurotransmitter receptors (e.g. opiate, dopamine). This suggests that benzodiazepine receptors may be involved in mediating and/or integrating multiple, complex physiological processes which might ultimately result in the expression of "anxious" behavior. The cellular and subcellular localization of the benzodiazepine receptor has been investigated using both anatomical (autoradiographic) (Young & Kuhar, 1979) and biochemical techniques. It is now generally accepted that benzodiazepine receptors are highly, if not exclusively, localized on neurons. Little or no "brain-specific" binding has been observed on glial elements (Syapin & Skolnick, 1979) or white matter. Subcellular fractionation of brain homogenates has shown a highly significant enrichment of the benzodiazepine receptor in synaptosomal membranes (Bosmann, Penny, Case, DiStefano, & Averill, 1978). Use of a photoaffinity label and electron microscopic autoradiography has demonstrated a predominence of receptors in areas of synaptic contacts, further supporting a neuronal localization (Mohler, Wu, and Richards, 1981).

Are There Endogenous Ligands for the Benzodiazepine Receptor?

The presence of benzodiazepine receptors in the CNS implies that endogenous substances may also be present which would interact with the receptor under physiological conditions. This hypothesis was supported by studies (Squires & Braestrup, 1977; Mackerer, 1978) demonstrating the lack of effect of a large number of putative neurotransmitters and amino acids, their agonists and antagonists, and many psychotropic drugs in displacing [^{3}H]diazepam from crude synaptosomal fractions or homogenates of rat brain.

Purines.   Initial studies using acidified-acetone extracts of bovine brain and subsequent chromatography on Sephadex G-25 resulted in the detection of three peaks which inhibited [^{3}H]diazepam binding in lysed synaptosomal fragments of rat brain (Marangos, Paul, Greenlaw, Goodwin, & Skolnick, 1978). Two of these peaks had a higher specific activity than the "crude extract", were dialyzable (molecular weight less than 5000 daltons), and resistant to proteolytic enzymes (such as trypsin and protease). These two peak fractions were competitive inhibitors of [^{3}H]diazepam binding and had little or no affinity for other neurotransmitter receptors (e.g. opiate, β-adrenergic, dopamine or cholinergic receptors). These peaks were subsequently identified by thin-layer chromatography, ultraviolet spectroscopy, high-pressure liquid chromatography, and mass spectral analysis as the purines inosine and hypoxanthine (Skolnick, Marangos, Goodwin, Edwards, & Paul, 1978). These results were subsequently confirmed and extended by other groups (Asano & Spector, 1979; Mohler, Polc, Cumin, Pieri, & Kettler, 1979). Asano and Spector (1979) employed both a radioimmunoassay and a radioreceptor to examine brain extracts for benzodiazepine-like activity. Inosine and hypoxanthine were the only endogenous factors which cross-reacted with a benzodiazepine specific antibody (as well as competitively inhibiting [^{3}H]diazepam binding in the radioreceptor assay). Subsequently, it was demonstrated that these purines may interact very weakly with GABA receptors (Ticku & Burch, 1980) and more potently to displace α-[^{3}H]dihydropicrotoxinin from binding sites which may be associated with a chloride ionophore (Olsen & Leeb-Lundberg, 1981). These observations may have important implications for the regulation of the benzodiazepine receptor as is discussed in a later section of this review.

In screening a large series of naturally-occurring and synthetic purines as inhibitors of [^{3}H]diazepam binding in vitro, several methylxanthines (including caffeine) were shown to be relatively potent inhibitors. In man, approximately 1 gram of caffeine will produce insomnia, restlessness, and excitement while higher doses produce a syndrome that is virtually indistinguishable from anxiety (Lutz, 1978). Assuming a body weight of 70 kg and a distribution of caffeine in total body water, doses of 1–2 grams are well within the range necessary to occupy between 10 to 25% of benzodiazepine receptors in vitro. It is tempting to speculate that the anxiogenic properties of caffeine may result from its interaction with benzodiazepine receptors (perhaps as an antagonist) at these sites. The fact that the benzodiazepines, which are the most widely prescribed drugs in current therapeutic use are relatively specific antagonists of the methylxanthines, which are among the most widely consumed psychotropic agents, may not simply be coincidence.

The in vitro affinities of inosine and hypoxanthine for the benzodiazepine receptor are low (K_i 800–900 μM) compared to K_i values of 1–600 nM for most pharmacologically active benzodiazepines. The low affinities of these purines for the benzodiazepine receptor made it difficult to reconcile with their proposed role as endogenous modulators or ligands, since whole brain concentrations of inosine and hypoxanthine have been estimated to be from 20–60 μM (Kleihues, Kobayashi, & Hossman, 1974; Saugstad & Shrader, 1978). However, studies by McIlwain and associates (Pull & McIlwain, 1972; Sun, McIlwain, & Pull, 1977) have demonstrated that levels of both inosine and hypoxanthine rise dramatically following electrical or chemical depolarization of brain. These increases are tetrodotoxin sensitive, suggesting the increased purine levels are associated with neuronal events. Furthermore, recent observations suggesting that only a small fraction of benzodiazepine receptors (less than 30%) need be occupied to fully manifest an anticonvulsant (Paul, Syapin, Paugh, Moncada, & Skolnick, 1979) or anxiolytic (Lippa, Critchett, Sano, Klepner, Greenblatt, Coupet, & Beer, 1979c) action of diazepam suggest the K_i (or IC_{50}) value obtained in vitro may not be a relevant measure of the ability of a compound to affect the benzodiazepine receptor function.

Since binding studies in vitro do not distinguish agonist from antagonist actions, a series of in vivo and pharmacologic and electrophysiologic experiments were conducted to determine the effects of exogenously administered purines. Inosine was found to partially antagonize pentylenetetrazole (PTZ) evoked seizures by increasing the latency to seizures, i.e. the period between injection of PTZ and the first appearance of tonic-clonic convulsions. Under the conditions of this in vivo assay (an ED_{99} of PTZ administered intraperitoneally), a frank protection against seizures was not observed (Skolnick, Syapin, Paugh, Moncada, Marangos, & Paul, 1979a). This increase in seizure latency was dependent upon both the injection interval between inosine and PTZ and the dose of inosine administered. Statistically significant increases in latency was observed with injection intervals of 1 and 2, but not 10 minutes. 7-Methylinosine, which is inactive in displacing [^{3}H]diazepam from receptor sites in vitro does not alter seizure latency. Relatively large doses of inosine (150 μg/mouse, administered intraventricularly) were necessary to afford this treatment protection against PTZ-induced seizures. The short-lived protection and large doses of inosine needed to elicit these effects may be explained in part by the rapid loss of intraventricularly administered inosine from the CNS. More than 80% of an administered dose of [^{14}C]inosine is no longer in the brain one minute after injection, and a significant amount of the radioactivity remaining after one minute is no longer inosine. The increased seizure latency produced by inosine has recently been confirmed (Lapin, 1980). Analogous experiments with centrally administered opioid peptides to elicit analgesia also require very large doses to elicit a significant effect (500 µg/animal). It was not until the development of an analogue of methionine-enkephalin which was not easily degraded (D-ala-me-enkephalin) that lower doses consistently produced analgesia. The transient effects of the benzodiazepines on PTZ-induced seizures may be thought of as being analogous to the actions of an "ultrashort acting" benzodiazepine. The short-lived effects may also be consonant with the actions of a physiologically relevant ligand which regulates events in a millisecond timeframe. In other experiments (Mohler et al., 1979), parenterally administered inosine (1000 mg/kg) protected 25% of mice against seizures induced by 3-mercaptopropionic acid, an inhibitor of GABA synthesis. Marangos, Martino, Paul, & Skolnick (1980) have observed that parenterally administered inosine protects mice against caffeine induced seizures in a dose-dependent fashion (500–1000 mg/kg). No protection was afforded by 7-methylinosine.

The electrophysiologic effects of inosine have been studied in primary cultures of fetal mouse spinal cord. Inosine produced two types of transmitter-like effects: a rapidly desensitizing excitatory response and a non-desensitizing inhibitory response. The benzodiazepine flurazepam produced a similar excitatory response that exhibited both cross-desensitization with the inosine response and blocked the inhibitory response. These results suggest inosine can activate at least two different conductances on spinal neurons and that flurazepam acts as an inosine agonist at one of these conductances and as an antagonist at the other (MacDonald, Barker, Paul, Marangos, & Skolnick, 1979). MacDonald and Barker (cf. Paul, Marangos, & Skolnick, 1980a) have also demonstrated that inosine can reverse the paroxysmal depolarizing events produced by the convulsant, picrotoxin. This property is shared by both benzodiazepines and barbiturates.

Nicotinamide. Nicotinamide has been reported to inhibit [^{3}H]diazepam binding with an IC_{50} of approximately 3.9 mM (Mohler et al., 1979). Intraperitoneal administration of large (500–1000 mg/kg) doses of this compound elicited an anticonflict (anxiolytic) effect in 50% of the animals tested and protected 25% of animals against 3-mercaptopropionic induced seizures. In addition, nicotinamide elicited a presynaptic inhibition of firing in cat spinal cord which was reversed by the GABA antagonist, bicuculline. Nicotinamide also produced a sedative action in both rodents and man. These effects are all reminiscent of the action of benzodiazepines. However, both the low levels of nicotinamide present in brain and the extremely low affinity for the benzodiazepine receptor in vitro make further study of this compound necessary in order to determine if this compound functions in the physiologic regulation of the benzodiazepine receptor. Recently, Lapin (1980) has reported no significant anticonvulsant effects of nicotinamide.

β-Carboline-3-Carboxylic Acid Ethyl Ester.   A factor isolated from human urine was found to potently inhibit [^{3}H]diazepam binding (Nielsen, Gredal, & Braestrup, 1979). Subsequent purification and mass spectral analysis of this factor yielded β-carboline-3-carboxylic acid ethyl ester (Braestrup, Nielsen and Olsen, 1980). The affinity of this compound (4–7 nM) in vitro makes it as potent as many clinically active benzodiazepines. However, there is good evidence to indicate this compound is formed non-enzymatically from tryptophan containing proteins subjected to the extraction and purification procedures employed. Squires (1981) has reported that extraction of many tryptophan containing proteins (e.g. liver, kidney, feathers) using an acidified-ethanol procedure will result in the formation of large quantities of this compound. Although the formation of this compound appears artifactual, Braestrup and co-workers maintain that this compound could be a precursor to an endogenous ligand. However, it appears that endogenously occurring β-carbolines (such as 6-hydroxy-β-carboline and tetrahydro β-carboline) have very low affinities for the benzodiazepine receptor (Skolnick, Paul, Rice, Barker, Cook, Weber, & Cain, 1980b). This observation, coupled with the reported hallucinogenic properties of some β-carbolines (cf. Ho, 1977) and the failure of the ethyl ester derivative to elicit behavioral or electrophysiological effects when administered either intraventricularly or by iontophoresis would argue against a role of β-carbolines in the physiologic regulation of the receptor.

High Molecular Weight Factors.   Two high molecular weight factors have been isolated from mammalian CNS which affect the benzodiazepine receptor. Collelo, Hockenberry, Bosmann, Fuchs, & Folkers (1978) have isolated a competitive inhibitor of [^{3}H]diazepam binding from porcine brain with a molecular weight estimated to be between 40,000–70,000 daltons. This factor is heat stable but degraded by trypsin. An endogenous ligand of this size would be extraordinary. These investigators have postulated that this factor may be a precursor of an endogenous ligand for the receptor. Costa and his colleagues (Guidotti, Toffano, & Costa, 1978; Toffano, Guidotti, & Costa, 1978) have purified a thermostable, acidic protein with a molecular weight of approximately 15,000 daltons from rat brain. This factor, referred to as "GABA-modulin" interacts with both GABA and benzodiazepine receptors. GABA-modulin will abolish the high affinity component of [^{3}H]GABA binding (obtained by treating membranes with Triton

X-100). This effect can be reversed by addition of benzodiazepines. GABA-modulin has also been reported to competitively inhibit [^{3}H]diazepam binding. Thus, these investigators have constructed a model wherein GABA-modulin regulates both GABA and benzodiazepine receptors. The isolation and kinetic properties of this factor have not been confirmed in at least two other laboratories (G. Johnston; R. Olsen, personal communications).

Low Molecular Weight Factors. Two laboratories have reported the presence of low molecular weight substances that competitively inhibit [^{3}H]diazepam binding. These compounds do not have the physicochemical characterisitics of inosine, hypoxanthine, or nicotinamide. Marangos, Clark, Martino, Paul, & Skolnick (1979) have isolated two factors from bovine brain using an aqueous extraction procedure. A large molecular weight factor (700–30,000 daltons) is only partially dialyzable and found in brain and pituitary extracts but not in peripheral tissue. The smaller factor (500–600 daltons) was found in highest concentrations in brain, pituitary, liver, and muscle. These factors are heat stable and resistant to proteolytic degradation. Using a similar extraction procedure, Davis and Cohen (1980) have partially purified a factor which is a weakly charged molecule with a weight of approximately 3,000 daltons. The factor is heat stable but can be destroyed by papain treatment. Further purification and identification of these factors is necessary before an assessment of their physiologic relevance can be made.

Relationship of the Benzodiazepine Receptor to Behavior

Labelling of benzodiazepine receptors in vivo permits the direct study of the relationship between receptor occupation and the behavioral (viz. pharmacological) effects of drugs. This type of experiment can definitively establish if a binding site for any given drug is a true pharmacological receptor since its occupation should be related to a pharmacological or physiological event. Studies of this kind are commonly done for peripheral hormone receptors but have only recently been attempted for CNS neurotransmitter receptors.

Administration of diazepam to mice produces a long-lasting protection against pentylenetetrazol (PTZ)-induced seizures, and the ability of a compound to protect mice against these seizures is a good predictor of anxiolytic activity (Lippa et al., 1979a). In an attempt to establish a relationship between occupation of benzodiazepine receptors by diazepam and anticonvulsant action, mice were administered an anticonvulsant dose of drug, and challenged at various intervals with PTZ. A parallel group of mice was sacrificed without the PTZ challenge and the number of receptors occupied by the injected diazepam was measured (Paul et al., 1979). An excellent correlation between receptor occupation and anticonvulsant activity was obtained (r = 0.98; p < .001). Furthermore, fewer than 30% of the receptors need be occupied to manifest a complete anticonvulsant response. Similar results have been obtained in the conflict avoidance paradigm where it was reported that only 15–20% of receptors need be occupied for benzodiazepine-induced anticonflict activity (Lippa et al., 1979b,c). These data suggest the presence of "spare" receptors or specific subpopulations of receptors that mediate the various behavioral actions of the benzodiazepines. These observations clearly demonstrate a very close relationship between receptors occupation and behavioral activity.

Although the pharmacological significance of benzodiazepine receptors is evident from numerous in vitro and in vivo studies, the physiological function(s) of these sites is unknown. Since the benzodiazepine receptor is a protein (or complex of functionally-related proteins) it is possible that there is both an inherited (i.e., genetic) and non-inherited (i.e. post-transcriptional) regulation of the receptor. Physiological or behavioral manipulations that result in alterations in either receptor number (density) or affinity have been attempted to provide insight into the possible physiological significance of the receptor. These studies have demonstrated a unique regulation of the benzodiazepine receptor in that significant alterations can be observed within minutes rather than days (or weeks) as is the case for other neurotransmitter/drug receptors.

Exposure of rats to stressful (and presumably anxiety-provoking) situations such as immersion in ice-water has been reported to increase cortical benzodiazepine receptors within 15 minutes. Both picrotoxin and pentylenetetrazol were less potent as convulsants in stressed rats when compared to non-stressed controls (Soubrie, Thiebot, Jobert, Monastruc, Hery, & Hamon, 1980). A similar increase (15–20%) in cerebral cortical benzodiazepine receptor density was observed 20 minutes after subjecting rats to either electroconvulsive or chemically-induced seizures (Paul & Skolnick, 1978). This increase in receptor number was fully manifest by 15 minutes, and returned to control levels by 60 minutes after the seizure. Repeated seizures, regardless of how they are induced, have been reported to elicit a long-lasting (> 24 hrs) increase in number of hippocampal benzodiazepine receptor (McNamara, Peper, & Patrone, 1980). The effects of experimental "stress" or seizures on benzodiazepine receptor density may represent adaptive changes in receptor protein that appears to be associated with a generalized reduction in neuronal excitability. It is of interest that administration of the anticonvulsant diphenylhydantoin also results in an increase (~ 20%) in receptor number approximately 30–60 minutes after injection (Gallager, Mallorga, & Tallman, 1980). It is tempting to speculate that the anticonvulsant properties of diphenylhydantoin may result from the drugs "inductive" effect on cortical benzodiazepine receptors. Nevertheless, adaptive increases in benzodiazepine receptors as a result of either environmental factors or drugs might be thought of as a homeostatic mechanism involved in attenuating pathological behavioral events such as stress-induced "anxiety" or seizures.

Experimental "anxiety" created by subjecting rats to the conflict avoidance paradigm results in a 20–25% decrease in [^{3}H]diazepam binding during exposure to foot shock (Lippa et al., 1979c). The decrease in [^{3}H]diazepam binding during experimental "anxiety" was not evident 15 minutes after cessation of the foot shock, indicating a close temporal association with the "anxiety-provoking" state. The Maudsley reactive rat, selectively bred for a high degree of fearfulness has been found to have significantly fewer benzodiazepine receptors throughout the brain when compared to the Maudsley non-reactive rat (Robertson, Martin, and Candy, 1978). Robertson (1979) has also studied benzodiazepine receptors in "emotional" and "non-emotional" strains of mice and reported that an "emotional" or "anxious" strain of mouse (Balb/cJ) had a significantly lower (by approximately 50%) density of benzodiazepine receptors compared to "non-emotional" strains (e.g. C57 Bl/6J or 10 J). Thus, both environmentally and genetically induced experimental anxiety is associated with a significant reduction in benzodiazepine receptors whereas adaptation to stressful situations results in the opposite effect. It is possible that a similar reduction of CNS benzodiazepine receptors may underlie a genetic predisposition or diathesis for the development of pathological anxiety in susceptible human beings. Alternatively the homeostatic regulation of receptor protein may be dysfunctional in such individuals.

If the anxiolytic actions of the benzodiazepines are mediated through this receptor, it may not be unreasonable to assume that non-benzodiazepine anxiolytics may also operate through a similar mechanism. Initial studies with both barbiturates and propanediol carbamates failed to demonstrate any significant interaction between these drugs and the benzodiazepine receptor (Mackerer et al., 1978). However, recently it has become apparent that the primary recognition site for benzodiazepines exists as a supramolecular complex with a number of potential regulatory sites. The components of the benzodiazepine receptor supramolecular complex and their apparent physiological regulation will be discussed in a subsequent section. Recent studies have now shown that both sodium pentobarbital (Skolnick, Barker, & Paul, 1980c) and meprobamate may produce at least some of their pharmacological effects by interacting with one or more of the regulatory sites of this complex. Both drugs significantly alter the affinity of benzodiazepine receptors for ligand at concentrations that are encountered during treatment with therapeutic doses. These observations strongly suggest a "GABA-benzodiazepine-chloride ionophore" receptor complex may be a common site of anxiolytic action (cf. Paul et al., 1981).

The GABA-Benzodiazepine Receptor-Chloride Ionophore Complex

Although there is a large body of neurophysiological evidence supporting a facilitatory role of benzodiazepines in GABAergic transmission (cf. Tallman et al., 1980), it is only within the past 2 years that important insights into the molecular mechanisms responsible for this interaction have been deduced. Initial reports on the interaction of exogenous GABA with the benzodiazepine receptor were negative (Squires & Braestrup, 1977). However, these studies were done in membrane preparations containing at least 30 μM GABA. Extensive washing of tissue preparations to remove endogenous GABA and subsequent readdition of GABA or the GABA-agonist muscimol results in a concentration dependent enhancement of [^{3}H]benzodiazepine binding to the benzodiazepine receptor (Briley & Langer, 1978; Tallman, Thomas & Galleger, 1978; Wastek, Speth, Reisine, & Yamamura, 1978). This increase in [^{3}H]benzodiazepine binding has been demonstrated to be due to increases in the apparent affinity of the receptor for radioligand rather than increases in receptor density. This effect was stereo-specifically blocked by the GABA-antagonist bicuculline and was reproduced in vivo by injection of the GABA precursor aminooxyacetic acid. These observations suggest interaction of GABA or a GABA mimetic agent with a recognition site alters the conformation of a benzodiazepine recognition site, thereby facilitating the binding of a benzodiazepine (or endogenous ligand) to this site. It is important to recognize that the sites responsible for this enhancement of benzodiazepine binding are not identical to sites described using [^{3}H]GABA or [^{3}H]-muscimol, being that substantial differences in pharmacologic potencies are obtained with a series of GABAergic compounds (Karobath, et al., 1979; Braestrup, Nielsen, Krogsgaard-Larsen, & Falch, 1979). In addition, significant differences in the regional responses to GABA-enhancement support the hypothesis that not all benzodiazepine receptors are functionally linked to these GABA-receptors (Karobath & Sperk, 1979).

These observations imply that drugs may affect the regulation of the benzodiazepine receptor not only by direct occupation of a "benzodiazepine recognition" site, but also via a GABA-benzodiazepine receptor coupling mechanism. Recent observations (Paul et al., 1981b; Marangos, Paul, & Parma, 1981) have shown that the GABA-enhanced increase in benzodiazepine binding is more sensitive to drug effects than is the benzodiazepine recognition site. In addition, an endogenous factor has been isolated that competitively inhibits the GABA-enhanced binding of [^{3}H]diazepam to receptor sites at approximately tenfold lower concentrations than it inhibits benzodiazepine binding in the absence of GABA (Paul, Marangos, Brownstein, & Skolnick, 1980b). Benzodiazepines and purines also interfere with GABA enhanced binding of [^{3}H]benzodiazepines more potently than at the benzodiazepine recognition site. The ability of such compounds to affect [^{3}H]GABA binding is quite weak (Ticku & Birch, 1980), suggesting that these effects could occur at a site other than the GABA receptor, perhaps at a chloride ionophore (Olsen & Leeb-Lundberg, 1981). For example, inosine and hypoxanthine have a K_i of approximately 800 μM for inhibition of [^{3}H]diazepam binding in the absence of GABA, less than 100 μM for inhibiting GABA-enhanced [^{3}H]diazepam binding, and approximately 200 μM for inhibition of [^{3}H]-α-dihydropicrotoxinin binding (a picrotoxin derivative which is reported to bind to the chloride ionophore). These observations suggest that

purines and other compounds) may not only affect the benzodiazepine at the "benzodiazepine recognition site", but may also affect receptor function by interacting at another recognition site of a functionally coupled unit.

Anxiolytics such as SQ 20009 (a pyrazolopyridine) (Placheta & Karobath, 1979) and pentobarbital (Skolnick et al., 1980c) enhance diazepam binding by increasing receptor affinity. These effects are antagonized by both picrotoxin and bicuculline, which suggests the presence of a functionally (if not physically) linked GABA-benzodiazepine-chloride ionophore receptor complex. Drugs may affect the entire supramolecular complex by interaction with one or more of these sites. Although it is not yet resolved as to whether drugs exert their pharmacologic effects by interacting with this complex, many drugs that were first thought not to alter the benzodiazepine receptor may do so by affecting one of the components of this complex. For example, pentobarbital enhances both basal (EC_{50} ca. 220 μM) and GABA-enhanced benzodiazepine binding (EC_{50} ca. 25 μM); these concentrations of pentobarbital are found in the sedative to anesthetic range. Meprobamate, which is an anxiolytic and anticonvulsant, has a very low affinity for the benzodiazepine recognition site (IC_{50} ca. 700 μM), but will inhibit GABA-enhanced [^{3}H]benzodiazepine binding at concentrations found in the brain after pharmacologically relevant doses (E. Williams, S. Paul, and P. Skolnick, unpublished observations).

Postulating a functional supramolecular complex in which purines have differential affinity at different loci may explain the dual electrophysiological effects of inosine on spinal neurons (MacDonald et al., 1979) as well as the recent observation that low doses of inosine administered parenterally disrupt diazepam-enhanced behaviors (Crawley, Marangos, Paul, Skolnick, & Goodwin, 1981). That is, low doses (or concentrations) of inosine may affect one locus resulting in disruption of GABA-enhanced coupling of drug (or endogenous ligand) to the receptor while higher doses may overcome this effect when inosine binds to the benzodiazepine recognition site (receptor). It is clear that we have begun to unravel the complexities of the molecular mechanisms of anxiolytic action as well as the physiological control of anxiety. However, further investigations will be required to precisely define the role(s) of each of these components of the supramolecular complex in the action of anxiolytic drugs and the physiologic regulation of anxiety.

Implications and Conclusions

Over the past 10 years, it has become apparent that many psychotropic drugs act by either directly or indirectly altering receptors for naturally-occurring neurohumoral substances. In retrospect, it is not surprising that similar recognition sites were found for the benzodiazepines since these agents have potent and specific psychopharmacological properties. Because of this relatively recent discovery, there is now compelling behavioral and pharmacological evidence that benzodiazepine receptors mediate the therapeutic effects of these drugs. Biochemical studies now strongly suggest that the recognition site for benzodiazepine are functionally (and perhaps structurally) related to a GABA receptor and an associated chloride channel. Furthermore, a number of anxiolytic and anticonvulsant drugs have been shown to alter benzodiazepine receptor affinity through indirect effects at these modulatory sites.

These findings have many practical applications. The screening of potential anxiolytics and anticonvulsants has been greatly facilitated by testing their ability to displace [^{3}H]benzodiazepine from receptor sites in vitro. Several new non-benzodiazepine drugs with a relatively high affinity for the benzodiazepine receptor have now been shown to have anxiolytic activity in animal screening tests. Some of these agents lack undesirable side effects such as sedation and potentiation of ethanol-induced narcosis and may therefore be more specific anxiolytics (Le Fur et al., 1981; Lippa et al., 1979b). The high affinity of benzodiazepines for the benzodiazepine receptor has been exploited for the development of a rapid, sensitive, and inexpensive assay for measuring benzodiazepines in blood and other biological specimens. This method has the advantage of simultaneously measuring all pharmacologically-active metabolites and can be performed without the use of complicated analytical equipment (Skolnick, Goodwin & Paul, 1979b).

Perhaps the most exciting aspect of the discovery of benzodiazepine receptors concerns their precise physiological (or pathophysiological) role(s). Is the concentration of benzodiazepine receptor in brain related to the behavioral and affectual manifestations of anxiety, as appears to be the case with the Maudsley reactive rat? Is the functional coupling of GABA and benzodiazepine receptors involved in the dissipation or attenuation of anxiety-provoking states? Are the purines or other endogenous ligands responsible for inhibiting neuronal excitability related to the pathogenesis of anxiety? Do anxiogenic drugs such as caffeine produce their effects by interacting with the benzodiazepine receptor, and as such does administration of caffeine represent a good experimental "model system" of anxiety? Although these questions remain unanswered, it is clear that the tools are now available to design appropriate experiments to answer them. Further insights into the neurobiology of anxiety should be forthcoming which may eventually result in the development of better therapeutic strategies for treating one of man's most common and incapacitating disorders.

CONCLUDING REMARKS

In this chapter, both the psychological and psychopharmacological approaches to the treatment of anxiety have been reviewed. Administration of minor tranquilizers such as the benzodiazepines has evolved as the major means of treating anxiety disorders. Although these tranquilizers are effective in reducing anxiety in many individuals, the use of minor tranquilizers without attempting to change the situational-interpersonal factors eliciting or exacerbating anxiety will usually not bring about any permanent resolution of this behavior. In addition to the lack of long-term improvement, drug therapy may produce unwanted side effects such as drowsiness and psychological, if not physiological dependence. In the first part of the review, we have surveyed a number of behavioral techniques shown to be effective in treating anxiety. The elimination of drug side effects, both psychological and pharmacological, may be the greatest advantage in the use of behavioral techniques as opposed to a chemotherapeutic effect.

There have been a number of studies evaluating the relative efficacy of psychopharmacologic and psychotherapeutic approaches to the treatment of anxiety. In a recent review of this literature, Freedman (1980) has concluded that a combination of pharmacologic agents *and* psychotherapy may be superior to either treatment alone. He also emphasizes the importance of individual differences in the manifestation of anxiety. This author has also devised a method for resolving somatic from cognitive symptoms of both anxiety and phobic neuroses when each of these categories are high and low, and suggests treatment modalities which may be most effective in each of these categories. For example, when both cognitive and somatic symptoms are high (as in a panic state), pharmacotherapy may be most important initially, with psychotherapy playing a less important role at the initial stages of treatment.

Further study is still needed to determine which treatments or combination of treatments are most effective in treating anxiety disorders. Recent developments in the biochemical psychopharmacology of anxiety will undoubtedly facilitate our understanding of both the causes and treatment of anxiety.

REFERENCES

Asano, T., & Spector, S. Identification of inosine and hypoxanthine as endogenous ligands for the brain benzodiazepine receptor sites. *Proceedings of the National Academy of Sciences (USA)*, 1979, *76*, 977-981.

Bandura, A. *Principles of Behavior Modification*. New York: Holt, Rinehart and Winston, 1969.

Berger, F. M., & Bradley, W. The pharmacological properties of hydroxy-2-(2-methylphenyloxy)propane (Myanesin). *British Journal of Pharmacology*, 1946, *1*, 265-277.

Berger, F. M. Meprobamate and other glycol derivatives. In E. Usdin and I. Forrest (Eds.), *Psychotherapeutic Drugs, Part II (Applications)*. New York: Marcel Dekker, 1977.

Bernstein, D. A. Anxiety management. In W. E. Craighead, A. E. Kazdin, & M. J. Mahoney (Eds.), *Behavior Modification: Principles, Issues, and Applications*. Boston: Houghton Mifflin, 1976.

Bosmann, H. B., Penney, D. P., Case, K. R., Di Stefano, P., & Averill, K. Diazepam receptor: Specific binding of [^{3}H]diazepam and [^{3}H]flunitrazepam to rat brain subpopulations. *FEBS Letters*, 1978, *87*, 199-202.

Braestrup, C., & Squires, R. F. Specific benzodiazepine receptors in rat brain characterized by high affinity [^{3}H]diazepam binding. *Proceedings of the National Academy of Sciences (USA)*, 1977, *74*, 3805-3838.

Braestrup, C., Nielsen, M., Krogsgaard-Larsen, P., & Falch, E. Partial agonists for brain GABA/benzodiazepine receptor complex. *Nature,* 1979, *280,* 331-333.

Braestrup, C., Nielsen, M., & Olsen, C. Urinary and brain β-carboline-3-carboxylates as potent inhibitors of brain benzodiazepine receptors. *Proc. Natl. Acad. Sci. (USA),* 1980, *77,* 2288-2292.

Briley, M. S., & Langer, S. Z. Influence of GABA receptor agonists and antagonists on the binding of [^{3}H]diazepam to the benzodiazepine receptor. *European Journal of Pharmacology,* 1978, *52,* 129-132.

Browne, T. R., & Penry, J. K. Benzodiazepines in the treatment of epilepsy. *Epilepsia,* 1973, *14,* 277-289.

Chang, R. S. L., & Snyder, S. H. Benzodiazepine receptors: Labelling in intact animals with [^{3}H]flunitrazepam. *European Journal of Pharmacology,* 1978, *48,* 213-218.

Colello, G. D., Hockenberry, D. M., Bosmann, H. B., Fuchs, S., & Folkers, K. Competitive inhibition of benzodiazepine binding by fractions from procine brain. *Proceedings of the National Academy of Sciences (USA),* 1978, *75,* 6319-6323.

Comar, O., Maziere, M., Godot, J. M., Berger, G., Soussaline, G., Menini, H., Arfel, G., & Naquet, R. Visualization of ^{11}C-flunitrazepam displacement in the brain of the live baboon. *Nature,* 1979, *280,* 329-331.

Comar, O., Maziere, M., Sargent, T., Naquet, R., Zarifian, E., Sechter, D., & Henri, F. J. Position emission tomography in psychopharmacological research. *Progress in Neuro-Psychopharmacology (Supplement),* 1980, Abstract 132, p. 111.

Cook, L., & Sepinwall, J. Behavioral analysis of the effects and mechanisms of action of benzodiazepines. In E. Costa & P. Greengard (Eds.), *Advances in Biochemistry and Pharmacology, Vol. 14.* New York: Raven Press, 1975.

Cook, L., & Sepinwall, J. Relationship of anticonflict activity of benzodiazepines to brain receptor binding, serotonin, and GABA. *Psychopharmacology Bulletin,* 1980, *16,* 30-32.

Crawley, J., & Goodwin, F. K. Preliminary report of a simple animal behavior model for the anxiolytic effects of benzodiazepines. *Pharmacology, Biochemistry and Behavior,* 1980, *13,* 167-170.

Crawley, J., Marangos, P., Paul, S., Skolnick, P., & Goodwin, F. Purine-benzodiazepine interaction: Inosine reverses diazepam-induced stimulation of mouse exploratory behavior. *Science,* 1981, in press.

Davidian, H. Aspects of anxiety in Iran. *Australian-New Zealand Journal of Psychiatry,* 1969, *3,* 254-258.

Davis, L. G., & Cohen, R. Identification of an endogenous peptide-ligand for the benzodiazepine receptor. *Biochemical Biophysical Research Communication,* 1980, *92,* 141-146.

Freedman, A. M. Psychopharmacology and psychotherapy in the treatment of anxiety. *Pharmakopsychiatric* 1980, *13,* 277-289.

Gallager, D., Mallorga, P., & Tallman, J. Interaction of diphenylhydantoin and benzodiazepines in the CNS. *Brain Research,* 1980, *189,* 209-220.

Garattini, S., Marcucci, F., & Mussini, E. In E. Usdin & I. S. Forrest (Eds.), *Psychotherapeutic Drugs, Part II (Applications).* New York: Marcel Dekker, 1977.

Gewirtz, J. L. A symposium of the Learning Research and Development Center. In *The Nature of Reinforcement.* New York: Academic Press, 1971.

Gschwend, H. W. Chemical approaches to the development of anxiolytics. In S. Fielding & H. Lal (Eds.), *Anxiolytics.* New York: Futura Publishing Co., 1979.

Guidotti, A., Toffano, G., & Costa, E. An endogenous protein modulates the affinity of GABA and benzodiazepine receptors in rat brain. *Nature,* 1978, *275,* 553-555.

Haefely, W., Kulcsor, A., Hohler, H., Pieri, L., Polc, P., & Schaffner, R. Possible involvement of GABA in the central actions of benzodiazepine. In E. Costa & P. Greengard (Eds.), *Advances in Biochemistry and Psypharmacology, Vol. 14.* New York: Raven Press, 1975.

Hagnell, O. *A Prospective Study of the Incidence of Mental Disorder.* Lund (Sweden): Scandinavian University Press, 1966.

Ho, B. T. Pharmacological and biochemical studies with beta-carboline analogs. In W. Essman & L. Valzelli (Eds.), *Current Developments in Psychopharmacology, Vol. 4.* New York: Spectrum Publishing, 1977.

Hollister, L. E. *Clinical Use of Psychotherapeutic Drugs.* Springfield: Charles C. Thomas, 1973.

Karobath, M., Placheta, P., Lippitsch, M., & Krogsgaard-Larsen, P. Is stimulation of benzodiazepine receptor binding mediated by a novel GABA receptor? *Nature,* 1970, *278,* 748–749.

Karobath, M., & Sperk, G. Stimulation of benzodiazepine receptor binding by α-aminobutyric acid. *Proceedings of the National Academy of Sciences (USA),* 1979, *76,* 1004–1006.

Kellogg, C., Tervo, D., Ison, J., Parisi, T., & Miller, R. K. Prenatal exposure to diazepam alters behavioral development in rats. *Science,* 1980, *207,* 205–207.

Kleihues, P., Kobayashi, K., & Hossman, K. Purine nucleotide metabolism in the cat brain after one hour of complete ischemia. *Journal of Neurochemistry,* 1974, *23,* 417–425.

Koe, B. K. Biochemical effects of antianxiety drugs on brain monoamines. In S. Fielding & H. Lal (Eds.), *Anxiolytics.* New York: Futura Publishing, Co., 1979.

Lapin, I. P. Dissimilar effects of nicotinamide and inosine, putative endogenous ligands of the benzodiazepine receptors, on pentylenetetrazol seizures in four strains of mice. *Pharmacology, Biochemistry and Behavior,* 1980, *13,* 337–341.

LeFur, G., Mizoule, J., Burgevin, M. C., Ferris, O., Heaulme, M., Gauthier, A., Gueremy, C., & Uzan, A. Multiple benzodiazepine receptors: Evidence of a dissociation between anticonflict and anticonvulsant properties by PK 8165 and PK 9084. *Life Sci.,* 1981, *28,* 1439–1448.

Lippa, A., Coupet, J., Greenblatt, E., Klepner, C., & Beer, B. A synthetic non-benzodiazepine ligand for benzodiazepine receptors: A probe for investigating neuronal substrates of anxiety. *Pharmacology, Biochemistry and Behavior,* 1979b. *11,* 99—106.

Lippa, A. S., Critchett, D., Sano, M., Klepner, C., Greenblatt, E., Coupet, J., & Beer, B. Benzodiazepine receptors: Cellular and behavioral characteristics. *Pharmacology, Biochemistry and Behavior,* 1979c, *10,* 831–843.

Lippa, A. S., Greenblatt, E. N., & Pelham, R. W. The use of animal models for delineating the mechanisms of action of anxiolytic agents. In E. Usdin & I. Hanin (Eds.), *Animal Models in Psychiatry and Neurology.* New York: Pergamon Press, 1977.

Lippa, A. S., Nash, P. A., & Greenblatt, E. N. Preclinical neuropsychopharmacological testing procedures for anxiolytic drugs. In S. Fielding & H. Lal (Eds.), *Anxiolytics.* New York: Futura Publishing Co., 1979a.

Lutz, E. G. Restless legs, anxiety, and caffeinism. *Journal of Clinical Psychiatry,* 1978, *39,* 693–698.

MacDonald, J. F., Barker, J., Paul, S., Marangos, P., & Skolnick, P. Inosine may be an endogenous ligand for benzodiazepine receptors on mouse cultured spinal neurons. *Science,* 1979, *205,* 715–717.

Mackerer, C., Kochman, R., Bierschenk, B., and Brema, S. The binding of [^{3}H]diazepam to rat brain homogenates. Journal of pharmacology an experimental therapeutic, 1978, *206,* 405–413.

Marangos, P., Clark, R., Martino, A., Paul, S., & Skolnick, P. Demonstration of two new endogenous "benzodiazepine-like" compounds from brain. *Psychiatry Research,* 1979, *1,* 121–130.

Marangos, P,, Martino, A., Paul, S., & Skolnick, P. *Psychopharmacology,* 1981, *72,* 269–274, in press. Benzodiazepines and inosine antagonize caffeine-induced seizures.

Marangos, P. J., Paul, S. M., Greenlaw, P., Goodwin, F. K., & Skolnick, P. Demonstration of an endogenous competitive inhibitor(s) of [^{3}H]diazepam binding in bovine brain. *Life Sciences,* 1978, *22,* 1893–1900.

Marangos, P., Paul, S. Parma, A., & Skolnick, P. Inhibition of GABA-enhanced [^{3}H]diazepam binding by purines and benzodiazepines. *Biochemical Pharmacology,* 1981, *30,* 2171–2173.

Marks, J. *The Benzodiazepines-Use, Overuse, Misuse*. Lancaster, England: MTP Press, Ltd., 1978.

Marks, I., & Lader, M. Anxiety states (anxiety neurosis). *Journal of Nervous and Mental Diseases*, 1973, *156*, 3–18.

Masserman, J. H. *Behavior and Neurosis: An Experimental Psycho-analytic Approach to Psychobiologic Principles*. Chicago: University of Chicago Press, 1943.

McNamara, J., Peper, A., & Patrone, V. Repeated seizures induced long-term increase in hippocampal benzodiazepine receptors. *Proceedings of the National Academy of Sciences (USA)*, 1980, *77*, 3029–3033.

Miles, H., Barrabee, E., & Finesinger, J. Evaluation of psychotherapy, with a follow-up study of 62 cases of anxiety neurosis. *Psychosomatic Medicine*, 1951, *13*, 83–105.

Mohler, H., & Okada, T. Benzodiazepine receptors: Demonstration in the central nervous system. *Science*, 1977a, *198*, 849–851.

Mohler, H., & Okada, T. Properties of [^{3}H]diazepam binding to benzodiazepine receptors in rat cerebral cortex. *Life Sciences*, 1977b, *20*, 2101–2109.

Mohler, H., Wu, J.-Y., & Richards, J. G. Benzodiazepine receptors: Autoradiographical and immunocytochemical evidence for their localization in regions of GABAergic synaptic contacts. In E. Cost, G. diChiara, & G. Gessa (Eds.), *GABA and Benzodiazepine Receptors*. New York: Raven Press, 1981. pp. 139–146.

Mohler, H., Okada, T., Ulrich, J., & Heitz, P. H. Biochemical identification of the site of action of benzodiazepines in human brain by [^{3}H]diazepam binding. *Life Sciences*, 1978, *22*, 985–996.

Mohler, H., Polc, P., Cumin, R., Pieri, L., & Kettler, R. Nicotinamide is a brain constituent with benzodiazepine-like actions. *Nature*, 1979, *278*, 563–565.

Nielsen, M., Gredal, O., & Braestrup, C. Some properties of [^{3}H]diazepam displacing activity from human urine. *Life Sciences.*, 1979, *25*, 679–686.

Noyes, R., Clancy, J., Hoenk, P., & Slymen, D. The prognosis of anxiety neurosis. *Archives of General Psychiatry*, 1980, *37*, 173–178.

Olsen, R. W., & Leeb-Lundberg, F. Convulsant and anticonvulsant drug binding sites related to GABA-regulated chloride ion channels. In E. Costa, G. diChiari & G. Gessa (Eds.), *GABA and Benzodiazepine Receptors*. New York: Raven Press, 1981, pp. 93–102.

Paul, S. M., & Skolnick, P. Rapid changes in brain benzodiazepine receptors after experimental seizures. *Science*, 1978, *202*, 892–894.

Paul, S., Marangos, P., & Skolnick, P. Are there endogenous ligands for benzodiazepine receptors? In H. Yamamura & R. Olsen (Eds.), *Psychopharmacology and Biochemistry of Neurotransmitters*. New York: Elsevier-North Holland, 1980a, pp. 661–676.

Paul, S., Marangos, P., & Skolnick, P. The GABA-benzodiazepine-Chloride ionophore receptor complex: Common locus of minor tranquilizer action. *Biological Psychiatry*, 1981, 213–229.

Paul, S., Marangos, P., Brownstein, M., & Skolnick, P. Demonstrating and characterization of an endogenous inhibitor of GABA-enhanced [^{3}H]diazepam binding from bovine cerebral cortex. In E. Costa, G. diChiara & G. Gessa (Eds.), *GABA and Benzodiazepine Receptors*. New York: Raven Press, in press, 1981b, pp. 103–110.

Paul, S., Syapin, P., Paugh, B., Moncada, V., & Skolnick, P. Correlation between benzodiazepine receptor occupation and anticonvulsant effects of diazepam. *Nature*, 1979, *281*, 688–689.

Placheta, P., & Karobath, M. *In vitro* modulation by SQ 20009 and SQ 65396 of GABA receptor binding in rat CNS membranes. *European Journal of Pharmacology*, 1979, *62*, 225–228.

Pull, I., & McIlwain, H. Adenine derivatives as neurohumoral agents in the brain. *Biochemical Journal*, 1972, *126*, 975–981.

Randall, L. O., & Kappell, B. Pharmacological activity of some benzodiazepines and their metabolites. In S. Garattini, E. Mussini & L. O. Randall (Eds.), *The Benzodiazepines*. New York: Raven Press, 1973.

Robertson, H. A. Benzodiazepine receptors in "emotional" and "non-emotional" mice: Comparison of four strains. *European Journal of Pharmacology*, 1979, *56*, 163–167.

Robertson, H., Martin, I. and Candy, J. Differences in benzodiazepine receptor binding in Maudsley reactive and Maudsley non-reactive rats. *European Journal of Pharmacology,* 1978, *50,* 455–457.

Saugstad, O. D., & Shrader, H. The determination of inosine and hypoxanthine in rat brain during normothermic and hypothermic anoxia. *Acta Neurologica Scandinavica,* 1978, *57,* 281–288.

Skolnick, P., & Paul, S. The mechanism(s) of action of the benzodiazepines. *Medicinal Research Reviews,* 1981, *1,* 3–21.

Skolnick, P., Barker, J., & Paul, S. Pentobarbital potentiates GABA-enhanced [³H]diazepam binding to benzodiazepine receptors. *European Journal of Pharmacology,* 1980c, *65,* 125–127.

Skolnick, P., Goodwin, F. K., & Paul, S.M. A rapid and sensitive radioreceptor assay for benzodiazepines in plasma. *Archives of General Psychiatry,* 1979b, *36,* 78–80.

Skolnick, P., Marangos, P. J., Goodwin, F. K., Edwards, M., & Paul, S. M. Identification of inosine and hypoxanthine as endogenous inhibitors of [³H]diazepam binding in the central nervous system. *Life Sciences,* 1978, *23,* 1473–1480.

Skolnick, P., Paul, S., & Marangos, P. J. Purines as endogenous ligands of the benzodiazepine receptor. *Federation Proceedings,* 1980a, *39,* 3050–3055.

Skolnick, P., Paul, S., Rice, K., Barker, S., Cook, J., Weber, R., & Cain, M. *In vitro* inhibition of [³H]diazepam binding to benzodiazepine receptors by β-carbolines. Abstracts of the American Chemical Society, 2nd Chemical Congress of North America. 1980b, Abstract No. 069 (Medicinal Chemistry).

Skolnick, P., Syapin, P., Paugh, B., Moncada, V., Marangos, P., & Paul, S. Inosine, an endogenous ligand of the brain benzodiazepine receptor antagonizes pentylenetetrazole-induced seizures. *Proceedings of the National Academy of Sciences (USA),* 1979a, *76,* 1515–1518.

Soubrie, P., Thiebot, M., Jobert, A., Montastruc, J., Hery, F., & Hamon, H. Decreases convulsant potency of picrotoxin and pentetrazol and enhanced [³H]flunitrazepam cortical binding following stressful manipulations in rats. *Brain Research,* 1980, *189,* 505–517.

Squires, R. & Braestrup, C. Benzodiazepine receptors in rat brain. *Nature,* 1977, *266,* 732–734.

Squires, R. GABA receptors regulate the affinities of anions required for brain specific benzodiazepine binding. In E. Costa, G. diChiara & G. Gessa (Eds.), *GABA and Benzodiazepine Receptors.* New York: Raven Press, 1981, 129–138.

Stein, L., Wise, C. D., & Berger, B. D. Effects of benzodiazepines on serotonergic mechanisms. In S. Garattini, E. Mussini, & L. O. Randall (Eds.), *The Benzodiazepines.* New York: Raven Press, 1973.

Sternbach, L. The benzodiazepine story. *Journal of Medicinal Chemistry,* 1979, *22,* 1–7.

Sun, M. C., McIlwain, H., & Pull, I. The metabolism of adenine derivatives in different parts of the brain of the rat, and their release from hypothalamic preparations on excitation. *Journal of Neurobiology,* 1977, *7,* 109–122.

Syapin, P. J., & Skolnick, P. J. Characterization of benzodiazepine binding sites in cultured cells of neural origin. *Journal of Neurochemistry,* 1979, *32,* 1047–1051.

Tallman, J. F., Thomas, J. W., & Gallager, D. W. GABAergic modulation of benzodiazepine binding site sensitivity. *Nature,* 1978, *274,* 383–385.

Tallman, J. F., Thomas, J. W., & Gallager, D. W. Identification of diazepam binding in intact animals. *Life Sciences,* 1979, *24,* 873–880.

Tallman, J., Paul, S., Skolnick, P., & Gallager, D. Receptors for the age of anxiety: Molecular pharmacology of the benzodiazepines. *Science,* 1980, *207,* 274–281.

Ticku, M., & Burch, T. Purine inhibition of [³H]α-aminobutyric acid receptor binding to rat brain membranes. *Biochemical Pharmacology,* 1980, *29,* 1217–1220.

Toffano, G., Guidotti, A., & Costa, E. Purification of an endogenous protein inhibitor of the high affinity binding of γ-aminobutyric acid to synaptic membranes of rat brain. *Proceedings National Academy of Sciences (USA),* 1978, *75,* 4024–4028.

Villeneuve, A. Differential psychopharmacology of anxiolytics and sedatives. In A. Villeneuve (Ed.), *Modern Problems in Pharmacopsychiatry,* Vol. 14. Basel: S. Karger, 1979.

Wastek, G. J., Speth, R. C., Reisine, T. D., & Yamamura, H. I. The effect of γ-aminobutyric acid on [^{3}H]flunitrazepam binding in rat brain. *European Journal of Pharmacology,* 1978, *50,* 445–447.

Weinryb, I., Beer, B., Proctor, E. B., & Hess, S. M. Studies *in vitro* and *in vivo* with SQ 20009: An inhibitor of cyclic nucleotide phosphodiesterase with central nervous system activity. *Journal de Pharmacologie (Paris),* 1974, *5,* (Suppl. 1), 114.

Wheeler, E. O., White, P., Reed, W., & Cohen, M. Neurocirculatory asthenia (anxiety neurosis, efford syndrome, nervous asthenia). *Journal of the American Medical Association,* 1950, *142,* 878–888.

Williamson, M. J., Paul, S. M., & Skolnick, P. Labeling of benzodiazepine receptors *in vivo. Nature,* 1978a, *275,* 551–553.

Williamson, M. J., Paul, S. M., & Skolnick, P. Demonstration of [^{3}H]diazepam binding to benzodiazepine receptors *in vivo. Life Sciences,* 1978b, *23,* 1935–1940.

Winokur, G., & Holeman, E. Chronic anxiety neurosis: Clinical and sexual aspects. *Acta Psychiatria Scandinavica,* 1963, *39,* 384–412.

Wolpe, J. *Psychotherapy by Reciprocal Inhibition.* Stanford: Stanford University Press, 1958.

Young, W. S., & Kuhar, M. J. Autoradiographic localization of benzodiazepine receptors in the brains of humans and animals. *Nature,* 1979, *280,* 393–395.

Zuckerman, M. In M. Zuckerman & C. D. Spielberger (Eds.), *Emotions and Anxiety.* Hillsdale, New Jersey: Lawrence Erlbaum Associates, 1976.

12 Affective Disorders

A. John Rush, M.D.
Carl Fulton, M.D.
University of Texas,
Health Science Center
Dallas, Texas

INTRODUCTION

This chapter reviews current methods for diagnosing, subclassifying, and measuring symptom severity in the affective disorders. Biological and psychological treatment methods are reviewed; suggestions for how to select patients for specific treatments in this heterogeneous group of disorders are offered.

The estimated lifetime prevalence for depression in the general population is 10–15%, whereas women may be at even higher risk (up to one chance in five). Nearly one fourth of all psychiatric hospitalizations in 1970 carried an admitting diagnosis of depression, but probably only one in five depressed persons receive treatment, one in five are hospitalized and one in 200 commit suicide. It is estimated that the male to female ratio for major depressive episode is 1:2–3. Finally, Major Depressive Disorders are more common among family members of a depressed patient than in the general population (Lehmann, 1971).

According to the Diagnostic and Statistical Manual, 3rd Edition (DSM-III) the essential feature of all affective disorders is a mood disturbance which is accompanied by a full or partial manic or depressive syndrome that is not due to other physical or psychiatric disorders (APA, 1980). The affective disorders include a number of distinct psychopathological conditions that differ in their response to different treatments. Given the wide range of available psychotherapeutic and biologic interventions, the need for careful clinical assessment cannot be overemphasized. Let us first consider the relevance and current status of diagnosis.

DIAGNOSIS

Purpose of Diagnosis

A diagnosis (to know through) is a hypothesis, the clinican's best judgment, about the nature of an ailment. It designates *what* the ailment is, and it often has etiological implications. It is a statement of both *what* the phenomenon is and *how* it might be explained. Thus, diagnosis involves both a classification and an explanation. The diagnostic process is designed to improve the matching of available treatments with the problems presented by the patient.

The descriptive diagnostic approach developed from work by Sydenham in the 17th century. It has led to the classification of disorders by signs, symptoms, and clinical course. The term "syndrome" refers to a constellation of signs (what the examiner sees) and symptoms (what the patient reports) that are known to recur with regularity in clinical populations. A syndrome is a description that does not imply a specific etiology or a common response to treatment. When available evidence suggests a distinct pathological process, then one speaks of a disease entity, or in psychiatry, a psychiatric disorder.

A second purpose of diagnosis is prognostication. Patients, relatives, and society often require a judgment about the ultimate outcome of a particular medical problem. A prognosis is derived from the recognition of particular syndromes or illnesses and from careful study of their ultimate courses and responses to treatments.

Other practical reasons also justify the diagnostic process: (a) the need to simplify complex data; (b) the need to communicate succinctly between professionals; and (c) the need to refine clinical research.

Historical Perspectives

Ancient and Biblical writings provide our earliest accounts of depression. Ancients generally considered deranged behaviors as curses from the gods, a curse afflicted upon sinners or as a sign of moral or personal weakness (Beck, Brady, & Quen, 1977). Hippocrates was the first clinician to describe depression carefully. He argued that psychiatric problems originated from natural causes rather than from supernatural forces and emphasized the critical role of the brain in the development of these disorders.

Artaeus of Cappacodia (A.D. 120–180) was the first to recognize organic (now called primary) and external (now called situational) types of depression as two separate illnesses. He recognized both manic and depressive episodes. He taught that some depressive illnesses included only recurrent episodes of depression (now called *unipolar depression*), whereas others involved both depression and mania (now called *bipolar* depressions) (Beck et al., 1977).

During the Dark Ages, Western Civilization returned to beliefs in possession and supernatural forces as explanations for psychiatric disorders. Not until the Renaissance was there a return to enlightened empiricism, observation and reasoned thought. Johann Weyer (1515–1588), a 16th century opponent of witchcraft, was the first physician to focus on the study of mental illness. He considered depression to be linked to somatic or bodily symptoms. Timothy Bright, a resident physician at London's St. Bartholomew's Hospital, was the first to recognize suicide as a manifestation of despair. Robert Burton summarized the existing theories of depression in his *Anatomy of Melancholia* (1630). He depicted a wide range of depressions from natural grief at death or separation to depressive illnesses.

In the 18th century there was the recognition of specific psychiatric disorders, and a tendency toward humane and enlightened treatments (Beck et al., 1977). The 19th and early 20th centuries focused on descriptive diagnosis (diagnosis based on the recognition of specific signs and symptoms) and on unconsciousness factors. Emil Kraepelin (1856–1926) established a system to diagnose specific disorders. He distinguished *manic-depressive insanity,* an episodic non-deteriorating disorder, from *dementia praecox,* later called "schizophrenia," a more progressive, deteriorating problem. Eugene Bleuler (1857–1939), a Swiss neurologist, proposed a more exact differentiation of various mental illnesses. He separated the "melancholias" or "affective disorders" from the "schizophrenias." He broadened the concept of "affective disorders" to include not only manic-depressive insanity, but also psychoneurotic depressive reactions, involutional melancholia, etc. However, he was unable to delineate subtypes of "affective disorders," a problem that persists today (Beck et al., 1977).

Sigmund Freud (1856–1939) focused attention on individual and personality development. Early psychoanalytic writers viewed depression as part of reparative mechanism: the loss of a loved person resulted in a psychic injury that could only be overcome by self-punishment. Melancholia was seen as a period of self-torment during which the emotional representation of the lost person received the negative portion of ambivalent feelings. Thus, depression represented anger turned on the self.

Bibring, a 20th Century psychoanalyst, believed that depression resulted from causes other than loss of a loved one by separation or death. He thought that helplessness in attaining a desired goal or person produced a loss of self-esteem and subsequent depression. This loss of self-esteem was seen as the common denominator for all depressions. Early in his career, Sando Rado (1890–1972) wrote of the adaptive qualities of depression but later noted that depressions were encountered in patients with neuroses, schizophrenia, syphillis and other physical illnesses, including drug dependencies.

Though the earlier psychoanalytic thinkers did not recognize different types or kinds of depressions and paid little attention to distinguishing between normal feelings of sadness and specific depressive disorders, later thinkers (e.g. Rado) began to recognize that these distinctions were critical to understanding the psychological aspects of depression. In other words, all depressions may not be explained by "anger turned inward" theory nor by a "loss in self-esteem." Perhaps some specific depressions are more likely to be accounted for by one or more of these hypothetical mechanisms (Beck et al., 1977).

The 1930's marked the discovery of the first specific biological treatment for severe mental disorders. In 1934, Von Meduna, a Hungarian psychiatrist, was the first to treat schizophrenia by inducing convulsions with an inhaled substance called camphor. In 1938, Cerletti and Bini, two Italian physicians, induced convulsions by passing an electric current between electrodes placed on the forehead.

In the 1950's came the discovery of antidepressant medications. These discoveries subsequently led to a host of investigations designed to identify the underlying neurophysiology and neurochemistry of depression. Specific "neurotransmitters" or chemical messengers in the brain that help nerve cells communicate with each other were identified. The idea that specific chemical changes in the brain may lead to depression was espoused. When specific chemicals in the brain were increased, depression was relieved, whereas when these chemicals were reduced, depression followed in some people.

In 1949, John Cade, an Australian psychiatrist, found that lithium was effective in the treatment of mania. In 1957, Kuhn, a Swiss psychiatrist discovered the so-called "tricyclic" antidepressants. In the 1970's, a new class of antidepressants, the four-ring, or "tetracyclic" agents were developed. New research now suggests several more chemically unique antidepressants will become available over the next 5-10 years (Beck et al., 1977).

The last decade has also witnessed the development of short-term psychotherapeutic methods that are specifically designed for the treatment of depression. These newer psychotherapies may help in the treatment of some depressions that respond poorly to currently available medications. It is hoped that such treatments will change psychological processes that make some persons particularly vulnerable to chronic or recurrent depressions.

Since treatments for the depressions have substantially improved as specific medications and psychotherapies have been developed, and, since these various biological and psychological interventions differ in their impact on different depressive disorders, improved diagnostic approaches for the depressions are called for. As therapeutic experiences with ECT, lithium, and the antidepressants have shown, the depressions are a heterogeneous group that includes a number of distinct psychopathological conditions. These conditions differ in their responsiveness to specific pharmacotherapies and probably to various specific psychotherapies (Mendels, 1974).

Although there is a general agreement that the depressions are heterogeneous, there is still no commonly agreed-upon single scheme for dividing the depressions. In Gillespie (1929) distinguished endogenous from reactive types of depression (Beck et al., 1977). This distinction was meant to differentiate depressions that arose in response to environmental events ("reactive") from those without a precipitant ("autonomous"). Other common diagnostic dualisms include: neurotic vs. psychotic (a distinction that refers to the evidence for a break with reality as manifested by hallucinations, delusions and ideas of reference); retarded versus agitated; unipolar versus bipolar, referring to the presence of mania or hypomania in the histories of bipolar patients. Unipolar and bipolar depressions are distinguished by clinical history, biology, physiology, genetics, and by response to treatment.

The primary versus secondary dichotomy is logically superordinate to the bipolar-unipolar subdivision (Beck et al., 1977). "Primary affective disorders" are depressions that occur in previously well patients or those with only previous psychiatric disorders have consisted of mania or depression. "Secondary depressions" are diagnosed if patients have previously suffered other psychiatric illnesses, not simply depression or mania. This dualism skirts questions of presence or absence of an environmental stress (i.e. reactive-endogenous) and of psychosis. However, it is unclear whether this dichotomy usefully predicts which patients will respond to psychotherapeutic and/or medication treatments.

In summary, then, depressions are syndromes that may have multiple causes, and that differ in their response to different therapies. Although our descriptive diagnostic system has been based on one or another significant "dimension" of the symptom pattern, recent evidence indicates that further differentiation among the depressions can be based on various dimensions including clinical-descriptive, biological, and possibly psychological parameters.

The Syndrome of Depression

A depressive episode is defined by DSM-III as the presence of a persistent and relatively prominent dysphoria (nearly every day for a period of at least two weeks), which is usually expressed in the form of sadness but may be expressed as irritability, anxiety, "not caring any more," or general feelings of being upset in association with other critical signs and symptoms of the depressive syndrome.

In major depressions this dysphoria is associated with four or more of the following eight symptoms: poor appetite or significant weight loss, or increased appetite or significant weight gain; insomnia or hypersomnia; psychomotor agitation or retardation; loss of interest or pleasure (anhedonia) in usual activities or decrease in sexual drive; loss of energy or easy fatiguability; feelings of worthlessness, self-reproach, or excessive or inappropriate guilt; difficulties in concentration, slowed thinking or indecisiveness, and recurrent thoughts of death or suicide or suicidal action.

The above symptomatology may not be superimposed on schizophrenia, schizophreniform disorder, or paranoid disorder; may not be due to any Organic

Mental Disorder or Uncomplicated Bereavement; and may not be absent when bizarre behavior is present.

A major depression may be associated with other symptoms such as depressed appearance, tearfulness, feelings of anxiety, fear, brooding, excessive concern with physical health, panic attacks, and phobias. In prepubertal children, separation anxiety may develop; children may cling, refuse to go to school and/or fear that they or their parents will die. In adolescence, negativistic or frankly antisocial behavior may appear. Aggression, sulkiness, withdrawal, and school difficulties are likely. Substance abuse may develop. In the elderly, symptoms suggesting dementia, such as memory loss, distractibility, disorientation, apathy, and inattentiveness may be associated with depression.

A major depression may begin at any age including infancy. Symptoms usually develop over a period of weeks or months; in some cases onset may be very sudden. It is estimated that over 50% of individuals with a Major Depression, Single Episode, will eventually have another major depressive episode, thus meeting the criteria for Major Depression, Recurrent Type. Depressive episodes typically last from weeks to months; they are longer and end less abruptly than do manic episodes. The course is variable, but usually functioning returns to the premorbid levels between episodes. However, in 20–35% of cases there is a chronic course with considerable residual symptomatic and social impairment (APA, 1980).

The most serious complication of a major depressive episode is suicide. Frequently, a Major Depressive episode follows a psychosocial stressor. If an individual has recurrent episodes, however, the subsequent episodes may occur without precipitating events. Predisposing factors include chronic physical illness, Alcohol Dependence, Cyclothymic and Dysthymic Disorders.

Endogenous or "endogenomorphic" depressions, or depressions with melancholia, are major depressions that are characterized by the presence of the full depressive syndrome plus the loss of pleasure in all or almost all activities; lack of reactivity to usually pleasurable stimuli; and at least three of the following: distinct quality of depressed mood (distinctly different from the kind of feelings experienced following the death of a loved one); depressed mood that is regularly worse in the morning; early morning awakening (at least 2 hours before usual time of awakening—terminal insomnia); marked psychomotor retardation or agitation; significant anorexia or weight loss; and excessive or inappropriate guilt. These depressions usually require biological treatment(s) (APA, 1980).

Bipolar Depressions.   Unipolar Disorders differ from Bipolar Disorders with regard to history, biology, and treatment. This dichotomy is the most well-documented descriptive subclassification (Fieve & Dunner, 1975). Bipolar depressives have a history of mania or hypomania, whereas unipolar depressives do not. Bipolar depressions have an earlier mean age of onset (28 years) than unipolar depressions (36 years). A higher frequency of affective illness is noted in extended families of bipolars (63%) as compared to unipolars (36%) (Winokur, Clayton, & Reich, 1969). Suicide rates are higher in families of bipolar (especially those with hypomania) than unipolar probands. Lower psychomotor activity and less anxiety are alleged to occur in bipolars compared to unipolars (Beigel & Murphy, 1971).

Biological studies also distinguish these two subgroups. Red blood cell enzyme (catechol-o-methyl transferase) and platelet enzyme (monoamine oxidase) distinguish the two groups (Cohn, Dunner, & Axelrod, 1970). Furthermore, turnover of specific central nervous system neurotransmitters (e.g. dopamine) differentiates the two depressions (Goodwin, Post, Dunner, & Gordon, 1973). Physiological investigations indicate that cortical evoked responses differentiate the two groups: bipolars augment while unipolars reduce evoked cortical responses (Buchsbaum, 1975). Flicker threshold and EEG response to photic stimulation may also differentiate bipolar and unipolar depressions. Furthermore, the evidence for genetic linkage including linkage to XG blood grouping and linkage to color blindness appears to characterize some bipolar illnesses (Rush, 1975).

Finally, response to various treatments differentiates these two groups: bipolars are particularly responsive to lithium for either the acute treatment or the prophylaxis for depression (Goodwin, Murphy, Dunner, & Bunney, 1972). Tricyclic agents are reported to precipitate mania in some bipolar patients. However, both bipolar and unipolar depressions both respond to electroconvulsive therapy (ECT), although bipolar depressions respond more rapidly (Mendels, 1974).

Organic Affective Syndrome.   This syndrome is a disturbance of mood due to specific organic factor(s). It may resemble either manic or major depressive episode(s). The severity of the disturbance may range from mild to severe. Certain substances (e.g. reserpine, methyldopa, some hallucinogens, etc.) can cause a depressive syndrome. Endocrine disorders may produce either depressive or manic syndromes. Examples are hyper- and hypothyroidism and hyper- and hypoadrenocorticolism. Carcinoma of the pancreas and viral illnesses may also cause depressive syndromes. Structural brain diseases are rare causes of Organic Affective Syndrome (APA, 1980).

Other Disorders Related to Depression.   Schizoaffective Disorder is diagnosed when patients exhibit signs of both an Affective Disorder and a Schizophreniform or Schizophrenic Disorder (APA, 1980).

Other disorders that may be confused with a depressive episode include organic brain syndrome (including but not limited to Primary Degenerative Dementia or Multi-infarct Dementia) in which decreased energy and difficulty in concentration may be prominent; a psychological reaction to the functional impairment associated with a physical illness; schizophrenia, catatonic type; Separation

Anxiety Disorder; Uncomplicated Bereavement; and other mental disorders, such as Obsessive-Compulsive Disorder, Alcoholism, Histrionic, Dependent or Borderline personality in which irritability and/or sadness is present. If a full depressive syndrome develops in these personalities, both the personality disorder and a Major Depression are diagnosed.

A minor depressive episode (Dysthymic Disorder) is expressed as a long-standing illness of at least 2 years' duration (one year for children and adolescents), with either sustained or intermittent mood of depression or loss of interest or pleasure in almost all usual activities and pastimes, along with specific associated symptoms that are not of sufficient severity and duration to meet the criteria for a Major Depression. A minor depression may be relatively persistent or separated by periods of normal mood lasting a few days to a few weeks, but no more than a few months at a time. There is never a history of delusions, hallucinations, or incoherence, or loosening of associations.

At least three of the following associated symptoms are present during the minor depressive period: insomnia or hypersomnia; chronic tiredness or low energy level; feelings of inadequacy, self-depreciation or loss of self-esteem; decreased productivity or effectiveness at school, work, at home; decreased attention, concentration or ability to think clearly; social withdrawal; loss of interest or enjoyment of pleasurable activities; irritability or excessive anger; inability to respond with apparent pleasure to praise or rewards; less active or talkative than usual or feels slowed down or restless; pessimistic attitude toward the future, brooding about past events, or feeling sorry for self; tearfulness or crying; recurrent thoughts of death or suicide (APA, 1980).

Atypical Depressive Disorder is a diagnosis reserved for individuals with depressive symptoms that cannot be classified as having a Major or Minor (Other Specific Affective Disorders) or Adjustment Disorder. These depressions lack the full symptom picture of a Major Depressive Episode and last less than 2 years (APA, 1980).

Mania

A Manic Episode is a distinct period lasting at least one week with feelings of euphoria and/or irritability in association with hyperactivity, pressure of speech, flight of ideas, inflated self-esteem, decreased need for sleep, distractibility, and excessive involvement in activities that have a high potential for painful consequences, that are not recognized.

Exclusion criteria are the same as for Major Depressive Episode. Associated symptoms may include an infectious quality to the elevated mood or a lability of mood with rapid shifts to anger or depression. Speech may be disorganized and incoherent especially when flight of ideas is severe. Delusions or hallucinations may be present in mania and their content is usually clearly consistent with the predominent mood. Persecutory delusions may be present. Less commonly, the content of the hallucinations or delusions can have no apparent relationship to the predominant mood (mood-incongruent). In children euphoria is frequently present with mania and is manifested as denial of any illness or problem. In addition, the characteristic appearance of depressive symptoms, such as hopelessness and helplessness, crying spells, death wishes, and beliefs of persecution can occur during mania in children.

Bipolar Disorder, Manic is diagnosed when a full manic episode is present. Bipolar Disorder, Depressed is diagnosed when the patient has a history of one or more full manic episodes and is currently in a major depression. Bipolar, Mixed is characterized by the presence of the full symptomatic picture of both manic and depressive episodes intermixed or rapidly alternating every few days.

The first manic episode of Bipolar Disorder typically occurs before age 30. Episodes begin suddenly, with a rapid escalation of symptoms over a few days and usually last from a few days to months and may end abruptly. Frequently, a manic or major depressive episode is immediately followed by a short episode of the other kind. In rare cases, over long periods of time, there is an alteration of the two kinds of episodes without an intervening period of normal mood (rapid-cycling).

The most common complications of manic episodes are substance abuse and social consequences from impaired judgment (e.g. financial losses and illegal activities). Predisposing factors for Bipolar illness are similar to those of Major Depressive Disorder. It is estimated that from 0.4% to 1.2% of the adult population has had Bipolar Disorder. It is equally common in women and in men. Bipolar Disorders are far more common among family members than in general population (APA, 1980).

Hypomania

A hypomanic episode is a pathological mood disturbance of distinct duration similar to but not as severe as a manic episode. Psychotic features are never present.

One of the clearest expressions of the minor manic or hypomanic disorder is found in Cyclothymic Disorders. Its logical counterpart among the depressive disorders is the Dysthymic Disorder. Cyclothymic Disorder is expressed as a longstanding illness of at least 2 years' duration involving numerous periods of depression and hypomania that are not of sufficient severity and duration to meet criteria for a Major Depression or Mania.

During the affective periods there are signs of depression and hypomania and the following pairs of symptoms are particularly common: feelings of inadequacy (during depressed periods) and inflated self-esteem (during hypomanic periods); social withdrawal and uninhibited people-seeking; sleeping too much and decreased need for sleep; diminished productivity at work and increased productivity, often associated with unusual and self-imposed work hours; decreased attention or concentration and sharpened and unusually creative thinking (APA, 1980).

Atypical Bipolar Disorder is diagnosed when manic features cannot be classified as Bipolar Disorder or as Cyclothymic Disorder. A major depressive episode may have been present historically, but the present episode presents with only a hypomanic symptom picture. Essentially, an Atypical Bipolar Disorder is an illness with a hypomanic symptom picture that lasts less than 2 years (APA, 1980).

Differential Diagnosis of Mania/Hypomania

Disorders that may be confused with a manic episode include Organic Affective Syndromes, especially secondary to substances such as amphetamines, steroids, or other organic factors, such as multiple sclerosis; Schizophrenia, paranoid type; Schizoaffective Disorder; or Cyclothymic Disorder.

Treatment Options

Various treatments are available for the affective disorders (i.e. major and minor depressive disorders, major depressive disorders with melancholia, mania and hypomania). They include electroconvulsive therapy (ECT), tricyclic antidepressants (TCA), monoamine oxidase inhibitors (MAOI), and various forms of psychotherapy. ECT is the treatment of choice for endogenous or melancholic depressions that have failed to respond to antidepressant medications. ECT may be a treatment of first choice in severely melancholic patients who require rapid response. (In general, ECT is both safer and more effective than TCA medication). Tricyclic antidepressants, a major advance in the treatment of certain depressive disorders, are especially effective in endogenous or melancholic depressions. Although some "neurotic" or nonmelancholic depressions also respond to TCAs. The monoamine oxidase inhibitors are particularly valuable in anxious depressions or in those with associated phobias.

Psychotherapeutic methods have recently been developed and carefully tested in populations of depressed patients. Cognitive and behavioral treatments have been perhaps the most clearly specified and extensively tested psychotherapies for depression (Rush and Beck, 1978). In addition, interpersonal psychotherapy has recently been developed, specified, and tested in depressed outpatients and shown to be effective (Di Mascio, Weisman, Prusoff, Neu, Zwilling & Klerman, 1971). Given this wide variety of treatment alternatives, and the known heterogeneity of the depressive disorders, the clinician is wise to diagnose carefully and reevaluate patients continually before and during treatment.

Adjuncts to Diagnosis

Descriptive Assessment.   Descriptive diagnoses are based on an evaluation of the patient's immediate observable and reportable signs and symptoms. The evaluator develops a picture of particular signs and symptoms that are involved in the criteria listed earlier to make descriptive diagnoses. The examiner asks about the patient's internal mood state, feelings of guilt and self-criticism, specific patterns must be elicited including bed time, time of sleep inception, number of awakenings during the night, and time of last awakening prior to arising. Specific inquiries about amount of weight loss, energy level, anhedonia, and diurnal variation in mood, etc. are made.

From that point, the examiner works backwards in time to determine when the present signs and symptoms began. Has this episode lasted a week, a month, 6 months, a year, 2 years, or 5 years? A life line methodology initially developed by Adolph Meyer is of value (Meyer, 1948–1952). The examiner uses a horizontal line to represent the patient's life in years. Various episodes of depression, mania, euthymia, hypomania, and other symptomatology are sought by careful questioning on a year-by-year basis. Thus, the number of episodes, lengths of episodes, symptomatology and severity within each episode lead to a descriptive diagnosis. Because a great deal of variance in descriptive diagnostic work has been attributed to interviewer's style, methodology and questions selected, a structured interview system is often used. An example of such a system is the SADS-L or Schizophrenia and Affective Disorder Survey, Lifetime Version (Endicott & Spitzer, 1978).

Once each episode has been characterized, a descriptive diagnosis is made based on signs, symptoms and history of present illness. The interviewer may also employ some type of rating scale to measure current symptom severity. Methods to assess the level of depression include interview-based ratings, self-reports, and behavioral observations.

The Hamilton Rating Scale for Depression (HRS-D) is the most popular interview-based rating. The HRS-D consists of 17, 21, or 24 items depending on the format. Each item is rated on a 3 to 4-point scale by a professional judge based on an interview. The sum of the items yields the severity of the depression. The scale has high interrater reliability when used by well-trained raters. It differentiates significantly between depressed and nondepressed patients and is sensitive to changing levels of depression in the same patient (Hamilton, 1960).

The Beck Depression Inventory (BDI) is an easily administered self-report measure that can be completed in the waiting room in 3–7 minutes. It consists of 21 items (range 0–63) with 4 possible alternatives stated as a sentence for each item group. The patient selects one statement under each item group that best describes him/her for a selected time interval (e.g. today, last week, etc.). It contains a greater number of "cognitive" items and fewer "vegetative" symptom items compared to the HRS-D. The BDI correlates significantly with the HRS ($r = 0.58–0.68$) and it is a sensitive measure of symptomatic change (Beck & Beamsderfer, 1974).

The Zung Self-Rating Scale (ZRS) is also an easily administered self-report consisting of 20 statements rated on a 4-point scale reflecting frequency of occurrence from "none or little of the time" to "most or all of the time." This scale has several items reflecting anxiety but has no item reflecting guilt (Zung, 1965).

The Carroll Rating Scale (CRS) is a 52-item self-report form. It reflects general severity of the depressive syndrome, like the HRS-D that requires yes-no responses to 52 items. It measures overall severity of depressive episode. High test-retest reliabilities and sensitivity to clinical change are reported (Carroll, Feinberg, Smouse, Rawson, & Greden, 1981). The BDI correlates 0.71 with the HRS-D and 0.68 with the CRS.

Medical Assessment.   A general medical assessment is absolutely essential in the evaluation of patients with minor or major depressive or manic symptomatology because of the many medical disorders that can imitate or be indistinguishable from psychiatric disorders. A careful medical history, physical examination, and selected laboratory tests are necessary to detect or exclude medical disorders such as thyroid, adrenal, and parathyroid dysfunctions, pernicious anemia, viral infections, cancer, epilepsy, vitamin deficiency, autoimmune diseases, rheumatoid arthritis, Parkinson's Disease, Huntington's Disease, and others. Finally, a number of medications are known to cause depressions (e.g. reserpine, alpha-methyldopa, propranol), birth control pills, steroids, and others) (Lipowski, 1975).

Recent reports suggest that as many as 25% of all patients who are self-referred or referred by other psychiatrists for depression may well be suffering from a medical disorder that is either causing or maintaining their "psychiatric" symptomatology. In addition, physical illness may well precipitate a psychiatric disorder, particularly depression. Studies of precipitating events related to the onset of severe depression show physical illness to be the fifth most common cause (Leff, Roatch, & Bunney, 1970). Often effective treatment for the physical illness relieves the depression. On the other hand, medical intervention may arrest or erradicate the disorder, yet the patient remains depressed.

Psychological Assessment.   While routine psychological testing with the MMPI, Rorschach and other standard tests may be of value in some depressed patients, recent research suggests that measurement of specific cognitive distortions and attitudes may also provide adjuncts to standard psychometric assessments.

Cognitions may be measured by the Cognitive Response Test (CRT-36), an open-ended sentence-completion format with 36 items. This test is designed to assess immediate cognitive responses to specific situations. A sample item is: when I think of an upcoming family reunion, I think to myself..." Responses are scored by Rational, Irrational Depressed, Irrational Other and Nonscorable categories. Scores may range from 0 to 36 for each subscale. The Irrational

Depressed (ID) category discriminates depressed from nondepressed subjects. Recent reports provides evidence of concurrent validity for both R and ID subscales (Watkins & Rush, unpublished manuscript).

The Automatic Thoughts Questionnaire (ATQ) is another self-report designed to measure cognitions. This 30-item questionnaire measures the frequency of occurrence of negative self-statements typically found in depression. The ATQ discriminates depressed and nondepressed subjects without a sex bias. A factor analysis reveals two major factors: personal maladjustment and negative concepts of future. Split-half reliability was 0.97 (p < .001). All ATQ item-to-total correlations were significant. The ATQ in 348 college student subjects correlated significantly with the BDI and MMPI-D. The test is now being validated in clinical samples (Hollon & Kendall, 1980). The ATQ provides an instrument that directly assesses automatic thoughts or conscious mental activity (i.e. cognition) hypothesized to exist in some depressions.

The Dysfunctional Attitude Scale is a vehicle to measure dysfunctional attitudes rather than cognitions. The DAS is a 40-item self-report that is available in two forms, A and B. Each form lists various beliefs to which the subject responds on a 7-point scale from "agree very much" to "disagree very much." The sum of these items reflects the degree to which the subject endorses dysfunctional attitudes hypothesized by Beck to contribute to a predisposition to depression. The items consist of assumptions or beliefs (schemas) by which the individual organizes and judges his/her experiences. The subject chooses from 40 attitudinal statements, such as "I can't find happiness without being loved by another person" or "I must be a useful, productive, creative person or life has no purpose." The score is based upon the number of maladaptive beliefs agreed to (Weissman, 1979).

DAS scores correlate with severity of depression as measured by the BDI (r = 0.48) and with the Story Completion Test (Hammen & Krantz, 1976) another measure of cognitive distortion in normal controls suggesting current validity. It has high internal consistency (0.93 alpha coefficient). A correlation of 0.79 is reported between Forms A and B. Test-retest reliability is 0.86 (Form A) and 0.87 (Form B).

Laboratory Tests for Depression. (a) Dexamethasone Suppression Test: Recently subtyping of depression has been significantly advanced by the development of biological measures that are relatively specific to certain affective disorders. The most well-developed of these is the Dexamethasone Suppression Test (DST) (Carroll et al., 1981). Hypothalamic-pituitary-adrenal (HPA) axis function is evaluated by challenging it with a synthetic glucocorticoid called dexamethasone. The hypothalamus normally drives the anterior pituitary gland to secrete adrenocorticotropic hormone (ACTH). ACTH circulates in the blood and activates certain sections of the adrenal glands to secrete cortisol and other glucocorticoids that can be measured in the blood stream. Secretory bursts or episodes occur with maximal cortisol secretory activity during the early morning hours and minimal secretion from 10:00 p.m. to 3:00 a.m. In many depressed patients, cortisol hypersecretion occurs, even during sleep.

When a nondepressed person is given dexamethasone, ACTH production is reduced to near zero. Thus, in normals, dexamethasone is followed by low or undetectable levels of cortisol in the blood for at least 24 hours.

However, in depressed patients, particularly those with melancholic or endogenous features, the dexamethsasone challenge is often followed by only a partial reduction in cortisol secretion and subsequent escape. This escape can be measured by serial blood samplings throughout the 24-hour period or by blood sampling at two points in time (4:00 and 11:00 p.m.) following dexamethasone.

Cortisol hypersecretion found in endogenous depressions is not simply stress related: hypersecretion is not reduced with sedative medications (Stokes, 1972); hypersecretion continues during sleep (Sacher, Hellman, Roffwarg, Halpern, Fukushima, & Gallagher, 1973); and hypersecretion is not induced with selective sleep deprivation schedules (i.e. it is not an epiphenomenon of sleep deprivation) (Ellman, Roffwarg, Sacher, Finkelstein, Kurti, & Hellman, 1970).

It is thought that the limbic system dysfunction, rather than stress and psychological defense patterns cause the hypothalamic-pituitary-adrenal (HPA) disturbances in depression. This limbic system dysfunction is associated with dysfunctional "affect, appetite, sleep, aggressive and sexual drive, and autonomic nervous system activity" (Sacher et al., 1973).

DST nonsuppression is a definite finding in 30–70% of patients with Endogenous Major Depressive Disorder or Melancholia. In fact, it has been stated that the DST is a specific dependent biological marker of melancholia (Carroll, Feinberg, Greden, Tarika, Aballa, Haskett, James, Krontrol, Lohr, Steiner, deVigne, & Young, 1981). However, a normal DST result does not rule out the diagnosis of melancholia, nor does it imply that TCAs or ECT will be ineffective.

Whether the DST can predict response to treatment is unclear. A few studies report that good treatment response to antidepressant drugs occurs with abnormal DST results. One group suggests that the DST might predict which antidepressant drug(s) will be most effective (Brown, Johnston, & Mayfield, 1974).

It is clear that effective treatment both reduces symptoms *and* normalizes the DST. Two studies have shown that DST will normalize before full clinical response occurs in many patients. Apparently, DST normalization is predictive of a good outcome with ECT (Albala, Greden, Tarika, & Carroll, 1980).

The most important finding has been that if significant clinical improvement occurs, without associated DST normalization, these patients are at serious risk of early relapse or suicide (Carroll, 1972). Failure to obtain DST normalization thus suggests that an incomplete resolution of underlying pathophysiological processes has been obtained. The DST appears to be a useful predictor of suicidal potential in melancholia (Carroll et al., 1981).

Bipolar patients also show DST nonsuppression when depressed, although in mania and hypomania, the DST is normal (Carroll et al., 1981). On the other hand, patients with a mixed picture of both depression and mania show DST nonsuppression.

However, the DST suffers from some shortcomings: Schizoaffective disorder, severe malnutrition, anorexia nervosa, acute medical-surgical illnesses (e.g. uncontrolled diabetes mellitus, myocardial infarction, and cardiac failure), Cushing's disease and hyperthyroidism may also produce DST nonsuppression, as can certain medications (estrogen, dilantin, and barbiturates).

DST nonsuppression is not found in schizophrenia (Carroll, 1972). Thus, the DST can be very helpful in identifying endogenous depressions. It may be especially useful in the assessment of problematic patients with catatonia, schizoaffective depression, or melancholia complicated by severe character disorders, as well as perpubertal and adolescent depressions (Rush, in press).

(b) The Sleep Electroencephalogram (EEG): The sleep EEG shows distinct changes in some depressions. The average adult has 4–5 rapid eye movement (REM) episodes during each night. The first REM period typically occurs about 90 minutes after the person falls asleep, and usually lasts 5–10 minutes. As the night continues, the episodes of REM sleep become more frequent and last longer.

While disorders other than depression may also interrupt sleep, the sleep EEG shows characteristic changes in many depressed patients. Dreaming sleep comes on much more rapidly and earlier in the night (decreased REM latency). Certain depressed patients will enter their first dream episode within 5–60 minutes after falling asleep, instead of taking the 90 minutes that are normally required. This reduced REM latency is most characteristic of endogenous primary Major Depressive Disorders (Rush, 1981; Kupfer, 1976). A reduced REM latency discriminates endogenous from nonendogenous depressions. In addition, a reduced REM latency is a more sensitive indicator of endogenous depressions than is the DST (Rush, Giles, Roffwarg, & Parker, 1982).

REM density (a reflection of REM activity during REM periods) distinguished depressions secondary to medical disease from primary depressions. The sleep EEG also appears to predict response to tricyclic antidepressants. Amitriptyline responders significantly increased REM latency and decreased REM sleep time after only 2 nights of drug treatment (Kupfer, Foster, Coble, McPartland, & Ulrich, 1978). These EEG changes provide evidence for alterations in brain physiology and biology during certain kinds of depressive episodes.

Thus, both REM latency and the DST are biological markers for certain types of depression, particularly endogenous depression. It has been suggested that a sequence of laboratory tests to confirm the diagnosis of Endogenous is now feasible. An initial DST is conducted. If nonsuppression occurs, no further testing is required, and Endogenous depression is confirmed. This test will detect 30–60% of outpatients and 50–70% of inpatients with Endogenous depressions.

For normal suppressors, the sleep EEG should be conducted. Data suggest that roughly 80% of all Endogenous depressions will be detected with these *two* procedures. The number of false positives will be low with DST nonsuppression. REM latency increases the sensitivity but can lead to more false positives (Rush et al., 1982).

(c) Other Biological Tests for Endogenous Depressions: The Thyrotropin-releasing hormone (TRH) stimulation test is an evaluation of the hypothalamic-pituitary-thyroid (HPT) axis function which uses a challenge synthetic thyrotropin-releasing hormone (protirelin) to provoke the production of thyroid stimulating hormone (thyrotropin or TSH). Thyrotropin releasing hormone (TRH) is produced in the hypothalamus and stimulates the anterior pituitary to secrete primarily thyroid stimulating hormone (TSH) which in turn stimulates the thyroid to produce triidothyronine (T3) and thyroxine (T4). The TRH stimulation test is conducted by giving TRH intravenously and measuring TSH prior to and during the hour following this injection. Roughly 30 to 40% of depressed patients have *blunted* or absent *TSH response to TRH.*

Takahasi, Kondo, Yoshimura, & Ochi (1974) suggested that a blunted TSH response to TRH is more likely if the depressive episode is longer (Takahasi et al., 1974). Kirkegaard, Bjorum, Cohn, & Lauridsen (1978) reported that the TSH response to TRH may be useful in diagnosis of bipolar disorders. In addition, Kirkegaard, Norlem, Lauridsen, & Borung (1975) reported that TSH response may predict relapse after treatment with ECT and drugs. These data suggest that adequate mobilization of thyroid function is associated with rapid clinical recovery from depression, whereas poor mobilization is associated with prolonged illness. Perhaps the TRH test may find a place in the clinical management of depressed patients (Kirkegaard et al., 1975).

Family History

Research findings support a familial-genetic factor in unipolar and bipolar illness. The disease rate in relatives of patients with genetic illness will be greater than the expectancy of the disease in the general population. The life-time expectancy in the general population is 1.32% to 3.58% for unipolar primary depressive illness (PDI) and 0.77% to 0.80% for bipolar primary depressive illness. The risk among the first-degree relatives of those affected is increased to 16% for unipolar PDI and 35% for bipolar PDI (Mendlewicz & Raines, 1974).

Determining the concordance rates in monozygotic as opposed to dizygotic twin pairs is another way of assessing the probability of a familial-genetic factor. Concordance among twin pairs for unipolar PDI is 43% and 74% for bipolar PDI. The concordance among twin pairs for dizygotic unipolar PDI is 19% and 17% for bipolar PDI. Therefore, the concordance among twin pairs is greater for monozygotic than for dizygotic pairs, another finding that indicates a familial-genetic factor at work (Allen, 1976).

Dorzah, Baker, Cadoret, & Winokur (1971) showed the frequency of alcoholic and/or antisocial brothers of unipolar patients is 11% and the frequency of alcoholic and/or antisocial personality in families of bipolar patients is even higher. The frequency of alcoholism and/or antisocial personality in normal controls is 6% (Robins, 1966). Winokur, Reich, Rimmer, & Pitts (1970) examined the female first-degree relatives (parents, siblings or children) of 259 alcoholics; the frequency of unipolar depression in these subjects was between 17% and 22%, which is considerably higher than expected in the general population (Winokur et al., 1970). Also, a higher frequency of the illness in the children of depressed patients who had been adopted away shortly after birth compared to adopted away children of well controls (37.5% vs. 7.0%) favors a familial-genetic factor in affective illness (Cadoret, 1978). Finally, half-siblings of patients with depression have a higher frequency of depression than normals but a lower frequency than full-siblings (Kallman, 1953).

Only half-siblings and adoption studies can be interpreted as firm evidence for a strictly genetic factor. Comparisons with the general population, unseparated twin studies, and the finding of a defect in the same functional system, must be considered as evidence in favor of a strictly familial factor. It seems reasonable, therefore, to consider a separation of depressive illness based on family history (Winokur, Behar, VanValkenburg, & Lowry, 1978). Recent reports suggest that for unipolar depressed patients with a positive history of depression in a first-degree relative, the probability of an endogenous depression is higher. Thus, a family history can be useful in choosing treatment.

Treatment

Electroconvulsive Therapy (ECT).   ECT is effective because of the seizure activity induced in parts of the brain. ECT is more effective than antidepressant medication in melancholic and psychotic depressions. ECT is safer than antidepressants, especially in pregnant women and in persons with heart disease or other medical illnesses (Avery & Winokur, 1976).

Over the last 10-15 years, ECT has received a negative reputation, in part due to its inappropriate use in illnesses for which it was basically ineffective. A similar process has been noted in the history of the development of therapeutic techniques in other medical specialities. We now know a great deal more about how to decide which depressed patients will respond to ECT. Furthermore, ECT was administered by methods that may have contributed to unwanted side effects. Present-day methods are far safer.

Today, patients are first put to sleep with a short-acting medication, such as sodium amytal. Then a paralyzing drug is given to prevent muscle contractions during the seizure (thereby preventing fractures and other injuries). Once the patient is asleep and paralyzed, an electric current is passed from one side of the head to the other for about 0.1-0.5 seconds. This current induces a generalized (grand mal) seizure. Since the patient is paralyzed, limb movement is minimal. The seizure ends after about 2 minutes, the paralytic agent wears off, and the patient awakens. The patient then returns to his room or may even return home. Seizures are induced 3 to 4 times per week and 5–10 seizures are usually required for the treatment of severe endogenous depression.

Since the late 1950's, ECT has been compared to antidepressant medication in over 153 studies involving over 5864 patients. Although different research methods were used in various studies, the mean percent improvement over all studies provides a clear picture of ECT's therapeutic effectiveness. On the average, ECT is effective in 75–90% of patients treated. Tricyclic antidepressant medications are effective in 60–80% of patients treated. Placebo is effective in 15–30% of patients with depression. In the "endogenous" depressions, ECT may be life-saving. It may even be effective in some patients for whom antidepressant medications do not work (McCabe, 1976). ECT is also effective in mania (Hesche & Raeder, 1976).

While mechanism of action of ECT is not fully understood, it is thought that the seizure produces a prolonged stimulation of the diencephalon in the brain. The seizure affects certain chemicals or neurotransmitters in the brain that restore specific chemical imbalances that are present in specific depressions. The limbic system, the part of the brain that controls emotions, appetite, weight, and sexual drives, is affected by these seizures (Crow & Johnstone, 1979).

The dangers of ECT must be weighed against the dangers of the illness and the risk of other types of treatment. In a recent study, 519 depressed patients were followed for 3 years after treatment. No one died during the treatment; 2.2% of the ECT-treated patients had died within 3 years following treatment, but not as a consequence of their treatment; 9.1% of the antidepressant-treated patients had died, and 11.4% of the patients who received neither ECT nor antidepressants had died. Thus, during the 3 years following treatment, fewer of those treated with ECT had died than those who were treated inadequately with antidepressants and than those who had received neither ECT nor antidepressants. The death rate associated with depression is quite significant, and treatment with ECT was associated with the best survival rate (Avery & Winokur, 1976). Hesche and Raeder (1976) studied the physical complications of 22,210 ECT treatments given in 3428 patients and found that ECT itself resulted in one death. This mortality rate (1 in 22,000) is much less than that associated with depression itself.

The side effects of ECT are surprisingly few. Long-lasting memory problems are relatively infrequent. As more seizures are induced, memory impairment appears to increase. Typically these are mild, fully reversible and last up to a week or two. They are rarely so severe that the patient doesn't remember what is happening to him. However, recent studies have clearly shown that depression itself impairs certain memory functions. Squire and Chance (1975) found no memory impairments in patients 6–9 months after ECT.

About one-half of those who develop a depression will have a recurrence. The relapse rate expected after successful treatment with antidepressant medication is stopped is roughly equal to that which follows ECT. Within 2 years about 18–40% of patients who respond to ECT will relapse unless maintained on antidepressant medication. Thus, ECT is often used to initially relieve the depression and antidepressants are added to prevent recurrences. These medications usually prevent relapses as long as patients take them (Frankel, 1977).

In summary, ECT is quite effective in selected depressions (severe endogenous or psychotic depressions). Recent methods have increased safety and significantly reduced side effects.

Tricyclic Antidepressants.   Since the historic identification of the antidepressant, imipramine, a number of drugs with antidepressant effects have been identified. The tricyclic medications, so called because of their three-ring chemical structure, dramatically changed the treatment of depression (Barchas, Berger, Ciarenello, & Elliott, 1977).

These medications act on parts of the brain that control emotion (the limbic system). A deficiency of certain neurotransmitters (the catechol and indole amines) within the central nervous system exists in endogenous depressions. Catecholamines include norepinephrine (NE), epinephrine, and dopamine, whereas serotonin is an indoleamine (Hollister, 1973).

The tricyclic antidepressants affect most specifically the metabolism of NE and 5HT. Almost all brain centers that control reward functions or pleasure contain both serotonergic and noradrenergic neurons. Thus, chemical imbalances in these systems could account for two prominent symptoms of depression, inability to cope, and inability to obtain enjoyment. If one is willing to assume a genetic-biochemical substrate for depression, then the obvious correlaries are that they may appear in many varying forms, at any age in life and may not necessarily only present as the extreme form (endogenous depression). Persons with deficiencies in central nervous system biogenic amines might be "depressive-prone." Given the proper environmental stresses, their coping mechanisms mediated by central catecholaminergic pathways would prove to be inadequate and a depressive disorder would ensue. A normal person subjected to the same stresses might merely experience a transient feeling of sadness without an incapacitating depression.

Tricyclic antidepressants (TCA's) act to make more neurotransmitter available for communication between neurons. When a nerve cell fires, neurotransmitter is released into the synapse, the space between nerve cells. After acting to initiate the firing of the next neuron, the remaining unused neurotransmitter is transported back into the presynaptic neuron for storage. TCA's slow down the rate at which neurotransmitter is transported out of the synaptic cleft and back into storage. This effect is called "blocking the reuptake of neurotransmitter." Thus, more neurotransmitter is made available to help initiate the firing of the next neuron and thereby to facilitate the propagation of nerve impulses. In essence, these drugs facilitate the chemical communication between nerve cells within the brain, particularly those parts of the brain that control emotion (Hollister, 1973).

The most common tricyclic antidepressants (TCAs) are amitriptyline, doxepin, imipramine, nortriptyline, desipramine, and protriptyline. These agents differ in their effect on various neurotransmitters.

While melancholic or endogenous depressions are most likely to respond to TCAs, these medications are also effective for some nonendogenous forms of depressions. In addition to reducing the signs and symptoms of the depression, these medications also prevent relapses or recurrences of depression in many patients if they continue to take TCAs.

In general, tricyclics are administered in gradually increasing dosages until a therapeutic effect or a particular therapeutic blood level is obtained. Patients must remain on therapeutic doses for at least 3 to 4 weeks to obtain a full medication effect. Then, if effective, the medication is usually continued for 6–12 months to prevent relapses.

Tricyclic antidepressnats differ in their side effects. Side effects do not occur in all patients; however, the most common side effects caused by this group of drugs are sedation and dry mouth. About 10% of patients complain of constipation, difficulty in focusing on near objects, blood pressure changes, urinary retention, or weight gain. The side effects of taking these medications for a long period of time (years) are remarkably low and not essentially different from those mentioned above. TCAs are neither addicting nor habit forming. Rather, they are specific treatments for depression (Hollister, 1973).

Monoamine Oxidase Inhibitors: The monoamine oxidases are enzymes that are widely distributed in the brain and many other organs. They help break down or metabolize neurotransmitters, those neurochemicals that help nerve cells to communicate.

The monoamine oxidase inhibitors (MAOIs) are antidepressnts that inhibit these enzymes. Specifically, they increase the functional amount of the neurotransmitters involved in the regulation of emotions and appetites: norepinephrine, serotonin, and dopamine. That is, instead of being broken down at a rapid rate, these neurotransmitters are broken down or metabolized more slowly; thereby, more neurotransmitter is available to assist in the nerve cell communication.

It has been over 25 years since the first reports suggested that the MAOI's had antidepressant properties. The MAOI's were fairly widely used in the treatment of depression in the 1950's and early 1960's before the discovery of TCAs. Even today they have a place in the treatment of some depressions. The two most widely used and studied of the available MAO inhibitors are phenelzine and tranylcypromine. Those depressed patients with marked features of anxiety, those who are very nervous, tense and unable to relax when depressed often respond well to MAOIs. Other patients who respond well to MAOIs have what are called "atypical" features such as: reversed diurnal mood variation (mood worse in the evening), hypersomnolence or initial insomnia, overeating, and weight gain, extreme sensitivity to perceived rejection and hyper-reactivity of mood (increased irritability and emotionality) (Hollister, 1973).

Like the TCAs, the MAOIs require 2–4 weeks at the appropriate dose to produce a full therapeutic effect. Once this acute response is obtained, MAOIs also prevent relapses if continued on a regular basis. Recently, a blood test has been developed that helps the clinician select the optimum dose for MAOIs (Robinson, Nies, Ravaris, Lamborn, 1978).

The MAOI's are more stimulating and less sedating than the TCAs. The most frequent side effects are drop in blood pressure, appetite loss, and insomnia.

Lithium Carbonate: Lithium, a metal, was discovered in 1817 and named after the Greek word for stone. It was first used for the treatment of mania in Australia in 1949. Subsequent investigations by Mogens Shou (Denmark) provided clearcut evidence of its effect in the treatment of mania and prophylaxis for Bipolar Depressions. In 1974, lithium was approved for the prevention of recurrent manic attacks in the United States (Frankel, 1977).

Lithium is unique in several respects. It is highly specific in its alleviation of manic symptoms, normalizing the mood of manic patients rather than producing sedation or tranquilization. In addition, it is the only drug in psychiatry for which a clear form of prophylaxis against disease recurrences and deterioration has been demonstrated. Finally, it is a simple inorganic salt that has no known function in normal metabolism though it is present at low levels in everyone's blood stream. Unlike most other antidepressant agents, it is not metabolized into other compounds. Lithium is excreted mainly by the kidneys.

Lithium appears to have several sites of action with various cells and organs in the body and eventually finds it way into various parts of the brain, particularly those parts that are involved in the manic-depressive illness. Which particular actions account for the therapeutic effect of the drug is still a matter of research. However, lithium affects the production, storage, and release of the neurotransmitters: norepinephrine, serotonin, and dopamine, which, as previously noted, are presumably involved in depression. Whether these neurotransmitter effects account for the therapeutic effect of lithium is still unclear. In addition, lithium is not used as a replacement for missing chemicals in the body. Patients with bipolar depression who respond to lithium are not lithium deficient. Rather, for some reason when used in large doses, lithium provides an effective treatment and is neither addicting nor habit-forming (Gershon & Shopsin, 1973).

Lithium is indicated in the treatment of acute mania. Eighty-five percent of patients with acute mania respond to lithium treatment in 5–10 days. Lithium is clearly superior to placebo and equal or more effective than other active medication in the treatment of acute mania. Furthermore, the evidence is overwhelming that lithium actually retards or prevents the recurrence of manic illness, and reduces both the symptoms and the episodes of mania.

In addition, lithium acts as an antidepressant in a small group of patients, particularly those who have relatives with a history of bipolar depression. Furthermore, lithium exceeds the effectiveness of antidepressants in preventing the recurrence of depression in bipolar illness (Jefferson & Griest, 1977).

Lithium is now widely used for the treatment of acute manic episodes and for prevention of recurrence of manic episodes. It may prevent recurrence of depressive episodes in patients with bipolar depressions and some studies suggest that lithium is an effective antidepressant in a few patients with unipolar recurrent depressions (Squire & Chance, 1975).

Lithium is taken in a daily oral dose that is adjusted to provide a therapeutic blood level. The patient is started on a low dose and the dosage is gradually increased until an adequate concentration of lithium in the blood stream is obtained. Blood levels of lithium are carefully monitored every few months.

Lithium has some unwanted effects or side effects. Toxic effects result if too much lithium is taken. That is, if the blood level is too high, patients will experience problems with nausea, vomiting, diarrhea, and abdominal pain; central nervous system side effects may include slurred speech, staggering gait, mental confusion and memory difficulties; cardiovascular effects may include irregular heart beats and defects in the electrical conduction of the heart. Toxic side effects can usually be prevented by careful monitoring of the lithium level in the blood and careful adherence to the lithium prescription.

A few long-term side effects have been recently reported. They may include a reduction in the function of the thyroid gland (hypothyroidism) or changes in other endocrine glands. These effects appear to occur in only 1% of patients. A few recent reports suggest that lithium may impair kidney function in some patients who have taken lithium for a number of years. In general, however, lithium is a drug that is surprisingly safe when taken properly and when blood level measurements are regularly used to evaluate the dosage schedule (Jefferson & Griest, 1977).

Psychological Treatment.   Antidepressant chemotherapy is reported to be at least partially effective in 70–80% of depressed outpatients. However, compared to a multitude of studies of chemotherapy, there is a relative dearth of clinical research indicating that behavioral or cognitive techniques are effective in moderate-severe depressions. The ultimate place of psychotherapy in the treatment of depression remains unclear.

On the other hand, recent clinical research data suggest that behavioral and cognitive therapies are effective in certain kinds of depressions. It is hoped that psychotherapy will provide prophylasis not available with chemotherapy, as the patient acquires new skills and/or develops new ways of thinking about himself/herself, and the world. If these patterns remain unchanged, they may well predispose to subsequent relapses (Hollon, Beck, Kovacs, & Rush, 1977). Secondly, cognitive and behavioral methods may significantly decrease the drop-out rate from outpatient treatment (Rush, Beck, Kovacs, & Hollon, 1977). Third, these methods may have an important place in the treatment of depressions which specifically require chemotherapy. More specific techniques might be developed to increase compliance with medication and to decrease premature termination from biological treatments. Furthermore, cognitive and behavioral methods may be usefully applied in the context of a couple or family system. These methods may reduce or even turn to therapeutic advantage angry, critical, or detached family member. This effect may provide improved prophylaxis, and/or earlier detection of a relapse, which facilitates earlier referral for additional treatment if necessary. Finally, there are a number of depressed patients who either refuse or cannot take antidepressant medication or who do not respond to adequate trials of chemotherapy. Although a few of these persons may require electroconvulsive or inpatient treatment, many may respond to cognitive or behavior therapies.

Behavioral Therapy.   Moss and Boren (1972) hypothesize that the essential characteristic of depression is a reduced frequency of positive reinforcements for adaptive behavior, usually as a consequence of the loss of a major reinforcer which results in reduction of the total behavioral repertoire, not just a reduction of one or two responses. A social skills deficit may prevent a depressed person from coping with such a reduced reinforcement schedule. In addition, aversive control (i.e., punishment, avoidance, and escape) may also be associated with depressive behavior (Moss and Boren, 1972). Lazarus (1974) supplements this viewpoint by considering depressives to be on an extinction schedule resulting in a weakened behavioral repertoire. Depression ensues when the missing reinforcer is a "pivotal link" in the person's reinforcement repertoire. He also notes that depressives undertake tasks they fail to complete, thereby failing to receive positive reinforcement. In addition, depressed behavior is reinforced by others (e.g. with sympathy, concern and attention), thereby facilitating further self-defeating behavior.

Costello argues that the general loss of interest in depression cannot be explained by the above theories which really only explain a loss of interest in those parts of the environment related to the reinforcer. He postulates a loss of reinforcer effectiveness, presumably due to biochemical or neurophysiological changes and/or to a disruption of a chain of behavior (Costello, 1972).

Seligman, Klein, and Miller (1976) offer a behavioral formulation for reactive depression based on an animal model termed "learned helplessness." They hypothesize that depression is a belief in one's own helplessness based on a conditioning history which fails to allow for positive control of the environment. Thus, after recurrent punishment or lack of positive reinforcement in the face of attempts at control, escape or avoidance, the individual comes to believe that his efforts are futile and does not assert himself; he becomes passive and hopeless. Furthermore, non-contingent positive events can produce helplessness and depression if the person believes that positive events are independent of his/her behavior. This is his explanation for "success depression." Seligman infers from this method that inducing the patient to discover that responding produces reinforcement is therapeutic; thus, therapy consists of reversing the negative cognitive set (Seligman et al., 1976). Blaney (1977) recently raised questions as to the specificity of the learned helplessness model for depression since increases in anxiety and/or hostility with a helplessness paradigm have been suggested by several studies. In addition, the usual helplessness-inducing manipulations may also decrease self-esteem (Blaney, 1977).

McLean conceptualizes depression as the consequence of ineffective coping used to remedy situational life problems. Thus, repeated goal frustrations lead to a feeling of little control over the environment, which in turn leads to anticipation of chronic failure and subsequent depressive symptomatology. His treatment consists of a highly structured, time-limited (12-week) package applied in 8–14 sessions. Depressed persons are presumed to be deficient in one or more of six skill problem areas: communication, behavioral productivity, social interaction, assertiveness, decision making and problem solving, and cognitive self-control, which are assessed with pretreatment questionnaires. Three skill deficit areas (communication, behavioral productivity, and social interactions) are treated in every patient, whereas the other three skill deficit areas are optionally treated depending on the assessment of the patient (McLean, 1976).

Lewinsohn and co-workers have approached depression through a social learning framework. Their model contains three assumptions: (1) a low rate of response-contingent positive reinforcement acts as an eliciting stimulus for some depressive behaviors; (2) the low rate of such reinforcements received by a person depends on the number of potentially reinforcing events in the environment, and the instrumental behavior (social skill) of the person to emit behaviors which will elicit reinforcements for him from his environment; (3) feelings of dysphoria occur when there is a lack of available reinforcers or when available reinforcers are not contingent on the person's behavior with social attention of others reinforcing "depressive" behavior (Lewinsohn & Graf, 1973).

Compared to non-depressed controls, depressives have a lower level of interpersonal activity in groups; reinforce others less frequently, skillfully and intelligently; emit shorter messages; elicit more negative than positive reactions from others; and interact with a more limited number of persons. However, whether these social skill deficits remain even when the individual is not depressed has not been answered. In addition, the causal relationship between activity and mood is doubtful since correlation studies have failed to show that drops in activities precede drops in mood level (Hammen & Glass, 1975). Furthermore, depressed subjects who were instructed to increase the frequency of pleasant activities showed less diminution of depression than subjects who only monitored their activity, although both groups maintained an equivalent level of pleasant activities. Further, those who increased activities reported a smaller frequency of "very enjoyable" activities. Thus, the conditions under which pleasant activities are increased seem to affect the impact of increased activity on mood (Lewinsohn, 1975).

Lewinsohn's model has given rise to a treatment strategy that is time-limited (up to 3-months), and involves home observation as an integral part of the treatment. Treatment is designed to increase the level of positive reinforcement for the patient. The guiding principle is to restore an adequate schedule of positive reinforcement for the quality, and the range of the patient's activities and interactions (Lewinsohn, 1975).

Cognitive Therapy   Beck's cognitive theory of depression views depression in terms of activation of three major thinking patterns (the cognitive triad) through which the person regards *himself,* his *experience* (his world) and his *future* in an unrealistically negative manner. These negative views are evident in the patient's moment-to-moment thinking and are hypothesized to maintain depression. In addition, these negative views are mutually reinforcing. The depressed person sees *himself* as deficient, inadequate, unworthy, and tends to attribute his unpleasant experiences to a physical, mental, or moral deficit in himself. He interprets his experiences in a distorted manner. He sees the *world* as making exorbitant demands on him or as presenting insurmountable obstacles to achieving his life goals. He systematically misinterprets situations in a negative way, construing his interactions with the environment as representing defeat or deprivation. Also, the depressed person anticipates that his current difficulties will continue indefinitely. He expects to fail and cannot see the *future* as more promising than his current reality (Beck, 1964).

The cognitive triad is viewed as explaining the signs and symptoms of the depressive syndrome. If the patient incorrectly thinks he is being rejected, he will react with the same affect that occurs with actual rejection. If he is pessimistic about the future and anticipates negative outcomes, he will feel low in energy, apathetic, and be reluctant to initiate various tasks. Suicidal wishes result from a desire to escape from what appears to be an unbearable situation or an insolvable problem. Seeing himself as inept, he overestimates the difficulty of normal tasks in life. He is indecisive because he believes any decisions he might make will be wrong (Beck, 1964).

These negative views are based on enduring concepts or *schemas,* which are inflexible, unspoken, general rules, beliefs or silent assumptions developed from early experience. These schemas form the basis for screening, weighing, categorizing and evaluating experiences, and for making judgments about situations. Judgments based on hypervalent schemas are distorted. Specific situations activate certain schemas and the activated schemas determine how the person evaluates the specific situation. Therefore, schemas increase a person's vulnerability to depression and account for the relapsing or recurrent nature of many depressions.

Finally, the cognitive model posits the existence of a number of logical errors in thinking that are evident in the depressed person's misinterpretation of events. *Arbitrary inference* refers to the process of drawing a conclusion in the absence of evidence to support the conclusion or when the evidence is contrary to the conclusion. *Selective abstraction* consists of focusing on a detail taken out of context and conceptualizing the whole experience on the basis of this element. *Over generalization* refers to a pattern of drawing a general conclusion the basis of a single incident. *Magnification or minimization* refers to assigning unusual importance to certain aspects of a situation and drawing an illogical conclusion from the situation. *Personalization* refers to the patient's tendency to relate external events (usually negative events) to himself without a basis for making such a connection. *Dichotomous thinking* refers to the tendency to think in terms of black and white or bipolar opposites (Beck, 1964, 1976).

A developmental hypothesis to explain the formation of a predisposition to depression is offered by the cognitive model. Accordingly, the child develops many attitudes about self and surroundings, some of which may be realistic and facilitate healthy adjustment while others deviate from reality and make the individual vulnerable to psychological disorders. An individual's concept about himself, the world and the future are based upon specific beliefs or assumptions derived from personal experience, identification with significant others, and perceptions of the attitudes of others. Once a particular belief is formed, it may form the basis for assumptions and cognitions that support these beliefs. Beliefs are reinforced by ongoing experience such that cognitions compatible with the beliefs are developed into enduring structures or schemas. An unpleasant life situation may then trigger schemas related to loss, negative expectancies, and self-blame. These schemas then stimulate related affective responses. These affects further energize the schemas to which they are connected. In phenomenological terms, the depressive's negative ideation leads to sadness; then sadness becomes a sign that life is painful and hopeless. Thus, negative interpretations of sadness further reinforce negative attitudes. Hence, a cycle is reproduced (Beck, 1974).

Correlational and experimental studies have shown that each of the elements of the cognitive triad is associated with depression (Hammen & Krantz, 1976). Several correlational studies show a relationship between depression and a negative interpretation of experience and that depression is associated with more frequent and rapid recall of negative events (Beck, 1964). Correlations between depression and a negative view of the future have been reported with projective testing (Hammen & Krantz, 1976). Evidence that negative cognitions precede mood in normals is offered by Weintraub, Segal, and Beck (1974). Finally, significant correlation between the severity of depression and the degree to which a person endorses these hypothesized dysfunctional depressogenic attitudes or schemas has been demonstrated (Weismann & Beck, 1977). Thus, there is empirical support for each of the ingredients of the cognitive model for depression (cognitive triad, structural errors of thinking and schemas), although more and particularly experimental studies are needed to test and expand this formulation.

Cognitive therapy for depression involves a short-term, time-limited intervention, usually requiring a maximum of 20 sessions in a period of 10–20 weeks. The therapist actively directs and focuses discussion on selected problem areas presented by the patient. Question, without argument or interrogation, is a major tool in the therapy. The therapeutic relationship is one of collaboration between the patient and the therapist. The technical approach to cognitive therapy is likened to a scientific investigation: (1) collecting data that are as reliable and valid as possible, (2) formulating hypotheses based on the data, (3) testing the hypotheses, and (4) revising hypotheses when indicated. The data on which cognitive therapy is based consists of the patients automatic thoughts, feelings and wishes which are referred to as the patient's cognitions. These are collected from oral reports of the patient's cognitions (including dreams) thoughts, images, and feelings experienced during therapy, and introspective material written by the patient as part of a homework assignment. Utilizing these automatic thoughts, the therapist helps the patient to identify or infer certain basic beliefs, attitudes and assumptions, which according to cognitive theory, shape automatic thoughts and images.

Cognitive therapy techniques are designed to facilitate changes in target symptoms of depression (e.g., inactivity, self-criticism, lack of gratification, suicidal wishes). In general, the therapy sessions proceed from a discussion of previously assigned homework to a focus on the patient's thinking and then to homework regarding treatment goals for the next session. Initially, behavioral changes (increased activity) is emphasized since severely depressed patients are often unable to engage in cognitive tasks. As the patient's concentration improves and the intensity of affect decreases, other cognitive techniques are introduced.

Specific cognitive therapy techniques include the Triple Column Technique in which the patient records the events associated with unpleasant affect as well as the actual cognitions or automatic thoughts associated with this dysphoria. He then attempts to answer these cognitions using concrete evidence (facts) to test the validity and reasonableness of each cognition. Then the evidence found against each specific cognition is examined. The therapist helps the patient categorize his cognitions under relevant themes that eventually tend to perseverate in a few stereotyped, self-defeating patterns. The patient learns to see his cognitions as psychological events or responses rather than as an accurate reflection of reality.

The later stages of cognitive therapy involve identification of chronic attitudes and assumptions by which the patient constructs and orders his/her experimental world. The content of these attitudes is inferred from the recurrent themes present in the patient's cognitive responses to specific situations. The patient learns to examine and assess the reasonableness of these attitudes based on the evidence for and against them. He/she is often asked to undertake homework to test out the validity or the degree to which the attitudes generally apply (Beck & Shaw, 1977).

The efficacy of cognitive therapy has been demonstrated in multiple studies. It has been reported to exceed or equal the therapeutic effects of imipramine (Rush et al., 1977) and amitriptyline (McLean & Hakstian, 1979). In addition, it exceeded the effects of relaxation training and short-term psychotherapy. Cognitive group therapy was more effective than wait list, behavioral, or client-centered therapy in group format (Shaw, 1977). Cognitive therapy appears to improve patients' views of themselves and their future and their cognitive distortions most uniquely (Blackburn & Bishop, 1979). In addition, cognitive therapy has a significantly lower drop-out rate than antidepressant pharmacotherapy at least in non-melancholic outpatients (Rush et al., 1977).

It is suspected that some, but clearly not all, patients are uniquely benefited by the combination of cognitive therapy and antidepressant medication. Other patients appear to benefit from cognitive therapy without medication. A third group do not respond at all to cognitive therapy. Clinical experience suggests that patients with impaired reality testing (e.g. hallucinations, delusions), reasoning abilities or memory functions (e.g. organic brain syndrome), those with borderline personality structures, and those with schizoaffective disorders will not respond to this treatment. In addition, melancholic depressions do not respond. In mild-moderately ill, nonpsychotic, non-bipolar depressed outpatients cognitive therapy effectively reduces the symptoms of the depressed syndrome.

Interpersonal Psychotherapy (IPT). IPT is another somewhat structured, treatment-manual-directed psychotherapy specifically designed for the treatment of depression. This treatment consists of at least once weekly 50-minute sessions. The therapy is time limited and focused on the social context of the depression rather than an exploration of intrapsychic material or past experiences. IPT is not yet as highly structured or specified as cognitive therapy, but it clearly provides more structure than "supportive," client-centered or psychodynamic therapies and appears to do as well or better in the treatment of depressed outpatients as pharmacotherapy in actually reducing the symptoms of the depressive syndrome (DiMascio, Weisman, Prusoff, Neu, Zwilling, & Klerman, 1971). Again, this conclusion is documented in nonendogenous depressions. IPT is not as effective as antidepressant medication in endogenous or melancholic depressions.

Relationship of Assessment to Treatment

Biological Indicators and Treatment Selection. Urinary 3-methyoxy-4-hydroxyphenylglycol (MHPG) is a major metabolite of brain norepinephrine (NE). Probably 50% of urinary MHPG is a direct product of brain NE metabolism and therefore may provide a useful index of brain NE. Pretreatment urinary MHPG concentration has been reported to be low in depressed patients who have a favorable response to the tricyclic antidepressants imipramine or desipramine, whereas amitriptyline responders have been reported to have normal or high pretreatment urinary MHPG (Beckman & Goodwin, 1975).

However, regardless of the urinary MHPG level, most patients with endogenous depression will respond to optimal treatment with a tricyclic drug. Thus, it is quite possible that many patients who fail to respond to a NE (noradrenergic) reuptake-blocking drug have normal or high urinary MHPG and may respond to a 5HT (serotonergic) reuptake-blocking drug, and vice versa.

The treatment implications of DST nonsuppression and sleep EEG findings in depression remain controversial. However, in one study, 41 patients were treated with tricyclic antidepressant medication of various types and their response was measured and then correlated with their pretreatment DST and sleep EEG findings. "Response" referred to complete or partial remission as judged by certain clinical rating scales. DST nonsuppression alone was associated with an 83% response rate, whereas a shortened REM latency of 60 minutes or less was associated with a 75% response rate. A 78% response rate was obtained when either or both biological markers were present. In patients without either marker, however, a 63% rate of response was noted. In summary then, these data suggest that biological treatments are more effective when (vegetative) endogenous symptoms and biological abnormalities are present (Beckman & Goodwin, 1975). A more thorough assessment of the relationship between particular biological markers and response to specific antidepressant medication is needed.

Psychological Indicators and Treatment Selection.   A history of "neurotic" traits has been reported by some to predict a poor response to antidepressants alone. However, those patients who suffer from a type of nonendogenous depression called "atypical" depression respond well to MAOI's. In general, however, cognitive symptoms, such as mood, ideation, helplessness, guilt, and a negative outlook, are affected by psychotherapy (Di Mascio, et al., 1979).

Some of the disagreement among investigators in this area may result from differing conceptions of "neurotic traits." Some patients who are diagnosed as having neurotic depression simply because the illness is relatively mild may also have weight loss, middle or late insomnia, and/or other endogenous symptoms and may well respond to antidepressants. In addition, chronic anxiety and obsessiveness when associated with endogenous depression have correlated with a positive response to antidepressants. It is clear then that a history of at least certain "neurotic" traits does not preclude a positive antidepressant response (VonZerson, 1977).

Combined Biological and Psychological Treatments.   Whether a combined approach offers unique advantages over either modality alone is far from answered. The answer will undoubtedly depend upon the types of disorders, the nature of the psychotherapy, and the choice of chemotherapy. Endogenous depressions may well respond best to a combination of individual psychotherapy or cognitive therapy plus chemotherapy. Nonendogenous depressions may respond well to either form of intervention alone. Apparently, chemotherapies are not as effective at addressing associated problems (e.g. social adjustment, marital discord) as are specific targeted psychotherapies. On the other hand, vegetative symptoms may improve with specific psychotherapies, but in general require and preferentially respond to chemotherapy.

Summary

It has become apparent that affective illness is heterogeneous with regard to history of present illness, clinical presentation, psychology, biology and treatment response. New biomedical techniques to improve the descriptive diagnosis and biological characterization of the affective disorders are now available. More will be forthcoming. New short-term psychotherapies have been developed and are being tested. Matching treatment to patient and illness will be an arena of future research and growing advantage to all patients concerned.

REFERENCES

Albala, A. A., Greden, J. F., Tarika, J., & Carroll, B. J. Changes in serial dexamethasone suppression tests among unipolar depressives receiving ECT. *Society of Biological Psychiatry Scientific Proceedings,* Abstract #2, P. 34, 1980.

Allen, M. Twin studies of affective illness. *Archives of General Psychiatry, 33,* 1476–1478, 1976.

American Psychiatric Association, *Diagnostic and Statistical Manual of Mental Disorders,* 3rd Ed. Washington, D.C., 1980.

Avery, D., & Winokur, G. Mortality in depressed patients treated with ECT and antidepressants. *Archives of General Psychiatry,* 1976, *33,* 1029.

Barchas, J. D., Berger, P. A., Ciaranello, R. D., & Elliott, G. R. (Eds.) *Psychopharmacology. From theory to practice.* New York: Oxford University Press, 1977.

Beck, A. T. Thinking and depression: II. Theory and therapy, *Archives General Psychiatry,* 1964, *10,* 561–571.

Beck, A. T. The development of depression: A cognitive model. In R. Friedman & M. Katz (Eds.), *Psychology of depression: Contemporary theory and research.* Washington, D.C.: Winston-Wiley, 1974.

Beck, A. T. Cognitive therapy and the emotional disorders. New York: International Universities Press, 1976.

Beck, A. T., & Beamsderfer, A. Assessment of depression: The depression inventory. In P. Pichot (Ed.), *Modern problems in pharmacopsychiatry,* (Vol. 7), Basal, Switzerland: Harger, 1974.

Beck, A. T., Brady, J. P., & Quen, J. M. *The history of depression.* New York: Insight Communications, Inc., 1977.

Beck, A. T., & Shaw, B. F. Cognitive approaches to depression. In A. Ellis & R. Grieger (Eds.), *Handbook of rational emotive theory and practice.* Springer: New York, 1977.

Beckman, H., & Goodwin, F. K. Antidepressant response to tricyclics and urinary MHPG in unipolar depressed patients. *Archives of General Psychiatry,* 1975, *32,* 17-21.

Beigel, A., & Murphy, D. L. Unipolar and bipolar affective illness: Differences in clinical characteristics accompanying depression. *Archives of General Psychiatry,* 1971, *24,* 215-229.

Blackburn, I., & Bishop, S. *A comparison of cognitive therapy, pharmacotherapy, and their combination in depressed outpatients.* Paper presented at the annual meeting of the Society for Psychotherapy Research, Oxford, England, July 1979.

Blaney, P. H. Contemporary theories of depression: Critique and comparison. *Journal of Abnormal Psychology,* 1977, *86,* 203-223.

Brown, W. A., Johnston, R., & Mayfield, D. The 24-hour dexamethasone suppression test in a clinical setting: relationship to diagnosis, symptoms, and response to treatment. *American Journal of Psychiatry, 136,* 543, 1979.

Buchsbaum, M. Average evoked response augmenting/reducing in schizophrenia and affective disorders. In D. X. Freedman (Ed.) *The Biology of the Major Psychoses: A Comparative Analysis,* New York: Raven Press, 1975.

Cadoret, R. J. Evidence for genetic inheritance of primary affective disorders in adoptees. *American Journal of Psychiatry, 135,* 463-466, 1978.

Carroll, B. J. Studies with hypothalmic-pituitary-stimulation tests in depression. In B. Davies, B. J. Carroll, & R. M. Mowbray (Eds.), *Depressive illness: Some research studies.* Springfield, Illinois: Thomas, 149-201, 1972.

Carroll, B. J. The dexamethasone suppression test for melancholia. *British Journal of Psychiatry,* in press.

Carroll, B. J., Feinberg, M., Greden, J. F., Tarika, J., Albala, A. A., Haskett, R. F., James, N. M. I., Krontrol, Z., Lohr, N., Steiner, M., deVigne, J. P., & Young, E. A specific laboratory test for the diagnosis of melcholia. *Archives of General Psychiatry, 38,* 15-22, 1981.

Carroll, B. J., Feinberg, M., Smouse, P. E., Rawson, S. G., & Greden, J. F. The Carroll Scale for Depression. *British Journal of Psychiatry, 138,* 194-209, 1981.

Cohn, C. K., Dunner, D. L., & Axelrod, J. Reduced catechol-o-methyltransfrase activity in red blood cells of women with primary affective disorder. *Science,* 1970, *170,* 1323-1324.

Costello, C. G. Depression: Loss of reinforcers or loss reinforcer effectiveness? *Behavior Therapy,* 1972, *3,* 240-247.

Crow, T. J., & Johnstone, E. C. Electroconvulsive therapy: efficacy, mechanisms of action, and adverse effects. In E. S. Paykel & A. Cooper (Eds.), *Psychopharmacology of affective disorders.* Oxford: Oxford University Press, 1979.

DiMascio, A., Weisman, M., Prusoff, B., Neu, C., Zwilling, M., & Klerman, G. Differential symptom reduction by drugs and psychotherapy in acute depression. *Archives of General Psychiatry,* 1979, *36,* 1450-1456.

Dorzah, J., Baker, M., Cadoret, R., & Winokur, G. Depressive disease: familial psychiatric illness. *American Journal of Psychiatry, 133,* 905-908, 1971.

Ellman, S. J., Roffwarg, H. P., Sachar, E. J., Finkelstein, J., Kurti, J., & Hellman, L. *Effects of REM deprivation on cortisol and growth hormone levels.* Paper delivered at the Association for the Psychophysiological Study of Sleep, Santa Fe, N.M., 1970.

Endicott, J., & Spitzer, R. L. A diagnostic interview: The schedule for affective disorders and schizophrenia. *Archives of General Psychiatry, 35,* 837-844, 1978.

Fieve, R. R., & Dunner, D. L. Unipolar and bipolar affective states in the nature and treatment of depression. In F. F. Flach & S. G. Draghi (Eds.), New York: Wiley, 1975.

Frankel, F. H. Current perspectives on ECT: A discussion. *American Journal of Psychiatry,* 1977, *134,* 9.

Gershon, S., & Shopsin, B. (Eds.) *Lithium: Its role in psychiatry research and treatment.* New York: Plenum Press, 1973.

Goodwin, F. K., Murphy, D. L., Dunner, D. L., & Bunney, W. E., Jr., Lithium response in unipolar versus bipolar depression. *American Journal of Psychiatry,* 1972, *129,* 44-47.

Goodwin, F. K., Post, R. M., Dunner, D. L., & Gordon, E. K. Cerebrospinal fluid amines metabolites in affective illness: the probenecid technique. *American Journal of Psychiatry*, 1973, *120*, 73–79.

Hamilton, M. a Rating Scale for depression symptoms. *J. Neurol. Neurosurg. Psychiatry 23*, 56–61, 1960.

Hammen, C. L., & Glass, D. R. Depression, activity, and evaluation of reinforcement. *Journal of Abnormal Psychology, 84*, 718–721, 1974.

Hammen, C. L., & Krantz, S. Effects of success and failure on depressive cognitions. *Journal of Abnormal Psychology, 85*, 577–586, 1976.

Hesche, J., & Raeder, E. Electroconvulsive therapy in Denmark. *British Journal of Psychiatry*, 1976, *128*, 241.

Hollister, L. E. *The Clinical Use of Psychotherapeutic Drugs*. Springfield, Illinois: Charles C Thomas, 1973.

Hollon, S. D., Beck, A. T., Kovacs, M., & Rush, A. J. *Cognitive therapy of depression: an outcome study with six-month followup*. Paper presented at the annual meeting of the Society for Psychotherapy Research, Madison, Wisc., June 1977.

Hollon, S. D., & Kendall, P. C. Cognitive self-statements in depression: development of an automatic thoughts questionnaire. *Cognitive Therapy & Research*, in press, 1980.

Jefferson, J. W., & Griest, J. H. *Primer of lithium therapy*. Baltimore: Williams and Wilkins, 1977.

Kallmann, F. *Heredity in health and mental disorder*. New York: Norton, 1953.

Kirkegaard, C., Bjorum, N., Cohn, D., & Lauridsen, U. Thyrotropin-Releasing Hormone (TRH) stimulation test in manic-depressive illness. *Archives of General Psychiatry, 35*, 1017–1021, 1978.

Kirkegaard, C., Norlem, N., Lauridsen, U. B., & Borung, N. Prognostic value of thyrotropin-releasing hormone stimulation test in endogenous depression. *Acta Psychiatrica Scandinavia*, 1975, *52*, 170–177.

Kupfer, D. J. REM latency: A psychobiologic marker for primary depressive disease. *Biological Psychiatry, 11*, 159–174, 1976.

Kupfer, D. J., Foster, F. G., Coble, P., McPartland, R. J., & Ulrich, R. F. The application of EEG sleep for the differential diagnosis of affective disorders. *American Journal of Psychiatry, 135*, 69–74, 1978.

Lazarus, A. A. Multimodel treatment of Depression. *Behavior Ther. 4*, 549–554, 1974.

Leff, M. J., Roatch, J. R., & Bunney, W. E. Environmental factors preceding the onset of severe depression. *Psychiatry*, 1970, *33*, 293–301.

Lehmann, H. Epidemiology of depressive disorders. In R. R. Fieve (Ed.), *Depression in the 70's*. Princeton: Exerpta Medica, 1971.

Lewinsohn, P. M. The behavioral study and treatment of depression. In M. Hersen, R. M. Eister, & P. M. Miller (Eds.), *Progress in behavior modification (Vol. 1)*. New York: Academic Press, 1975.

Lewinsohn, P. M., & Graf, M. Pleasant activities and depression. *Journal of Consulting and Clinical Psychology*, 1973, *41*, 216–268.

Lipowski, Z. J. Psychiatry of somatic diseases: epidemiology, pathogenesis, classification. *Comprehensive Psychiatry*, 1975, *16*, 105–124.

McCabe, M. S. ECT in the treatment of mania: a controlled study. *American Journal of Psychiatry*, 1976, *133*, 6.

McLean, P. Decision-making in the behavioral treatment of depression. In P. O. Davidson (Ed.), *Behavioral management of anxiety, depression and pain*. New York: Brunner/Mazel, 1976.

McLean, P. D., & Hakstian, A. R. Clinical depression: Comparative efficacy of outpatient treatments. *Journal of Consulting and Clinical Psychology*, 1979, *47*(5), 818–836.

Mendels, J. Biological aspects of affective illness. In S. Arieti & E. B. Brady (Eds.), *American handbook of psychiatry*. New York: Basic Books, 1974, 491–523.

Mendlewicz, J., & Raines, J. Morbidity risk and genetic transmission in manic depressive illness. *American Journal of Human Genetics, 26,* 692–701, 1974.

Meyer, A. *Collected papers of Adolf Meyer.* (4 Vols.) Baltimore: Johns Hopkins Press, 1948–1952.

Moss, G. R., & Boren, J. J. Depression as a model for behavioral analysis. *Comp. Psychiatry,* 1972, *13,* 581–590.

Robins, L. *Deviant children grown up.* Baltimore: Williams & Wilkins, 1966.

Robinson, D. S., Nies, A., Ravaris, C. L., Lamborn, K. Treatment response to MAO inhibitors. In M. Lipton, A. DiMascio, & K. E. Killan (Eds.), *Psychopharmacology : a generation of progress.* New York: Raven Press, 1978.

Rush, A. J. The why's and how's of diagnosing the depressions. *Biological Psychology Bulletin,* 1975, *4,* 47–61.

Rush, A. J. *Biological markers and treatment response in affective disorders.* Paper presented at the McLean Hospital Symposium at the APA, New Orleans, Louisiana, May, 1981.

Rush, A. J., & Beck, A. T. Adults with affective disorders. In M. Hersen & Bellack, A. S. (Eds.), *Behavioral therapy in the psychiatric setting.* Baltimore: Williams and Wilkins, 1978. Chapter 10.

Rush, A. J., Beck, A. T., Kovacs, M., & Hollon, S. Comparative efficacy of cognitive therapy and pharmacotherapy in the treatment of depressed outpatients. *Cognitive Therapy and Research, 1,* 17–37, 1977.

Rush, A. J., Giles, D. E., Roffwarg, H. P., & Parker, C. R. Sleep EEG and dexamethasone suppression test findings in outpatients with unipolar major depressive disorder. *Biological Psychiatry, 17,* 327–341, 1982.

Sacher, E. J., Hellman, L., Roffwarg, H. P., Halpern, F. S., Fukushima, D., & Gallagher, T. E. Disrupted 24-Hour patterns of cortisol secretion in psychotic depression. *Archives of General Psychiatry, 28,* 19–24, 1973.

Seligman, M. E., Klein, D. C., & Miller, W. R. Depression. In H. Leitenberg (Ed.), *Handbook of behavior modification and behavior therapy.* Englewood Cliffs, N.J.: Prentice-Hall, 1976.

Shaw, B. F. Comparison of cognitive therapy and behavior therapy in the treatment of depression. *Journal of Consulting and Clinical Psychology,* 1977, *45,* 543–551.

Stokes, P. E. Studies on the control of adrenocortical function in depression. In T. A. Williams, M. M. Katz, & J. A. Shield (Eds.), *Recent advances in the psychobiology of depressive illness.* Washington, D.C.: U.S. Department of Health, Education, and Welfare Publication 70-9053, 199–220, 1972.

Squire, L. R., & Chance, P. M. Memory functions in six to nine months after electroconvulsive therapy. *Archives of General Psychiatry,* 1975, *32,* 1557.

Takahashi, S., Kondo, H., Yoshimura, M., & Ochi, Y. Thyrotropin responses to TRH in depressive episodes. *Folia Psychiatrica Neurologica* Japan 28, 335–365, 1974.

Von Zersen, D. Premorbid personality and affective psychoses. In G. D. Burrows (Ed.), *Handbook of studies in depression.* New York: Excepta Medica, 1977.

Watkins, J. T., & Rush, A. J. Cognitive Response Test. Unpublished manuscript.

Weintraub, M., Segal, R. M., & Beck, A. T. An investigation of cognition and affect in the depressive experiences of normal men. *Journal of Consulting and Clinical Psychology, 42,* 211, 1974.

Weissman, A. N. *The Dysfunctional Attitude Scale: An Inventory designed to measure the relationship between cognitive distortions and emotional disorders.* Unpublished manuscript, University of Pennsylvania, *Dissertation Abstracts* International, 40, 1389–1390B, 1979 (University Microfilm No. 79-19533).

Weissman, A. W., & Beck, A. T. *A preliminary investigation of the relationship between dysfunctional attitudes and depression.* Unpublished manuscript, University of Pennsylvania, 1977.

Winokur, G., Behar, D., VanValkenburg, C., & Lowry, M. Is a familial definition of depression both feasible and valid? *The Journal of Nervous and Mental Disease, 166*(11), 764–768, 1978.

Winokur, G., Clayton, P., & Reich, J. *Manic Depressive Illness*. St. Louis: C. V. Mosbey, 1969.

Winokur, G., Reich, T., Rimmer, J., & Pitts, Ferris N. Alcoholism: III. Diagnosis and familial psychiatric illness in 250 alcoholic probands. *Archives of General Psychiatry, 23,* 104–111, 1970.

Zung, W. W. K. A self-rating depression scale. *Archives of General Psychiatry, 12,* 63–70, 1965.

13 Lifestyle, Behavioral Health, and Heart Disease

Jack F. Hollis
William E. Connor
Joseph D. Matarazzo
Departments of Medical Psychology and Medicine
University of Oregon School of Medicine
Portland, Oregon

INTRODUCTION

Behavioral health appears to represent a challenging and rapidly developing area of application for behavioral specialists (Matarazzo, 1982). In his review of some historical precursors of these recent developments, Matarazzo (1980) offered the following description of the field:

> Behavioral health is an interdisciplinary field dedicated to promoting a philosophy of health that stresses *individual responsibility* in the application of behavioral and biomedical science knowledge and techniques to the *maintenance* of health and the *prevention* of illness and dysfunction by a variety of self-initiated individual or shared activities (p. 813).

As in many new areas, opportunities for innovation abound, as do barriers to effective action. A first step for psychologists and other professionals who are preparing themselves to work at the interface of such diverse fields as psychology, medicine, nutrition, and exercise is to become familiar with the basic terminology, concepts and issues central to the interdisciplinary effort they will be concerned with. As an aid toward that end, our purpose here is to acquaint the reader with some of the background and rationale and a few of the practical issues related to the prevention of disease and promotion of health through lifestyle modification. In the first section, we consider some of the evidence implicating various habits and lifestyles in the etiology of disease in general and heart disease in particular. We concentrate on those habits and their related conditions that seem particularly ammenable to change. In the next section, representative strategies, models, and ideas relevant to the promotion of healthier lifestyles are discussed along with their particular applications and limitations. Finally, a community-based nutrition intervention project known as the Family Heart Study Alternative Diet Program, is described briefly as one prototype (involving psychology, cardiology, and nutrition) for effecting health behavior change on a relatively large scale.

THE CARDIOVASCULAR DISEASE EPIDEMIC

Americans currently devote nearly 10% of the gross national product (GNP), or roughly $1,000 per person, each year on health care (Kristein, Arnold, & Wynder, 1977; Vischl, Jones, Shank, & Lima, 1980). The fact that we invest more per capita on health than any other nation testifies to the importance that Americans place on good health and longevity. Paradoxically, the National Heart and Lung Institute Task Force on Arteriosclerosis (1971) has ranked the United States far below the healthiest of the industrialized countries. It appears that even sophisticated treatment approaches have not adequately dealt with the prevalent diseases of our time. In this regard, the evidence is overwhelming that many of our current health problems (e.g., heart disease, lung cancer, etc.) are largely the result of complex culturally-embedded behaviors and environmental influences; in short, our modern way of life.

Historically, prevention rather than treatment has been responsible for society's major advances in the control of disease. For example, early in this century, rampant infectious diseases such as tuberculosis, influenza and poliomyelitis were among the major public health problems. Improved sanitation, nutrition, and general living conditions as well as the introduction of specific vaccines have been responsible for a dramatic decline in mortality due to these diseases (Califano, 1979b; McKeown, 1979). Thus, these prevention oriented approaches required input from many elements of society including physicians, agriculturalists, policy makers, and others to bring about the individual and environmental changes that were called for.

Unfortunately, the health gains achieved during the first half of the century have been offset by a dramatic increase in mortality due to chronic degenerative diseases such as coronary heart disease (CHD), cancer and stroke. Potential artifacts such as changes in death-reporting procedures or our country's increasing numbers of adult persons cannot fully account for the 50% increase in CHD mortality that occurred between 1940 and 1960 (Gordon & Thom, 1975; Lewis, 1980). Age-adjusted increases were greatest among white men (26%), nonwhite men (48%) and nonwhite women (34%). No increase was noted for white women despite their changing roles in the society (Haynes & Feinleib, 1980).

The increase in CHD peaked in 1963 and then appeared to plateau until 1967. While revisions of the 1968 Eighth International Classification of Diseases make subsequent comparisons difficult, it is clear that age-adjusted death rate from ischemic (i.e. coronary) heart disease actually *declined* 21% between 1968 and 1976 (Rosenberg & Klebba, 1979). The fact that death rates from other cardiovascular diseases and "all causes" also decreased, suggests that this decline is also real and not an artifact of reclassification. Explanations of these favorable trends have been offered (Gordon & Thom, 1975; Lancet Editorial, 1980; Walker, 1977) and though no clear consensus has been reached, large scale lifestyle changes may, in part, be responsible.

It should be emphasized that whereas the decline in CHD is significant and certainly welcomed, it should not blind us to the considerable toll this disease continues to take. At age 50, for example, Americans still have a 50% chance of dying of CHD. Thus, CHD clearly remains the primary cause of mortality in the United States. Together, the vascular diseases (CHD, stroke and arteriosclerosis) accounted for over 50% of all deaths in 1973 (Gordon, Kannel, McGee, & Dawber, 1974). Many of these deaths may be considered "premature" (Gordon & Kannel, 1971) in that they strike during the middle years of peak productivity and vitality. It has been estimated (Cooper & Rice, 1976) that in 1972 diseases of the circulatory system cost the U.S. $40 billion in both direct (the largest component) and indirect costs such as lost work years. The next most costly health conditions were accidents ($27 billion) and cancer ($17 billion). The total direct cost of health services in this country in 1972 was about $75 billion which represents a 300% increase since 1963. The costs in 1980 now exceed $200 billion (Rogers, 1980).

Whereas such increased expenditures have undoubtedly improved medical treatment for many patients, it is not clear that proportionally greater health benefits and reduced mortality have always been realized. For example, the results of randomized, controlled trials comparing sophisticated coronary care units for the treatment of uncomplicated myocardial infarctions (i.e. heart attacks) to less expensive and disruptive "home management" techniques have consistently shown no overall benefit for these more expensive approaches in terms of lives saved (Hill, Hampton, & Mitchell, 1978; Mather, Morgan, Pearson, Read, Shaw, Steed, Thorne, Lawrence, & Riley, 1976; Mather, Pearson, Read, Shaw, Steed, Thorne, Jones, Guerrier, Eraut, McHugh, Chowdhury, Jafary, & Wallace, 1971). Even if elaborate medical treatments were completely effective, about 60% of those now dying from CHD would still not benefit since they succumb suddenly, outside the hospital, before medical assistance arrives (Feinleib & Davidson, 1972; Gordon & Kannel, 1971).

The nature and causes of heart disease are such that most experts are coming to realize that effective solutions are likely to be found at the interface of the behavioral and medical sciences rather than through further advances in traditional medical care alone. Psychologists, nutritionists, health educators, communications specialists and policy makers must now join physicians if significant progress is to be made. In the Forward Plan for Health, the Department of Health, Education and Welfare (1978) has indicated: "It has become clear that only by preventing disease, rather than treating it later, can we hope to achieve any major improvement in the Nation's health." To this end, the core of the matter becomes the alteration of those individual behaviors and conditions which foster atherosclerosis.

Habits and Heart Disease

A variety of factors have been repeatedly associated with an increased risk of cardiovascular disease (Pooling Project Research Group, 1978; Report of Inter-Society Commission For Heart Disease Resources, 1970). These include hereditary factors such as hyperlipidemia (e.g., high plasma cholesterol levels) and being male, as well as the aging process which provides for a longer exposure to the cummulative effects of the atherogenic process. Of greater interest to the readers of this chapter are those factors that are potentially modifiable. Converging lines of epidemiologic, clinical, and laboratory evidence have all underlined the independent etiologic significance of several such factors. Those best documented include cigarette smoking (Califano, 1979a; Gordon et al., 1974), elevated levels of serum cholesterol and the low density lipoprotein (LDL) fraction of cholesterol along with decreased levels of high density lipoprotein (HDL) (Connor & Connor, 1972; Lewis, 1980; Report of Inter-Society Commission, 1970), and mild to severe hypertension (e.g., Dawber, 1975). There remains little question that these factors bear powerful, independent and almost certainly causal relationships to the development and onset of CHD. Their impact in terms of potential morbidity and mortality seems to increase synergistically rather than additively when two or more are present in the same individual (Gordon, Sorlie, & Kannel, 1971). Other characteristics associated with an increased CHD risk include obesity (Dawber, 1975), sedentary living (Frank, Weinblatt, Shapiro, & Sager, 1966; Paffenbarger, Hale, Brand, & Hyde, 1977), and a chronically stressed Type A lifestyle (Haynes, Manning, & Kannel, 1980; Rosenman, Brand , Jenkins, Friedman, Straus, & Wurm, 1975). Figure 13.1 represents a schemata of the major risk factors and the three stages of development of CHD. The first key stage is the presence of elevated cholesterol (i.e., hyperlipidemia) which is brought on by both genetic and dietary factors. The second stage occurs with time and involves actual vascular pathology; atherosclerosis itself. This stage is largely asymptomatic. The third stage represents clinical CHD. Other risk factors such as hypertension, cigarette smoking, stress, and lack of exercise impinge upon both stages II and III to accelerate the basic disease process. All are important risk factors and, although the precise pathogenic mechanisms remain to be specified, there is a growing body of evidence that a generally prudent style

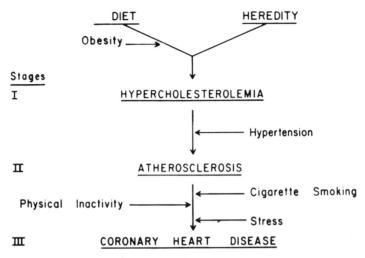

FIG. 13.1.   Factors in the Development of Coronary Heart Disease.

of life is related to lower age-specific mortality and improved overall health (Belloc, 1973; Belloc & Breslow, 1972; Lalonde, 1974; Lewis, 1980).

A perusal of the above list of established risk factors confirms the dominant role of personal habits and appetites in the development of the most frequent causes of death. Considering the top four causes of mortality (CHD, cancer, stroke, and accident), lifestyle emerges as the largest single contributor eclipsing inherited bodily dysfunctions, the environment and the organization of health service delivery (Dever, 1975). But what evidence is there that people, dissatisfied with their current or future profiles, have real options for change available to them that will improve their risk status?

People certainly have quit smoking. In the years following the 1964 Surgeon General's report (DHEW, 1964), the percentage of American *men* smoking cigarettes decreased from 53% to 32% (Califano, 1979a). The importance of this trend is highlighted in a recent report (Friedman, Dales, & Ury, 1979) of an 11-year prospective study of over 4000 individuals in a health care system. Smokers were 4.7 times as likely to develop CHD as nonsmokers, even after controlling for 48 other risk factors and characteristics. For ex-smokers, the relative odds were only 1.86 greater than that of nonsmokers. Assuming these results apply to the general population, then the over 30 million Americans who have given up tobacco since 1964 already have dramatically reduced their risk status.

It is well known that hypertension is frequently associated with a chronic overconsumption of salt (sodium) (Tobian, 1979) and obesity (Reisin, Abel, Modan, Silverberg, Eliahou, & Modan, 1978) and that adherence to a combined approach involving the maintenance of ideal weight, sodium restriction, and medication when necessary, effectively controls high blood pressure in most patients with this problem. A randomized 5-year controlled clinical trial has recently been concluded (Hypertension Detection and Follow-up Program Cooperative Group, 1979) showing that the effective control of even borderline hypertension produced a 20% drop in overall mortality, a 26% drop in mortality due to CHD, and a 45% decrease in cerebrovascular mortality during the study period. The "control" group was not a no-treatment control inasmuch as these individuals were referred to their physicians for standard (i.e., less aggressive) hypertensive treatment. These results then, impressive as they are, still vastly underestimate the importance of lowering elevated blood pressure.

Similarly, sedentary living has been associated with increased coronary risk. For example, the mortality rate of men with more sedentary jobs was shown to be one-third higher than that for active cargo handlers (Paffenbarger, Laughlin, Gima, & Black, 1970). Physical exercise has been shown to contribute to weight control (Stalonas, Johnson, & Christ, 1978), the protective high density lipoprotein (HDL) cholesterol, (Wood, Haskell, Klein, Lewis, Stern, & Farquhar, 1976) and reduction of triglyceride levels (Oscai, Patterson, Bogard, Beck, & Rothermel, 1972).

The causal role of diet in the development of CHD has been the subject of continuing controversy despite a large body of supportive evidence. First, cultures around the world are known to vary markedly in both their rates of CHD and their per capita intake of certain nutrients. In addition, strong positive associations have been observed between CHD mortality rates and the average consumption of dietary cholesterol, animal protein, animal fat, total fat, meat, eggs, and total number of calories (Connor, 1979b; Hegsted, McGanely, Myers, & Stare, 1965; Keys & Parlin, 1966). In laboratory experiments, altering these same dietary factors has been found to consistently affect plasma cholesterol concentrations in man (Connor & Connor, 1972) and in animals (e.g., Moore & Williams, 1964) and to accelerate the development of atherosclerotic lesions in sub-human species (Taylor, Paton, & Cox, 1963). Recent work also indicates that substantial modification of a habitual high-fat high-cholesterol diet can lead to regression of atherosclerotic plaques in animals (Armstrong, Warner, & Connor, 1970). Epidemiological investigations have, in addition, repeatedly shown an important independent relationship between level of plasma cholesterol and risk of developing CHD. This is true both cross culturally (Keys, 1980) and within our own population (Kannel, McGee, & Gordon, 1976).

Current evidence leaves little question that (1) dietary intake of fats and cholesterol affect plasma cholesterol levels, and (2) that higher levels of plasma cholesterol are predictive of increased risk. The primary element of the "diet-heart" hypothesis which remains to be adequately tested is the effectiveness of altering diet to prevent new cases of CHD. Nevertheless, the evidence of the role of diet in the development of disease was sufficient to lead the American Heart Association, in 1964, to recommend a mass change in the American diet in order

TABLE 13.1
The Effects of Various Nutrients upon the
Plasma Cholesterol Concentration

Nutrient	Effect on Cholesterol
Cholesterol	Increases
Saturated fat	Increases
Polyunsaturated fat	Decreases
Total fat	Increases
Carbohydrates (starch and sugars)	Minimal long-term effect
Fiber*	No effect
Protein	No effect

*In amounts normally consumed by humans.

to prevent CHD and other diseases of overconsumption. Connor and Connor (1977) have proposed an "Alternative Diet" consistent with these recommendations. This eating pattern is low in cholesterol, saturated fat, and total calories. The effects of these and other factors on plasma cholesterol levels are summarized in Table 13.1. Animal products such as meat, egg yolk, and high fat dairy products are deemphasized in favor of whole grains, legumes, vegetables, fruits, and skim milk products. Further details of the Alternative Diet will be provided in a later section. In conclusion, it is now clear that safe, sensible, and satisfying eating styles are available which do reduce plasma cholesterol and predicted risk of disease.

It is worth noting that since the 1964 Surgeon General's smoking and American Heart Association's dietary recommendations, the U.S. per capita consumption of tobacco, animal fats, butter, milk, cream and eggs have all decreased, whereas the use of vegetable oils has increased (Department of Agriculture, 1976; Taylor, Romo, Jacobs, & Blackburn, 1975). Regular exercise is also more in evidence, having become a daily routine for many Americans. Concurrent with these lifestyle changes, the National Center for Health Statistics (Abraham, Johnson, & Carroll, 1977) has uncovered an associated systematic decline in average serum cholesterol for the general population. Options for lifestyle change clearly do exist and large segments of our population have already acted on them to some degree. For now, we may only speculate about the cause and effect contribution these changes may have made to the declining CHD mortality.

Controversy, Cost, and Common Sense

In summary, it is now possible to identify a number of common behaviors associated with conditions that elevate one's risk of premature death or disability. We know that it is practical and safe, although admittedly difficult, to intervene and alter these behaviors that are associated with high risk. We also know that a large segment of our population has already made significant progress in this respect. And yet, in spite of an enormous research effort and the wealth of evidence implicating the role of habits in disease, some authorities still question the value of primary prevention programs at the present time (Ahrens, 1979; Borhani, 1977; Corday & Corday, 1975). One basis for this skepticism is a perceived lack of clear-cut evidence that it is possible, much less cost effective, to implement and maintain long-term health behavior change in most target groups. Herein lies the challenge for the behavioral scientist; for unless it is demonstrated that behavioral technology and social action are capable of fostering stable health-promoting lifestyles in a cost efficient fashion, the prospect for preventive medicine in these areas will be dim.

Experts also disagree on whether to apply prevention efforts only to those identified as high risk (or otherwise susceptible) or to the population as a whole. However, a strong case has been made (Connor, 1979a; Epstein, 1977) that our entire population is at risk and that efforts directed at, for example, the top 10% of those at risk would miss the majority (75%) of Americans who die of CHD but who have lower, though still not optimal, levels of various risk factors. Furthermore, by singling out only those with very high risk levels for intervention, a prescription for healthy living becomes a kind of treatment for a special condition which few see themselves as having. For example, it is not uncommon for families to cook special foods for a member "afflicted" with a high risk profile (e.g., high blood pressure or cholesterol) while the eating habits of the rest of the family remain unchanged. Besides making change difficult for the high risk individual, preparation of different meals for different family members works against the recommended general acceptance of a prudent lifestyle.

From a public health standpoint, what is called for is a large-scale community approach that will impact both the younger, healthy and less susceptible person, as well as those currently at risk. The goal of such programs should be to encourage entire families (especially children and young adults) to develop patterns early on that will minimize the risk of disease and maximize the quality of life over the entire age span.

Another controversy over the value of prevention centers around the fact that, as yet, we have no scientific demonstration that lowering most risk factors actually decreases mortality. One might argue, for example, that atherosclerosis is a progressive disease and that by middle age, the damage is already done and mostly irreversible. If this is true, efforts to alter risk factors might then best be confined to children who have not yet sustained significant arterial damage. In the absence of hard experimental "proof," we simply have no way to rule out the possibility that even a successful intervention program would still have little or no effect on disease rates.

One must then ask, however, what constitutes proof or acceptable evidence of the value of primary prevention. When will such evidence be available and what measures are called for in the meantime to react responsibly to our continuing health crisis? Ideally, the demonstration of the value of intervention would consist of several randomized single factor, controlled clinical trials in which one factor (e.g., serum cholesterol) is manipulated within a large group over many years and the effects on long-term morbidity and mortality are evaluated. A specific example is the Hypertension Detection and Follow-up Program (Hypertension Detection and Follow-up Program Cooperative Group, 1979), described earlier. This demonstration of the value of controlling even mild hypertension will almost certainly encourage more aggressive treatment of borderline hypertension in the community and thereby significantly reduce mortality.

Unfortunately, a similar study on the control of elevated cholesterol was considered by the NIH and then rejected (Diet-Heart Review Panel of the National Heart Institute, 1969) because of the enormous sample size, extended follow-up period, and the prohibitive costs that would be required. Instead, a combined cholesterol, smoking, and blood pressure intervention program was recommended. Such a multifactor approach has a substantially greater predicted power to quickly influence disease outcomes and it thereby greatly reduces the cost of demonstrating the efficacy of primary prevention. The disadvantage is that, while the effects of the overall program may be evaluated at its conclusion, the specific effects of altering any one risk factor (e.g., plasma cholesterol levels) may not be.

Based upon this recommendation and cognizant of the drawbacks, the National Heart, Lung and Blood Institute provided the funding to initiate the largest clinical trial in history—the Multiple Risk Factor Intervention Trial (MRFIT) (Multiple Risk Factor Intervention Trial Group, 1977). The MRFIT program is now into its fifth year and the initial results should be available early in 1982. Although answers about the precise role of specific risk factors may not be forthcoming (Kuller, Neaton, Caggiula, & Falvo-Gerard, 1980), MRFIT will go a long way toward demonstrating the value and feasibility of concurrently altering multiple risk behaviors if, in fact, it does have a positive outcome.

PROMOTING HEALTHY LIFESTYLES: SOME CHALLENGES

Certain aspects of fostering healthier lifestyles have, of course, been of interest to psychologists for some time. Extensive literatures on how to bring about weight loss (Leon, 1977; Mahoney & Mahoney, 1976; Stuart, 1980; Stuart & Davis, 1972; Stunkard & Mahoney, 1976) and help smokers quit (Hunt & Matarazzo, 1973; Leventhal & Cleary, 1980) testify to the considerable and important progress that has been made and to the challenges that yet remain. Our intent is not to review the record of behavioral approaches in these and related areas. Instead, we shall consider from a broader perspective a variety of important issues relevant to prevention programs in general.

The accumulating knowledge on the control of obesity and smoking will, no doubt, provide valuable information about how to alter other health-related behaviors (Carmody, Fey, Pierce, Connor, & Matarazzo, 1982) such as atherogenic diets, chronic inactivity, and the overly harried Type A lifestyle. Whereas the basic principles of behavioral self-management will generally apply, specific target areas each have their unique problems and requirements and call for a specialized language, unique skills and intervention approaches, and a highly specific base of empirical knowledge.

In this section we first consider some of the conditions that make the modification of disease-fostering habits difficult and, in some areas, different from other target behaviors psychologists are accustomed to working with. We will then review models of what leads people to undertake action to regain, preserve or promote their health. Also, a variety of practical issues that often arise during the initiation and maintenance of new health behaviors are discussed. Finally, ideas will be presented which may help address the challenge of long-term maintenance. Throughout, the focus will be on presenting relevant practical concepts drawn from paradigms in behavioral, clinical, and social psychology and health education with examples of how they have been used in actual behavioral prevention programs.

Barriers to Change

Historically, behavioral treatment approaches primarily have emphasized the task of changing maladaptive behaviors. Those individuals who seek out traditional psychologists and other mental health professionals are often depressed, fearful, or unhappy with their marriage, their excessive weight or an unfulfilling life. Whatever the reason, they are generally dissatisfied and are looking for a change. Although therapists may not always agree with the client about what needs to change, some initial motivation for such change generally exists. Quite appropriately, the strategy of the behavioral therapist has been to provide such motivated clients with the tools and atmosphere that will help the individual learn to more effectively reach his or her self-chosen goals.

In contrast, the initial orientation, assumptions, and level of motivation of individuals encountered in a prevention setting are frequently quite different. Such individuals are often approached or referred as a result of a medical screening that indicates the presence of, or potential for, risk-elevating conditions or behaviors (i.e., so-called "silent" risks). Before being informed of the implications of their current lifestyle, such persons may be quite content with the status quo. The first step, then, is to provide relevant information, feedback, and explanations that will maximize the impact and personalization of an unexpected and unwelcome message. Generally, the message is that certain cherished habits are increasing one's future vulnerability to disease, suffering, and premature death, and that by enduring some minor discomfort, deprivation, inconvenience or expense now, the predicted probability of such an event may be substantially reduced. Thus, one who is initially unconcerned is suddenly asked to process a great deal of complex, abstract and potentially fear-arousing information, engage in a difficult cost-benefit analysis, and ultimately come to some decision about how to live. In effect, the internalization of this message requires that the individual confront and acknowledge the unsettling possibility of premature death. The disequilibrium or dissonance (Festinger, 1957) which is aroused may create what Milsum (1980) has termed the "teachable moment," or instead may generate any number of less adaptive cognitive defenses that restore consonance and a comfortable sense of safety. Although it is prudent to assume that humans are motivated to reduce or avoid the discomfort of fear-producing messages, from the scientific knowledge accumulated to date it is more difficult to predict whether constructive behavior change or potentially more costly behaviors such as avoidance, rationalization or denial, will be chosen following the presentation of such a message (Leventhal & Watts, 1966).

In a truly rational world where health and life are of value, the rather straightforward approach of informing persons of why and how they can promote their health should suffice. In the real world, however, the provision of even highly credible information and recommendations have been notoriously ineffective in altering health practices (Bergman & Werner, 1963; Leventhal & Cleary, 1980; Mitchell, 1974; Sexton-McDill, 1975; Thompson, 1978). Although probably necessary, knowledge alone seems insufficient to overcome the many and potent forces maintaining unhealthy patterns. Nevertheless, the wholesale dissemination of information continues to be the method of choice in many health education campaigns (Thompson, 1978).

Working with asymptomatic persons to alter risk factors offers very different problems and therefore requires intervention models which go beyond those used in the traditional treatment of patients motivated by sickness or other dysfunction. Barie (1969) has provided a compelling portrayal of what it means for a person to adopt an "at risk," as opposed to a "sick" role (Kasl & Cobb, 1966). The at-risk individual "feels fine" but is often asked to comply with an unpleasant behavioral, dietary, or medical regimen on an indefinite and often permanent basis. Compliance produces little or no rewarding physical feedback (e.g., reduction in pain) and typically elicits only minimal or short-term acknowledgement and support in the family, social, or work setting. Thus, the person must suffer the responsibilities and aggravations of a chronic treatment in the absence of overt signs and symptoms of disease, sympathy, and tangible signs of the value of compliance. This lack of naturally occurring reinforcers is consistent with the observed difficulties associated with compliance and adherence.

It comes as no surprise that people are reluctant to alter patterns that represent powerful, predictable, and immediate sources of gratification which are deeply ingrained in the social and cultural contexts in which they live. For many, the consumption of rich foods, alcohol and cigarettes provides both sensual gratification and a wide variety of potent psychological, social, and economic rewards. For health educators, a high fat meal (e.g., prime rib) may represent an elevated risk of hyperlipidemia and heart disease, but for the success-seeking executive, it may instead symbolize a well-deserved, dependable delight and a public measure of having "made it." Food, thus, becomes a way to impress friends and pamper business associates. Another example is the female homemaker who sees her role and much of her power as based on her ability to serve up sumptuous feasts and tantalizing "treats" that keep the family content and appreciative. Similarly, smokers sometimes report that cigarettes provide a "legitimate" excuse for a break which they would otherwise feel uncomfortable about taking. Still another example is alcohol which can signal, as well as produce, a period of relaxation, distraction and reverie.

Increasingly, Americans are enjoying the luxury and convenience of dining out, of frequenting fast-food establishments, and relying on easy-to-prepare processed food products at home. This trend, reflected in today's popular slogan "You deserve a break today," frequently works against efforts to lead a healthier lifestyle. Thus, habits are rarely just superficial behavioral patterns devoid of emotional investments. More frequently, they are deeply and inextricably woven into the individual's unique needs, motives, beliefs, ethnic background, culture, social structure, and environment. That these important, but complex and infinitely varied, physical, social, and psychological interconnections are so poorly understood and difficult to measure may account for the scarcity of reliable methods of prevention and treatment designed to address them. But unless the important functions and meanings of each individual's unique behavioral style are considered in order that they may learn alternate ways to meet their needs and reduce the personal cost of change, the likelihood for long-term maintenance of healthier lifestyles will remain low.

Another source of resistance to change is simple inertia. People tend to enjoy and feel comfortable with the familiar and avoid that which is new, different, or unknown. Although exotic ethnic cuisines are gaining popularity, many Americans still regard themselves as "meat and potato" types. Alteration of the atherogenic character of the American diet requires that new and often unusual foods and cooking practices become familiar and comfortable. Patiently encouraging experimentation over time through modeling (e.g., cooking and food demonstrations) and regular practice with new menus (e.g., potlucks), appears to be useful in broadening culinary horizons and options.

In addition to these intra-individual influences, a variety of powerful external forces also work in concert to undermine the potential for effecting prudent lifestyle change. One such impediment has been the inability of the various constituencies of American medicine and health services to adopt a coherent public policy and make consistent recommendations for healthier living. Whereas the scientific controversies are legitimate, and important questions remain to be clarified, the social costs of such "mixed medical messages" are great in that they confuse the public and undermine the credibility and potential social power of medical science. The inconsistencies of those scientists, educators, and policymakers who demand hard "proof" before recommending preventive action has been pointed out cogently by noted physician and epidemiologist, Henry Blackburn (1978), who observed that:

> Distinguished physicians and surgeons who daily employ dangerous invasive diagnostic procedures, prescribe toxic medications, and perform untested surgical hydraulics, protest that the simple, safe, rational, and palatable hygienic lowering of risk characteristics and bad habits, by means tested for centuries in natural populations, is unproven, adventuresome folly! (p. 106)

It is indeed commendable that numerous national and international agencies and commissions have recognized the need for a consensus and have struggled to present clear and reasonable guidelines based on the considerable evidence already available. The Surgeon Generals' Reports (DHEW, 1964; Califano, 1979a, 1979b) and the Senate Select Committee's (1977) United States Dietary Goals are fine examples. However, a lack of real commitment to the concept of healthier living as communicated by the private physician will frequently engender doubt and rationalization in the patient which, in turn, undermines motivation and long-term success during the difficult process of change. As interested physicians continue to turn more of their attention from acute care in order to promote and maintain optimal levels of health, the credibility, authority and personal example of such physicians will constitute an increasingly powerful public health message. What is called for is not that physicians necessarily become the agents of change (a role for which some may have neither the training, time, nor interest) but, instead, that they support and help legitimize the efforts of other professionals working in preventive medicine. Highly motivated interdisciplinary teams composed of physicians, psychologists, nutritionists and other specialists working in unison have a tremendous, but as yet, mostly unrealized potential to affect health by modeling, guiding and working with the motivations and behaviors of patients.

In trying to sway the public's health practices, health educators must also take into account at least one other major counterforce—the economics of big business. As examples, the fiscal viability of the cigarette industry and certain elements of the food industry will likely suffer if mass prevention efforts are successful. Advertising is their primary vehicle for sales and their counter-weapon against prevention efforts. Although the impact of advertisements on actual health practices is difficult to assess (Klapper, 1969), the food industry is clearly optimistic. Each year advertisers spend approximately $1.2 billion (Senate Select Committee, 1977) to persuade Americans to consume targeted food products. Unfortunately, decisions about which products to push are based on economic rather than health or humanistic considerations.

As Americans' preferences for healthier products evolve, so too will the targets of advertising. In the meantime, attempts to alter health behaviors should incorporate techniques that innoculate the public (Evans, Rozelle, Mittlemark,

Hansen, Bane, & Havis, 1978; Lumsdaine & Janis, 1953) against this pervasive and often destructive force. The current unavailability of many healthful food choices in stores and restaurants (e.g., low fat, low sodium cheeses), the numerous outmoded regulations regarding the labeling and content of specific foods, and the understandable but no longer defensible governmental support of the various manufacturers of illness (e.g., the tobacco industry) represent just a few of the many challenges which must be surmounted.

Models of Motivation

Despite these many forces working against change, many people do quit smoking, alter their diets, use seat belts, and engage in other practices for the sake of their health. Sometimes these changes are relatively easy and economical (e.g., seat belts), sometimes they entail considerable time and energy (e.g., jogging) or monetary expense (e.g., regular medical and dental check-ups). A number of conceptually similar theoretical paradigms have been offered by behavioral scientists to describe conditions under which such health-related actions are more likely to be practiced (Anderson & Bartkus, 1973; Fabrega, 1973; Mechanic, 1968; Rosenstock, 1966; Suchman, 1966). A well-documented example is the Health Belief Model (Becker, Drachman & Kirscht, 1972; Becker & Maiman, 1975). In essence, the model suggests that an individual's readiness to engage in health actions depends on the extent to which that person regards health as important, feels susceptible to an illness which has severe consequences and sees the likely benefits of that action as subjectively worth the bother or cost. Also important is an external "cue to action" which might include, for example, a physician's recommendation that the individual eat less fat, the death of a friend, or a publicized community "Quit Smoking Day."

The heuristic value of the Health Belief Model is attested to by the large number of studies it has spawned. Beliefs and attitudes regarding disease susceptibility and severity and the benefits and costs of action have been investigated as determinants of actual behavior in a wide variety of health settings. Health issues which have been considered include tuberculosis, cancer, heart disease, genetic anomalies, dental check-ups, immunization for polio and influenza, accident prevention, weight loss, smoking cessation, and hypertension control, to name a few. Reviews (e.g., Becker, 1974; Cummings, Becker, & Maile, 1980) have generally indicated that the variables in the model account for a substantial portion of the variance in individual differences in health behaviors, but also that certain inconsistencies have been noted.

A case in point occurred in a study of participation in a screening program for the Tay-Sachs trait (Becker, Kaback, Rosenstock, & Ruth, 1975), a relatively rare and unknown genetic disorder. Areas of Baltimore and Washington were first exposed to an intensive campaign designed to provide information about the disorder, its consequences, and methods of detection. A screening program was then made available and all interested persons were invited to participate. A random sample of 500 participants and an equal number of those refusing to participate completed a questionnaire assessing each individual's health beliefs and attitudes. As predicted, those participating in the program reported more interest in having children (which provides a health motive), perceived themselves as more susceptible to being a carrier, and felt screening offered greater benefits than did non-participants. The perceived costs of action were not measured in this study. The one inconsistent finding was that the perceived severity of the consequences of the Tay-Sachs trait was *inversely* related to participation in the screening program. To explain this finding, the authors suggested that those perceiving the consequences as most severe may have been too threatened to go through the screening procedure. Results such as these suggest that health belief variables are important but that they do not always operate in a simple, linear, or additive fashion. It is likely that their influence depends on their interactions as well as the specific populations and different health issues being targeted. Understanding these complexities will undoubtedly add to the usefulness of the Health Belief Model and to our ability to promote better health behavior.

A related line of research undertaken by social psychologists interested in the general determinants of attitude change (Hovland, Janis, & Kelley, 1953; Insko, 1967; Kiesler, Collins, & Miller, 1969; Leventhal, 1974) may provide some additional understanding. Unfortunately, much of this work occurred in highly controlled and somewhat artificial settings and relied on self-report rather than actual behavioral indices of attitude change. Generalizing from the conclusions of many of these studies to other settings is therefore risky. Several paradigms, however, are more convincing and raise important considerations relevant to the practical task of disease prevention. A large number of studies have addressed the question of whether threat or fear appeals are useful in motivating adaptive behavior change. The answer appears to be a complex one, dependent on a variety of personality and contextual factors. The earliest work (Janis & Feshbach, 1953; Janis & Terwilliger, 1962) was consistent with the findings cited above in suggesting that highly fear-arousing communications may functionally paralyze or reduce effective coping and therefore be counterproductive. Subsequently, a curvilinear relationship between level of fear and degree of change was postulated which indicated that increasing amounts of threat will initially motivate action until a subjective threshold is reached. After this point, additional threat becomes increasingly dysfunctional. The optimal level of arousal was thought to depend on a variety of other individual and situation-specific factors.

Reviews (Janis, 1967; Leventhal, 1970; McGuire, 1969) of more recent work sugguest that the presentation of threatening information may be useful in producing behavior change but primarily when directed at persons initially at low levels of concern or arousal (Janis, 1967), who have confidence in their general ability to cope (Leventhal & Watts, 1966), and who have a highly reassuring set of specific, acceptable and effective options immediately available to them (Chu, 1966; Leventhal & Cleary, 1980). When used insensitively or in isolation as a quick and easy way to manipulate behavior, the more likely outcomes of threatening messages are upset, avoidance, and defensiveness. Another problem in the use of fear to induce behavior change appears to be that the effects of a threatening message fade rather quickly unless reinstated (Leventhal & Niles, 1965). For this reason, smokers are sometimes asked to rehearse on a regular schedule their reasons for quitting in order to prolong the motivational impact.

In intervention settings, ethical considerations often make it necessary to inform high risk persons of the health-threatening implications of their present risk status and habits. It also appears that within a well-designed, comprehensive intervention program, the presentation of threatening information can be a useful tool as long as there is an awareness of the unique needs of the audience and the possible dangers. When individuals are already fearful and yet feel unable to comply with a health recommendation, the emphasis should be on reducing anxiety to a more manageable level and on decreasing the perception of helplessness (Seligman, 1975). Bandura's model of "self-efficacy" (1977), as well as the cognitive-behavioral analysis of the relapse phenomenon offered by Marlatt and Gordon (1980), suggest valuable approaches that may increase the likelihood of effective coping in the face of threatening information. These will be considered in a later section.

Whereas theoretical work rarely gives unambiguous answers to practical questions, it does serve to sensitize the interventionist to important, often counter-intuitive processes that may be operating. Models of health beliefs and attitude change tell us not so much what to do, as what to look for in the intervention process. Above all, the many complexities involved serve to emphasize the importance of thorough client assessments, individually tailored approaches and good general counseling skills on the part of those attempting to promote better health practices.

Issues in Intervention

Behavioral specialists, biomedical personnel, and lay health educators often rely on quite different approaches to promote healthy lifestyles. These alternative approaches sometimes derive from differing assumptions about the theoretical and empirical determinants of behavior and behavior change, but probably more often arise merely as a result of the interventionist's professional orientation, training, biases, and needs. While diversity is desirable, it is unfortunate when such diversity arises from lack of insight into the limitations of one's own approach and ignorance of the complimentary advantages of the methods and frameworks utilized by allied workers. For example, the presentation of facts, motivational arguments, and recommendations are important and necessary but are not likely to be effective if the individual lacks the skills needed to implement new behaviors on a lasting basis. Similarly, a headlong rush to teach the latest behavioral techniques before an individual has the necessary information or motivation needed for change will also be unproductive in most cases. Today, interdisciplinary teams are often well equipped to provide the broad spectrum of talents and techniques which are called for. In addition, the team approach serves well as fertile ground for the professional's continuing development. We shall next consider some of the important practical issues that often are encountered within a health risk intervention program.

The Role of Information and Information-Giver.   To make sound lifestyle decisions, people need appropriate facts, a firm rationale, and clear instructions and guidelines for change. It is a common and not implausible assumption that destructive personal habits stem from specific maladaptive attitudes which are based on a lack of knowledge. This view implies that as knowledge deficits and misconceptions are corrected, first attitudes and then behaviors will change accordingly. Unfortunately, the popularity of this approach may be related more to the personal needs of health educators, than to fact. It can be quite satisfying for an interventionist to take on the role of "purveyor of truth," to be the knowing expert and to have quick and ready answers to every question, excuse or counter-argument a client offers. The academic training of many health professionals reinforces the perceived value of accumulating and presenting facts and ideas. This is then further reinforced each day as the professional displays his or her considerable expertise before the impressed and appreciative program participant. However, the task is not to elicit mere verbal acceptance or even a shift in subjective attitude. The appropriate goal is to translate both of these into meaningful lifestyle modification and its maintenance over a lifetime.

Though knowledge, in and of itself, rarely leads to lasting habit change, it unquestionably serves a necessary function. A crucial issue, then, is how to package information so that it is meaningful and palatable to the targeted consumer or audience. A presentation regarding the long-range health consequences of a given diet that is compelling to nutritionists and physicians may be quite incomprehensible or irrelevant to their patients. Before bombarding people with facts, their interests, goals, health belief systems and current level of understanding should be assessed and taken into account. Unless information is relevant to a value or goal the *client* or *patient* regards as important, its impact will be minimal, regardless of the quality of its presentation.

Although most people value good health, increasing risk of disease may not be a particularly salient issue for many who view themselves as currently healthy. As previously discussed, attempts to increase a person's sense of perceived vulnerability to disease may make health more salient or, instead, increase discomfort or dissonance and lead to denial, selective forgetting, repression, or other forms of avoidance. An alternative approach is to appeal to other values currently more relevant to the individual. For example, if long-range health consequences are not sufficient to motivate adoption of a low-fat diet, perhaps other more immediate benefits such as weight loss, feeling in control of one's physical being, economics, or ecological considerations could be emphasized (Mausner, 1973). The key is to discover and respond to that which is important and of value to that individual (Rokeach, 1960).

Probably the most crucial consideration in presenting relevant information and recommendations is the *complexity* of the message (Svarstad, 1976). For example, altering traditional eating patterns entails learning a great deal of new, complex and detailed information. Special efforts are therefore required to insure that important concepts are presented in simple, systematic and concrete terms at a rate that can be absorbed. A large body of research (Ley, 1977) has shown that 35% to 50% of what physicians in general practice tell their patients about a diagnosis or prescribed treatment *cannot* be recalled by the patient. Shockingly, this is as true 5 minutes after a consultation as it is 1 to 4 weeks later (Joyce, Caple, Mason, Reynolds, & Mathews, 1969; Ley, Bradshaw, Eaves, & Walker, 1973). However, a patient's memory for such medical information has been shown to improve (Ley, 1977) if the following suggestions are implemented:

1. Short words and sentences are used.
2. Instructions, advice and recommendations are provided first and their importance is stressed later.
3. Recommendations are as specific, detailed and concrete as possible.
4. Important ideas are repeated.

For example, a simplified vocabulary (i.e., low complexity on the Flesch Index) has been found to increase the retention of both dietary (Bradshaw, Ley, Kincey, & Bradshaw, 1975) and x-ray instructions (Ley, Goldman, Bradshaw, Kincey, & Walker, 1972). It is interesting that the mere order of presentation of such physician-dispensed information is important. The usual practice among physicians is to first describe the patient's condition in general terms, followed by specific instructions and advice. However, evidence suggests that in some cases recall (and the potential for compliance) is increased if the health practitioner reverses this procedure and gives the advice and instructions first and stresses their importance later.

Repeated exposure and practice are, no doubt, essential when complex behavioral patterns (e.g., a high fat eating style) are being altered. Periodic assessment of the level and accuracy of understanding helps point up deficits and specific needs that may be addressed during follow-up sessions. Complexity may be minimized but it is especially important that people know exactly what is being recommended and that they have some means of assessing their level of compliance or noncompliance on an ongoing basis. Accurate feedback (acknowledging what "is") in no way diminishes and, indeed, is essential to the exercise of free choice.

Certain characteristics of the individual who makes a recommendation also have been shown to influence an audience's acceptance of the persuasive message in important ways. For example, mothers of sick children have been found to be more compliant with medical recommendations when they view their physicians as friendly and understanding rather than business-like (Francis, Dorsch, & Morris, 1969). As summarized by McGuire (1964), two additional important factors determining receptivity to a persuasive communication are credibility and attractiveness of the source of the message. Credibility is a function of both perceived expertise and perceived trustworthiness. It is not surprising to learn that experts are more believable, but it also appears that their influence is dependent upon the motives they are assumed to have (Hovland & Mandell, 1952). If the communicator appears to have a vested interest in the audience's acceptance of the message (e.g., the health advocate's intervention research program will be a success), influence will be less likely. Other work (Brehm, 1966) indicates that when persons perceive attempts to manipulate or control their behavior, psychological reactance is elicited along with a motivation to demonstrate autonomy and personal freedom. Such reassertion of freedom may come as a direct refusal to comply or may take on more indirect or symbolic forms such as forgetting appointments or making small changes while compensating in other ways.

Both the early work of Lewin (1943) and later studies (Festinger, 1957; Festinger & Carlsmith, 1959) indicate the importance of individuals making public commitments to newly advocated positions, but only when they feel they have done so free of external pressure or coercion. The implication here is that we should avoid making clients passive recipients of information and should instead foster a "therapeutic alliance" in which we invite them to openly weigh the personal advantages and disadvantages of change, draw their own conclusions, affirm these publicly, and then act on this self-determined resolve (Evans & Hall, 1978).

In summary, a broad body of evidence on the role of information suggests that health experts who believe in the value of their recommendations, who are respected and well-liked, and whose overriding concern is their patients' welfare, are most likely to be persuasive. Persuasion, however, is only the first step in altering health behaviors.

Behavioral Implementation. Behavioral approaches to changing habits commonly utilize multiple techniques including some or all of the following: self-assessment, goal setting, modeling, operant consequences (i.e., reinforcement), aversive conditioning, cognitive restructuring, and stimulus control procedures. Techniques such as these are well grounded in laboratory-derived learning principles and most have been evaluated, either alone or in combination, and have been found to be useful within a variety of settings (Mahoney, 1975). The most meaningful measure of therapeutic effectiveness is successful long-term maintenance of the desired treatment effects. In this regard, some reviewers have questioned (Franks & Wilson, 1975; Hunt & Matarazzo, 1973; Stunkard & Mahoney, 1976), whereas others have supported (Leon, 1977; Stuart, 1980), the relative superiority of behavioral over nonbehavioral approaches. There is, however, widespread agreement on two points. First, that behavioral approaches are generally the most effective means of *initiating* habit change. Second, as currently applied, behavior change programs routinely fail to adequately equip most clients for the *maintenance* of change over time (e.g., Hunt & Matarazzo, 1973; Leventhal & Cleary, 1980; Matarazzo & Saslow, 1960).

Behavior strategies can only be effective to the extent that individuals are willing to initiate and to adhere to the steps they entail. Behavioral expertise does not endow therapists with special powers to change another's life, even if that is what both the client and therapist would like to believe. Behavioral techniques are merely useful tools that therapists can help individuals learn to utilize once the latter are willing to devote time and energy to the task of self-directed change. An essential requirement is a level of motivation and commitment that will allow the person to tolerate the inevitable frustrations and setbacks and see them as learning experiences that will be useful in their future planning. Overly passive clients who endow therapists or techniques per se with "the power" to change their lives for them are destined to dependency, helplessness, and ultimate failure.

Progress within a behavior change program is unlikely when self-monitoring is neglected, when prearranged reward schedules are overlooked, or when self-determined behavioral contracts are broken. However, it is often difficult to ascertain whether behavioral progress (e.g., weight loss) is interrupted by a lapse in adherence to behavioral strategies or the reverse. Activities such as keeping daily records are often regarded as time-consuming and otherwise annoying and, while graphic evidence of improvement is gratifying, discouraging downward trends can result in abandonment of the technique in the absence of adequate supports. As described by Bandura (1977), continued motivation towards a specific goal depends, in part, on the person's: (1) level of perceived self-efficacy (i.e., perceived ability to perform the behavior), and (2) outcome expectation (i.e., conviction that the behavior, if performed, will result in the desired outcome). Tests of the self-efficacy theory and a related expectancy-based model offered by Seligman (1975) highlight the central motivational importance of the individual's expectation or perception of personal control.

Poor adherence to a mutually agreed upon behavioral plan is not necessarily a reflection on either the value of the technique or the individual's level of motivation to achieve the desired outcome. Rather, resistance often is a cue that some important aspect (Mausner, 1973) of the complex of factors maintaining the target behavior has not been dealt with adequately. A lack of adherence may reflect unexpressed fears or anxiety due to expectations of failure or, alternatively, a perceived inability to cope with the social implications of success.

Resistance may also stem from reactance (Brehm, 1966) or a distaste for "gimmicks" and outside assistance. Issues such as these are best dealt with when they are openly expressed. This, however, requires that individuals take the risk of admitting attitudes they may regard as socially or therapeutically unacceptable. Trust and an atmosphere of mutual problem-solving are needed if individuals are to disclose the important needs their resistance protects. Disclosure, however, is only the first critical step. The individual must next be encouraged to alter those forces that perpetuate his or her current maladaptive habit patterns.

Stuart (1980) discusses this problem in detail in relation to the treatment of obesity. He proposes an "indirect" model of intervention involving the following steps: (1) encourage the selection of positive change goals (e.g., increase acceptable, rather than decrease unacceptable, food choices); (2) identify the various physiological, habitual, cognitive, affective, and situational forces that strengthen the *desire* or *urge* for the overeating or other problem behavior; (3) instigate behavioral plans to alter these forces and the urges they maintain without attempting to directly change the target behavior itself (e.g., first help foster more supportive family relationships before introducing a family diet change); and finally, (4) engage in direct efforts to alter the target behavior (e.g., serve smaller portions or make better meal choices). The individual is considered the best source of information about the basis of his or her own problematic urges. Also, it is recommended that multiple contributing forces and multiple behavioral strategies be addressed concurrently when possible. Other writers have echoed this call for a broader conceptual framework (Hunt & Matarazzo, 1973; Wilson, 1980) and techniques that more fully address the complex motivational factors which underlie highly resistant habits (Leventhal & Cleary, 1980; Mausner, 1973).

Family Patterns. As alluded to earlier, an individual's attempt to change will inevitably affect the entire family unit in important ways (Stuart, 1978) that are frequently ignored in behavior change programs. For example, much of the burden of dietary change often falls not on the patient or target person, but on the one who prepares the family meals. The meal planner may try to help but may also resent altering favorite family recipes and taking the extra time to learn to shop for and prepare different foods. In other cases, parents' eating habits are influenced remarkably by the whims and tastes of their children. It is unrealistic to expect even the most motivated family member to maintain difficult new patterns in the face of loved ones who directly or indirectly ignore, resist or even ridicule his or her efforts.

The importance of family support has been demonstrated in the control of obesity. For example, Mahoney and Mahoney (1976) found that spouse attendance and cooperation at treatment sessions was closely associated with treatment success. Other work indicates that mere attendance by the spouse is not enough (Wilson & Brownell, 1978). However, when both partners have been trained in the use of modeling, record-keeping, and reinforcement procedures, the target person's treatment outcomes and maintenance have been improved substantially (Brownell, Heckerman, Westlake, Hayes, & Monti, 1978; Pearce, LeBow, & Orchard, 1979; Stuart & Davis, 1972). Thus, family support appears to serve a vital function and, for this reason, family units may be the most effective targets for intervention. In addition, the well documented familial-genetic aspects of coronary risk also argue for a family intervention model designed to foster health-promoting values, norms, and habits early in life.

Group Dynamics.   During World War II, Kurt Lewin (1943) pioneered research which showed the potential for altering the American diet. His aim was to increase the use of plentiful organ meats such as beef hearts, sweetbreads, and kidneys by Iowa housewives. His research compared the effectiveness of a well-presented lecture versus an open-ended group discussion format and demonstrated that the latter was clearly more effective in moving larger numbers of homemakers to make the desired behavior change. Today, Lewin's method, if not his target behavior, is as appropriate as ever.

In addition to the economic advantages, groups such as those used by Lewin provide a setting where participants may receive consensual validation and support as they consider and attempt change. As groups develop their unique character and increase in cohesiveness, they become micro-social systems or reference groups that can help establish new health norms for the individual members. An important function of groups is that they allow their individual members to observe others as they question, make tentative efforts, falter, share mistakes, and then ultimately succeed. Thus, group interaction often leads to valuable experiences that interventionists working one-on-one simply cannot provide.

Maintenance

Threat of disease, the physician's authority or a desire to take up a new lifestyle are all capable of motivating a change in health behavior. Too often, however, temptation and other pressures to relapse abound. When major shifts in daily habit patterns occur rapidly, frustration and feelings of deprivation are typical and often lead first to occasional and then permanent slips back into old patterns. Relapse curves for various treatment areas (e.g., smoking, weight-loss, dietary change, and alcohol use) are amazingly consistent (Hunt, Barnett, & Branch, 1971; Hunt & Matarazzo, 1973) and the search for a quick easy method of altering complex behaviors is now recognized as unrealistic by most experts. Maintenance is a difficult problem and one that deserves primary attention rather than the perfunctory concern it has received in many intervention programs.

With few exceptions, lifestyle intervention programs offered commercially or by health practitioners tend to be of brief duration ranging from short physician consultations, to 5-day smoking plans, to weight loss sessions lasting several weeks. Such approaches, by necessity, must encourage rapid change in behavioral patterns and little attention can be devoted to the individual's unique habit-controlling variables. When intervention ends, the individual is left to face the difficulties of long-term maintenance without the needed professional support or guidance.

A basic principle of Skinner's behaviorism is the method of successive approximation or shaping. Surprisingly, this concept all too rarely figures prominently in lifestyle modification programs. The alteration of well-learned patterns and appetites in small graduated steps allows for adaptation to occur and increases the probability of early success experiences which, in turn, foster increased self-efficacy and continued motivation to persevere. In practice, participants often voice an enthusiastic urge to go "cold turkey" when attempting to quit smoking, alter their diet or make other major changes. This desire for instant success is probably rooted in an implicitly held treatment model of change and the notion that once old habits are corrected, new behaviors will be self-maintaining. The frequency of the relapse phenomenon, however, suggests that such attitudes are often far from realistic; particularly with complex behavioral patterns where it is important to encourage progressive short-term goals that are large enough to matter and small enough to achieve.

Periodic, even if infrequent, contact with the health professional over an extended time period may be one way to provide the support needed to facilitate continued maintenance. The optimal contact frequency may well differ with the habit being modified. For example, "cold turkey" approaches to smoking cessation may call for a briefer and more intense contact schedules than the alteration of the more complex dietary behaviors. Treatment for the use of alcohol may require both frequent initial contact and continued long-term support to be effective. Clearly, additional research is called for to clarify this important issue.

Long-term maintenance ultimately requires that individuals internalize the value and methods of implementing health behaviors in their lives. Encouraging participants to make their *own* decisions about what, when, and how to change can help foster commitment to the actions taken and reduces the likelihood of reactance (Brehm, 1966). To the extent that interventionists communicate strong personal or emotional investments in their participants' change (e.g., as a measure of their effectiveness as leaders), participants are likely to feel obligated to "try" to change in order to please the leader. It is the experience of many interventionists that such changes typically do not endure. Externally-motivated change may be valuable when the initial experimentation is likely to be reinforced quickly by the natural environment (e.g., a more assertive coping style). However, when environmental supports for new patterns are expected to develop slowly following a considerable period of adjustment (e.g., as in long-term weight control), external motives such as pleasing the group leader are less likely to be effective and may even undermine existing internal motivations for health change.

Individuals encounter many of the same problems and barriers as they attempt to change and interventionists quickly develop an arsenal of all too ready-made solutions which they are eager to share. In many cases, the latter might well consider restraining their impulse to offer solutions and, instead, offer support to the person in the struggle to find his or her own solution. While initially more time consuming and frustrating for all concerned, this client-centered approach increases the participant's self-reliance, commitment, and sense of personal responsibility for the change process, each of which is important for maintenance.

Methods of improving maintenance and avoiding the relapse phenomenon are receiving increased attention. Marlatt and Gordon (1980) have characterized models of relapse prevention as either multi-modal (i.e., the "shotgun" approach) or self-control-oriented (i.e., individual-as-therapist). Multi-modal approaches are based on the assumption that a combination of techniques will be more effective and longer lasting than any one technique alone. The self-control approach attempts to give clients the tools and skills needed to analyze and alter their own habits and ever-changing environments in order to prevent relapse. A third tact was also suggested in which the therapist helps the client anticipate and prepare for specific conditions likely to result in relapse.

Research in alcohol treatment programs (Marlatt, 1976) has indicated that most cases of relapse occur in situations involving anger or frustration or in the face of social pressure from family and friends. Similarly, in a smoking treatment program, Condiotte and Lichtenstein (1982) have demonstrated that exsmokers can specify, with considerable accuracy, the nature of the circumstances in which they will eventually relapse. Subjects who had recently quit smoking were asked to rate the probability that they would smoke in each of 48 potentially high-risk situations. Cluster analysis revealed seven basic clusters or types of such situations. Subjects were assigned self-efficacy scores (i.e., ratings of their own self-effectiveness in dealing with different types of potentially tempting situations) for each of the clusters based on their self-ratings. After 3 months, the results indicated that 44 of 78 (56%) subjects had resumed smoking and that the overall self-efficacy ratings were found to be strong inverse predictors of the probability of relapse. Of special interest was the finding that subjects' ratings of low self-efficacy (or low ability to resist temptation) in a specific situation cluster were highly congruent with their actual relapse experience months later. If replicated, these initial findings suggest important implications for the prevention of relapse. Specifically, if individuals can accurately identify the situations in which they are likely to relapse, highly *individualized* skills training programs can be developed, prescribed, and implemented.

The effectiveness of any such relapse prevention training would be expected to depend on the effects of the training experience on participants' perceived self-efficacy. In one program for alcoholics (Chaney, O'Leary, & Marlatt, 1978), small group sessions were utilized to teach specific coping skills to individuals to upgrade their abilities to deal with problem areas. Participants were presented with hypothetical situations involving social pressure, upset, loneliness, boredom and so on, and were asked to role play their likely responses. The leaders and other group members provided feedback and discussed alternate coping strategies. The coping responses were rehearsed until they were considered acceptable and likely to be effective in vivo. Compared to a control group and a group whose members merely discussed their emotional reactions to similar high-risk situations, the skills-training program was found to be more effective on several relapse-related measures during the following year. Similarly, Evans and his co-workers (1978) in Houston have found that role playing the refusal of a cigarette helps protect (i.e., "inocculate") fifth-grade children in peer pressure situations likely to lead to the initiation of smoking in these youngsters.

In practice, discussing the probability of relapse can be difficult and is often actively avoided by participants and interventionists alike. Preparing for relapse implies that it is likely to be forthcoming and the process itself may threaten the individual's already fragile self confidence. The powerful influence of the expectations of authority figures in social situations has been aptly demonstrated by Milgram (1974) and the possibility remains that emphasizing the risk of relapse may actually decrease perceived ability to cope. If relapse prevention is to succeed, it must provide experiences that leave participants with both adequate coping skills and the confidence to apply them.

A variety of training methods have been suggested (Marlatt & Gordon, 1980) including rehearsal, in vivo guided practice, programmed relapse and stress management techniques, among others. Each of these approaches acts to increase either specific or more global feelings of self-efficacy. Early results suggest that they each have promise, but their long-term utility remains to be demonstrated. Although refinements in self-efficacy theory and relapse prevention are to be anticipated, these trends represent an encouraging and significant response to the formidable challenge of the maintenance of healthier lifestyles.

THE FAMILY HEART STUDY: A COMMUNITY DIET INTERVENTION PROGRAM

The assumptions and aims of participants in lifestyle intervention programs combine with the resources and limitations of the particular setting to dictate how techniques will translate into actual practice. The best approaches are those that fit into the setting considered. Their value lies not so much in themselves, but in the creativity and skill of their application. Rarely does one have the degree of participant contact and cooperation that would be ideal and, thus, the eloquence and promise of any approach to behavior change must be tempered with common sense and a sensitivity to the constraints that exist. Much of the real challenge and frustration of the multidisciplinary prevention approach centers around the task of effectively implementing promising approaches that co-workers from different health disciplines find unfamiliar, counter-intuitive or even threatening.

Whatever the approach, care should be taken to insure that the representatives of various disciplines have reached a consensus about how to proceed and have helped one another become as skilled as possible in the individual roles they each are to play.

A practical illustration of many of the concepts we have discussed in this chapter is offered by the Portland-based Family Heart Study. The purpose of the project is to foster and evaluate the acceptance of the low-fat, low-cholesterol "Alternative Diet" (Connor & Connor, 1977) designed to reduce serum cholesterol and overall risk of disease.

Overview and Objectives

The Family Heart Study (FHS) differs from other intervention programs in several important ways. First, the intervention effort is directed at intact family units rather than specific individuals. Both intervention and data collection have been tailored, as appropriate, to the adults, teenagers, children and infants in the study. Since many of the participants do not have high risk profiles, the emphasis is on concepts such as optimum or relative health risks as well as the many other motives relevant to dietary change (e.g., economy).

A second feature is the use of a group approach in an attempt to develop and then utilize an increasingly cohesive group network to foster healthier habits and attitudes. The 233 participating families meet on a monthly basis with others from their neighborhood in small groups co-led by a psychologist and a nutritionist. The goal is to provide a blend of medical-nutritional information, behavioral skills and the group and family support needed to effect a permanent dietary change. The format of each meeting varies according to an overall plan which was designed to provide dietary and health information at an optimal rate. Regular group discussion and feedback provide a gauge as to the needs of the families at each point over the 5-year study period.

A third important aspect of the program is the use of a gradual or *phased* approach to dietary change. The dietary guidelines are based on an appreciation of the difficulty most people encounter when attempting to alter their typical American diet to a healthier alternative. The phased approach is designed to allow "easy" initial changes to become routine before proceeding to more difficult challenges (e.g., reducing consumption of meat and cheese). This aspect of the program is especially appealing to those participants who are interested in adopting a better diet but who are initially leery of being pressured into a radical or unacceptable change. The phased approach allows participants infinite flexibility and freedom in choosing the eating style which is right for them. The emphasis is on a noncoercive approach that communicates both the ideal diet as well as an "improved" eating pattern which may be more realistic for many. A patient, empathetic attitude on the part of the staff is encouraged in order to minimize the participants' sense of guilt, struggle and fear and to maintain their motivation and desire to remain involved. At the same time, this climate of acceptance places both the responsibility and the credit for change squarely on the shoulders of the family members themselves as they work to improve their eating style. We anticipate that this gradual evolution of dietary behaviors will foster changes in both appetites and group norms that will minimize transition stress, resistance and backsliding following the intervention period.

The FHS dietary changes may be viewed in terms of three logical phases although, in practice, the nature and rate of change varies with each individual. Figure 13.2 illustrates how certain nutrients change as one progresses from the standard American diet (AD) through the three phases of the Alternative Diet. *Phase* I is emphasized during the first 6–12 months of intervention. The primary aim is to eliminate or decrease the use of high-cholesterol and high-fat foods through the use of substitute products and related minor changes that most families find easy to accomplish. Recommendations include the use of alternate foods such as low-fat dairy products, vegetable oils, egg whites or substitutes, and so on. Such substitute foods can be readily accepted by most individuals without substantially modifying the character, appearance or taste of foods normally consumed by the family. Adherence to Phase I results in a 150 mg. drop in dietary cholesterol and a reduction of fat to 35% of total calories. Carbohydrates are increased from 45% to approximately 50% of calories.

Phase II calls for changes during years two and three that are more central to the basic eating patterns of most Americans. The consumption of meat is gradually reduced from the American average of the up to a pound per day to less than 6 oz daily. Red meats are generally avoided in favor of poultry and fish. The use of cheese is limited to less than 3 oz of low fat cheese per day. Important in terms of immunizing against later relapse, the emphasis during intervention is

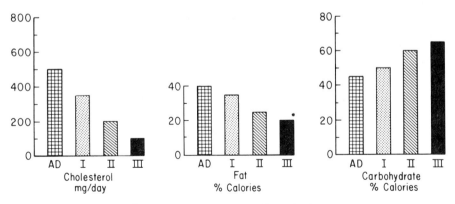

*Saturated fat not to exceed 6% total calories

FIG. 13.2. The Cholesterol, Fat and Carbohydrate Content of the American Diet (AD) and the Phases (I, II, III) of the Alternative Diet.

less on "giving up" favorite foods than it is on increasing the use of equally tasty but healthier alternatives. Some "positive change goals" (Stuart, 1980) include eating more whole grain breads, pasta, rice, legumes, fresh vegetables and fruits, all of which are low in cholesterol, fat and calories. At this point carbohydrates make up 60% of total calories while fats have been reduced to 25%. Cholesterol is limited to 250 mg. Many traditional and foreign cuisines are compatible with these guidelines and are emphasized through discussion, handouts, cooking demonstrations, taste tests, and the sampling of such foods at each group meeting. Also, Alternative Diet recipes, shopping excursions, visits to restaurants, and potlucks with members of the groups are utilized.

Phase III is designed for those individuals who are interested in the optimum well-balanced diet for Americans that will produce a maximal reduction of plasma cholesterol. The endpoint Alternative Diet calls for 100 mg of cholesterol and 20% of calories due to fat, with 65% of calories derived from carbohydrate sources. These additional changes are introduced in years four and five and include limiting the daily consumption of animal products to 3–4 oz of lean meat, fish or poultry *or* 2 oz of low-fat cheese. At this point, meats and cheese represent condiments, as has been the case for most populations around the world for centuries, rather than the central focus of the meal. Exciting new low-fat foods, spices and cooking styles are introduced (initially by the nutritionist leaders but later by group members themselves) from the cuisines of the Orient, Mexico, Italy, India and the Middle East. Meatless days each week are encouraged. Traditional menus, extra cheese, high-fat baked goods, chocolate and coconut are reserved only for infrequent festive occasions. Participants often report that these "feast days" serve as potent reminders of the relatively painless changes in behaviors and tastes which they have already accomplished.

A complete description of the guidelines and a precise nutrient analysis for the Alternative Diet has been presented elsewhere along with a number of useful tables, menu plans, and recipes (Connor & Connor, 1977). The composition of the diet exceeds all recommended daily allowances (i.e., RDA guidelines) and has been thoroughly tested for nutritional adequacy, lipid-lowering effectiveness, and palatability.

Group Process and Family Interaction.   The FHS population consists of 233 families (742 individuals) recruited by means of a door-to-door health survey conducted by professional pollsters in a single district representative of the larger community of Portland, Oregon. Eligible families included those with at least two persons between the ages of 6 and 65 who generally share meals and consume a typical American diet. At least two family members had to agree to participate for the family to be considered. Almost half (47%) of the eligible families contacted agreed to participate. The dietary, demographic and other measured characteristics of those refusing and those entering the program were similar. In all respects, the participants in the program appear to represent a cross-section of middle class Americans (Matarazzo, Connor, Fey, Carmody, Pierce, Brischetto, Baker, Connor, & Sexton, 1982).

Three separate control groups have been selected from other districts in Portland matched for socio-economic, demographic and health variables. One group of 80 families is being monitored three times at 2-year intervals. Two other control groups are being monitored only once; one near the middle and one near the end of the 5-year study period. The three control groups will provide estimates of spontaneous population drift in cholesterol and other values as well as the effects of repeated measurement and contact by FHS personnel.

Intervention families undergo extensive biomedical, dietary, psychological and behavioral assessments three times each year. The biomedical measurements include plasma lipids (cholesterol and triglycerides), lipoproteins (e.g., low density and high density lipoproteins), blood pressure, weight, tricep skinfold thickness and 24-hour urinary sodium and potassium excretion tests. Dietary measures include 24-hour dietary recalls, a more behavioral dietary habit survey, a 2-week grocery shopping assessment and a restaurant (i.e., eating-out) assessment. Behavioral and psychological measures include a structured clinical interview and a large battery of standardized instruments designed to assess the use of tobacco, alcohol and drugs, exercise patterns, Type A behavior, psychosocial stress, cognitive style, overall coping skills and the organization and interaction of the family.

The monthly evening group meetings led by psychologist-nutritionist teams are the primary means of dietary intervention. These family group sessions generally entail the following elements: (1) a review of recent individual dietary progress, setbacks and any new coping strategies which were devised; (2) the presentation of that evening's topic or discussion theme; (3) group discussion and reactions with an emphasis on how these new dietary ideas and concepts might be applied; and (4) clarification of specific behavioral steps and approaches, if any, that each person intends to pursue during the coming month.

During the first months of intervention, participants receive a good deal of information about diet, coronary heart disease, and the specifics of an improved eating pattern. As the members become better acquainted and more comfortable in sharing their experiences, the focus of the discussion is shifted increasingly to the group. The leaders become facilitators whose goal is to stimulate group members to think about and evaluate their personal food habits and motives for change. The option not to change is explicitly respected from the beginning.

The second year represents a shift from a strong informational approach to a more behavioral emphasis. Didactic presentations are minimized to encourage group discussion. When problems develop (e.g., "My kids won't drink skim milk."), the individual voicing this obstacle to change and the other group members are asked to work together as peer-consultants to one another to identify potential solutions. Suggestions derived by the group are often highly appropriate, creative and more readily received than are those the group leaders could provide. Those members offering suggestions derive the added benefits of the groups' reinforcement for their creativity and the consolidation of their own motivation to improve their diet.

Whenever possible, group members are encouraged to take an active role in the planning of present and future group meetings. Many, for example, have suggested individualized monthly homework assignments (e.g., restock the cupboards), exploring natural food stores as a group or having group meetings or potlucks in one of their homes rather than at the clinic. These cohesion-building actions do much to increase the participants' sense of involvement and commitment to the project and their health in general.

The content of the monthly group meetings may be discerned by the list of topics presented. These included Food Buying, Main Dishes, Stress, Family Support, Changing Habits, and Fats of Life. Some group members have overriding personal needs or conditions that do not pertain to the group as a whole. Therefore, special interest groups have been organized to meet these needs. Examples include a group for teenagers as well as special sessions or series for those with unusually elevated lipids (i.e., Hyperlipidemia Group) and for those families with pregnant or lactating mothers. Other groups interested in dealing with stress management and weight loss are presently being considered.

Every monthly meeting is seen as a valuable opportunity to expose group members to unfamiliar foods and preparation techniques and, usually, some snack or dish is available to taste. Frank discussion and feedback are encouraged to help people express their feelings about the dietary changes making up the Alternative Diet. For example, some women feel that being a ''good mother'' means giving out frequent treats. Expression of such reactions as well as fears about protein deficiency, weight gain or possible negative social consequences of attempting a new eating pattern are difficult at first, but become routine as cohesion and mutual trust develop. The group members' support for each other serves to legitimize the importance of each person's concerns, but also provides the encouragement to persist, re-examine and to take small steps until the desired solutions are found. Also, group leaders frequently disclose their own dilemmas and struggles with dietary change. Group members appear relieved to know that their professional colleagues are not the nutritional demigods they sometimes imagine them to be.

Finally, the popular press is replete with overstated controversy, financially-motivated claims for certain products, and a plethora of confusing fads and easy answers. Participants in the FHS groups have good reason to be confused and skeptical of what they hear ''out there'' as well as from the staff. Participants' reports and questions regarding these controversial issues frequently illuminate key barriers to change. They are responded to in a serious and nondefensive manner that addresses blatant misconceptions while acknowledging the limits of scientific information and the validity of the questions that yet remain.

Progress and Prospects

At the time of this writing, the majority of the participants are in their second year of the program although some have been involved for up to 36 months. A particularly gratifying indication of the program's initial effectiveness has been the level of attendance and participation seen in the monthly group meetings. Preliminary data at 12 months indicate that approximately 70% of the primary adults are in attendance at each meeting and no significant drop off over time is in evidence. The percentage of families represented at each meeting is, of course, even higher. Recall that these normal urban families have predominantly low to moderate risk profiles, are typically young (mean age of the adults is 37 years) and have no other obvious external incentives. The intrinsic value of the social support offered by the group milieu may, indeed, provide the necessary context for the gradual long-term alteration of important aspects of the way we live. However, the general public's willingness to enter and continue with a large scale community intervention program of this sort speaks to the widespread and considerable societal concern about optimum diet and the promotion of a health ier lifestyle.

Analyses of the first year behavioral and physiological outcomes are currently underway and will soon be available. The nature and design of the program precludes, of course, dramatic initial results in terms of cholesterol lowering. Rather, the first year represents the foundation for the progressive adoption and long-term maintenance of the Alternative Diet. While the main purpose of the FHS is to evaluate the intervention program, the rich pool of psychological, dietary, and biomedical information which is being collected is making possible numerous ancillary research projects. Of particular interest are the psychosocial characteristics associated with elevated risk profiles and their successful modification during the study period. (cf. Brischetto, Pierce, Matarazzo, Carmody, & Connor, 1982; Carmody, Matarazzo, Fey, Pierce, & Connor, 1982; Matarazzo et al., 1982). As intervention proceeds, this wealth of information will increasingly add to the understanding of individual and family health behavior, as well as the process and challenge of community lifestyle intervention.

ACKNOWLEDGMENTS

Preparation of this chapter was supported, in part, by National Heart, Lung and Blood Institute Grants HL20910, HL07332, and HL07295 and RR334 from the General Clinical Research Center of the National Institute of Health.

REFERENCES

Abraham, S., Johnson, C. L., & Carroll, M. D. A comparison of levels of serum cholesterol of adults 18–74 years of age in the U.S. in 1960–62 and 1971–74. *Advance data from Vital and*

Health Statistics of the National Center for Health Statistics (DHEW No. 5). Washington, D.C.: Government Printing Office, 1977.

Ahrens, E. H. Dietary fats and coronary heart disease: Unfinished business. *Lancet,* 1979, *2,* 1345–1348.

Anderson, J., & Bartkus, D. Choice of medical care: A behavioral model of health and illness behavior. *Journal of Health and Social Behavior,* 1973, *14,* 348–362.

Armstrong, M. L., Warner, E. D., & Connor, W. E. Regression of coronary atheromatosis in rhesus monkeys. *Circulation Research,* 1970, *27,* 59–67.

Bandura, A. Self-efficacy: Towards a unifying theory of behavioral change. *Psychological Review,* 1977, *84,* 191–215.

Barie, L. Recognition of the "at-risk" role: A means to influence behavior. *International Journal of Health Education,* 1969, *12,* 24–34.

Becker, M. H. (Ed.) The health belief model and personal health behavior. *Health Education Monographs,* 1974, *2,* 326–508.

Becker, M. H., Drachman, R. H., & Kirscht, J. P. Motivations as predictors of health behavior. *Health Service Reports,* 1972, *87,* 852–861.

Becker, M., Drachman, R., & Kirscht, J. A field experiment to evaluate various outcomes of continuity of physical care. *American Journal of Public Health,* 1974, *64,* 1062–1070.

Becker, M. H., Haefner, O. P., Kasl, S. V., Kirscht, J. P., Maiman, L. A., & Rosenstock, I. M. *Medical Care,* 1977, *15*(5), Supplement, 27–47.

Becker, M. H., Kaback, M. M., Rosenstock, I. M., & Ruth, M. V. Some influences on public participation in a genetic screening program. *Journal of Community Health,* 1975, *1,* 3–14.

Becker, M. H., & Maiman, L. A. Sociobehavioral determinants of compliance with health and medical care recommendations. *Medical Care,* 1975, *13,* 10–24.

Belloc, N. B. Relationship of health practices and mortality. *Preventive Medicine,* 1973, *2,* 67–81.

Belloc, N. B., & Breslow, H. Relationship of physical health status and health practices. *Preventive Medicine,* 1972, *1,* 409–421.

Bergman, A. B., & Werner, R. J. Failure of children to receive penicillin by mouth. *New England Journal Medicine,* 1963, *268,* 1334–1338.

Blackburn, H. Prevention of coronary heart disease: The need, potential, strategy, impediments, and implications. In G. Schettler, J. Drews, & H. Greten (Eds.), *Changes in the Medical Panorama.* Stuttgart: Georg Thieme, 1978.

Borhani, N. O. Primary prevention of coronary heart disease: A critique. *American Journal of Cardiology,* 1977, *40,* 251–259.

Bradshaw, P. W., Ley, P., Kincey, J. A., & Bradshaw, J. Recall of medical advice: Comprehensibility and specificity. *British Journal of Social and Clinical Psychology,* 1975, *14,* 55–62.

Brehm, J. W. *A theory of psychological reactance.* New York: Academic, 1966.

Brischetto, C. S., Pierce, D. K., Matarazzo, J. D., Carmody, T. P., & Connor, W. E. *Psychological and behavioral correlates of smoking.* Submitted for publication, 1981.

Brownell, K. D., Heckerman, C. L., Westlake, R. J., Hayes, S. C., & Monti, P. M. The effect of couples training and partner cooperativeness in the behavioral treatment of obesity. *Behavioral Research Therapy,* 1978, *16,* 323–333.

Califano, J. A., Jr. *Smoking and health: A report of the Surgeon General.* Washington, D.C.: Superintendent of Documents, Government Printing Office, Stock Number 017-000-0218-0, 1979 (a).

Califano, J. A., Jr. *Healthy People: The Surgeon General's report on health promotion and disease prevention.* Washington, D.C.: Superintendent of Documents, Government Printing Office, Stock Number 017-001-00416-2, 1979 (b).

Carmody, T. P., Fey, S. G., Pierce, D. K., Connor, W. E., & Matarazzo, J. D. Behavioral treatment of hyperlipidemia: Techniques, results and future directions. *Journal of Behavioral Medicine,* 1982.

Carmody, T. P., Matarazzo, J. D., Fey, S. G., Pierce, D. K., & Connor, W. E. *Symptom, report on the Cornell Medical Index, and cardiovascular risk detection*, 1982.

Chaney, E. F., O'Leary, M. R., & Marlatt, G. A. Skills training with alcoholics. *Journal of Consulting and Clinical Psychology*, 1978, *46*, 1092-1104.

Chu, G. C. Fear arousal, efficacy, and imminency. *Journal of Personality and Social Psychology*, 1966, *4*, 517-524.

Condiotte, M. M., & Lichtenstein, E. Self-efficacy and relapse in smoking cessation programs. *Journal of Consulting and Clinical Psychology*, 1982, *49*, 648-658.

Connor, W. E. Too little or too much: The case for preventive nutrition. *The American Journal of Clinical Nutrition*. 1979a, *32*, 1975-1978.

Connor, W. E. The relationship of hyperlipoproteinemia to atherosclerosis: The decisive role of dietary cholesterol and fat. In A. M. Scann, R. W. Wissler, & G. S. Getz, (Eds.), *The Biochemistry of Atherosclerosis*. New York: Marcel Dekker, 1979b.

Connor, W. E., & Connor, S. L. The key role of nutritional factors in the prevention of coronary heart disease. *Preventive Medicine, 1972, 1,* 49-83.

Connor, W. E., & Connor, S. L. Dietary Treatment of Hyperlipidemia. In B. M. Rifkind & R. I. Levy, (Eds.), *Hyperlipidemia: Diagnosis and Therapy*. New York: Grune & Stratton, Inc., 1977.

Cooper, B. S., & Rice, D. P. The economic costs of illness revisited. *Social Security Bulletin, 1976, 39,* 21-36.

Corday, E., & Corday, S. R. Prevention of heart disease by control of risk factors: The time has come to face the facts. *American Journal of Cardiology, 1975, 35,* 330-333.

Cummings, K. M., Becker, M. H., & Maile, M. C. Bringing the models together: An empirical approach to combining variables used to explain health actions. *Journal of Behavioral Medicine,* 1980, *3,* 123-145.

Dawber, T. R. *Risk factors for atherosclerotic disease*. Kalamazoo, Michigan: The Upjohn Company, 1975.

Department of Agriculture. *Agriculture statistics*. Washington, D.C., Government Printing Office, 1976.

Department of Health, Education and Welfare. *Smoking and health report of the advisory committee to the Surgeon General of the public health service*. Washington, D.C.: Government Printing Office, 1964.

Department of Health, Education and Welfare. *Public Health Service: Forward Plan for Health* (FY 1978-1982). Washington, D.C.: Government Printing Office, 1978.

Dever, G. E. A. *An epidemiological model for health policy analysis*. Atlanta, Georgia: Georgia Department of Human Resources, 1975.

Diet-Heart Review Panel of the National Heart Institute. Mass field trials of the diet-heart question: Their significance, timeliness, feasibility and applicability. *American Heart Association Monograph* (No. 28). New York: American Heart Association, 1969.

Epstein, F. H. Preventive trials and the "diet-heart" question: Wait for results or act now? *Atherosclerosis*, 1977, *26*, 515-523.

Evans, R. I., & Hall, Y. Social-psychological perspective in motivating changes in eating behavior. *Journal of the American Dietetic Association*, 1978, *72*, 378-383.

Evans, R., Rozelle, R., Mittlemark, M., Hansen, W., Bane, A., & Havis, J. Deterring the onset of smoking in children: Knowledge of immediate physiological effects and coping with peer pressure, media, pressure, and parent modeling. *Journal of Applied Social Psychology*, 1978, *8*, 126-135.

Fabrega, H. Towards a model of illness behavior. *Medical Care*, 1973, *11*, 470-484.

Feinleib, M., & Davidson, M. J. Coronary heart disease mortality: A community perspective. *Journal of the American Medical Association*, 1972, *222*, 1129-1134.

Festinger, L. *A theory of cognitive dissonance*. Evanston, Illinois: Row Peterson, 1957.

Festinger, L., & Carlsmith, J. M. Cognitive consequences of forced compliance. *Journal of Abnormal and Social Psychology*, 1959, *58*, 203–211.

Francis, V., Dorsch, B. M., & Morris, M. J. Gaps in doctor-patient communication: Patients' response to medical advice. *New England Journal of Medicine*, 1969, *280*, 535–540.

Frank, C. W., Weinblatt, E., Shapiro, S., & Sager, R. V. Physical inactivity as a lethal factor in myocardial infarction among men. *Circulation*, 1966, *34*, 1022–1033.

Franks, C. M., & Wilson, G. T. *Annual review of behavioral therapy: Theory and practice*. New York: Brunner-Mazel, 1975.

Friedman, G. D., Dales, L. G., & Ury, A. K. Mortality in middle-aged smokers and non-smokers. *New England Journal of Medicine*, 1979, *300*, 213–217.

Gordon, T., & Kannel, W. B. Premature mortality from coronary heart disease: The Framingham Study. *Journal of the American Medical Association*, 1971, *215*, 1617–1625.

Gordon, T., Kannel, W. B., McGee, D., & Dawber, T. R. Death and coronary attacks in men after giving up cigarette smoking: A report from the Framington Study. *Lancet*, 1974, *2*, 1345–1348.

Grodon, T., Sorlie, P., & Kannel, W. B. Coronary heart disease, atherothrombotic brain infarction, intermittent claudication: A multivariate analysis of some factors related to their incidence. *Framington Study, 16-year Followup* (Section 27). Washington, D.C.: Government Printing Office, 1971.

Gordon, T., & Thom, T. The recent decrease in CHD mortality. *Preventive Medicine*, 1975, *4*, 115–125.

Haynes, S. G., & Feinleib, M. Women, Work and Coronary Heart Disease: Prospective Findings from the Framington Heart Study. *American Journal of Public Health*, 1980, *70*, 133–141.

Haynes, S. G., Manning, F., & Kannel, W. B. The relationship of psychosocial factors to coronary heart disease in the Framington Study. *American Journal of Epidemiology*, 1980, *111*, 37–58.

Hegsted, D. M., McGandy, R. B., Myers, M. L., & Stare, F. J. Quantitative effects of dietary fat on serum cholesterol in man. *American Journal of Clinical Nutrition*, 1965, *17*, 281–295.

Hill, J. D., Hampton, J. R., & Mitchell, J. R. A. A randomized trial of home-versus-hospital management for patients with suspected myocardial infarction. *Lancet*, 1978, *1*, 837–841.

Hovland, C. I., Janis, I. L., & Kelley, H. H. *Communication and persuasion*. New Haven: Yale University Press, 1953.

Hovland, C. I., Lumsdaine, A. A., & Sheffield, F. D. *Experiments on mass communications*. Princeton: Princeton University Press, 1949.

Hovland, C. I., & Mandell, W. An experimental comparison of conclusion-drawing by communicator and the audience. *Journal of Abnormal and Social Psychology*, 1952, 47, 581–588.

Holder, L. Effects of source, message, and audience characteristics on health behavior compliance. *Health Service Reports*, 1972, *87*, 343–350.

Hunt, W. A., Barnett, L. W., & Branch, L. G. Relapse rates in addiction programs. *Journal of Clinical Psychology*, 1971, *27*, 455–456.

Hunt, W., & Matarazzo, J. D. Three years later: Recent developments in the experimental modification of smoking behavior. *Journal of Abnormal Psychology*, 1973, *81*, 107–114.

Hypertension Detection and Follow-up Program Cooperative Group. Five-Year Findings of the Hypertension Detection and Follow-up Program. *Journal of the American Medical Association*, 1979, *242*, 2562–2577.

Insko, C. A. *Theories of attitude change*. New York: Appleton-Century-Crofts, 1967.

Janis, I. L. Effects of fear arousal on attitude change: Recent developments in theory and experimental research. In L. Berkowitz (Ed.), *Advances in Experimental Social Psychology*, (Vol. 3), New York: Academic Press, 1967.

Janis, I. L., & Feshbach, S. Effects of fear arousing communications. *Journal of Abnormal and Social Psychology*, 1953, *48*, 78–92.

Janis, I. L., & Terwilliger, R. An experimental study of psychological resistance to fear-arousing communication. *Journal of Abnormal and Social Psychology*, 1962, *65*, 403–410.

Joyce, C. R. B., Caple, G., Mason, M., Reynolds, E., & Mathews, J. A. Quantitative study of doctor-patient communication. *Quarterly Journal of Medicine,* 1969, *38,* 183-194.

Kannel, W. R., McGee, D., & Gordon, T. A general cardiovascular risk profile: the Framingham Study. *American Journal of Cardiology,* 1976, *38,* 46-51.

Kasl, S. V., & Cobb, S. Health behavior, illness behavior, and sick role behavior. *Archives of Environmental Health,* 1966, *12,* 246-266.

Keys, A. *Seven Countries: A Multivariate analysis of death and coronary heart disease.* Cambridge: Harvard University Press, 1980.

Keys, A., & Parlin, R. W. Serum Cholesterol response to changes in dietary lipids. *American Journal Clinical Nutrition,* 1966, *19,* 175-181.

Kiesler, C. A., Collins, B. A., & Miller, N. *Attitude change: A critical analysis of theoretical Approaches.* New York: Wiley, 1969.

Klapper, J. T. *The effects of mass communication.* New York: Free Press, 1969.

Kristein, M. M., Arnold, C. B., & Wynder, E. L. Health economics and preventive care. *Science,* 1977, *195,* 457-462.

Kuller, L., Neaton, J., Caggiula, A., & Falvo-Gerard, L. Primary prevention of heart attacks: The Multiple Risk Factor Intervention Trial. *American Journal of Epidemiology,* 1980, *112,* 185-199.

Lalonde, M. *A new perspective on the health of Canadians.* Ottawa: Information Canada, 1974.

Lancet Editorial. Why the American decline in coronary heart disease? *Lancet,* 1980, *1,* 183-184.

Leon, G. R. A behavioral approach to obesity. *The American Journal of Clinical Nutrition,* 1977, *30,* 785-789.

Leventhal, H. Findings and theory in the study of fear communications. In L. Berkowitz (Ed.), *Advances in Experimental Social Psychology* (Vol. 5). New York: Academic Press, 1970.

Leventhal, H. Attitudes: Their nature, growth, and change. In C. Nemeth (Ed.), *Social Psychology: Classic and Contemporary Integrations.* Chicago: Rand McNally, 1974.

Leventhal, H., & Cleary, P. D. The smoking problem: A review of the research and theory in behavioral risk modification. *Psychological Bulletin,* 1980, *88,* 370-405.

Leventhal, H., & Niles, P. Persistence of influence for varying durations of exposure to threat stimuli. *Psychological Reports,* 1965, *16,* 223-233.

Leventhal, H., & Watts, J. Sources of resistance to fear-arousing communications on smoking and lung cancer. *Journal of Personality,* 1966, *34,* 155-175.

Ley, P. Psychological studies of doctor-patient communication. In S. Rachman (Ed.), *Contributions to Medical Psychology* (Vol. 1). New York: Pergman Press, 1977.

Ley, P., Bradshaw, P. W., Eaves, D. E., & Walker, C. M. A method for increasing patients' recall of information presented to them. *Psychological Medicine,* 1973, *3,* 217-220.

Ley, P., Goldman, M., Bradshaw, P. W., Kincey, J. A., & Walker, C. M. The comprehensibility of some x-ray leaflets. *Journal of the Institute of Health Education,* 1972, *10,* 47-55.

Ley, P., & Spelmann, M. S. Communications in an out-patient setting. *British Journal of Social and Clinical Psychology,* 1965, *4,* 114-116.

Lewin, K. Forces behind food habits and methods of change. *Bulletin of the National Research Council,* 1943, *108,* 35-65.

Lewis, B. Dietary prevention of ischaemic heart disease: A policy for the '80s. *British Medical Journal,* 1980, *281,* 177-180.

Lumsdaine, A. A., & Janis, I. L. Resistance to counter propaganda presentations. *Public Opinion Quarterly,* 1953, *17,* 311-318.

Mahoney, M. J. Behavioral Treatment of Obesity. In A. J. Enelow & J. B. Henderson (Eds.), *Applying Behavioral Science to Cardiovascular Risk.* Seattle, Washington: American Heart Association, 1975.

Mahoney, M. J., & Mahoney, K. *Permanent weight control.* New York: W. W. Norton, 1976.

Marlatt, G. A. The Drinking Profile: A questionnaire for the behavioral assessment of alcoholism. In

E. J. Mash & L. G. Terdal (Eds.), *Behavioral therapy assessment: Diagnosis, design, and evaluation.* New York: Springer, 1976.

Marlatt, G. A., & Gordon, J. R. Determinants of relapse: Implication for the maintenance of behavior change. In P. O. Davidson & S. M. Davidson, (Eds.), *Behavioral Medicine: Changing Health Lifestyles.* New York: Brunner-Mazel, 1980.

Matarazzo, J. D. Behavioral health and behavioral medicine: Frontiers for a new health psychology. *American Psychologist*, 1980, *35*, 807–817.

Matarazzo, J. E. *Behavioral health's challenge to academic, scientific and professional psychology. American Psychologist*, 1982, *37*, 1–14.

Matarazzo, J. D., & Saslow, G. Psychological and related characteristics of smokers and non-smokers. *Psychological Bulletin*, 1960, *57*, 493–513.

Matarazzo, J. D., Connor, W. E., Fey, S. G., Carmody, T. P., Pierce, D. K., Brischetto, C. S., Baker, L. H., Connor, S. L., & Sexton, G. Behavioral cardiology with emphasis on The Family Heart Study: Fertile ground for psychological and biomedical research. In T. Millon, C. J. Green, & R. B. Meagher, (Eds.), *Handbook of Health Care Psychology.* New York: Plenum, 1982, in press.

Mather, H. G., Morgan, D. C., Pearson, N. G., Read, K. L. Q., Shaw, D. B., Steed, G. A., Thorne, M. G., Lawrence, C. J., & Riley, F. S. Myocardial infarction: A comparison between home and hospital care for patients. *British Medical Journal*, 1976, *1*, 925–929.

Mather, H. G., Pearson, N. G., Read, K. L., Shaw, D. B., Steed, G. R., Thorne, M. G., Jones, S., Guerrier, C. I., Eraut, C. D., McHugh, P. M., Chowdhury, N. R., Jafary, M. H., & Wallace, T. J. Acute myocardial infarction: Home and hospital treatment. *British Medical Journal*, 1971, *3*, 334–338.

Mausner, B. An ecological view of cigarette smoking. *Journal of Abnormal Psychology*, 1973, *81*, 115–126.

McGuire, W. J. Inducing resistance to persuasion: Some contemporary approaches. In L. Berkowitz (Ed.) *Advances in Experimental Social Psychology* (Vol. 1). New York: Academic Press, 1964.

McGuire, W. J. The nature of attitudes and attitude change. In G. Lindzey & E. Aronson, (Eds.), *The Handbook of Social Psychology* (Vol. 3). Reading, Mass.: Addison-Wesley, 1969.

McKeown, T. *The Role of Medicine: Dream, Mirage or Nemesis?* Princeton, New Jersey: Princeton University Press, 1979.

Mechanic, D. *Medical Sociology: A Selective View.* New York: The Free Press, 1968.

Milgram, S. *Obedience to Authority: An Experimental View.* New York: Harper & Row, 1974.

Milsum, J. H. Lifestyle changes for the whole person: Stimulation through health hazard appraisal. In P. O. Davidson & S. M. Davidson, (Eds.), *Behavioral Medicine: Changing Health Lifestyles.* New York: Brunner/Mazel, Inc., 1980.

Mitchell, J. H. Compliance with medical regimens: An annotated bibliography. *Health Education Monographs*, 1974, *2*, 75–87.

Moore, J. H., & Williams, D. L. The effect of diet on the level of plasma cholesterol and the degree of atheromatous degeneration in the rabbit. *British Journal of Nutrition*, 1964, *18*, 253–262.

Multiple Risk Factor Intervention Trial Group. Statistical design considerations in the NHLBI multiple risk factor intervention trial (MRFIT). *Journal of Chronic Disease*, 1977, *30*, 261–275.

National Diet-Heart Study Research Group. The National Diet-Heart Study Final Report. *Circulation*, 1968, *38* (Suppl. I), 1–412.

National Heart and Lung Institute Task Force on Arteriosclerosis. Arteriosclerosis, Volume I. Washington, D.C.: Government Printing Office, DHEW (NIH) 72–137, 1971.

Oscai, L. B., Patterson, J. A., Bogard, D. L., Beck, R. J., & Rothermel, B. L. Normalization of serum triglycerides and lipoprotein electrophoretic patterns by exercise. *American Journal of Cardiology*, 1972, *30*, 775–780.

Paffenbarger, R. S., Jr., Hale, W. E., Brand, K. J., & Hyde, R. T. Work-energy level, personal characteristics and fatal heart attack: A birth-cohort effect. *American Journal Epidemiology*, 1977, *105*, 200–213.

Paffenbarger, R. S., Laughlin, M. E., Gima, A. S., & Black, R. A. Work activity of longshoremen as related to death from coronary heart disease and stroke. *New England Journal of Medicine,* 1970, *282,* 1109–1114.

Pearce, J. W., LeBow, M. D., & Orchard, J. *The role of spouse involvement in the behavioral treatment of obese women.* Paper presented at a meeting of the Canadian Psychological Association, 1979.

Pooling Project Research Group. Relationship of blood pressure, serum cholesterol, smoking habit, relative weight and ECG abnormalities to incidence of major coronary events: Final report of the Pooling Project. *Journal of Chronic Disease,* 1978, *31,* 201–306.

Reisin, E., Abel, R., Modan, M., Silverberg, D. S., Eliahou, H. E., & Modan, B. Effects of weight loss without salt restriction on the reduction of blood pressure in overweight hypertensive patients. *New England Journal of Medicine,* 1978, *298,* 1–6.

Report of Inter-Society Commission for Heart Disease Resources. Primary prevention of atherosclerotic disease. *Circulation,* 1970, *42,* 1–44.

Rogers, D. E. Adjusting to a no-growth future: Imperative for academic medicine in the 1980's. *Cornell University Medical College Alumni Quarterly,* 1980, *43,* 3–9.

Rokeach, M. *Open and closed mind,* New York: Basic Books, 1960.

Rosenberg, M. M., & Klebba, A. J. Trends in cardiovascular mortality with focus on ischemic heart disease: United States 1950–76. In R. Havilik & M. Feinleib, (Eds.), *Proceedings of the Conference on the Decline in Coronary Heart Disease Mortality.* Bethesda, MD: Department of Health, Education and Welfare, 1979.

Rosenman, R. H., Brand, R. J., Jenkins, C. D., Friedman, M., Straus, R., & Wurm, M. Coronary heart disease in the Western Collaborative Group Study: Final follow-up of 8-½ years. *Journal of the American Medical Association,* 1975, *233,* 872–877.

Rosenstock, I. M. Why people use health services. *Milbank Memorial Fund Quarterly,* 1966, *44,* 94–127.

Seligman, M. E. P. *Helplessness.* San Francisco: Freeman, 1975.

Senate Select Committee on Nutrition and Human Needs. *Dietary Goals for the United States.* Washington, D.C.: Government Printing Office, 1977.

Sexton-McDill, M. Structure of social systems determining attitude, knowledge, and behavior toward disease: Micro social structures. In A. J. Enelow & J. B. Henderson (Eds.), *Applying Behavioral Science to Cardiovascular Risk.* Seattle, Washington: American Heart Association, Inc., 1975.

Stalonas, P. M., Johnson, W. G., & Christ, M. Behavior modification for obesity: The evaluation of exercise, contingency management and program adherence. *Journal of Consulting and Clinical Psychology,* 1978, *46,* 463–469.

Stuart, R. B. *Act thin: Stay thin.* New York: W. W. Norton, 1978.

Stuart, R. B. Weight loss and beyond: Are they taking it off and keeping it off? In P. O. Davidson & S. M. Davidson, (Eds.), *Behavioral Medicine: Changing Health Lifestyles.* New York: Brunner-Mazel, 1980.

Stuart, R. B., & Davis, B. *Slim chance in a fat world: Behavioral control of obesity.* Champaign, Ill.: Research Press, 1972.

Stunkard, A. J., & Mahoney, M. M. Behavioral treatment of the eating disorders. In H. Leitenberg, (Eds.), *Handbook of Behavior Modification and Behavior Therapy.* Englewood Cliffs, N.J.: Prentice-Hall, 1976.

Suchman, E. A. Health orientation and medical care. *American Journal of Public Health,* 1966, *56,* 97–105.

Svarstad, B. Physician-patient communication and patient conformity with medical advice. In D. Mechanic, (Ed.), *The Growth of Bureaucratic Medicine: An Inquiry into the Dynamics of Patient Behavior and the Organization of Medical Care.* New York: John Wiley & Sons, 1976.

Taylor, C. B., Paton, D. E., & Cox, G. E. Atherosclerosis in rhesus monkeys: Fatal myocardial infarction in a monkey fed fat and cholesterol. *Archives of Pathology,* 1963, *76,* 404–412.

Taylor, H. L., Romo, M., Jacobs, D. R., & Blackburn, H. Secular changes in coronary heart disease risk factors. *Circulation,* (abstract), 1975, *51* (Suppl. II), 96.

Thompson, E. L. Smoking education programs, 1960-76. *American Journal of Public Health,* 1978, *68,* 250-257.

Tobian, L. The relationship of salt to hypertension. *American Journal of Clinical Nutrition,* 1979, *32,* 2739-2748.

Vischl, T. R., Jones, K. R., Shank, E. L., & Lima, L. H. *The alcohol, drug abuse, and mental health national data book.* Washington, D.C.: Superintendent of Documents, Government Printing Office, Stock Number 017-024-00983-1, 1980.

Walker, W. J. Changing United States lifestyle and declining vascular mortality: Cause or coincidence? *New England Journal of Medicine,* 1977, *297,* 163-165.

Wilson, G. T. Cognitive factors in lifestyle changes: A social learning perspective. In P. O. Davidson & S. M. Davidson, (Eds.), *Behavioral Medicine: Changing Health Lifestyles.* New York: Brunner-Mazel, 1980.

Wilson, G. T., & Brownell, K. D. Behavior therapy for obesity including family members in the treatment process. *Behavior Therapy,* 1978, *9,* 943-945.

Wood, P. D., Haskell, W., Klein, H., Lewis, S., Stern, M. P., & Farquhar, J. W. The distribution of plasma lipoproteins in middle-aged male runners. *Metabolism,* 1976, *25,* 1249-1257.

Author Index

Numbers in italic indicate the page on which the complete reference appears.

A

Abate, F., 290, 291, *326*
Abel, G. G., 42, 44, *67*
Abel, R., 469, *501*
Abikoff, H., 265, 297, 314, 316, *316, 319*
Abraham, S., 471, *495*
Abram, H. S., 345, *365*
Abramovici, H., 361, *367*
Abrams, B., 287, *326*
Abrams, D., 136, *169*
Abramson, P. R., 333, *369*
Achenbach, T. M., 263, 267, 268, 270, *316, 317*
Ackerman, P., 278, *318*
Adams, H. E., 50, 51, *67, 69*
Adams, K. M., 19, *34*
Adams, R. D., 12, *34, 36*
Ader, R., 389, *394*
Adesso, V., 136, *166*
Ad Hoc Committee on Classification of Headache, 63, *67*
Adkins, D., 143, 158, *168,* 193, *207*
Adkins, J., 379, *397*
Adler, C. S., 63, *68*
Adolphe, A., 358, *366*
Agle, D. P., 347, *366*
Agnew, H. W., 221, *260*
Ahn, H., 291, 295, *317*
Ahrens, E. H., 472, *496*

Aiken, P. P., 189, *202*
Albala, A. A., 444, *460, 461*
Albert, M., 12, *34*
Alcoholics Anonymous World Services, 129, *163*
Alexander, A. B., 53, *67*
Alexander, F., 382, *394*
Alexander, J., 178, *206*
Allen, M. T., 390, *396, 460*
Allen, R. P., 275, 301, *324*
Allen, T., 291, 292, *324*
Allison, T., 55, *70,* 223, *255*
Allport, G. W., 192, *202*
Altman, K., 349, *367*
Ambuel, J., 296, *324*
American Psychiatric Association, 3, *34, 122, 163,* 263, *317,* 339, *366, 460*
Anastasi, A., 23, *34*
Anch, A. M., 229, *258*
Anderson, D. E., 43, *73*
Anderson, E. E., 354, *368*
Anderson, J., 478, *496*
Anderson, L., 136, *164*
Andrasik, F., 63, *67*
Andreasen, N. J., 388, *394*
Andres, R., 103, 105, 107, 108, *118*
Andrew, J. M., 386, 388, *394*
Andreychuk, T., 49, *67*
Andrulonis, P., 287, *318*
Anglin, B., 190, *207*

503

Subject Index